The Courage and Suffering, the Triumph and Tragedy, of the Climactic Years

Volume Two of The Blue and the Gray *opens with Lee and the Southern army at the peak of strength, moving north in a great and desperate gamble for decisive victory. It ends with the last bloody days of futile resistance and inevitable surrender as the Union was preserved at a staggering cost.*

These dramatic years of bitter struggle come to life in the writings of those who lived through them, participated in the momentous actions, and recorded them with the agonies of choice and the din of battle still fresh and vivid. This was the Civil War as it really was. This is history as it was seen by those who made it.

HENRY STEELE COMMAGER has had a long and distinguished career as a teacher and historian. His academic credentials include posts at New York University, Duke, Harvard, the University of Chicago, the University of California, and Columbia. Simultaneously, he has had a remarkable literary output since his first widely acclaimed book in 1930, *The Growth of the American Republic,* written in collaboration with Samuel Eliot Morison.

The Blue and the Gray

THE STORY OF THE CIVIL WAR AS TOLD BY PARTICIPANTS

Volume Two: The Battle of Gettysburg
to Appomattox

Edited by Henry Steele Commager

(Revised and Abridged)

Foreword by Douglas Southall Freeman

A MENTOR BOOK
NEW AMERICAN LIBRARY
TIMES MIRROR
NEW YORK AND SCARBOROUGH, ONTARIO
THE NEW ENGLISH LIBRARY LIMITED, LONDON

MENTOR TRADEMARK REG. U.S. PAT. OFF. AND FOREIGN COUNTRIES
REGISTERED TRADEMARK—MARCA REGISTRADA
HECHO EN CHICAGO, U.S.A.

SIGNET, SIGNET CLASSICS, MENTOR, PLUME AND MERIDIAN BOOKS
are published *in the United States* by
The New American Library, Inc.,
1633 Broadway, New York, New York 10019,
in Canada by The New American Library of Canada Limited,
81 Mack Avenue, Scarborough, Ontario M1L 1M8
in the United Kingdom by
The New English Library Limited,
Barnard's Inn, Holborn, London, EC1N 2JR, England.

First Printing, December, 1973
2 3 4 5 6 7 8 9 10

Printed in Canada

To
the memory of

HENRY STEELE COMMAGER
Colonel, 67th Ohio

DAVID HEDGES COMMAGER
Captain, 184th Ohio

JAMES ALEXANDER WILLIAM THOMAS
Captain, 21st South Carolina

DUNCAN DONALD MCCOLL
1st Heavy Artillery, North Carolina

JAMES THOMAS CARROLL
North Carolina Volunteers

and to
my children

HENRY STEELE
NELLIE THOMAS MCCOLL
ELISABETH CARROLL

That they may remember their forebears
and the causes for which they fought

Foreword

Many hands filled the storehouse from which Henry Steele Commager drew the treasures that appear in the fascinating pages of this long-desired collection. Some survivors wrote of the eighteen-sixties because they had tarnished reputations to repolish or grudges to satisfy. Other participants set down the history of their old Regiment to please comrades who met annually at a G.A.R. encampment or at a Confederate reunion to live again in memory their great hours. In a few instances, most notably that of General Grant, memoirs were prepared because the public literally demanded them. Hundreds of books and brochures were the work of those who sought, consciously or otherwise, to associate themselves with the mighty men and the decisive conflict of their generation. The failure of some Southern writers to find a publisher was responsible for the private printing of numerous books and for the allegation, never justified, that the North would not give Southern writers a hearing. One forgotten phase of this had its origin in the persistent effort of certain schoolbook publishers to procure the "adoption" in the South of texts on American history written in partizan spirit for Northern readers. This salesmanship was met repeatedly with pleas for the establishment in Richmond, Atlanta or New Orleans of a publishing house that would be "fair to the South." Where a response was made to this appeal, the fruit sometimes was a text as extreme as the one that provoked it. A long-popular Southern school history contained 590 pages, of which more than 200 were devoted to the preliminaries of the War between the States and to the events of that struggle. A study of the disputes of the eighteen-nineties involving rival books of this type would startle a generation that assumes an author's non-partizan approach as a matter of course.

Many contrasts are offered in the literature of the American war of 1861-65, and most notably in what Mr. Commager remarks in his introduction—that "the Confederate narratives seem to be of a higher literary quality than the Federal." This is meant, of course, to be subject at the outset to qualification as respects some notable books. The list of Union brigade histories, for example, may contain no single volume better than Caldwell's charming story of Gregg's South Carolinians; but Mr. Commager most surely is correct in saying that Charles E. Davis's account of the Thirteenth Massachusetts is definitely the most interesting regimental history on either side.

If there is general, or average superiority in Southern memoirs and personal narratives, this doubtless is due to a number of circumstances that raise no questions of rival "cultures." Nearly always there is glamor to a "lost cause." Cromwell's body on the Tyburn gallows, "Bonnie Prince Charlie" in exile, and Bonaparte dying of cancer at Longwood never fail to arouse sympathy the Puritan Revolution, the Jacobite cause and Napoleonic imperialism cannot stir. It manifestly has been so with the South which had, in addition, a most unusual number of picturesque leaders. These men possessed the "color" and the peculiarities that inspire the *causerie de bivouac* the Little Corporal said every general should provide if he wished to be successful. Lee had a magnificence that awed his soldiers, who seldom cheered him; when Stonewall Jackson came in sight, riding awkwardly on a poor horse, the rebel yell nearly always would be raised. He fired the imagination of his troops as Lee never did until the *post-bellum* years. Albert Sidney Johnston, Forrest, Morgan, "Jeb" Stuart—these, too, were men to arouse enthusiasms that echoed in the memoirs of their followers. The North had soldiers and seamen of like appeal, but somehow the memory of nearly all these leaders was forgotten in the changes of population incident to the Westward movement and to expanded immigration. Static Southern society had longer memory.

Besides this, the South chanced to produce early a "war book" that set a standard which perhaps was considered representative, though actually it could not be maintained. This was Lieutenant General Richard Taylor's *Destruction and Reconstruction,* parts of which appeared in *The North American Review* in January-April 1878, the year before the memoirs were published in book form. Anyone reading that superb narrative would get an exalted conception of the literary skill of Southern military wirters, a conception not borne out by later works of other authors. This is not derogatory because Taylor's book remains to this day the most exciting narrative of its kind by an American commander. It would be difficult to find anywhere a better told story of a military movement than Taylor's account of "Stonewall" Jackson's Valley Campaign of 1862 (Vol. I p. 150ff).

If these and other circumstances bear out Mr. Commager's statement regarding the excellence of some Confederate narratives, fair play requires a Southerner to put the emphasis on that word *narratives*. There certainly is not a like superiority in the poetry. Thomas De Leon, from whom Mr. Commager takes several diverting episodes, remarked in his *Four Years in Rebel Capitals* that he had accumulated 1,900 wartime poems of the South, and later added greatly to his list: "There were battle odes, hymns, calls to arms, paeans and dirges and prayers for peace—many of them good, few of them great; and the vast majority, alas! wretchedly poor."

De Leon could have carried his scrutiny of Southern literature twenty years further and would have found few Confederate poems besides those of the Catholic priest, Father Abram Joseph Ryan, that voiced impressively the full emotion of the Southern people. Frequently Theodore O'Hara's "The Bivouac of the Dead" is put forward with Father Ryan's "Conquered Banner," but O'Hara wrote in 1847 of the Kentuckians killed in the Battle of Buena Vista. It is a singular fact that John R. Thompson's verses on the Confederacy, though written, as it were, to the pulsing of the guns on the Richmond defenses, seldom reached the level of his best work. Simms, Hayne, Lanier, Timrod, Randall—none of these wrote of "the war" as their admirers might have expected. No theme seemed to elicit their finest utterance, not even "Marse Robert" himself. Lee remains the demigod of the South and has there a place even Washington does not hold, but where may be found a poem on Lee that anyone would wish to make a permanent part of one's mental acquisition? In contrast, Lowell outdid himself in the "Harvard Commemoration Ode"; Whitman's "O Captain! My Captain!" and his "When Lilacs Last in the Dooryard Bloomed" are among the author's most successful works; and as Mr. Commager says, the North produced the "one great battle hymn of our literature."

Perhaps the most remarkable feature of the 300 and more articles reproduced in this notable collection is the humor that runs through nearly all of them and particularly through those of Southern origin. Doubtless there was an Erich Remarque somewhere on the Rappahannock front; letters written home by Billy Yank and Johnny Reb contained the

usual number of complaints and requests; but when the
column was in motion, there were more jests than oaths on
the lips of the soldiers. Laughter was the medicine for most
of the ills visible to the men next in line, though fear and
rebellious wrath and homesickness might be gnawing at the
heart.

Good cheer was not unnatural in the Union Regiments
after July 1863, but its persistence until the autumn of 1864
in most of the Southern forces, and particularly in the Army
of Northern Virginia, is a phenomenon of morale. The same
thing may be said of the attitude of the men toward the
manifest inferiority of Southern military equipment. The
graycoats laughed at their wagons and their harness, their
tatters and their gaping shoes. Again and again this stirs one
who opens these volumes at random and reads the first
paragraph on which the eye falls: were these men mocking
death as a foe long outwitted, or were they assuming a
heroism they did not possess? Were they valiant or merely
pretending? It scarcely seemed to matter where some of
them were or what they were doing: they laughed their way
from Manassas to Appomattox and even through the hospitals. Except for the military prisons, the Confederates, for
instance, could have had few places of darker tragedy, written
in tears and anguish, than Chimborazo Hospital in Richmond,
where as many as 7,000 soldiers sometimes suffered together;
yet it was life there that Mrs. Phoebe Pember described in
some of the most humorous writing of the war.

These Confederate soldiers and nurses and citizens of beleaguered towns had one inspiration that twentieth-century
America has not credited to them—the vigorous Revolutionary
tradition. The men who fought at Gettysburg were as close
in time to the turning point of that earlier struggle, the
Trenton-Princeton campaign of 1777, as readers of 1950 are
to the *dies irae* described by Colonel Frank Haskell in his famous account of the repulse of Pickett's charge. Many men
in the ranks, North and South, had seen old soldiers of the
Continental Army; thousands had heard stories of the sacrifices
of 1777 and of the hunger and nakedness at Valley Forge.
From its very nature, freedom was born in travail. Ignorant
men sensed this vaguely, if at all; the literate reread William
Gordon and Washington Irving and steeled themselves to like
hardship. To some of the commanders, and above all to Lee,
there daily was an inspiring analogy between the struggle of
the Confederacy and that of Revolutionary America under
the generalship of Lee's great hero, Washington. Many an-

other Southern soldier told himself the road was no more stony than the one that had carried his father and his grandfather at last to Yorktown. If independence was to be the reward, patience, good cheer and the tonic of laughter would bring it all the sooner.

Those Confederates believed they were as good judges of humor as, say, of horses; and both they and their adversaries in blue regarded themselves as strategists or, at least, as competent critics of strategy. Quick to perceive the aim of the marches they were called upon to make, they discussed by every campfire and on every riverbank the shrewdness or the blunders of the men who led them. After the manner of youth in every land and of every era, they made heroes of the officers they admired and they denounced the martinets, but, in time, most of them learned from their discussion and, considering the paucity of their information, came to broad strategical conclusions their seniors would not have been ashamed to own.

Many of the diarists and letter writers were observant, too, and not infrequently recorded important fact no officer set down in any report. If some of these writers let their vanity adorn their tale, the majority were of honest mind. One somewhat renowned *post-bellum* lecturer who should have been an invaluable witness, progressively lost the truth of his narrative as he made it more and more dramatic and egocentric, but he did not have many fellow offenders outside the ranks of those known and branded prevaricators who bored their comrades of the U.C.V. or the G.A.R. as they told how "they won" the battle or the war. On the other hand, Mr. Commager quotes in these pages several veterans who wrote long after the conflict, without access to records, and yet were so astonishingly accurate that any psychologist, chancing on their memoirs, will wish he might have studied in person the mentality of the authors.

These men and women had no literary inhibitions other than those of a decency that is to be respected both for itself and for the contrasts it suggests with certain later writing on war and warriors. If, incidentally, the restraint and modesty of most of the soldiers' letters of the eighteen-sixties were Victorian, then so much the better for Victorianism. This apart, every man felt free to write of anything—and considered himself as competent as free—with the result that the source materials of the conflict are opulently numerous and almost bewilderingly democratic. Private Casler may dispute in a footnote the pronouncements of the learned Dr.

Dabney on the strategy of "Old Jack"; the testimony of a boy who saw Grant once only may be preferred to that of a corps commander who conferred so often with "Unconditional Surrender" that, in retrospect, he confused the details of the various interviews.

Historically, then, it may be hoped that one result of the appearance of this book will be the use of other authorities than the few, such as "Rebel War Clerk" Jones and Mrs. Chesnut, for example, who have been overworked and, on some subjects, have been uncritically cited. The student will find that new witnesses have been made available, and that stirring tales have been assembled and prefaced sagely by an editor whose knowledge of the literature of 1861-65 in unexcelled. Henry Steele Commager has the admiration as well as the personal affection of all students who appreciate the catholicity of his scholarship and the penetrating justice of his judgment. Had members of his profession been asked by the publishers to name the individual best equipped to present "a history of the Civil War in the words of those who fought it," their choice would have been the man who flawlessly has rendered here that welcome service to the American people.

DOUGLAS SOUTHALL FREEMAN

Westbourne,
Richmond, Virginia,
August 14, 1950.

Introduction

We have fought six major wars in the last century or so, and four since Appomattox, but of them all it is the Civil War that has left the strongest impression on our minds, our imagination, and our hearts. It is the Civil War songs that we sing—who does not know "Marching Through Georgia" or "Tramp, Tramp, Tramp" or "Dixie"?—and that war gave us the one great battle hymn of our literature. It furnished our best war poetry, both at the time and since; no other war has produced anything as good as "Drum Taps" or the "Harvard Commemoration Ode," nor has any other been celebrated by an epic poem comparable to Stephen Benét's *John Brown's Body*. It has inspired more, and better, novels than any other of our wars and occasionally it excites even Hollywood to rise above mediocrity. It has furnished our standards of patriotism, gallantry, and fortitude; it has given us our most cherished military heroes—Lee and Jackson, Grant and Sherman, and Farragut, and a host of others, and it has given us, too, our greatest national hero and our greatest sectional one, Lincoln and Lee. No other chapter in our history has contributed so much to our traditions and our folklore. The very words—whether they are Civil War or War between the States—conjure up for us a hundred images: Jackson standing like a stone wall; U. S. Grant becoming Unconditional Surrender Grant; Lee astride Traveller, "It is well war is so terrible, or we should get too fond of it"; Barbara Frietchie waving her country's flag; A. P. Hill breaking through the wheat fields at Antietam; Thomas standing like a rock at Chickamauga; Pickett's men streaming up the long slope of Cemetery Ridge; Farragut lashed to the mast at Mobile Bay, "Damn the torpedoes, full steam ahead"; the Army of the Cumberland scrambling up the rugged heights of Missionary Ridge; Hood's Texans forcing Lee to the rear before they would close the gap at Spotsylvania; Sheridan dashing down the Winchester Pike; Lincoln pardoning the sleeping sentinels, reading Artemus Ward to his Cabinet, dedicating the battlefield of Gettysburg; Grant and Lee at Appomattox Court House.

It was, in many respects, a curious war, one in which amenities were often preserved. It could not begin until high-ranking officers of the army and navy had been permitted to resign and help organize a rebellion. Southerners tolerated outspoken Unionists, like Petigru or Botts; Northerners permitted Vallandigham to campaign openly against the war, and at the crisis of the conflict almost two million of them voted for a party that had formally pronounced the war a failure. Journalists seemed to circulate at will, and Northern papers had correspondents in the South while Confederates got much of their information about Federal army movements from the Northern newspapers. There was an immense amount of trading back and forth, some of it authorized or at least tolerated by the governments, and Sherman could say that Cincinnati furnished more supplies to the Confederacy than did Charleston. Officers had been trained in the same schools and fought in the same armies and most of them knew one another or knew of one another; Mrs. Pickett tells us that when her baby was born Grant's staff celebrated with bonfires. There was a great deal of fraternization both among soldiers and civilians. Pickets exchanged tobacco, food, and news; if Yankee officers did not marry Southern beauties as often as novelists imagined, there was at least some basis for the literary emphasis on romance. Confederates cheered Meagher's Irish Brigade as it charged up Marye's Heights, and the Yankees almost outdid the Confederates in admiration for Jackson and Pelham. There were plenty of atrocity stories, but few atrocities. There was a good deal of pillaging and vandalism—as in all wars—but little of that systematic destruction we know from two world wars or from the war in Vietnam. On the whole, civilians were safe; there were crimes against property but few against persons, and women everywhere were respected. When Butler affronted the ladies of New Orleans he was transferred to another command, and Sherman engaged in a wordy correspondence with the mayor of Atlanta seeking to justify what he thought a military necessity. Whether Sherman burned Columbia is still a matter of controversy; the interesting thing is that there should be a controversy at all. Both peoples subscribed to the same moral values and observed the same standards of conduct. Both displayed that "decent respect to the opinions of mankind" to which Jefferson had appealed three quarters of a century earlier. Both were convinced that the cause for which they fought was just—and their descendants still are.

Nor did the war come to an end, psychologically or emotionally, with Appomattox. Politicians nourished its issues; patriotic organizations cherished its memories; scholars refought its battles with unflagging enthusiasm. No other war has started so many controversies and for no other do they flourish so vigorously. Every step in the conflict, every major political decision, every campaign, almost every battle, has its own proud set of controversies, and of all the military figures only Lee stands above argument and debate. Was the election of Lincoln a threat to the South, and was secession justified? Was secession a revolutionary or a constitutional act, and was the war a rebellion or an international conflict? Was the choice of Davis a mistake, and did Davis interfere improperly in military affairs? Should the Confederacy have burned its cotton, or exported it? Was the blockade a success, and if so at what point? Should Britain have recognized the Confederacy, or did she go too far toward the assistance of the South as it was? Who was responsible for the attack on Fort Sumter, Lincoln or Beauregard, and was the call for 75,000 men an act of aggression? Was Jackson late at Seven Days? Was Grant surprised at Shiloh? Did the radicals sabotage McClellan's Peninsular campaign? Who was responsible for the disaster of Second Bull Run and was Fitz John Porter a marplot or a scapegoat? Should Lee have persisted in his offensive of the autumn of 1862 even after the discovery of the Lost Order? Should McClellan have renewed battle after Antietam? Why did Pemberton fail to link up with Johnston outside Vicksburg and why did Johnston fail to relieve Pemberton? Would Gettysburg have been different had Jackson been there, or had Longstreet seized Little Round Top on the morning of the second day, or had Pickett been properly supported on the third? Who was responsible for the Confederate failure at Stones River and who for the debacle of Missionary Ridge, and why did Davis keep Bragg in command so long? Could Johnston have saved Atlanta, and did Hood lose it? Was Hood's Tennessee campaign strategically sound but tactically mismanaged, or was it the other way around? Was Lee deceived during those critical June days when Grant flung his army across the James? And why did the Federals fail to break through the thin lines of Petersburg? Who burned Columbia, and was Sherman's theory of war justified? What really happened at Five Forks, and would the outcome have been different had Pickett been more alert?

What explains the failure to have supplies at Amelia Court House and could Lee have made good his escape and linked up with Johnston had the supplies been there? Could the Confederacy ever have won the war, or was defeat foredoomed; if defeat was not foredoomed what caused it? These and a thousand other questions are still avidly debated by a generation that has already forgotten the controversies of the Spanish War and the First World War.

Nor is it by chance that the cause lost on the battlefield should be celebrated in story and in history, or that victors and vanquished alike should exalt its heroism and cherish its leaders. Lee is only less of a hero than Lincoln, and the Federal Army boasts no figure so glamorous as Stonewall Jackson. Novelists have been kinder to the Confederacy than to the Union, and so, too, in our own day, the moving pictures and television. There is no literary monument to any Union general comparable to that erected to Lee by Douglas Freeman, and for a generation Northern historians found themselves apologizing for Appomattox.

From the point of view of the student of military history, too, the Civil War is inexhaustibly interesting, and it is no wonder that English, French, and German strategists and historians have assiduously studied its battles and campaigns. It was, in a sense, the last of the old wars and the first of the new. It had many of the characteristics of earlier wars—the chivalry that animated officers and men, and the mutual esteem in which the combatants held each other, for example; the old-fashioned weapons and tactics such as sabers and cavalry charges; the woeful lack of discipline; the pitiful inadequacy of medical and hospital services, of what we would now call service of supply, of any provision for welfare and morale; the almost total absence of any proper Intelligence service or adequate staff work, and the primitive state of maps; the casual and amateur air that prevaded it all. But it was, too, in many and interesting respects, a modern war, one that anticipated the "total" wars of the twentieth century. It was the first in which the whole nation was involved, and it is probable that a larger proportion of the population, North as well as South, was actually in uniform than in any previous war of modern history. It was the first in which there was an even partial control of the economy—this largely in the South rather than in the more fortunate North. It was the first in which a large-scale blockade was really effective if not indeed a decisive weapon. It was the first in which the railroad and the telegraph played a major role. It involved almost every known form of warfare: large-scale battles, guerrilla fighting, trench warfare, sieges and investments, bold forays into enemy country and large-scale invasions, amphibious warfare along coastal and inland waters, blockade, privateering, surface and sub-surface naval war, the war of propaganda and of nerves. It produced in Lee one of the supreme military geniuses of history, in Farragut one of the great naval captains; in Grant a major strategist; in Sherman, Thomas, Jackson, A. P. Hill, and Joseph E. Johnston captains whose tactics are still worthy of study; in Thomas a master of artillery; in Forrest and Stuart, Buford, Sheridan and Wilson, cavalry leaders whose exploits have rarely been surpassed.

Every war dramatizes the ordinary and accentuates the characteristic; more than any other in which we have ever been engaged the Civil War brought out in sharp relief those qualities that we think of as distinctively American. The American was practical, experimental, inventive, intelligent, self-reliant, opportunistic, energetic, careless, undisciplined, amateurish, equalitarian, sentimental, humorous, generous and moral. He believed that the civil was superior to the military even in war, and that privates were as good as officers, that it was wrong to begin a war or to fight in a cause that was not just, that a war should be fought according to rules, and that moral standards should obtain in war as in peace. Most of these qualities and principles were carried over from the civil to the military arena.

Thus the war discovered a people wholly unprepared, and never willing to prepare, either materially or psychologically. Neither side ever really organized for war; neither ever used the whole of its resources—though the South came far closer to this than the North; neither accepted the iron discipline which modern war imposes. The war required the subordination of the individual to the mass, of the particular to the general interest, and of the local to the central government; but both Federals and Confederates indulged their individualism in the army and out, rejected military standards and discipline, selected officers for almost any but military reasons, pursued local and state interest at the expense of the national. The war required organization and efficiency, but both sides conducted the war with monumental inefficiency—witness the shambles of conscription, or of the procurement of ordnance or of finances. The war required the husbanding of resources, but both sides wasted their resources, human and material—witness the medical services, or desertion, or the indulgence of business as usual, especially in the North.

The Americans were an educated, informed, self-reliant and resourceful people, and the Civil War armies probably boasted the highest level of intelligence of any armies in modern history up to that time. It took foreigners to remark this quality, however; Americans themselves took it for granted. Everyone, as both Dicey and Trollope remarked in wonder, read newspapers, followed political debates, and had opinions on the war, slavery, politics, and everything else; almost everyone—as an editor knows—kept a diary or a journal. Resourcefulness was almost their most striking quality. This resourcefulness appeared in Grant, who kept at it until he had found the road to Vicksburg; it appeared in Lee, who was able to adjust his plans to his shifting opponents, and to count on the understanding and co-operation of his lieutenants; it appeared in the engineers, who built dams and bridges, laid railroad tracks—or tore them up—solved problems of transport and supply that appeared insoluble; it appeared in the privates of both armies, who improvised breastworks or camp shelters, foraged for food and supplies, chose their own officers, voted in the field, provided their own newspapers, theatricals, and religious services, and often fought their own battles with such weapons as they could piece together. It appeared, too, in civilians, especially in the South, who managed somehow to improvise most of the weapons of war and the essentials of domestic economy, to make do with such labor and such materials as they had, and to hold society together through four years of strife and want.

Thus the conduct of the war confounded both the critics and the prophets. It was thought a people as unmilitary as the Americans could not fight a long war, or would not—but they did. It was thought that an agricultural South could not produce the matériel of war, but no single Southern defeat could be ascribed to lack of arms or equipment. It was supposed that neither side could finance a major war, but both managed somehow, and though Confederate finances were a shambles the North emerged from the conflict richer than she had entered it. To blockade thousands of miles of coast line, to invade an area of continental dimensions—these had never been done successfully in modern times, but the Union did them. Curiously, Europe was not convinced; the same basic errors of judgment that distinguished England and France during the Civil War reappeared in Germany in 1917 and in Germany, Italy, and France in 1940.

The Americans were a good-natured people, easygoing and

careless, and in a curious sense these qualities carried over
even into war. Lincoln set the tone here, for the North—
Lincoln, who somehow managed to mitigate the wrath of war
and his own melancholy with his humor, and who never referred to the Confederates as rebels; and Lee for the South,
Lee, who always called the enemy "those people." Relations
between the two armies were often good-natured: the very
names the combatants had for each other, Johnny Reb and
Billy Yank, testified to this. Only occasionally were relations
between these enemies who so deeply respected each other
exacerbated by official policy or by the prejudices of an officer. The soldiers themselves—boys for the most part, for it
was a boy's war—were high-spirited and amiable, and endured
endless discomforts and privations with good humor. Their
good humor emerged in their songs—"Goober Peas," "Mister,
Here's Your Mule," "Grafted into the Army," "We are the
Boys of Potomac's Ranks"—their stories, their campfire
jokes, so naïve and innocent for the most part; it spilled over
into their letters home and into the diaries and journals they
so assiduously kept. There was bitterness enough in the war,
especially for the South and for the women of the South, but
probably no other great civil war was attended by so little
bitterness during the conflict, and no other recorded so many
acts of kindness and civility between enemies; certainly no
other was so magnanimously concluded. Read over, for example, that moving account of the surrender at Appomattox by
Joshua Chamberlain:

Before us in proud humiliation stood the embodiment of manhood: men whom neither toils and sufferings, nor the fact
of death, nor disaster, nor hopelessness could bend from their
resolve; standing before us now, thin, worn, and famished, but
erect, and with eyes looking level with ours, waking memories
that bound us together as no other bond;—was not such manhood to be welcomed back into a Union so tested and assured? . . . How could we help falling on our knees, all of
us together, and praying God to pity and forgive us all!

The Americans thought themselves a moral people and
carried their ordinary moral standards over into the conduct
of war. They thought aggressive warfare wrong—except
against Indians—and the war could not get under way until
Beauregard had fired on Fort Sumter; Southerners insisted
that the firing was self-defense against Yankee aggression.
Every war is barbarous, but—the conduct of Sherman, Hunter,

and Sheridan to the contrary notwithstanding—there was less barbarism in the Civil than in most other wars, certainly less than in our own current wars. Both peoples, as Lincoln observed, read the same Bible and prayed to the same God; both armies were devout; leaders on both sides managed to convince themselves that they stood at Armageddon and battled for the Lord. When the end came there was no vengeance and no bloodshed; this was probably the only instance in modern history where rebellion was crushed without punishing its leaders.

Above all, the generation that fought the war had that quality which Emerson ascribed pre-eminently to the English —character. It is an elusive word, as almost all great words are elusive—truth, beauty, courage, loyalty, honor—but we know well enough what it means and know it when we see it. The men in blue and in gray who marched thirty miles a day through the blistering heat of the Bayou Teche, went without food for days on end, shivered through rain and snow in the mountains of Virginia and Tennessee, braved the terrors of hospital and prison, charged to almost certain death on the crest of Cemetery Ridge, closed the gap at the Bloody Angle, ran the batteries of Vicksburg and braved the torpedoes of Mobile Bay, threw away their lives on the hills outside Franklin for a cause they held dear—these men had character. They knew what they were fighting for, as well as men ever know this, and they fought with a tenacity and a courage rarely equaled in history. So, too, their leaders, civil and military. It is, in last analysis, grandeur of character that assures immortality to Lincoln as to Lee, and it is character, too, we admire in Grant and Jackson, Sherman and Thomas, the brave Reynolds and the gallant Pelham, and a thousand others. Winston Churchill tells us, in his account of Pearl Harbor, that there were some in England who feared the consequences of that fateful blow and doubted the ability of Americans to stand up to the test of modern war. "But I had studied the American Civil War," he says, "fought out to the last desperate inch," and "I went to bed and slept the sleep of the saved and thankful."

But it is a veteran of the war itself who paid the finest tribute to his comrades in blue and in gray. "Through our great good fortune," said Justice Oliver Wendell Holmes— and he spoke for his whole generation—

in our youth our hearts were touched with fire. It was given us to learn at the outset that life is a profound and passionate thing. While we are permitted to scorn nothing but indifference, and do not pretend to undervalue the worldly rewards of ambition, we have seen with our own eyes, beyond and above the gold fields, the snowy heights of honor, and it is for us to bear the report to those who come after us.

What I have tried to do in these volumes is very simple, but the execution of the task has been far from simple. I have tried to present a well-rounded—I cannot call it complete— history of the Civil War in the words of those who fought it. From the three hundred-odd narratives which are presented here there will emerge, I hope, a picture of the war that is authentic, coherent, and interesting. All depends, to be sure, on the selection and the editing of the material, and it is relevant therefore to say something about the principles that have governed that selection and about editorial practices.

Only those who have worked in the rich fields of Civil War history know how apparently inexhaustible the material is, and how unorganized. Only the Puritan Revolution and the French Revolutionary and Napoleonic wars boast a comparable literature, and even here the literature is not really comparable. For the American Civil War affected the whole population and, as Edward Dicey remarked in astonishment, it was a highly literate population. Almost everyone could write, and almost everyone, it seems, did. Surely no other chapter of modern history has been so faithfully or so elaborately recorded by ordinary men and women; in the American Civil War Everyman was, indeed, his own historian. A disproportionate body of the available material is, to be sure, from officers or from statesmen; these were the more articulate members of the population and those who could better arrange for the publication of what they wanted to say. But to a remarkable degree the privates kept records, and so too did the folks back home. Their reminiscences, recollections, and journals are to be found not in the handsomely published volumes from the great publishing houses, but in the pages of regimental histories, of state, local, and patriotic historical societies, of magazines that printed letters from veterans or from their families. The richness of this literature is the delight and the despair of every student.

My point of departure has not, however, been literature but history. My concern has been the particular battle or campaign, the particular military or social institution, and I have worked out from these to the available literature, selecting not primarily what was interesting for its own sake, or dramatic or eloquent, but what illuminated the subject and the problem. I do not mean to imply that I have been immune to the purely literary appeal, or to the appeal of drama or of personality. Needless to say it is not for authenticity alone that I have preferred Haskell's to a score of other accounts of Pickett's charge, or Chamberlain's to a dozen others of the surrender at Appomattox.

I have tried to cover the whole war; not only the military, which has attracted disproportionate attention, and the naval, but the economic, social, political, and diplomatic as well. The war was not all fighting; it was public opinion, it was the draft, it was prison and hospital, ordnance and supplies, politics and elections, religion, and even play. Approximately half the material in these volumes records the actual fighting; another half is devoted to the other aspects of the war. I have tried to hold even the balance between Union and Confederate, the East and the West, the military and the civil, and to give some representation to women and to foreign observers. I cannot suppose that I have wholly succeeded in all this, for the available material has not always lent itself to a balanced picture. As every student knows, good battle accounts are voluminous but accounts of Intelligence or ordnance or supply or the roles of the Blacks, North and South, are meager, and there are at least two capital descriptions of fighting for every one of politics or diplomacy or even of social conditions. Nor is the balance between the material available from officer and private really even. Almost every leading officer wrote his reminiscences or at least contributed them to the *Battles and Leaders* series, and the temptation to draw on these magisterial accounts has been irresistible. Nor do I feel unduly apologetic about drawing on Grant and Sherman, Longstreet and Hood and others; think what we would give for the war memoirs of R. E. Lee!

Even in the matter of proper representation from Federal and Confederate participants and from the East and the West I have not been entirely a free agent. There are considerably more Union than Confederate narratives—quite naturally, considering the relative numbers involved and the mechanics and economy of publishing. Again, the literature on the fighting in the East, especially in Northern Virginia, is far more voluminous and more interesting than that on the fighting in the West; the reasons for this are not wholly clear, but the fact will not, I think, be disputed by any student of the war and it is one to which an editor must accommodate himself as best he can.

There are, of course, many gaps in these volumes, and these will doubtless pain some readers. Those whose grandfathers were wounded at Perryville will object, quite properly, that that battle is neglected; others whose forebears fought at Fort Pillow will wonder why the massacre is not included; students of economic or social history will doubtless feel that these important subjects have been slighted, while military historians, alive to the importance in our own day of Intelligence or logistics, will feel that the fighting war has been overemphasized. In extenuation I can only plead the obvious. Some of the gaps in these volumes are dictated by considerations of space, others by availability of material. I could not put in everything; I could not even put in everything that was important. That is part of the story. The other part is that many of the things that interest us most did not appear to interest the generation that fought the war—or that read about it. There are descriptions enough of food and cooking, but no systematic account of the services of supply. There must be a hundred narratives of prison life and prison escape for every one of the organization and administration of prisons. If there is any good analysis of what we now call Intelligence, outside voluminous official correspondence, I do not know it.

I have tried in every case to get actual participants and observers to contribute to this co-operative history. Most of the contributors were participants in the physical sense; they experienced what Oliver Wendell Holmes called "the crush of Arctic ice." Others, and among them some of the most sagacious, were "behind the lines": poets who interpreted the significance of the war; diplomats who pleaded their country's cause abroad; women who lived "the lives which women have lead since Troy fell"; surgeons who treated the wounded and chaplains who comforted the dying. All these were participants even though they may not have held a musket, and all have something to tell us of the war.

It would be naïve for me, or for the reader, to suppose that the accounts here reproduced are in every case authentic, or that even the most authentic are wholly reliable. Most of those who claimed to be participants indoubtedly were so, but it would strain our imagination to suppose that all of our reporters actually witnessed everything they described. As every student of evidence knows, people do not always see what they think they see and they do not remember what they saw. There are doubtless many instances where soldiers, writing fifteen or twenty years after the event, deluded themselves, as well as their readers. They embroidered on their original stories; they incorporated into their accounts not only what they had experienced but what they had heard or read elsewhere; they went back and consulted official records and doctored their manuscripts. Soldiers whose companies did not actually get into a battle appear, in written recollections, in the thick of it; hangers-on, who have entertained their friends with the gossip of the capital for years, remember through the haze of time that they themselves directed great affairs of state.

All this is a commonplace of historical criticism, and there is no wholly effective safeguard against it. Diaries, journals, and letters are obviously to be preferred to later recollections, but there is no guarantee that diaries and letters conform to the strictest standards of accuracy and objectivity, or that they come to us untouched by the editorial pen, while many volumes of reminiscences, otherwise suspect for age, are based on diaries and letters and have claims on our confidence. Official reports are doubtless more reliable than merely personal accounts, but even official reports were often written months after the event and colored by imagination or wishful thinking, and there is no sound reason for supposing that the average officer, writing an official report, really knew the whole of what he was writing about.

We must keep in mind, too, that the Civil War was a far more casual affair than more recent wars. There was no proper organization for keeping records or for writing history. Even the most elementary facts are in dispute, and the statistical picture is a chaos. We do not know the numbers of those who fought on either side, or of those who took part in particular battles, or of casualties, and Confederate figures in these fields are mostly guesswork. Take so simple a matter as executions. Our literature tells us of innumerable executions. But Phisterer, author of a statistical handbook of the war, gives us three widely varying official figures, and historians who have gone into the matter accept none of them. Or take the matter of desertion. Both Ella Lonn and Fred Shannon have dealt with this at length, but about the best they can do for us is to give broad estimates. For what was desertion, after all? Were those who failed to register for conscription deserters, or those who having registered failed to show up? Were bounty jumpers deserters, and how often should one of them be counted? Were those who went home to visit their wives or to help get in the crops, and later returned to the army, deserters? Or what shall we say of the blockade? Was it ever really effective? How many blockade-runners were there, and how many of them got through the blockade? With the most elementary facts of the war in this state of confusion it is perhaps excessive to strain overmuch at discrepancies in accounts of the conduct of a company or a regiment in a particular battle.

Something should be said about the principles governing the reproduction of source material in these volumes. There has been no tinkering with the text except in three very minor details. First, in some instances where paragraphs seemed intolerably long, they have been broken up. Second, while I have faithfully indicated all omissions within any excerpt I have not thought it necessary to put the customary dots at the beginning and end of excerpts: these can usually be taken for granted. Third, in deference to modern usage I have capitalized the word Negro wherever it appears. Aside from these insignificant modifications the text appears here as it appears in the original source to which credit is given in the bibliography.

That authors themselves, or editors—often devoted wives or daughters—have sometimes tinkered with the text is, however, painfully clear. There is no protection against this, and nothing to be done about it short of going back to the original manuscript where that is available; ordinarily it is not available. And this leads me to a more important matter. Not only have I not presumed to correct spelling or punctuation, I have not attempted to correct factual statements or misstatements. To have done so would have involved both me and the reader in a wilderness of controversy. There are, after all, hundreds of histories that attempt to set the facts straight. Careful readers will therefore note many glaring errors in these accounts. Almost every soldier, for example, consistently exaggerated enemy strength, and enemy losses, and two accounts of the same battle will confidently submit wholly inconsistent statistical information. The reader must keep in mind that our contributors are not writing as scholarly historians. They are giving their story from their own point of view—a point of view at once circumscribed and biased. They are not only limited in their knowledge; they are often ignorant, prejudiced, and vain. Sometimes they are on the defensive; sometimes they are repeating rumor and gossip; sometimes they are yielding to the temptation of the purple passage; sometimes they are trying to make a good impression on the folks back home, or on posterity. The reader is warned: they are not always to be trusted. But there are some consolations and some safeguards. As we give both Federal and Confederate accounts the errors often cancel out. The vainglorious give themselves away, and so too the ignorant and the timid, while those who write with an eye on the verdict of history proclaim that fact in every line.

An enterprise of this nature, stretching over more than a decade, naturally incurs a great many debts and obligations. I could not have completed this work without the help of the staff of the Columbia University Library, who endured with patience and good humor continuous raids upon their collections and who co-operated generously in making their Civil War collection one of the best in the country. I am indebted, too, to libraries and librarians elsewhere: the Library of Congress, the New York Public Library, the libraries of Harvard University, the University of Virginia, the University of North Carolina, New York University, the University of California, to name but a few. To my graduate students who have helped in the arduous work of tracking down elusive books, transcribing and photostating, I am deeply indebted, and especially to Mrs. Elizabeth Kelley Bauer, Mr. Wilson Smith, and Mr. Leonard Levy. The editorial and production departments of The Bobbs-Merrill Company have co-operated far beyond the call of duty, and I owe a great deal to the sagacious judgment of Mr. Laurance Chambers, the astute editorial eye of Miss Judith Henley, the imaginative co-operation of Mr. Walter Hurley. To the many publishers, historical societies, university presses, and private individuals who have so generously given me permission to reproduce material in their control I am deeply grateful. To my wife, who magnanimously permitted the Yankees to win an occasional victory in these pages, my debt is, of course, beyond expression.

HENRY STEELE COMMAGER

Williamsville, Vermont
August, 1950
Amherst, Massachusetts
February, 1971

Contents

Foreword: *Douglas Southall Freeman*   **vii**

Introduction: *Henry Steele Commager*   **xiii**

Chapter

I. GETTYSBURG   **1**

  1. General Lee Decides to Take the Offensive:
     Robert E. Lee   **3**

  2. General Lee Invades Pennsylvania:
     William S. Christian   **6**

  3. The Armies Converge on Gettysburg:
     Henry J. Hunt   **8**

  4. Buford and Reynolds Hold up the Confederate
     Advance: *Joseph G. Rosengarten*   **13**

  5. A Boy Cannoneer Describes Hard Fighting
     on the First Day: *Augustus Buell*   **16**

  6. The Struggle for Little Round Top   **22**

     A. General Warren Seizes Little Round Top:
       Porter Farley   **23**

     B. Colonel Oates Almost Captures Little Round Top:
       William C. Oates   **27**

     C. The 20th Maine Saves Little Round Top:
       Theodore Gerrish   **32**

  7. High Tide at Gettysburg   **35**

     A. Alexander Gives the Signal to Start:
       E. P. Alexander   **37**

     B. Armistead Falls Beside the Enemy's Battery:
       James Longstreet   **42**

     C. "The Crest Is Safe": *Frank A. Haskell*   **44**

     D. "All This Will Come Right in the End":
       A. J. Fremantle   **51**

  8. General Lee Offers to Resign after Gettysburg:
     Robert E. Lee and Jefferson Davis   **53**

  9. "Bells Are Ringing Wildly":
     William Thompson Lusk   **57**

  10. "A New Birth of Freedom": *Abraham Lincoln*   **58**

Chapter

II. VICKSBURG AND PORT HUDSON   60

  1. "Onward to Vicksburg": *Charles E. Wilcox*   62

  2. A Union Woman Suffers Through the Siege
     of Vicksburg: *Anonymous*   71

  3. Vicksburg Surrenders: *U. S. Grant*   79

  4. General Banks Takes Port Hudson   85

    A. Eating Mules at Port Hudson: *Anonymous*   85

    B. Blue and Gray Fraternize after the Surrender
      of Port Hudson: *Anonymous*   87

  5. "The Father of Waters Again Goes Unvexed
     to the Sea": *Abraham Lincoln*   88

  6. General Morgan Invades the North   89

    A. Morgan's Cavalrymen Sweep Through Kentucky:
      Colonel Alston   90

    B. Morgan's Raid Comes to an Inglorious End:
      James B. McCreary   94

III. PRISONS, NORTH AND SOUTH   97

  1. Abner Small Suffers in Danville Prison:
     Abner Small   98

  2. Suffering in Andersonville Prison:
     Eliza F. Andrews   101

  3. The Bright Side of Libby Prison: *Frank E. Moran* 103

  4. The Awful Conditions at Fort Delaware:
     Randolph Abbott Shotwell   107

  5. The Privations of Life in Elmira Prison:
     Marcus B. Toney   111

IV. BEHIND THE LINES: THE NORTH   116

  1. Washington as a Camp: *Noah Brooks*   117

  2. Walt Whitman Looks Around in Wartime
     Washington: *Walt Whitman*   120

  3. Anna Dickinson Sees the Draft Riots in
     New York City: *Anna E. Dickinson*   124

  4. The Army of Lobbyists and Speculators:
     Régis de Trobriand   130

  5. Charles A. Dana Helps Stop Frauds in the
     War Department: *Charles A. Dana*   132

  6. Colonel Baker Outwits Bounty Jumpers and
     Brokers: *L. C. Baker*   135

  7. Confederate Plots Against the North   140

    A. A Confederate Plan to Seize Johnson's Island
      Is Frustrated: *H. B. Brown*   141

    B. The Confederates Attempt to Burn New York:
      John W. Headley   142

Chapter

V. BEHIND THE LINES: THE SOUTH   **146**

1. A War Clerk Suffers Scarcities in Richmond:
    J. B. Jones   147
2. Mr. Eggleston Recalls When Money Was Plentiful:
    George C. Eggleston   153
3. Parthenia Hague Tells How Women Outwitted
    the Blockade: *Parthenia A. Hague*   157
4. The Confederates Burn Their Cotton:
    Sarah Morgan Dawson   161
5. "The Yankees Are Coming": *Mary A. Ward*   163
6. "The Lives Which Women Have Lead Since
    Troy Fell": *Julia LeGrand*   166
7. "They Must Reap the Whirlwind":
    William T. Sherman   167
8. Georgia's Governor Laments Davis' Despotism:
    Joseph E. Brown   168
9. Peace at Any Price: *Jonathan Worth*   170
10. "The Man Who Held His Conscience Higher Than
    Their Praise": *Petigru Monument*   171

VI. HOSPITALS, SURGEONS, AND NURSES   **173**

1. George Townsend Describes the Wounded on the
    Peninsula: *George A. Townsend*   174
2. The Sanitary Commission to the Rescue:
    Katharine Wormeley   178
3. Clara Barton Surmounts the Faithlessness of
    Union Officers: *Clara Barton*   182
4. Susan Blackford Nurses the Wounded at Lynchburg:
    Susan Blackford   184
5. Cornelia Hancock Nurses Soldiers and Contrabands:
    Cornelia Hancock   187
6. The Ghastly Work of the Field Surgeons   191
    A. The Heartlessness of the Surgeons:
       Samuel Edmund Nichols   191
    B. The Horrors of the Wilderness:
       Augustus C. Brown   193
7. The Regimental Hospital: *Charles B. Johnson*   194

VII. THE COAST AND INLAND WATERS   **199**

1. The *Merrimac* and the *Monitor*   201
    A. The *Minnesota* Fights for Her Life in Hampton
       Roads: *Captain Van Brunt*   202

Chapter

    B. The *Monitor* Repels the *Merrimac: S. D. Greene*   205

  2. Commodore Farragut Captures New Orleans:
      George H. Perkins   208

  3. New Orleans Falls to the Yankees   212

    A. Julia LeGrand Describes the Surrender of
       New Orleans: *Julia LeGrand*   212

    B. General Butler Outrages the Moral Sentiment
       of the World: *Benjamin F. Butler*   214

    C. Palmerston Protests Butler's Proclamation:
       Viscount Palmerston   215

    D. "A More Impudent Proceeding Cannot Be
       Discovered": *Benjamin Moran*   215

  4. Ellet's Steam Rams Smash the Confederate Fleet at
     Memphis: *Alfred W. Ellet*   217

  5. Attack and Repulse at Battery Wagner:
     New York Tribune   222

  6. Farragut Damns the Torpedoes at Mobile Bay:
     John C. Kinney   228

  7. Lieutenant Cushing Torpedoes the *Albemarle:*
     W. B. Cushing   237

  8. The Confederates Repulse an Attack on
     Fort Fisher: *William Lamb*   239

  9. "It Beat Anything in History": *Augustus Buell*   245

VIII. THE BLOCKADE AND THE CRUISERS   250

  1. The United States Navy Blockades the Confederacy:
     Horatio L. Wait   252

  2. The *Robert E. Lee* Runs the Blockade:
     John Wilkinson   260

  3. The *Rob Roy* Runs the Blockade out of Havana:
     William Watson   264

  4. Blockade-Runners Supply Charleston:
     W. F. G. Peck   268

  5. Confederate Privateers Harry Northern
     Merchantmen   270

    A. The *Ivy* Prowls Outside New Orleans: *M. Repard* 271

    B. The *Jefferson Davis* Takes a Prize off Delaware:
       Captain Fitfield   271

  6. The *Georgia* Fires the *Bold Hunter:*
     James M. Morgan   273

  7. The *Kearsarge* Sinks the *Alabama* off Cherbourg:
     John McIntosh Kell   275

Chapter

IX. CHICKAMAUGA AND CHATTANOOGA   282

   1. The Federals Oppose Hood with Desperation:
     James R. Carnahan   284
   2. Thomas Stands Like a Rock at Chickamauga   288
     A. Longstreet Breaks the Federal Line:
       Daniel H. Hill   289
     B. Thomas Holds the Horseshoe Ridge:
       Gates P. Thruston   291
   3. Chattanooga under Siege: *W. F. G. Shanks*   294
   4. Hooker Wins the "Battle above the Clouds":
     Joseph G. Fullerton   301
   5. The Army of the Cumberland Carries Missionary
     Ridge   303
     A. "First One Flag, Then Another, Leads":
       William A. Morgan   304
     B. "Amid the Din of Battle 'Chickamauga' Could
       Be Heard": *James Connolly*   307
   6. "The Disaster Admits of No Palliation":
     Braxton Bragg   313
   7. Burnside Holds out at Knoxville: *Henry S. Burrage*   314

X. ATLANTA AND THE MARCH TO THE SEA   321

   1. General Sherman Takes Command:
     John Chipman Gray   323
   2. Sherman Marches from Chattanooga to Atlanta:
     William T. Sherman   325
   3. Johnston Halts Sherman at New Hope Church:
     Joseph E. Johnston   330
   4. Joe Johnston Gives Way to Hood   333
     A. President Davis Removes General Johnston
       before Atlanta: *Jefferson Davis*   334
     B. General Johnston Justifies Himself:
       Joseph E. Johnston   335
   5. Hardee Wins and Loses the Battle of Atlanta:
     Richard S. Tuthill   337
   6. "You Might as Well Appeal against the
     Thunder-Storm": *William T. Sherman*   341
   7. Sherman Marches from Atlanta to the Sea:
     William T. Sherman   344
   8. Sherman's "Bummers"   348
     A. A Good Word for the Bummers:
       Henry O. Dwight   349
     B. "We Were Proud of Our Foragers":
       Daniel Oakey   349

Chapter

    9. "The Heavens Were Lit Up with Flames from
        Burning Buildings": *Dolly Sumner Lunt*   **351**
  10. Eliza Andrews Comes Home Through the Burnt
        Country: *Eliza F. Andrews*   **354**
  11. The Burning of Columbia   **357**
    A. "A Scene of Shameful Confusion":
        George Ward Nichols   **357**
    B. Major Hitchcock Explains the Burning of
        Columbia: *Henry Hitchcock*   **360**
  12. General Sherman Thinks His Name May Live:
        William T. Sherman   **361**

XI. THE WILDERNESS   **364**

    1. U. S. Grant Plans His Spring Campaign: *U. S. Grant* **366**
    2. Colonel Porter Draws a Portrait of General Grant:
       Horace Porter   **368**
    3. Private Goss Describes the Battle of the Wilderness:
       Warren Lee Goss   **372**
    4. "Texans Always Move Them": *Anonymous*   **377**
    5. "Their Dead and Dying Piled Higher Than the
       Works": *Robert Stiles*   **380**
    6. Spotsylvania and the Bloody Angle: *Horace Porter* **383**
    7. "These Men Have Never Failed You on Any Field":
       John B. Gordon   **388**
    8. Grant Hurls His Men to Death at Cold Harbor:
       William C. Oates   **392**

XII. THE SIEGE OF PETERSBURG   **395**

    1. Grant's Army Crosses the James: *U. S. Grant*   **396**
    2. Beauregard Holds the Lines at Petersburg:
       G. T. Beauregard   **398**
    3. "A Hurricane of Shot and Shell":
       Augustus C. Brown   **404**
    4. The Mine and the Battle of the Crater: *John S. Wise* **408**
    5. Lee Stops Hancock at the Gates of Richmond:
       Richard W. Corbin   **413**
    6. The Iron Lines of Petersburg: *Luther Rice Mills*   **416**

XIII. THE VALLEY IN 1864   **420**

    1. V.M.I. Boys Fight at New Market: *John S. Wise*   **421**
    2. General Hunter Devastates the Valley:
       John D. Imboden   **428**

Chapter

3. General Ramseur Fights and Dies for His Country:
   S. D. Ramseur   431

4. Early Surprises the Federals at Cedar Creek:
   S. E. Howard   439

5. Sheridan Rides Down the Valley Pike to Victory
   and Fame: *P. H. Sheridan*   443

6. "The Valley Will Have Little in It for Man or Beast":
   P. H. Sheridan   448

XIV. LEE AND LINCOLN   450

1. Robert E. Lee Goes with His State   452
   A. "My Relatives, My Children, My Home":
      Robert E. Lee   452
   B. "I Never Desire Again to Draw My Sword":
      Robert E. Lee   453

2. "A Splendid Specimen of an English Gentleman":
   Lord Wolseley   454

3. "It Is Well War Is So Terrible, Or We Should Get
   Too Fond of It": *W. N. Pendleton*   456

4. Dr. Parks's Boy Visits Lee's Headquarters:
   Leighton Parks   457

5. "A Sadness I Had Never Before Seen upon His
   Face": *John B. Imboden*   462

6. Lee and Traveller Review the Army of Northern
   Virginia: *Robert E. Lee, Jr.*   464

7. "He Looked as Though He Was the Monarch of
   the World": *William C. Oates*   465

8. "The Field Resounded with Wild Shouts of Lee,
   Lee, Lee": *J. Catlett Gibson*   467

9. Lee Bids Farewell to the Army of Northern Virginia:
   Robert E. Lee   469

10. Nathaniel Hawthorne Calls on President Lincoln:
    Nathaniel Hawthorne   470

11. John Hay Lives with "The Tycoon" in the
    White House: *John Hay*   473

12. "My Paramount Object Is to Save the Union"   475
    A. "The Prayer of Twenty Millions":
       Horace Greeley   476
    B. "I Would Save the Union": *Abraham Lincoln*   477

13. "We Shall Nobly Save or Meanly Lose the Last,
    Best Hope of Earth": *Abraham Lincoln*   478

14. Lincoln Becomes the Great Emancipator   479
    A. Secretary Chase Recalls a Famous Cabinet
       Meeting: *Salmon P. Chase*   480

Chapter

  B. "Forever Free": *Abraham Lincoln*   482
15. Lincoln and Hay Follow the Election Returns:
    John Hay   483
16. Lincoln Replies to a Serenade: *Abraham Lincoln*   487
17. Lincoln Visits the Colored Soldiers at City Point:
    Horace Porter   488
18. "With Malice Toward None": *Abraham Lincoln*   491
19. Abraham Lincoln Is Assassinated: *Gideon Welles*   493

XV. THE SUNSET OF THE CONFEDERACY   498

  1. Thomas Annihilates Hood at Nashville:
     James H. Wilson   500
  2. "The Last Chance of the Confederacy":
     Alexander C. McClurg   506
  3. "Now Richmond Rocked in Her High Towers to
     Watch the Impending Issue":
     George A. Townsend   513
  4. "The Most Superb Soldier in All the World" Falls at
     Five Forks: *William Gordon McCabe*   519
  5. The Confederates Abandon Richmond   521
     A. "A Great Burst of Sobbing All over the Church":
        Constance C. Harrison   521
     B. "The Poor Colored People Thanked God that
        Their Sufferings Were Ended": *R. B. Prescott*   524
  6. The White Flag at Appomattox: *J. L. Chamberlain*   528
  7. General Lee Surrenders at Appomattox:
     Charles Marshall   536
  8. "The Whole Column Seemed Crowned with Red":
     J. L. Chamberlain   540
  9. The Stars and Stripes Are Raised over Fort Sumter:
     Mary Cadwalader Jones   544
 10. "Bow Down, Dear Land, for Thou Hast Found
     Release": *James Russell Lowell*   547

Bibliography and Acknowledgments   549
Index   564

NOTE: This volume represents Chapters xvii–xxxi of the hardcover edition published by The Bobbs-Merrill Company, Inc.

List of Maps

The Seat of the War in Pennsylvania and Maryland   11

The Battle of Gettysburg   24

The Vicksburg Campaign   64

Charleston Harbor   224

The Blockaded Coast   255

Chattanooga and Its Approaches   297

From Chattanooga to Atlanta   328

Savannah to Bentonville   356

The Wilderness   385

Defenses of Richmond and Petersburg   401

Franklin and Nashville   503

Petersburg to Appomattox   531

I

Gettysburg

THE *Battle of Gettysburg is commonly regarded as the turning point of the war. In a sense it was. Certainly it was high tide for the Confederacy; had Lee won at Gettysburg he might have gone on to Harrisburg, Philadelphia, Baltimore, or Washington, and while it is almost inconceivable that he could have captured and held any of these cities or transferred the theater of the war permanently to the North, a successful invasion might have had far-reaching consequences. It might have brought that foreign recognition so important to the survival of the Confederacy; it might have strengthened the peace party in the North, The Copperheads, and the draft rioters, and created a widespread demand for a negotiated peace. Needless to say all of these possibilities were in Lee's mind, and in the minds of Confederate leaders, in planning the invasion.*

Yet from the strategical point of view Gettysburg was not decisive. It was strategically far less important than Vicksburg, which cleared the Mississippi and cut off the West from the heart of the Confederacy. It is well to remember that there were almost two years of hard fighting ahead, and that in these months the South could still have won the war— won it not by successful invasion or even by overwhelming victories on the battlefield, but by wearing down the Northern will to fight. The draft riots came after Gettysburg; greenbacks and government bonds were lower in 1864 than in 1863; Lincoln thought that he was going to be defeated for re-election in the summer of 1864. It was, after all, the campaigns of 1864 that were decisive—Sherman's capture of

1

*Atlanta and the March to the Sea, and the attrition of Lee's
forces in the Wilderness.*

Yet Gettysburg remains the great battle of the war—the
one that everyone knows, the one that has inspired more
historical investigation—and more controversy, more fiction
and more poetry, than any other; it is wholly appropriate
that it gave its name to the most memorable of Lincoln's
addresses. The reason is not hard to find. It was the greatest
single battle ever fought in North America, both in numbers
actually involved and in casualties. It was marked by some
of the hardest fighting in the war, and as long as Americans
cherish courage such names as Peach Orchard, Little Round
Top, and Cemetery Ridge will quicken their pulses. There were
other fights as fierce as that for Culp's Hill—the Bloody
Angle for instance; there were other charges as gallant as
Pickett's—the Union charge up Missionary Ridge or the Con·
federate charge at Franklin; there were other battles whose
outcome was as uncertain—Shiloh or Antietam; there were
other days which exacted heavier casualties than any one
day of Gettysburg—Shiloh again. But no other single battle
combined so dramatically so many memorable scenes and
events.

Gettysburg was, in many respects, a curious battle, but
this might be said of most battles. It was, in a sense, an
accident: neither Lee nor Hooker wanted to fight at Gettysburg, though once the fighting had begun Meade—who suc·
ceeded Hooker—saw the advantages of the Gettysburg terrain
for defensive fighting. Neither strategically nor tactically
was it a well-fought battle, though Meade, whose task was
simpler, appears to better advantage in these matters than
Lee. That it was Lee's "worst-fought" battle is generally
agreed. He had allowed Stuart to go off on one of his junkets,
and was without his eyes. He missed those lieutenants who
had brought him victory in the past, especially the in·
comparable Jackson. Once the battle was joined the Confederates made a series of mistakes—mistakes that in the
end proved fateful: the failure to push on and seize Cemetery
Hill the first day, to occupy either Big or Little Round Top
early on the second day, to attempt a flanking movement
around the Union left, the delay in the assault on the third
day and the inability to concentrate all available forces for
that assault. Meade, too, fought a somewhat disorganized
battle. There was confusion on the first day, even in the
matter of command; there was a failure to use all potential
strength—four of seven Union corps bore the brunt of the

*battle; there was above all an egregious failure to follow up
victory by energetic pursuit.*

*The literature on Gettysburg is voluminous, and we can
only skim its surface. Here are accounts of the preliminary
skirmishing in the Valley, the invasion of Maryland and
Pennsylvania, the high points of each of the three days of
fighting, and the retreat. Wherever possible we have presented
Union and Confederate accounts of the same engagements.*

1. GENERAL LEE DECIDES TO TAKE THE OFFENSIVE

*After Fredericksburg and Chancellorsville, Lee decided once
more to carry the war to the North. Many considerations led
to this resolution, which he urged successfully on Davis and
his Cabinet. He wanted to take his army north of the Potomac
where he could find provisions for both men and horses. He
wanted to get clear of the Wilderness, to where he could
maneuver more effectively against the enemy. He hoped
that an invasion of the North would encourage Copperheads
and the peace movement in that section and that, if successful, it would hasten foreign recognition.*

*"I considered the problem in every possible phase," he
later recalled, "and to my mind, it resolved itself into a choice
of one of two things—either to retire to Richmond and stand
a siege, which must ultimately have ended in surrender, or to
invade Pennsylvania." We can follow, in his letters, the
crystallization of his plans.*

(CONFIDENTIAL.) HDQRS. ARMY OF NORTHERN VIRGINIA

June 8, 1863

Hon. JAMES A. SEDDON
    Secretary of War, Richmond, Va.:
    SIR:
    . . . As far as I can judge, there is nothing to be gained
by this army remaining quietly on the defensive, which it must
do unless it can be re-enforced. I am aware that there is
difficulty and hazard in taking the aggressive with so large
an army in its front, intrenched behind a river, where it
cannot be advantageously attacked. Unless it can be drawn
out in a position to be assailed, it will take its own time to

prepare and strengthen itself to renew its advance upon Richmond, and force this army back within the intrenchments of that city. This may be the result in any event; still, I think it is worth a trial to prevent such a catastrophe. Still, if the Department thinks it better to remain on the defensive, and guard as far as possible all the avenues of approach, and await the time of the enemy, I am ready to adopt this course. You have, therefore, only to inform me.

R. E. LEE,
General.

HEADQUARTERS ARMY OF NORTHERN VIRGINIA

June 10, 1863

His Excellency JEFFERSON DAVIS, *Richmond:*

MR. PRESIDENT: . . . Conceding to our enemies the superiority claimed by them in numbers, resources, and all the means and appliances for carrying on the war, we have no right to look for exemptions from the military consequences of a vigorous use of these advantages, excepting by such deliverance as the mercy of Heaven may accord to the courage of our soldiers, the justice of our cause, and the constancy and prayers of our people. While making the most we can of the means of resistance we possess, and gratefully accepting the measure of success with which God has blessed our efforts as an earnest of His approval and favor, it is nevertheless the part of wisdom to carefully measure and husband our strength, and not to expect from it more than in the ordinary course of affairs it is capable of accomplishing. We should not, therefore, conceal from ourselves that our resources in men are constantly diminishing, and the disproportion in this respect between us and our enemies, if they continue united in their efforts to subjugate us, is steadily augmenting.

The decrease of the aggregate of this army, as disclosed by the returns, affords an illustration of this fact. Its effective strength varies from time to time, but the falling off in its aggregate shows that its ranks are growing weaker and that its losses are not supplied by recruits.

Under these circumstances, we should neglect no honorable means of dividing and weakening our enemies, that they may feel some of the difficulties experienced by ourselves. It seems to me that the most effectual mode of accomplishing this object, now within our reach, is to give all the encouragement we can, consistently with truth, to the rising peace party of the North.

Nor do I think we should, in this connection, make nice distinction between those who declare for peace unconditionally and those who advocate it as a means of restoring the Union, however much we may prefer the former.

We should bear in mind that the friends of peace at the North must make concessions to the earnest desire that exists in the minds of their countrymen for a restoration of the Union, and that to hold out such a result as an inducement is essential to the success of their party.

Should the belief that peace will bring back the Union become general, the war would no longer be supported, and that, after all, is what we are interested in bringing about. When peace is proposed to us, it will be time enough to discuss its terms, and it is not the part of prudence to spurn the proposition in advance, merely because those who wish to make it believe, or affect to believe, that it will result in bringing us back to the Union. We entertain no such apprehensions, nor doubt that the desire of our people for a distinct and independent national existence will prove as steadfast under the influence of peaceful measures as it has shown itself in the midst of war. . . .

I am, with great respect, your obedient servant,

R. E. Lee,
General.

After Chancellorsville both armies marked time for a while. Hooker was too badly hurt to resume the offensive; Lee awaited reinforcement by Longstreet's corps. During May he carried through a reorganization of the command, dividing the army into three corps and appointing A. P. Hill commander of the new corps. Early in June, reinforced by Longstreet and by new recruits and conscripts, he embarked on the most famous of his offensives. Leaving A. P. Hill temporarily at Fredericksburg to tie down Hooker's vast army, Lee began to move his other two corps into the Valley. Hooker, who suspected that something was up, sent his cavalry under Pleasonton to probe out the Confederates; the clash with Stuart at Brandy Station was the largest cavalry engagement of the war, but ended in a draw.

Meantime Ewell moved down the Valley toward Winchester, which Milroy held with 9,000 men. Warned of the Confederate approach, Milroy decided to stay and fight it out. With an élan reminiscent of Stonewall Jackson, Ewell struck Milroy on June 14, drove him out of Winchester, bagged over 3,300 prisoners, and sent the Federals scurrying toward Harpers Ferry.

2. GENERAL LEE INVADES PENNSYLVANIA

The defeat of Milroy at Winchester and the withdrawal of the Federals from Harpers Ferry to Maryland Heights cleared the Valley; on the seventeenth Ewell forded the Potomac and occupied Hagerstown and Sharpsburg. Meantime Longstreet was swinging up on the east side of the Blue Ridge Mountains while Stuart's cavalry protected the passes on his right. Realizing that Lee had left Richmond practically undefended, Hooker wanted to launch an attack on that city, but was overruled by Lincoln, who insisted that Lee's army and not Richmond was his proper objective. "If the head of Lee's army is at Martinsburg and the tail of it on the plank road between Fredericksburg and Chancellorsville," he wrote, "the animal must be very slim somewhere. Could you not break him?" But by that time it was too late to "break him." Ewell was well into Pennsylvania; Longstreet's corps was splashing across the fords of the Potomac; Stuart had repulsed the Federals in several sharp cavalry engagements—Aldie, Middleburg, and Upperville—and was off on his foraging expedition.

This letter from William Christian reveals something of the spirit of Lee's troops as they invaded the North in that fateful June of 1863.

Camp near Greenwood, Pa., June 28, 1863.—My own darling wife: You can see by the date of this that we are now in Pennsylvania. We crossed the line day before yesterday and are resting today near a little one-horse town on the road to Gettysburg, which we will reach tomorrow. We are paying back these people for some of the damage they have done us, though we are not doing them half as bad as they done us. We are getting up all the horses, etc., and feeding our army with their beef and flour, etc., but there are strict orders about the interruption of any private property by individual soldiers.

Though with these orders, fowls and pigs and eatables don't stand much chance. I felt when I first came here that I would like to revenge myself upon these people for the desolation they have brought upon our own beautiful home, that home where we could have lived so happy, and that we loved so much, from which their vandalism has driven you and my helpless little ones. But though I have such severe wrongs and grievances to redress and such great cause for revenge, yet when I got among these people I could not find it in my heart to molest them. They looked so dreadfully scared and talked so humble that I have invariably endeavored to protect their property and have prevented soldiers from taking chickens, even in the main road; yet there is a good deal of plundering going on, confined principally to the taking of provisions. No houses were searched and robbed, like our houses were done by the Yankees. Pigs, chickens, geese, etc., are finding their way into our camp; it can't be prevented, and I can't think it ought to be. We must show them something of war. I have sent out today to get a good horse; I have no scruples about that, as they have taken mine. We took a lot of Negroes yesterday. I was offered my choice, but as I could not get them back home I would not take them. In fact my humanity revolted at taking the poor devils away from their homes. They were so scared that I turned them all loose.

I dined yesterday with two old maids. They treated me very well and seemed greatly in favor of peace. I have had a great deal of fun since I have been here. The country that we have passed through is beautiful, and everything in the greatest abundance. You never saw such a land of plenty. We could live here mighty well for the next twelve months, but I suppose old Hooker will try to put a stop to us pretty soon. Of course we will have to fight here, and when it comes it will be the biggest on record. Our men feel that there is to be no back-out. A defeat here would be ruinous. This army has never done such fighting as it will do now, and if we can whip the armies that are now gathering to oppose us, we will have everything in our own hands. We must conquer a peace. If we can come out of this country triumphant and victorious, having established a peace, we will bring back to our own land the greatest joy that ever crowned a people. We will show the Yankees this time how we can fight.

Be of good cheer, and write often to your fondly attached husband.

—Letter of William S. Christian

3. THE ARMIES CONVERGE ON GETTYSBURG

"It had not been intended to deliver a general battle so far from our base unless attacked," wrote General Lee later. "But coming unexpectedly upon the whole Federal army, to withdraw through the mountains with our extensive trains would have been difficult and dangerous." This was accurate enough, but not comprehensive. Had Stuart's cavalry been on the job, Lee would have known where the Federal army was, and how widely it was scattered. After being surprised at Brandy Station Stuart was eager to redeem himself and once more suggested riding around the Federal army. On June 22 Lee gave him somewhat ambiguous instructions to "move into Maryland and take position on Ewell's right." This was what Stuart wanted and off he went into Maryland and Pennsylvania. Not until July 1 did he learn that Lee's army was concentrated around Gettysburg.

Meantime Gordon Meade had supplanted Hooker in command of the Army of the Potomac. As General Hunt makes clear, both Hooker and Meade had hoped to fight behind Pipe Creek, in Maryland, and the seven corps of the army were spread out over a wide area south of Gettysburg. Only Buford's cavalry was in the town, and it was Buford who held up Heth when that general, hearing that there was a supply of shoes at Gettysburg, sent Pettigrew's brigade down the Chambersburg Pike on June 30.

General Hunt, who here recalls the beginnings of the great battle, was a veteran of the Mexican War and of the Peninsular, Antietam, and Fredericksburg campaigns. At this time he was chief of artillery of the Army of the Potomac.

Hearing nothing from Stuart, and therefore believing that Hooker was still south of the Potomac, Lee, on the afternoon of the 28th, ordered Longstreet and A.P. Hill to join Ewell at Harrisburg; but late that night one of Longstreet's scouts came in and reported that the Federal army had crossed the river, that Meade had relieved Hooker and was at Frederick. Lee thereupon changed the rendezvous of his army to Cashtown, which place Heth reached on the 29th. Next day Heth sent Pettigrew's brigade on to Gettysburg, nine miles, to procure a supply of shoes. Nearing this place, Pettigrew discovered the advance of a large Federal force and returned to Cashtown. Hill immediately notified Generals Lee and Ewell, informing the latter that he would advance next morning on Gettysburg. Buford, sending Merritt's brigade to

Mechanicstown as guard to his trains, had early on the morning of the 29th crossed into and moved up the Cumberland valley via Boonsboro' and Fairfield with those of Gamble and Devin, and on the afternoon of Tuesday, June 30th, under instructions from Pleasonton, entered Gettysburg, Pettigrew's brigade withdrawing on his approach.

From Gettysburg, near the eastern base of the Green Ridge, and covering all the upper passes into the Cumberland valley, good roads lead to all important points between the Susquehanna and the Potomac. It is therefore an important strategic position. On the west of the town, distant nearly half a mile, there is a somewhat elevated ridge running north and south, on which stands the "Lutheran Seminary." The ridge is covered with open woods through its whole length, and is terminated nearly a mile and a half north of the seminary by a commanding knoll, bare on its southern side, called Oak Hill. From this ridge the ground slopes gradually to the west, and again rising forms another ridge about 500 yards from the first upon which, nearly opposite the seminary, stand McPherson's farm buildings. The second ridge is wider, smoother, and lower than the first, and Oak Hill, their intersection, has a clear view of the slopes of both ridges and of the valley between them. West of McPherson's ridge Willoughby Run flows south into Marsh Creek. South of the farm buildings and directly opposite the seminary, a wood borders the run for about 300 yards, and stretches back to the summit of McPherson's ridge. From the town two roads run: one south-west to Hagerstown via Fairfield, the other northwesterly to Chambersburg via Cashtown. The seminary is midway between them, about 300 yards from each. Parallel to and 150 yards north of the Chambersburg pike, is the bed of an unfinished railroad, with deep cuttings through the two ridges. Directly north of the town the country is comparatively flat and open; on the east of it, Rock Creek flows south. On the south, and overlooking it, is a ridge of bold, high ground, terminated on the west by Cemetery Hill and on the east by Culp's Hill, which, bending to the south, extends half a mile or more and terminates in low grounds near Spangler's Spring. Culp's Hill is steep toward the east, is well wooded, and its eastern base is washed by Rock Creek.

Impressed by the importance of the position, Buford, expecting the early return of the enemy in force, assigned to Devin's brigade the country north, and to Gamble's that west of the town; sent out scouting parties on all the roads to collect information, and reported the condition of affairs to

Reynolds. His pickets extended from below the Fairfield road, along the eastern bank of Willoughby Run, to the railroad cut, then easterly some 1500 yards north of the town, to a wooded hillock near Rock Creek.

On the night of June 30th Meade's headquarters and the Artillery Reserve were at Taneytown; the First Corps at Marsh Run, the Eleventh at Emmitsburg, Third at Bridgeport, Twelfth at Littlestown, Second at Uniontown, Fifth at Union Mills, Sixth and Gregg's cavalry at Manchester, Kilpatrick's at Hanover. A glance at the map will show at what disadvantage Meade's army was now placed. Lee's whole army was nearing Gettysburg, while Meade's was scattered over a wide region to the east and south of that town.

Meade was now convinced that all designs on the Susquehanna had been abandoned; but as Lee's corps were reported as occupying the country from Chambersburg to Carlisle, he ordered, for the next day's moves, the First and Eleventh corps to Gettysburg, under Reynolds, the Third to Emmitsburg, the Second to Taneytown, the Fifth to Hanover, and the Twelfth to Two Taverns, directing Slocum to take command of the Fifth in addition to his own. The Sixth Corps was left at Manchester, thirty-four miles from Gettysburg, to await orders. But Meade, while conforming to the current of Lee's movement, was not merely drifting. The same afternoon he directed the chiefs of engineers and artillery to select a field of battle on which his army might be concentrated, whatever Lee's lines of approach, whether by Harrisburg or Gettysburg, —indicating the general line of Pipe Creek as a suitable locality. Carefully drawn instructions were sent to the corps commanders as to the occupation of this line, should it be ordered; but it was added that developments might cause the offensive to be assumed from present positions. These orders were afterward cited as indicating General Meade's intention not to fight at Gettysburg. They were, under any circumstances, wise and proper orders, and it would probably have been better had he concentrated his army behind Pipe Creek rather than at Gettysburg; but events finally controlled the actions of both leaders.

At 8 A.M., July 1st, Buford's scouts reported Heth's advance on the Cashtown road, when Gamble's brigade formed on McPherson's Ridge, from the Fairfield road to the railroad cut; one section of Calef's battery A, 2d United States, near the left his line, the other two across the Chambersburg or Cashtown pike. Devin formed his disposable squadrons from Gamble's right toward Oak Hill, from which he had afterward to trans-

THE SEAT OF THE WAR IN PENNSYLVANIA AND MARYLAND

fer them to the north of the town to meet Ewell. As Heth advanced, he threw Archer's brigade to the right, Davis's to the left of the Cashtown pike, with Pettigrew's and Brockenbrough's brigades in support. The Confederates advanced skirmishing heavily with Buford's dismounted troopers. Calef's battery, engaging double the number of its own guns, was served with an efficiency worthy of its former reputation as "Duncan's battery" in the Mexican war, and so enabled the cavalry to hold their long line for two hours. When Buford's report of the enemy's advance reached Reynolds, the latter, ordering Doubleday and Howard to follow, hastened toward Gettysburg with Wadsworth's small division (two brigades, Meredith's and Cutler's) and Hall's 2d Maine battery. As he approached he heard the sound of battle, and directing the troops to cross the fields toward the firing, galloped himself to the seminary, met Buford there, and both rode to the front, where the cavalry, dismounted, were gallantly holding their ground against heavy odds. After viewing the field, he sent back to hasten up Howard, and as the enemy's main line was now advancing to the attack, directed Doubleday, who had arrived in advance of his division, to look to the Fairfield road, sent Cutler with three of his five regiments north of the railroad cut, posted the other two under Colonel Fowler, of the 14th New York, south of the pike, and replaced Calef's battery by Hall's, thus relieving the cavalry. Cutler's line was hardly formed when it was struck by Davis's Confederate brigade on its front and right flank, where upon Wadsworth, to save it, ordered it to fall back to Seminary Ridge. This order not reaching the 147th New York, its gallant major, Harney, held that regiment to its position until, having lost half its numbers, the order to retire was repeated. Hall's battery was now imperiled, and it withdrew by sections, fighting at close canister range and suffering severely. Fowler thereupon changed his front to face Davis's brigade, which held the cut, and with Dawes's 6th Wisconsin—sent by Doubleday to aid the 147th New York—charged and drove Davis from the field. The Confederate brigade suffered severely, losing all its field-officers but two, and a large proportion of its men killed and captured, being disabled for further effective service that day.

—HUNT, "The First Day at Gettysburg"

4. BUFORD AND REYNOLDS HOLD UP THE CONFEDERATE ADVANCE

Lee concentrated his army more rapidly than Meade, Hill pushing on from the west of Gettysburg down the Chambersburg Pike, and Ewell coming down from the north. Only Buford's cavalry division was there to resist the Confederate advance—but that was a formidable force. There was some skirmishing on June 30; the real fighting got under way the next morning when, as we have seen, Buford's cavalrymen, fighting as dismounted troopers, put up a stiff resistance to Heth's and Pender's divisions, giving Reynolds time to hurry up with the I and XI Corps. At about midmorning Wadsworth's division took up position on Seminary Ridge, and from there sallied forth to capture a good part of Arthur's brigade. It was at this time that General Reynolds was killed.

Few officers in the Union Army had longer military experience than John Reynolds. He had served with distinction in the Mexican War and in the Mormon and Indian campaigns of the fifties, and the skill with which he commanded his troops at Fredericksburg and Chancellorsville marked him as one of the coming leaders of the Union forces. He was in command of the left wing of the Union army at Gettysburg, and the rapidity with which he brought up his scattered forces and the discernment which led him to order the occupation of Cemetery Hill contributed largely to ultimate Union victory.

Joseph Rosengarten was a major in the Army of the Potomac.

Reynolds knew Buford thoroughly, and knowing him and the value of cavalry under such a leader, sent them through the mountain passes beyond Gettysburg to find and feel the enemy. The old rule would have been to keep them back near the infantry, but Reynolds sent Buford on, and Buford went on, knowing that wherever Reynolds sent him, he was sure to be supported, followed, and secure. It was Buford who first attracted Reynolds' attention to the concentration of roads that gave Gettysburg its strategic importance, and it was Reynolds who first appreciated the strength and value of Cemetery Hill, and the plateau between that point and Round Top, as the stronghold to be secured for the concentration of the scattered corps and as the place where Meade could put his army to meet and overthrow the larger body he was pursuing. Together they found Gettysburg and made it the spot upon which the Union forces won a victory that was bought with his among the precious lives lost there. Buford and Reynolds were soldiers of the same order, and each found in the other just the qualities that were most needed to perfect and complete the task intrusted to them. The brilliant achievement of Buford, with his small body of cavalry, up to that time hardly appreciated as to the right use to be made of them, is but too little considered in the history of the battle of Gettysburg. It was his foresight and energy, his pluck and self-reliance, in thrusting forward his forces and pushing the enemy, and thus inviting, almost compelling their return, that brought on the engagement of the first of July.

Buford counted on Reynolds' support, and he had it fully, faithfully, and energetically. Reynolds counted in turn on having within his reach and at his immediate service at least the three corps that belonged to him, and there can be little question that if they had been up as promptly as he was in answer to Buford's call, the line he had marked out would have been fully manned and firmly held, while Meade's concentration behind Gettysburg would have gone on easily, and the whole of the Army of the Potomac would have done briefly and effectually what was gained only at the end of three days of hard fighting, with varying successes that more than once threatened to turn against us, and the loss on our side would have been so much less that the pursuit of Lee's forces could have been made promptly and irresistibly. It is not, however, given to all men to be of the same spirit, and the three corps that were under Reynolds followed his orders in a very different way from that in which he always did his work. When he got Buford's demand for infantry support on the morning of the first, it was just what Reynolds expected, and with characteristic energy, he went forward, saw Buford, accepted at once the responsibility, and returning to find the leading division of the First Corps (Wadsworth's), took it in hand, brought it to the front, put it in position, renewed his orders for the rest of the corps, assigned the positions for the other divisions, sent for his other corps, urged their coming with the greatest speed, directed the point to be held by the reserve, renewed his report to Meade that Buford had found the place for a battle, and that he had begun it, then calmly and coolly hurried some fresh troops forward to fill a gap in his lengthening lines, and as he returned to find fresh divisions, fell at the first onset.

The suddenness of the shock was in itself, perhaps, a relief to those who were nearest to Reynolds. In the full flush of life and health, vigorously leading on the troops in hand, and energetically summoning up the rest of his command, watching and even leading the attack of a comparatively small body, a glorious picture of the best type of military leader, superbly mounted, and horse and man sharing in the excitement of the shock of battle, Reynolds was, of course, a shining mark to the enemy's sharpshooters. He had taken his troops into a heavy growth of timber on the slope of a hill-side, and, under their regimental and brigade commanders, the men did their work well and promptly. Returning to join the expected divisions, he was struck by a Minnie ball, fired by a sharpshooter hidden in the branches of a tree almost overhead, and killed at once; his horse bore him to the little clump of trees, where a cairn of stones and a rude mark on the bark, now almost overgrown, still tells the fatal spot. The battle went on in varying fortune, and so long as the influence of his orders that had inspired men and officers could still be felt, all went well; but when the command had been changed by the successive arrival of generals who outranked each other, what there was of plan could hardly be made out, and the troops of the First Corps, without reinforcements and worn out and outnumbered, fell back at first with some show of order, and then as best they could, to find shelter in the lines pointed out by Reynolds for the concentration of his fresh troops. Thus even after his death, his military foresight had provided for the temporary defeat, which prepared the way for the great victory.

It is a striking proof of the discipline he had taught his own corps, that the news of the death, although it spread rapidly and that at a time when the inequality of numbers became apparent, produced no ill effect, led to no disorder, changed no disposition that he had directed, and in itself made the men only the more eager to carry out his orders. At the moment that his body was taken to the rear, for his death was instantaneous, two of his most gallant staff officers, Captain Riddle and Captain Wadsworth, in pursuance of his directions, effected a slight movement which made prisoners of Archer's Brigade, so that the rebel prisoners went to the rear almost at the same time, and their respectful conduct was in itself the highest tribute they could pay to him who had thus fallen.

—ROSENGARTEN, "General Reynolds' Last Battle"

5. A BOY CANNONEER DESCRIBES HARD FIGHTING ON THE FIRST DAY

The great battles of the second and third days of Gettysburg have overshadowed the fighting on the first. Had the battle ended with the retreat of the Federals on the afternoon of the first, it would still have gone down in history as one of the hardest fought engagements of the war. The stout resistance of Buford, the charge of Archer's brigade, the sharp fighting along Willoughby's Run, the desperate struggle for the railway cut, the final victorious advance of Pender's and Heth's divisions that hurled the Federals back through Gettysburg to Cemetery and Culp's hills—all these engagements added up to a major battle.

By late afternoon of July 1 the Union front had collapsed, but Schurz and Doubleday managed to retire in good order through Gettysburg and to the hills south of the town. The Confederates had bagged almost 5,000 prisoners and were confidently anticipating another Chancellorsville.

There is no better account of the first day's fighting than that by "cannoneer" Augustus Buell, member of a famous artillery brigade attached to the 1st division of the I Corps of the Army of the Potomac.

We were turned out the next morning about daybreak [July 1, 1863], harnessed up, and, after crossing the creek, halted to let the infantry of Wadsworth's Division file by. There was no mistake now. While we stood there watching these splendid soldiers file by with their long, swinging "route-step," and their muskets glittering in the rays of the rising sun, there came out of the northwest a sullen "boom! boom! boom!" of three guns, followed almost immediately by a prolonged crackling sound, which, at that distance, reminded one very much of the snapping of a dry brush-heap when you first set it on fire. We soon reasoned out the state of affairs up in front. Buford, we calculated, had engaged the leading infantry of Lee's army, and was probably trying to hold them with his cavalry in heavy skirmish line, dismounted, until our infantry could come up. They said that the enemy had not yet developed more than a skirmish line, because if he had shown a heavy formation Buford would be using his artillery, of which he had two or three batteries, whereas we had thus far heard only the three cannon shots mentioned. These apparently trifling incidents show how the men in our

Army were in the habit of observing things, and how unerring their judgment was, as a rule, even in matters of military knowledge far beyond their sphere or control.

But my eyes were riveted on the infantry marching by. No one now living will ever again see those two brigades of Wadsworth's Division—Cutler's and the Iron Brigade—file by as they did that morning. The little creek made a depression in the road, with a gentle ascent on either side, so that from our point of view the column, as it came down one slope and up the other, had the effect of huge blue billows of men topped with a spray of shining steel, and the whole spectacle was calculated to give nerve to a man who had none before. Partly because they had served together a long time, and, no doubt, because so many of their men were in our ranks, there was a great affinity between the Battery and the Iron Brigade, which expressed itself in cheers and good-natured chaffing between us as they went by. "Find a good place to camp; be sure and get near a good dry rail fence; tell the Johnnies we will be right along," were the salutations that passed on our part, while the infantry made such responses as "All right; better stay here till we send for you; the climate up there may be unhealthy just now for such delicate creatures as you," and all that sort of thing. It was probably 8 o'clock when the last brigade had passed, and then we got the order to march, moving with Doubleday's Division. As we moved up the road we could see the troops of the next division coming close behind. By this time the leading regiments of Wadsworth's infantry had got on the ground, and the sounds of battle were increasing rapidly. . . .

The sounds of the cavalry fight had been distinct ever since we left Marsh Creek—a fitful crackle—but now we heard fierce, angry crash on crash, rapidly growing in volume and intensity, signifying that our leading infantry—Cutler's and the Iron Brigade—had encountered the "doughboys" of Lee's advance. It is well known that the men of the Iron Brigade always preferred slouch hats (Western fashion), and seldom or never wore caps. At the time this heavy crashing began we were probably half way up from Marsh Creek, and, as the Battery was marching at a walk, most of us were walking along with the guns instead of riding on the limbers. Among the Cannoneers was a man from the 2d Wisconsin (John Holland) who took great pride in the Iron Brigade. So, when that sudden crash! crash! crash! floated over the hills to our ears, John said, with visible enthusiasm, "Hear that, my

son! That's the talk! The old slouch hats have got there, you
bet!!"

Now the artillery began to play in earnest, and it was
evident that the three batteries which had preceded us were
closely engaged, while the musketry had grown from the
crackling sound of the skirmishing we had heard early in
the morning to an almost incessant crash, which betokened
the file firing of a main line of battle. Just before reaching the
brow of the hill, south of the town, where we could get our
first sight of the battle itself, there was a provoking halt of
nearly half an hour. We could hear every sound, even the
yells of the troops fighting on the ridge beyond Gettysburg,
and we could see the smoke mount up and float away lazily
to the northeastward; but we could not see the combatants.
While halted here Doubleday's Division passed up the road,
each regiment breaking into double quick as it reached the
top of the hill. The Eleventh Corps also began by this time to
arrive from Emmittsburg. Finally, when the last of the Second
Brigade of Doubleday's (Stone's) had passed, we got the order
to advance again, and in two minutes the whole scene burst
upon us like the lifting of the curtain in a grand play. The
spectacle was simply stupendous. It is doubtful if there was
ever a battle fought elsewhere of which such a complete
view was possible from one point as we got of that battle
when we reached the top of the hill abreast of Round
Top. . . .

Our guns pointed about due west, taking the Cashtown Pike
en echarpe. The right half-battery was in line with us on the
north side of the cut. Its right gun rested on the edge of a
little grove, which extended some distance farther to the
right, and was full of infantry (the 11th Pennsylvania) supporting us. There was also infantry in our rear, behind the
crest and in the Railroad Cut (the 6th Wisconsin). One of our
squad volunteered the facetious remark that these infantry
"were put there to shoot the recruits if they flinched," for
which he was rebuked by Corp'l Packard, who told him to
"see that he himself behaved as well as the recruits." As
Stewart commanded the right half-battery in person, he did
not have much to do with us, directly, during the action that
followed.

At this time, which was probably about noon, all the infantry of the First Corps, except that massed immediately
about our position, together with Hall's, Reynolds's and one of
the cavalry horse-batteries—Calef's—had been struggling desperately in the fields in our front, and for a few moments

we had nothing to do but witness the magnificent scene. The enemy had some batteries firing down the pike, but their shot—probably canister—did not reach us. In a few minutes they opened with shell from a battery on a high knoll to the north of us (Oak Hill), and, though at long range, directly enfilading our line. But they sent their shells at the troops who were out in advance. We stood to the guns and watched the infantry combat in our front. Over across the creek (Willoughby's) we could see the gray masses of the Rebel infantry coming along all the roads and deploying in the fields, and it seemed that they were innumerable. At this time some 200 or 300 Rebel prisoners passed by our position on their way to our rear. They were a tough-looking set. Some had bloody rags tied round their limbs or heads, where they had received slight wounds.

In the meantime our infantry out in the field toward the creek was being slowly but surely overpowered, and our lines were being forced in toward the Seminary. It was now considerably past noon. In addition to the struggle going on in our immediate front, the sounds of a heavy attack from the north side were heard, and away out beyond the creek, to the south, a strong force could be seen advancing and overlapping our left. The enemy was coming nearer, both in front and on the north, and stray balls began to zip and whistle around our ears with unpleasant frequency. Then we saw the batteries that had been holding the position in advance of us limber up and fall back toward the Seminary, and the enemy simultaneously advance his batteries down the road. All our infantry out toward the creek on both sides of the pike began to fall back.

The enemy did not press them very closely, but halted for nearly an hour to reform his lines, which had been very much shattered by the battle of the forenoon. At last, having reformed his lines behind the low ridges in front, he made his appearance in grand shape. His line stretched from the railroad grading across the Cashtown Pike, and through the fields south of it half way to the Fairfield Road—nearly a mile in length. First we could see the tips of their color-staffs coming up over the little ridge, then the points of their bayonets, and then the Johnnies themselves, coming on with a steady tramp, tramp, and with loud yells. It was now apparent that the old Battery's turn had come again, and the embattled boys who stood so grimly at their posts felt that another page must be added to the record of Buena Vista and Antietam. The term "boys" is literally true, because of our gun detachment alone, consisting of a Sergeant, two Corporals, seven Cannoneers and six Drivers, only four had hair on their faces, while the other 12 were beardless boys whose ages would not average 19 years, and who, at any other period of our history, would have been at school! The same was more or less true of all the other gun detachments. But if boys in years they were, with one or two exceptions not necessary to name, veterans in battle, and braver or steadier soldiers than they were never faced a foe! A glance along our line at that moment would have been a rare study for an artist. As the day was very hot many of the boys had their jackets off, some with sleeves rolled up, and they exchanged little words of cheer with each other as the gray line came on. In quick, sharp tones, like successive reports of a repeating rifle, came Davison's orders: "Load—Canister—Double!" There was a hustling of Cannoneers, a few thumps of the rammer-heads, and then "Ready!—By piece!—At will!—Fire!!" . . .

Directly in our front—that is to say, on both sides of the pike—the Rebel infantry, whose left lapped the north side of the pike quite up to the line of the railroad grading, had been forced to halt and lie down by the tornado of canister that we had given them from the moment they came in sight over the bank of the creek. But the regiments in the field to their right (south side) of the pike kept on, and kept swinging their right flanks forward as if to take us in reverse or cut us off from the rest of our troops near the Seminary. At this moment Davison, bleeding from two desperate wounds, and so weak that one of the men had to hold him up on his feet (one ankle being totally shattered by a bullet), ordered us to form the half-battery, action left, by wheeling on the left gun as a pivot, so as to bring the half-battery on a line with the Cashtown Pike, muzzles facing south, his object being to rake the front of the Rebel line closing in on us from that side.

Of the four men left at our gun when this order was given two had bloody heads, but they were still "standing by," and Ord. Serg't Mitchell jumped on our off wheels to help us. "This is tough work, boys" he shouted, as we wheeled the gun around, "but we are good for it."

And Pat Wallace, tugging at the near wheel, shouted back: "If we ain't, where'll you find them that is!"

Well, this change of front gave us a clean rake along the Rebel line for a whole brigade length, but it exposed our right flank to the raking volleys of their infantry near the pike, who at that moment began to get up again and come on. Then for seven or eight minutes ensued probably the most desperate fight ever waged between artillery and infantry at close range without a particle of cover on either side. They gave us volley after volley in front and flank, and we gave them double canister as fast as we could load. The 6th Wisconsin and 11th Pennsylvania men crawled up over the bank of the cut or behind the rail fence in rear of Stewart's caissons and joined their musketry to our canister, while from the north side of the cut flashed the chainlightning of the Old Man's half-battery in one solid streak!

At this time our left half-battery, taking their first line *en echarpe,* swept it so clean with double canister that the Rebels sagged away from the road to get cover from the fences and trees that lined it. From our second round on a gray squirrel could not have crossed the road alive.

How those peerless Cannoneers sprang to their work! Twenty-six years have but softened in memory the picture of "Old Griff" (Wallace), his tough Irish face set in hard lines with the unflinching resolution that filled his soul, while he sponged and loaded under that murderous musketry with the precision of barrack drill; of the burly Corporal, bareheaded, his hair matted with blood from a scalp wound, and wiping the crimson fluid out of his eyes to sight the gun; of the steady Orderly Sergeant, John Mitchell, moving calmly from gun to gun, now and then changing men about as one after another was hit and fell, stooping over a wounded man to help him up, or aiding another to stagger to the rear; of the dauntless Davison on foot among the guns, cheering the men, praising this one and that one, and ever and anon profanely exhorting us to "Feed it to 'em, G— d— em; feed it to 'em!" The very guns became things of life—not implements, but comrades. Every man was doing the work of two or three. At our gun at the finish there were only the Corporal, No. 1 and No. 3, with two drivers fetching ammunition. The water in Pat's bucket was like ink. His face and hands were smeared all over with burnt powder. The thumbstall of No. 3 was burned to a crisp by the hot vent-field. Between the black of the burnt powder and the crimson streaks from his bloody head, Packard looked like a demon from below! Up and down the line men reeling and falling; splinters flying from wheels and axles where bullets hit; in rear, horses tearing and plunging, mad with wounds or terror; drivers yelling, shells bursting, shot shrieking overhead, howling about our ears or throwing up great clouds of dust where they struck; the musketry crashing on three sides of us; bullets hissing, humming and whistling everywhere; cannon roaring; all crash on crash and peal on peal, smoke, dust, splinters, blood, wreck and carnage indescribable; but the brass guns of Old B still bellowed and not a man or boy flinched or faltered! Every man's shirt soaked with sweat and many of them sopped with blood from wounds not severe enough to make such bulldogs "let go"—bareheaded, sleeves rolled up, faces blackened—oh! if such a picture could be spread on canvas to the life! Out in front of us an undulating field, filled almost as far as the eye could see with a long, low, gray line creeping toward us, fairly fringed with flame! . . .

For a few moments the whole Rebel line, clear down to the Fairfield Road, seemed to waver, and we thought that maybe we could repulse them, single-handed as we were. At any rate, about our fifth or sixth round after changing front made their first line south of the pike halt, and many of them sought cover behind trees in the field or ran back to the rail fence parallel to the pike at that point, from which they resumed their musketry. But their second line came steadily on, and as Davison had now succumbed to his wounds Ord. Serg't Mitchell took command and gave the order to limber to the rear, the 6th Wisconsin and the 11th Pennsylvania having begun to fall back down the railroad track toward the town, turning about and firing at will as they retreated.

—BUELL, *"The Cannoneer"*

6. THE STRUGGLE FOR LITTLE ROUND TOP

Gettysburg was won, and lost, on the second day, and the outcome of that day's fighting was determined largely by geography, or by the enterprise of Union commanders in taking advantage of geography. The terrain of the second and third days of the battle is familiar enough. Immediately to the south of Gettysburg lies an irregular string of hills forming, as has often been noted, a giant fishhook almost four miles in length: the eye at Round Top, the shank along Cemetery Ridge, the bend at Cemetery Hill, the barb curving around Culp's Hill. The approach to these hills was everywhere difficult. The slope up to Cemetery Ridge was covered by wheat fields, orchards and patches of woods; the fields in front of the Round Tops, Cemetery and Culp's hills were littered with boulders and underbrush.

On the afternoon of the first Lee, who saw the strategical importance of Cemetery and Culp's hills, ordered Ewell to seize them "if possible." That evening, before Ewell could carry out these instructions, Wadsworth entrenched himself on Culp's Hill and Steinwehr and Schurz took position on Cemetery Hill; Ewell did not find it possible to advance. Longstreet's corps came up during the night, and Lee planned a general assault on the Union lines early the next morning. But Meade, too, had some appreciation of terrain, and as brigade after brigade marched in during the night and next morning—many of them exhausted with long marches—they were assigned positions all along Cemetery Ridge and Culp's Hill. Not until three o'clock in the afternoon did Longstreet's offensive get under way. By that time the Union positions were bristling with guns and men.

Prompt action might still have given victory to the Confederates. For there was an Achilles' heel in the Union position: the Round Tops. Sickles had been ordered to occupy the Round Tops but had chosen, instead, to probe the ground in front of Little Round Top and there—at the Peach Orchard—ran into Longstreet's corps and suffered severe losses. Meantime the Round Tops were all but undefended. Late in the afternoon Hood, who had begged hard to be allowed to swing south of the Federal position and outflank it—a perfectly feasible plan—started for Little Round Top. Just in time General Warren discovered its defenseless position and ordered elements of the V Corps to hurry to its defense. There ensued one of the fiercest fights not only of the battle but of the entire war. It was a touch and go affair, but in the end the Federals held the hill.

We give here three accounts of the struggle for Little Round Top. The first is by Captain Porter Farley, a Rochester boy who enlisted in the 140th New York Volunteers, fought through the last years of the war, and later became one of the most distinguished of upstate New York surgeons; it tells how Warren's instant understanding of the importance of Little Round Top came just in time to save the Union position. The second is by William Oates, colonel of the 15th Alabama Infantry and later governor of his state. The third is by Theodore Gerrish of the 20th Maine Volunteers—a regiment which bore the brunt of the fighting.

A. GENERAL WARREN SEIZES LITTLE ROUND TOP

The leading regiments of our brigade were just passing over that slightly elevated ground north of Little Round Top

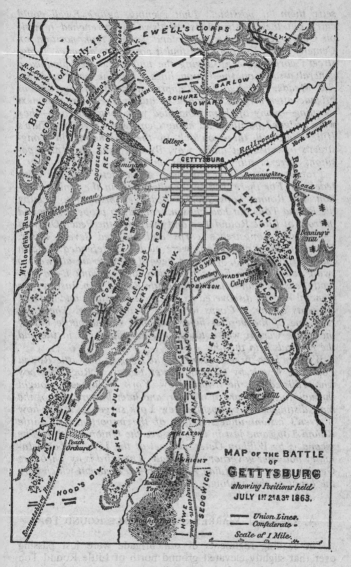

MAP of the BATTLE
OF
GETTYSBURG

showing Positions held
JULY 1ST 2ND & 3RD 1863.

Union Lines.
Confederate.

Scale of 1 Mile.

when down its slopes on our left, accompanied by a single
mounted officer and an orderly, rode General G. K. Warren,
our former brigade commander, then acting as General
Meade's chief engineer. Warren came straight toward the head
of the regiment, where I was riding with the colonel. He called
out to O'Rorke, beginning to speak while still some eight or
ten rods from us, that he wanted us to come up there, that the
enemy were advancing unopposed up the opposite side of the
hill, down which he had just come, and he wanted our regiment to meet them. He was evidently greatly excited and spoke
in his usual impulsive style.

O'Rorke answered, "General Weed is ahead and expects me
to follow him."

'Never mind that," said Warren, "bring your regiment up
here and I will take the responsibility."

It was a perplexing situation, but without hesitating O'Rorke
turned to the left and followed the officer who had been riding with Warren, while Warren himself rode rapidly down the
stony hill, whether in the direction from which we had just
come or to overtake the rest of our brigade I cannot say, but
evidently to find and order up more troops. . . .

We turned off the road to our left and rushed along the
wooded, rocky, eastern slope of Little Round Top, ascending
it while at the same time moving toward its southern extremity.
It was just here that some of the guns of Hazlett's battery came
rapidly up and plunged directly through our ranks, the horses
being urged to frantic efforts by the whips of their drivers and
the cannoniers assisting at the wheels, so great was the effort
necessary to drag the guns and caissons up the ragged hill-
side.

As we reached the crest a never to be forgotten scene
burst upon us. A great basin lay before us full of smoke and
fire, and literally swarming with riderless horses and fighting,
fleeing and pursuing men. The air was saturated with the sul-
phurous fumes of battle and was ringing with the shouts and
groans of the combatants. The wild cries of charging lines, the
rattle of musketry, the booming of artillery and the shrieks of
the wounded were the orchestral accompaniments of a scene
like very hell itself—as terrific as the warring of Milton's
fiends in Pandemonium. The whole of Sickles's corps, and
many other troops which had been sent to its support in that
ill-chosen hollow, were being slaughtered and driven before
the impetuous advance of Longstreet. But fascinating as was
this terrible scene we had no time to spend upon it. Bloody
work was ready for us at our very feet.

Round Top, a conical hill several hundred feet in height, lay just to the south of us, and was separated from Little Round Top, on whose crest we were now moving, by a broad ravine leading down into the basin where the great fight was raging. Right up this ravine, which offered the easiest place of ascent, a rebel force, outflanking all our troops in the plain below, was advancing at the very moment when we reached the crest of the hill. Vincent's brigade of the First division of our corps, had come up through the woods on the left and were just getting into position, and the right of their line had opened fire in the hollow on our left when the head of our regiment came over the hill. As soon as we reached the crest bullets came flying in among us. We were moving with the right in front and not a musket was loaded, a fact which Warren of course knew nothing about when he rushed us up there. The enemy were coming from our right and to face them would bring our file closers in front. The order, "On the right, by file into line," would have brought us into proper position; but there was no time to execute it, not even time to allow the natural impulse which manifested itself on the part of the men to halt and load the instant we received the enemy's fire.

O'Rorke did not hesitate a moment. "Dismount," he said to me, for the ground before us was too rough to ride over. We sprung from our horses and gave them to the sergeant major. O'Rorke shouted, "Down this way, boys," and following him we rushed down the rocky slope with all the same moral effect upon the rebels, who saw us coming, as if our bayonets had been fixed and we ready to charge upon them. Coming abreast of Vincent's brigade, and taking advantage of such shelter as the huge rocks lying about there afforded, the men loaded and fired, and in less time than it takes to write it the onslaught of the rebels was fairly checked, and in a few minutes the woods in front of us were cleared except for the dead and wounded. Such of the rebels as had approached so near as to make escape almost impossible dropped their guns, threw up their hands, and upon a slight slackening of our fire rushed in upon us, and gave themselves up as prisoners, while those not so near took advantage of the chance left them and retreated in disorder.

—FARLEY, "Reminiscences of the 140th New York Volunteers"

B. COLONEL OATES ALMOST CAPTURES
LITTLE ROUND TOP

General Law rode up to me as we were advancing, and informed me that I was then on the extreme right of our line and for me to hug the base of Great Round Top and go up the valley between the two mountains, until I found the left of the Union line, to turn it and do all the damage I could, and that Lieutenant-Colonel Bulger would be instructed to keep the Forty-seventh closed to my regiment, and if separated from the brigade he would act under my orders.

Just after we crossed Plum Run we received the first fire from the enemy's infantry. It was Stoughton's Second Regiment United States sharp-shooters, posted behind a fence at or near the southern foot of Great Round Top. They reached that position as we advanced through the old field. No other troops were there nor on that mountain at that time. I did not halt at the first fire, but looked to the rear for the Forty-eighth Alabama, and saw it going, under General Law's order, across the rear of our line to the left, it was said, to reenforce the Texas brigade, which was hotly engaged. That left no one in my rear or on my right to meet this foe. They were in the woods and I did not know the number of them.

I received the second fire. Lieutenant-Colonel Feagin and one or two of the men fell. I knew it would not do to go and leave that force, I knew not how strong, in our rear with no troops of ours to take care of them; so I gave the command to change direction to the right. The seven companies of the Forty-seventh swung around with the Fifteenth and kept in line with it. The other three companies of that regiment were sent forward as skirmishers before the advance began. The sharp-shooters retreated up the south front of the mountain, pursued by my command.

In places the men had to climb up, catching to the rocks and bushes and crawling over the boulders in the face of the fire of the enemy, who kept retreating, taking shelter and firing down on us from behind the rocks and crags which covered the side of the mountain thicker than grave-stones in a city cemetery. Fortunately they usually over-shot us. We could see our foe only as they dodged back from one boulder to another, hence our fire was scattering. As we advanced up the mountain they ceased firing about half way up, divided, and a battalion went around the mountain on each side. Those who went up to the right fired a few shots at my flank. To meet this I deployed Company A, and moved it by the left flank to protect my right, and continued my rugged ascent until we reached the top.

Some of my men fainted from heat, exhaustion, and thirst. I halted and let them lie down and rest a few minutes. . . . I saw Gettysburg through the foliage of the trees. Saw the smoke and heard the roar of battle which was then raging at the Devil's Den, in the peach orchard, up the Emmitsburg road, and on the west and south of the Little Round Top. I saw from the highest point of rocks that we were then on the most commanding elevation in that neighborhood. I knew that my men were too much exhausted to make a good fight without a few minutes' rest. . . .

When we formed line of battle before the advance began, a detail was made of two men from each of the eleven companies of my regiment to take all the canteens to a well about one hundred yards in our rear and fill them with cool water before we went into the fight. Before this detail could fill the canteens the advance was ordered. It would have been infinitely better to have waited five minutes for those twenty-two men and the canteens of water, but generals never ask a colonel if his regiment is ready to move. The order was given and away we went. The water detail followed with the canteens of water, but when they got into the woods they missed us, walked right into the Yankee lines, and were captured, canteens and all. My men in the ranks, in the intense heat, suffered greatly for water. The loss of those twenty-two men and lack of the water contributed largely to our failure to take Little Round Top a few minutes later. About five minutes after I halted, Captain Terrell, assistant adjutant-general to General Law, rode up by the only pathway on the southeast side of the mountain and inquired why I had halted. I told him. He then informed me that General Hood was wounded, Law was in command of the division, and sent me his compliments, said for me to press on, turn the Union left, and capture Little Round Top, if possible, and to lose no time.

I then called his attention to my position. A precipice on the east and north, right at my feet; a very steep, stony, and wooded mountain-side on the west. The only approach to it by our enemy, a long wooded slope on the northwest. Within half an hour I could convert it into a Gibraltar that I could hold against ten times the number of men that I had, hence in my judgment it should be held and occupied by artillery as soon as possible, as it was higher than the other mountain and would command the entire field. Terrell replied that

probably I was right, but that he had no authority to change
or originate orders, which I very well knew; but with his
sanction I would have remained at that point until I could
have heard from Law or some superior in rank. I inquired
for Law. Terrell said that as senior brigadier he was commanding the division, and along the line to the left. He then
repeated that General Law had sent him to tell me to lose no
time, but to press forward and drive everything before me as
far as possible. General Meade did not then know the importance of the Round Tops. . . .

Just as the Forty-seventh companies were being driven back,
I ordered my regiment to change direction to the left, swing
around, and drive the Federals from the ledge of rocks, for
the purpose of enfilading their line, relieving the Forty-seventh
—gain the enemy's rear, and drive him from the hill. My
men obeyed and advanced about half way to the enemy's
position, but the fire was so destructive that my line wavered
like a man trying to walk against a strong wind, and then
slowly, doggedly, gave back a little; then with no one upon
the left or right of me, my regiment exposed, while the
enemy was still under cover, to stand there and die was
sheer folly; either to retreat or advance became a necessity.
The Lieutenant-Colonel, I. B. Feagin, had lost his leg at
Plum Run; the heroic Captain Ellison had fallen; while Captain
Brainard, one of the bravest and best officers in the regiment,
in leading his company forward, fell, exclaiming, "O God!
that I could see my mother," and instantly expired. Lieutenant John O. Oates, my dear brother, succeeded to the command of the company, but was pierced through by a number
of bullets, and fell mortally wounded. Lieutenant Cody fell
mortally wounded, Captain Bethune and several other officers
were serious wounded, while the carnage in the ranks was
appalling.

I again ordered the advance, and knowing the officers and
men of that gallant old regiment, I felt sure they would
follow their commander anywhere in the line of duty. I
passed through the line waving my sword, shouting, "Forward,
men, to the ledge!" and was promptly followed by the
command in splendid style. We drove the Federals from their
strong defensive position; five times they rallied and charged
us, twice coming so near that some of my men had to use
the bayonet, but in vain was their effort. It was our time now
to deal death and destruction to a gallant foe, and the account
was speedily settled. I led this charge and sprang upon the
ledge of rock, using my pistol within musket length, when

the rush of my men drove the Maine men from the ledge along the line. . . . At this angle and to the southwest of it is where I lost the greatest number of my men. The Twentieth Maine was driven back from this ledge, but not farther than to the next ledge on the mountain-side.

I recall a circumstance which I recollect. I, with my regiment, made a rush forward from the ledge. About forty steps up the slope there is a large boulder about midway the Spur. The Maine regiment charged my line, coming right up in a hand-to-hand encounter. My regimental colors were just a step or two to the right of that boulder, and I was within ten feet. A Maine man reached to grasp the staff of the colors when Ensign Archibald stepped back and Sergeant Pat O'Connor stove his bayonet through the head of the Yankee, who fell dead. I witnessed that incident, which impressed me beyond the point of being forgotten.

There never were harder fighters than the Twentieth Maine men and their gallant Colonel. His skill and persistency and the great bravery of his men saved Little Round Top and the Army of the Potomac from defeat. Great events sometimes turn on comparatively small affairs. My position rapidly became untenable. The Federal infantry were reported to be coming down on my right and certainly were closing in on my rear, while some dismounted cavalry were closing the only avenue of escape on my left rear. I sent my sergeant-major with a request to Colonel Bowles, of the Fourth Alabama, the next in line to the left, to come to my relief. He returned within a minute and reported that none of our troops were in sight, the enemy to be between us and the Fourth Alabama, and swarming the woods south of Little Round Top. The lamented Captain Park, who was afterwards killed at Knoxville, and Captain Hill, killed near Richmond in 1864, came and informed me that the enemy were closing in on our rear. I sent Park to ascertain their number. He soon returned, and reported that two regiments were coming up behind us, and just then I saw them halt behind a fence, some two hundred yards distant, from which they opened fire on us. These, I have since learned from him, were the battalions of Stoughton's sharpshooters, each of which carried a flag, hence the impression that there were two regiments. They had been lost in the woods, but, guided by the firing, came up in our rear. At Balaklava Captain Nolan's six hundred had cannon to the right of them, cannon to the left of them, cannon in front of them, which volleyed and thundered. But at this moment the Fifteenth Alabama had infantry in front of them, to the right of them, dismounted cavalry to the left of them, and infantry in the rear of them. With a withering and deadly fire pouring in upon us from every direction, it seemed that the regiment was doomed to destruction. While one man was shot in the face, his right-hand or left-hand comrade was shot in the side or back. Some were struck simultaneously with two or three balls from different directions. Captains Hill and Park suggested that I should order a retreat; but this seemed impracticable. My dead and wounded were then nearly as great in number as those still on duty. They literally covered the ground. The blood stood in puddles in some places on the rocks; the ground was soaked with the blood of as brave men as ever fell on the red field of battle.

I still hoped for reenforcements or for the tide of success to turn my way. It seemed impossible to retreat and I therefore replied to my captains, "Return to your companies; we will sell out as dearly as possible."

Hill made no reply, but Park smiled pleasantly, gave me the military salute, and said, "All right, sir."

On reflection a few moments later I saw no hope of success and did order a retreat, but did not undertake to retire in order. I sent Sergeant-Major Norris and had the officers and men advised the best I could that when the signal was given that we would not try to retreat in order, but every one should run in the direction from whence we came, and halt on the top of the Big Round Top Mountain. I found the undertaking to capture Little Round Top too great for my regiment unsupported. I waited until the next charge of the Twentieth Maine was repulsed, as it would give my men a better chance to get out unhurt, and then ordered the retreat. . . .

When the signal was given we ran like a herd of wild cattle, right through the line of dismounted cavalrymen. Some of the men as they ran through seized three of the cavalrymen by the collar and carried them out prisoners. As we ran, a man named Keils, of Company H, from Henry County, who was to my right and rear had his throat cut by a bullet, and he ran past me breathing at his throat and the blood spattering. His wind-pipe was entirely severed, but notwithstanding he crossed the mountain and died in the field hospital that night or the next morning.

—OATES, *The War between the Union and the Confederacy*

C. The 20th Maine Saves Little Round Top

At daylight, on the morning of July 2d, we resumed our march, and in a few hours halted within supporting distance of the left flank of our army, about a mile to the right of Little Round Top. The long forenoon passed away, and to our surprise the enemy made no attack. This was very fortunate for our army, as it enabled our men to strengthen our lines of fortifications, and also to obtain a little rest, of which they were in great need. The rebels were also engaged in throwing up rude lines of defenses, hurrying up reinforcements, and in dicussing the line of action they should pursue. . . .

The hour of noon passed, and the sun had measured nearly one-half the distance across the western sky, before the assault was made. Then, as suddenly as a bolt of fire flies from the storm cloud, a hundred pieces of rebel artillery open upon our left flank, and under the thick canopy of screaming, hissing, bursting shells, Longstreet's corps was hurled upon the troops of General Sickles. Instantly our commanders discerned the intention of General Lee. It was to turn and crush our left flank, as he had crushed our right at Chancellorsville. It was a terrible onslaught. The brave sons of the South never displayed more gallant courage than on that fatal afternoon of July 2d. But brave Dan Sickles and the old Third corps were equal to the emergency, and stood as immovable against the surging tides as blocks of granite. But a new and appalling danger suddenly threatened the Union army. Little Round Top was the key to the entire position. Rebel batteries planted on that rocky bluff could shell any portion of our line at their pleasure. For some reason Sickles had not placed any infantry upon this important position. A few batteries were scattered along its ragged side, but they had no infantry support.

Lee saw at a glance that Little Round Top was the prize for which the two armies were contending, and with skillful audacity he determined to wrest it from his opponent. While the terrible charge was being made upon the line of General Sickles, Longstreet threw out a whole division, by extending his line to his right, for the purpose of seizing the coveted prize. The danger was at once seen by our officers, and our brigade was ordered forward, to hold the hill against the assault of the enemy. In a moment all was excitement. Every soldier seemed to understand the situation, and to be inspired by its danger. "Fall in! Fall in! By the right flank! Double-quick! March!" and away we went, under the terrible artillery fire. It was a moment of thrilling interest. Shells were exploding on every side. Sickles' corps was enveloped in sheets of flame, and looked like a vast windrow of fire. But so intense was the excitement that we hardly noticed these surroundings. Up the steep hillside we ran, and reached the crest. "On the right by file into line," was the command, and our regiment had assumed the position to which it had been assigned. We were on the left of our brigade, and consequently on the extreme left of all our line of battle. The ground sloped to our front and left, and was sparsely covered with a growth of oak trees, which were too small to afford us any protection. Shells were crashing through the air above our heads, making so much noise that we could hardly hear the commands of our officers; the air was filled with fragments of exploding shells and splinters torn from mangled trees; but our men appeared to be as cool and deliberate in their movements as if they had been forming a line upon the parade ground in camp.

Our regiment mustered about three hundred and fifty men. Company B, from Piscataquis county, commanded by the gallant Captain Morrill, was ordered to deploy in our front as skirmishers. They boldly advanced down the slope and disappeared from our view. Ten minutes have passed since we formed the line; the skirmishers must have advanced some thirty or forty rods through the rocks and trees, but we have seen no indications of the enemy; "But look!" "Look!" "Look!" exclaimed half a hundred men in our regiment at the same moment; and no wonder, for right in our front, between us and our skirmishers, whom they have probably captured, we see the lines of the enemy. They have paid no attention to the rest of the brigade stationed on our right, but they are rushing on, determined to turn and crush the left of our line. Colonel Chamberlain with rare sagacity understood the movement they were making, and bent back the left flank of our regiment until the line formed almost a right angle with the colors at the point, all these movements requiring a much less space of time than it requires for me to write of them.

How can I describe the scenes that followed? Imagine, if you can, nine small companies of infantry, numbering perhaps three hundred men, in the form of a right angle, on the extreme flank of an army of eighty thousand men, put there to hold the key of the entire position against a force at least ten times their number, and who are desperately de-

termined to succeed in the mission upon which they came.
Stand firm, ye boys from Maine, for not once in a century are
men permitted to bear such responsibilities for freedom and
justice, for God and humanity, as are now placed upon you.

The conflict opens. I know not who gave the first fire, or
which line received the first lead. I only know that the carnage
began. Our regiment was mantled in fire and smoke. I wish
that I could picture with my pen the awful details of that
hour,—how rapidly the cartridges were torn from the boxes
and stuffed in the smoking muzzles of the guns; how the
steel rammers clashed and clanged in the heated barrels;
how the men's hands and faces grew grim and black with
burning powder; how our little line, baptized with fire, reeled
to and fro as it advanced or was pressed back; how our
officers bravely encouraged the men to hold on and recklessly
exposed themselves to the enemy's fire,—a terrible medley of
cries, shouts, cheers, groans, prayers, curses, bursting shells,
whizzing rifle bullets and clanging steel. And if that was all,
my heart would not be so sad and heavy as I write. But the
enemy was pouring a terrible fire upon us, his superior
forces giving him a great advantage. Ten to one are fearful
odds where men are contending for so great a prize. The
air seemed to be alive with lead. The lines at times were
so near each other that the hostile gun barrels almost
touched. As the contest continued, the rebels grew desperate
that so insignificant a force should so long hold them in check.
At one time there was a brief lull in the carnage, and our
shattered line was closed up, but soon the contest raged again
with renewed fierceness. The rebels had been reinforced, and
were now determined to sweep our regiment from the crest
of Little Round Top.

Many of our companies have suffered fearfully. . . .
But there is no relief, and the carnage goes on. Our line is
pressed back so far that our dead are within the lines of
the enemy. The pressure made by the superior weight of the
enemy's line is severely felt. Our ammunition is nearly all
gone, and we are using the cartridges from the boxes of our
wounded comrades. A critical moment has arrived, and we
can remain as we are no longer; we must advance or retreat.
It must not be the latter, but how can it be the former?
Colonel Chamberlain understands how it can be done. The
order is given "Fix bayonets!" and the steel shanks of the
bayonets rattle upon the rifle barrels. "Charge bayonets,
charge!" Every man understood in a moment that the movement was our only salvation, but there is a limit to human

endurance, and I do not dishonor those brave men when I write that for a brief moment the order was not obeyed, and the little line seemed to quail under the fearful fire that was being poured upon it. O for some man reckless of life, and all else save his country's honor and safety, who would rush far out to the front, lead the way, and inspire the hearts of his exhausted comrades!

In that moment of supreme need the want was supplied. Lieut. H. S. Melcher, an officer who had worked his way up from the ranks, and was then in command of Co. F, at that time the color company, saw the situation, and did not hesitate, and for his gallant act deserves as much as any other man the honor of the victory on Round Top. With a cheer, and a flash of his sword, that sent an inspiration along the line, full ten paces to the front he sprang—ten paces—more than half the distance between the hostile lines. "Come on! Come on! Come on, boys!" he shouts. The color sergeant and the brave color guard follow, and with one wild yell of anguish wrung from its tortured heart, the regiment charged.

The rebels were confounded at the momvent. We struck them with a fearful shock. They recoil, stagger, break and run, and like avenging demons our men pursue. The rebels rush toward a stone wall, but, to our mutual surprise, two scores of rifle barrels gleam over the rocks, and a murderous volley was poured in upon them at close quarters. A band of men leap over the wall and capture at least a hundred prisoners. Piscataquis has been heard from, and as usual it was a good report. This unlooked-for reinforcement was Company B, whom we supposed were all captured.

Our Colonel's commands were simply to hold the hill, and we did not follow the retreating rebels but a short distance. After dark an order came to advance and capture a hill in our front. Through the trees, among the rocks, up the steep hillside, we made our way, captured the position, and also a number of prisoners.

—GERRISH, *Army Life*

7. HIGH TIDE AT GETTYSBURG

Both Pickett and Stuart had come up during the afternoon of the second. With his army at full strength, and undaunted by the repulses of the second day's fighting, Lee determined to renew the next morning, hurling Longstreet and Hill against the Union center on Cemetery Ridge and Ewell against Culp's Hill. Again ill fortune plagued him. Ewell's attack came off almost as planned, but was thrown back. Longstreet once more had what Lincoln called "the slows," but whether because of natural difficulties of co-ordinating so many forces for attack or because of reluctance to launch an attack which he disapproved is still a subject of controversy.

Meanwhile two of the greatest artillerists of the war—Alexander and Hunt—made ready. Although the Federals had artillery superiority, Alexander was able to bring over 100 guns to bear on the Union position, while Hunt could not mass more than about 80 on Cemetery Ridge and the Round Tops. At one o'clock the greatest artillery duel ever seen on the continent began, and for 40 minutes the roar of cannon shook the earth. Then—with both sides low on artillery ammunition—silence fell over the battlefield.

Now Pickett and Pettigrew were ready for that famous charge which was to live forever in history. "Up men and to your posts!" cried Pickett. "Don't forget today that you are from old Virginia." And Pettigrew called to Colonel Marshall, "Now, Colonel, for the honor of the good Old North State, forward!" Forward they swept, 15,000 men in gray, the colors of 47 regiments fluttering in the breeze, up the long slope of Cemetery Ridge. The Federals, too, were ready, General Gibbon—a Southerner with three brothers in the Confederate ranks—riding up and down encouraging his men to stand firm.

But let our chroniclers tell the great story. They need little introduction. First comes the lionhearted General Alexander, chief of artillery of Longstreet's corps and—as the event proved—a distinguished stylist. Next comes Lee's war horse, James Longstreet, the focal figure in the controversies that raged around Gettysburg for a generation after the battle. We have only one Union historian—but what an historian he is! Frank Haskell had been born in Vermont and educated at Dartmouth; he moved out to Wisconsin and it was there that he joined the famous Iron Brigade, was promoted from lieutenant to colonel, and in time became aide-de-camp to General Gibbon. During the two weeks after the repulse of Pickett's charge he composed a book-length letter to his brother giving a history of the battle. A year later he was killed at Cold Harbor. Haskell's Gettysburg has become a classic of American literature—the only American military account to find its way into the Harvard Classics. Our final account is from

he gifted pen of the English observer, Colonel Fremantle,
who tells of the aftermath of the charge and gives us an un-
forgettable picture of Lee at this crisis of his career.

A. Alexander Gives the Signal to Start

Before daylight on the morning of the 3d I received orders to
post the artillery for an assault upon the enemy's position, and
later I learned that it was to be led by Pickett's division and
directed on Cemetery Hill. Some of the batteries had gone
back for ammunition and forage, but they were all brought
up immediately, and by daylight all then on the field were
posted. Dearing's batallion (with Pickett's division) reported
sometime during the morning. The enemy fired on our movements and positions occasionally, doing no great damage, and
we scarcely returned a shot. The morning was consumed in
waiting for Pickett's division, and possibly other movements
of infantry. . . .

About 11 A.M. the skirmishers in A. P. Hill's front got to
fighting for a barn in between the lines, and the artillery on
both sides gradually took part until the whole of Hill's artillery in position, which I think was 63 guns, were heavily engaged with about an equal number of the enemy's guns for
over a half hour, but not one of the 75 guns which I then had
in line was allowed to fire a shot, as we had at best but a
short supply of ammunition for the work laid out. . . .

Gradually the cannonade just referred to died out as it began, and the field became nearly silent, but writers have frequently referred to "the cannonade preceding the assault" as
having begun at 11 o'clock and lasted for some hours, being
misled by this affair. About 12 M. General Longstreet told
me that when Pickett was ready, he would himself give the
signal for all our guns to open (which was to be two guns
from the Washington Artillery, near the center of our line),
and meanwhile he desired me to select a suitable position for
observation, and to take with me one of General Pickett's
staff, and exercise my judgment in selecting the moment
for Pickett's advance to begin. Complying, I selected the advanced salient angle of the wood in which Pickett's line was
now formed, just on the left flank of my line of 75 guns. While
occupying this position and in conversation with General A.
R. Wright, commanding a Georgia brigade in A. P. Hill's
corps, who had come out there for an observation of the posi-

tion, I received a note from General Longstreet, which copy from the original still in my possession, as follows:

HD. QRS., *July 3rd*, 1863

COLONEL:

If the artillery fire does not have the effect to drive off the enemy or greatly demoralize him so as to make our efforts pretty certain, I would prefer that you should not advise General Pickett to make the charge. I shall rely a great deal on your good judgment to determine the matter, and shall expect you to let General Pickett know when the moment offers.

Respectfully,

J. LONGSTREET, Lieut.-General.

To Colonel E.P. ALEXANDER, *Artillery.*

This note at once suggested that there was some alternative to the attack, and placed me on the responsibility of deciding the question. I endeavored to avoid it by giving my views in a note, of which I kept no copy, but of which I have always retained a vivid recollection, having discussed its points with General A. R. Wright as I wrote it. It was expressed very nearly as follows:

GENERAL:

I will only be able to judge of the effect of our fire on the enemy by his return fire, for his infantry is but little exposed to view and the smoke will obscure the whole field. If, as I infer from your note, there is any alternative to this attack, it should be carefully considered before opening our fire, for it will take all the artillery ammunition we have left to test this one thoroughly, and, if the result is unfavorable, we will have none left for another effort. And even if this is entirely successful it can only be so at a very bloody cost.

Very respectfully, &c.,

E. P. ALEXANDER, *Colonel Artillery.*

To this note I soon received the following reply:

HD. QRS., *July 3rd*, 1863

COLONEL:

The intention is to advance the infantry if the artillery has the desired effect of driving the enemy's off, or having other effect such as to warrant us in making the attack. When that moment arrives advise General P., and of course advance such artillery as you can use in aiding the attack.

Respectfully,

J. LONGSTREET, *Lieut.-General, Commanding.*

To Colonel ALEXANDER.

This letter again placed the responsibility upon me, and I felt it very deeply, for the day was rapidly advancing (it was about 12 M., or a little later), and whatever was to be done was to be done soon. Meanwhile I had been anxiously discussing the attack with General A. R. Wright, who said that the difficulty was not so much in *reaching* Cemetery Hill, or taking it—that his brigade had carried it the afternoon before —but that the trouble was to hold it, for the whole Federal army was massed in a sort of horse-shoe shape and could rapidly reinforce the point to any extent, while our long, enveloping line could not give prompt enough support. This somewhat reassured me, as I had heard it said that morning that General Lee had ordered "every brigade in the army to charge Cemetery Hill," and it was at least certain that the question of supports had had his careful attention. Before answering, however, I rode back to converse with General Pickett, whose line was now formed or forming in the wood, and without telling him of the question I had to decide, I found out that he was entirely sanguine of success in the charge, and was only congratulating himself on the opportunity. I was convinced that to make any half-way effort would insure a failure of the campaign, and that if our artillery fire was once opened, after all the time consumed in preparation for the attack, the only hope of success was to follow it up promptly with one supreme effort, concentrating every energy we possessed into it, and my mind was fully made up that *if the artillery opened Pickett must charge.* After the second note from General Longstreet, therefore, and the interview with Pickett, I did not feel justified in making any delay, but to acquaint General Longstreet with my determination. I wrote him a note, which I think I quote verbatim, as follows: "General: When our artillery fire is doing its best I shall advise General Pickett to advance." It was my intention, as he had a long distance to traverse, that he should start not later than fifteen minutes after our fire opened. . . .

It was 1 P.M. by my watch when the signal guns were fired, the field at that time being entirely silent, but for light picket firing between the lines, and as suddenly as an organ strikes up in a church, the grand roar followed from all the

guns of both armies. The enemy's fire was heavy and sever
and their accounts represent ours as having been equally s
though our rifle guns were comparatively few and had on
very defective ammunition. . . .

I had fully intended giving Pickett the order to advance a
soon as I saw that our guns had gotten their ranges, say, i
ten or fifteen minutes, but the enemy's fire was so severe tha
when that time had elapsed I could not make up my mind t
order the infantry out into a fire which I did not believe the
could face, for so long a charge, in such a hot sun, tired a
they already were by the march from Chambersburg. I ac
cordingly waited in hopes that our fire would produce some
visible effect, or something turn up to make the situation
more hopeful; but fifteen minutes more passed without any
change in the situation, the fire on neither side slackening for
a moment. Even then I could not bring myself to give a
peremptory order to Pickett to advance, but feeling that the
critical moment would soon pass, I wrote him a note to this
effect: "If you are coming at all you must come immediately
or I cannot give you proper support; but the enemy's fire
has not slackened materially, and at least 18 guns are still
firing from the Cemetery itself."

This note (which, though given from memory, I can vouch
for as very nearly verbatim) I sent off at 1:30 P.M., consulting my watch. I afterwards heard what followed its receipt from members of the staff of both Generals Pickett and
Longstreet, as follows: Pickett on receiving it galloped over to
General Longstreet, who was not far off, and showed it to
General L. The latter read it and made no reply. (General
Longstreet himself, speaking of it afterwards, said that he
knew the charge had to be made, but could not bring himself
to give the order.) General Pickett then said: "General, shall
I advance?" Longstreet turned around in his saddle and would
not answer. Pickett immediately saluted, and said: "I am going
to lead my division forward, sir," and galloped off to put it
in motion; on which General L. left his staff and rode out
alone to my position.

Meanwhile, five minutes after I sent the above note to
Pickett, the enemy's fire suddenly slackened materially, and
the batteries in the Cemetery were limbered up and were
withdrawn. As the enemy had such abundance of ammunition and so much better guns than ours that they were not
compelled to reserve their artillery for critical moments (as we
almost always had to do), I knew that they must have felt
the punishment a good deal, and I was a good deal elated

by the sight. But to make sure that it was a withdrawal for good, and not a mere change of position or relieving of the batteries by fresh ones, I waited for five minutes more, closely examining the ground with a large glass. At that time I sent my courier to Pickett with a note: "For God's sake come quick; the 18 guns are gone"; and, going to the nearest guns, I sent a lieutenant and a sergeant, one after the other, with other messages to same effect.

A few minutes after this, Pickett still not appearing, General Longstreet rode up alone, having seen Pickett and left his staff as above. I showed him the situation, and said I only feared I could not give Pickett the help I wanted to, my ammunition being very low, and the seven guns under Richardson having been taken off. General Longstreet spoke up promptly: "Go and stop Pickett right where he is, and replenish your ammunition." I answered, that the ordnance wagons had been nearly emptied, replacing expenditures of the day before, and that not over 20 rounds to the gun were left—too little to accomplish much—and that while this was being done the enemy would recover from the effect of the fire we were now giving him. His reply was: "I don't want to make this charge; I don't believe it can succeed. I would stop Pickett now, but that General Lee has ordered it and expects it," and other remarks, showing that he would have been easily induced, even then, to order Pickett to halt.

It was just at this moment that Pickett's line appeared sweeping out of the wood, Garnett's brigade passing over us. I then left General Longstreet and rode a short distance with General Garnett, an old friend, who had been sick, but, buttoned up in an old blue overcoat, in spite of the heat of the day, was riding in front of his line. I then galloped along my line of guns, ordering those that had over 20 rounds left to limber up and follow Pickett, and those that had less to maintain their fire from where they were. I had advanced several batteries or parts of batteries in this way, when Pickett's division appeared on the slope of Cemetery Hill, and a considerable force of the enemy were thrown out, attacking his unprotected right flank. Meanwhile, too, several batteries which had been withdrawn were run out again and were firing on him very heavily. We opened on these troops and batteries with the best we had in the shop, and appeared to do them considerable damage, but meanwhile Pickett's division just seemed to melt away in the blue musketry smoke which now covered the hill. Nothing but stragglers came back. As soon as it was clear that Pickett was "gone up," I ceased firing, saving what little ammunition was left for fear of an advance by the enemy. About this time General Lee came up to our guns alone and remained there a half hour or more, speaking to Pickett's men as they came straggling back, and encouraging them to form again in the first cover they could find.

—Letter from General E. P. Alexander to the Reverend
J. Wm. Jones

B. ARMISTEAD FALLS BESIDE THE ENEMY'S BATTERY

The signal guns broke the silence, the blaze of the second gun mingling in the smoke of the first, and salvoes rolled to the left and repeated themselves, the enemy's fine metal spreading its fire to the converging lines, plowing the trembling ground, plunging through the line of batteries, and clouding the heavy air. The two or three hundred guns seemed proud of their undivided honors and organized confusion. The Confederates had the benefit of converging fire into the enemy's massed position, but the superior metal of the enemy neutralized the advantage of position. The brave and steady work progressed. . . .

General Pickett rode to confer with Alexander, then to the ground upon which I was resting, where he was soon handed a slip of paper. After reading it he handed it to me. It read:

"If you are coming at all, come at once, or I cannot give you proper support, but the enemy's fire has not slackened at all. At least eighteen guns are still firing from the cemetery itself.

—ALEXANDER"

Pickett said, "General, shall I advance?"

The effort to speak the order failed, and I could only indicate it by an affirmative bow. He accepted the duty, with seeming confidence of success, leaped on his horse, and rode gaily to his command. I mounted and spurred for Alexander's post. He reported that the batteries he had reserved for the charge with the infantry had been spirited away by General Lee's chief of artillery, that the ammunition of the batteries of position was so reduced that he could not use them in proper support of the infantry. He was ordered to stop the march at once and fill up his ammunition chests. But, alas! there was no more ammunition to be had.

The order was imperative. The Confederate commander had

fixed his heart upon the work. Just then a number of the enemy's batteries hitched up and hauled off, which gave a glimpse of unexpected hope. Encouraging messages were sent for the columns to hurry on—and they were then on elastic springing step. The officers saluted as they passed, their stern smiles expressing confidence. General Pickett, a graceful horseman, sat lightly in the saddle, his brown locks flowing quite over his shoulders. Pettigrew's division spread their steps and quickly rectified the alignment, and the grand march moved bravely on. As soon as the leading columns opened the way, the supports sprang to their alignments. General Trimble mounted, adjusting his seat and reins with an air and grace as if setting out on a pleasant afternoon ride. When aligned to their places solid march was made down the slope and past our batteries of position.

Confederate batteries put their fire over the heads of the men as they moved down the slope, and continued to draw the fire of the enemy until the smoke lifted and drifted to the rear, when every gun was turned upon the infantry columns. The batteries that had been drawn off were replaced by others that were fresh. Soldiers and officers began to fall, some to rise no more, others to find their way to the hospital tents. Single files were cut here and there; then the gaps increased, and an occasional shot tore wider openings, but, closing the gaps as quickly as made, the march moved on. . . .

Colonel Latrobe was sent to General Trimble to have his men fill the line of the broken brigades, and bravely they repaired the damage. The enemy moved out against the supporting brigade in Pickett's rear. Colonel Sorrel was sent to have that move guarded, and Pickett was drawn back to that contention. McLaws was ordered to press his left forward, but the direct line of infantry and cross fire of artillery was telling fearfully on the front. Colonel Fremantle ran up to offer congratulations on the apparent success, but the big gaps in the ranks grew until the lines were reduced to half their length. I called his attention to the broken, struggling lines. Trimble mended the battle of the left in handsome style, but on the right the massing of the enemy grew stronger and stronger. Brigadier Garnett was killed; Kemper and Trimble were desperately wounded; Generals Hancock and Gibbon were wounded. General Lane succeeded Trimble and with Pettigrew held the battle of the left in steady ranks.

Pickett's lines being nearer, the impact was heaviest upon them. Most of the field officers were killed or wounded.

Colonel Whittle, of Armistead's brigade, who had been shot through the right leg at Williamsburg and lost his left arm at Malvern Hill, was shot through the right arm, then brought down by a shot through his left leg.

General Armistead, of the second line, spread his steps to supply the places of fallen comrades. His colors cut down, with a volley against the bristling line of bayonets, he put his cap on his sword to guide the storm. The enemy's massing, enveloping numbers held the struggle until the noble Armistead fell beside the wheels of the enemy's battery. Pettigrew was wounded but held his command.

General Pickett, finding the battle broken while the enemy was still reinforcing, called the troops off. There was no indication of panic. The broken files marched back in steady step. The effort was nobly made and failed from blows that could not be fended.

—LONGSTREET, *From Manassas to Appomattox*

C. "THE CREST IS SAFE"

Half-past two o'clock, an hour and a half since the commencement, and still the cannonade did not in the least abate; but soon thereafter some signs of weariness and a little slacking of fire began to be apparent upon both sides. . . . All things must end, and the great cannonade was no exception to the general law of earth. In the number of guns active at one time, and in the duration and rapidity of their fire, this artillery engagement, up to this time, must stand alone and pre-eminent in this war. It has not been often, or many times, surpassed in the battles of the world. Two hundred and fifty guns, at least, rapidly fired for two mortal hours. . . .

At three o'clock almost precisely, the last shot hummed, and bounded and fell, and the cannonade was over. The purpose of General Lee in all this fire of his guns—we know it now, we did not at the time so well—was to disable our artillery and break up our infantry upon the position of the Second Corps, so as to render them less an impediment to the sweep of his own brigades and divisions over our crest and through our lines. . . . There was a pause between acts, with the curtain down, soon to rise upon the great final act, and catastrophe of Gettysburg. We have passed by the left of the Second Division, coming from the First; when we crossed the crest the enemy was not in sight, and all was still—we walked slowly along in the rear of the troops, by the ridge cut off now from a view of the enemy on his position, and were returning to the spot where we had left our horses. . . . In a moment afterwards we met Captain Wessels and the orderlies who had our horses; they were on foot leading the horses. Captain Wessels was pale, and he said, excited: "General, they say the enemy's infantry is advancing." We spring into our saddles, a score of bounds brought us upon the all-seeing crest.

To say that men grew pale and held their breath at what we and they there saw, would not be true. Might not six thousand men be brave and without shade of fear, and yet, before a hostile eighteen thousand, armed, and not five minutes' march away, turn ashy white? None on that crest now need be told that *the enemy is advancing*. Every eye could see his legions, an overwhelming resistless tide of an ocean of armed men sweeping upon us! Regiment after regiment and brigade after brigade moved from the woods and rapidly take their places in the lines forming the assault. Pickett's proud division, with some additional troops, hold their right; Pettigrew's (Worth's) their left. The first line at short interval is followed by a second, and that a third succeeds; and columns between support the lines. More than half a mile their front extends; more than a thousand yards the dull gray masses deploy, man touching man, rank pressing rank, and line supporting line. The red flags wave, their horsemen gallop up and down; the arms of eighteen thousand men, barrel and bayonet, gleam in the sun, a sloping forest of flashing steel. Right on they move, as with one soul, in perfect order, without impediment of ditch, or wall or stream, over ridge and slope, through orchard and meadow, and cornfield, magnificent, grim, irresistible.

All was orderly and still upon our crest; no noise and no confusion. The men had little need of commands, for the survivors of a dozen battles knew well enough what this array in front portended, and, already in their places, they would be prepared to act when the right time should come. The click of the locks as each man raised the hammer to feel with his fingers that the cap was on the nipple; the sharp jar as a musket touched a stone upon the wall when thrust in aiming over it, and the clicking of the iron axles as the guns were rolled up by hand a little further to the front, were quite all the sounds that could be heard. Cap-boxes were slid around to the front of the body; cartridge boxes opened, officers opened their pistol-holsters. Such preparations, little more was needed. The trefoil flags, colors of the brigades and divisions moved to their places in rear; but along the lines in front the grand old ensign that first waved in battle at Saratoga in 1777, and which these people coming would rob of half its stars, stood up, and the west wind kissed it as the sergeants sloped its lance towards the enemy. I believe that not one above whom it then waved but blessed his God that he was loyal to it, and whose heart did not swell with pride towards it, as the emblem of the Republic before that treason's flaunting rag in front.

General Gibbon rode down the lines, cool and calm, and in an unimpassioned voice he said to the men, "Do not hurry, men, and fire too fast, let them come up close before you fire, and then aim low and steadily." The coolness of their General was reflected in the faces of his men. Five minutes has elapsed since first the enemy have emerged from the woods—no great space of time surely, if measured by the usual standard by which men estimate duration—but it was long enough for us to note and weigh some of the elements of mighty moment that surrounded us; the disparity of numbers between the assailants and the assailed; that few as were our numbers we could not be supported or reinforced until support would not be needed or would be too late; that upon the ability of the two trefoil divisions to hold the crest and repel the assault depended not only their own safety or destruction, but also the honor of the Army of the Potomac and defeat or victory at Gettysburg. Should these advancing men pierce our line and become the entering wedge, driven home, that would sever our army asunder, what hope would there be afterwards, and where the blood-earned fruits of yesterday? It was long enough for the Rebel storm to drift across more than half the space that had at first separated it from us. None, or all, of these considerations either depressed or elevated us. They might have done the former, had we been timid; the latter had we been confident and vain. But, we were there waiting, and ready to do our duty—that done, results could not dishonor us.

Our skirmishers open a spattering fire along the front, and, fighting, retire upon the main line—the first drops, the heralds of the storm, sounding on our windows. Then the thunders of our guns, first Arnold's then Cushing's and Woodruff's and the rest, shake and reverberate again through the air, and their sounding shells smite the enemy. . . . All our available guns are now active, and from the fire of shells, as the range grows shorter and shorter, they change to shrapnel, and from shrapnel to canister; but in spite of shells, and shrapnel and canister, without wavering or halt, the hardy lines of the enemy continue to move on. The Rebel guns make no reply to ours, and no charging shout rings out to-day, as is the Rebel wont; but the courage of these silent men amid our shots seem not to need the stimulus of other noise.

The enemy's right flank sweeps near Stannard's bushy crest, and his concealed Vermonters rake it with a well-delivered fire of musketry. The gray lines do not halt or reply, but withdrawing a little from that extreme, they still move on. And so across all that broad open ground they have come, nearer and nearer, nearly half the way, with our guns bellowing in their faces, until now a hundred yards, no more, divide our ready left from their advancing right. The eager men there are impatient to begin. Let them. First, Harrow's breastworks flame; then Hall's; then Webb's. As if our bullets were the fire coals that touched off their muskets, the enemy in front halts, and his countless level barrels blaze back upon us. The Second Division is struggling in battle. The rattling storm soon spreads to the right, and the blue trefoils are vieing with the white. All along each hostile front, a thousand yards, with narrowest space between, the volleys blaze and roll; as thick the sound as when a summer hail-storm pelts the city roofs; as thick the fire as when the incessant lightning fringes a summer cloud.

When the Rebel infantry had opened fire our batteries soon became silent, and this without their fault, for they were foul by long previous use. They were the targets of the concentrated Rebel bullets, and some of them had expended all their canister. But they were not silent before Rhorty was killed, Woodruff had fallen mortally wounded, and Cushing, firing almost his last canister, had dropped dead among his guns shot through the head by a bullet. The conflict is left to the infantry alone. . . .

The conflict was trememdous, but I had seen no wavering in all our line. Wondering how long the Rebel ranks, deep though they were, could stand our sheltered volleys, I had come near my destination, when—great heaven! were my senses mad? The larger portion of Webb's brigade—my God, it was true—there by the groups of trees and the angles of the wall, was breaking from the cover of their works, and, without orders or reason, with no hand lifted to check them, was falling back, a fear-stricken flock of confusion! The fate of Gettysburg hung upon a spider's single thread!

A great magnificent passion came on me at the instant, not one that overpowers and confounds, but one that blanches the face and sublimes every sense and faculty. My sword, that

had always hung idle by my side, the sign of rank only in
every battle, I drew, bright and gleaming, the symbol of
command. Was not that a fit occasion, and these fugitives the
men on whom to try the temper of the Solinzen steel? All
rules and proprieties were forgotten; all considerations of
person, and danger and safety despised; for, as I met the
tide of these rabbits, the damned red flags of the rebellion
began to thicken and flaunt along the wall they had just
deserted, and one was already waving over one of the guns
of the dead Cushing. I ordered these men to "halt," and "face
about" and "fire," and they heard my voice and gathered my
meaning, and obeyed my commands. On some unpatriotic
backs of those not quick of comprehension, the flat of my sabre
fell not lightly, and at its touch their love of country returned,
and, with a look at me as if I were the destroying angel, as I
might have become theirs, they again faced the enemy.

General Webb soon came to my assistance. He was on foot,
but he was active, and did all that one could do to repair the
breach, or to avert its calamity. The men that had fallen
back, facing the enemy, soon regained confidence in themselves, and became steady. This portion of the wall was lost to
us, and the enemy had gained the cover of the reverse side,
where he now stormed with fire. But Webb's men, with their
bodies in part protected by the abruptness of the crest, now
sent back in the enemies' faces as fierce a storm. Some scores
of venturesome Rebels, that in their first push at the wall had
dared to cross at the further angle, and those that had dese-
crated Cushing's guns, were promptly shot down, and speedy
death met him who should raise his body to cross it again.

At this point little could be seen of the enemy, by reason of
his cover and the smoke, except the flash of his muskets and
his waving flags. These red flags were accumulating at the wall
every moment, and they maddened us as the same color does
the bull. Webb's men are falling fast, and he is among them
to direct and encourage; but, however well they may now
do, with that walled enemy in front, with more than a dozen
flags to Webb's three, it soon becomes apparent that in
not many minutes they will be overpowered, or that there will
be none alive for the enemy to overpower. Webb has but
three regiments, all small, the 69th, 71st and 72nd Pennsylvania—the 106th Pennsylvania, except two companies, is
not here to-day—and he must have speedy assistance, or
this crest will be lost.

Oh, where is Gibbon? where is Hancock?—some general—
anybody with the power and the will to support that wast-

ing, melting line? No general came, and no succor! . . . As a last resort I resolved to see if Hall and Harrow could not send some of their commands to reinforce Webb. I galloped to the left in the execution of my purpose, and as I attained the rear of Hall's line, from the nature of the ground and the position of the enemy it was easy to discover the reason and the manner of this gathering of Rebel flags in front of Webb.

The enemy, emboldened by his success in gaining our line by the group of trees and the angle of the wall, was concentrating all his right against and was further pressing that point. There was the stress of his assault; there would he drive his fiery wedge to split our line. In front of Harrow's and Hall's Brigades he had been able to advance no nearer than when he first halted to deliver fire, and these commands had not yielded an inch. To effect the concentration before Webb, the enemy would march the regiment on his extreme right of each of his lines by the left flank to the rear of the troops, still halted and facing to the front, and so continuing to draw in his right, when they were all massed in the position desired, he would again face them to the front, and advance to the storming. This was the way he made the wall before Webb's line blaze red with his battle flags, and such was the purpose there of his thick-crowding battalions.

Not a moment must be lost. Colonel Hall I found just in rear of his line, sword in hand, cool, vigilant, noting all that passed and directing the battle of his brigade. The fire was constantly diminishing now in his front, in the manner and by the movement of the enemy that I have mentioned, drifting to the right.

"How is it going?" Colonel Hall asked me, as I rode up.

"Well, but Webb is hotly pressed and must have support, or he will be overpowered. Can you assist him?"

"Yes."

"You cannot be too quick."

"I will move my brigade at once."

"Good."

He gave the order, and in the briefest time I saw five friendly colors hurrying to the aid of the imperilled three; and each color represented true, battle-tried men, that had not turned back from Rebel fire that day nor yesterday, though their ranks were sadly thinned; to Webb's brigade, pressed back as it had been from the wall, the distance was not great from Hall's right. The regiments marched by the right flank. . . . The movement, as it did, attracting the enemy's fire, and executed in haste, as it must be, was difficult; but in reasonable time, and in order that is serviceable, if not regular, Hall's men are fighting gallantly side by side with Webb's before the all important point.

I did not stop to see all this movement of Hall's, but from him I went at once further to the left, to the 1st brigade. Gen'l Harrow I did not see, but his fighting men would answer my purpose as well. The 19th Me., the 15th Mass., the 32d N. Y. and the shattered old thunderbolt, the 1st Minn.—poor Farrell was dying then upon the ground where he had fallen —all men that I could find I took over to the right at the *double quick*.

As we were moving to, and near the other brigade of the division, from my position on horseback, I could see that the enemy's right, under Hall's fire, was beginning to stagger and to break. "See," I said to the men, "See the *chivalry!* See the gray-backs run!" The men saw, and as they swept to their places by the side of Hall and opened fire, they roared, and this in a manner that said more plainly than words—for the deaf could have seen it in their faces, and the blind could have heard it in their voices—*the crest is safe!*

The whole Division concentrated, and changes of position, and new phases, as well on our part as on that of the enemy. having as indicated occurred, for the purpose of showing the exact present posture of affairs, some further description is necessary. Before the 2d Division the enemy is massed, the main bulk of his force covered by the ground that slopes to his rear, with his front at the stone wall. Between his front and us extends the very apex of the crest. All there are left of the White Trefoil Division—yesterday morning there were three thousand eight hundred, this morning there were less than three thousand—at this moment there are somewhat over two thousand;—twelve regiments in three brigades are below or behind the crest, in such a position that by the exposure of the head and upper part of the body above the crest they can deliver their fire in the enemy's face along the top of the wall.

By reason of the disorganization incidental in Webb's brigade to his men's having broken and fallen back, as mentioned, in the two other brigades to their rapid and difficult change of position under fire, and in all the divisions in part to severe and continuous battle, formation of companies and regiments in regular ranks is lost; but commands, companies, regiments and brigades are blended and intermixed—an irregular extended mass—men enough, if in order, to form a line of four or five ranks along the whole front of the division. The twelve flags of the regiments wave defiantly at intervals along the front; at the stone wall, at unequal distances from ours of forty, fifty or sixty yards, stream nearly double this number of the battle flags of the enemy.

These changes accomplished on either side, and the concentration complete, although no cessation or abatement in the general din of conflict since the commencement had at any time been appreciable, now it was as if a new battle, deadlier, stormier than before, had sprung from the body of the old—a young Phoenix of combat, whose eyes stream lightning, shaking his arrowy wings over the yet glowing ashes of his progenitor. The jostling, swaying lines on either side boil, and roar, and dash their flamy spray, two hostile billows of a fiery ocean. Thick flashes stream from the wall, thick volleys answer from the crest. No threats or expostulation now, only example and encouragement. All depths of passion are stirred, and all combatives fire, down to their deep foundations. Individuality is drowned in a sea of clamor, and timid men, breathing the breath of the multitude, are brave. The frequent dead and wounded lie where they stagger and fall—there is no humanity for them now, and none can be spared to care for them. The men do not cheer or shout; they growl, and over that uneasy sea, heard with the roar of musketry, sweeps the muttered thunder of a storm of growls. Webb, Hall, Devereux, Mallon, Abbott among the men where all are heroes, are doing deeds of note.

Now the loyal wave rolls up as if it would overleap its barrier, the crest. Pistols flash with the muskets. My "Forward to the wall" is answered by the Rebel counter-command, "Steady, men!" and the wave swings back. Again it surges, and again it sinks. These men of Pennsylvania, on the soil of their own homesteads, the first and only to flee the wall, must be the first to storm it. . . . "Sergeant, forward with your color. Let the Rebels see it close to their eyes once before they die." The color sergant of the 72d Pa., grasping the stump of the severed lance in both his hands, waved the flag above his head and rushed towards the wall. "Will you see your color storm the wall alone?" One man only starts to follow. Almost half way to the wall, down go color bearer and color to the ground—the gallant sergeant is dead. The line springs—the crest of the solid ground with a great roar, heaves forward its maddened load, men, arms, smoke, fire, a fighting mass. It rolls to the wall—flash meets flash, the wall is crossed—a moment ensues of thrusts, yells, blows, shots, and undistinguishable conflict, followed by a shout uni-

versal that makes the welkin ring again, and the last and
bloodiest fight of the great battle of Gettysburg is ended and
won.

—HASKELL, *The Battle of Gettysburg*

D. "ALL THIS WILL COME RIGHT IN THE END"

July 3d.—The distance between the Confederate guns and
the Yankee position—i.e. between the woods crowning the
opposite ridges—was at least a mile, quite open, gently undulating, and exposed to artillery the whole distance. This was
the ground which had to be crossed in today's attack. Pickett's
division, which had just come up, was to bear the brunt in
Longstreet's attack, together with Heth and Pettigrew in Hill's
corps. Pickett's division was a weak one (under five thousand),
owing to the absence of two brigades.

At noon all Longstreet's dispositions were made; his troops
for attack were deployed into line and lying down in the
woods; his batteries were ready to open. The General then dismounted and went to sleep for a short time. . . .

Finding that to see the actual fighting it was absolutely
necessary to go into the thick of the thing, I determined to
make my way to General Longstreet. It was then about two-
thirty. After passing General Lee and his staff, I rode on
through the woods in the direction in which I had left Longstreet. I soon began to meet many wounded men returning
from the front; many of them asked in piteous tones the way
to a doctor or an ambulance. The farther I got, the greater
became the number of the wounded. At last I came to a
perfect stream of them flocking through the woods in numbers as great as the crowd in Oxford Street in the middle of
the day. Some were walking alone on crutches composed of
two rifles, others supported by men less badly wounded than
themselves, and others were carried on stretchers by the ambulance corps; but in no case did I see a sound man helping
the wounded to the rear unless he carried the red badge of the
ambulance corps. They were still under a heavy fire; the shells
were continually bringing down great limbs of trees and
carrying further destruction amongst this melancholy procession. I saw all this in much less time than it takes to write
it, and although astonished to meet such vast numbers of
wounded, I had not seen enough to give me any idea of the
real extent of the mischief.

When I got close up to General Longstreet, I saw one of

his regiments advancing through the woods in good order; so, thinking I was just in time to see the attack, I remarked to the General that "I wouldn't have missed this for anything."

Longstreet was seated at the top of a snake fence at the edge of the wood and looking perfectly calm and unperturbed. He replied, laughing: "The devil you wouldn't! I would like to have missed it very much; we've attacked and been repulsed; look there!"

For the first time I then had a view of the open space between the two positions and saw it covered with Confederates, slowly and sulkily returning toward us in small broken parties, under a heavy fire of artillery. But the fire where we were was not so bad as farther to the rear, for although the air seemed alive with shell, yet the greater number burst behind us. The General told me that Pickett's division had succeeded in carrying the enemy's position and capturing his guns, but after remaining there twenty minutes, it had been forced to retire, on the retreat of Heth and Pettigrew on its left. . . .

Soon afterward I joined General Lee, who had in the meanwhile come to the front on becoming aware of the disaster. If Longstreet's conduct was admirable, that of Lee was perfectly sublime. He was engaged in rallying and in encouraging the broken troops and was riding about a little in front of the wood, quite alone, the whole of his staff being engaged in a similar manner farther to the rear. His face, which is always placid and cheerful, did not show signs of the slightest disappointment, care, or annoyance; and he was addressing to every soldier he met a few words of encouragement, such as: "All this will come right in the end; we'll talk it over afterwards; but in the meantime, all good men must rally. We want all good and true men just now," etc. He spoke to all the wounded men that passed him, and the slightly wounded he exhorted to "bind up their hurts and take up a musket" in this emergency. Very few failed to answer his appeal, and I saw many badly wounded men take off their hats and cheer him.

He said to me, "This has been a sad day for us, Colonel— a sad day; but we can't expect always to gain victories." . . . I saw General Willcox come up to him and explain, almost crying, the state of his brigade. General Lee immediately shook hands with him and said cheerfully: "Never mind, General, all this has been *my* fault—it is I that have lost this fight, and you must help me out of it in the best way you can."

In this way I saw General Lee encourage and reanimate his somewhat dispirited troops and magnanimously take upon his own shoulders the whole weight of the repulse. It was impossible to look at him or to listen to him without feeling the strongest admiration.

—[FREMANTLE], "The Battle of Gettysburg"

8. GENERAL LEE OFFERS TO RESIGN AFTER GETTYSBURG

"It is all my fault," said Lee, on the afternoon of the third. History does not agree with that verdict, but it was characteristic of Lee that he should shoulder the blame for the failure of the invasion. On August 8 he sent Davis his offer to resign. In his reply Davis referred finely to those "achievements which will make you and your army the subject of history and object of the world's admiration for generations to come."

CAMP ORANGE, *August 8, 1863*

His Excellency JEFFERSON DAVIS,
    President of the Confederate States:
    MR. PRESIDENT: Your letters of July 28 and August 2 have been received, and I have waited for a leisure hour to reply, but I fear that will never come. I am extremely obliged to you for the attention given to the wants of this army, and the efforts made to supply them. Our absentees are returning, and I hope the earnest and beautiful appeal made to the country in your proclamation may stir up the virtue of the whole people, and that they may see their duty and perform it. Nothing is wanted but that their fortitude should equal their bravery to insure the success of our cause. We must expect reverses, even defeats. They are sent to teach us wisdom and prudence, to call forth greater energies, and to prevent our falling into greater disasters. Our people have only to be true and united, to bear manfully the misfortunes incident to war, and all will come right in the end.
    I know how prone we are to censure and how ready to blame others for the non-fulfillment of our expectations. This is unbecoming in a generous people, and I grieve to see its expression. The general remedy for the want of success in a military commander is his removal. This is natural, and, in many instances, proper. For, no matter what may be the

ability of the officer, if he loses the confidence of his troops disaster must sooner or later ensue.

I have been prompted by these reflections more than once since my return from Pennsylvania to propose to Your Excellency the propriety of selecting another commander for this army. I have seen and heard of expression of discontent in the public journals at the result of the expedition. I do not know how far this feeling extends in the army. My brother officers have been too kind to report it, and so far the troops have been too generous to exhibit it. It is fair, however, to suppose that it does exist, and success is so necessary to us that nothing should be risked to secure it. I therefore, in all sincerity, request Your Excellency to take measures to supply my place. I do this with the more earnestness because no one is more aware than myself of my inability for the duties of my position. I cannot even accomplish what I myself desire. How can I fulfill the expectations of others? In addition I sensibly feel the growing failure of my bodily strength. I have not yet recovered from the attack I experienced the past spring. I am becoming more and more incapable of exertion, and am thus prevented from making the personal examinations and giving the personal supervision to the operations in the field which I feel to be necessary. I am so dull that in making use of the eyes of others I am frequently misled. Everything, therefore, points to the advantages to be derived from a new commander, and I the more anxiously urge the matter upon Your Excellency from my belief that a younger and abler man than myself can readily be attained. I know that he will have as gallant and brave an army as ever existed to second his efforts, and it would be the happiest day of my life to see at its head a worthy leader—one that would accomplish more than I could perform and all that I have wished. I hope Your Excellency will attribute my request to the true reason, the desire to serve my country, and to do all in my power to insure the success of her righteous cause.

I have no complaints to make of any one but myself. I have received nothing but kindness from those above me, and the most considerate attention from my comrades and companions in arms. To Your Excellency I am specially indebted for uniform kindness and consideration. You have done everything in your power to aid me in the work committed to my charge, without omitting anything to promote the general welfare. I pray that your efforts may at length be crowned with success, and that you may long live to enjoy the thanks of grateful people.

With sentiments of great esteem, I am, very respectfully and truly, yours,

R.E. LEE,
General.

RICHMOND, VA., *August* 11, 1863
General R. E. LEE,
Commanding Army of Northern Virginia:

Yours of 8th instant has been received. I am glad that you concur so entirely with me as to the want of our country in this trying hour, and am happy to add that after the first depression consequent upon our disaster in the west, indications have appeared that our people will exhibit that fortitude which we agree in believing is alone needful to secure ultimate success.

It well became Sidney Johnston, when overwhelmed by a senseless clamor, to admit the rule that success is the test of merit; and yet there has been found nothing which I have found to require a greater effort of patience than to bear the criticisms of the ignorant, who pronounce everything a failure which does not equal their expectations or desires, and can see no good result which is not in the line of their own imaginings. I admit the propriety of your conclusions, that an officer who loses the confidence of his troops should have his position changed, whatever may be his ability, but when I read the sentence I was not at all prepared for the application you were about to make. Expressions of discontent in the public journals furnish but little evidence of the sentiment of an army. I wish it were otherwise, even though all the abuse of myself should be accepted as the results of honest observation. I say I wish I could feel that the public journals were not generally partisan nor venal.

Were you capable of stooping to it, you could easily surround yourself with those who would fill the press with your laudations, and seek to exalt you for what you had not done, rather than detract from the achievements which will make you and your army the subject of history and object of the world's admiration for generations to come.

I am truly sorry to know that you still feel the effects of the illness you suffered last spring, and can readily understand the embarrassments you experience in using the eyes of others, having been so much accustomed to make your own reconnaissances. Practice will, however, do much to relieve that embarrassment, and the minute knowledge of the country which you have acquired will render you less dependent for topographical information.

But suppose, my dear friend, that I were to admit, with all their implications, the points which you present, where am I to find that new commander who is to possess the greater ability which you believe to be required? I do not doubt the readiness with which you would give way to one who could accomplish all that you have wished, and you will do me the justice to believe that if Providence should kindly offer such a person for our use, I would not hesitate to avail of his services.

My sight is not sufficiently penetrating to discover such hidden merit, if it exists, and I have but used to you the language of sober earnestness when I have impressed upon you the propriety of avoiding all unnecessary exposure to danger, because I felt our country could not bear to lose you. To ask me to substitute you by some one in my judgment more fit to command, or who would possess more of the confidence of the army, or of the reflecting men of the country, is to demand an impossibility.

It only remains for me to hope that you will take all possible care of yourself, that your health and strength may be entirely restored, and that the Lord will preserve you for the important duties devolved upon you in the struggle of our suffering country for the independence which we have engaged in war to maintain.

As ever, very respectfully and truly, yours,

JEFFERSON DAVIS.

—War of the Rebellion . . . Official Records

9. "BELLS ARE RINGING WILDLY"

The day after Gettysburg was the greatest Fourth of July since the Declaration. Vicksburg had fallen, Lee had been defeated, the Union was safe! So, at least, thought most Northerners, and the North was swept with enthusiasm and jubilation.

William Lusk tells of the reception of the news in Wilmington.

HEADQUARTERS DELAWARE DEPARTMENT,
WILMINGTON, DEL., July 7th, 1863

Dear, dear Cousin Lou:

I said I would write you so soon as the full purport of the good news was ascertained. And now that it has all broken upon us, although my heels are where my head ought to be, I will try and fulfil my engagement as coherently as possible. We have had the dark hour. The dawn has broken, and the collapsed confederacy has no place where it can hide its head. Bells are ringing wildly all over the city. Citizens grin at one another with fairly idiotic delight. One is on the top of his house frantically swinging a dinner bell, contributing thus his share of patriotic clamor to the general ding-dong. Bully for him! How I envy the heroes of Meade's Army. It would be worth while to die, in order that one's friends might say, "He died at Gettysburg." But to live to hear all the good news, and now to learn that Vicksburg has surrendered, is a little too much happiness for poor mortal men. I can laugh, I can cry with joy. All hysterical nonsense is pardonable now. Manassas, twice repeated, Fredericksburg and Chicka-hominy! Bless them as the cruel training that has made us learn our duties to our country. Slavery has fallen, and I believe Heaven as well as earth rejoices. Providence has tenderly removed that grand old hero, Jackson, before the blow came, that the one good, earnest, misguided man might be spared the sight of the downfall of a cause fanaticism led him to believe was right. . . . These enthusiastic citizens of Wilmington, not content with bell-ringing, have taken to firing cannon, and the boys, to help matters, are discharging pistols into empty barrels. The people in a little semi-slave-holding State, when not downright traitors, are noisily, ob-streperously loyal, to a degree that New England can hardly conceive of. My letter must be short and jubilant, I cannot do anything long to-day.

Just dance through the house for me, and kiss every one you meet. So I feel now. Goody-bye.

Affec'y.,
WILL.

—*War Letters of William Thompson Lusk*

10. "A NEW BIRTH OF FREEDOM"

On July 4 Lincoln had announced to the country the victory of the Army of the Potomac, and invoked "the con-

dolences of all for the many gallant fallen." That November part of the battlefield of Gettysburg was made a permanent cemetery for the soldiers who had fallen there. Edward Everett of Massachusetts delivered the principal oration. The superintendent of the enterprise, David Wills, asked Lincoln to make "a few appropriate remarks" and the result was the most memorable of all American addresses.

Fourscore and seven years ago our fathers brought forth on this continent a new nation, conceived in Liberty, and dedicated to the proposition that all men are created equal.

Now we are engaged in a great civil war, testing whether that nation or any nation so conceived and so dedicated can long endure. We are met on a great battlefield of that war. We have come to dedicate a portion of that field as a final resting place for those who here gave their lives that that nation might live. It is altogether fitting and proper that we should do this.

But in a larger sense we cannot dedicate—we cannot consecrate—we cannot hallow—this ground. The brave men, living and dead, who struggled here, have consecrated it, far above our poor power to add or detract. The world will little note nor long remember what we say here, but it can never forget what they did here. It is for us the living, rather, to be dedicated here to the unfinished work which they who fought here have thus far so nobly advanced. It is rather for us to be here dedicated to the great task remaining before us—that from these honored dead we take increased devotion to that cause for which they gave the last full measure of devotion —that we here highly resolve that these dead shall not have died in vain—that this nation, under God, shall have a new birth of freedom—and that government of the people, by the people, for the people, shall not perish from the earth.

—LINCOLN, "The Gettysburg Address"

II

Vicksburg and Port Hudson

THE *Vicksburg campaign, which lasted from November 1862 to July 1863, was the most confused and confusing of all Civil War campaigns. The confusion, however, is in the tactics rather than in the grand strategy. That strategy was simple enough. It was to clear the Mississippi, thus cutting off the Trans-Mississippi West from the rest of the Confederacy, and opening a channel from the Gulf to the North. By midsummer 1862 these grand objectives had been largely achieved. Farragut had taken New Orleans; Columbus had been evacuated; New Madrid and Island No. 10 had fallen; the Confederates had abandoned Fort Pillow and Memphis. In the thousand-mile stretch from the Gulf to the Ohio, only Vicksburg and Port Hudson were still in Confederate hands.*

In June 1862 Farragut had steamed northward toward the gunboat flotilla under Davis; he had been able to run the batteries of Vicksburg, but unable to take the city. Such an operation required a combined land and water attack. Had Halleck moved promptly on Vicksburg after Shiloh he could probably have captured it; he failed to do so and the Confederates, alert to its importance, hastened to reinforce it. As early as October 1862 Grant asked permission to attack Vicksburg, but not until December was that permission granted, and even then it was not clear whether the operation was to be by Grant, Sherman, or McClernand.

The Vicksburg campaign opened in November when Grant

established a base at Holly Springs, Mississippi, and prepared to move down the Yazoo on Vicksburg. Forrest attacked Grant's communications and then Van Dorn captured Holly Springs and destroyed his stores, and the plan was abandoned. Late the next month Sherman moved down the Mississippi to the mouth of the Yazoo, and up the Yazoo to Chickasaw Bluffs; on December 29 he attacked the Confederates at the Bluffs and was repulsed.

Thus the first attempt to take Vicksburg from the rear—a joint operation by Grant and Sherman—ended in failure. It was, as events were to prove, the sound approach, and had Grant been properly supported it might have worked. Balked in the attempt to take Vicksburg from Memphis, Grant moved his forces to the west side of the Mississippi and began to probe for a crossing. We cannot follow in detail the long and complex story of the effort to find a crossing below Vicksburg and ferry the great army very for an attack from the south. Eventually Grant moved his army down a series of rivers and bayous west of the Mississippi—Lake Providence, the Bayou Macon, the Tensas, and the Washita—to Hard Times on the Red River. An attempt to cross at Grand Gulf—about 50 miles below Vicksburg—was frustrated by stiff Confederate opposition. Meantime Porter's gunboats had run the batteries of Vicksburg and steamed south to where Grant's army lay waiting. On April 30 Grant began ferrying his army across the Mississippi at Bruinsburg. Pemberton, now in command at Vicksburg, hurried reinforcements south to Port Gibson, a few miles from Bruinsburg; there was a sharp fight but the Confederates were worsted and retreated. During the next week the whole of Grant's army crossed the river and prepared to move against Vicksburg.

The next two weeks saw a swift development of Grant's campaign, and some of the hottest fighting of the war. Pemberton had some 25,000 men at Vicksburg and along the Vicksburg and Jackson Railway; Joseph E. Johnston had about the same number at and around Jackson. It was Grant's purpose to prevent these two forces from combining, and to defeat them separately. It was a formidable task. He had broken his communications and was forced to live off the country; the terrain—muddy and swampy and with wretched roads—was not favorable to swift movements; if Grant was defeated his army would be lost in enemy territory.

On May 12 Grant moved one wing of his army under McPherson on Jackson, capital of the state and important railroad center. There was a fight at Raymond; the Confeder-

*ates fell back; and on the fourteenth McPherson defeated
Johnston, and seized Jackson. Then the army turned westward
to deal with Pemberton. That hapless general, who did everything at the wrong time, had moved out to harry Grant's rear
and his nonexistent line of communications. Grant caught him
at Champion's Hill on May 15 and defeated him. Pemberton
retreated to the Black River, where there was another sharp
fight. Once more the Confederates withdrew, this time to the
strong works outside Vicksburg. Reluctant to embark on a
siege Grant tried, on May 19, to storm the works—and
failed. Undaunted he tried another general assault on the
twenty-second, only to be repulsed with heavy losses.*

*Clearly Vicksburg could be taken only by a siege. Method-
ically Grant collected a large army of some 70,000, over 200
guns, and set about to invest the city. The siege lasted 47
days. Just as Grant was preparing for a final grand attack,
Pemberton surrendered. Johnston, who had been preparing
to go to Pemberton's aid, fell back with Sherman in pursuit.
Port Hudson surrendered on July 9. Once more the Mississippi
went unvexed to the sea.*

1. "ONWARD TO VICKSBURG"

*High on a bluff the guns of Vicksburg commanded the
Mississippi approaches from both north and south. As
Grant feared to run the batteries he decided to move his
army to the western side of the river and attack the great
fortress city from the south and rear. A long-drawn-out
attempt to by-pass Vicksburg by building a canal across the
peninsula in the great curve of the Mississippi failed when
the Confederates planted batteries below the city and commanding the canal. By the end of April, however, Grant had
succeeded in getting his army of some 40,000 down the river
system to the west of the Mississippi and across to the east
side of the Mississippi at Bruinsburg. Now, as Sergeant
Charles Wilcox tells us, the cry was "On to Vicksburg!"*

*The campaign that followed was one of the most brilliant
of the war, both in tactics and in strategy. In three weeks
Grant's armies won five victories—Port Gibson, Raymond,
Jackson, Champion's Hill, and Big Black River; captured the
capital of the state; separated the armies of Johnston and
Pemberton; and invested Vicksburg.*

Charles Wilcox, whose diary tells something of this story, was a student at Illinois State Normal University when the war opened. He enlisted in the 33rd Illinois Volunteers, fought in Missouri, at Vicksburg, and in Louisiana, and ended up as captain of the 92nd Colored Infantry.

Thursday, [April] 23d [1863]—We are jubilant over the success of our boats (transports) which came past Vicksburg last night. Six transports made the attempt and all got past—this side of the battery (rebel) fartherest down the river when one—the *Tigress*—was sunk, it having sprung a leak from the effect of the enemy's fire; the other five came down past Carthage though one (the *Empire City*) being so disabled it floated all the way from Vicksburg. The other four are somewhat injured but will soon be fitted for our use. Talked with several of those who came down on the boats. Only three or four out of the crews of the six boats were wounded—none killed—some fatally wounded though. These crews were nearly all soldiers who volunteered their services. . . . The crew of the *Tigress* were all saved. The *Empire City* was under fire one hour and a half; this long time is accounted for by she being totally disabled before she got half way past the batteries.

Some of our baggage came up. Gen. Osterhaus' Division is on transports to go and attack Grand Gulf. Our Brigade is ordered to be ready with 3 days cooked rations to march to the support of Osterhaus' Division.

Sunday, [April] 26th . . . Weather cloudy—it commenced raining about sunset and still continues. The private news is that we march sometime to-night, and are to make the attack upon Grand Gulf sometime to-morrow. The rebels have been, of late, reinforcing their force at that place. O God, protect us.

Monday, [April] 27th—Got orders about noon to embark immediately, which we very soon prepared to do, but did not succeed in getting aboard the boat (*Forest Queen*, the Flag Boat) till after dark. We leave behind everything save the well men with their knapsacks, guns and accoutrements with 80 rounds of ammunition to the man, three days rations in our haversacks, and horses for the main staff officers and their orderlies. Everybody is jolly and each one has a good word of cheer for his friend or comrade—all are in a bustle; every one is confident of victory in the coming contest. It rained in the night and some this forenoon; it is very mudy. . . .

Tuesday, [April] 28th—Did not leave the landing last night

THE VICKSBURG CAMPAIGN

as all the boats were not loaded till about eleven o'clock this A.M. Troops are coming in from Milliken's Bend; a part of McPherson's *Corps de Armie* is already here waiting to embark which they will do as soon as the boats can take us down and return. Seven transports and four or five barges, each loaded with a regiment or more, left Perkin's Plantation about noon, we disembarking on the Louisiana side, four or five miles above the fortifications at Grand Gulf, about two o'clock P.M. The rebels' position is in plain view. Judging from appearances they have a strong position. We found six of our gunboats just above Grand Gulf, lying out of reach of the rebels' guns. As the day was closing our gunboats threw three shells into the enemy's position, to learn the range of the guns; the enemy did not reply. The weather is very warm, sky clear. It is said that the ball opens in the morning. The transports and barges are all back after more troops. All of Carr's Division and part of Osterhaus' are here. When we were landing there were some Negroes near by who appeared to be very happy indeed upon seeing us. They clapped their hands in joy, prostrated themselves, shook hands with each other, and thanked the Lord as a Negro only can. 'Twas interesting, affecting, and impressive to witness these manifestations of joy. Col. Lippincott, who, until this war has always been a proslavery man, seeing them remarked "I was never more tempted to be an abolitionist." I carry a gun, and have no horse to ride while on this expedition.

Wednesday, [April] 29th—The sun arose throwing an impressive splendor upon the exciting scenes of the early morn. Every boat—transport and barge—lies at the landing, about five miles above Grand Gulf, covered till they are black with troops. Every heart here is full of anxiety and emotion; wondering eyes and eyes not altogether tearless, gaze ever and anon upon the *Father of Waters* where lie the formidable fleet of gunboats and rams, transports and barges, the latter heavily loaded with troops whose courage and valor are sufficient when combined with that of the rest of this mighty army, to redeem this lovely valley of the Mississippi from fiends and traitors who are desecrating it.

Now it is 7½ o'clock, A.M. Each gunboat and transport has gotten up full steam. The black smoke curls up from the blacker smoke-pipes, and moves towards the rebels, seeming to tell them of their black deeds and warns them of their portion when we attack them. It is like that which comes from the lower regions, scented with brimstone and issuing as it does from those gunboats, the traitors may well think, as they see it, that that fleet from which it comes has a portion of hell to give them, and that too, ere long, if they do not surrender or run. And now what means that? Every gunboat is steaming up the river. Can it be that the attack is not to be made? Every one is surprised. No; 'tis only the preparation for the attack. They are now "rounding to" and there they go. Thousands of eyes are looking upon. The first gun is fired by the enemy; the *Benton*, I believe, replies. 'Tis 8 o'clock. The contest has fairly begun; every gunboat is engaged. We all know when the enemy fires his heaviest guns as they make a sharper report than any of ours, though we have as large guns as he; this is probably accounted for by ours being on the water.

Eleven o'clock, A.M. Several of the enemy's batteries are silenced. The gunboats ply around and close to his strongest battery which gives them a round every opportunity, but as they near that battery they, one after another, give him broadsides which are terrible and produce a marked effect. The *Benton* "lays off" nearly across the river and just opposite and within good range of this powerful battery; every few minutes she sends an 84 or 64 pounder with nice precision at it; the dust flies and the enemy is quiet for a minute. This boat makes the most of the best shots that are fired. It seems to me that the enemy shoots wildly.

A few minutes after 12 M. The bombardment is over. Every one of the enemy's batteries save one, of three heavy guns are silenced, and we tried in vain to silence it.

The fleet has retired. Gen. Grant who was in a messenger boat during the bombardment, has come ashore. A little while passes and we get orders to start immediately down the levee, past Grand Gulf. The transports are being unloaded. At two P.M. we started for below; all the boats are to run the gauntlet to-night. We are now (evening) three or four miles below the enemy's works, though we only marched about three miles to get from five miles above them. The generals, colonels, and privates all lie down together, one faring no better than another. . . .

Friday, May 1st [1863]—A bright, clear and warm day, with a very slight breeze. This has been a glorious day for the Union, and for the despondent hearts in the North. We have fought a battle and won a complete victory. Having partaken our suppers last evening we again set forth upon our march, the Second Brigade going in the advance on account of our much wearied skirmishers. We came along slowly, carefully feeling our way though the moon shone brightly, and twice dispersing the enemy's pickets, till two o'clock A.M. when we came upon the enemy in force who *saluted* us with several rounds of grape and cannister, though not hurting us very much. . . .

A little after sunrise Major Potter in command of companies A, C, F and G of our regiment was ordered to go out on the road to our left (our line of battle at this time was north and south, facing to the east) and hold it till Gen. Osterhaus could relieve him. I asked permission of the Colonel to go with comp. "A," and carry a gun, but was refused so I had to stay with the regiment to be ready to carry and repeat orders. The Major with his pet soldiers had not gone far ere the enemy opened fire upon him with his cannon. This was really the beginning of the battle. Soon the skirmishers in front come in contact and the roar of musketry is heard. . . . We have not *all* got our positions yet, but the battle commences in earnest, the artillery on both sides firing smartly. The enemy has a cross fire upon us and we double quick into line or cover ourselves under the brow of a ridge of land. Our regiment being divided the six companies are ordered to stay back till the other four companies come up.

And now I see Major Potter with his gallant band coming; I tell the fact to Col. Lippincott. He orders me to bring the Major and his command to join the regiment. I go but dear me! how the shells and shot whiz around me. One shell bursts just over me; I shrink and dodge with the flash, but hasten on very soon, and after some difficulty, helping right up capsized caissons and crowding through the excited troops, I find the Major and direct him to the regiment, but on our way the grape, cannister, shells and solid shot drop about us and go over us in storms. I hear a ball whizzing towards me; I fall to the earth for safety and just in time for it to go about three feet over me. It strikes the ground a few yards from me; I dare not turn to look at it, but am up and off.

Now our regiment hastens to its post in the line of battle. Meanwhile the small arms of the other regiments send forth terrible volleys. The line of battle having moved forward it is now just behind the brow of a hill. As our regiment comes up into the line the rebels fire upon it, but our boys pour a deadly fire into them and make them get behind a ridge beyond the one we are on. *"Cease firing"* is ordered; *"Lie down"* follows. Gen. Benton comes along the line and orders us to fix bayonet for he's going to charge. All is quiet for several minutes, and then a few rebel sharpshooters fire at our heads and our flags.

When our boys see a rebel they give him a round, the same as they do us.

The 99th Ill, and the 18th and 24th Ind. make a charge, the order don't reach us so we lie quiet. A furious yell is sent up by those who are charging. The rebels break and run but we capture many of them and take two of their cannons. This ends the fight for the forenoon with us, and it is nearly noon now. Osterhaus continues the fight on the left; Hovey's and our Division pursue the rebels that we routed, and we find them, after traveling two miles towards Port Gibson, where they found their reinforcements.

It is a little after noon; again we are thrown into a line of battle, facing as before, to the east, meanwhile the fight is progressing. The enemy masses his troops and try to break our line, but fail. He throws a heavy force upon our right, then centre, and then left. He has but two cannons working upon us and ere night we capture those two. Our artillery fires with powerful effect at them; we have to go over an open field before our musketry can reach them, but there is a ridge, upon which are our cannon, behind which we lie in almost perfect safety. Now we have about 30 pieces of artillery all at work; their booming is not unfamiliar to our ears. With now and then a cessation in firing the battle is thus kept up till night fall when our regiment with some others retires to get a bite to eat, but as soon as we are through eating we return to the field, stack our arms on the line of battle and lie down to sleep, and oh, how thankful we are, for we have slept but about four hours within the last sixty.

We don't know our whole success, but we know this, that we drove the enemy in every close contact.

Sunday, [May] 3d—Reveille at three and was to march at five A.M. but did not get started till nearer seven. Our Division then moved one mile and a half directly towards Grand Gulf when, finding we could not cross Bayou Perre with our artillery as the enemy had burnt the bridges, we about faced and came back to Port Gibson and then came on seven miles from there towards Rocky Spring, having traveled in all ten miles. Saw about 20000 lbs of bacon and shoulders and hams that the enemy had endeavored to secrete. The enemy evacuated Grand Gulf last night, first spiking the cannons and blowing up two of their magazines, our gunboats making it too unpleasant for them to blow up the third. We are bivouaced in line of battle, and live upon what we can forage. The weather was warm—road very dusty. Came through a fine tract of country. Negroes are flocking to our lines with mules, horses, and wagons.

Tuesday, [May] 19th—"Onward to Vicksburg" is the cry. Came up within rifle shot of the enemy's works in rear of Vicksburg. The fight began our our right in the morning. It is stated that Sherman has taken Hanes' Bluff and that we therefore have direct communication with the [Yazoo] river and can get ample supplies. We, too, began the fight at about 2 P.M. and continued it till night closed in upon us. Some of our Regt. were wounded by shell from the enemy. The enemy used his cannon freely upon us. We have now completely invested this place and believe we'll take it with the whole garrison within a day or two. Sherman's Corps is on the right, his right resting on the Yazoo River between Haines' Bluff & Vicksburg, McPherson's in the center and McClernand's on the left. Our provisions are cooked in our rear and brought up to us. Our (Division) Hospital is a mile and a half directly in our rear and near the railroad. Smith's Division is just to the right of the railroad, ours just to the left and Osterhaus' to the left of us; Hovey is our reserve. Weather warm.

Friday, [May] 22nd—Now that we have tried to take the enemy's works by storm we suffering terribly and doing the enemy but little harm, we are all—generals and privates— content to lay a regular siege to the place. This has been a sad day for the 33d as well as for this whole army. The army's loss to-day will I think exceed 4000 killed and wounded while the enemy has repulsed us his loss, undoubtedly being trifling. At ten we were all ready for the charge and though not very confident of success we put on an air of confidence. Our Brigade filed down the hollow in which we lay last night till it intersected a larger hollow which we followed up to its head, and then, still marching by the flank, we mounted the ridge within 4 rods of the enemy who poured a deadly fire into us till we reached the opposite side of the ridge. To do this we had to run along the brow of the ridge in a direct line of the enemy's fire, for 15 rods.

Here is where our poor boys suffered terribly, the ridge being covered with the dead and wounded. A part of the Brigade halted and lay down in the wagon road which runs along on the ridge; I was among this lot. We lay there about eight minutes and yet it seemed an age to me, for showers of bullets and grape were passing over me and not a foot above me, and on my right and left were my comrades dying and dead as well as living. What an awful eight minutes that was, we having to lay there not allowed to fire a single shot at the enemy who was sending to eternity by scores our brave boys souls! Oh, how my heart palpitated! It seemed to thump the ground (I lay on my face) as hard as the enemy's bullets. The sweat from off my face run in a stream from the tip ends of my whiskers. God only knows all that passed through my mind. Twice I exclaimed aloud, that my comrades might here *"My God, why don't they order us to charge,"* and then I thought perhaps all of our officers were killed and there was no one to order us forward. I thought of dear friends, of home and of heaven, but never wished, as did some who were near me that, *I* had never attempted to charge, and, indeed, wished that I had not become a soldier. Some who were wounded groaned and shrieked, others were calm and resigned. Generally those that were the slightest wounded shrieked the loudest, thinking they were wounded the worst.

One fellow whose performance was the most pleasing thing I saw during the day was wounded slightly just as he got near where I lay. He immediately started to go back, his officers trying in vain to make him stay with us. After stepping a few steps he, it seemed to me, purposely dropped on the ground and then rolled as if the lightning had set him going, clear back into the ravine, a distance of about two and a half rods. Though under such precarious circumstances and in such peril I could not refrain from smiling when seeing the "rolling man."

Receiving orders from Colonel Roe all of our regiment who could arose and made for over the ridge where we could get under cover; meantime Col. Roe fell just before me, wounded in the leg. The regiment was then divided, all of us who lay down in the road being in one place and the rest in another. The right wing of the 8th Ind. soon coming up our little band joined them and we all charged over the railroad where we were again exposed to an awful fire, though but few were hit as we were exposed but a minute. Here on the south side of the railroad we took a position within three rods of one of the enemy's forts upon which the 77th Ill. had its flag planted, and from which it was taken, by the enemy. Here we lay sharpshooting whenever the enemy showed himself, till after dark when we all fell back without molestation to the position we occupied early in the morning. There were only six companies of the 33d in the charge, (three being out sharpshooting and one on provost guard), about one hundred and fifty men. Out of this number there were 76 killed and wounded. Am wearied and can't tell more of the sad tale. The fragment of the regiment is this evening still a unit and if

we are attacked to-night we will be able to give the enemy
a warm reception, though our hearts are sad.

    —ERICKSON, ed., "With Grant at Vicksburg—From the
    Civil War Diary of Captain Charles E. Wilcox"

2. A UNION WOMAN SUFFERS THROUGH THE SIEGE OF VICKSBURG

*After two futile assaults, May 19 and 22, Grant settled
down to reducing Vicksburg by siege. While his batteries
hurled shells into the beleaguered city, the gunboats attacked
it from the river. Pemberton had failed adequately to provision the city, and its inhabitants were soon enduring near
starvation.*

*This diary by an unknown Union lady, caught in the siege,
tells of the hardships and perils that the civilian inhabitants
endured.*

    March 20.—The slow shelling of Vicksburg goes on all
the time, and we have grown indifferent. It does not at present
interrupt or interfere with daily avocations, but I suspect they
are only getting the range of different points; and when they
have them all complete, showers of shot will rain on us all
at once. Non-combatants have been ordered to leave or
prepare accordingly. Those who are to stay are having caves
built. Cave-digging has become a regular business; prices range
from twenty to fifty dollars, according to size of cave. Two
diggers worked at ours a week and charged thirty dollars.
It is well made in the hill that slopes just in the rear of the
house, and well propped with thick posts, as they all are.
It has a shelf also, for holding a light or water. When we
went in this evening and sat down, the earthy, suffocating
feeling, as of a living tomb, was dreadful to me. I fear I shall
risk death outside rather than melt in the dark furnace. The
hills are so honeycombed with caves that the streets look like
avenues in a cemetery.

    The hill called the Sky-parlor has become quite a fashion-
able resort for the few upper-circle families left there. Some
officers are quartered there, and there is a band and a field-
glass. Last evening we also climbed the hill to watch the shelling, but found the view not so good as on a quiet hill nearer
home. Soon a lady began to talk to one of the officers: "It is
such folly for them to waste their ammunition like that. How

can they ever take a town that has such advantages for defense and protection as this? We'll just burrow into these hills and let them batter away as hard as they please." . . .

It is strange I have met no one yet who seems to comprehend an honest difference of opinion, and stranger yet that the ordinary rules of good breeding are now so entirely ignored. As the spring comes one has the craving for fresh, green food that a monotonous diet produces. There was a bed of radishes and onions in the garden that were a real blessing. An onion salad, dressed only with salt, vinegar, and pepper, seemed fit for a king; but last night the soldiers quartered near made a raid on the garden and took them all.

April 2.—We have had to move, and thus lost our cave. The owner of the house suddenly returned and notified us that he intended to bring his family back; did n't think there 'd be any siege. The cost of the cave could go for the rent. That means he has got tired of the Confederacy and means to stay here and thus get out of it. . . .

April 28.—I never understood before the full force of those questions—What shall we eat? what shall we drink? and wherewithal shall we be clothed? We have no prophet of the Lord at whose prayer the meal and oil will not waste. Such minute attention must be given the wardrobe to preserve it that I have learned to darn like an artist. Making shoes is now another accomplishment. Mine were in tatters. H. came across a moth-eaten pair that he bought me, giving ten dollars, I think, and they fell into rags when I tried to wear them; but the soles were good, and that has helped me to shoes. A pair of old coat-sleeves saved—nothing is thrown away now—was in my trunk. I cut an exact pattern from my old shoes, laid it on the sleeves, and cut out thus good uppers and sewed them carefully; then soaked the soles and sewed the cloth to them. I am so proud of these home-made shoes, think I'll put them in a glass case when the war is over, as an heirloom. . . .

I have but a dozen pins remaining, so many I gave away. Every time these are used they are straightened and kept from rust. All these curious labors are performed while the shells are leisurely screaming through the air; but as long as we are out of range we don't worry. For many nights we have had but little sleep, because the Federal gunboats have been running past the batteries. The uproar when this is happening is phenomenal. The first night the thundering artillery burst the bars of sleep, we thought it an attack by the river. To get into garments and rush up-stairs was the work of a moment. From the upper gallery we have a fine view of the river, and soon a red glare lit up the scene and showed a small boat, towing two large barges, gliding by. The Confederates had set fire to a house near the bank. Another night, eight boats ran by, throwing a shower of shot, and two burning houses made the river clear as day. One of the batteries has a remarkable gun they call "Whistling Dick," because of the screeching, whistling sound it gives, and certainly it does sound like a tortured thing. Added to all this is the indescribable Confederate yell, which is a soul-harrowing sound to hear. . . . Yesterday the *Cincinnati* attempted to go by in daylight, but was disabled and sunk. It was a pitiful sight; we could not see the finale, though we saw her rendered helpless.

May 1, 1863.—It is settled at last that we shall spend the time of siege in Vicksburg. Ever since we were deprived of our cave, I had been dreading that H. would suggest sending me to the country, where his relatives lived. As he could not leave his position and go also without being conscripted, and as I felt certain an army would get between us, it was no part of my plan to be obedient. A shell from one of the practising mortars brought the point to an issue yesterday and settled it. Sitting at work as usual, listening to the distant sound of bursting shells, apparently aimed at the court-house, there suddenly came a nearer explosion; the house shook, and a tearing sound was followed by terrified screams from the kitchen. I rushed thither, but met in the hall the cook's little girl America, bleeding from a wound in the forehead, and fairly dancing with fright and pain, while she uttered fearful yells. I stopped to examine the wound, and her mother bounded in, her black face ashy from terror. "Oh! Miss V., my child is killed and the kitchen tore up." Seeing America was too lively to be a killed subject, I consoled Martha and hastened to the kitchen. Evidently a shell had exploded just outside, sending three or four pieces through. When order was restored I endeavored to impress on Martha's mind the necessity for calmness and the uselessness of such excitement. Looking round at the close of the lecture, there stood a group of Confederate soldiers laughing heartily at my sermon and the promising audience I had. They chimed in with a parting chorus:

"Yes, it's no use hollerin', old lady." . . .

May 17.—Hardly was our scanty breakfast over this morning when a hurried ring drew us both to the door. Mr. J., one of H.'s assistants, stood there in high excitement.

"Well, Mr. L., they are upon us; the Yankees will be here by this evening."

"What do you mean?"

"That Pemberton has been whipped at Baker's Creek and Big Black, and his army are running back here as fast as they can come, and the Yanks after them, in such numbers nothing can stop them." . . .

What struck us both was the absence of that concern to be expected, and a sort of relief or suppressed pleasure. After twelve some worn-out-looking men sat down under the window.

"What is the news?" I inquired.

"Retreat, retreat!" they said, in broken English—they were Louisiana Acadians.

About three o'clock the rush began. I shall never forget that woeful sight of a beaten, demoralized army that came rushing back,—humanity in the last throes of endurance. Wan, hollow-eyed, ragged, foot-sore, bloody, the men limped along unarmed, but followed by siege-guns, ambulances, guncarriages, and wagons in aimless confusion. At twilight two or three bands on the court-house hill and other points began playing "Dixie," "Bonnie Blue Flag," and so on, and drums began to beat all about; I suppose they were rallying the scattered army.

May 28.—Since that day the regular siege has continued. We are utterly cut off from the world, surrounded by a circle of fire. Would it be wise like the scorpion to sting ourselves to death? The fiery shower of shells goes on day and night. H.'s occupation, of course, is gone; his office closed. Every man has to carry a pass in his pocket. People do nothing but eat what they can get, sleep when they can, and dodge the shells. There are three intervals when the shelling stops, either for the guns to cool or for the gunners' meals, I suppose,—about eight in the morning, the same in the evening, and at noon. In that time we have both to prepare and eat ours. Clothing cannot be washed or anything else done. On the 19th and 22d, when the assaults were made on the lines, I watched the soldiers cooking on the green opposite. The half-spent balls coming all the way from those lines were flying so thick that they were obliged to dodge at every turn. At all the caves I could see from my high perch, people were sitting, eating their poor suppers at the cave doors, ready to plunge in again. As the first shell again flew they dived, and not a human being was visible. The sharp crackle of the musketry-firing was a strong contrast to the scream of the bombs. I think all the dogs and cats must be killed or starved: we don't see any more pitiful animals prowling around. . . .

The cellar is so damp and musty the bedding has to be carried out and laid in the sun every day, with the forecast that it may be demolished at any moment. The confinement is dreadful. To sit and listen as if waiting for death in a horrible manner would drive me insane. I don't know what others do, but we read when I am not scribbling in this. H. borrowed somewhere a lot of Dickens's novels, and we reread them by the dim light in the cellar. When the shelling abates, H. goes to walk about a little or get the "Daily Citizen," which is still issuing a tiny sheet at twenty-five and fifty cents a copy. It is, of course, but a rehash of speculations which amuses a half hour. To-day he heard while out that expert swimmers are crossing the Mississippi on logs at night to bring and carry news to Johnston.

I am so tired of corn-bread, which I never liked, that I eat it with tears in my eyes. We are lucky to get a quart of milk daily from a family near who have a cow they hourly expect to be killed. I send five dollars to market each morning, and it buys a small piece of mule-meat. Rice and milk is my main food; I can't eat the mule-meat. We boil the rice and eat it cold with milk for supper. Martha runs the gauntlet to buy the meat and milk once a day in a perfect terror. The shells seem to have many different names: I hear the soldiers say, "That 's a mortar-shell. There goes a Parrott. That 's a rifle-shell." They are all equally terrible. A pair of chimney-swallows have built in the parlor chimney. The concussion of the house often sends down parts of their nest, which they patiently pick up and reascend with.

Friday, June 5. In the cellar. . . . Yesterday morning a note was brought H. from a bachelor uncle out in the trenches, saying he had been taken ill with fever, and could we receive him if he came? H. sent to tell him to come, and I arranged one of the parlors as a dressing-room for him, and laid a pallet that he could move back and forth to the cellar. He did not arrive, however.

It is our custom in the evening to sit in the front room a little while in the dark, with matches and candle held ready in hand, and watch the shells, whose course at night is shown by the fuse. H. was at the window and suddenly sprang up, crying, "Run!"—"Where?"—"*Back!*"

I started through the back room, H. after me. I was just within the door when the crash came that threw me to the floor. It was the mose appalling sensation I'd ever known—

worse than an earthquake, which I've also experienced.
Shaken and deafened, I picked myself up; H. had struck a
light to find me. I lighted mine, and the smoke guided us to
the parlor I had fixed for Uncle J. The candles were useless in
the dense smoke, and it was many minutes before we could
see. Then we found the entire side of the room torn out. The
soldiers who had rushed in said, "This is an eighty-pound
Parrott." . . .

June 7. (In the cellar.)—There is one thing I feel especially
grateful for, that amid these horrors we have been spared
that of suffering for water. The weather has been dry a long
time, and we hear of others dipping up the water from
ditches and mud-holes. This place has two large underground cisterns of good cool water, and every night in my
subterranean dressingroom a tub of cold water is the nerve-
calmer that sends me to sleep in spite of the roar. One cistern
I had to give up to the soldiers, who swarm about like hungry
animals seeking something to devour. Poor fellows! my heart
bleeds for them. They have nothing but spoiled, greasy bacon,
and bread made of musty pea-flour, and but little of that. The
sick ones can't bolt it. They come into the kitchen when Martha puts the pan of corn-bread in the stove, and beg for the
bowl she mixed it in. They shake up the scrapings with water,
put in their bacon, and boil the mixture into a kind of soup,
which is easier to swallow than pea-bread. When I happen in,
they look so ashamed of their poor clothes. I know we saved
the lives of two by giving a few meals.

To-day one crawled on the gallery to lie in the breeze. He
looked as if shells had lost their terrors for his dumb and
famished misery. I've taught Martha to make first-rate corn-
meal gruel, because I can eat meal easier that way than in
hoe-cake, and I fixed him a saucerful, put milk and sugar and
nutmeg—I've actually got a nutmeg! When he ate it the
tears ran from his eyes. "Oh, madam, there was never anything so good! I shall get better."

June 13.—Shell burst just over the roof this morning.
Pieces tore through both floors down into the dining-room.
The entire ceiling of that room fell in a mass. We had just
left it. Every piece of crockery on the table was smashed up.
The "Daily Citizen" to-day is a foot and a half long and six
inches wide. It has a long letter from a Federal officer, P. P.
Hill, who was on the gunboat *Cincinnati,* that was sunk May
27. Says it was found in his floating trunk. The editorial says,
"The utmost confidence is felt that we can maintain our posi-

tion until succor comes from outside. The undaunted Johnston is at hand."

June 18.—To-day the "Citizen" is printed on wallpaper; therefore has grown a little in size. It says, "But a few days more and Johnston will be here"; also that "Kirby Smith has driven Banks from Port Hudson," and that "the enemy are throwing incendiary shells in."

June 21.—I had gone up-stairs to-day during the interregnum to enjoy a rest on my bed, and read the reliable items in the "Citizen," when a shell burst right outside the window in front of me. Pieces flew in, striking all around me, tearing down masses of plaster that came tumbling over me. When H. rushed in I was crawling out of the plaster, digging it out of my eyes and hair. When he picked up a piece as large as a saucer beside my pillow, I realized my narrow escape. The window-frame began to smoke, and we saw the house was on fire. H. ran for a hatchet and I for water, and we put it out. Another [shell] came crashing near, and I snatched up my comb and brush and ran down here. It has taken all the afternoon to get the plaster out of my hair, for my hands were rather shaky.

June 25.—A horrible day. The most horrible yet to me, because I've lost my nerve. We were all in the cellar, when a shell came tearing through the roof, burst up-stairs, tore up that room, and the pieces coming through both floors down into the cellar, one of them tore open the leg of H.'s pantaloons. This was tangible proof the cellar was no place of protection from them. On the heels of this came Mr. J. to tell us that young Mrs. P. had had her thigh-bone crushed. When Martha went for the milk she came back horror-stricken to tell us the black girl there had her arm taken off by a shell. For the first time I quailed. I do not think people who are physically brave deserve much credit for it; it is a matter of nerves. In this way I am consitutionally brave, and seldom think of danger till it is over; and death has not the terrors for me it has for some others. Every night I had lain down expecting death, and every morning rose to the same prospect, without being unnerved. It was for H. I trembled. But now I first seemed to realize that something worse than death might come: I might be crippled, and not killed. Life, without all one's powers and limbs, was a thought that broke down my courage. I said to H., "You must get me out of this horrible place; I cannot stay; I know I shall be crippled." Now the regret comes that I lost control, because H. is worried, and has lost his composure, because my coolness has broken down.

July 3.—To-day we are down in the cellar again, shells flying as thick as ever; provisions so nearly gone, except the hogshead of sugar, that a few more days will bring us to starvation indeed. Martha says rats are hanging dressed in the market for sale with mule-meat: there is nothing else. The officer at the battery told me he had eaten one yesterday. We have tried to leave this Tophet and failed, and if the siege continues I must summon that higher kind of courage— moral bravery—to subdue my fears of possible mutilation.

July 4.—It is evening. All is still. Silence and night are once more united. I can sit at the table in the parlor and write. Two candles are lighted. I would like a dozen. We have had wheat supper and wheat bread once more. H. is leaning back in the rocking-chair; he says:

"G., it seems to me I can hear the silence, and feel it, too. It wraps me like a soft garment; how else can I express this peace?"

But I must write the history of the last twenty-four hours. About five yesterday afternoon, Mr. J., H.'s assistant, who, having no wife to keep him in, dodges about at every change and brings us the news, came to H. and said:

"Mr. L., you must both come to our cave to-night. I hear that to-night the shelling is to surpass everything yet. An assault will be made in front and rear. You know we have a double cave; there is room for you in mine, and mother and sister will make a place for Mrs. L. Come right up; the ball will open about seven."

We got ready, shut up the house, told Martha to go to the church again if she preferred it to the cellar, and walked up to Mr. J.'s. When supper was eaten, all secure, and ladies in their cave night toilet, it was just six, and we crossed the street to the cave opposite. As I crossed a mighty shell flew screaming right over my head. It was the last thrown into Vicksburg. We lay on our pallets waiting for the expected roar, but no sound came except the chatter from neighboring caves, and at last we dropped asleep. I woke at dawn stiff. A draft from the funnel-shaped opening had been blowing on me all night. Every one was expressing surprise at the quiet. We started for home and met the editor of the "Daily Citizen." H. said:

"This is strangely quiet, Mr. L."

"Ah, sir," shaking his head gloomily, "I'm afraid (?) the last shell has been thrown into Vicksburg."

"Why do you fear so?"

"It is surrender. At six last evening a man went down to the river and blew a truce signal; the shelling stopped at once."

—Cable, ed., "A Woman's Diary of the Siege of Vicksburg"

3. VICKSBURG SURRENDERS

On May 18, 1863, Johnston had ordered Pemberton to abandon Vicksburg and escape, if possible. Pemberton decided that escape was impossible, and retired behind the formidable works of the city. By the end of June it was clear that he could not hold out much longer, and Grant's army was by that time so large that it appeared unlikely that Johnston could break through to his aid. He therefore decided to surrender. That decision was probably inevitable; what inspired a good deal of criticism was the decision to make the formal surrender on July 4. Altogether over 30,000 Confederates were surrendered at Vicksburg—the largest force, it is alleged, in the history of modern warfare up to that time. General Grant himself here tells the story of the surrender.

On July 1st Pemberton, seeing no hope of outside relief, addressed the following letter to each of his four division commanders:

"Unless the siege of Vicksburg is raised, or supplies are thrown in, it will become necessary very shortly to evacuate the place. I see no prospect of the former, and there are many great, if not insuperable, obstacles in the way of the latter. You are, therefore, requested to inform me with as little delay as possible as to the condition of your troops, and their ability to make the marches and undergo the fatigues necessary to accomplish a successful evacuation."

Two of his generals suggested surrender, and the other two practically did the same; they expressed the opinion that an attempt to evacuate would fail. Pemberton had previously got a message to Johnston suggesting that he should try to negotiate with me for a release of the garrison with their arms. Johnston replied that it would be a confession of weakness for him to do so; but he authorized Pemberton to use his name in making such an arrangement.

On the 3d, about 10 o'clock A.M., white flags appeared on a
portion of the rebel works. Hostilities along that part of the
line ceased at once. Soon two persons were seen coming toward our lines bearing a white flag. They proved to be General Bowen, a division commander, and Colonel Montgomery,
aide-de-camp to Pemberton, bearing the following letter to
me:

"I have the honor to propose an armistice for — hours,
with the view to arranging terms for the capitulation of
Vicksburg. To this end, if agreeable to you, I will appoint
three commissioners, to meet a like number to be named by
yourself, at such place and hour to-day as you may find convenient. I make this proposition to save the further effusion
of blood, which must otherwise be shed to a frightful extent,
feeling myself fully able to maintain my position for a yet
indefinite period. This communication will be handed you,
under a flag of truce, by Major-General John S. Bowen."

It was a glorious sight to officers and soldiers on the line
where these white flags were visible, and the news soon
spread to all parts of the command. The troops felt that their
long and weary marches, hard fighting, ceaseless watching by
night and day in a hot climate, exposure to all sorts of
weather, to diseases, and, worst of all, to the gibes of many
Northern papers that came to them, saying all their suffering
was in vain, Vicksburg would never be taken, were at last at an
end, and the Union sure to be saved.

Bowen was received by General A. J. Smith, and asked to
see me. I had been a neighbor of Bowen's in Missouri, and
knew him well and favorably before the war; but his request
was refused. He then suggested that I should meet Pemberton. To this I sent a verbal message saying that if Pemberton
desired it I would meet him in front of McPherson's corps, at
3 o'clock that afternoon. I also sent the following written reply to Pemberton's letter:

"Your note of this date is just received, proposing an armistice for several hours, for the purpose of arranging terms of
capitulation through commissioners to be appointed, etc. The
useless effusion of blood you propose stopping by this course
can be ended at any time you may choose, by the unconditional surrender of the city and garrison. Men who have
shown so much endurance and courage as those now in
Vicksburg will always challenge the respect of an adversary,

and I can assure you will be treated with all the respect due to prisoners of war. I do not favor the proposition of appointing commissioners to arrange the terms of capitulation, because I have no terms other than those indicated above."

At 3 o'clock Pemberton appeared at the point suggested in my verbal message, accompanied by the same officers who had borne his letter of the morning. Generals Ord, McPherson, Logan, A. J. Smith, and several officers of my staff accompanied me. Our place of meeting was on a hill-side within a few hundred feet of the rebel lines. Near by stood a stunted oak-tree, which was made historical by the event. It was but a short time before the last vestige of its body, root, and limb had disappeared, the fragments being taken as trophies. Since then the same tree has furnished as many cords of wood, in the shape of trophies, as "The True Cross."

Pemberton and I had served in the same division during a part of the Mexican war. I knew him very well, therefore, and greeted him as an old acquaintance. He soon asked what terms I proposed to give his army if it surrendered. My answer was the same as proposed in my reply to his letter. Pemberton then said, rather snappishly, "The conference might as well end," and turned abruptly as if to leave. I said, "Very well." General Bowen, I saw, was very anxious that the surrender should be consummated. His manners and remarks while Pemberton and I were talking showed this. He now proposed that he and one of our generals should have a conference. I had no objection to this, as nothing could be made binding upon me that they might propose. Smith and Bowen accordingly had a conference, during which Pemberton and I, moving some distance away toward the enemy's lines, were in conversation. After a while Bowen suggested that the Confederate army should be allowed to march out, with the honors of war, carrying their small-arms and field-artillery. This was promptly and unceremoniously rejected. The interview here ended, I agreeing, however, to send a letter giving final terms by 10 o'clock that night. I had sent word to Admiral Porter soon after the correspondence with Pemberton had commenced, so that hostilities might be stopped on the part of both army and navy. It was agreed on my parting with Pemberton that they should not be renewed until our correspondence should cease.

When I returned to my headquarters I sent for all the corps and division commanders with the army immediately confronting Vicksburg. (Half the army was from eight to

twelve miles off, waiting for Johnston.) I informed them of
the contents of Pemberton's letters, of my reply, and the substance of the interview, and was ready to hear any suggestion; but would hold the power of deciding entirely in my
own hands. This was the nearest to a "council of war" I ever
held. Against the general and almost unanimous judgment of
the council I sent the following letter:

"In conformity with agreement of this afternoon I will
submit the following proposition for the surrender of the city
of Vicksburg, public stores, etc. On your accepting the terms
proposed I will march in one division as a guard, and take
possession at 8 A.M. to-morrow. As soon as rolls can be made
out of our lines, the officers taking with them their side-arms
and clothing; and the field, staff, and cavalry officers one horse
each. The rank and file will be allowed all their clothing, but
no other property. If these conditions are accepted, any
amount of rations you may deem necessary can be taken
from the stores you now have, and also the necessary cook-
ing-utensils for preparing them. Thirty wagons also, counting
two-horse or mule teams as one, will be allowed to transport
such articles as cannot be carried along. The same conditions
will be allowed to all sick and wounded officers and soldiers as
fast as they become able to travel. The paroles for these latter
must be signed, however, whilst officers present are authorized
to sign the roll of prisoners."

. . . Late at night I received the following reply to my last
letter:

"I have the honor to acknowledge the receipt of your
communication of this date, proposing terms of capitulation
for this garrison and post. In the main, your terms are accepted; but, in justice both to the honor and spirit of my
troops manifested in the defense of Vicksburg, I have to
submit the following amendments, which, if acceded to by
you, will perfect the agreement between us. At 10 o'clock A.M.
to-morrow I propose to evacuate the works in and around
Vicksburg, and to surrender the city and garrison under my
command, by marching out with my colors and arms, stacking them in front of my present lines, after which you will
take possession. Officers to retain their side-arms and personal property, and the rights and property of citizens to be
respected."

This was received after midnight; my reply was as follows:

"I have the honor to acknowledge the receipt of your communication of 3d July. The amendment proposed by you cannot be acceded to in full. It will be necessary to furnish every officer and man with a parole signed by himself, which, with the completion of the roll of prisoners, will necessarily take some time. Again, I can make no stipulations with regard to treatment of citizens and their private property. While I do not propose to cause them any undue annoyance or loss, I cannot consent to leave myself under any restraint by stipulations. The property which officers will be allowed to take with them will be as stated in my proposition of last evening; that is, officers will be allowed their private baggage and side-arms, and mounted officers one horse each. If you mean by your proposition for each brigade to march to the front of the lines now occupied by it, and stack arms at 10 o'clock A.M., and then return to the inside and there remain as prisoners until properly paroled, I will make no objection to it. Should no notification be received of your acceptance of my terms by 9 o'clock A.M., I shall regard them as having been rejected, and shall act accordingly. Should these terms be accepted, white flags should be displayed along your lines to prevent such of my troops as may not have been notified from firing upon your men."

Pemberton promptly accepted these terms.

During the siege there had been a good deal of friendly sparring between the soldiers of the two armies, on picket and where the lines were close together. All rebels were known as "Johnnies"; all Union troops as "Yanks." Often "Johnny" would call, "Well, Yank, when are you coming into town?" The reply was sometimes: "We propose to celebrate the 4th of July there." Sometimes it would be: "We always treat our prisoners with kindness and do not want to hurt them"; or, "We are holding you as prisoners of war while you are feeding yourselves." The garrison, from the commanding general down, undoubtedly expected an assault on the 4th. They knew from the temper of their men it would be successful when made, and that would be a greater humiliation than to surrender. Besides it would be attended with severe loss to them.

The Vicksburg paper, which we received regularly through the courtesy of the rebel pickets, said prior to the 4th, in speaking of the "Yankee" boast that they would take dinner in Vicksburg that day, that the best receipt for cooking rabbit was, "First ketch your rabbit." The paper at this time, and for some time previous, was printed on the plain side of wall paper. The last was issued on the 4th and announced that we had "caught our rabbit."

I have no doubt that Pemberton commenced his correspondence on the 3d for the twofold purpose; first, to avoid an assault, which he knew would be successful, and second, to prevent the capture taking place on the great national holiday,—the anniversary of the Declaration of American Independence. Holding out for better terms, as he did, he defeated his aim in the latter particular.

At the 4th, at the appointed hour, the garrison of Vicksburg marched out of their works, and formed line in front, stacked arms, and marched back in good order. Our whole army present witnessed this scene without cheering. . . .

Pemberton says in his report: "If it should be asked why the 4th of July was selected as the day for surrender, the answer is obvious. I believed that upon that day I should obtain better terms. Well aware of the vanity of our foe, I knew they would attach vast importance to the entrance, on the 4th of July, into the stronghold of the great river, and that, to gratify their national vanity, they would yield then what could not be extorted from them at any other time." This does not support my view of his reasons for selecting the day he did for surrendering. But it must be recollected that his first letter asking terms was received about 10 o'clock, A.M., July 3d. It then could hardly be expected that it would take 24 hours to effect a surrender. He knew that Johnston was in our rear for the purpose of raising the siege, and he naturally would want to hold out as long as he could. He knew his men would not resist an assault, and one was expected on the 4th. In our interview he told me he had rations enough to hold out some time—my recollection is two weeks. It was this statement that induced me to insert in the terms that he was to draw rations for his men from his own supplies. . . .

As soon as our troops took possession of the city, guards were established along the whole line of parapet, from the river above to the river below. The prisoners were allowed to occupy their old camps behind the intrenchments. No restraint was put upon them, except by their own commanders. They were rationed about as our own men, and from our supplies. The men of the two armies fraternized as if they had been fighting for the same cause. When they passed out of the works they had so long and so gallantly defended, between lines of their late antagonists, not a cheer went up, not a remark was made that would give pain. I believe there was a feeling of sadness among the Union soldiers at seeing the dejection of their late antagonists.

—U. S. GRANT, "The Vicksburg Campaign"

4. GENERAL BANKS TAKES PORT HUDSON

Port Hudson, just above Baton Rouge, was the last remaining Confederate fort on the Mississippi. As early as December 1862 Banks had made a demonstration against it, but had not been strong enough to take it. Feeling that he could not undertake a full-scale attack on the fort while the Confederates were in strength in the Bayou Teche and Red River country, Banks undertook several expeditions west of the Mississippi. These were for the most part. inconclusive. When Grant succeeded in crossing the river at Bruinsburg, Banks was ordered to co-operate by reducing Port Hudson. He arrived there with some 30,000 men in mid-May. It was the story of Vicksburg over again. Like Grant, Banks launched two futile assaults on the strong works of the fort, then settled down to a siege. By July the defenders of the fort were reduced to eating mules; the surrender of Vicksburg made the Confederate position untenable, and on July 9 General Gardner surrendered.

We have here two accounts of the Port Hudson operations from the pen of an unknown Confederate officer.

A. EATING MULES AT PORT HUDSON

The last quarter ration of beef had been given out to the troops on the 29th of June [1863]. On the 1st of July, at the request of many officers, a wounded mule was killed and cut up for experimental eating. All those who partook of it spoke highly of the dish. The flesh of mules is of a darker color than beef, of a finer grain, quite tender and juicy, and has a flavor something between that of beef and venison. There was an immediate demand for this kind of food, and the number of mules killed by the commissariat daily increased. Some horses were also slaughtered, and their flesh was found to be very good eating, but not equal to mule.

Rats, of which there were plenty about the deserted camps,
were also caught by many officers and men and were found
to be quite a luxury—superior, in the opinion of those who
eat them, to spring chicken; and if a philosopher of the
Celestial Empire could have visited Port Hudson at the time,
he would have marveled at the progress of the barbarians
there toward the refinements of his own people.

Mule meat was regularly served out in rations to the
troops from and after the 4th of July, and there were very
few among the garrison whose natural prejudices were so
strong as to prevent them from cooking and eating their
share. The stock of corn was getting very low, and besides
that nothing was left but peas, sugar, and molasses. These
peas were the most indigestible and unwholesome articles
that were ever given to soldiers to eat, and that such a large
quantity was left on hand was probably accounted for by
the fact that most of the troops would not have them on
any consideration. To save corn they were issued out to horses
and mules and killed a great many of these animals. All of
the horses and mules which were not needed for hauling
or other imperative duties had been turned out to graze,
where numbers of them were killed or disabled by the enemy's
cannonade and rain of Minie balls and the rest nearly starved
to death.

The sugar and molasses were put to good use by the
troops in making a weak description of beer which was constantly kept at the lines by the barrelful and drunk by the
soldiers in preference to the miserable water with which
they were generally supplied. This was a very pleasant and
healthful beverage and went far to recompense the men for
the lack of almost every other comfort or luxury. In the
same way, after the stock of tobacco had given out, they
substituted sumac leaves, which grew wild in the woods. It
had always been smoked by the Indians under the name of
killickinnic and when properly prepared for the pipe is a
tolerably good substitute for tobacco.

There was a small proportion of the garrison who could
not, however, reconcile themselves so easily to the hardships
and dangers of the siege. Some one hundred and fifty or
more men, almost entirely foreigners of a low class or ignorant conscripts from western Louisiana, men who were
troubled with none of that common feeling usually styled
patriotism, deserted us for the better-provided commissariats
of the enemy, slinking away by couples and squads during
the night time. Their loss was not wept over, nor could the

information they carried with them concerning our position enable the enemy to capture it.

—*Port Hudson . . . As Sketched from the Diary of an Officer*

B. Blue and Gray Fraternize after the Surrender of Port Hudson

At two o'clock on the morning of the 8th of July [1863] General Gardner sent to General Banks by flag of truce for confirmation of the fall of Vicksburg, which was accorded him. About nine o'clock the same morning he dispatched commissioners to treat for the surrender of the post [Port Hudson]. They did not return until afternoon and then announced that an unconditional surrender of the place and garrison had been agreed upon and that the ceremony would take place at seven o'clock the next morning.

A cessation of hostilities had already taken place, and immediately that it was known that the capitulation had been agreed upon, a singular scene was presented to the observer, particularly upon the extreme right, where the contending patries, almost near enough to clutch each other by the throat, had been engaged in a desperate struggle for the mastery.

Soldiers swarmed from their places of concealment on either side and met each other in the most cordial and fraternal spirit. Here you would see a group of Federal soldiers escorted round our works and shown the effects of their shots and entertained with accounts of such part of the siege operations as they could not have learned before. In the same way our men went into the Federal lines and gazed with curiosity upon the work which had been giving them so much trouble, escorted by Federal soldiers, who vied with each other in courtesy and a display of magnanimous spirit. The subject of the attack and defense seemed to be a tireless one with both sides, and the conversations that ensued between them were of so cheerful and pleasant a character that one could hardly believe it possible these men had just before been fighting with the ferocity of tigers and striving by every art to slaughter the men they were now fraternizing with.

Not a single case occurred in which the enemy, either officers or privates, exhibited a disposition to exult over their victory, but on the contrary, whenever the subject came up in conversation it elicited from them only compliments upon the

skill and bravery of the defense. Nor was their conduct
limited to mere expressions. They were liberal in making
presents of tobacco and other luxuries, asking of the garrison
only such articles as they could retain as relics of the siege.
One of their surgeons came in during a heavy rainstorm and
brought medicines for our sick, repeating his visit the next
morning and bringing a large quantity of quinine, which he
dosed out to the fever patients. During the afternoon and
evening of the 8th a large number of Federals were within our
lines visiting at our camps, whither most of our men had
repaired to pack up their little stock of clothing prepara-
tory to an expected departure on the morrow.

> —*Port Hudson . . . As Sketched from the*
> *Diary of an Officer*

5. "THE FATHER OF WATERS AGAIN GOES UNVEXED TO THE SEA"

Lincoln had been invited to address a meeting of Union
men at Springfield, Illinois; finding it impossible to leave
Washington he sent, instead, a long letter to the chairman of
the meeting, James Conkling. Most of the letter argued the
necessity of emancipation; the concluding paragraphs—some
of the most felicitous words Lincoln ever wrote—discussed
some of the implications of the war and of victory.

Executive Mansion, Washington, August 26, 1863
HON. JAMES C. CONKLING
My Dear Sir.
. . . The signs look better. The Father of Waters again goes
unvexed to the sea. Thanks to the great Northwest for it.
Nor yet wholly to them. Three hundred miles up they met
New England, Empire, Keystone, and Jersey, hewing their way
right and left. The sunny South, too, in more colors than one,
also lent a hand. On the spot, their part of the history was
jotted down in black and white. The job was a great national
one; and let none be banned who bore an honorable part in
it. And while those who have cleared the great river may well
be proud, even that is not all. It is hard to say that anything has been more bravely and well done than at Antietam,
Murfreesboro', Gettysburg, and on many fields of lesser note.
Nor must Uncle Sam's web-feet be forgotten. At all the watery
margins they have been present. Not only on the deep sea,
the broad bay, and the rapid river, but also up the narrow

muddy bayou, and wherever the ground was a little damp, they have been, and made their tracks. Thanks to all. For the great republic—for the principle it lives by, and keeps alive —for man's vast future—thanks to all.

Peace does not appear so distant as it did. I hope it will come soon, and come to stay; and so come as to be worth the keeping in all future time. It will then have been proved that, among free men, there can be no successful appeal from the ballot to the bullet; and that they who take such an appeal are sure to lose their case, and pay the cost. And then, there will be some black men who can remember that, with silent tongue, and clenched teeth, and steady eye, and well-poised bayonet, they have helped mankind on to this great consummation; while, I fear, there will be some white ones, unable to forget that with malignant heart, and deceitful speech, they strove to hinder it.

Still, let us not be over-sanguine of a speedy final triumph. Let us be quite sober. Let us diligently apply the means, never doubting that a just God, in his own good time, will give us the rightful result.

Yours very truly

A. LINCOLN.

—Complete Works of Abraham Lincoln

6. GENERAL MORGAN INVADES THE NORTH

After Stones River (December 31, 1862) General Bragg had fallen back on Tullahoma, and then to Chattanooga. To cover his retreat he ordered General Morgan to raid the railroads in Kentucky and, if possible, threaten Louisville. Morgan wanted to invade Ohio, but to this plan Bragg refused his consent. Starting out on July 2, 1863—just as Pemberton was getting ready to surrender Vicksburg—Morgan swept through Kentucky, crossed the Green River, captured Lebanon, and on July 9 reached the banks of the Ohio. Contrary to orders he then went ahead with his own plan of an invasion—with disastrous results.

Morgan himself was one of the most galmorous figures in the Confederacy. He had fought in the Mexican War and as early as 1857 had organized the Lexington (Kentucky) Rifles. Commissioned captain in 1861 he began the series of raids that were so effective in disrupting Federal communications in the West. By the time of Shiloh he was a colonel, and

*in June a brigadier. With Forrest and Wheeler he was one of
the three great cavalry leaders of the Army of Tennessee.
Captured at the end of this raid Morgan was imprisoned
in the Ohio State Penitentiary; we will read elsewhere how
he escaped. In 1864 he was sent to western Virginia to deal
with the attack launched by Averell and Crook, and was killed
at Greenville, Tennessee, in September of that year.*

*We have here two accounts of the Morgan raid. The first,
by Colonel Alston, Morgan's chief of staff, carries the story
up through July 5, 1863; the second, by Colonel James B.
McCreary, continues the story to its end. McCreary was later
Governor of Kentucky and served for six terms in Congress.*

A. Morgan's Cavalrymen Sweep through Kentucky

July 1st, 1863.—On the banks of the Cumberland. The river
very high. No boats. General M. obliged to build a number
of boats, which he accomplished with very little delay, and
commenced crossing at sundown.

July 2d.—Bucksville. He had great difficulty in making the
horses swim, but by united and systematic exertion succeeded
in getting the entire command of— —regiments over by ten
A.M., though the command was very much scattered. At
eleven o'clock, scouts came into Bucksville and reported the
enemy advancing, and within four miles of the town. It was
supposed to be only a scouting party, and a portion of Dick
Morgan's command was sent out to make a reconnoissance.
The report of the scouts of the enemy advancing proved to
be correct, and a message was received from Colonel Ward
that he was attacked. Colonel Grigsby was sent to reënforce
him, and succeeded in driving the Yankees back in great
confusion upon their reënforcements. My regiment lost two
mortally wounded and two others slightly. Five of the Yankees were known to be killed and a number wounded, with
about fifteen prisoners. No tidings heard of the Second
brigade until dark, when they arrived and reported that
Colonel Johnson, commanding, had experienced great difficulty in crossing, and that in addition to the precipitous banks
and absence of all boats or other means of transportation,
the enemy were hovering on the river and harassing him as far
as they could. He was, however, quite successful in driving
them back. Yesterday a young man, calling himself Charles
Rogers, dressed in full confederate uniform, came into our
lines and expressed a desire to join our command. I suspi-

cioned him, and, after a few questions, I was convinced that he was a spy. I threatened to shoot him, when he confessed that he had been lying, and that his name was Simon Blitz— in fact he convicted himself of being a spy. I hated to shoot him, although he deserved it.

July 3d.—My regiment behaved very gallantly in yesterday's fight with the enemy, frequently having hand-to-hand encounters. To-day we experienced the same difficulty in getting the artillery on, and had to press a number of oxen for the purpose. After two halts for the column to close up, our advance proceeded to Columbia. They were met by detachments from three regiments said to be under command of Colonel Wolford. A brief engagement followed, in which we drove the enemy in great haste through the town, capturing six prisoners, killing two, among them Captain Carter, and wounding three. Our loss was two killed and two wounded, among them Captain Cassel, a most dashing and daring officer, wounded in the thigh. Our men behaved badly at Columbia, breaking open a store and plundering it. I ordered the men to return the goods, and made all the reparation in my power. These outrages are very disgraceful, and are usually perpetrated by men accompanying the army simply for plunder. They are not worth a— —, and are a disgrace to both armies. Passed through Columbia, and camped six miles from Green River Bridge.

July 4th.—New-Market, Ky. A day of gloom, deep gloom, to our entire command. How many who rose this morning full of enthusiasm and hope now "sleep the sleep that knows no waking." The sun rose bright and beautiful, the air was cool and balmy, all nature wore the appearance of peace and harmony. While riding along, affected by the stillness of all around, Captain Magennis, the Adjutant-General, rode up and remarked how dreadful to reflect that we were marching on to engage in deadly strife, and how many poor fellows would pass into eternity before the setting of yonder sun. I have no doubt the poor fellow was moved to these reflections by one of those unaccountable presentiments which are so often the harbingers of evil. (Before dark he was a corpse.) About sunrise we drove in the enemy's pickets and were soon near their fortifications, which had been erected to prevent our crossing. General Morgan sent in a flag of truce and demanded the surrender, but the Colonel quietly remarked: "If it was any other day he might consider the demand, but the Fourth of July was a bad day to talk about surrender, and he must therefore decline." This

Colonel is a gallant man, and the entire arrangement of his defence entitles him to the highest credit for military skill. We would mark such a man in our army for promotion.

We attacked the place with two regiments, sending the remainder of our force across at another ford. The place was judiciously chosen and skilfully defended, and the result was that we were repulsed with severe loss—about twenty-five killed and twenty wounded. . . . Our march thus far has been very fatiguing—bad roads, little rest or sleep, little to eat, and a fight every day. Yet our men are cheerful, even buoyant, and to see them pressing along barefooted, hurrahing and singing, would cause one to appreciate what those who are fighting in a just and holy cause will endure.

About three o'clock, as I rode on about forty yards in advance, I heard the General exclaim something in a very excited tone, which I could not understand, and heard at the same time the report of a pistol. I turned, and, great God! to my horror I saw Captain Magennis falling from his horse, with the blood gushing out of his mouth and breast. His only remark was: "Let me down easy." In another moment his spirit had fled. He was killed by Captain Murphy because Magennis, by the direction of General Morgan, had ordered Murphy to restore a watch taken from a prisoner. Thus was the poor fellow's language of the morning dreadfully realized. I was terribly affected. I had seen blood flow freely on many a battlefield—my friends had been killed in the morning—but this caused a deeper impression and shock than any occurrence I ever witnessed. Truly this has been a sad day. General Morgan looks haggard and weary, but he never despairs. May to-morrow dawn more bright than to-day closes.

July 5th.—Another day of gloom, fatigue, and death. Moved on Lebanon at sunrise—placed our men in line. Sent around Colonel J—— —— with his brigade to the Danville road to cut off reënforcements, which we knew were expected from Danville. I went in with a flag of truce. It was fired on five times. Officer apologized, saying he thought it was a man with a white coat on. Very dangerous mistake, at least for me. Demanded unconditional surrender. Told Colonel Hanson we had his reënforcements cut off, and resistance was useless. He refused to surrender, and I then ordered him to send out the non-combatants, as we would be compelled to shell the town. He posted his regiment in the dépôt and in various houses, by which he was enabled to make a desperate resistance. After a fight of seven hours, General Morgan, finding the town could be taken in no other way, ordered a charge to be made. This ought to have been done at first, but General Morgan said, when it was urged on him, that he wished to avoid the destruction of private property as much as possible, and he would only permit it as a last and final resort. Colonel Hanson still held out in hopes of receiving reënforcements, and only surrendered after we had fired the buildings in which he was posted. . . .

By this surrender we obtained a sufficient quantity of guns to arm all our men who were without them; also a quantity of ammunition, of which we stood sorely in need. At the order to charge, Duke's regiment rushed forward, and poor Tommy Morgan, who was always in the lead, ran forward and cheered the men with all the enthusiasm of his bright nature. Almost at the first volley he fell back, pierced through the heart. His only words were: "Brother Cally, they have killed me." Noble youth! how deeply lamented by all who knew you! This was a crushing blow to General Morgan, as his affection for his brother exceeded the love of Jonathan to David. It caused a terrible excitement, and the men were in a state of frenzy. It required the utmost energy and promptitude on the part of the officers to prevent a scene of slaughter, which all would deeply have lamented. Our men behaved badly here, breaking open stores and plundering indiscriminately. All that officers could do was done to prevent, but in vain. These occurrences are very disgraceful, and I am truly glad that they form exceptions to the general conduct.

While I was paroling the prisoners, a courier arrived, informing me that the enemy were approaching with two regiments of cavalry and a battery of artillery, and that skirmishing was then going on with our pickets. I was therefore obliged to order the prisoners to Springfield on the double-quick. Soon after we left Lebanon, the hardest rain I ever experienced commenced to fall, and continued till nine o'clock. Arrived at Springfield at dark, when I halted the prisoners in order to parole those who were not paroled at Lebanon, and formally dismissed them. This detained me at Springfield two hours after the command had passed. Wet and chilly, worn out, horse tired and hungry. Stopped to feed her. Falling asleep, was aroused by one of the men. Started on to the command. When I reached the point on the Bardstown road where I had expected the Second brigade to encamp, was halted by a party of cavalry. Supposing them to be our own pickets, I rode up promptly to correct them for standing in full view of any one approaching, when lo! to my mortification, I found myself a prisoner. My God! how I hated it, no one can understand.

—"Journal of Lieutenant-Colonel Alston"

B. MORGAN'S RAID COMES TO AN INGLORIOUS END

8 July, 1863. The great Ohio River, the dividing line between the North and the South, is reached. The command is crossing. Here I met Capt. Heady. The enemy are pressing us in the rear, and their gunboats kept up a steady fire on the two stern boats, in which Morgan's command is crossing. Thoughts, hopes and anxieties chase each other in wild succession through my mind, but my Regiment is again guarding the rear and vigilance is the price of liberty. At 12 o'clock tonight, it being moonrise, the enemy pressed upon us and drove our pickets in, but again fell back.

July 9. This morning I am left with half of the Regiment one mile from the river as rear guard, and at daylight the Yankees moved down upon me. It was a critical and trying moment. By the interposition of Divine Providence, a heavy fog suddenly, and whilst hot skirmishing was going on, enveloped friends and foes, and the Yankees halted. Under this fog I crossed my command over the river. As I moved up the hills of Indiana, the enemy moved down the hills of Kentucky. We are now fairly into Yankee land. What the result will be God only knows. We attacked Corydon this evening, and, after a tolerable severe fight of two hours, took the place and several hundred prisoners. Thence to Salsberry, where we bivouacked for a few hours.

July 10. Attacked Palmyra and captured a small force of the enemy. Then moved on Salem, where, after some fighting, a considerable force surrendered to us. Here we destroyed heavy supplies, a depot, and several bridges. Then we captured Canton, tore up the railroad, and tore down the telegraph, and then rapidly moved on, like an irresistable storm, to the vicinity of Vienna, where, for a brief period, we bivouacked. The citizens seemed frightened almost to death, for Federal papers have published the wildest tales about us. The Governors of Indiana and Ohio have ordered out all able-bodied men, and we have already fought decrepit, white-haired age and buoyant, blithe boyhood.

July 11. Marched without any hindrance through Vienna, New Philadelphia, Lexington, and Paris, and came to Vernon, where we found the enemy in great force. The enemy consisted of a large force of Volunteers and Militia. We made a flank movement, tore up all the railroads around Vernon, and then traveled all night to Dupont, where we rested and fed our horses. Like an irresistable avalanche we are sweeping over this country. Man never knows his powers of endurance 'till he tries himself. The music of the enemy's balls is now as familiar and common as the carol of the spring bird which, unknowing of death and carnage around, sings today the same song that gladdened our forefathers.

July 12. We move rapidly through six or seven towns without any resistance, and tonight lie down for a little while with our bridles in our hands.

July 13. Today we reach Harrison, the most beautiful town I have yet seen in the North—a place, seemingly, where love and beauty, peace and prosperity, sanctified by true religion, might hold high carnival. Here we destroyed a magnificent bridge and saw many beautiful women. From here we moved to Miami Town, where we destroyed another splendid bridge over the Miami River. The bridge at Harrison was across Whitewater River. From Miami Town we passed through the most fertile and lovely region of Ohio. For hours the column moved at full speed, for we were now moving around Cincinnati. County seat after county seat reared itself in stately splendor, now scarcely distinguishable for the clouds of dust. Town after town and city after city are passed. A part of Morgan's command makes a feint on Cincinnati, and we move at this rate a distance of eighty-three miles, and all in sixteen hours. If there be a man who boasts of a march, let him excel this. After this Gilpin race we rested by capturing a train of cars on the Little Miami and a considerable number of prisoners. Then we surrounded Camp Dennison, captured a large train of wagons, and about two hundred mules. From there we moved on Winchester, where we destroyed a fine bridge, and thence to Jackson.

July 15. Today we traveled through several unimportant towns, destroyed one bridge, and bivouacked at Walnut Grove.

July 16. Today we find the first obstruction in our way, consisting of felled trees. The enemy are now pressing us on all sides, and the woods swarm with militia. We capture hundreds of prisoners, but, a parole being null, we can only sweep them as chaff out of our way. Today we crossed the Scioto to Piketon, and, as usual, destroyed the bridge. Thence we moved to Jackson.

July 17. Today we find our road badly blockaded and "axes to the front" is now the common command. We have today passed through many little dutch towns with which this country abounds. Tonight we halt near Pomeroy. The enemy are in considerable force in front. We attacked them and drove them from our front, and then moved rapidly in the direction of Buffington, where we intend to cross.

July 18. All are now on the qui vive, for the Ohio River is full of gunboats and transports, and an immense force of cavalry is hovering in our rear. We reached Buffington tonight. All was quiet. A dense fog wrapped this woodland scene. Early in the morning of the 19th the Yankees guarding the ford were attacked by our force, and driven away and their artillery captured. Immediately after this, and whilst we were trying the river to ascertain if it was fordable, the gunboats steamed up the river. The transports landed their infantry, thousands of cavalry moved down upon us, and the artillery commenced its deadly work. We formed and fought here to no purpose. The river was very full in consequence of a heavy rain away up the river. Shells and minie balls were ricocheting and exploding in every direction, cavalry were charging, and infantry with its slow, measured tread moved upon us, while broadside after broadside was poured upon our doomed command from the gunboats. It seemed as if our comparatively small command would be swallowed up by the innumerable horde. About half of it was here captured or killed. I made my way out by charging through the enemy's lines with about one-half the Regiment, and finally formed a juncture with the remnant of our command under Gen. Morgan, now numbering about 1,200. With these we moved towards Cheshire, traveling rapidly all night, and passing around the enemy's pickets, over cliffs and ravines, which under ordinary circumstances, would have been considered insurmountable.

July 20. Today reached Cheshire. There Buffington was entrenched to a certain extent. The Yankees pressed us in the rear and fired on us from their gunboats in front, thus forcing us back to a high hill, where, after exhausting our ammunition, we surrendered, 700 men. I saw General Shackelford and arranged the terms of surrender. He allowed all field officers to retain side arms and horses, all other to retain private property. This proposition I announced to all the officers, and all voted to surrender, and thus ended the saddest day of my life.

—McCreary, "The Journal of My Soldier Life"

III

Prisons,
North and South

THIS *is doubtless the darkest chapter in the history of the war. No other, certainly, reveals so clearly American unreadiness for war or the failure to take in, early enough, its true nature or to anticipate its problems. In a sense the war took both sides by surprise. Neither government was prepared for it, neither anticipated its long duration. There was, consequently, no adequate preparation either for prisoners or for medical services. At the beginning authorities on both sides improvised prisons. The North was fairly well supplied with prisons of a sort—the existing penitentiaries, and military prisons—and others were speedily set up well behind the lines. The South used the meager facilities it already had, took over factories and warehouses, and eventually fell back on open stockades such as the notorious Andersonville.*

From the very beginning there were perplexing problems relating to the treatment of prisoners. From the strictly legal point of view all Confederates were rebels—and thus traitors —and subject to the extreme penalty. Circumstances, however, forced the Union to recognize the de facto *belligerency of the South, and Confederate prisoners were accorded the customary treatment of prisoners of war. There was a brief attempt to make an exception of sailors on privateers—to regard them as pirates—but a threat of reprisal took care of that. Some Southern officers were inclined to regard Negro troops as beyond the pale and there was a gesture of turning*

*them over to state authorities for such treatment as was
thought appropriate; this, too, yielded to the threat of reprisal and there is no evidence that Negro prisoners were
maltreated. The most serious problem was that of prisoner
exchange. Under the cartel of July 1862 both sides agreed to
exchange or parole all prisoners within ten days, and if this
cartel had been observed it would have eliminated the whole
prisoner problem, for captures (up to the very end of the war)
were roughly equal. Unfortunately both sides violated the
cartel, and in 1863 Grant suspended further exchange of
prisoners—technically on the ground of Confederate violations of the cartel but actually because the Confederacy had
more to gain by exchange than the Union.*

*Conditions in prisons, North and South, were uniformly
bad. Most of them were overcrowded; few provided adequate
food, shelter or clothing, and the medical and sanitary
services were about as bad as they could be. The result was
a shockingly high mortality rate. Of 194,743 Union soldiers
actually imprisoned, 30,128 died in captivity; of 214,865
Confederate soldiers actually imprisoned, 25,976 died. The
different mortality rate was a measure not of wickedness or
neglect on the part of the Confederacy but of shortages of
food, clothing, medical supplies, and manpower. If approximately one third of all the prisoners at Andersonville died,
it must be remembered that the mortality rate in Camp
Douglas in Chicago ran as high as 10 per cent a month,
at times, while that at such comparatively well built camps
as Elmira ran to 5 per cent a month.*

1. ABNER SMALL SUFFERS IN
DANVILLE PRISON

*Abner Small was a boy in Waterville, Maine, when the war
broke out. Enlisting as a private in the 3rd Maine Volunteers
he eventually rose to be major of the 16th Maine, whose
history he subsequently wrote. He fought through Fredericksburg, Chancellorsville, Gettysburg, and the Wilderness, was
captured in August 1864, and imprisoned in Libby and Danville prisons in Virginia, and in Salisbury, North Carolina. His
is one of the best, and one of the least embittered, accounts
of prison life in the South.*

[November 1864]. Our quarters were so crowded that
none of us had more space to himself than he actually oc-

cupied, usually a strip of the bare, hard floor, about six feet
by two. We lay in long rows, two rows of men with their
heads to the side walls and two with their heads together
along the center of the room, leaving narrow aisles between
the rows of feet. The wall spaces were preferred because a
man could brace his back there and sit out the long day or the
longer night. There was a row of posts down the center of the
room, but these were too few and too narrow to give much
help; I know, because I had a place by one of them.

I remember three officers, one a Yankee from Vermont,
one an Irishman from New York, and one a Dutchman from
Ohio, who messed together by the wall opposite me. When
they came to Danville they were distinct in feature and personality. They became homesick and disheartened. They lost
all interest in everything, and would sit in the same attitude
hour after hour and day after day, with their backs against the
wall and their gaze fixed on the floor at my feet. It grew upon
me that they were gradually being merged into one man
with three bodies. They looked just alike; truly, I couldn't tell
them apart. And they were dying of nostalgia. . . .

Some of the prisoners played chess, checkers, and back-
gammon. Captain Conley and I had made a set of checkers in
Libby, and we still had them, but the game palled on us. Like
the ungodly majority, we killed time and escaped insanity
with cards. A few of our associates, pursuing the consolations
of religion, found none too much time to study the Scriptures;
games had no fascinating power over them. A few others,
remembering what they had learned at college, engaged in
the study of classical or modern languages. Many tried to
read, but reading somehow ceased to be a comfort in prison; at
least, that was my experience. Our library, moreover, was a
small one; it consisted of a few books and some back numbers
of monthlies brought to us by the Reverend Charles K. Hall,
a Methodist minister of Danville, who occasionally preached to
us.

Many of our comrades developed a wonderful talent at
handicraft and made hundreds of ornaments from bone and
wood. Crosses, rings, and pins were artistically fashioned and
most beautifully chased. Busts were carved from bricks
taken from the walls. Checkers with monograms and raised
figures were cut from bone and bits of wood. Altogether,
there was output enough to stock a respectable museum. These
objects were not made wholly in the cause of art, nor to
while away the time; they were valuable for barter and exchange.

As our money gave out, we sold the things to get more, or swapped articles of value or works of art for necessities. Boots, spurs, watches, rings, jack-knives, buttons, even toothpicks, were commodities of traffic. Boots were a quick commodity and brought high prices in debased rebel currency; but we hated to part with them. Captain Conley's pride in a pair of nice boots lasted until his luxurious habit of smoking demanded a sacrifice. The officer of the guard, an inveterate haggler with the general manner and appearance of a Malay pirate, offered one hundred Confederate dollars and finally a pair of shoes also, for the boots, and the offer was accepted. The cash was paid, and the captain, almost in tears, gave up his fine footwear. After a wait of two weeks there was passed into the prison a package addressed to Captain Conley. "My shoes!" he cried. He tore off the wrapper, and for an hour sat and swore at two old army brogans, of different sizes and both for the same foot. My own boots went for cash the day after Christmas. I fared better than Conley; I got a hundred dollars and a pair of shoes that I could wear.

All sorts of makeshifts were adopted to cover our persons as decency demanded. When I was captured, I was the proud possessor of a new staff uniform ornamented with gold lace. Five months later, my most intimate friends would have failed to recognize me in the ragged tramp who sat naked on the floor at Danville and robbed the ends of his trousers in order to reseat them. It was not until after I was paroled that I took those trousers off; I couldn't have done so before, because after sewing up the legs while I had them on, I couldn't get my feet through.

Although we all became disreputable in appearance, some of us kept up as best we could our proper relations of mutual respect. I am sorry to say that military rank was soon ignored by the majority of officers in Prison No. 3, and that selfishness and dishonesty added to our cup of humiliation and suffering; yet I know that much should be forgiven in men who had almost lost their natural humanity. Our nerves were worn ragged. The slightest of provocations would cause a quarrel. Two cavalry officers, Captain Harris and Lieutenant McGraw, fought over the possession of a few rusty cans. The captain's shirt was torn to shreds, and since it was the only shirt he had, and the remainder of his wardrobe consisted of a well-ventilated pair of trousers, he was to be pitied. . . .

Life became so unbearable, and the prospects of a general exchange so delusive, that on December 10th about a hundred of the prisoners, the most courageous, or the most wanting in judgment, made an attempt to break prison and escape, and failed miserably. Unaware of the attempt to be made, I, with five others, was walking on the ground floor for exercise when I saw two officers close in on the sentry by the door that opened into the yard, one seizing his gun and the other taking him by the throat to prevent him from giving an alarm. At the same moment another officer tried to choke into silence the sentry by the stairs, but his grip was too weak, and the brave rebel, in spite of threats, shouted, "Turn out the guard!" The cry was at once repeated outside, and muskets were thrust in through the sashless windows. I have outlived the sensation of that moment, but I know that I was never more conscious of being in the presence of death than when I caught a glimpse of eternity in the black muzzle of a gun held within six feet of my breast. The other promenaders were as helplessly exposed, and we all might have been the victims of nervous and frightened sentries, but Colonel Smith came running and shouted, "Cease firing!" He was not quick enough, however, to save the officer who had grappled with the sentry by the stairs. That unfortunate prisoner was shot through the bowels, and his wound was cruelly aggravated as he made his way up the two flights to the top floor, hurriedly helped along by some of his associates. Colonel Smith came inside, ordered a number of prisoners into close confinement, and told us that a keg of powder was buried under the prison, and that if another attempt to escape should be made, he would blow us all to hell.

—SMALL, *The Road to Richmond*

2. SUFFERING IN ANDERSONVILLE PRISON

Andersonville, in southwestern Georgia, was the largest and the most dreaded of Confederate prisons. The first captured Federals arrived there early in 1864; by midsummer the number of prisoners had increased to some 32,000, and this though the prison was originally designed to accommodate only 10,000. In no other prison were conditions so crowded or so wretched; the prisoners lived in tents on the bare ground or in improvised huts; the food was woefully insufficient; the water polluted; sanitary facilities wholly inadequate. By the end of the war about 50,000, prisoners—all of them privates—had been received at Andersonville, and about one third of these had died. After peace the superintendent, Captain Henry Wirz, was tried for murder and executed.

This account differs from most prison narratives in that it comes from a friendly source. Eliza Andrews was one of that notable galaxy of Confederate woman diarists who tell us so much about social life in the South during the war. After the war she wrote two books on botany and three novels.

January 27, 1865.—While going our rounds in the morning we found a very important person in Peter Louis, a paroled Yankee prisoner, in the employ of Captain Bonham. The captain keeps him out of the stockade, feeds and clothes him, and in return reaps the benefit of his skill. Peter is a French Yankee, a shoemaker by trade, and makes as beautiful shoes as I ever saw imported from France. My heart quite softened toward him when I saw his handiwork, and little Mrs. Sims was so overcome that she gave him a huge slice of her Confederate fruitcake. I talked French with him, which pleased him greatly, and Mett and I engaged him to make us each a pair of shoes. I will feel like a lady once more, with good shoes on my feet. I expect the poor Yank is glad to get away from Anderson on any terms. Although matters have improved somewhat with the cool weather, the tales that are told of the condition of things there last summer are appalling. Mrs. Brisbane heard all about it from Father Hamilton, a Roman Catholic priest from Macon, who has been working like a good Samaritan in those dens of filth and misery. It is a shame to us Protestants that we have let a Roman Catholic get so far ahead of us in this work of charity and mercy. Mrs. Brisbane says Father Hamilton told her that during the summer the wretched prisoners burrowed in the ground like moles to protect themselves from the sun. It was not safe to give them material to build shanties as they might use it for clubs to overcome the guard. These underground huts, he said, were alive with vermin and stank like charnel houses. Many of the prisoners were stark naked, having not so much as a shirt to their backs. He told a pitiful story of a Pole who had no garment but a shirt, and to make it cover him better, he put his legs into the sleeves and tied the tail around his neck. The others guyed him so on his appearance and the poor wretch was so disheartened by suffering that one day he deliberately stepped over the dead line and stood there till the guard was forced to shoot him. But what I can't understand is that a Pole, of all people in the world, should come over here and try to take away our liberty when his own country is in the hands of oppressors. One would think that the Poles, of all nations in the world, ought to sympathize with a people fighting for their liberties.

Father Hamilton said that at one time the prisoners died at the rate of a hundred and fifty a day, and he saw some of them die on the ground without a rag to lie on or a garment to cover them. Dysentery was the most fatal disease, and as they lay on the ground in their own excrements, the smell was so horrible that the good father says he was often obliged to rush from their presence to get a breath of pure air. It is dreadful. My heart aches for the poor wretches, Yankees though they are, and I am afraid God will suffer some terrible retribution to fall upon us for letting such things happen. If the Yankees ever should come to southwest Georgia and go to Anderson and see the graves there, God have mercy on the land! And yet what can we do? The Yankees themselves are really more to blame than we, for they won't exchange these prisoners, and our poor, hard-pressed Confederacy has not the means to provide for them when our own soldiers are starving in the field. Oh, what a horrible thing war is when stripped of all its pomp and circumstance!

—ANDREWS, *The War-Time Journal of a Georgia Girl*

3. THE BRIGHT SIDE OF LIBBY PRISON

Next to Andersonville Libby was the most famous, or notorious, of Confederate prisons. Originally a vacant warehouse in Richmond, it was taken over by General Winder, provost marshal of the city, and made into a prison for commissioned officers; privates from the Virginia battles were housed at Belle Isle in the James. There were a number of spectacular escapes from Libby, and after the Dahlgren Raid of 1864, designed to free the prisoners, Libby was largely abandoned in favor of prisons farther to the south.

Frank Moran, who here tells something of the brighter side of prison life, was a captain of the 73rd New York Volunteers who was captured at Gettysburg and imprisoned first at Libby and later at Macon, Georgia, and Charleston, South Carolina.

The building had a frontage from east to west of 145 feet, and a depth from north to south of 105 feet. It stood isolated from other buildings, with streets passing its front, rear, and west ends, and with a vacant space on the east of about sixty feet in width. The portion of the building devoted to the use of the prisoners consisted of nine rooms, each 102 feet in length by forty-five feet in breadth. The ceiling was eight feet high, except in the upper rooms, which were higher, better lighted, and better ventilated, owing to the pitch of the roof. Rickety, unbanistered stairs led from the lower to the upper rooms, and all the rooms of the upper floors were connected by doors, leaving free access from one to the other. With the exception of a few rude bunks and tables in the upper and lower west rooms, which were respectively termed "Streight's room" and "Milroy's room," and four long tables in the lower middle or "kitchen room," there was no furniture in the prison. The north windows commanded a partial view of the hilly portion of the city. From the east the prisoners could look off toward the Rocketts and City Point. The south windows looked out upon the canal and James river, with Manchester opposite and Belle Isle, while from the windows of the upper west room could be seen Castle Thunder, Jefferson Davis's mansion, and the Confederate capital.

Libby prison was a vast museum of human character, where the chances of war had brought into close communion every type and temperament; where military rank was wholly ignored, and all shared a common lot. At the time referred to, there were about 1200 Union officers there, of all ranks, and representing every loyal state. They were not men who would have sought each other's society from natural or social affinity, but men who had been involuntarily forced together by the fortunes of war, which, like politics, often "makes strange bedfellows." There were men of all sizes and nationalities. Youth and age, and titled men of Europe, who had enlisted in our cause, might be found among the captives. There were about thirty doctors, as many ministers, a score of journalists and lawyers, a few actors, and a proportionate representation from all trades and professions that engage men in civil life. Among them were travelers and scholars, who had seen the world, and could entertain audiences for hours with narratives of their journeyings; indeed, among the attractions of the prison was the pleasure derived by intimate association with men of bright and cultured minds; men who had often led their squadrons on the tough edge of battle and who in their history presented the best types of modern chivalry. It was indeed a remarkable gathering and the circumstances are not likely to arise that will reassemble its counterpart again in this generation. All in all, Libby prison, from the vast mixture of its inmates, and from all its peculiar surroundings, was doubtless the best school of human nature ever seen in this country.

It will not seem strange, therefore, that men of such varied talents, tastes, and dispositions, shipwrecked in this peculiar manner, should begin to devise ways and means to turn the tedious hours of prison life to some account. To this end meetings and consultations were held to set on foot amusements and instruction for the prisoners.

A minstrel troupe was organized, and its talent would compare favorably with some professional companies of to-day. A number of musical instruments were purchased, forming a respectable orchestra.

Refreshing music often enlivened the place when the weary-souled prisoner had laid down for the night. If there ever was a time and place when that old melody, "Home Sweet Home," touched the tenderest chords of the soldier's heart, it was on Christmas Eve of 1863, behind the barred windows of Libby prison. Chess, checkers, cards, or such other games occupied much of our time. Some busied themselves with making bone rings or ornaments, many of them carved with exquisite skill. . . .

At night the prisoners covered the floor completely, lying in straight rows like prostrate lines of battle, and when one rolled over all must necessarily do the same. It was inevitable that among such large numbers there should appear the usual infliction of snorers, whose discord at times drew a terrific broadside of boots, tin cans, and other convenient missiles, which invariably struck the wrong man. Among our number was one officer whose habit of grinding his teeth secured him a larger share of room at night than was commonly allowed to a prisoner, and his comrades hoped that a special exchange might restore him to his family; for certainly he was a man that would be missed wherever he had lodged. On a memorable night when this gentleman was entertaining us with his "tooth solo," one comrade who had been kept awake for the three previous nights, after repeatedly shouting to the nocturnal minstrel to "shut up," arose in wrath, and, picking his steps in the dark among his prostrate comrades, arrived at last near a form which he felt certain was that of the disturber of the peace. With one mighty effort, he bestowed a kick in the ribs of the victim, and hurriedly retreated to his place. Then arose the kicked officer, who was not the grinder at all, and made an address to his invisible assailant, employing terms and vigorous adjectives not seen in the New Testament, vehemently declaring in a brilliant peroration that it was enough to be compelled to spend wakeful nights beside a man who made nights hideous with serenades, without being kicked for him. He resumed his bed amid thunderous applause, during which the grinder was awakened and was for the first time made aware of the cause of the enthusiasm.

The spirit of Yankee enterprise was well illustrated by the publication of a newspaper by the energetic chaplain of a New York regiment. It was entitled *The Libby Prison Chronicle*. True, there were no printing facilities at hand, but, undaunted by this difficulty, the editor obtained and distributed quantities of manuscript paper among the prisoners who were leaders in their several professions, so that there was soon organized an extensive corps of able correspondents, local reporters, poets, punsters, and witty paragraphers, that gave the chronicle a pronounced success. Pursuant to previous announcement, the "editor" on a stated day each week, would take up his position in the center of the upper east room, and, surrounded by an audience limited only by the available space, would read the articles contributed during the week.

"The Prison Minstrels" were deservedly popular. The troupe was organized and governed by strictly professional rules. Nothing but the possession and display of positive musical or dramatic talent could command prominence, and as a natural consequence it was a common occurrence to see a second lieutenant carrying off the honors of the play, and the colonel of his regiment carrying off the chairs as a "supe." Our elephant, by the way, deserves especial mention, not only because of his peculiar construction, but because both intellectually and physically he differed from all elephants we had previously seen. The animal was composed of four United States officers, which certainly gave him unusual rank. One leg was a major, a second a naval officer, a third a captain of cavalry, and the last leg was by the happy thought of the astute manager an army surgeon. A quantity of straw formed the body; the tusks and trunk were improvised from the meager resources of our "property room." The whole was covered ingeniously by five army blankets. Indeed the elephant, seen by the "footlights" (four candles set in bottles), was pronounced by the critics of *The Libby Prison Chronicle* "a masterpiece of stage mechanism."

—MORAN, "Libby's Bright Side"

4. THE AWFUL CONDITIONS AT FORT DELAWARE

Fort Delaware was the Andersonville of the North—the most dreaded of Northern prisons. Located on an island in the Delaware River, much of it was below water—which was held back by dykes—and the flimsy barracks in which the men lived were cold and damp. Unlike most prisons, Fort Delaware housed both officers and privates. Young Shotwell whom we have met before, was captured on the eve of the battle of Cold Harbor and imprisoned first at Point Lookout and later at Fort Delaware.

July 12, 1864.—I have just witnessed a sight that made my blood boil. When I first arrived here I made the acquaintance of a handsome young officer; Captain William H. Gordon, from West Virginia, a native of Brooke County, not far from Wheeling. After some years' service he went home on furlough and was captured while returning to the Army.

His captors were renegades, Southern born, but wearing Yankee blue; and to furnish an excuse for their malevolent treatment, they charged him with being on a recruiting expedition inside of their lines; just as I was put in irons as a spy, tho' simply on a legitimate scouting expedition with arms in my hands, and wearing our uniform.

On Saturday, Captain Gordon, and Mr. E. J. Debett, a Democrat, held as a "political prisoner," were marched out of the pen, stripped of their clothes, and dressed in the castoff blue trousers of the Yankees; after which they were put in the "Chain gang," or gang of condemned felons from the Yankee Army, underoing sentence to hard labor for various crimes. Several hundred of this class are on the island; deserters, bounty jumpers, murderers, thieves, etc., all of whom are compelled to haul heavy loads of stone or lumber for the repair of dykes or buildings. In strange contrast of cause and effect, a handsome Gothic Chapel was built for the use of the garrison, by the labor of these miserable malefactors —hardened old sinners, who never before were inside of a church even as workmen. Into such companionship was young Gordon thrust, and today I saw his tall figure clad in shabby rags, and "paired" with a greasy looking convict, dragging at the rope of a heavy cart together with about fifty other men; while a low-browed brutal looking Yankee, with a long stick or goad, sat atop the load of bricks of granite, and continuously yelled at the team, thus: "Pull, d— —n you, pull! What the h— —l you hanging back for? Who's that making signs at them windows?" The last speech was meant for Captain Gordon, who as he passed our windows looked up with a sad smile as if to say: "This is hard! but I shall endure to the end." . . .

August 10th:—How strange a thing it is to be hungry! actually craving something to eat, and constantly thinking about it from morning till night, from day to day; for weeks and months!

It did not seem possible for a man thus to worry over lack of nourishment, keeping his mind continually engrossed with anger against those who starve us, and with longing for food, the German philosopher's "earnest aspirations after the unattainable."

For the past month our rations have been six, sometimes four hard crackers and 1/10 of a pound of rusty bacon (a piece the size of a hen's egg) for the twenty-four hours.

But for five days past we have not had a morsel of meat of any kind; the cooks alleging that the supply ran short and "spoiled." (For a fortnight before it ceased to be issued, the rations were so full of worms, and stank so that one had to hold his nose while eating it!) But now we receive *none at all!* Talk about Andersonville! We would gladly exchange rations with the Yankees there!

For my part I cannot swallow very fat meat, or any that is in the very least tainted, so that for a long time I have subsisted on little else than hard tack and water. And such water! There has been no rain for some time; the tanks are no longer adequate for the supply of the pen even when full; therefore the Yankees have a small vessel that is used as a water boat, and is designed to ascend the creek sufficiently far to obtain fresh water. But the boat doesn't go above tide water, hence brings back a brackish *briny* fluid scarcely one whit better than the water from the Delaware, which oozes through the ditches in the pen.

The standing rain water of course breeds a dense swarm of animalculae, and when the hose pipes from the water boat are turned into the tanks the interior sediment is stirred up, and the whole contents become a turgid, salty, jellified mass of waggle tails, worms, dead leaves, dead fishes, and other putrescent abominations, most of which is visibile to the eye in a cup of it.

The *smell* of it is enough to revolt the stomach of a fastidious person; to say nothing of the thought of making one's throat a channel for such stuff. Yet, when the tanks are empty—as they are for half a day once or oftener in the week—the cry for this briny liquid is universal, because it creates a thirst equally as much as it quenches it, but if it were not so, the intense heat which beats upon this flat, parched island would make us swallow soluble salts for temporary relief.

The surface of the Pea Patch being of alluvial mud, becomes very porous and damp in wet weather, but parched and as hard as rock in the long dry season. No shade is there, no elevation, no breeze; only a low, flat, sultry, burning oven! Today the heat is so intense that men by hundreds are seen sweltering on their backs, fairly gasping for breath, like fish dying on a sand beach.

August 11th:—Shocking reports of the ravage of pestilence both in this pen and the other. I remain so closely in my bunk, or walking to and fro in the yard that I had no idea there was so much sickness prevailing until two cases of smallpox had been taken from my own division.

Horrible to relate, the hospital is full and men are no longer taken out until dying or dead. One of the smallpox cases (since dead I learn) was poor C., who slept directly over my bunk. He was very dirty and annoying while in health, and we had some words about his stepping on my blankets with muddy boots while climbing to his bunk; but after he took the fearful disease I felt sorry for him, and helped to lift him down from his tier and carry him to the gate. Strange to say, I cannot realize the danger, though most of the prisoners are getting nervous. So are the garrison. . . .

Oct. 4th:—The catching and eating of the huge rats which infest the island has become a common thing. It is a curious sight; grown men, whiskered and uniformed officers who have already "set a squadron in the field," lurking, club in hand, near one of the many breathing holes, which the long tailed rodents have cut in the hard earth, patiently awaiting a chance to strike a blow for "fresh meat and rat soup"—for dinner! They generally succeed in getting one or more rats at a sitting. Indeed the surface of the earth in some portions of the yard seems to be honeycombed by these amphibious burrowers, which are not the ordinary house rat, but a larger species of water rat, something like the Norway variety.

They are eaten by fully a score of the officers, and apparently with relish. When deviled or stewed, they resemble young squirrels *in looks*. I have not yet mustered stomach enough to nibble at one—though once—three years ago on the Potomac island—their brethren nibbled at me in no pleasant fashion. The flesh of these rodents is quite white, and when several are on a plate with plenty of dressing, they look so appetizing one cannot help regretting his early mis-education, or prejudice. That our antipathy to rats is all prejudice the rat eaters firmly assert. "Why," quoth one of them—"you eat wagon loads of hogs, and everybody knows a rat is cleaner than a hog. Rats are just as dainty as squirrels or chickens. Try a piece?" "No, thanks, my 'prejudices' unfortunately, are not yet abated." . . .

Oct. 9th:—Ugh! Fingers are too cold to hold the pen! Dozens of us have lain since breakfast, curled up under our blankets—thinking, thinking, and shivering with intense chilliness; not comfortable a moment in the day!

The wintry blasts sweep up the broad river, and across the flat island, with the keenness of an ocean cyclone; roaring round the prison yard, whistling through thousands of crevices in the open barracks with a chill rasping sound that increases the cold by imagination.

As for comfort, it is out of the question for the well and hearty. How much worse for the sick and debilitated! God help us this dreary winter! I dread to see night come, for then I must surrender the blankets borrowed from my comrades, and I have only half of one to sleep on and half for a covering.

And yet we are much better off than many of the poor fellows in the Privates' Pen! There are ten, or more, thousand men packed into a square of about six acres—thousands of them *barefooted*, not one in twenty supplied with undercloth-ing. Even of those taken out to work the greater number are shoeless and hatless, and yet they gladly consent to go out and drag the heavy stone carts as long as they can stand, simply *for a few extra crusts of bread* to appease their constant, unsatisfied hunger! . . .

Stoves have been put up, one in each shed, but there is not fuel enough furnished to keep up even a semblence of fire more than half the time, and with a crowd of one hundred and ten shivering men to make a double circle around it, there is not much chance for a diffident person to get anywhere near it.

For three weeks I have not been comfortably warm during the day, nor able to sleep over two hours any night; have not tasted warm food; have not been free from the pangs of actual hunger any moment during the time. Our ration is still three hardtacks at 9 A.M. and three more at 3 P.M. with a morsel of rusty meat, and an occasional gill of rice soup. Stuff at which no ordinary respectable Negro's *dog* would condescend to sniff at, down South.

The hardships that we, officers and gentlemen, *prisoners of war*, not criminals, suffer, and which have tumbled nearly ten thousand Southerners into the pits on yonder Jersey shore, are not *necessary;* are not the result of poverty, blockade, lack of supplies, nor from necessary vigor of discipline to prevent escape. It is sheer cruelty!

> —HAMILTON, ed., "The Papers of
> Randolph Abbott Shotwell"

5. THE PRIVATIONS OF LIFE IN
ELMIRA PRISON

Elmira, opened in May 1864 to relieve pressure on the older prisons, was one of the largest of the Northern prisons, housing, by the end of the war, over 12,000 Confederates. At first the prisoners had only tents; with the coming of winter rude barracks were constructed and as these were equipped with stoves they protected the Southern boys from the worst rigors of an upstate New York winter. A feud between the commandant and the surgeon was partly responsible for bad conditions and a high sickness and mortality rate: altogether some 3,000 of Elmira's inmates died during one year of operation.

Marcus Toney was a Tennessee boy whose Privations of a Private *is one of the better of the little-known Civil War narratives.*

The prison camp contained some forty acres of land about one mile above the city [of Elmira, New York], and near the Chemung River, a beautiful, clear, limpid mountain stream of very pure water. The stockade that surrounded the camp was much like the one at Point Lookout, but built of heavier material, and the ends of the upright planks going some eighteen inches into the ground. The planks were about sixteen feet high, and nailed to heavy sills, which were supported by large posts set deep in the ground. The stockade was about sixteen feet high, and three feet from the top was the parapet walkway or beat of the guards, who were stationed some forty feet apart, and were relieved every two hours by other guards.

Commencing at nine o'clock at night, or taps, they would cry out their posts all through the hours of the night, as "Post No. 1, nine o'clock; all is well" which would be taken up by all posts and repeated all around the stockade. Inside the stockade about fifty feet apart were large coal oil lamps nailed near the center of the stockade, with large reflectors, which were lit after nightfall, and the guards on the parapet would be able to see any one approaching.

The tents in which we slept were struck every morning in order for inspection. The prisoners in one of the tents had a false floor laid and covered with dirt hard packed so it would have the same appearance as the ground floor in the other tents. Under this false floor was one of the prisoners digging day and night. There were six occupants of this particular tent and by making a detail one man was digging all the time. They were tunneling to get under the fence. The tunnel was only about two feet under the ground and they had to go about sixty feet distance to get under the fence; the only implement they had was a large knife. They had a small box to which was attached a string at both ends and when the fellow at the farther side had filled his box he gave a pull of the string and the other fellow just under the false floor of the tent would pull the box under the floor, pile up the dirt and at night they would remove the false floor, gather the dirt in their hands, fill their haversacks, and scatter the dirt along the new-made streets. When they reached the upright planks of the stockade they had to go over a foot lower than the tunnel in order to get under the end of the planks. Finally the tunnel was completed and one of the boys crawled through poked his head on the outside and came and reported bright moonshine disclosed the camp of the guards under patrol across the street and a number of pieces of artillery in position along the camp; so they waited for the moon to go down before they commenced their underground journey. The plan was that the last of the six to leave should notify as many of the prisoners as he could in order that they might take advantage of it; but only fifteen got out and we heard that they reached Canada in safety. . . .

In a military prison it was very difficult to get information from the outside world. No papers were allowed, and the papers received had been opened and read; if there was anything contraband, you did not get it. When you wrote a letter it was left unsealed, and when the prison authorities examined it they stamped it "Prisoner's letter, approved," and then sealed and mailed it. Money was contraband of war, for a fellow might bribe his way out; therefore, whenever a remittance came to a prisoner it was turned over to the sutler who opened an account with the owner, and he could purchase all he wished so long as the funds held out; but when money went, a prisoner's credit was *non est.*

Until I reached prison I did not know what a slave to habit man was. I have seen men go hungry a day and save their rations and trade them for tobacco. I have seen a prisoner discharge a quid of tobacco from his mouth and other one pick it up, dry and smoke it. They used the black navy tobacco, sold in prison at the rate of one dollar per pound. They would cut it into little squares; each square would be called a chew, and five chews five cents. We had all kinds of trade and traffics, and tobacco was one of the mediums of exchange. We had many barbers, and they would shave you for five chews of tobacco. When the barber would get more tobacco than he needed, he would sell five chews for a small loaf of bread, valued at five cents, or he could purchase a small piece of meat or a fresh rat each valued at five cents. These barbers carried square boxes with them, upon which they set their patients; and a fellow would have to be very patient, as they never used a hone or strap except their boots and shoes, and it was hard to tell which was the worst sufferer, the barber or his customer. . . .

Adjoining the cook house was a large shed with tables that would accommodate three hundred men, and there were in the shed about twenty tables which were higher than my waist when standing. . . . Seats were not allowed. The men were marched in in two ranks, and separated at the head of the table, making one rank face the other. Each man had a plate and spoon; in the plate were his bean soup and beans, by the side of his plate was a small piece of light bread, and on the bread a thin ration of salt pork. The rations were thus prepared: a baker who lived outside would come in daily and superintend the baking. In the cook house were a large number of iron kettles or caldrons in which the meat and beans were boiled. I suppose these caldrons would hold fifty gallons. The salt pork was shipped in barrels and rolled up to the caldrons, and with a pitchfork tossed in, then the beans—I have heard the boys say four beans to a gallon of water. Now when this is boiled down it gets very salty, and after three weeks of a diet of this kind a prisoner will commence to get sick. I thought for a while that the government was retaliating on us on account of Andersonville, but I afterwards believed that it was done by the army contractors. . . . I can say without hesitancy that the death rate here was higher than at any other prison North or South. . . .

A prisoner eating this diet will crave any kind of fresh meat. Marching through the camp one day was a prisoner in a barrel shirt, with placard, "I eat a dog"; another one bearing a barrel, with placard, "Dog Eater." The barrel shirt was one of the modes of punishment. The shirt was made by using a whisky or coal oil barrel knocking out one end and in the other boring a hole so as to get his head through, and then putting on a placard to indicate the crime. It appeared that these prisoners had captured a lapdog owned by the baker who came into camp daily to bake the bread. The baker made complaint to Colonel Beall, and said that his wife and children would not have taken one hundred dollars for the dog. As the prisoners had nothing to pay with, they were treated to the barrel shirt. The punishment was a two hours' march followed by a soldier with a boyonet, and they were not allowed much rest till the two hours were completed.

I saw another barrel shirt, "I told a lie." A prisoner did not have much compunction of conscience, especially if he had lied to deceive the commandant, which he conceived to be his religious duty. A prisoner carrying a barrel shirt, "I stole my messmate's rations," was hissed all around the camp; and deservedly so, because a man who would steal from his messmates in prison deserved the most severe punishment; while the ones who carried the placard, "Dog Eater" had the sympathies of the entire camp, because many of them would have enjoyed a piece of fresh meat. When twitted about it they said: "It was not a common cur, but a Spitz, and tasted like mutton."

On account of the waste from the commissary a great many rodents from Elmira ran into the prison. As there were not any holes in which they could hide it was an easy catch for the boys by knocking them over with sticks, and there was quite a traffic in them. As there was very little currency in prison, tobacco, rats, pickles, pork, and light bread were mediums of exchange. Five chews of tobacco would buy a rat, a rat would buy five chews of tobacco, a loaf of bread would buy a rat, a rat would buy a loaf of bread, and so on. . . .

The bunks extended the length of the ward on each side, leaving an aisle in the center and two stoves in each ward, and the prisoners were not allowed to get very close to them in zero weather. With an open building, the heat was not very intense. The bunks were three high, and the boys occupying the top bunk had to do some climbing. They were wide enough to sleep two medium-sized men. Each one was allowed only a pair of blankets, and so had to sleep on the hard board; therefore, in extreme weather four slept in the space of two, using one pair of blankets to sleep on, which gave three for cover. Two of them slept with their heads toward the east, and two with their heads toward the west, and of course had to be on their sides; and when ready to change positions, one would call out, "All turn to the right"; and the next call would be, "All turn to the left." The turns had to be made as stated, or there would be collisions. Of course the men did not disrobe in extreme cold weather, and on awakening in the morning their feet would be in each other's faces.

—TONEY, *The Privations of a Private*

IV

Behind the Lines:
The North

TOTAL war is a twentieth-century concept. The Civil War was
very far from a total war, either North or South. Neither side
ever mustered its full strength; neither side achieved anything like the unity we take for granted in our own time.
Because the war was fought almost entirely in the South,
and because the Confederacy, as the smaller and weaker of
the belligerents, was required to organize a larger part of her
resources, the impact of the war on the South was far
deeper than it was on the North. To an extraordinary degree
life went on, in the North, almost on a peacetime basis.
Industry boomed; farmers expanded into the West; immigration kept up and with it city growth; colleges flourished;
for the most part there was politics as usual. The war itself
was fought haphazardly and inefficiently. The potential man
power of the North was never effectively exploited; conscription was long delayed and, when it came, was badly administered. Business as usual was the order of the day, and profits
and cost of living soared.

What is perhaps most striking, to the contemporary student,
is the pervasiveness in the North of disunity and disloyalty,
fraud and corruption, incompetence and confusion in both
the civilian and the military. Large segments of the population were unalterably opposed to the war; men like
Vallandigham denounced it in language that was treasonable,
and organizations like the Knights of the Golden Circle

planned revolution, while the draft was sabotaged, bounty jumping was common, and desertion ran to over 10 per cent. Only because the Confederacy was afflicted by comparable disunity and disorganization did the Union eventually triumph.

It would require a whole volume to do justice to this large theme of the Union and the Confederacy—behind the lines. We have, of necessity, contented ourselves here with some of the more interesting and illuminating narratives.

1. WASHINGTON AS A CAMP

A political compromise dating back to the beginning of the Republic had located the capital city on the banks of the Potomac; with Maryland seething with secessoin sentiment and Virginia in the Confederacy, Washington was from the beginning peculiarly vulnerable, and its defense remained, throughout the war, a major strategical consideration. The location of the Confederate capital, too, was dictated by political considerations that deeply and adversely affected military strategy; had the capital remained at Montgomery, the whole strategy of the war, North and South, might have been different.

Noah Brooks, who here describes the capital as a camp, was a journalist who was in Washington during the war as correspondent of the Sacramento Union; *long-standing friendship wtih Lincoln gave him access to the White House and to many of the political leaders of the Republic. After the war he served as editor of the* New York Tribune *and the* New Tork Times, *and wrote a number of juveniles, the best of which are* The Boy Emigrants *and* The Fairport Nine.

Washington was then a military camp, a city of barracks and hospitals. The first thing that impressed the newly arrived stranger, especially if he came, as I did, from the shores of the Peaceful Sea, where the waves of war had not reached, was the martial aspect of the capital. Long lines of army wagons and artillery were continually rumbling through the streets; at all hours of the day and night the air was troubled by the clatter of galloping squads of cavalry; and the clank of sabers, and the measured beat of marching infantry, were ever present to the ear. The city was under military government and the wayfarer was liable to be halted anywhere in public buildings, or on the outskirts of the city, by an armed sentry, who curtly asked, "What is your business here?" Army blue was the predominating color on the sidewalks, sprinkled here and there with the gold lace of officers. In the galleries of the Senate and House of Representatives, especially during the cold weather,—when the well-warmed Capitol was a convenient refuge for idle people,—great patches of the light blue of military overcoats were to be marked among more somber colors of the groups of visitors.

It was contrary to army regulations to supply soldiers with liquors, and in most bar-rooms cards were conspicuous, bearing the legend, "Nothing sold to soldiers." At some of the drinking-places, as if to soften the severity of the dictum, was displayed an artistically painted group of the three arms of the military service, over which were printed the words, "No liquors sold to."

Now and again, just after some great battle near at hand, like that of Fredericksburg, or Chancellorsville, or Grant's long struggles in the Wilderness, the capital afforded a most distressful spectacle. Then, if at no other time, the home-staying citizen realized something of the horrors of war. The Washington hospitals were never empty, but at such times they were crowded with the maimed and wounded, who arrived by hundreds as long as the waves of sorrow came streaming back from the fields of slaughter. One occasionally met a grim procession of the slightly wounded coming up from the railway station at Alexandria or the steamboat landing from Aquia Creek. They arrived in squads of a hundred or more, bandaged and limping, ragged and disheveled, blackened with smoke and powder, and drooping with weakness. They came groping, hobbling, and faltering, so faint and so longing for rest that one's heart bled at the piteous sight. Here and there were men left to make their way as best they could to the hospital, and who were leaning on the iron railings or sitting wearily on the curbstones; but it was noticeable that all maintained the genuine American pluck in the midst of sorrow and suffering. As a rule, they were silent and unmurmuring; or if they spoke, it was to utter a grim joke at their own expense.

At the height of the war there were twenty-one hospitals in and about Washington. Some were in churches, public halls, the Patent Office, and other public buildings; but many were temporary wooden structures built for this special purpose. One of the representative hospitals was that of Harewood, erected by the government on the private grounds of

W. W. Corcoran, in the outskirts of the city. There was a highly ornamented barn filled with hospital stores, clothing, and sanitary goods. A long row of cattlesheds was boarded in and transformed into a hospital bakery. The temporary buildings constructed by the government were one story high, arranged in the form of a hollow square, row within row, and kept very neat and clean. . . .

Convalescents who had been discharged from the hospitals and who were not fit for military duty were assembled at a rendezvous in Alexandria, known as Camp Convalescent. This camp eventually became so crowded with the vast numbers of those who had been discharged from the hospitals or were stragglers from the army, that its condition was properly characterized as "infamous." More than ten thousand men, some of whom in the depth of winter were obliged to sleep on the cold ground, under canvas shelter and without fire or suitable covering, were massed together there, in the company of healthy reprobates who were "bummers," deserters, and stragglers—the riffraff of the Federal and Confederate armies. There were two of these curious improvised institutions—Camp Convalescent and Camp Straggle—both of which were crammed full. . . .

The Washington of the war was a very different city from the present stately capital. Before the war the city was as drowsy and as grass-grown as any old New England town. Squalid Negro quarters hung on the flanks of fine old mansions, and although in the centers of this "city of magnificent distances" there were handsome public buildings, with here and there a statue or some other work of art, the general aspect of things was truly rural. The war changed all that in a very few weeks. Temporary hospitals and other rude shelters arose as if by magic on every hand. The streets were crowded by night and day, and the continual passage of heavily loaded quartermasters' trains, artillery, and vehicles of kinds before unknown in Washington, churned the unpaved streets into muddy thoroughfares in winter, or cut them deep with impalpable dust in summer. It was a favorite joke of Washingtonians that "real estate was high in dry weather, as it was for the most part all in the air."

Over the flats of the Potomac rose the then unfinished white obelisk of the Washington monument, a truncated cone; and in the weather-beaten sheds around its base were stored the carved and ornamented blocks that had been contributed to the structure by foreign governments, princes, potentates, and political and social organizations. On its hill rose the unfinished dome of the Capitol, whose bare ribs were darkly limned against the sky. It was a feeling of pride, or perhaps of some tenderer sentiment, that induced the government to insist that work on the Capitol should go on in the midst of the stress and strain of civil war, just as though nothing had happened to hinder the progress of the magnificent undertaking. It is no metaphor to say that the sound of the workman's hammer never ceased on that building, even in the dark times when it was not certain that "Washington was safe." The completion of the pediments of the House and Senate wings went on without delay during all these perilous times. The colossal statue of Freedom which now adorns the apex of the central dome (designed by Crawford and cast in bronze by Clark Mills) was at first set up on a temporary base in the Capitol grounds, where it was an object of curiosity and interest to visitors. . . .

The frequent appearance in Washington of paroled rebel officers, who usually wore their own uniform with evident pride and pleasure, and sometimes with a swagger, generally threw loyalists into a fever of excitement. More than once I saw ultra-loyal newsboys or boot-blacks throw a lump of mud, or a brickbat, at the passing Confederate. One of these officers, a Lieutenant Garnett, being on parole, sent in his card to Representative Wickliffe, of Kentucky, and was by him introduced upon the floor of the House, where he attracted attention, as well as indignation, from the members present. Presently a wave of excitement seemed to sweep over the galleries, the spectators being visibly affected by the appearance of an officer in full Confederate uniform sitting on one of the sofas of the House of Representatives. This was intensified when a door-keeper spoke to the visitor, who rose from his seat, gave a profound and sweeping bow, and withdrew to the outer corridor. It appeared that the door-keeper had told the Confederate that it was contrary to the rules of the House for him to be present.

—Brooks, "Washington in Lincoln's Time"

2. WALT WHITMAN LOOKS AROUND IN WARTIME WASHINGTON

Here is another, and very different, impression of wartime Washington, and from an even more famous pen. Walt Whitman was writing for New York and Brooklyn news-

papers when, in December 1862, he got word that his young brother George had been wounded at Fredericksburg. He left at once for the front, found his brother at Falmouth, Virginia; and then returned to Washington, where he earned a meager living copying documents and devoted most of his time to visiting wounded soldiers in the Washington hospitals. It was during this experience as a "wound dresser" that—so he always believed—he contracted the infection which later led to paralysis. At the very end of the war Whitman got a clerkship in the Department of the Interior, only to lose it when the Secretary discovered that he was the author of a "scandalous" book—Leaves of Grass.

Washington, March 19, 1863

DEAR NAT AND FRED GRAY:

Since I left New York I was down in the Army of the Potomac in front with my brother a good part of the winter, commencing time of the battle of Fredericksburgh—have seen *"war-life,"* the real article—folded myself in a blanket, lying down in the mud with composure—relished salt pork and hard tack— have been on the battlefield among the wounded, the faint and the bleeding, to give them nourishment—have gone over with a flag of truce the next day to help direct the burial of the dead— have struck up a tremendous friendship with a young Mississippi captain (about 19) that we took prisoner badly wounded at Fredericksburgh (he has followed me here, is in the Emory hospital here minus a leg—he wears his confederate uniform, proud as the devil—I met him first at Falmouth, in the Lacy house middle of December last, his leg just cut off, and cheered him up—poor boy, he has suffered a great deal, and still suffers—has eyes bright as a hawk, but face pale—our affection is an affair quite romantic—sometimes when I lean over to say I am going, he puts his arms around my neck, draws my face down, etc., quite a scene for Rappahannock.—During January came up hither, took a lodging room here. Did the 37th Congress, especially the night sessions the last three weeks, explored the Capitol, meandering the gorgeous painted interminable Senate corridors, getting lost in them (a new sensation, rich and strong, that endless painted interior at night)—got very much interested in some particular cases in Hospitals here—go now steadily to more or less of said Hospitals by day or night—find always the sick and dying soldiers forthwith begin to cling to me in a way that makes a fellow feel funny enough. These Hospitals, so different from all others—there thousands, and tens and twenties of thousands of American young men, badly wounded, all sorts of wounds, operated on, pallid with diarrhoea, languishing, dying with fever, pneumonia, etc., open a new world somehow to me, giving closer insights, new things, exploring deeper mines, than any yet, showing our humanity (I sometimes put myself in fancy in the cot, with typhoid, or under the knife) tried by terrible, fearfullest tests, probed deepest, the living soul's, the body's tragedies, bursting the petty bonds of art. To these, what are your dramas and poems, even the oldest and the fearfullest? Not old Greek mighty ones; where man contends with fate (and always yealds)—not Virgil showing Dante on and on among the agonized and damned, approach what here I see and take part in. For here I see, not at intervals, but quite always, how certain man, our American man—how he holds himself cool and unquestioned master above all pains and bloody mutilations. It is immense, the best thing of all—nourishes me of all men. This then, what frightened us all so long. Why, it is put to flight with ignominy—a mere stuffed scarecrow of the fields. Oh death, where is thy sting? Oh grave, where is thy victory?

In the Patent Office, as I stood there one night, just off the cot-side of a dying soldier, in a large ward that had received the worst cases of Second Bull Run, Antietam, and Fredricksburgh, the surgeon, Dr. Stone (Horatio Stone the Sculptor) told me, of all who had died in that crowded ward the past six months, he had still to find the first man or boy who had met the approach of death with a single tremor or unmanly fear. But let me change the subject—I have given you screed enough about Death and the Hospitals—and too much—since I got started. Only I have some curious yarns I promise you my darlings and gossips, by word of mouth whene'er we meet.

Washington and its points I find bear a second and a third perusal, and doubtless many. My first impressions, architectural, etc., were not favorable: but upon the whole, the city, the spaces, buildings, etc., make no unfit emblem of our country, so far, so broadly planned, everything in plenty, money and materials staggering with plenty, but the fruit of the plans, the knit, the combination yet wanting—Determined to express ourselves greatly in a Capitol but no fit Capitol yet here (time, associations, wanting I suppose) many a hiatus yet—many a thing to be taken down and done over again yet—perhaps an entire change of base—maybe a succession of changes.

Congress does not seize very hard upon me: I studied it and its members with curiosity, and long—much gab, great fear of public opinion, plenty of low business talent, but no masterful man in Congress (probably best so). I think well of the President. He has a face like a Hoosier Michael Angelo, so awful ugly it becomes beautiful, with its strange mouth, its deep cut, crisscross lines, and its doughnut complexion.—My notion is too, that underneath his outside smutched mannerism, and stories from third-class county barrooms (it is his humor), Mr. Lincoln keeps a fountain of first-class practical telling wisdom. I do not dwell on the supposed failures of his government: he has shown, I sometimes think an almost supernatural tact in keeping the ship afloat at all, with head steady, not only not going down, and now certain not to, but with proud and resolute spirit, and flag flying in sight of the world, menacing and high as ever. I say never yet captain, never ruler, had such a perplexing dangerous task as his, the past two years. I more and more rely upon his idiomatic western genius, careless of court dress or court decorum.

Friday morning, 20th—I finish my letter in the office of Major Hapgood, a paymaster, and a friend of mine. This is a large building filled with paymasters' offices, some thirty or forty or more. This room is up on the fifth floor (a most noble and broad view from my window) curious scenes around here —a continual stream of soldiers, officers, cripples, etc., some climbing wearily up the stairs. They seek their pay—and every hour, almost every minute, has its incident, its hitch, its romance, farce or tragedy. There are two paymasters in this room. A sentry at the street door, another halfway up the stairs, another at the chief clerk's door, all with muskets and bayonets—sometimes a great swarm, hundreds around the side walk in front waiting (everybody is waiting for something here). I take a pause, look up a couple of minutes from my pen and paper—see spread, off there the Potomac, very fine, nothing pretty about it—the Washington monument, not half finished—the public grounds around it filled with ten thousand beeves on the hoof—to the left the Smithsonian with its brown turrets—to the right far across, Arlington Heights, the forts, eight or ten of them—then the long bridge, and down a ways but quite plain, the shipping of Alexandria. Opposite me and in a stone throw is the Treasury Building, and below the bustle and life of Pennsylvania Avenue. I shall hasten with my letter, and then go forth and take a stroll down "the avenue" as they call it here.

Now you boys, don't you think I have done the handsome

thing by writing this astoundingly magnificent letter—certainly the longest I ever wrote in my life. Fred, I wish you to present my best respects to your father, Bloom and all; one of these days we will meet, and make up for lost time, my dearest boys.

WALT.

—HALLOWAY, ed., *The Uncollected Poetry and Prose of Walt Whitman*

3. ANNA DICKINSON SEES THE DRAFT RIOTS IN NEW YORK CITY

The Confederacy had resort to conscription as early as April 1862; not until March 1863 did the Federal Congress enact a conscription act, and it proved so full of loopholes and exemptions as to be practically useless. The act was widely denounced as unconstitutional and despotic, and first attempts to enforce it met with resistance in various Northern cities. By all odds the worst disturbances were the great "draft riots" that swept New York City from the thirteenth to the seventeenth of July. For three or four days New York was in the grip of hoodlums who rioted, pillaged, and burned almost at will; the local authorities were all but helpless and Governor Seymour gave aid and comfort to the rioters by promising to get the obnoxious law repealed. The most disgraceful feature of the riots was the savage attack on Negroes; even the Negro Orphan Asylum was burned down by the mob.

Anna Dickinson, who here describes these outbreaks, was at the time a young woman but already well known as writer and lecturer on antislavery, temperance and woman's rights.

On the morning of Monday, the thirteenth of July [1863], began this outbreak, unparalleled in atrocities by anything in American history and equaled only by the horrors of the worst days of the French Revolution. Gangs of men and boys, composed of railroad employees, workers in machine shops, and a vast crowd of those who lived by preying upon others, thieves, pimps, professional ruffians, the scum of the city, jailbirds, or those who were running with swift feet to enter the prison doors, began to gather on the corners and in streets and alleys where they lived; from thence issuing forth, they visited the great establishments on the line of their advance, commanding their instant close and the companionship of the workmen—many of them peaceful and orderly men—on pain of the destruction of one and a murderous assault upon the other, did not their orders meet with instant compliance.

A body of these, five or six hundred strong, gathered about one of the enrolling offices in the upper part of the city, where the draft was quietly proceeding, and opened the assault upon it by a shower of clubs, bricks, and paving stones torn from the streets, following it up by a furious rush into the office. Lists, records, books, the drafting wheel, every article of furniture or work in the room, was rent in pieces and strewn about the floor or flung into the streets, while the law officers, the newspaper reporters—who are expected to be everywhere—and the few peaceable spectators, were compelled to make a hasty retreat through an opportune rear exit, accelerated by the curses and blows of the assailants.

A safe in the room, which contained some of the hated records, was fallen upon by the men, who strove to wrench open its impregnable lock with their naked hands, and, baffled, beat them on its iron doors and sides till they were stained with blood, in a mad frenzy of senseless hate and fury. And then, finding every portable article destroyed—their thirst for ruin growing by the little drink it had had—and believing, or rather hoping, that the officers had taken refuge in the upper rooms, set fire to the house, and stood watching the slow and steady lift of flames, filling the air with demoniac shrieks and yells, while they waited for the prey to escape from some door or window, from the merciless fire to their merciless hands. One of these, who was on the other side of the street, courageously stepped forward and, telling them that they had utterly demolished all they came to seek, informed them that helpless women and little children were in the house and besought them to extinguish the flames and leave the ruined premises—to disperse or at least to seek some other scene.

By his dress recognizing in him a government official, so far from hearing or heeding his humane appeal, they set upon him with sticks and clubs and beat him till his eyes were blind with blood, and he, bruised and mangled, succeeded in escaping to the handful of police who stood helpless before this howling crew, now increased to thousands. With difficulty and pain the inoffensive tenants escaped from the rapidly-spreading fire, which, having devoured the house originally lighted, swept across the neighboring buildings till the whole block stood a mass of burning flames. The firemen came up tardily and reluctantly, many of them of the same class as the miscreants who surrounded them and who cheered at their approach, but either made no attempt to perform their duty or so feeble and farcical a one as to bring disgrace upon a service they so generally honor and ennoble.

At last, when there was here nothing more to accomplish, the mob, swollen to a frightful size, including myriads of wretched, drunken women and the half-grown vagabond boys of the pavements, rushed through the intervening streets, stopping cars and insulting peaceable citizens on their way, to an armory where were manufactured and stored carbines and guns for the government. In anticipation of the attack, this, earlier in the day, had been fortified by a police squad capable of coping with an ordinary crowd of ruffians, but as chaff before fire in the presence of these murderous thousands. Here, as before, the attack was begun by a rain of missiles gathered from the streets, less fatal, doubtless, than more civilized arms, but frightful in the ghastly wounds and injuries they inflicted. Of this no notice was taken by those who were stationed within. It was repeated. At last, finding they were treated with contemptuous silence and that no sign of surrender was offered the crowd swayed back, then forward, in a combined attempt to force the wide entrance doors. Heavy hammers and sledges which had been brought from forges and workshops, caught up hastily as they gathered the mechanics into their ranks, were used with frightful violence to beat them in at last successfully. The foremost assailants began to climb the stairs but were checked and for the moment driven back by the fire of the officers, who at last had been commanded to resort to their revolvers. A halfscore fell wounded, and one who had been acting in some sort as their leader—a big, brutal Irish ruffian—dropped dead.

The pause was but for an instant. As the smoke cleared away there was a general and ferocious onslaught upon the armory; curses, oaths, revilings, hideous and obscene blasphemy, with terrible yells and cries, filled the air in every accent of the English tongue save that spoken by a native American. Such were there mingled with the sea of sound, but they were so few and weak as to be unnoticeable in the roar of voices. The paving stones flew like hail until the street was torn into gaps and ruts and every windowpane and sash and doorway was smashed or broken. Meanwhile divers attempts were made to fire the building but failed through haste or ineffectual materials or the vigilant watchfulness of the besieged. In the midst of this gallant defense word was brought to the defenders from headquarters that nothing

could be done for their support and that if they would save
their lives they must make a quick and orderly retreat.
Fortunately there was a side passage with which the mob was
unacquainted, and one by one they succeeded in gaining
this and vanishing.

The work was begun, continued, gathering in force and
fury as the day wore on. Police stations, enrolling offices,
rooms or buildings used in any way by government authority
or obnoxious as representing the dignity of law, were gutted,
destroyed, then left to the mercy of the flames. Newspaper
offices whose issues had been a fire in the rear of the nation's
armies by extenuating and defending treason and through
violent and incendiary appeals stirring up "lewd fellows of
the baser sort" to this very carnival of ruin and blood were
cheered as the crowd went by. Those that had been faithful
to loyalty and law were hooted, stoned, and even stormed
by the army of miscreants, who were only driven off by the
gallant and determined charge of the police and in one place
by the equally gallant and certainly unique defense which
came from turning the boiling water from the engines upon
the howling wretches, who, unprepared for any such warm
reception as this, beat a precipitate and general retreat. Before night fell it was no longer one vast crowd collected in a
single section, but great numbers of gatherings, scattered over
the whole length and breadth of the city, some of them
engaged in actual work of demolition and ruin, others, with
clubs and weapons in their hands, prowling round apparently
with no definite atrocity to perpetrate, but ready for any
iniquity that might offer, and, by way of pastime, chasing
every stray police officer or solitary soldier or inoffensive
Negro who crossed the line of their vision; these three objects—the badge of a defender of the law, the uniform of the
Union army, the skin of a helpless and outraged race—acted
upon these madmen as water acts upon a rabid dog.

Late in the afternoon a crowd which could have numbered
not less than ten thousand, the majority of whom were
ragged, frowzy, drunken women, gathered about the Orphan
Asylum for Colored Children—a large and beautiful building
and one of the most admirable and noble charities of the
city. When it became evident from the menacing cries and
groans of the multitude that danger, if not destruction, was
meditated to the harmless and inoffensive inmates, a flag of
truce appeared, and an appeal was made in their behalf, by
the principal, to every sentiment of humanity which these
beings might possess—a vain appeal! Whatever human feel-

ing had ever, if ever, filled these souls was utterly drowned and washed away in the tide of rapine and blood in which they had been steeping themselves. The few officers who stood guard over the doors and manfully faced these demoniac legions were beaten down and flung to one side, helpless and stunned, whilst the vast crowd rushed in. All the articles upon which they could seize—beds, bedding, carpets, furniture, the very garments of the fleeing inmates, some of these torn from their persons as they sped by—were carried into the streets and hurried off by the women and children who stood ready to receive the goods which their husbands, sons, and fathers flung to their care. The little ones, many of them assailed and beaten—all, orphans and caretakers, exposed to every indignity and every danger—driven on to the street, the building was fired. This had been attempted whilst the helpless children, some of them scarce more than babies, were still in their rooms; but this devilish consummation was prevented by the heroism of one man. He, the chief of the fire department, strove by voice and arm to stay the endeavor; and when, overcome by superior numbers, the brands had been lit and piled, with naked hands and in the face of threatened death he tore asunder the glowing embers and trod them underfoot. Again the effort was made and again failed through the determined and heroic opposition of this solitary soul. Then on the front steps, in the midst of these drunken and infuriated thousands, he stood up and besought them, if they cared nothing for themselves nor for those hapless orphans, that they would not bring lasting disgrace upon the city by destroying one of its noblest charities, which had for its object nothing but good.

He was answered on all sides by yells and execrations and frenzied shrieks of "Down with the nagurs!" coupled with every oath and every curse that malignant hate of the blacks could devise and drunken Irish tongues could speak. It had been decreed that this building was to be razed to the ground. The house was fired in a thousand places, and in less than two hours the walls crashed in, a mass of smoking, blackened ruins, whilst the children wandered through the streets, a prey to beings who were wild beasts in everything save the superior ingenuity of man to agonize and torture his victims.

Frightful as the day had been, the night was yet more hideous, since to the horrors which were seen was added the greater horror of deeds which might be committed in the darkness—or, if they were seen, it was by the lurid glare

of burning buildings, the red flames of which, flung upon the
stained and brutal faces, the torn and tattered garments, of
men and women who danced and howled around the scene
of ruin they had caused, made the whole aspect of affairs seem
more like a gathering of fiends rejoicing in pandemonium
than aught with which creatures of flesh and blood had to
do. . . .

The next morning's sun rose on a city which was ruled
by a reign of terror. Had the police possessed the heads of
Hydra and the arms of Briareus and had these heads all
seen, these arms all fought, they would have been powerless
against the multitude of opposers. Outbreaks were made,
crowds gathered, houses burned, streets barricaded, fights
enacted, in a score of places at once. Where the officers
appeared they were irretrievably beaten and overcome, their
stand, were it ever so short, but inflaming the passions of
the mob to fresh deeds of violence. Stores were closed, the
business portion of the city deserted, the large works and
factories emptied of men, who had been sent home by their
employers or were swept into the ranks of the marauding
bands. The city cars, omnibuses, hacks, were unable to run
and remained under shelter. Every telegraph wire was cut,
the posts torn up, the operators driven from their offices. The mayor, seeing that civil power was helpless to
stem this tide, desired to call the military to his aid and place
the city under martial law, but was opposed by the Governor
—a governor who, but a few days before, had pronounced the
war a failure and not only predicted but encouraged this mob
rule which was now crushing everything beneath its heavy
and ensanguined feet. This man, through almost two days
of these awful scenes, remained at a quiet seaside retreat but
a few miles from the city. Coming to it on the afternoon of
the second day, instead of ordering cannon planted in the
streets, giving these creatures opportunity to retire to their
homes, and, in the event of refusal, blowing them there by
powder and ball, he first went to the point where was collected
the chiefest mob and proceeded to address them. Before him
stood incendiaries, thieves, and murderers, who even then
were sacking dwelling houses and butchering powerless and
inoffensive beings. These wretches he apostrophized as "my
friends," repeating the title again and again in the course of
his harangue, assuring them that he was there as a proof
of his friendship, which he had demonstrated by "sending
his adjutant general to Washington to have the draft stopped,"
begging them to "wait for his return," "to separate now as

good citizens," with the promise that they "might assemble again whenever they wished to so do"; meanwhile he would "take care of their rights." This model speech was incessantly interrupted by tremendous cheering and frantic demonstrations of delight, one great fellow almost crushing the Governor in his enthusiastic embrace.

His allies in newspaper offices attempted to throw the blame upon the loyal press and portion of the community. This was but a repetition of the cry raised by traitors in arms that the government, struggling for life in their deadly hold, was responsible for the war: "If thou wouldst but consent to be murdered peaceably, there could be no strife."

It was absurd and futile to characterize this new reign of terror as anything but an effort on the part of Northern rebels to help Southern ones at the most critical moment of the war, with the state militia and available troops absent in a neighboring commonwealth and the loyal people unprepared. These editors and their coadjutors, men of brains and ability, were of that most poisonous growth—traitors to the government and the flag of their country—renegade Americans.

—ANNA DICKINSON, *What Answer?*

4. THE ARMY OF LOBBYISTS AND SPECULATORS

No one has ever told the full story of graft and corruption in the Civil War, but we know that it was pervasive and constant—far more so in the North than in the South, for the Confederacy offered little opportunity for large-scale corruption. Régis de Trobriand was one of those foreigners whom McClellan saluted in his Story. He was colonel of the 54th New York Volunteers, a French unit raised in the summer of 1861, and fought bravely through the war, winning the brevet rank of major general. His Four Years with the Army of the Potomac was based on a diary.

Besides the army formed to act against the enemy, there was another army—of lobbyists, contractors, speculators, which was continually renewed and never exhausted. These hurried to the assault on the treasury, like a cloud of locusts alighting down upon the capital to devour the substance of the country. They were everywhere: in the streets, in the hotels, in the offices, at the Capitol, and in the White House. They continually besieged the bureaus of administration, the doors of the Senate and House of Representatives, wherever there was a chance to gain something.

Government, obliged to ask the aid of private industry, for every kind of supply that the army and navy must have without delay, was really at the mercy of these hungry spoilers, who combined with one another to make the law for the government. From this arose contracts exceedingly burdensome, which impoverished the treasury, to enrich a few individuals.

As a matter of course, these latter classes, strangers to every patriotic impulse, saw in the war only an extraordinary opportunity of making a fortune. Every means for obtaining it was a good one to them; so that corruption played a great part in the business of contracting. Political protection was purchased by giving an interest in the contracts obtained. Now, as these contracts must be increased or renewed, according to the duration of the war, its prolongation became a direct advantage to a certain class of people disposing of large capital and of extended influence. What was the effect on events? It would be difficult to state precisely. But, in any case, this was evidently one of the causes which embarrassed the course of affairs, and delayed, more or less, the reëstablishment of the Union.

The government—that is, the people, who, in the end, support the weight of public expenses—was, then, fleeced by the more moderate and robbed by the more covetous. The army suffered from it directly, as the supplies, which were furnished at a price which was much above their value if they had been of a good quality, were nearly all of a fraudulent inferiority. For example, instead of heavy woolen blankets, the recruits received, at this time, light, open fabrics, made I do not know of what different substances, which protected them against neither the cold nor the rain. A very short wear changed a large part of the uniform to rags, and during the winter spent at Tenally-town the ordinary duration of a pair of shoes was no longer than twenty or thirty days.

This last fact, well attested in my regiment, was followed by energetic remonstrances, on account of which the general commanding the brigade appointed, according to the regulations, a special *Board of Inspection*, with the object of obtaining the condemnation of the defective articles. Amongst the members of the board was an officer expert in these matters, having been employed, before the war, in one of the great shoe factories of Massachusetts. The report was very precise. It showed that the shoes were made of poor leather, not having been properly tanned, that the inside of the soles was filled with gray paper, and that the heels were so poorly fastened that it needed only a little dry weather following a few days of rain to have them drop from the shoes. In fine, the fraud was flagrant in every way.

The report was duly forwarded to the superior authorities. Did it have any consideration? I never knew. However, it was necessary to exhaust the stock in hand before obtaining a new supply, and the price charged the soldier was not altered.
—DE TROBRIAND, *Four Years with the Army of the Potomac*

5. CHARLES A. DANA HELPS STOP FRAUDS
IN THE WAR DEPARTMENT

Charles A. Dana had gone from Brook Farm to the New York Tribune under Greeley, and had become, by the time of the Civil War, one of the most influential of American editors. A disagreement with Greeley led to his resignation in 1862; he was promptly appointed by the War Department a sort of field inspector, attached himself to Grant's headquarters, and did inestimable service to the Union cause by his shrewd championship of Grant and Sherman. In 1863 he became Assistant Secretary of War, dividing his time between Washington and the battle front. After the war he bought the New York Sun and lived to become the most powerful editor of his generation. The frauds he recounts here were typical of many that were being perpetrated at the time.

At the time that I entered the War Department for regular duty, it was a very busy place. Mr. Stanton frequently worked late at night, keeping his carriage waiting for him. I never worked at night, as my eyes would not allow it. I got to my office about nine o'clock in the morning, and I stayed there nearly the whole day, for I made it a rule never to go away until my desk was cleared. When I arrived I usually found on my table a big pile of papers which were to be acted on, papers of every sort that had come to me from the different departments of the office.

The business of the War Department during the first winter that I spent in Washington was something enormous. Nearly $285,000,000 was paid out that year (from June, 1863, to

June, 1864) by the quartermaster's office, and $221,000,000
stood in accounts at the end of the year awaiting examination
before payment was made. We had to buy every conceivable
thing that an army of men could need. We bought fuel,
forage, furniture, coffins, medicine, horses, mules, telegraph
wire, sugar, coffee, flour, cloth, caps, guns, powder, and
thousands of other things. Sometimes our supplies came by
contract; again by direct purchase; again by manufacture. Of
course, by the fall of 1863 the army was pretty well supplied; still, that year we bought over 3,000,000 pairs of
trousers, nearly 5,000,000 flannel shirts and drawers, some
7,000,000 pairs of stockings, 325,000 mess pans, 207,000
camp kettles, over 13,000 drums, and 14,830 fifes. It was my
duty to make contracts for many of these supplies.

In making contracts for supplies of all kinds, we were
obliged to take careful precautions against frauds. I had a
colleague in the department, the Hon. Peter H. Watson,
the distinguished patent lawyer, who had a great knack
at detecting army frauds. One which Watson had spent much
time in trying to ferret out came to light soon after I went
into office. This was an extensive fraud in forage furnished to
the Army of the Potomac. The trick of the fraud consisted
in a dishonest mixture of oats and Indian corn for the
horses and mules of the army. By changing the proportions of the two sorts of grain, the contractors were able to
make a considerable difference in the cost of the bushel, on
account of the difference in the weight and price of the
grain, and it was difficult to detect the cheat. However,
Watson found it out, and at once arrested the men who were
most directly involved.

Soon after the arrest Watson went to New York. While he
was gone, certain parties from Philadelphia interested in the
swindle came to me at the War Department. Among them was
the president of the Corn Exchange. They paid me thirty-three
thousand dollars to cover the sum which one of the men
confessed he had appropriated; thirty-two thousand dollars
was the amount restored by another individual. The morning
after this transaction the Philadelphians returned to me, demanding both that the villians should be released, and that
the papers and funds belonging to them, taken at the time of
their arrest, should be restored. It was my judgment that,
instead of being released, they should be remanded to solitary confinement until they could clear up all the forage
frauds and make complete justice possible. Then I should
have released them, but not before. So I telegraphed to

Watson what had happened, and asked him to return to prevent any false step.

Now, it happened that the men arrested were of some political importance in Pennsylvania, and eminent politicans took a hand in getting them out of the scrape. Among others, the Hon. David Wilmot, then Senator of the United States and author of the famous Wilmot proviso, was very active. He went to Mr. Lincoln and made such representations and appeals that finally the President consented to go with him over to the War Department and see Watson in his office. Wilmot remained outside, and Mr. Lincoln went in to labor with the Assistant Secretary. Watson eloquently described the nature of the fraud, and the extent to which it had already been developed by his partial investigation. The President, in reply, dwelt upon the fact that a large amount of money had been refunded by the guilty men, and urged the greater question of the safety of the cause and the necessity of preserving united the powerful support which Pennsylvania was giving to the administration in suppressing the rebellion. Watson answered:

"Very well, Mr. President, if you wish to have these men released, all that is necessary is to give the order; but I shall ask to have it in writing. In such a case as this it would not be safe for me to obey a verbal order; and let me add that if you do release them the fact and the reason will necessarily become known to the people."

Finally Mr. Lincoln took up his hat and went out. Wilmot was waiting in the corridor, and came to meet him.

"Wilmot," he said, "I can't do anything with Watson; he won't release them."

The reply which the Senator made to this remark can not be printed here, but it did not affect the judgment or the action of the President.

The men were retained for a long time afterward. The fraud was fully investigated, and future swindles of the kind were rendered impossible. If Watson could have had his way, the guilty parties—and there were some whose names never got to the public—would have been tried by military commission and sternly dealt with. But my own reflections upon the subject led me to the conclusion that the moderation of the President was wiser than the unrelenting justice of the Assistant Secretary would have been.

—DANA, *Recollections of the Civil War*

6. COLONEL BAKER OUTWITS BOUNTY JUMPERS AND BROKERS

It is difficult to imagine how the enlistment and conscription laws of the Federal government could have been drawn more badly than they were. By the law of July 1861 Congress promised a bounty of $100 for three-year enlistments, and this bounty was later extended to conscripts who agreed to serve for a long term. The act of March 3, 1863, gave a bounty of $300 to three-year enlisters. At the same time many states and localities filled their quotas by offering generous bounties. Altogether, it is estimated, the Federal government paid out some $300,000,000 in bounties, and state and local governments a comparable sum. Inevitably many soldiers enlisted just for the bounty, deserted, and re-enlisted elsewhere; some professional bounty jumpers managed to enlist and collect bounty ten or twenty times. Along with bounty jumping went bounty brokers—crooks who recruited men, and then robbed them of their bounties.

Colonel LaFayette C. Baker, who here tells us how he caught bounty jumpers and brokers red-handed, was Chief of the United States Secret Service, notorious alike for his high-handed and illegal methods and for his success in feathering his own nest while serving his government. President Johnson dismissed him for maintaining an espionage system in the White House. One historian observes that Baker's "habitual carelessness in mixing truth and fiction was not overcome in his History of the Secret Service," but, however unreliable his general account of his own distinguished services, this story of bounty jumping in January 1865 would seem to be authentic enough.

The great demand for recruits during the war, the large bounties offered for them, and the manifold facilities for fraudulent transactions, presented temptations of great power, even to reputable citizens, to evade the plain letter of the law, and traffic in substitutes, or, by bribery and deception, personally to keep out of the hands of the recruiting officer.

The majority of the officers assigned to recruiting service were guilty of great dereliction of duty, inasmuch as, instead of endeavoring to check the growing evil, they rather pretended ignorance, or allowed it to pass unnoticed. . . .

The Department at Washington was constantly urging upon me the necessity for forming some plan, which, in a summary and successful manner, would frustrate the designs of these dishonest parties, and bring them to justice. Several attempts had been made for this purpose, but had all proved unsuccessful.

A number of plans were submitted to me, each of which I considered objectionable, on certain accounts. The shortest way to catch these deserters, which was tracking them to their haunts, it would have been folly to pursue, as such a course would result in a general alarm and stampede of the guilty. . . .

I took up my headquarters at the Astor House, and let the brokers know that I was an agent or supervisor for the interior of the State, having several large quotas to fill. I was at once besieged by applications to purchase credits. The third day I purchased sixteen sets of these enlistment-papers; and on the fourth, twenty-two, when a proposition was made by a broker to purchase forged papers, saying, those I had were such, and would answer the same purpose; that so skillfully were they prepared detection was impossible. The offer was accepted, and placed me on the most friendly terms with my associates in business. For a number of days I continued the purchase of spurious papers for less than half the price of the genuine documents. This feature of the swindling came near causing a quarrel among the brokers; some of them insisting that I should not have been informed that I bought forged papers, because I might then have paid full price. The other party contended, that by committing me to the forgery I was secured against betrayal of the cause. The former further claimed, that forged papers were worth as much to me as the genuine. These negotiations were carried on four days, when I decided to arrest the whole company. It will be understood, that the arrest of a single broker in the city would create an alarm, and end the investigation. The greatest strategy and concealment were therefore indispensible to success. The knowledge of my presence in the metropolis would have defeated my plans. On a certain day I requested nine brokers, with whom I had business, to come to my room at the same hour, bringing their papers. I had concealed, in an adjoining room, a number of my assistants. I instructed them that the signal I should use to bring them to my aid, would be a knock on the door of the apartment in which they were placed.

The illustrious nine stood around me, forged papers in hand, eagerly waiting for the checks which would bring the reward of their villainy. To fasten the guilt upon the criminals, be-

yond dispute, I had written receipts for the money to be
paid each broker. As they walked up in line, and made their
marks, for most of them could not write, I stepped to the
folding-doors and gave the signal. Instantly a detective came
in, and I said to my broker-friends: "Gentlemen, this joke
has gone far enough; you are my prisoners. I am General
Baker, the Chief of the Detective Bureau."

It would be futile for tongue or pen to attempt to describe
the effect of my words upon the assemblage before me. The
change that passed over it was very marked, and to me, who
was the cause of it, irresistibly entertaining. The explosion
of a bomb-shell in the battle-ranks could not have startled
and dismayed the soldiery more suddenly than this unexpected
exposure of their crimes, and the powerful grasp of justice, did the discomfited brokers, who had anticipated a very
different fate. . . .

It has been sufficiently demonstrated, by incidents recorded,
that monstrous frauds were perpetrated by the manufacture
and sale of enlistment papers.

Indeed, it is very evident, from knowledge thus far obtained, that not a small proportion of all such documents, on
which credits were given, were forged.

I shall only add to the record a few incidents, which com-
bine in their character both comic and tragic qualities.

I had been told that soldiers would receive the bounty, re-
enlist the same day, be sent to the Island, and repeat the
process the day following. I was, at the time, skeptical respect-
ing such facility in deception and incredible assurance, and
to satisfy myself in regard to the truth of the matter, I
dressed myself in the garb of a regular jumper and repaired,
February 9th, to a recruiting office in the public square
near the Astor House, New York. Assuming the air of a veteran in the business, I asked the officer what he was paying
for recruits.

Before the question could be answered, the gentlemanly
broker, always at hand, inquired of me my name and place of
residence, which I gave him. In a low tone of voice, and with
a knowing wink, he said: "Have you been through before
in New York?"

I answered: "Not since last fall."

He added: "All right; come inside." And in less time than
it has taken to relate the incident, I was one of "Uncle Sam's
boys."

My friend gave me one hundred dollars, promising the remainder due me when I should arrive at the Island; then directing me to remain where I was for a while, he left me.

Returning within an hour, he opened the following conversation with me: "Have you ever been on the Island?"

I replied, "Yes."

Evidently enlightened in regard to the matter, he immediately remarked: "You know how to get off, then? When you *do*, come up to Tammany Hall, and I will put you through up town": meaning, of course, he would enlist me again.

While this conversation was passing between us another broker stepped up, and said: "Gentlemen, let us take a drink." We accepted the invitation, and they conducted me across the Park to a saloon, where I saw, at a glance, they were quite at home. Liquor was called for, and while the vender was getting it, one of the brokers quietly stepped behind the bar and addressed some conversation to him.

We then all drank to the success of the Union, or rather, all of us *appeared* to do so.

I raised the glass to my lips, and, unobserved by the rest, poured its contents into my bosom, as I had done many times before when compelled to join the convivial ring. I was convinced that my potation had been drugged. Next followed a proposition to repair to an adjoining room and engage in a game of cards.

We played until I thought it necessary to affect drowsiness and insensibility. My eyes began to close, until at length my head rested on the table in front of me, and my whole appearance indicated to my betrayers my entire helplessness in their hands.

At this juncture one of them left the room, but soon returning, exclaimed, "All right." Immediately I caught the sound of carriage wheels, and, as I anticipated, was carried to the door, and, supported by broker number one, lifted into a vehicle, and driven rapidly to the Cedar Street rendezvous. My hat was then unceremoniously pushed over my face, and I was hurried into the presence of the recruiting officer in attendance, who asked me, "Do you wish to enlist?"

Number two answered, in a tone to represent my own voice, "Ye-e-s."

I was again declared to be one of the volunteers, taken into another room, and laid on a bench, where I remained an hour, in company with three other recruits, who had been drugged in the same manner, my friends the brokers supposing they had disposed of me.

In the mean time broker number one returned, and said:

"Well, old fellow, how do you feel?" to which I replied, "Very sick." Then remarking, "You'll be all right by-and-by," he left me.

I looked about me to judge of the possibility of escape. I saw at once that I could not pass out by the door, as a sentry was stationed there, and came to the conclusion that I would have to try my chances at a window.

I opened one which overlooked a back yard, sprang out, and after walking through a long passage-way, which led me into the open street, I went deliberately to my room in the Astor House.

Here I masked my face, disguised myself anew, and proceeded directly to the office of Mr. Blunt, where I offered myself to the army service, to make my third enlistment for that day.

I was hardly seated, when broker number three approached me, saying: "You want to enlist, do you?"

"Yes, I am thinking of it. What are you paying recruits now?"

"Six hundred dollars. Where are you from?"

"Steuben County. I would like to enlist if I could get a situation as clerk. I can write a pretty good hand, and am hardly able to go into the ranks."

He replied quickly, "Oh, I can fix that all right."

A conversation then followed between him and the recruiting officer, when I was made a soldier of the Union army once more. I was requested to be seated for a few moments. Soon after the broker asked me to take "a glass." I went with him to an old drinking-saloon in Cherry Street, where I found brokers numbers one and two, who immediately recognized me, but expressed no surprise at the meeting. My successful escape from the Cedar Street headquarters convinced my friends that I was an old expert in the tricks of the trade.

Their admiration for me became so great that they received me into full fellowship, regarded me as a shrewd member of the bounty jumping brotherhood, and, after freely discussing their plans and prospects, declared me to be a "perfect trump." Propositions were made to enter into partnership at once.

I was greatly amused while listening to the exploits of each, as he in turn detailed them. One related, that at a certain period he left New York, and having enlisted at Albany, Troy, Utica, Buffalo, and Chicago, returned *via* Elmira, at which place he likewise enlisted. Another had enlisted at every rendezvous from New York to Portland, Maine; while a third boasted of the amounts he had received, and mentioned those paid to recruiting officers, surgeons, brokers, and detectives. The den in which I spent the evening was a favorite haunt of the bounty jumpers. It contained a wardrobe of wearing apparel, consisting of both soldiers' and citizens' outfits. The idea of this I easily comprehended; here the jumpers could assume whatever dress they pleased, to carry out their designs. Three times that night, before two o'clock, I saw the interesting operation performed.

I selected one of my assistants to experiment in this military lottery. He dressed himself in the appropriate apparel, and in one day enlisted three times; he was sent to the Island, bought himself off, and reported for duty the following day.

The scenes described were followed by numberless arrests of bounty brokers, bounty jumpers, and others in the business, and consequently by the disclosures of their crimes, which have since attracted much public attention.

—BAKER, *The Secret Service in the Late War*

7. CONFEDERATE PLOTS AGAINST THE NORTH

It was entirely natural that the Confederacy, which was on the defensive militarily, should have sought to attack the Union from behind the lines. For in the end the only hope of Confederate victory—and it was a persistent hope—lay in encouraging discontent and disunity to the point where the Northern people would weary of the war. To this end Confederate secret agents, working closely with such treasonable organizations as the Knights of the Golden Circle and the Sons of Liberty, planned a series of attacks and uprisings in the fall of 1864. The immediate objective was to release Confederate prisoners at such places as Camp Douglas, in Chicago, and Johnson's Island, in Lake Erie, to burn Northern cities, and to distract the strength of the North by border raids; the ultimate purpose was to encourage the peace movement and defeat Lincoln in the 1864 elections. The plan to seize Camp Douglas miscarried and the leaders of the Knights implicated in the plan were captured and tried for treason. A border raid on St. Albans, Vermont, was a minor success. The two plots described in these excerpts were both fiascos.

A. A CONFEDERATE PLAN TO SEIZE JOHNSON'S ISLAND IS FRUSTRATED

On the 20th of September, 1864, the Lake cities were suddenly aroused from their imagined security by the news that a passenger steamer upon Lake Erie had been seized by a squad of Confederates, her crew overpowered, the steamer captured and her course directed to Johnson's Island, with the avowed purpose of rescuing the prisoners confined there and taking them to the Ohio shore, whence it was hoped they might make their way South through the state of Ohio. The plot was carefully planned, and perhaps might have been carried to a successful conclusion had it not been for the abundant precautions taken by the Federal forces.

The steamer, the *Philo Parsons*, left Detroit at her usual hour in the morning, and at the request of one Bennett G. Burleigh, who had come on board the night before stopped at Sandwich in Canada, nearly opposite Detroit, to take on board three friends of Burleigh, one of whom he said was lame and unable to cross the ferry. Proceeding down the river, the steamer stopped at Amherstberg, where sixteen roughish-looking men came aboard with an old trunk tied with a rope. They did not seem to be connected with Burleigh, but were supposed to be refugees from the draft returning home; and little attention was paid to them.

Nothing occurred to excite suspicion until the boat was well within American waters, when one Beall, the leader of the gang, while engaged in conversation with the mate in the pilot house, suddenly drew his revolver, and demanded possession of the boat as a Confederate officer. Recognizing the force of this argument, the mate surrendered the wheel. The crew and passengers were overpowered, driven into the cabin, and the old trunk, which proved to be a small arsenal, opened, hatchets and revolvers distributed among the conspirators, and the course of the boat continued toward Sandusky, near which lay Johnson's Island.

But at this point the success of the expedition culminated. Failing to meet a messenger who was to have been sent to meet them at Kelley's Island, on the route of the steamer, or to receive an expected signal, all the conspirators but three mutinied, refused to go further, and returned at top speed to Amherstberg, where the boat was scuttled and abandoned and the conspirators dispersed. Another steamer was captured and scuttled on the Lake. All of the men were arrested,

taken before a Justice of the Peace and discharged, although
the officers were sufficiently alert to seize certain property
which had been landed and detain it for customs dues.

It was fortunate the steamer turned about when she did. The
officers of the *Michigan* had been apprised that the raid
would be made that day. The *Michigan*, a man-of-war of
fifteen guns, lay off the island, cleared for action, her guns
shotted, her anchor hove short, and every preparation made to
receive the expected guests. The messenger who was sent to
Kelley's Island to join the conspirators had already been arrested and put in custody. There was an available force of nine
hundred men at the Island to put down any insurrection. That
twenty men, armed only with revolvers and hatchets, should
have been able to capture the *Michigan* and release the
prisoners was simply preposterous. A single broadside from the
Michigan would probably have sunk the steamer.
—BROWN, "The Lake Erie Piracy Case"

B. THE CONFEDERATES ATTEMPT TO BURN NEW YORK

At 6 o'clock promptly on the evening of November 25,
1864, our party met in our cottage headquarters, two failing
to report.

The bottles of Greek fire having been wrapped in paper
were put in our coat pockets. Each man took ten bottles. It
was agreed that after our operations were over we should secrete ourselves and meet here the next night at 6 o'clock to
compare notes and agree on further plans.

I had rooms at the Astor House, City Hotel, Everett House,
and the United States Hotel. Colonel Martin occupied rooms
at the Hoffman, Fifth Avenue, St. Denis, and two others.
Lieutenant Ashbrook was at the St. Nicholas, La Farge, and
several others. Altogether nineteen hotels were fired, namely:
Hoffman House, Fifth Avenue, St. Denis, St. James, La
Farge, St. Nicholas, Metropolitan, Howard, Tammany,
Brandreth's, Gramercy Park, Hanford, New England, Belmont,
Lovejoy's, City Hotel, Astor, United States, and Everett.

I reached the Astor House at 7.20 o'clock, got my key, and
went to my room in the top story. It was the lower corner
front room on Broadway. After lighting the gas jet I hung
the bedclothes loosely on the headboard and piled the chairs,
drawers of the bureau and washstand on the bed. Then stuffed
some newspapers about among the mass and poured a bottle of turpentine over it all. I concluded to unlock my door

and fix the key on the outside, as I might have to get out in a hurry, for I did not know whether the Greek fire would make a noise or not. I opened a bottle carefully and quickly and spilled it on the pile of rubbish. It blazed up instantly and the whole bed seemed to be in flames, before I could get out. I locked the door and walked down the hall and stairway to the office, which was fairly crowded with people. I left the key at the office, as usual and passed out.

Across at the City Hotel I proceeded in the same manner. Then in going down to the Everett House I looked over at my room in the Astor House. A bright light appeared within but there were no indications below of any alarm. After getting through at the Everett House I started to the United States Hotel, when the fire bells began to ring up town. I got through at the United States Hotel without trouble, but in leaving my key the clerk, I thought, looked at me a little curiously. It occurred to me that it had been discovered that my satchel had no baggage in it and that perhaps the clerk had it in mind to mention the fact.

As I came back to Broadway it seemed that a hundred bells were ringing, great crowds were gathering on the street, and there was general consternation. I concluded to go and see how my fires were doing. There was no panic at the Astor House, but to my surprise a great crowd was pouring out of Barnum's Museum nearly opposite the Astor. It was now a quarter after nine o'clock by the City Hall tower clock. Presently the alarm came from the City Hotel and the Everett. The surging crowds were frantic. But the greatest panic was at Barnum's Museum. People were coming out and down ladders from the second and third floor windows and the manager was crying out for help to get his animals out. It looked like people were getting hurt running over each other in the stampede, and still I could not help some astonishment for I did not suppose there was a fire in the Museum.

In accordance with our plan I went down Broadway and turned across to the North River wharf. The vessels and barges of every description were lying along close together and not more than twenty yards from the street. I picked dark spots to stand in, and jerked a bottle in six different places. They were ablaze before I left. One had struck a barge of baled hay and made a big fire. There were wild scenes here the last time I looked back. I started straight for the City Hall.

There was still a crowd around the Astor House and everywhere, but I edged through and crossed over to the City Hall, where I caught a car just starting up town. I got off on Bowery street opposite the Metropolitan Hotel to go across and see how Ashbrook and Harrington had succeeded. After walking half a square I observed a man walking ahead of me and recognized him. It was Captain Kennedy. I closed up behind him and slapped him on the shoulder. He squatted and began to draw his pistol, but I laughed and he knew me. He laughed and said he ought to shoot me for giving him such a scare.

We soon related to each other our experience. Kennedy said that after he touched off his hotels he concluded to go down to Barnum's Museum and stay until something turned up, but had only been there a few minutes when alarms began to ring all over the city. He decided to go out, and coming down the stairway it happened to be clear at a turn and the idea occurred to him that there would be fun to start a scare. He broke a bottle of Greek fire, he said, on the edge of a step like he would crack an egg. It blazed up and he got out to witness the result. He had been down there in the crowd ever since and the fires at the Astor House and the City Hotel had both been put out. But he had listened to the talk of the people and heard the opinion expressed generally that rebels were in the city to destroy it. He thought our presence must be known. Harrington had broken a bottle in the Metropolitan Theater at 8 o'clock, just after he fired the Metropolitan Hotel adjoining; and Ashbrook had done likewise in Niblo's Garden Theater adjoining the La Farge Hotel.

We went into the crowd on Broadway and stopped at those places to see what had happened. There was the wildest excitement imaginable. There was all sorts of talk about hanging the rebels to lamp posts or burning them at the stake. Still we discovered that all was surmise apparently. So far as we could learn the programme had been carried out, but it appeared that all had made a failure. It seemed to us that there was something wrong with our Greek fire.

All had observed that the fires had been put out in all the places as easily as any ordinary fire. We came to the conclusion that Longmire and his manufacturing chemist had put up a job on us after it was found that we could not be dissuaded from our purpose.

Martin and I got together as agreed and found lodging about 2 o'clock. We did not awake until 10 o'clock next day. We went into a restaurant on Broadway near Twelfth street for breakfast. It was crowded, but every one was reading a newspaper. After giving our order we got the *Herald*, *World, Tribune,* and *Times,* and to our surprise the entire front pages were given up to sensational accounts of the attempt to burn the city. It was plainly pointed out that rebels were at the head of the incendiary work, and quite a list of names was given of parties who had been arrested. All our fictitious names registered at the different hotels were given and interviews with the clerks described us all. The clerk of the United States Hotel especially gave a minute description of my personal appearance, clothing, manners and actions. He said I did not eat a meal at the hotel, though I had been there two days as a guest, and had nothing in my black satchel.

It was stated in the papers that the authorities had a full knowledge of the plot and the ring-leaders would be captured during the day. One paper said the baggage of two of them had been secured, and all avenues of escape being guarded the villains were sure to be caught, the detectives having a full knowledge of the rebels and their haunts.

—HEADLEY, *Confederate Operations in Canada and New York*

V

Behind the Lines: The South

WHY *did the Confederacy lose the war? Historians are still discussing this engrossing question, and they are still unable to agree on the answer. There is pretty general agreement, though, that the South did not lose the war on the battlefield. To be sure the Confederates were beaten at Vicksburg and Gettysburg, Chattanooga and Atlanta, decimated in the Wilderness, and shattered by Sherman's march from Atlanta to the sea and beyond. But these military defeats—so runs the argument—were consequences, not causes.*

The most varied causes are assigned to explain these defeats: the blockade and shortages of essential materials; failure to win the foreign recognition so confidently anticipated; the breakdown of finance and of transportation; the incompetence of the President and of Congress; the disintegrating impact of State rights. Yet had the Confederacy used such resources of man power as it had, it might not have suffered defeat. There was food enough in the Confederacy; finances could have been controlled; the transportation system was not beyond repair; the blockade was not effective until 1863; foreign intervention would have followed upon military success and a statesmanlike policy toward such things as cotton and slavery; State rights denied to the Confederacy resources that promised victory; a wiser government would have made Lee commander in chief and permitted him to control the grand strategy of the war, and so forth. So the argument runs, and most students fall back, in the end, on the vague phrase "breakdown of morale"—a phrase which merely begs the question.

But what all this adds up to is that the Confederate cause was lost in the Confederacy itself—that is, behind the lines. The internal history of the Confederacy thus becomes a matter of paramount interest. This chapter is not designed, primarily, to illuminate the breakdown of the Confederacy, but there can be little doubt that it does so. Successive excerpts describe the inadequacy of food and of other necessities, runaway inflation, the incompetence of the medical services, the short-sighted cotton policy, the effectiveness of the blockade, the impact of invasion and of defeat on morale, dissatisfaction with the conduct of the war, the role of State rights, and the growth of defeatism.

1. A WAR CLERK SUFFERS SCARCITIES IN RICHMOND

Concentration on staple crops at the expense of grains and dairy products made the agricultural South far from self-sufficient, while industrially the South was almost wholly dependent on the North or on Britain. These basic economic factors, plus state competition for such foodstuffs and industrial products as could be found, contributed largely to the growing shortages that harassed the Confederacy.

After the war was fairly under way the Confederate government tried to meet nearly all its expenses by issues of paper money. This money steadily depreciated in value, so that every new issue was followed by a rise in prices which had to be met, in turn, by another new issue. By the end of 1864 the paper currency in circulation had reached about one billion dollars.

Other factors, too, contributed to inflation: the blockade by shutting off imports from abroad; the breakdown of the transportation system by making it hard to move merchandise; the decline in farm and factory production. All this meant that prices soared, that wages—especially the sorry wages of the soldiers—became almost worthless, and that the poor everywhere and the city-folk suffered sharp hardships.

John Beauchamp Jones, whose Rebel War Clerk's Diary *we have used before, was an editor and novelist who obtained a clerkship in the War Department for the express purpose of being at the center of things and writing about them. His book, verbose and prejudiced, is an authentic record of day-by-day life in the capital.*

May 23, 1862.—Oh, the extortioners! Meats of all kinds are selling at fifty cents per pound; butter, seventy-five cents; coffee, a dollar and half; tea, ten dollars; boots, thirty dollars per pair; shoes, eighteen dollars; ladies' shoes, fifteen dollars; shirts, six dollars each. Houses that rented for five hundred dollars last year are a thousand dollars now. Boarding, from thirty to forty dollars per month. General Winder has issued an order fixing the maximum prices of certain articles of marketing, which has only the effect of keeping a great many things out of market. The farmers have to pay the merchants and Jews their extortionate prices and complain very justly of the partiality of the general. It does more harm than good.

October 1st.—How shall we subsist this winter? There is not a supply of wood or coal in the city—and it is said that there are not adequate means of transporting it hither. Flour at sixteen dollars per barrel and bacon at seventy-five cents per pound threaten a famine. And yet there are no beggars in the streets. We must get a million of men in arms and drive the invader from our soil. We are capable of it, and we must do it. Better die in battle than die of starvation produced by the enemy.

The newspapers are printed on half sheets—and I think the publishers make money; the extras (published almost every day) are sold to the newsboys for ten cents and often sold by them for twenty-five cents. These are mere slips of paper, seldom containing more than a column—which is reproduced in the next issue. The matter of the extras is mostly made up from the Northern papers, brought hither by persons running the blockade. The supply is pretty regular, and dates are rarely more than three or four days behind the time of reception. We often get the first accounts of battles at a distance in this way, as our generals and our government are famed for a prudential reticence.

6th.—. . . This evening Custis and I expect the arrival of my family from Raleigh, N.C. We have procured for them one pound of sugar, eighty cents; four loaves of bread, as large as my fist, twenty cents each; and we have a little coffee, which is selling at two dollars and a half per pound. In the morning some one must go to market, else there will be short-commons. Washing is two dollars and a half per dozen pieces. Common soap is worth seventy-five cents per pound.

November 7th.—Yesterday I received from the agent of the City Councils fourteen pounds of salt, having seven persons in my family, including the servant. One pound to each member, per month, is allowed at five cents per pound. The extortionists sell it at seventy cents per pound. One of *them* was drawing for his family. He confessed it but said he paid fifty cents for the salt he sold at seventy cents. Profit ten dollars per bushel! I sent an article today to the *Enquirer*, suggesting that fuel, bread, meat, etc. be furnished in the same manner. We shall soon be in a state of siege.

21st.—Common shirting cotton and Yankee calico that used to sell at twelve and a half cents per yard is now a dollar seventy-five! What a temptation for the Northern manufacturers! What a rush of trade there would be if peace should occur suddenly! And what a party there would be in the South for peace (and unity with Northern Democrats) if the war were waged somewhat differently. The excesses of the Republicans *compel* our people to be almost a unit. This is all the better for us. Still, we are in quite a bad way now, God knows!

Mr. Dargan, M.C., writes to the President from Mobile that the inhabitants of that city are in an awful condition—meal is selling for three dollars and a half per bushel and wood at fifteen dollars per cord—and that the people are afraid to bring supplies, apprehending that the government agents will seize them. The President (thanks to him!) has ordered that interference with domestic trade must not be permitted.

December 1st.—God speed the day of peace! Our patriotism is mainly in the army and among the ladies of the South. The avarice and cupidity of the men at home, could only be excelled by the ravenous wolves; and most of our sufferings are fully deserved. Where a people will not have mercy on one another, how can they expect mercy? They depreciate the Confederate notes by charging from $20 to $40 per bbl. for flour; $3.50 per bushel of meal; $2 per lb. for butter; $20 per cord for wood, etc. When we shall have peace let the extortionists be remembered! let an indelible stigma be branded upon them.

A portion of the people look like vagabonds. We see men and women and children in the streets in dingy and dilapidated clothes; and some seem gaunt and pale with hunger—the speculators, and thieving quartermasters and commissaries only, looking sleek and comfortable. If this state of things continue a year or so longer, they will have their reward. There will be governmental bankruptcy, and all their gains will turn to dust and ashes, dust and ashes!

January 18, 1863.—We are now, in effect, in a state of siege, and none but the opulent, often those who have defrauded the government, can obtain a sufficiency of food and raiment. Calico, which could once be bought for twelve and a half cents per yard, is now selling at two dollars and a quarter, and a lady's dress of calico costs her about thirty dollars. Bonnets are not to be had. Common bleached cotton shirting brings a dollar and a half per yard. All other dry goods are held in the same proportion. Common tallow candles are a dollar and a quarter per pound; soap, one dollar; hams, one dollar; opossum, three dollars; turkeys, four to eleven dollars; sugar, brown, one dollar; molasses, eight dollars per gallon; potatoes, six dollars per bushel, etc.

These evils might be remedied by the government, for there is no great scarcity of any of the substantials and necessities of life in the country, if they were only equally distributed. The difficulty is in procuring transportation, and the government monopolizes the railroads and canals.

January 30th.—I cut the following from yesterday's *Dispatch:*

"*The Results of Extortion and Speculation.*—The state of affairs brought about by the speculating and extortion practiced upon the public cannot be better illustrated than by the following grocery bill for one week for a small family, in which the prices before the war and those of the present are compared:

1860		1863	
Bacon, 10 lbs. at 12½¢	$1.25	Bacon, 10 lbs. at $1	$10.00
Flour, 30 lbs. at 5¢	1.50	Flour, 30 lbs. at 12½¢	3.75
Sugar, 5 lbs. at 8¢	.40	Sugar, 5 lbs. at $1.15	5.75
Coffee, 4 lbs. at 12½¢	.50	Coffee, 4 lbs. at $5	20.00
Tea (green), ½ lb. at $1	.50	Tea (green), ½ lb. at $16	8.00
Lard, 4 lbs. at 12½¢	.50	Lard, 4 lbs. at $1	4.00
Butter, 3 lbs. at 25¢	.75	Butter, 3 lbs. at $1.75	5.25
Meal, 1 pk. at 25¢	.25	Meal, 1 pk. at $1	1.00
Candles, 2 lbs. at 15¢	.30	Candles, 2 lbs. at $1.25	2.50
Soap, 5 lbs. at 10¢	.50	Soap, 5 lbs. at $1.10	5.50
Pepper and salt (about)	.10	Pepper and salt (about)	2.50
Total	$6.55	Total	$68.25

"So much we owe the speculators, who have stayed at home to prey upon the necessities of their fellow-citizens."

February 11th.—Some idea may be formed of the scarcity of

food in this city from the fact that, while my youngest daughter was in the kitchen today, a young rat came out of its hole and seemed to beg for something to eat; she held out some bread, which it ate from her hand, and seemed grateful. Several others soon appeared and were as tame as kittens. Perhaps we shall have to eat them!

18th.—One or two of the regiments of General Lee's army were in the city last night. The men were pale and haggard. They have but a quarter of a pound of meat per day. But meat has been ordered from Atlanta. I hope it is abundant there.

All the necessaries of life in the city are still going up higher in price. Butter, three dollars per pound; beef, one dollar; bacon, a dollar and a quarter; sausage meat, one dollar; and even liver is selling at fifty cents per pound.

By degrees, quite perceptibly, we are approaching the condition of famine. What effect this will produce on the community is to be seen. The army must be fed or disbanded, or else the city must be abandoned. How we, "the people," are to live is a thought of serious concern.

March 30th.—The gaunt form of wretched famine still approaches with rapid strides. Meal is now selling at twelve dollars per bushel and potatoes at sixteen. Meats have almost disappeared from the market, and none but the opulent can afford to pay three dollars and a half per pound for butter. Greens, however, of various kinds, are coming in; and as the season advances, we may expect a diminution of prices. It is strange that on the 30th of March, even in the "sunny South," the fruit trees are as bare of blossoms and foliage as at midwinter. We shall have fire until the middle of May— six months of winter!

I am spading up my garden and hope to raise a few vegetables to eke out a miserable subsistence for my family. My daughter Ann reads Shakespeare to me o' nights, which saves my eyes.

April 17th.—Pins are so scarce and costly that it is now a pretty general practice to stoop down and pick up any found in the street. The boardinghouses are breaking up, and rooms, furnished and unfurnished, are renting out to messes. One dollar and fifty cents for beef leaves no margin for profit even at a hundred dollars per month, which is charged for board, and most of the boarders cannot afford to pay that price. Therefore they take rooms and buy their own scanty food. I am inclined to think provisions would not be deficient to an alarming extent if they were equally distributed. Wood is no scarcer than before the war, and yet thirty dollars per load (less than a cord) is demanded for it and obtained.

August 22nd.—Night before last all the clerks in the city post-office resigned, because the government did not give them salaries sufficient to subsist them. As yet their places have not been filled, and the government gets no letters—some of which lying in the office may be of such importance as to involve the safety or ruin of the government. To-morrow is Sunday, and of course the mails will not be attended to before Monday—the letters lying here four days unopened! This really looks as if we had no Postmaster-General.

October 22nd.—A poor woman yesterday applied to a merchant in Carey Street to purchase a barrel of flour. The price he demanded was $70.

"My God!" exclaimed she, "how can I pay such prices? I have seven children; what shall I do?"

"I don't know, madam," said he, coolly, "unless you eat your children."

Such is the power of cupidity—it transforms men into demons. And if this spirit prevails throughout the country, a just God will bring calamities upon the land, which will reach these cormorants, but which, it may be feared, will involve all classes in a common ruin.

January 26, 1864—The prisoners on Belle Isle (8000) have had no meat for eleven days. The Secretary says the Commissary-General informs him that they fare as well as our armies, and so he refused the commissary (Capt. Warner) of the prisoners a permit to buy and bring to the city cattle he might be able to find. An outbreak of the prisoners is apprehended: and if they were to rise, it is feared some of the inhabitants of the city would join them, for they, too, have no meat—many of them—or bread either. They believe the famine is owing to the imbecility, or worse of the government. A riot would be a dangerous occurrence now: the city battalion would not fire on the people—and if they did the army might break up, and avenge their slaughtered kindred. It is a perilous time.

March 18th.—My daughter's cat is staggering to-day, for want of animal food. Sometimes I fancy I stagger myself. We do not average two ounces of meat daily; and some do not get any for several days together. Meal is $50 per bushel. I saw adamantine candles sell at auction to-day (box) at $10 per pound; tallow, $6.50. Bacon brought $7.75 per pound by the 100 pounds.

April 8th.—Bright and warm—really a fine spring day. It is the day of *fasting*, humiliation, and prayer, and all the offices are closed. May God put it into the hearts of the extortioners to relent, and abolish, for a season, the insatiable greed for gain! I paid $25 for a half cord of wood to-day, new currency. I fear a nation of extortioners are unworthy of independence, and that we must be chastened and purified before success will be vouchsafed us.

What enormous appetites we have now, and how little illness, since food has become so high in price! I cannot afford to have more than an ounce of meat daily for each member of my family of six; and to-day Custis's parrot, which has accompanied the family in all their flights, and, it seems, will *never* die, stole the cook's ounce of fat meat and gobbled it up before it could be taken from him. He is permitted to set at one corner of the table, and has lately acquired a fondness for meat. The old cat goes staggering about from debility, although Fannie often gives him her share. We see neither rats nor mice about the premises now. This is famine. Even the pigeons watch the crusts in the hands of the children, and follow them in the yard. *And, still, there are no beggars.*

August 13th.—Flour is falling: It is now $200 per barrel—$500 a few weeks ago; and bacon is falling in price also, from $11 to $6 per pound. A commission merchant said to me, yesterday, that there was at least eighteen months' supply (for the people) of breadstuffs and meats in the city; and pointing to the upper windows at the corner of Thirteenth and Cary Streets, he revealed the ends of many barrels piled above the windows. He said that flour had been there two years, held for "still higher prices." Such is the avarice of man. Such is war. And such the greed of extortioners, even in the midst of famine—and famine in the midst of plenty!

—JONES, *A Rebel War Clerk's Diary*

2. MR. EGGLESTON RECALLS WHEN MONEY WAS PLENTIFUL

Eggleston's account of the impact of inflation on the life of the South—and especially of Richmond—parallels and supplements that of the Rebel war clerk, but is more genial and optimistic. Certainly his conclusion that municipal regulations wiped out gambling in the Confederate capital is not borne out by other evidence. George Cary Eggleston was, himself,

*a romantic character. Born in Indiana—brother of that Edward
Eggleston who wrote the famous* Hoosier Schoolmaster—*he
early inherited a plantation in Amelia County, Virginia, and
wholly identified himself with the life of the South. At the
outbreak of the war he joined the 1st Virginia Cavalry, fought
under Stuart, Fitzhugh Lee, and Longstreet and, for a time, in
the South Carolina field artillery.*

*After the war Eggleston had a long career as journalist
and man of letters. He was literary editor of the* New York
Evening Post, *served on the staff of the* New York World,
*wrote scores of novels and boy's stories, compiled his recol-
lections, and contributed a two-volume* History of the Confederate War *that is still valuable.*

The financial system adopted by the Confederate government
was singularly simple and free from technicalities. It consisted
chiefly in the issue of treasury notes enough to meet all the
expenses of the government, and in the present advanced
state of the art of printing there was but one difficulty incident
to this process; namely, the impossibility of having the notes
signed in the Treasury Department as fast as they were needed.
There happened, however, to be several thousand young
ladies in Richmond willing to accept light and remunerative
employment at their homes, and as it was really a matter of
small moment whose names the notes bore, they were given
out in sheets to these young ladies, who signed and returned
them for a consideration. I shall not undertake to guess how
many Confederate treasury notes were issued. Indeed, I am
credibly informed by a gentleman who was high in office in
the Treasury Department that even the secretary himself did
not certainly know. The acts of Congress authorizing issues
of currency were the hastily formulated thought of a not
very wise body of men, and my informant tells me they were
frequently susceptible of widely different construction by different officials. However that may be, it was clearly out of the
power of the government ever to redeem the notes, and
whatever may have been the state of affairs within the treasury, nobody outside its precincts ever cared to muddle his
head in an attempt to get at exact figures.

We knew only that money was astonishingly abundant. Provisions fell short sometimes, and the supply of clothing was
not always as large as we should have liked, but nobody found
it difficult to get money enough. It was to be had almost for
the asking. And to some extent the abundance of the currency
really seemed to atone for its extreme badness. Going the

rounds of the pickets on the coast of South Carolina one day in 1863, I heard a conversation between a Confederate and a Union soldier, stationed on opposite sides of a little inlet, in the course of which this point was brought out.

Union Soldier. Aren't times rather hard over there, Johnny?

Confederate Soldier. Not at all. We've all the necessaries of life.

U.S. Yes, but how about luxuries? You never see any coffee nowadays, do you?

C.S. Plenty of it.

U.S. Isn't it pretty high?

C.S. Forty dollars a pound, that's all.

U.S. Whew! Don't you call that high?

C.S. (after reflecting). Well, perhaps it is a trifle uppish, but then you never saw money so plentiful as it is with us. We hardly know what to do with it and don't mind paying high prices for things we want.

And that was the universal feeling. Money was so easily got and its value was so utterly uncertain that we were never able to determine what was a fair price for anything. We fell into the habit of paying whatever was asked, knowing that tomorrow we should have to pay more. Speculation became the easiest and surest thing imaginable. The speculator saw no risks of loss. Every article of merchandise rose in value every day, and to buy anything this week and sell it next was to make an enormous profit quite as a matter of course. So uncertain were prices, or rather so constantly did they tend upward, that when a cargo of cadet-gray cloths was brought into Charleston once, an officer in my battery, attending the sale, was able to secure enough of the cloth to make two suits of clothes without any expense whatever, merely by speculating upon an immediate advance. He became the purchaser at auction of a case of the goods and had no difficulty, as soon as the sale was over, in finding a merchant who was glad to take his bargain off his hands, giving him the cloth he wanted as a premium. The officer could not possibly have paid for the case of goods, but there was nothing surer than that he could sell again at an advance the moment the auctioneer's hammer fell on the last lot of cloths. . . .

The prices which obtained were almost fabulous, and singularly enough there seemed to be no sort of ratio existing between the values of different articles. I bought coffee at forty dollars and tea at thirty dollars a pound on the same day.

My dinner at a hotel cost me twenty dollars, while five dollars gained me a seat in the dress circle of the theater. I paid one dollar the next morning for a copy of the *Examiner*, but I might have got the *Whig, Dispatch, Enquirer,* or *Sentinel* for half that sum. For some wretched tallow candles I paid ten dollars a pound. The utter absence of proportion between these several prices is apparent, and I know no way of explaining it except upon the theory that the unstable character of the money superinduced a reckless disregard of all value on the part of both buyers and sellers. A facetious friend used to say prices were so high that nobody could see them and that they "got mixed for want of supervision." He held, however, that the difference between the old and the new order of things was a trifling one. "Before the war," he said, "I went to market with the money in my pocket and brought back my purchases in a basket; now I take the money in the basket and bring the things home in my pockets." . . .

The effects of the extreme depreciation of the currency were sometimes almost ludicrous. One of my friends, a Richmond lady, narrowly escaped very serious trouble in an effort to practise a wise economy. Anything for which the dealers did not ask an outrageously high price seemed wonderfully cheap always, and she, at least, lacked the self-control necessary to abstain from buying largely whenever she found anything the price of which was lower than she had supposed it would be. Going into market one morning with "stimulated ideas of prices," as she phrased it, the consequence of having paid a thousand dollars for a barrel of flour, she was surprised to find nearly everything selling for considerably less than she had expected. Thinking that for some unexplained cause there was a temporary depression in prices, she purchased pretty largely in a good many directions, buying, indeed, several things for which she had almost no use at all and buying considerably more than she needed of other articles. As she was quitting the market on foot—for it had become disreputable in Richmond to ride in a carriage, and the ladies would not do it on any account—she was tapped on the shoulder by an officer who told her she was under arrest, for buying in market to sell again. As the lady was well known to prominent people she was speedily released, but she thereafter curbed her propensity to buy freely of cheap things. Buying to sell again had been forbidden under severe penalities—an absolutely necessary measure for the protection of the people against the rapacity of the hucksters, who, going early into the markets, would buy literally everything there and by agreement among themselves double or quadruple the already exorbitant rates.

It became necessary also to suppress the gambling houses in the interest of the half-starved people. At such a time, of course, gambling was a very common vice, and the gamblers made Richmond their headquarters. It was the custom of the proprietors of these establishments to set costly suppers in their parlors every night for the purpose of attracting visitors likely to become victims. For these suppers they must have the best of everything without stint, and their lavish rivalry in the poorly-stocked markets had the effect of advancing prices to a dangerous point. To suppress the gambling houses was the sole remedy, and it was only by uncommonly severe measures that the suppression could be accomplished. It was therefore enacted that any one found guilty of keeping a gambling house should be publicly whipped upon the bare back, and as the infliction of the penalty in one or two instances effectually and permanently broke up the business of gambling, even in the disorganized and demoralized state in which society then was, it may be said with confidence that whipping is the one certain remedy for this evil. Whether it be not, in ordinary cases, worse than the evil which it cures, it is not our business just now to inquire.

—EGGLESTON, *A Rebel's Recollections*

3. PARTHENIA HAGUE TELLS HOW WOMEN OUTWITTED THE BLOCKADE

Probably not until 1863 was the blockade really effective, but even before that date the South began to feel the pinch for ordinary domestic necessities. Now the South was paying the price of neglecting to develop even local industries. Probably the best of all accounts of what life was like for a Southern family from day to day, is that by Parthenia Hague, a Georgia lady who went to live on an Alabama plantation during the war.

As no shoe-blacking or polish could be bought during the blockade, each family improvised its own blacking, which was soot and oil of some variety (either cottonseed, ground peas, or oil of compressed lard) mixed together. The shoes would be well painted with the mixture of soot and oil, with brushes made of the bristles of swine. Then a thin paste made of flour, bolted meal, or starch, was applied all over the blackened shoe with another brush, which paste, when dry, gave the shoe as bright and glossy an appearance as if "shined" by the best of bootblacks. Palnters were very careful in killing their hogs to save a good supply of bristles, from which shapely brushes were manufactured.

The obtaining of salt became extremely difficult when the war had cut off our supply. This was true especially in regions remote from the sea-coast and border States, such as the interior of Alabama and Georgia. Here again we were obliged to have recourse to whatever expedient ingenuity suggested. All the brine left in troughs and barrels, where pork had been salted down, was carefully dipped up, boiled down, and converted into salt again. In some cases the salty soil under old smoke-houses was dug up and placed in hoppers, which resembled backwoods ash-hoppers, made from leaching ashes in the process of soap-manufacture. Water was then poured upon the soil, the brine which percolated through the hopper was boiled down to the proper point, poured into vessels, and set in the sun, which by evaporation completed the rude process. Though never of immaculate whiteness, the salt which resulted from these methods served well enough for all our purposes, and we accepted it without complaining.

Before the war there were in the South but few cotton mills. These were kept running night and day, as soon as the Confederate army was organized, and we were ourselves prevented by the blockade from purchasing clothing from the factories at the North, or clothing from France or England. The cotton which grew in the immediate vicinity of the mills kept them well supplied with raw material. Yet notwithstanding the great push of the cotton mills, they proved totally inadequate, after the war began, to our vast need for clothing of every kind. Every household now became a miniature factory in itself, with its cotton, cards, spinning-wheels, warping frames, looms, and so on. Wherever one went, the hum of the spinning wheel and the clang of the batten of the loom was borne on the ear.

Great trouble was experienced, in the beginning, to find dyes with which to color our stuffs; but in the course of time, both at the old mills and at smaller experimental factories, which were run entirely by hand, barks, leaves, roots, and berries were found containing coloring properties. I was well acquainted with a gentleman in southwestern Georgia who owned a small cotton mill, and who, when he wanted coloring substances, used to send his wagons to the woods and freight them with a shrub known as myrtle, that grew teeming in low moist places near his mill. This myrtle yielded a nice gray for woolen goods.

That the slaves might be well clad, the owners kept, according to the number of slaves owned, a number of Negro women carding and spinning, and had looms running all the time. Now and then a planter would be so fortunate as to secure a bale or more of white sheeting and osnaburgs from the cotton mills, in exchange for farm products, which would be quite a lift, and give a little breathing-spell from the almost incessant whirr, hum, and clang of the spinning wheel and loom. . . .

I have often joined with neighbors, when school hours for the day were over, in gathering roots, barks, leaves, twigs, sumach berries, and walnuts, for the hulls, which dyed wool a beautiful dark brown. Such was the variety we had to choose from, to dye our cloth and thread. We used to pull our way through the deep tangled woods, by thickly shaded streams, through broad fields, and return laden with the riches of the Southern forest! Not infrequently clusters of grapes mingled with our freight of dyes. The pine-tree's roots furnished a beautiful dye, approximating very closely to garnet, which color I chose for the sheeting for my dress. A strong decoction of the roots of the pine-tree was used. Copperas of our own production was used as the mordant. A cask or some small vessel was set convenient to the dwelling-house and partly filled with water, in which a small quantity of salt and vinegar had been mingled; then pieces of rusty, useless iron, such as plows too much worn to be used again, rusty broken rails, old horse-shoes, and bits of old chains were picked up and cast into the cask. The liquid copperas was always ready, and a very good substance we found it to fix colors in cloth or thread. The sheeting for the dress was folded smoothly and basted slightly so as to keep the folds in place. It was first thoroughly soaked in warm soapsuds, then dipped into the dye, and afterwards into a vessel containing liquid lye from wood-ashes; then it went again into the dye, then the lye, and so on till the garnet color was the required shade. By varying the strength of the solution any shade desirable could be obtained. My garnet-colored dress of unbleached sheeting was often mistaken for worsted delaine. . . .

One of our most difficult tasks was to find a good substitute for coffee. This palatable drink, if not a real necessary of life, is almost indespensable to the enjoyment of a good meal, and some Southerners took it three times a day. Coffee soon rose to thirty dollars per pound; from that it went to sixty and seventy dollars per pound. Good workmen received thirty dollars per day; so it took two days' hard labor to buy one pound of coffee, and scarcely any could be had even at that fabulous price. Some imagined themselves much better in health for the absence of coffee, and wondered why they had ever used it at all, and declared it good for nothing any way; but "Sour grapes" would be the reply for such as they. Others saved a few handfuls of coffee, and used it on very important occasions, and then only as an extract, so to speak, for flavoring substitutes for coffee.

There were those who planted long rows of the okra plant on the borders of their cotton or corn fields, and cultivated this with the corn and cotton. The seeds of this, when mature and nicely browned, came nearer in flavor to the real coffee than any other substitute I now remember. Yam potatoes used to be peeled, sliced thin, cut into small squares, dried and then parched brown; they were thought to be next best to okra for coffee. Browned wheat, meal, and burnt corn made passable beverages; even meal-bran was browned and used for coffee if other substitutes were not obtainable.

We had several substitutes for tea which were equally as palatable, and, I fancy, more wholesome, than much that is now sold for tea. Prominent among these substitutes were raspberry leaves. Many during the blockade planted and cultivated the raspberry-vine all around their garden palings, as much for tea as the berries for jam or pies; these leaves were considered the best substitute for tea. The leaves of the blackberry bush, huckleberry leaves, and the leaves of the holly-tree when dried in the shade, also made a palatable tea.

Persimmons dried served for dates.

Each household made its own starch, some of the bran of wheat flour. Green corn and sweet potatoes were grated in order to make starch. This process was very simple. The grated substance was placed to soak in a large tub of water; when it had passed through the process of fermentation and had risen to the surface, the grated matter was all skimmed off, the water holding the starch in solution was passed through a sieve, and then through a thin cloth to free altogether from any foreign substance. A change of clear water twice a day for three or four days was made to more thoroughly bleach the starch. It would then be put on white cloth, placed on scaffolds in the yard, and left to drip and dry. Starch of wheat bran was made in the same manner. It was as white and fine as any ever bought.

A good makeshift had soon been devised for putty and cement, and the artlessness of it will perhaps cause a smile to flit across the face of glaziers. But no cement could be bought, and this was useful in many ways, as panes of glass had to be set in, or a break to be mended; the handle broken from a pitcher to be placed on anew, or repairing done to table ware. When it was necessary to repair any such breaks, a Spanish potato (none other of the species of that esculent root answered so well) was roasted in hot ashes, peeled while yet hot, immediately mashed very fine, and mixed with about a tablespoonful of flour; it was then, while warm, applied to whatever need there was. This paste, when it had become hardened, remained fixed and firm, and was as durable as putty.

In place of kerosene for lights, the oil of cotton seed and ground peas, together with the oil of compressed lard, was used, and served well the need of the times. For lights we had also to fall back on moulding candles, which had long years lain obsolete. When beeswax was plentiful it was mixed with tallow for moulding candles. Long rows of candles so moulded would be hung on the lower limbs of widespreading oaks, where, sheltered by the dense foliage from the direct rays of the sun, they would remain suspended day and night until they were bleached as white as the sperm candles we had been wont to buy, and almost as transparent as wax candles. When there was no oil for the lamps or tallow for moulding candles, which at times befell our households, mother-wit would suggest some expedient by which the intricate problem of light could be solved.

—HAGUE, *A Blockaded Family*

4. THE CONFEDERATES BURN THEIR COTTON

Two considerations persuaded the Confederacy to try to limit cotton production: the necessity of growing enough food for her needs, and the desire to create an artificial cotton scarcity for purposes of bargaining for foreign recognition. The result of Confederate and state laws—the latter by all odds the most effective—and of invasion and the general derangement of war was a reduction in the cotton crop from over four million bales in 1861 to only three hundred thousand bales in 1864. In addition to this reduction of planting,

*the Confederate Congress required owners to destroy all cotton
that might fall into enemy hands, and it has been estimated
that some two and one half million bales were destroyed
by planters or by the Confederate armies. When Farragut
forced the entrance to the Mississippi on April 24, 1862, the
Confederates destroyed the cotton piled up in New Orleans
to prevent it falling into Federal hands.*

*Sarah Dawson, whom we have met elsewhere, was the
daughter of Judge Thomas Gibbes Morgan, whose home
in Baton Rouge was sacked by the Federals in 1862. She
later married Francis Warringtone Dawson, English journalist
and littérateur, who ran the blockade to join the Confederacy,
fought in the Army of Northern Virginia, and later edited
the famous* Charleston News and Courier.

April 26, 1862.—We went this morning to see the cotton
burning—a sight never before witnessed and probably never
again to be seen. Wagons, drays—everything that can be
driven or rolled—were loaded with the bales and taken a few
squares back to burn on the commons. Negroes were running
around, cutting them open, piling them up, and setting them
afire. All were as busy as though their salvation depended on
disappointing the Yankees. Later Charlie sent for us to come
to the river and see him fire a flatboat loaded with the precious
material for which the Yankees are risking their bodies and
souls. Up and down the levee, as far as we could see, Negroes
were rolling it down to the brink of the river where they
would set the bales afire and push them in to float burning
down the tide. Each sent up its wreath of smoke and looked
like a tiny steamer puffing away. Only I doubt that from the
source to the mouth of the river there are as many boats
afloat on the Mississippi. The flatboat was piled with as many
bales as it could hold without sinking. Most of them were cut
open, while Negroes staved in the heads of barrels of alcohol,
whisky, etc., and dashed bucketfuls over the cotton. Others
built up little chimneys of pine every few feet, lined with
pine knots and loose cotton, to burn more quickly. There,
piled the length of the whole levee or burning in the river, lay
the work of thousands of Negroes for more than a year past.
It had come from every side. Men stood by who owned the
cotton that was burning or waiting to burn. They either
helped or looked on cheerfully. Charlie owned but sixteen
bales—a matter of some fifteen hundred dollars; but he was
the head man of the whole affair and burned his own as well
as the property of others. A single barrel of whisky that was

thrown on the cotton cost the man who gave it one hundred and twenty-five dollars. (It shows what a nation in earnest is capable of doing.) Only two men got on the flatboat with Charlie when it was ready. It was towed to the middle of the river, set afire in every place, and then they jumped into a little skiff fastened in front and rowed to land. The cotton floated down the Mississippi one sheet of living flame, even in the sunlight. It would have been grand at night. But then we will have fun watching it this evening anyway, for they cannot get through today, though no time is to be lost. Hundreds of bales remained untouched. An incredible amount of property has been destroyed today, but no one begrudges it. Every grogshop has been emptied, and gutters and pavements are floating with liquors of all kinds. So that if the Yankees are fond of strong drink, they will fare ill.

—Dawson, *A Confederate Girl's Diary*

5. "THE YANKEES ARE COMING"

It was the fate of the South to know invasion—and the ruth of war. Sometimes—as with Sheridan and Hunter in the Valley or Sherman in Georgia and the Carolinas—invasion meant pillaging and destruction; sometimes it was orderly enough. Occasionally, as in Mrs. Ward's account, it turned out to be merely the coming of Federal prisoners. We have met Mrs. Ward before; she was twenty-three when the events which she described took place; her description came in the form of testimony before the Congressional committee 20 years later. Of this testimony Margaret Mitchell wrote, "If I had had that book, I'm sure I would not have had to read hundreds of memoirs, letters and diaries to get the background of Gone with the Wind *accurately."*

In the fall of 1863 we were very much menaced by General Rosecrans' army up about Dalton and Resaca, and every little while we would have an alarm that a raid was coming. A raid was a very amusing thing, or rather, it is amusing to think of now. We would wake up out of our sleep and everybody would spring out of bed saying, "The Yankees are coming; they are only 10 miles out of town; they are coming with a sword in one hand and a torch in the other." That was the watchword. Then we would all try to think what we

had that was valuable, although at that time we didn't have
much except the family silver and furniture, which were
rapidly wearing out. The supply of bed linen was also getting
small. The blankets had been all sent to the soldiers long
before. Very few housekeepers had blankets as late as 1863.
On these occasions the ladies would put on three or four
dresses and tie around under the dresses everything that could
be suspended and hidden in that way. Hams would be jerked
out of the smoke-house, and holes would be dug and everything thrown in pell mell. Then we would begin to imagine
that because *we* knew where those things were, the first
Yankee that appeared would know, too, and often we would
go and take them all up from there and dig another hole
and put them in that; so that our yards came to look like
graveyards. It is very funny to think of now, but it wasn't
funny then—to be flying around in the middle of the night
that way. Then, to add to the confusion, the children would
wake up and would stare around with a vacant look, and
begin saying, "What is the matter? What is the matter?"
And then we would tell them "The Yankees are coming." . . .

The ideas of the children about the Yankees was very
funny. As soon as they heard the Yankees were coming they
would jump up and get under the bed, or run out of
the house. In fact they would have no idea of what they
ought to do to preserve themselves. If you told them the
house was on fire of course their first impulse would have
been to get out of the house, but when you told them the
Yankees were coming they didn't know what to do or which
way to turn—whether to run out of the house or to get under
the bed or go up the chimney.

I remember one night—all these things come up to me
now so vividly—I remember just such a night as I have been
describing, when all the children jumped up and got under
the bed. We asked what was the matter. Well, "the Yankees
were coming." There was one little girl who was terribly
frightened. She had no idea whether the Yankees were men,
or horses, or what kind of animals they were. She just knew
that they were something dreadful. That business went on
through the whole of that night; we would hear that the
Yankees were six miles off; that they were two miles off,
and every sound we heard, whether it was the baker's cart,
or anything else, we would think it was the Yankees; that
they were actually in town.

On these occasions, after we had secured the things, as we
thought, there would be consultations as to which of the serv-

ants would be the most trustworthy to do the manual labor —which ones we could take into our confidence, for of course it was necessary to have a Negro man around to lift things. We were obliged to take them into our confidence, and yet we mistrusted them on such occasions, because this was in 1863, and by that time there had been a great many stories told among us of the disloyalty of servants in such emergencies.

On the night I am now speaking of this excitement continued until morning came. Everybody had been up all night, and it would have been a relief to us to have known that the Yankees had come; but after awhile we ascertained that it was an unmistakable demonstration; that the Yankees were really down here about Gadsden, and that the report brought to Rome had come from a very reliable man, who had traveled all night to carry the news. The first alarm came from somebody who had heard of the matter but was not able to report the entire truth. That night and the next morning all was suspense. . . .

Just as we were all expecting the Yankees to come in, and expecting that we were just literally going to be butchered— in fact I don't know what we did think—a courier came rushing into town with the news that Forrest had captured the Yankees and was bringing them in with him as captives. Then there was a reaction, and the excitement was worse than any camp-meeting you ever saw. Everybody was flying from one end of the town to the other. Suppers that were just ready to be cooked were never cooked or eaten; there was a general jollification. Everybody in town felt relieved from a terrible pressure. Forrest came into town and every lady insisted on going up and speaking to the general and shaking hands with him and his forces. My daughter Minnie was a baby at the time, and I took her with me and went up and spoke to him and he took her and kissed her. He told us that his prisoners were coming into town, and he wanted them to eat at once. Everybody went home and there was just a regular wholesale cooking of hams and shoulders and all sorts of provisions that we had, and everything was sent down to the respective camps. We were quite willing to feed the Yankees when they had no guns.

—Testimony of Mrs. Mary A. Ward

6. "THE LIVES WHICH WOMEN HAVE LEAD SINCE TROY FELL"

The Union had no such galaxy of woman diarists and memoir writers as the Confederacy—women like Mrs. Chesnut, Sarah Morgan, Judith McGuire, Parthenia Hague, Eliza Andrews, and others. To this brilliant group belongs Julia LeGrand. Her father had been a colonel in the War of 1812 and one of the lordly planters of Louisiana, and Julia grew up in the world of fashion and of culture. Impoverished by her father's death, and by the war. Miss LeGrand and her sister opened a girls' school in New Orleans, and were there when the Federals captured the city. Later they took refuge in Georgia and in Texas. Only fragments of the wartime diary have been preserved.

To Mrs. SHEPARD BROWN.

New Orleans, Nov. 17th, 1862

Dear Mrs. B——:

I have nothing to say, and might not say it if I did have it, for you know there is a heaviness prevailing in this latitude, which is not favorable to expansion of idea. I only send a line to remind you that I live and wish you to remember me. A dull and heavy anxiety has settled upon us. We hear nothing to which we can cling with comfort. Those who come in say there is much joy beyond the lines, but no one can give the why and wherefore. In the meantime we are leading the lives which women have lead since Troy fell; wearing away time with memories, regrets and fears; alternating fits of suppression, with flights, imaginary, to the red fields where great principles are contended for, lost and won; while men, more privileged, are abroad and astir, making name and fortune and helping to make a nation.

There was a frolic on board the English ship a few nights since for the benefit, the *Delta* says, of Secession women. I did not go, though Miss Betty Callender offered her services in the way of invitation. I am told that the contraband "bonny-blue flag" waved freely over seas of red wine and promontories of sugar-work. The ship represents secessiondom just now; it has not a stronghold in the city. Many a lady opened her vial of wrath, I suppose, for all were told that freedom of speech should be the order of the night. There was acting and dancing, and fish, flesh and fowl suffered in the name of our cause. Toasts were drunk to our great spirits to whom it seems the destiny of a nation is entrusted. How my heart warms to the weary, battle-stained heroes. I never fancied carpet knights even before the stern trial came.

I can't tell you what a life of suppression we lead. I feel it more because I know and feel all that is going on outside. I am like a pent-up volcano. I wish I had a field for my energies. I hate common life, a life of visiting, dressing and tattling, which seems to devolve on women, and now that there is better work to do, real tragedy, real romance and history weaving every day, I suffer, suffer, leading the life I do. . . .

Things go on just as they did. Daily life presents the same food for sorrowful reflection. Tiger, Jake and Emma hold their own within doors, and nothing has happened to prevent us from parading the streets without. A shrill horn breaks often upon my sad speculations. I rush out perhaps and sometimes find a train of striped and bestarred cavalry and sometimes only an orange cart. "What an age we live in," says philosophy, and goes in again to repine and wonder. The *Advocate* was suppressed an hour or two ago, but the pliant Jacob made haste to smooth his phrases. A quarrel is reported between the French admiral and the General. There has been a great commotion about the money sent from the New Orleans bank. Lemore has gone to prison and some others. Where are our people? Can't you contrive to let me into the secret, if you have any? You can't read if I keep on, so good-bye, with best wishes to all.

Ever your friend,
J.E. LeGrand.

—Rowland and Croxall, eds., *The Journal of Julia LeGrand*

7. "THEY MUST REAP THE WHIRLWIND"

This brief excerpt from a letter of General Sherman's to his wife is a fitting commentary on the two preceding items. The "enmity of the women of the South" is a familiar theme in Civil War literature. Mrs. Chesnut herself wrote that "we hate our enemies and love our friends," and Stephen Vincent Benét, whose John Brown's Body *is in some ways the most faithful of all interpretations of the war, has written of*

The terrible hate of women's ire
The smoky, the long-consuming fire. †

To his wife.

Camp on Bear Creek, 20 Miles N.W. of Vicksburg,
June 27, 1863

I doubt if history affords a parallel to the deep and bitter enmity of the women of the South. No one who sees them and hears them but must feel the intensity of their hate. Not a man is seen; nothing but women with houses plundered, fields open to the cattle and horses, pickets lounging on every porch, and desolation sown broadcast, servants all gone and women and children bred in luxury, beautiful and accomplished, begging with one breath for the soldiers' ration and in another praying that the Almighty or Joe Johnston will come and kill us, the despoilers of their homes and all that is sacred. Why cannot they look back to the day and hour when I, a stranger in Louisiana, begged and implored them to pause in their career, that secession was death, was everything fatal, and that their seizure of the public arsenals was an insult that the most abject nation must resent or pass down to future ages an object of pity and scorn? Vicksburg contains many of my old pupils and friends; should it fall into our hands I will treat them with kindness, but they have sowed the wind and must reap the whirlwind. Until they lay down their arms and submit to the rightful authority of the government they must not appeal to me for mercy or favors.

—HOWE, ed., *Home Letters of General Sherman*

8. GEORGIA'S GOVERNOR LAMENTS DAVIS' DESPOTISM

If Lincoln had his Seymours and Vallandighams, Davis had men like Governor Brown and Governor Vance to contend with. There was, if anything, more discontent and positive disloyalty in the Confederacy than in the Union. Part of it was inspired by sincere State-rights sentiment, part by personal hostility to President Davis, part by dissatisfaction with the conduct of the war. State-righters like Stephens and Brown and Vance thought the tyranny of Richmond worse than

† From *John Brown's Body* in *The Selected Works of Stephen Vincent Benét*, published by Rinehart and Company, Inc. Copyright 1927, 1928 by Stephen Vincent Benét.

*that of Washington; they were particularly outraged by such
things as conscription and the suspension of the writ of habeas
corpus. Others were sure that Davis was a monster of wickedness and of incompetence, and exhausted their energies
denouncing him and his administration.*

*The letter given here is from the egregious Governor Brown
of Georgia, the most powerful of all the state governors, and
one who by his policy of putting Georgia interests first
effectively sabotaged the Confederacy.*

Joseph E. Brown to Alexander H. Stephens
                    (Private)

                              Canton [Georgia], Sept. 1st, 1862
    Dear Sir: I have the pleasure to acknowledge the receipt
of your letter of the 26th ult. and am gratified that you take
the view which you have expressed about the action of Genl.
Bragg in his declaration of martial law over Atlanta and
his appoint[ment], as the newspapers say, of a civil governor
with aids, etc.
    I have viewed this proceeding as I have others of our mili-
tary authorities of late with painful apprehensiveness for the
future. It seems military men are assuming the whole powers
of government to themselves and setting at defiance con-
stitutions, laws, state rights, state sovereignty, and every other
principle of civil liberty, and that our people engrossed in the
struggle with the enemy are disposed to submit to these bold
usurpations tending to military despotism without murmur,
much less resistance. I should have called this proceeding into
question before this time but I was hopeful from the indications which I had noted that Congress would take such action
as would check these dangerous usurpations of power, and
for the further reasons that I have already come almost into
conflict with the Confederate authorities in vindication of
what I have considered the rights of the State and people of
Georgia, and I was fearful, as no other governor seems to
raise these questions, that I might be considered by good and
true men in and out of Congress too refractory for the times.
I had therefore concluded to take no notice of this matter
till the meeting of the legislature when I expect to ask the
representatives of the people to define the bounds to which
they desire the Governor to go in the defense of the rights
and sovereignty of the state. I confess I have apprehensions
that our present General Assembly does not properly reflect
the sentiments of our people upon this great question, but if

the Executive goes beyond the bounds where he is sustained by the representatives of the people he exposes himself to censure without the moral power to do service to the great principles involved. I fear we have much more to apprehend from military despotism than from subjugation by the enemy. I trust our generals will improve well their time while we have the advantage and the enemy are organizing another army. Hoping that your health is good and begging that you will write me when your important duties are not too pressing to permit it, I am very truly your friend.

—PHILLIPS, ed., *"The Correspondence of Robert Toombs, Alexander H. Stephens, and Howell Cobb"*

9. PEACE AT ANY PRICE

Jonathan Worth was an old-line Whig politician who fought nullification in the thirties and secession in 1861 but—like so many others—went with his state when the crisis materialized. During the war he was State Treasurer of North Carolina; in 1865 he was elected to the governorship, and re-elected again the following year.

Jonathan Worth to Jesse G. Henshaw   Raleigh Aug. 24, 1863
     I hardly know whether I am in favor of the peace meetings or not. On the one hand, it is very certain that the President and his advisers will not make peace, if not forced into it by the masses and the privates in the army. Their cry echoed by almost every press is: "Independence, or the last man and the last dollar." The North will not make peace on the basis of Independence. The real question which nobody—not even Holden—will squarely present is, shall we fight on with certain desolation and impoverishment and probably ultimate defeat; or make peace on the basis of reconstruction? Nearly every public man—every journal, political and religious, and every politician, in the fervor of their patriotism, has vociferously declared in favor of "the last man and the last dollar" cry. These classes cannot be consistent unless they still cry war. Many believe the masses in their saner hours never approved the war and would rather compromise on the basis of the Constitution of the U.S. with such additional securities against any future rupture as could be agreed on. If there be any sense in peace meetings they mean reconstruction. They may

rather do mischief if they are not so imposing as to force the administration to reconstruction. They will be impotent and mischievous if the army is still for war to the last man and the last dollar. I do not know the sentiments of the rank and file of the army.

I am for peace on almost any terms and fear we shall never have it until the Yankees dictate it. Upon the whole I would not go into a peace meeting now or advise others to go into one, particularly in Randolph—but I have no repugnance to them in other places and see no other chance to get to an early end of this wicked war, but by the action of the masses who have the fighting to do. If an open rupture occur between Gov. V[ance] and Mr. Holden, it will be ruinous to us. There ought to be none and I trust there will be none. There is no difference between them that justifies a breach. The Governor concedes the right of the people to hold meetings and express their wishes, but he deems such meetings inexpedient and tending to dissatisfaction and disorganization in the army and that no honorable peace can be made, after we cease to present a strong military front. The Gov. acts consistently and in the eminent difficult position he occupied, I doubt whether any pilot could manage the crippled ship in such a storm with more skill. Repress all expressions of dissatisfaction against him. He values the extravagant eulogiums of the fire-eaters at their worth. They are playing an adroit game. They would get up dissention between the Gov. and Holden and then break up the Conservative party and seize the helm of Government.

—HAMILTON, ed., *The Correspondence of Jonathan Worth*

10. "THE MAN WHO HELD HIS CONSCIENCE HIGHER THAN THEIR PRAISE"

Unionist sentiment was weaker in South Carolina than in any other Southern state and weaker, probably, in Charleston than in any other city. This epitaph on the Petigru monument in St. Michael's churchyard, Charleston, is included as evidence of the respect with which the South, even in wartime, respected honest difference of opinion. Member of a famous Charleston family, lawyer and public servant, James Petigru was probably the most distinguished of South Carolina Unionists. The toleration accorded him was a product in part of the sophistication of Charleston, in part of that class con-

sciousness which accepted eccentricity in its aristocracy, in part of a respect for intellectual independence commoner in the Civil War generation than in our own.

JAMES LOUIS PETIGRU

Born at
Abbeville May 10th 1789
Died at Charleston March 9th 1863

JURIST. ORATOR. STATESMAN. PATRIOT.

Future times will hardly know how great a life
This simple stone commemorates—
The tradition of his Eloquence, his
Wisdom and his Wit may fade:
But he lived for ends more durable than fame,
His Eloquence was the protection of the poor and wronged;
His Learning illuminated the principles of Law—
In the admiration of his Peers,
In the respect of his People,
In the affection of his Family
His was the highest place;
The just meed
Of his kindness and forbearance
His dignity and simplicity
His brilliant genius and his unwearied industry
Unawed by Opinion,
Unseduced by Flattery,
Undismayed by Disaster,
He confronted Life with antique Courage
And Death with Christian Hope.

In the great Civil War
He withstood his People for his Country
But his People did homage to the Man
Who held his conscience higher than their praise
And his Country
Heaped her honors on the grave of the Patriot,
To whom living,
His own righteous self-respect sufficed
Alike for Motive and Reward.

"Nothing is here for tears, nothing to wail,
Or knock the breast; no weakness, no contempt,
Dispraise or blame; nothing but well and fair
And what may quiet us in a life so noble."
—CARSON, *Life and Letters of James Petigru*

VI

Hospitals, Surgeons, and Nurses

THE *story of Civil War medicine is only less depressing than the story of Civil War prisons; if the first is lighted by flashes of heroism, the second is ameliorated by generosity and self-sacrifice on the part of doctors and nurses. As we have seen, one reason for the high mortality rate in prisons was the low state of medical and nursing services and the primitive standards of sanitation that obtained generally. This situation reflected in part conditions in civil life, in part the wholly inadequate preparation for war, in part the conditions of medicine and public health at mid-century.*

At the outbreak of the war the United States Surgeon General's office consisted of a total of 115 surgeons; 24 of these resigned to form the nucleus of the Confederate medical services. Eventually both services were vastly—but quite inadequately—expanded. Nursing services, too, were primitive. The army still relied on male nurses, most of them quite untrained. At the outbreak of the war the famous humanitarian, Dorothea Dix, hurried to Washington to offer her services; she was appointed Superintendent of Women Nurses, but never allowed any real independence. Most of the nursing service on both sides was voluntary; the United States Sanitary Commission did invaluable work in nursing and relief both at the front and in hospitals behind the line. Hospitals were mostly hastily improvised and inadequate. It is sobering to read that inspection of hospitals in the Union Army at the mid-war period (November 1862 to March 1863) reported a total of 589 as good and no less than 303 as bad or very bad, while inspections of medical officers from the beginning of the war to March 1863 found 2,727 good and 851 bad! It is to be remembered, too, when we read of the work of the surgeons and contemplate the mortality figures, that antiseptics were unknown, the relation of dirt to infection was generally not understood, anesthesia was just coming into general use, and drugs were inadequate.

It is not surprising in the light of all this that mortality from disease and wounds was far higher than from bullets, and that hospitalization was often regarded as equivalent to a death sentence. While no statistics are satisfactory and those for the Confederacy in a state of total confusion, it is a safe generalization that deaths from wounds were as numerous as deaths on the battlefield and that deaths from disease were more than twice both these combined. Perhaps the least unreliable statistics for the Union armies give 67,000 killed in action, 43,000 died of wounds, and 224,000 died of disease; an additional 24,000 are listed as dead from other causes—doubtless either wounds or disease. Confederate statistics indicate a comparable situation. Fortunately most of the soldiers were young—the largest single age group was eighteen—and from the country, and had therefore high powers of resistance and recuperation; otherwise the situation would have been even more appalling.

1. GEORGE TOWNSEND DESCRIBES THE WOUNDED ON THE PENINSULA

George Alfred Townsend was only twenty when he began to report the Civil War for the New York Herald, *but he quickly established himself as one of the most brilliant of all the many war correspondents. We have already read his account of Fitz John Porter's ascent in a balloon; we shall meet him again describing the Battle of Five Forks. Townsend followed McClellan's army up the Peninsula and through that campaign to its inglorious close. There are few more graphic accounts of wounds, disease and death than those from his gifted pen.*

It was evening, as I hitched my horse to a stake near-by, and pressed up to the receptacle for the unfortunates. Sentries enclosed the pen, walking to-and-fro with loaded muskets; a throng of officers and soldiers had assembled to gratify their curiosity; and new detachments of captives came in hourly, encircled by sabremen, the Southerners being disarmed and on foot.

The scene within the area was ludicrously moving. It reminded me of the witch-scene in Macbeth, or pictures of brigands or Bohemian gypsies at rendezvous, not less than five hundred men, in motley, ragged costumes, with long hair, and lean, wild, haggard faces, were gathered in groups or in pairs, around some fagot fires. In the glowing darkness their expressions were imperfectly visible; but I could see that most of them were weary, and hungry, and all were depressed and ashamed. Some were wrapped in blankets of rag-carpet, and others wore shoes of rough, untanned hide. Others were without either shoes or jackets, and their heads were bound with red handkerchiefs. Some appeared in red shirts; some in stiff beaver hats; some were attired in shreds and patches of cloth; and a few wore the soiled garments of citizen gentlemen; but the mass adhered to homespun suits of gray, or "butternut," and the coarse blue kersey common to slaves. In places I caught glimpses of red Zouave breeches and leggings; blue Federal caps, Federal buttons, or Federal blouses; these were the spoils of anterior battles, and had been stripped from the slain. Most of the captives were of the appearances denominated "scraggy" or "knotty." They were brown, brawny, and wiry, and their countenances were intense, fierce, and animal. They came from North Carolina, the poorest and least enterprising Southern State, and ignorance, with its attendant virtues, were the common facial manifestations. Some lay on the bare ground, fast asleep; others chatted nervously as if doubtful of their future treatment; a few were boisterous, and anxious to beg tobacco or coffee from idle Federals; the rest—and they comprehended the greater number—were silent, sullen, and vindictive. They met curiosity with scorn, and spite with imprecations.

A child—not more than four years of age, I think—sat sleeping in a corner upon an older comrade's lap. A gray-bearded pard was staunching a gash in his cheek with the tail of his coat. A fine-looking young fellow sat with his face in his hands, as if his heart were far off, and he wished to shut out this bitter scene. In a corner, lying morosely apart, were a Major, three Captains, and three Lieutenants,—young athletic fellows, dressed in rich gray cassimere, trimmed with black, and wearing soft black hats adorned with black ostrich-

feathers. Their spurs were strapped upon elegantly fitting
boots, and they looked as far above the needy, seedy privates,
as lords above their vassals. . . .

I rode across the fields to the Hogan, Curtis, and Gaines
mansions; for some of the wounded had meantime been deposited in each of them. All the cow-houses, wagon-sheds,
hay-barracks, hen-coops, Negro cabins, and barns were turned
into hospitals. The floors were littered with "corn-shucks" and
fodder; and the maimed, gashed, and dying lay confusedly
together. A few slightly wounded, stood at windows, relating incidents of the battle; but at the doors sentries stood
with crossed muskets, to keep out idlers and gossips. The
mention of my vocation was an "open sesame," and I went
unrestrained, into all the largest hospitals. In the first of these
an amputation was being performed, and at the door lay a
little heap of human fingers, feet, legs, and arms. I shall not
soon forget the bare-armed surgeons, with bloody instruments,
that leaned over the rigid and insensible figure, while the
comrades of the subject looked horrifiedly at the scene.

The grating of the murderous saw drove me into the open
air, but in the second hospital which I visited, a wounded man
had just expired, and I encountered his body at the threshold.
Within, the sickening smell of mortality was almost insup-
portable, but by degrees I became accustomed to it. The
lanterns hanging around the room streamed fitfully upon the
the red eyes, and half-naked figures. All were looking up, and
saying, in pleading monotone: "Is that you, doctor?" Men
with their arms in slings went restlessly up and down, smarting with fever. Those who were wounded in the lower extrem-
ities, body, or head, lay upon their backs, tossing even in sleep.
They listened peevishly to the wind whistling through the
chinks of the barn. They followed one with their rolling eyes.
They turned away from the lantern, for it seemed to sear
them. Soldiers sat by the severely wounded, laving their sores
with water. In many wounds the balls still remained, and the
discolored flesh was swollen unnaturally. There were some who
had been shot in the bowels, and now and then they were
frightfully convulsed, breaking into shrieks and shouts. Some
of them iterated a single word, as, "doctor," or "help," or
"God," or "oh!" commencing with a loud spasmodic cry,
and continuing the same word till it died away in cadence.
The act of calling seemed to lull the pain. Many were unconscious and lethargic, moving their fingers and lips mechanically, but never more to open their eyes upon the light; they
were already going through the valley and the shadow.

I think, still, with a shudder, of the faces who were told mercifully that they could not live. The unutterable agony; the plea for somebody on whom to call; the longing eyes that poured out prayers; the looking on mortal as if its resources were infinite; the fearful looking to the immortal as if it were so far off, so implacable, that the dying appeal would be in vain; the open lips, through which one could almost look at the quaking heart below; the ghastliness of brow and tangled hair; the closing pangs; the awful *quietus*. I thought of Parrhasius, in the poem, as I looked at these things:—

> "Gods!
> Could I but paint a dying groan—"

And how the keen eye of West would have turned from the reeking cockpit of the *Victory*, or the tomb of the Dead Man Restored, to this old barn, peopled with horrors. I rambled in and out, learning to look at death, studying the manifestations of pain,—quivering and sickening at times, but plying my avocation, and jotting the names for my column of mortalities. . . .

Ambulances, it may be said, incidentally, are either two-wheeled or four-wheeled. Two-wheeled ambulances are commonly called "hop, step, and jumps." They are so constructed that the forepart is either very high or very low, and may be both at intervals. The wounded occupants may be compelled to ride for hours in these carriages, with their heels elevated above their heads, and may finally be shaken out, or have their bones broken by the terrible jolting. The four-wheeled ambulances are built in shelves, or compartments, but the wounded are in danger of being smothered in them.

It was in one of these latter that I rode, sitting with the driver. We had four horses, but were thrice "swamped" on the road, and had to take out the wounded men once, till we could start the wheels. Two of these men were wounded in the face, one of them having his nose completely severed, and the other having a fragment of his jaw knocked out. A third had received a ball among the thews and muscles behind his knee, and his whole body appeared to be paralyzed. Two were wounded in the shoulders, and the sixth was shot in the breast, and was believed to be injured inwardly, as he spat blood, and suffered almost the pain of death.

The ride with these men, over twenty miles of hilly, woody

country, was like one of Dante's excursions into the Shades. In the awful stillness of the dark pines, their screams frightened the hooting owls, and the whirring insects in the leaves and tree-tops quieted their songs. They heard the gurgle of the rills, and called aloud for water to quench their insatiate thirst. One of them sang a shrill, fierce, fiendish ballad, in an interval of relief, but plunged, at a sudden relapse, in prayers and curses. We heard them groaning to themselves, as we sat in front, and one man, it seemed, was quite out of his mind. These were the outward manifestations; but what chords trembled and smarted within, we could only guess. What regrets for good resolves unfulfilled, and remorse for years misspent, made hideous these sore and panting hearts? The moonlight pierced through the foliage of the wood, and streamed into our faces, like invitations to a better life. But the crippled and bleeding could not see or feel it,—buried in the shelves of the ambulance.

—TOWNSEND, *Campaigns of a Non-Combatant*

2. THE SANITARY COMMISSION TO THE RESCUE

The United States Sanitary Commission, the leading private relief organization of the Civil War period, was created— against strong opposition in the army—in June 1861. A distinguished Unitarian divine, the Reverend Henry W. Bellows, was President; the famous landscape architect, Frederick Law Olmsted, was Secretary; and the Commission enlisted scores of physicians and literally hundreds of public-spirited men and women. Its object, wrote Mary Livermore, "was to do what the Government could not." The "could" here is, of course, relative; it was merely that governments had not yet conceived it their responsibility to take care of the health, comfort, and general welfare of soldiers.

The Commission did a little bit of everything. Its inspectors looked into the sanitary arrangements in camps—hence its name—and brought about reforms. It reviewed matters of diet, cooking, clothing; provided private aid to soldiers and to their dependents; took care of fugitives; collected and forwarded boxes of food to the soldiers—a combination, as we have said elsewhere, of YMCA, Red Cross, and USO— and helped out even with nursing and hospital care. At the

*time of the Peninsular campaign the Commission obtained
some hospital transports for the wounded.*

*We give an account here of the use of these hospital trans-
ports. Katharine Wormeley, who tells the story, was one of
the many women who worked heroically for the Sanitary
Commission. Born in England, the daughter of an admiral,
she later distinguished herself in philanthropy and literature.
She is remembered today for her remarkable translations of
Balzac and of other modern French writers.*

"WILSON SMALL," 5 *June,* 1862

DEAR MOTHER: I finished my last letter on the afternoon of
the day when we took eighty men on the *Small,* and transferred them to the *Webster.*

We had just washed and dressed, and were writing letters
when Captain Sawtelle came on board to say that several
hundred wounded men were lying at the landing; that the
Daniel Webster No. 2 had been taken possession of by the
medical officers, and was already half full of men, and that
the surplus was being carried across her to the *Vanderbilt;*
that the confusion was terrible; that there were no stores on
board the *Daniel Webster No. 2* (she was being seized
the moment she reached the landing on her return from
Yorktown, without communicating with the Commission),
nor were there any stores or preparations, not even mattresses,
on board the *Vanderbilt.*

Of course the best in our power had to be done. Mrs.
Griffin and I begged Mr. Olmsted not to refrain from sending us, merely because we had been up all night. He said he
wouldn't send us, but if we chose to offer our services to the
United States surgeon, he thought it would be merciful. Our
offer was seized. We went on board; and such a scene as we
entered and lived in for two days I trust never to see again.
Men in every condition of horror, shattered and shrieking,
were being brought in on stretchers borne by "contrabands,"
who dumped them anywhere, banged the stretchers against
pillars and posts, and walked over the men without compas-
sion. There was no one to direct what ward or what bed
they were to go into. Men shattered in the thigh, and even
cases of amputation, were shovelled into top berths without
thought or mercy. The men had mostly been without food
for three days, but there was *nothing* on board either boat for
them; and if there had been, the cooks were only engaged to
cook for the ship, and not for the hospital.

We began to do what we could. The first thing wanted by

wounded men is something to drink (with the sick, stimulants are the first thing). Fortunately we had plenty of lemons, ice, and sherry on board the *Small*, and these were available at once. Dr. Ware discovered a barrel of molasses, which, with vinegar, ice, and water, made a most refreshing drink. After that we gave them crackers and milk, or tea and bread. It was hopeless to try to get them into bed; indeed, there were no mattresses on the *Vanderbilt*. All we could do at first was to try to calm the confusion, to stop some agony, to revive the fainting lives, to snatch, if possible, from immediate death with food and stimulants. Imagine a great river or Sound steamer filled on every deck,—every berth and every square inch of room covered with wounded men; even the stairs and gangways and guards filled with those who are less badly wounded; and then imagine fifty well men, on every kind of errand, rushing to and fro over them, every touch bringing agony to the poor fellows, while stretcher after stretcher came along, hoping to find an empty place; and then imagine what it was to keep calm ourselves, and make sure that every man on both those boats was properly refreshed and fed. We got through about 1 A.M., Mrs. M. and Georgy having come off other duty and reënforced us.

We were sitting for a few moments, resting and talking it over, and bitterly asking why a Government so lavish and perfect in its other arrangements should leave its wounded almost literally to take care of themselves, when a message came that one hundred and fifty men were just arriving by the cars. It was raining in torrents, and both boats were full. We went on shore again: the same scene repeated. The wretched *Vanderbilt* was slipped out, the *Kennebec* brought up, and the hundred and fifty men carried across the *Daniel Webster No. 2* to her, with the exception of some fearfully wounded ones, who could not be touched in the darkness and rain, and were therefore made as comfortable as they could be in the cars. We gave refreshment and food to all, Miss Whetten and a detail of young men from the *Spaulding* coming up in time to assist, and the officers of the *Sebago*, who had seen how hard pressed we were in the afternoon, volunteering for the night-watch. Add to this sundry Members of Congress, who, if they talked much, at least worked well. One of them, the Hon. Moses F. Odell, proposed to Mr. Olmsted that on his return to Washington he should move that the thanks of Congress be returned to us! Mr. Olmsted, mindful of our feelings, promptly declined.

We went to bed at daylight with *breakfast* on our minds,

and at six o'clock we were all on board the *Daniel Webster No. 2*, and the breakfast of six hundred men was got through with in good time. Captain Sawtelle kindly sent us a large wall-tent, twelve caldrons and camp-kettles, two cooks, and a detail of six men. The tent was put up at once, Dr. Ware giving to its preparation the only hour when he might have rested during that long nightmare. We began to use it that (Tuesday) morning. It is filled with our stores; there we have cooked not only the sick-food, but *all* the food needed on the Government boats. It was hard to get it in sufficient quantity; but when everything else gave out, we broke up "hard-tack" into buckets full of hot milk and water a little sweetened,— "bread and milk" the men called it. Oh, that precious condensed milk, more precious to us at that moment than beef essence!

Tuesday was very much a repetition of Monday night. The men were cleared from the main-deck and gangways of the *Daniel Webster No. 2* onto the *Kennebec*. The feeding business was almost as hard to manage as before. But still it was done, and we got to bed at 1 A.M. Mrs. M. and I were to attend to the breakfast at 6 next morning. By some accident Mrs. M., who was ready quite as soon as I was, was carried off by the *Small*, which started suddenly to run down to the *Spaulding*. I had, therefore, to get the breakfast alone. I accomplished it, and then went ashore and fed some men who were just arriving in cars, and others who were in tents near the landing. The horrors of that morning are too great to speak of. The men in the cars were brought on board the *Daniel Webster No. 2* and laid about the vacant main-deck and guards and on the dock of a scow that lay alongside. I must not, I ought not to tell you of the horrors of that morning. One of the least was that I saw a "contraband" step on the amputated stump of a wretched man. I took him by the arm and walked him into the tent, where I ordered them to give him other work, and forbade that he should come upon the ships again. I felt white with anger, and dared not trust myself to speak to *him*. While those awful sights pass before me I have comparatively no feeling, except the anxiety to alleviate as much as possible. I do not suffer under the sights; but oh! the sounds, the screams of men. It is when I think of it afterwards that it is so dreadful. . . .

About nine hundred wounded remain to be brought down. Mr. Olmsted says *our* boats have transported one thousand seven hundred and fifty-six since Sunday; the Government and Pennsylvania boats together about three thousand. Mr.

Clement Barclay was with us on Monday night on the *Vanderbilt*. I believe he went with her to Fortress Monroe. He was working hard, with the deepest interest and skill. I went with him to attend to a little "Secesh" boy, wounded in the thigh; also to a Southern colonel, a splendid-looking man, who died, saying to Mr. Barclay, with raised hand: "Write to my wife and tell her I die penitent for the part I have taken in this war." I try to be just and kind to the Southern men. One of our men stopped me, saying: "*He's* a rebel; give that to me." I said: "But a wounded man is our brother!" (rather an obvious sentiment, if there is anything in Christianity); and they both touched their caps. The Southerners are constantly expressing surprise at one thing or another, and they are shy, but not surly, at receiving kindness. Our men are a noble set of fellows, so cheerful, uncomplaining, and generous.

Remember that in all I have written, I have told you only about ourselves—the women. What the gentlemen have seen, those of our party, those of the *Spaulding* and of the other vessels, is beyond my power to relate. Some of them fainted from time to time.

Last night, shining over blood and agony, I saw a lunar rainbow; and in the afternoon a peculiarly beautiful effect of rainbow and stormy sunset,—it flashed upon my eyes as I passed an operating-table, and raised them to avoid seeing anything as I passed.

—Wormeley, *The Other Side of War*

3. CLARA BARTON SURMOUNTS THE FAITHLESSNESS OF UNION OFFICERS

It was not only doctors and nurses who were, at times, incompetent but army officers as well. At least so Clara Barton often thought. She was a strong-minded woman, and a bit inclined to think the worst of her superiors and associates. When the war broke out Miss Barton was working in the Patent Office in Washington. Deeply moved by the distress of the soldiers after First Bull Run she wrote a letter to the Worcester (Massachusetts) Spy asking for food, clothing, and bandages for the soldiers. Provisions poured in—and she had found her mission. Never formally associated either with the Sanitary Commission or, except for a brief interlude, with the army, she conducted something of a one-woman relief organization. She carried on her beneficent activities with the

Army of the Potomac, the Army of the James, around Charleston, and in and around Washington. After the war she was the moving spirit in the establishment of the American Red Cross, and for over twenty years its director.
This excerpt comes from her war diary.

No one has forgotten the heart-sickness which spread over the entire country as the busy wires flashed the dire tidings of the terrible destitution and suffering of the wounded of the Wilderness whom I attended as they lay in Fredericksburg. But you may never have known how many hundredfold of these ills were augmented by the conduct of improper, heartless, unfaithful officers in the immediate command of the city and upon whose actions and indecisions depended entirely the care, food, shelter, comfort, and lives of that whole city of wounded men. One of the highest officers there has since been convicted a traitor. And another, a little dapper captain quartered with the owners of one of the finest mansions in the town, boasted that he had changed his opinion since entering the city the day before; that it was in fact a pretty hard thing for refined people like the people of Fredericksburg to be compelled to open their homes and admit "these dirty, lousy, common soldiers," and that he was not going to compel it.

This I heard him say, and waited until I saw him make his words good, till I saw, crowded into one old sunken hotel, lying helpless upon its bare, wet, bloody floors, five hundred fainting men hold up their cold, bloodless, dingy hands, as I passed, and beg me in Heaven's name for a cracker to keep them from starving (and I had none); or to give them a cup that they might have something to drink water from, if they could get it (and I had no cup and could get none); till I saw two hundred six-mule army wagons in a line, ranged down the street to headquarters, and reaching so far out on the Wilderness road that I never found the end of it; every wagon crowded with wounded men, stopped, standing in the rain and mud, wrenched back and forth by the restless, hungry animals all night from four o'clock in the afternoon till eight next morning and how much longer I know not. The dark spot in the mud under many a wagon, told only too plainly where some poor fellow's life had dripped out in those dreadful hours.

I remembered one man who would set it right, if he knew it, who possessed the power and who would believe me if I told him I commanded immediate conveyance back to Belle Plain. With difficulty I obtained it, and four stout horses with a light army wagon took me ten miles at an unbroken gallop, through field and swamp and stumps and mud to Belle Plain and a steam tug at once to Washington. Landing at dusk I sent for Henry Wilson, chairman of the Military Committee of the Senate. A messenger brought him at eight, saddened and appalled like every other patriot in that fearful hour, at the weight of woe under which the Nation staggered, groaned, and wept.

He listened to the story of suffering and faithlessness, and hurried from my presence, with lips compressed and face like ashes. At ten he stood in the War Department. They could not credit his report. He must have been deceived by some frightened villain. No official report of unusual suffering had reached them. Nothing had been called for by the military authorities commanding Fredericksburg.

Mr. Wilson assured them that the officers in trust there were not to be relied upon. They were faithless, overcome by the blandishments of the wily inhabitants. Still the Department doubted. It was then that he proved that my confidence in his firmness was not misplaced, as, facing his doubters he replies: "One of two things will have to be done—either you will send some one to-night with the power to investigate and correct the abuses of our wounded men at Fredericksburg, or the Senate will send some one tomorrow."

This threat recalled their scattered senses.

At two o'clock in the morning the Quartermaster-General and staff galloped to the 6th Street wharf under the orders; at ten they were in Fredericksburg. At noon the wounded men were fed from the food of the city and the houses were opened to the "*dirty, lousy* soldiers" of the Union Army.

Both railroad and canal were opened. In three days I returned with carloads of supplies.

No more jolting in army wagons! And every man who left Fredericksburg by boat or by car owes it to the firm decision of one man that his grating bones were not dragged ten miles across the country or left to bleach in the sands of that city.

—*The Diary of Clara Barton*

4. SUSAN BLACKFORD NURSES THE WOUNDED AT LYNCHBURG

The South had no organization comparable to the Sanitary Commission, but a Women's Relief Society dedicated itself to

*collecting money to help sick and wounded soldiers, and
thousands of Southern women volunteered for nursing duty.
Mrs. Arthur Hopkins for example not only contributed
some $200,000 to hospital work but went to the front and
was wounded at Seven Pines; others, like Mrs. Ella Newsom
and Miss Kate Cumming, worked indefatigably in the makeshift hospitals of the Confederacy; Mrs. Phoebe Yates Pember—superintendent of a division of the vast Chimborazo
Hospital in Richmond—was tireless in hospital and nursing
home and even at the front.*

Mrs. Blackford, was a member of one of Virginia's first
families, wife to the distinguished Charles Blackford, judge
advocate under Longstreet.*

May 7th [1864]. The wounded soldiers commenced arriving
on Saturday, and just as soon as I heard of it, which was before
breakfast, I went to see Mrs. Spence to know what I could do
for them. She said the ladies had been so shamefully treated by
the surgeons that she was afraid to take any move in the matter. I told her I would go and see Dr. Randolph and ask him
if we could not do something. I went down and did so at once
and asked him what we could do. He said we might do anything we pleased in the way of attention to them; send or carry
anything to them we wished and he would be glad of our help.
As soon as I reported to Mrs. Spence what he said she started
messengers in every direction to let it be known and I went
to eleven places myself. We then determined to divide our provisions into two divisions: the bread, meat, and coffee to be sent
to the depot, the delicacies to the hospitals. The reception of
wounded soldiers here has been most hospitable. You would
not believe there were so many provisions in town as have
been sent to them.

On Saturday evening I went up to Burton's factory, where
most of the wounded were taken, and found the committee of
ladies who had been selected, of whom I was one, just going
in with the supper. I went in with them. We had bountiful
supplies of soup, buttermilk, tea, coffee, and loaf bread, biscuits, crackers, and wafers. It did my heart good to see how
the poor men enjoyed such things. I went around and talked
to them all. One man had his arm taken off just below the
elbow and he was also wounded through the body, and his
drawers were saturated with blood. I fixed his pillow com-

* Letter reprinted from *Letters from Lee's Army* by Susan Lee
Blackford; copyright 1947 by Charles Scribner's Sons; used by permission of the publishers.

fortably and stroked his poor swelled and burning arm. Another I found with his hand wounded and his nose bleeding. I poured water over his face and neck, and after the blood ceased to flow wiped his pale face and wounded hand which was black from blood and powder. They were very grateful and urged us to come and see them again.

On Sunday evening news came that six hundred more would arrive and Mrs. Spence sent me word to try and do something. The servants were away and I went into the kitchen and made four quarts of flour into biscuits and two gallons of coffee, and Mrs. Spence gave me as much more barley, so I made, by mixing them, a great deal of coffee. I am very tired.

May 12th. My writing desk has been open all day, yet I have just found time to write to you. Mrs. Spence came after me just as I was about to begin this morning and said she had just heard that the Taliaferro's factory was full of soldiers in a deplorable condition. I went down there with a bucket of rice milk, a basin, towel, soap, etc. to see what I could do. I found the house filled with wounded men and not one thing provided for them. They were lying about the floor on a little straw. Some had been there since Tuesday and had not seen a surgeon. I washed and dressed the wounds of about fifty and poured water over the wounds of many more. The town is crowded with the poor creatures, and there is really no preparations for such a number. If it had not been for the ladies many of them would have starved to death. The poor creatures are very grateful, and it is a great pleasure to us to help them in any way. I have been hard at work ever since the wounded commenced coming. I went to the depot twice to see what I could do. I have had the cutting and distribution of twelve hundred yards of cotton cloth for bandages, and sent over three bushels of rolls of bandages, and as many more yesterday. I have never worked so hard in all my life and I would rather do that than anything else in the world. I hope no more wounded are sent here as I really do not think they could be sheltered. The doctors, of course, are doing much, and some are doing their full duty, but the majority are not. They have free access to the hospital stores and deem their own health demands that they drink up most the brandy and whiskey in stock, and, being fired up most the time, display a cruel and brutal indifference to the needs of the suffering which is a disgrace to their profession and to humanity.

—BLACKFORD, ed., *Letters from Lee's Army*

5. CORNELIA HANCOCK NURSES SOLDIERS AND CONTRABANDS

Of the many nursing narratives this is probably the best. Cornelia Hancock was a young lady of twenty-three when she responded to the call of her brother-in-law, Dr. Henry Child of Philadelphia, to help out as a nurse. A New Jersey Quaker, she found in nursing her vocation; after the war she worked with Southern Negroes and among the Philadelphia poor.

Her letters, covering her nursing and hospital experience from Gettysburg to the Wilderness and beyond, are simple, vivid and sincere.

Gettysburg—July 8th, 1863

My Dear Sister

We have been two days on the field; go out about eight and come in about six—go in ambulances or army buggies. The surgeons of the Second Corps had one put at our disposal. I feel assured I shall never feel horrified at anything that may happen to me hereafter. There is a great want of surgeons here; there are hundreds of brave fellows, who have not had their wounds dressed since the battle. Brave is not the word; more, more Christian fortitude never was witnessed than they exhibit, always say—"Help my neighbor first he is worse." The Second Corps did the heaviest fighting, and, of course, all who were badly wounded, were in the thickest of the fight, and, therefore, we deal with the very best class of the men—that is the bravest. My name is particularly grateful to them because it is Hancock. General Hancock is very popular with his men. The reason why they suffer more in this battle is because our army is victorious and marching on after Lee, leaving the wounded for citizens and a very few surgeons. The citizens are stripped of everything they have, so you must see the exhausting state of affairs. The Second Army Corps alone had two thousand men wounded, this I had from the Surgeon's head quarters.

I cannot write more. There is no mail that comes in, we send letters out: I believe the Government has possession of the road. I hope you will write. It would be very pleasant to have letters to read in the evening, for I am so tired I cannot write them. Get the Penn Relief to send clothing here; there are many men without anything but a shirt lying in poor shelter tents, calling on God to take them from this world of suffering; in fact the air is rent with petitions to deliver them from their sufferings. . . .

I do not know when I shall go home—it will be according to how long this hospital stays here and whether another battle comes soon. I can go right in an ambulance without being any expense to myself. The Christian Committee support us and when they get tired the Sanitary is on hand. Uncle Sam is very rich, but very slow, and if it was not for the Sanitary, much suffering would ensue. We give the men toast and eggs for breakfast, beef tea at ten o'clock, ham and bread for dinner, and jelly and bread for supper. Dried rusk would be nice if they were only here. Old sheets we would give much for. Bandages are plenty but sheets very scarce. We have plenty of woolen blankets now, in fact the hospital is well supplied, but for about five days after the battle, the men had no blankets nor scarce any shelter.

It took nearly five days for some three hundred surgeons to perform the amputations that occurred here, during which time the rebels lay in a dying condition without their wounds being dressed or scarcely any food. If the rebels did not get severely punished for this battle, then I am no judge. We have but one rebel in our camp now; he says he never fired his gun if he could help it, and, therefore, we treat him first rate. One man died this morning. I fixed him up as nicely as the place will allow; he will be buried this afternoon. We are becoming somewhat civilized here now and the men are cared for well.

On reading the news of the copperhead performance, in a tent where eight men lay with nothing but stumps (they call a leg cut off above the knee a "stump") they said if they held on a little longer they would form a stump brigade and go and fight them. We have some plucky boys in the hospital, but they suffer awfully. One had his leg cut off yesterday, and some of the ladies, newcomers, were up to see him. I told them if they had seen as many as I had they would not go far to see the sight again. I could stand by and see a man's head taken off I believe—you get so used to it here. I should be perfectly contented if I could receive my letters. I have the cooking all on my mind pretty much. I have torn almost all my clothes off of me, and Uncle Sam has given me a new suit. William says I am very popular here as I am such a contrast to some of the office-seeking women who swarm around hospitals. I am black as an Indian and dirty as a pig and as well as I ever was in my life—have a nice bunk and tent about twelve feet square. I have a bed that is made of four crotch sticks and some sticks laid across and pine boughs laid on that with blankets on top. It is equal to any mattress ever made. The tent is open at night and sometimes I have laid in the damp all night long, and got up all right in the morning.

The suffering we get used to and the nurses and doctors, stewards, etc., are very jolly and sometimes we have a good time. It is very pleasant weather now. There is all in getting to do what you *want* to do and I am doing that. . . .

Pads are terribly needed here. Bandages and lint are plenty. I would like to see seven barrels of dried rusk here. I do not know the day of the week or anything else. Business is slackening a little though—order is beginning to reign in the hospital and soon things will be right. One poor fellow is hollowing fearfully now while his wounds are being dressed.

There is no more impropriety in a *young* person being here provided they are sensible than a sexagenarian. Most polite and obliging are all the soldiers to me.

It is a very good place to meet celebrities; they come here from all parts of the United States to see their wounded. Senator Wilson, Mr. Washburn, and one of the Minnesota Senators have been here. I get beef tenderloin for dinner.— Ladies who work are favored but the dress-up palaverers are passed by on the other side. I tell you I have lost my memory almost entirely, but it is gradually returning. Dr. Child has done very good service here. All is well with me; we do not know much war news, but I know I am doing all I can, so I do not concern further. Kill the copperheads. Write everything, however trifling, it is all interest here.

From thy affectionate
C. HANCOCK

Contraband Hospital, Washington, Nov. 15th, 1863
My dear Sister:

I shall depict our wants in true but ardent words, hoping to affect you to some action. Here are gathered the sick from the contraband camps in the northern part of Washington. If I were to describe this hospital it would not be believed. North of Washington, in an open, muddy mire, are gathered all the colored people who have been made free by the progress of our Army. Sickness is inevitable, and to meet it these rude hospitals, only rough wooden barracks, are in use —a place where there is so much to be done you need not remain idle. We average here one birth per day, and have no baby clothes except as we wrap them up in an old piece of muslin, *that* even being scarce. Now the Army is advancing it is not uncommon to see from 40 to 50 arrivals in one day. They go at first to the Camp but many of them being *sick* from exhaustion soon come to us. They have nothing that any one in the North would call clothing. I always see them as soon as they arrive, as they come here to be vaccinated; about 25 a day are vaccinated.

This hospital is the reservoir for all cripples, diseased, aged, wounded, infirm, from whatsoever cause; all accidents happening to colored people in all employs around Washington are brought here. It is not uncommon for a colored driver to be pounded nearly to death by some of the white soldiers. We had a dreadful case of Hernia brought in today. A woman was brought here with three children by her side; said she had been on the road for some time; a more forlorn, wornout looking creature I never beheld. Her four eldest children are still in Slavery, her husband is dead. When I first saw her she laid on the floor, leaning against a bed, her children crying around her. One child died almost immediately, the other two are still sick. She seemed to need most, food and rest, and those two comforts we gave her, but clothes she still wants. I think the women are more trouble than the men. One of the white guards called to me today and asked me if I got any pay. I told him no. He said he was going to be paid soon and he would give me 5 dollars. I do not know what was running through his mind as he made no other remark. I ask for clothing for women and children, both boys and girls. Two little boys, one 3 years old, had his leg amputated above the knee the cause being his mother not being allowed to ride inside, became dizzy and had dropped him. The other had his leg broken from the same cause. This hospital consists of all the lame, halt, and blind escaped from slavery. We have a man and woman here without any feet, theirs being frozen so they had to be amputated. Almost all have scars of some description and many have very weak eyes.

There were two very fine looking slaves arrived here from Louisiana, one of them had his master's name branded on his forehead, and with him he brought all the instruments of torture that he wore at different times during 39 years of very hard slavery. I will try to send you a Photograph of him he wore an iron collar with 3 prongs standing up so he could not lay down his head; then a contrivance to render one leg entirely stiff and a chain clanking behind him with a bar weighing 50 lbs. This he wore and worked all the time hard.

At night they hung a little bell upon the prongs above his head so that if he hid in any bushes it would tinkle and tell his whereabouts. The baton that was used to whip them he also had. It is so constructed that a little child could whip them till the blood streamed down their backs. This system of proceeding has been stopped in New Orleans and may God grant that it may cease all over this boasted free land, but you may readily imagine what development such a system of treatment would bring them to. With *this* class of beings, those who wish to do good to the contrabands must labor. Their standard of morality is very low.

—JAQUETTE, ed., *South after Gettysburg*

6. THE GHASTLY WORK OF THE FIELD SURGEONS

These two descriptions of the work of the surgeons could be matched in letter after letter, diary after diary, North and South. One Kentucky editor charged that the doctors had "slain more of our troops than all of Lincoln's minions," and a Richmond one characterized the Medical Department as "unfeeling, shameful and brutal." We must remember however that it is the exceptionally bad conduct that gets recorded; routine work is taken for granted. On the whole the surgeons and nurses did about as well as they could. Certainly many of those who worked all through the war, at great peril to themselves, were distinguished members of a distinguished profession.

The first of these critics, Samuel Nichols, was an Amherst College student who enlisted in the 37th Massachusetts Volunteers; served through the war; and later edited the Pittsfield (Massachusetts) Sun. The second is Augustus Brown, captain in the 4th New York Heavy Artillery.

A. THE HEARTLESSNESS OF THE SURGEONS

Hd. Qtrs. 37th Regiment Mass. Vols.
Camp near Stafford Court House
Nov. 23rd 1862

My Dear Cousin Phebe:
As yet only four of our number have died and some six have been discharged, two of the latter of whom were officers.

Lieut. Eli T. Blackmer, a son of the Blackmer that moved from Hodges Corner in Warren, is discharged and has gone to his home in Chicopee. His health is much impaired, and his discharge was merited. Everything here concerning sickness and its management seems so repulsive that the thought of being sick or of having one of your friends in the Hospital, is filled with gloom. I will relate an instance. It is probably an instance more censurable to those having charge than usually occurs; but if the whole history of this war were brought to light more such facts would be revealed, in my mind, than would be pleasing to men (no, brutes) whose duty it is to look after the physical health of the soldier.

In our regiment was a man, private of course, who came under my notice while we were at New Baltimore, a little over one week since. He was emaciated and almost spiritless. He, to be sure, was not as cleanly as he should have been; but I know that it requires much exertion where water is scarce (and it always is in the vicinity of an army like ours) to keep decent. He looked as though he had been sick for some time. He like many others had acquired a dislike to reporting himself to the surgeons, as they have an idea the surgeons are destitute of feeling and unjust. I will not say how far this feeling is just. He at length came with those of his company who reported sick that day to the Surgeon's office within a few steps of where I sleep. I stood at the mouth of my tent and saw and heard the treatment each patient received. This fellow was treated as the rest. He took his turn and came to the front of the Doctor's tent, and received the customary question, "What's the matter with you?" (pretty question for a doctor). "What are you here for? Let's see your tongue. Shall return you to duty."

He was returned to duty. He refused to do duty and as punishment was sentenced to stand on the barrel (a very severe punishment), and added to this, to hold a heavy stone in his hand, two hours on and two off. This was the Doctor's work and not the Colonel's. I admit that it was the Colonel's duty to stop an unjust punishment if he saw one being exacted, but he would probably refer the whole case to the Doctor. To continue my story: after this I watched that young man. All energy seemed absent from him, and he acted as if he was unable to stir. I went to him and advised him to go to the Surgeon again, knowing that by tiring out the M.D. he might receive attention. I could not induce him. I saw during my conversation that he was really sick; and I was anxious to find out what ailed him, knowing if I did, I could find him medicine. I went to another regiment to get a doctor with whom I was acquainted to come and see him; but the regiment had moved that morning, and so I let the matter go for the time being. Two mornings after I saw him again at the Doctor's tent. With the usual flourishes he was reported for duty, and the next morning he was brought to the Hospital to die almost immediately. The same day he was buried with soldier's honors; and with the last volleys fired over his grave died all feelings of remissness or regret, if any such feelings were entertained.

—UNDERHILL, ed., *"Your Soldier Boy Samuel"*

B. THE HORRORS OF THE WILDERNESS

Tuesday, May 10th [1864]. Heavy cannonading from 8 A.M. to 1 P.M. The Pontoon train has been sent back to Fredericksburg, apparently to get it out of the way, and the army horses are put on half-rations, that is, five pounds of food. Ambulances and army wagons with two tiers of flooring, loaded with wounded and drawn by four and six mule teams, pass along the plank, or rather, corduroy road to Fredericksburg, the teamsters lashing their teams to keep up with the train, and the wounded screaming with pain as the wagons go jolting over the corduroy. Many of the wounds 'are full of maggots. I saw one man with an arm off at the shoulder, with maggots half an inch long crawling in the sloughing flesh, and several poor fellows were holding stumps of legs and arms straight up in the air so as to ease the pain the rough road and the heartless drivers subjected them to. These men had been suffering in temporary field hospitals, as no opportunity had been afforded to send them to the rear until we got within reach of the road running to Fredericksburg.

And this reminds me of a scene I witnessed a day or two since which seemed to me to cap the climax of the horrors of war. Passing along a little in the rear of the lines when a battle was raging in which my battalion was not engaged, I came upon a field-hospital to which the stretcher-bearers were bringing the men wounded in the conflict. Under three large "tent flies," the center one the largest of all, stood three heavy wooden tables, around which were grouped a number of surgeons and their assistants, the former bareheaded and clad in long linen dusters reaching nearly to the ground, which were covered with blood from top to bottom and had the arms cut off or rolled to the shoulders. The stretcher-bearers deposited their ghastly freight side by side in a winrow on the ground in front of the table under the first tent fly. Here a number of assistants took charge of the poor fellows, and as some of them lifted a man on to the first table others moved up the winrow so that no time nor space should be lost. Then some of the surgeons administered as anaesthetic to the groaning and writhing patient, exposed his wound and passed him to the center table. There the surgeons who were operating made a hasty examination and determined what was to be done and did it, and more often than not, in a very few moments an arm or a leg or some other portion of the subject's anatomy was flung out upon a pile of similar fragments behind the hospital, which was then more than six feet wide and three feet high, and what remained of the man was passed on to the third table, where other surgeons finished the bandaging, resuscitated him and posted him off with others in an ambulance. Heaven forbid that I should ever again witness such a sight!

—BROWN, *Diary of a Line Officer*

7. THE REGIMENTAL HOSPITAL

Although Charles Johnson wrote this many years after the war, it is one of the best of the comparatively few accounts of military field hospitals. Johnson had enlisted as a boy of eighteen, and was assigned to hospital duty in the West; he was with Grant in the siege of Vicksburg and later took part in the expedition into the Bayou Teche country. His account goes far to explain the failure of medical services in the war and to place responsibility not on the medical officers but on the state of medical science at the time.

In the field the Regimental Hospital department was allowed two small tents for the officers, medicines, etc., another small tent for the kitchen department and supplies, and a larger one for the sick. This last, known as the hospital tent, was about fourteen feet square and was capable of containing eight cots with as many patients.

In the field we almost never had sheets and white pillow cases, but made use of army blankets that were made of the coarsest, roughest fiber imaginable. In warm weather the walls of the tent were raised, which made it much more pleasant for the occupants.

However, the policy that obtained was to send those who were not likely to recover quickly to the base hospitals, though this was not always to the patient's best interests, for these larger hospitals were oftentimes centers of infection of one kind or another, especially of hospital gangrene, which seldom attacked the wounded in the field.

During a campaign our stock of medicines was necessarily limited to standard remedies, among which could be named opium, morphine, Dover's powder, quinine, rhubarb, Rochelle salts, castor oil, sugar of lead, tannin, sulphate of copper, sulphate of zinc, camphor, tincture of opium, tincture of iron, tincture opii, camphorata, syrup of squills, simple syrup, alcohol, whiskey, brandy, port wine, sherry wine, etc. Upon going into camp, where we were likely to remain a few days, these articles were unpacked and put on temporary shelves made from box-lids; and, on the other hand, when marching orders came, the medicines were again packed in boxes, the bottles protected from breaking by old papers, etc.

Practically all the medicines were administered in powder form or in the liquid state. Tablets had not yet come into use, and pills were very far from being as plentiful as they are today. The result was that most powders were stirred in water and swallowed. In the case of such medicine as quinine, Dover's powder, tannin, etc., the dose, thus prepared, was a bitter one. The bromides, sulfonal, trional and similar soporifices and sedatives, had not come in use, and asafetida, valerian and opium and its derivatives were about all the Civil War surgeon had to relieve nervousness and induce sleep.

Among the surgical supplies were chloroform, ether, brandy, aromatic spirits of ammonia, bandages, adhesive plaster, needles, silk thread for ligatures, etc. There were, also, amputating cases well supplied with catlins, artery forceps, bone forceps, scalpels, scissors, bullet probes, a tourniquet, etc. But while all the instruments were washed in water and wiped dry to keep from rusting, such an idea as making them aseptic never entered the head of the most advanced surgeon.

There was an emergency case, about the size of a soldier's knapsack, and, indeed, intended to be carried on an attendant's back like a knapsack. In this emergency case were bandages, adhesive plaster, needles, artery forceps, scalpels, spirits of ammonia, brandy, chloroform, ether, etc. This emergency case, or hospital knapsack, was always taken with the regi-

ment when the firing-line was about to be approached, and
where the First Assistant Surgeon was in charge and was
ready to render first aid to any who might be wounded.

This first aid, however, never went further than staunching bleeding vessels and applying temporary dressings. Thus
attended to, the wounded were taken to an ambulance, and
in this conveyed to the field hospital in the rear, generally out
of musket range, but almost never beyond the reach of shells
and cannon balls.

Arrived at the larger field hospital the patient was cared
for by the surgeons and male nurses. The wounds were examined and dressed, but never antiseptically, for no one
knew the importance of antisepsis or how to put it in practise;
consequently, every wound suppurated, and so-called *laudable
pus* was welcomed by those in charge as an indication that
the patient had reached one of the mile-posts that had to be
passed on his road to recovery. Careful handwashing and
nail scrubbing was never practised before operations or in
dressing recent wounds. And yet, for the most part, the
wounds in the end healed satisfactorily. The fact that those
receiving them were, in the great majority of cases, vigorous
young men had much to do with the good results. Here it may
be proper to say that in the Civil War by far the largest
proportion of wounds were made with bullets from what
were called minie balls. There were fired, in most instances,
from single-shooters and muzzle-loaders, such as the Springfield rifled musket, the Enfield rifled musket, the Austrian
rifled musket, etc. These bullets weighed an ounce or more,
and the guns from which they were fired would kill a man
nearly a mile away, and that they produced large, ugly wounds
goes without saying.

When a minie ball struck a bone it almost never failed to
fracture and shatter the contiguous bony structure, and it
was rarely that only a round perforation, the size of the bullet,
resulted. When a joint was the part the bullet struck, the
results were especially serious in Civil War days. Of course,
the same was true of wounds of the abdomen and head,
though to a much greater degree. Indeed, recovery from
wounds of the abdomen and brain almost never occurred. One
of the prime objects of the Civil War surgeon was to remove
the missile, and, in doing this, he practically never failed to
infect the part with his dirty hands and instrument.

When Captain William M. Colby of my company was
brought from the firing-line to our Division Hospital he was
in a comatose state from a bullet that had penetrated his

brain through the upper portion of the occipital bone. The first thing our surgeon did was to run his index finger its full length into the wound; and this without even ordinary washing. Next he introduced a dirty bullet probe. The patient died a day or two later. . . . These facts are narrated to show the frightful handicap Civil War surgery was under from a lack of knowledge of asepsis and antisepsis; and it is needless to say that no reflection is intended to be made on our surgeon, for he was making use of the very best lights of his day, dangerous as some of these were. . . .

I think wounds from bullets were five times as frequent as those from all other sources. Shell wounds were next in frequency, and then came those from grape and canister. I never saw a wound from a bayonet thrust, and but one made by a sword in the hands of an enemy. In another chapter a reference is made to a man who received a deep wound in the upper part of his thigh, which, after some days, proved fatal. Not long after the wound was received the parts began to assume a greenish tinge and this became of a deeper hue, and when after death the parts were cut down upon, a copper tap from an exploding shell was found to be the ugly missile which had inflicted the injury that, in the end, proved fatal.

Where so many men are grouped together accidents of greater or less gravity are liable to occur. On the whole, however, our regiment was fortunate. We lost two or three by drowning and one by a steamboat explosion . . . , and I can recall but three who received accidental bullet wounds. One of these was a pistol shot of small caliber . . . , and the other was from one of the Springfield guns that was supposed not to be loaded. Looking back, I can but regard our record in this direction as especially fortunate, when the handling of so many loaded guns through so long a period is taken into account.

The only light vehicle in the regiment was our hospital ambulance, . . . a four-wheeled vehicle with bed on springs and covered with strong ducking. The rear end-gate opened with hinges at its lower part for the convenience of putting in and taking out very sick or severely injured patients. The driver of our hospital ambulance was a soldier by the name of Throgmorton, who knew his business, and attended to it. He was an expert horseman, and kept the pair of bays under his care well-groomed and properly attended to in every way. They were, to a degree, spirited, and when the occasion called for it, were good steppers. Besides serving its purpose in conveying sick and wounded, our ambulance proved useful as a sort of family carriage, upon several occasions taking *certain* of us *well ones* "here-and-yon."

For service about the hospital men were detailed from the regiment to serve in the several capacities of nurses, cooks, and ambulance drivers, etc. Service of this kind was known as "special duty," and not a few came to have no little aptness in their new duties. Especially was this true of the men who cared for the sick, some of whom developed quite a little insight into disease, and were frequently able to make tolerable diagnoses and prognoses.

—JOHNSON, *Muskets and Medicine*

VII

The Coast and Inland Waters

SEA *power played a decisive role in the Civil War. It was the blockade, as much as any other single factor, that assured Union victory; had the Confederacy been able to break the blockade, or to persuade European nations to do so, she could probably have held out indefinitely. Almost equally important was Federal control of the major ports along the Atlantic and the Gulf coasts and of the river systems that led deep into the heart of the Confederacy. This control of coast and inland waters not only enabled the Union to supply its own forces and to move along interior lines of communication, but cut off the flow of supplies from one part of the Confederacy to another and broke Confederate lines of communication.*

In the nature of the case naval supremacy rested, from the beginning, with the Union. It was possible, after a fashion, to improvise an army, and certainly to improvise a defense; it was not possible to improvise a navy, though here the Confederacy almost did the impossible. Although the Union Navy numbered less than 40 effective vessels at the beginning of the war, it was rapidly built up to really effective strength. The Confederacy had nothing to start with—only two navy yards, no merchant marine, no seafaring population on which to draw. It was something of a miracle that the Confederacy did as well as it did on water.

The war found the Union Navy as unprepared as the army. The total number of vessels on the navy list was about 90; of these 50 were obsolete sailing ships. Most of the 40 steamers comprising the fleet were scattered around the globe; only 12 were actually available in the Home Squadron. Naval personnel was equally inadequate. Of the almost 1,500 officers, over 300 had resigned at the beginning of the war, and there were less than 7,500 seamen to man the fleet. Yet this fleet was expected to blockade over 3,000 miles of coast and cooperate with the army in attacks on coastal ports and along the inland rivers.

The Confederacy was in an even worse situation. It had no navy, and no naval personnel except such as had resigned from the Union Navy at the outbreak of the war. Both its navy yards fell to the Union before the end of the war. Yet somehow it managed to create a navy. It captured some ships, built others, raised several that had been sunk at Norfolk, converted a few merchant ships into warships, fitted out privateers, bought and built vessels abroad. At the same time it greatly strengthened its habor defenses: Fort Fisher did not fall until January 1865; Charleston resisted every assault by sea.

The United States Navy faced a twofold task. First it had to enforce the blockade. This actually proved less difficult than had been anticipated, for there were comparatively few ports which combined adequate harbors, harbor defenses, and connections with the interior. The most important were Norfolk (James River), Roanoke Island, New Bern (Neuse River), Beaufort, Wilmington (Cape Fear River), Charleston, Beaufort (South Carolina), Savannah, and, on the Gulf, Pensacola, Mobile, New Orleans, and Galveston. Obviously it was easier to capture these ports, once and for all, than to blockade them throughout the war, and it was to this task of reducing coastal forts and capturing ports that the Federal Army-Navy team first addressed itself.

One after another the ports fell: first Hilton Head, Port Royal, and Beaufort (South Carolina); then Roanoke Island, controlling Albemarle Sound; then—after the Monitor had forced the Merrimac to withdraw—Norfolk at the mouth of the James; and then James Island, outside Charleston. The great prize was, however, New Orleans, greatest city in the Confederacy and key to the Gulf and the Mississippi. After that the Confederacy had only a few good ports to which the swift blockade-runners could sail: Charleston, Wilmington, Mobile, and Galveston. It took longer to capture these, and Charleston was never captured from the sea, but it is no ex-

*aggeration to say that by the end of 1862 the Confederacy
was pretty well bottled up.*

Even more arduous was the task of clearing the Mississippi
and co-operating with the army in warfare along its
tributaries—the Tennessee, the Cumberland, the Arkansas, and
the Red—which Federal strategy imposed upon the navy. For
most of the victories in the West the army got the credit, yet
without the navy the story of Fort Donelson, Shiloh, New
Madrid, Vicksburg, Port Hudson, and even the Red River
campaign would have been very different.

What we have here is amphibious warfare, and the
problem of allocating its history to the services is a perplexing
one. Certainly it does some violence to history to place the
attack on Battery Wagner, for example, in a chapter devoted
to the navy, or to separate the naval and the military history
of the Vicksburg campaign. To break up this story, however,
inserting its various segments into the history of military campaigns, would be to lose sight of the remarkable achievement
of the Union Navy—and the interesting achievement of the
Confederate Navy, in the war; and that would be a pity.

1. THE *MERRIMAC* AND THE *MONITOR*

This is one of the half-dozen most famous engagements in
American history. If it did not revolutionize naval warfare, as
is often erroneously asserted, it did dramatize the advent of
the revolution that had taken place—the substitution of iron
or steel for oak.

When the Federals abandoned Norfolk they fired and sank
a number of their ships there; among them was the 350-
ton frigate, Merrimac. The Confederates raised this ship and
converted her into an ironclad—renaming her, but in vain,
the Virginia. Alarmed by rumors of progress on the Merrimac, the Navy Department asked for bids for the building of
armored vessels. The well-known naval engineer, John Ericsson, who had been born in Sweden, was among those who
submitted plans. These were accepted, and Ericsson began
building his armored ship in October 1861. It was launched
at the end of January, ready for sea on February 19, and
sailed from New York March 6, under the command of Lieutenant John L. Worden. It arrived off Hampton Roads just
in the nick of time—or perhaps a bit too late. For on March

8 the Merrimac *had come out and attacked the Union fleet off Fortress Monroe.*

We give here the account of the terrible destruction wrought by the Merrimac *on the eighth and of the tremendous duel between the two ironclads the following day. Our first historian is Captain Van Brunt of the* Minnesota; *our second the intrepid Lieutenant S. Dana Greene, who succeeded the blinded Worden in command of the* Monitor.

A. The *Minnesota* Fights for Her Life in Hampton Roads

UNITED STATES STEAMER *Minnesota,*
March 10, 1862

SIR: On Saturday, the eighth instant, at forty-five minutes after twelve o'clock P.M., three small steamers, in appearance, were discovered rounding Sewall's Point, and as soon as they came into full broadside view, I was convinced that one was the iron-plated steam-battery *Merrimac,* from the large size of her smoke-pipe. They were heading for Newport News, and I, in obedience to a signal from the senior officer present, Capt. John Marston, immediately called all hands, slipped my cables, and got under way for that point, to engage her. While rapidly passing Sewall's Point, the rebels there opened fire upon us from a rifle-battery, one shot from which going through and crippling my mainmast. I returned the fire with my broadside-guns and forecastle-pivot. We ran without further difficulty within about one and a half miles of Newport News, and there, unfortunately, grounded. The tide was running ebb, and although in the channel there was not sufficient water for this ship, which draws twenty-three feet, I knew the bottom was soft and lumpy, and endeavored to force the ship over, but found it impossible so to do. At this time it was reported to me that the *Merrimac* had passed the frigate *Congress* and run into the sloop-of-war *Cumberland,* and in fifteen minutes after, I saw the latter going down by the head. The *Merrimac* then hauled off, taking a position, and about half-past two o'clock P.M., engaged the *Congress,* throwing shot and shell into her with terrific effect, while the shot from the *Congress* glanced from her iron-plated sloping sides, without doing any apparent injury. At half-past three o'clock P.M., the *Congress* was compelled to haul down her colors. Of the extent of her loss and injury, you will be informed from the official report of her commander.

At four o'clock P.M., *the Merrimac, Jamestown* and *Patrick Henry,* bore down upon my vessel. Very fortunately, the iron battery drew too much water to come within a mile of us. She took a position on my starboard bow, but did not fire with accuracy, and only one shot passed through the ship's bow. The other two steamers took their position on my port bow and stern, and their fire did most damage in killing and wounding men, inasmuch as they fired with rifled guns; but with the heavy gun that I could bring to bear upon them, I drove them off, one of them apparently in a crippled state. I fired upon the *Merrimac* with my ten-inch pivot-gun, without any apparent effect, and at seven o'clock P.M., she too hauled off, and all three vessels steamed toward Norfolk.

The tremendous firing of my broadside guns had crowded me further upon the mud-bank, into which the ship seemed to have made herself a cradle. From ten P.M., when the tide commenced to run flood, until four A.M., I had all hands at work, with steamtugs and hawsers, endeavoring to haul the ship off the bank; but without avail, and as the tide had then fallen considerably, I suspended further proceedings at that time.

At two A.M. the iron battery *Monitor,* Com. John L. Worden, which had arrived the previous evening at Hampton Roads, came alongside and reported for duty, and then all on board felt that we had a friend that would stand by us in our hour of trial.

At six A.M. the enemy again appeared, coming down from Craney Island, and I beat to quarters; but they ran past my ship, and were heading for Fortress Monroe, and the retreat was beaten, to allow my men to get something to eat. The *Merrimac* ran down near the Rip Raps, and then turned into the channel through which I had come. Again all hands were called to quarters, and opened upon her with my stern-guns, and made signal to the *Monitor* to attack the enemy. She immediately ran down in my wake, right within the range of the *Merrimac,* completely covering my ship, as far as possible with her diminutive dimensions, and, much to my astonishment, laid herself right alongside of the *Merrimac,* and the contrast was that of a pigmy to a giant. Gun after gun was fired by the *Monitor,* which was returned with whole broadsides from the rebels, with no more effect, apparently, than so many pebble-stones thrown by a child. After a while they commenced manœuvering, and we could see the little battery point her bow for the rebel's, with the intention, as I thought, of sending a shot through her bow-porthole; then she would shoot by her, and rake her through her stern. In the mean time the rebels were pouring broadside after broadside, but almost all her shot flew over the little submerged propeller; and when they struck the bomb-proof tower, the shot glanced off without producing any effect, clearly establishing the fact that wooden vessels cannot contend successfully with iron-clad ones, for never before was anything like it dreamed of by the greatest enthusiast in maritime warfare.

The *Merrimac*, finding that she could make nothing of the *Monitor*, turned her attention once more to me in the morning. She had put one eleven-inch shot under my counter, near the water-line, and now, on her second approach, I opened upon her with all my broadside-guns and ten-inch pivot —a broadside which would have blown out of water any timber-built ship in the world. She returned my fire with her rifled bow-gun, with a shell which passed through the chief engineer's state-room, through the engineer's mess-room amidships, and burst in the boatswain's room, tearing four rooms all into one, in its passage exploding two charges of powder, which set the ship on fire, but it was promptly extinguished by a party headed by my first lieutenant. Her second went through the boiler of the tugboat *Dragon*, exploding it, and causing more consternation on board my ship for the moment, until the matter was explained. This time I had concentrated upon her an incessant fire from my gun-deck, spar-deck and forecastle pivot-guns, and was informed by my marine officer, who was stationed on the poop, that at least fifty solid shot struck her on her slanting side, without producing any apparent effect. By the time she had fired her third shell, the little *Monitor* had come down upon her, placing herself between us, and compelled her to change her position, in doing which she grounded, and again I poured into her all the guns which could be brought to bear upon her.

As soon as she got off, she stood down the bay, the little battery chasing her with all speed, when suddenly the *Merrimac* turned around, and ran full speed into her antagonist. For a moment I was anxious, but instantly I saw a shot plunge into the iron roof of the *Merrimac*, which surely must have damaged her, for some time after the rebels concentrated their whole battery upon the tower and pilot-house of the *Monitor*, and soon after the latter stood down for Fortress Monroe, and we thought it probable she had exhausted her supply of ammunition, or sustained some injury. Soon after the *Merrimac* and the two other steamers headed for my ship, and I then felt to the fullest extent my condition. I was hard and im-

movable aground, and they could take position under my
stern and rake me. I had expended most of my solid shot,
and my ship was badly crippled, and my officers and men
were worn out with fatigue; but even in this extreme dilemma
I determined never to give up the ship to the rebels, and after
consulting my officers, I ordered every preparation to be made
to destroy the ship, after all hope was gone to save her. On
ascending the poop-deck, I observed that the enemy's vessels
had changed their course, and were heading for Craney Island; then I determined to lighten the ship by throwing overboard my eight-inch guns, hoisting out provisions, starting
water, etc.

At two P.M. I proceeded to make another attempt to save
the ship, by the use of a number of powerful tugs and the
steamer *S. R. Spaulding* . . . and succeeded in dragging her
half a mile distant, and then she was again immovable, the
tide having fallen. At two A.M. this morning I succeeded in
getting the ship once more afloat, and am now at anchor opposite Fortress Monroe.

It gives me great pleasure to say that, during the whole of
these trying scenes, the officers and men conducted themselves
with great courage and coolness.

I have the honor to be your very obedient servant,

G. J. VAN BRUNT,

Captain U. S. N., Commanding Frigate *Minnesota*.

HON. GIDEON WELLES,

Secretary of the Navy, Washington, D. C.

—"Report of Captain Van Brunt"

B. THE *Monitor* REPELS THE *Merrimac*

U.S. Steamer *Monitor,* Hampton Roads, Va.—At 4 P.M.
[March 8, 1862] we passed Cape Henry and heard heavy
firing in the direction of Fortress Monroe. As we approached,
it increased, and we immediately cleared ship for action. When
about halfway between Fortress Monroe and Cape Henry we
spoke the pilot boat. He told us the *Cumberland* was sunk and
the *Congress* was on fire and had surrendered to the *Merrimac.* We could not credit it at first, but as we approached
Hampton Roads, we could see the fine old *Congress* burning
brightly; and we knew it must be true. Sad indeed did we
feel to think those two fine old vessels had gone to their
last homes with so many of their brave crews. Our hearts
were very full, and we vowed vengeance on the *Merrimac* if

it should be our lot to fall in with her. At 9 P.M. we anchored near the frigate *Roanoke*, the flagship, Captain Marston. Captain Worden immediately went on board and received orders to proceed to Newport News and protect the *Minnesota* (then aground) from the *Merrimac*.

We got under way and arrived at the *Minnesota* at 11 P.M. I went on board in our cutter and asked the captain what his prospects were of getting off. He said he should try to get afloat at 2 A.M., when it was high water. I asked him if we could render him any assistance, to which he replied, "No!" I then told him we should do all in our power to protect him from the *Merrimac*. He thanked me kindly and wished us success. Just as I arrived back to the *Monitor* the *Congress* blew up, and certainly a grander sight was never seen; but it went straight to the marrow of our bones. Not a word was said, but deeply did each man think and wish we were by the side of the *Merrimac*. At 1 A.M. we anchored near the *Minnesota*. The captain and myself remained on deck, waiting for the appearance of the *Merrimac*. At 3 A.M. we thought the *Minnesota* was afloat and coming down on us; so we got under way as soon as possible and stood out of the channel. After backing and filling about for an hour, we found we were mistaken and anchored again. At daylight we discovered the *Merrimac* at anchor with several vessels under Sewall's Point. We immediately made every preparation for battle. At 8 A.M. on Sunday the *Merrimac* got under way, accompanied by several steamers, and started direct for the *Minnesota*. When a mile distant she fired two guns at her. By this time our anchor was up, the men at quarters, the guns loaded, and everything ready for action. As the *Merrimac* came close, the captain passed the word to commence firing. I triced up the port, ran out the gun, and fired the *first* gun, and thus commenced the great battle between the *Monitor* and the *Merrimac*.

Now mark the condition our men and officers were in. Since Friday morning, forty-eight hours, they had had no rest and very little food, as we could not conveniently cook. They had been hard at work all night, and nothing to eat for breakfast except hard bread, and were thoroughly worn out. As for myself, I had not slept a wink for fifty-one hours and had been on my feet almost constantly.

But after the first gun was fired we forgot all fatigues, hard work, and everything else and fought as hard as men ever fought. We loaded and fired as fast as we could. I pointed and fired the guns myself. Every shot I would ask the captain the effect, and the majority of them were encouraging. The captain was in the pilothouse, directing the movements of the vessel; Acting Master Stodder was stationed at the wheel which turns the tower but, as he could not manage it, was relieved by Steiners. The speaking trumpet from the tower to the pilothouse was broken; so we passed the word from the captain to myself on the berth deck by Paymaster Keeler and Captain's Clerk Toffey.

Five times during the engagement we touched each other, and each time I fired a gun at her, and I will vouch the hundred and sixty-eight pounds penetrated her sides. Once she tried to run us down with her iron prow but did no damage whatever. After fighting for two hours we hauled off for half an hour to hoist shot in the tower. At it we went again as hard as we could, the shot, shell, grape, canister, musket, and rifle balls flying in every direction but doing no damage. Our tower was struck several times, and though the noise was pretty loud it did not affect us any. Stodder and one of the men were carelessly leaning against the tower when a shot struck it exactly opposite them and disabled them for an hour or two.

At about 11:30 A.M. the captain sent for me. I went forward, and there stood as noble a man as lives, at the foot of the ladder to the pilothouse, his face perfectly black with powder and iron, and apparently perfectly blind. I asked him what was the matter. He said a shot had struck the pilothouse exactly opposite his eyes and blinded him, and he thought the pilothouse was damaged. He told me to take charge of the ship and use my own discretion. I led him to his room, laid him on the sofa, and then took his position. On examining the pilothouse I found the iron hatch on top, on the forward side, was completely cracked through.

We still continued firing, the tower being under the direction of Steiners. We were between two fires, the *Minnesota* on one side and the *Merrimac* on the other. The latter was retreating to Sewall's Point, and the *Minnesota* had struck us twice on the tower. I knew if another shot should strike our pilothouse in the same place, our steering apparatus would be disabled, and we should be at the mercy of the batteries on Sewall's Point. We had *strict* orders to act on the defensive and protect the *Minnesota*. We had evidently finished the *Merrimac* as far as the *Minnesota* was concerned. Our pilothouse was damaged, and we had orders *not* to follow the *Merrimac* up; therefore, after the *Merrimac* had retreated. I went to the *Minnesota* and remained by her until she was afloat. General Wool and Secretary Fox both commended me for acting as I did and said it was the strict military plan to follow. This is the reason we did not sink the *Merrimac,* and every one here capable of judging says we acted perfectly right.

—POST, ed., *Soldiers' Letters from Camp, Battle-field and Prison*

2. COMMODORE FARRAGUT CAPTURES NEW ORLEANS

From the beginning of the war the government had appreciated the paramount importance of capturing New Orleans and sealing up the Mississippi from blockade-runners. New Orleans was, however, a very tough nut to crack. Well up from the mouth of the river, it was defended by formidable forts, and across the river the Confederates had built a powerful boom consisting of chains, hulks of ships, and other obstacles.

In December 1861 the President selected David G. Farragut to command the West Gulf Blockading Squadron and directed him "to proceed up the Mississippi River and reduce the defenses which guard the approaches to New Orleans, when you will appear off that city and take possession of it." Farragut was, at the time, sixty years old—and a veteran with 49 years of service at sea; his career, so far, had been exemplary rather than brilliant.

On February 2 Farragut sailed from Hampton Roads with 17 wooden vessels and a mortar flotilla of 20 schooners under the command of David D. Porter. On April 18, 1862, he began the bombardment of Forts Jackson and St. Philip, but was unable to make any impression on them. He then decided to run the forts, smash the boom, and sail up to New Orleans—an audacious feat which he carried through with spectacular success.

The story is told here by the New Hampshire lieutenant, George H. Perkins, of the gunboat Cayuga; *Perkins later commanded the monitor* Chickasaw *at Mobile Bay, and retired from the navy with the rank of captain in 1881.*

NEW ORLEANS, April 27, 1862

We arrived here two days ago, after what was "the most desperate fight and greatest naval achievement on record," so every one says. Wednesday night, April 23, we were ordered to lead the way, and be ready to run by the forts at two o'clock in the morning; and at two o'clock precisely the signal was made from the *Hartford* to "get underweigh."

Captain Harrison paid me the compliment of letting me pilot the vessel, and though it was a starlight night we were not discovered until we were well under the forts; then they opened a tremendous fire on us. I was very anxious, for the steering of the vessel being under my charge gave me really the whole management of her. The *Cayuga* received the first fire, and the air was filled with shells and explosions which almost blinded me as I stood on the forecastle trying to see my way, for I had never been up the river before. I soon saw that the guns of the forts were all aimed for the mid-stream, so I steered close under the walls of Fort St. Philip, and although our masts and rigging got badly shot through, our hull was but little damaged.

After passing the last battery and thinking we were clear, I looked back for some of our vessels, and my heart jumped up into my mouth, when I found I could not see a *single one*. I thought they all must have been sunk by the forts. Then looking ahead I saw eleven of the enemy's gunboats coming down upon us, and it seemed as if we were "*gone*" sure. Three of these made a dash to board us, but a heavy charge from our eleven-inch gun settled the *Gov. Moore*, which was one of them. A ram, the *Manasses*, in attempting to butt us, just missed our stern, and we soon settled the third fellow's "hash." Just then some of our gunboats, which had passed the forts, came up, and then all sorts of things happened. There was the wildest excitement all round. The *Varuna* fired a broadside into *us*, instead of the enemy. Another of our gunboats attacked one of the *Cayuga's* prizes,—I shouted out, "Don't fire into that ship, she has surrendered!" Three of the enemy's ships had surrendered to us before any of our vessels appeared, but when they did come up we all pitched in, and settled the eleven rebel vessels, in about twenty minutes. Our short fight with the *Gov. Moore*—it used to be the *Morgan* —was very exciting. We were alongside of each other, and had both fired our guns, and it all depended on which should get reloaded first. The large forward gun on the *Gov. Moore* was a ten-inch shell, ours an eleven-inch, and we were so near, they were almost muzzle to muzzle.

Ours was fired first, and Beverly Kennon, the Captain of the *Gov. Moore*, is now a prisoner on board the *Cayuga*. He tells me our shot was the one that ruined him,—disabled his vessel, capsized his gun, and killed thirteen of the gun's crew. Beverly Kennon used to be an officer in our navy.

The *Cayuga* still led the way up the river, and at daylight we discovered a regiment of infantry encamped on shore. As we were very close in, I shouted to them to come on board and deliver up their arms, or we would blow them all to pieces. It seemed rather odd for a regiment on shore to be surrendering to a ship! They hauled down their colors, and the Colonel and command came on board and gave themselves up as prisoners of war. The regiment was called the Chalmette Regiment, and has been quite a famous one. The officers were released on parole and allowed them to retain their side-arms, all except one Captain, who I discovered was from New Hampshire. His name is Hickery, and he came from Portsmouth. I took his sword away from him and have kept it.

The next thing that happened was the sinking of the *Varuna,* which had been disabled by one of the enemy's vessels running into her. Soon after this the Commodore came up in the *Hartford* and ordered us all to anchor and take a little rest before attacking New Orleans, which was now within twenty miles.

By this time our ship had received forty-two shots in masts and hull, and six of our men had been wounded; one of the boys had to have one of his legs cut off. All this time, night and day, firerafts and ships loaded with burning cotton had been coming down the river and surrounded us everywhere. Besides these, the bombardment was continuous and perfectly awful. I do not believe there ever was anything like it before, and I never expect to see such a sight again. The river and shore were one blaze, and the sounds and explosions were terrific. Nothing I could say would give you any idea of these last twenty-four hours!

The next morning, April 25, we all got underweigh again, the *Cayuga* still leading, and at about nine o'clock New Orleans hove in sight. We called all hands and gave three cheers and a tiger!

There were two more fortifications still between us and New Orleans, called the Chalmette Batteries, but Captain Bailey thought they could not be of much account, and that we had best push on. When we arrived in sight of these batteries, no flag floated over them, and there was not a man to be seen—nothing but the guns, which seemed abandoned. In fact, though, there were a lot of treacherous rascals concealed in these batteries, and when we had come close enough to make them feel sure they could sink us, they opened a heavy fire. We gave them back as well as we could, but they were too much for one gunboat; so, after getting hit fourteen times, and the shot and shell striking all about us, we decided not to advance any further until some of the ships came up. Soon we had the *Hartford* on one side and the *Pensacola* on the other, and then the rebel battery was silenced very quick.

After this, there were no further obstacles between us and the city, and the fleet were soon anchored before it. The Commodore ordered Captain Bailey to go on shore, and demand its surrender, and he asked me to go with him. We took just a boat and a boat's crew, with a flag of truce, and started off. When we reached the wharf there were no officials to be seen; no one received us, although the whole city was watching our movements, and the levee was crowded in spite of a heavy rain-storm. Among the crowd were many women and children, and the women were shaking rebel flags, and being rude and noisy.

They were all shouting and hooting as we stepped on shore, but at last a man, who, I think, was a German, offered to show us the way to the councilroom, where we should find the mayor of the city.

As we advanced, the mob followed us in a very excited state. They gave three cheers for Jeff Davis and Beauregard, and three groans for Lincoln. Then they began to throw things at us, and shout, "Hang them!" "Hang them!" We both thought we were in a *bad fix*, but there was nothing for us to do, but just go on.

We reached the city hall, though, in safety, and there we found the mayor and council. They seemed in a very solemn state of mind, though I must say, from what they said, they did not impress me as having much *mind* about anything, and certainly not much sense. The mayor said *he* had nothing to do with the city, as it was under martial law, and we were obliged to wait till General Lovell could arrive.

In about half an hour this gentleman appeared. He was very pompous in his manner and silly and wiry in his remarks. He had about fifteen thousand troops under his command, and said he would "never surrender," but would withdraw his troops from the city as soon as possible, when the city would fall into the hands of the mayor and he could do as he pleased with it.

The mob outside had by this time become perfectly infuriated. They kicked at the doors and swore they would have us out and hang us! Of course Captain Bailey and I *felt per-*

fectly at our ease all this while! Indeed, every person about us, who had any sense of responsibility, was frightened for our safety. As soon as the mob found out that General Lovell was not going to surrender, they swore they would have us out anyway; but Pierre Soule and some others went out and made speeches to them, and kept them on one side of the building, while we went out the other, and were driven to the wharf in a close carriage. Finally we got on board ship all right; but of all the blackguarding I ever heard in my life that mob gave us the worst.

—BELKNAP, ed., *Letters of Capt. Geo. Hamilton Perkins*

3. NEW ORLEANS FALLS TO THE YANKEES

Farragut's fleet appeared before New Orleans about noon of April 25. The Confederate General Lovell had already fled, the coal, cotton, and ships at the levee were ablaze, the city in a state of excitement bordering on frenzy. On the afternoon of the twenty-fifth the city surrendered; on May 1 General Benjamin Butler arrived and the control of the city was turned over to the army.

Butler's rule in New Orleans was highhanded, and possibly corrupt; it is still an article of faith throughout the South that Butler stole all the silver spoons in the city! The insults which Union soldiers suffered from the men and women of New Orleans impelled Butler to issue his notorious Order No. 28. Although there appeared to be justification for this order, it excited dismay in the North and indignation abroad. Palmerston, who made it the occasion for an unofficial protest, had to be put in his place by Minister Adams.

We give here Julia LeGrand's account of the surrender of New Orleans; General Butler's Order; Palmerston's protest against the Order; and Secretary Moran's account of the exchange between Palmerston and Adams.

A. JULIA LEGRAND DESCRIBES THE SURRENDER OF NEW ORLEANS

Behold, what has now come to the city! Never can I forget the day that the alarm bell rang. I never felt so hopeless and forsaken. The wretched generals, left here with our troops, ran away and left them. Lovell knew not what to do; some say he was intoxicated, some say frightened. Of course the greatest confusion prevailed, and every hour, indeed almost every moment, brought its dreadful rumor. After it was known that the gunboats had actually passed, the whole city, both camp and street, was a scene of wild confusion. *The Women only* did not seem afraid. They were all in favor of resistance, *no matter how hopeless* that resistance might be.

The second day matters wore a more favorable aspect, and the Mayor and the City Council assumed a dignified position toward the enemy. Flag Officer Farragut demanded the unconditional surrender of the town. He was told that as brute force, and brute force only, gave him the power that he might come and take it. He then demanded that we, with our own hands, pull down the flag of Louisiana. This I am happy to say, was refused. Four days we waited, expecting to be shelled, but he concluded to waive the point; so he marched in his marines with two cannons and our flag was taken down and the old stars and stripes lifted in a dead silence. We made a great mistake here; we should have shot the man that brought down the flag, and as long as there was a house-top in the city left, it should have been hoisted. The French and English lay in the Gulf and a French frigate came up the river to protect French subjects.

Farragut allowed the women and children but forty-eight hours to leave the city, but the foreign consuls demanded a much longer time to move the people of their respective nations. If we had been staunch and dared them to shell, the Confederacy would have been saved. The brutal threat would never have been carried out, for England and France would never have allowed it. The delay would have enabled us to finish our boat, and besides a resistance would have showed the enemy and foreign nations, too, what stuff we were made of and how very much we were in earnest.

I never wished anything so much in my life as for resistance here. I felt no fear—only excitement. The ladies of the town signed a paper, praying that it should never be given up. We went down to put our names on the list, and met the marines marching up to the City Hall with their cannon in front of them. The blood boiled in my veins—I felt no fear—only anger. I forgot myself and called out several times: "Gentlemen, don't let the State Flag come down," and, "Oh, how can you men stand it?" Mrs. Norton was afraid of me, I believe, for she hurried me off.

I have forgotten to mention—at first, the Germans at the fort mutinied and turned their guns on their officers. In the first place, several gunboats had passed the fort at night because a traitor had failed to give the signal. He was tried and shot, and Duncan telegraphed to the city that no more should pass—then came a report that the Yankee vessels were out of powder and coal and they could not get back to their transports which they had expected to follow them. We were quite jubilant at the idea of keeping them in a sort of imprisonment, and this we could have done but for the German mutineers. The wives of these men were allowed to visit the fort, and they represented the uselessness of the struggle, because the city had already surrendered. They were told, too, that Duncan intended to blow up the fort over their heads rather than surrender. So they spiked their cannon and threatened the lives of their officers and then the Yankee fleet poured up.

These people have complimented us highly. To quell a small "rebellion," they have made preparations enough to conquer a world. This is a most cowardly struggle—these people can do nothing without gunboats. Beauregard in Tennessee can get no battle from them where they are protected by these huge block steamers. These passive instruments do their fighting for them. It is at best a dastardly way to fight. We should have had gunboats if the Government had been efficient, wise or earnest. We have lost our city, the key to this great valley, and my opinion is that we will never, never get it more, except by treaty.

—ROWLAND AND CROXALL, eds., *The Journal of Julia Le-Grand*

B. GENERAL BUTLER OUTRAGES THE MORAL SENTIMENT OF THE WORLD

ORDER NO. 28

Headquarters, Department of Gulf
New-Orleans, May 15 [1862]

As officers and soldiers of the United States have been subject to repeated insults from women calling themselves ladies, of New-Orleans, in return for the most scrupulous non-interference and courtesy on our part, it is ordered hereafter, when any female shall by mere gesture or movement insult, or show contempt for any officers or soldiers of the

United States, she shall be regarded and held liable to be treated as a woman about town plying her avocation.

By command of Major-Gen. BUTLER

GEO. C. STRONG, A. A. G.

—MOORE, ed., *The Rebellion Record*

C. PALMERSTON PROTESTS BUTLER'S PROCLAMATION

Brocket, 11 June, 1862

Confidential.

My Dear Sir,—I cannot refrain from taking the liberty of saying to you that it is difficult if not impossible to express adequately the disgust which must be excited in the mind of every honorable man by the general order of General Butler given in the inclosed extract from yesterday's *Times.* Even when a town is taken by assault it is the practice of the Commander of the conquering army to protect to his utmost the inhabitants and especially the female part of them, and I will venture to say that no example can be found in the history of civilized nations till the publication of this order, of a general guilty in cold blood of so infamous an act as deliberately to hand over the female inhabitants of a conquered city to the unbridled license of an unrestrained soldiery.

If the Federal Government chuses to be served by men capable of such revolting outrages, they must submit to abide by the deserved opinion which mankind will form of their conduct. My dear Sir, Yours faithfully,

PALMERSTON

—*Proceedings of the Massachusetts Historical Society*

D. "A MORE IMPUDENT PROCEEDING CANNOT BE DISCOVERED"

Wednesday, June 25, 1862. A serious correspondence has just taken place between Lord Palmerston and Mr. Adams which is destined to become historical. His Lordship with that impudence that only an Englishman can be guilty of wrote a private and confidential note to Mr. Adams on the 11th Inst., about Gen'l Butler's late order at New Orleans in which he said he could not "express adequately the disgust which must be excited in the mind of every honorable man" at that regulation "of a General guilty of so infamous an act as to deliberately hand over the female inhabitants of a conquered city to the unbridled license of an unrestrained soldiery."

Mr. Adams replied on the 12th refusing to recognise the note, unless he was assured it was official, and expressing surprise at such an unusual proceeding on the part of the Prime Minister, instead of the Minister of Foreign Affairs,—with whom Foreign Ministers carry on their correspondence on matters connected with the duties of their Mission.

To this Ld. Palmerston rejoined on the 15th by saying his note was official.

In the interview Mr. Adams saw Lord Russell and stated the case to him. He was much offended, & said Ld. Palmerston had exceeded the bounds of good behavior—a thing he had often done of late, and had no business to write such a note.

Mr. Adams renewed the subject on the 16th and after commenting on the nature of his Lordship's letter, said that "the Government he represented would visit with just indignation upon its servants abroad their tame submission to receive under the seal of privacy any indignity which it might be the disposition of the servants of any sovereign however exalted, to offer to it in that form."

Palmerston with his usual insolence answered this in a sophistical strain on the 19th, & on the 20th Mr. Adams closed the affair by a note in which he said he would decline while here to receive such communications from him. This severe reprimand had its intended effect, and his Lordship has remained silent under it.

The incident placed Mr. Adams in a very critical position, and for a few days we considered things so serious as to strongly anticipate a sudden rupture of all intercourse. Fortunately, Mr. Adams' decision saved such a result.

A more impudent proceeding than that of Palmerston in this case cannot be discovered in the whole range of political life. Knowing the brutality of his own officers and soldiers he readily imagined ours of the same stamp, and insolently presumed to lecture Mr. Adams on a thing which was not his business. His ill-manners were properly rebuked. American soldiers, he will find out, are not beasts, altho' English soldiers are; and he will also learn that it is only a debased mind that would construe Gen'l Butler's order as he has done. He has defined it according to English practice. That is all.

This proceeding of Lord Palmerston is one of the most remarkable, and probably without a parallel in Diplomatic history. Mr. Adams was placed in a most awkward predica-

ment & managed the affair with great skill. When the story shall be made public, it will create astonishment in certain quarters. Had not Palmerston taken the course he did, it was Mr. Adams' intention to have published the correspondence privately and sent it to his colleagues so that they might know what they might at some time or other expect from his Lordship should he remain in office.
—WALLACE AND GILLESPIE, eds., *The Journal of Benjamin Moran*

4. ELLET'S STEAM RAMS SMASH THE CONFEDERATE FLEET AT MEMPHIS

At the beginning of the war Commander John Rodgers was instructed to prepare a naval force for the Mississippi. He bought three river steamers, authorized J. B. Eads of St. Louis to build seven gunboats, built a fleet of mortar boats, and prepared to co-operate with the army in its advance into the South. In January 1862 he was succeeded in command by Flag Officer Andrew Foote, who took part in the Fort Donelson expedition, and after the reduction of that fort preached in Cairo on the text "Ye believe in God; believe also in me." Foote's river fleet ran the batteries of Island No. 10 and helped reduce that island and New Madrid. Foote was disabled in action, and command of the river fleet was turned over to Captain Charles H. Davis.

Meantime an army engineer, Colonel Charles Ellet, had been authorized by the War Department to build a fleet of rams for service on the Mississippi. Two of these, the Queen of the West and the Monarch, participated in the attack on the Confederate River Defense Fleet at Memphis, on June 6. Ellet himself was mortally wounded in action.

The story of the battle is told by Colonel Ellet's brother, Alfred W. Ellet, who succeeded to the command of the rams.

Upon the startling verification of his neglected admonitions afforded by the *Merrimac,* Mr. Ellet was called to the War Department, and, after a short conference with Secretary Stanton, was given authority to purchase, refit, man, and command, with the rank of colonel, any number of vessels deemed, in his judgment, necessary to meet and defeat the fleet of iron-clad rams then known to be in process of construction on the lower Mississippi River.

Never was work more promptly or more effectually performed. Colonel Ellet purchased a number of steamboats at different points on the Ohio River, the best he could find in the short time at his disposal. He took some old and nearly worn-out boats, strengthened their hulls and bows with heavy timbers, raised bulkheads of timber around the boilers, and started them down the river to Cairo as fast as they could be got off the ways. They were the *Dick Fulton, Lancaster, Lioness, Mingo, Monarch, Queen of the West, Samson, Switzerland,* and *T. D. Horner.*

While the work was progressing, and before any one of the rams was nearly completed, information was received that the Confederate fleet had come out from under the batteries of Fort Pillow, had attacked our fleet of gun-boats lying near Craighead's Point, and had disabled two of them. Colonel Ellet received most urgent telegrams from the Secretary of War to hurry the rams forward at the earliest possible moment. In consequence of these demands, five of them were immediately dispatched down the river under my command, work upon them being continued as they proceeded and for several days after their arrival at Fort Pillow. The other rams followed, and about the 25th of May Colonel Ellet joined the fleet on board the *Switzerland,* and the ram-fleet was now ready for action.

Colonel Ellet at once conferred with Flag-Officer Charles H. Davis on the propriety of passing Fort Pillow, and engaging the enemy's fleet wherever found. Flag-Officer Davis did not approve the plan suggested, but offered no objection to Colonel Ellet's trying the experiment. Accordingly, immediate preparations were begun for running the batteries with the entire ram-fleet.

During this period of preparation, constant watch was kept upon the fort and the enemy's fleet. On the night of the 4th of June [1862] I crossed the timber point in front of the fort, and reported to the colonel commanding my conviction that the fort was being evacuated. About 2 o'clock in the morning I obtained permission, with many words of caution from Colonel Ellet, to run down opposite the fort in a yawl and, after lying off in order to become assured that the place was abandoned, to land, with the assurance that the rams would follow in case my yawl did not return before daylight. I landed with my little band, only to find the fort entirely deserted; and after planting the National colors upon the ruins of one of the magazines, we sat down to wait for the coming of daylight and the rams. They came, followed by the entire fleet, and after a short stop all proceeded down the river, the rams taking the lead, to Fort Randolph, where they delayed long enough to plant the National flag and to examine the abandoned fortifications, the gun-boats at this point taking the advance.

After leaving Fort Randolph the ram-fleet proceeded without incident to within about twenty-five miles of Memphis, where they all rounded to and tied up for the night, with orders of sailing issued to each commander; instructions to be ready to round out at the signal from the flag-ship, and that "each boat should go into the anticipated fight in the same order they maintained in sailing." At the first dawn of day (June 6th) the fleet moved down the river, and at sunrise the flag-ship rounded the bend at "Paddy's Hen and Chickens," and immediately after came in sight of the Federal gun-boats anchored in line across the river, about a mile above Memphis. Colonel Ellet promptly signaled his vessels to tie up on the Arkansas shore, in the order of their sailing, as he desired to confer with Flag-Officer Davis before passing further.

The *Queen of the West* came to first, followed by the *Monarch* and other rams in regular succession. The *Queen of the West* had made the land, and passed out line to make fast; the *Monarch* was closing in just above, but had not yet touched the shore. At this moment, and as the full orb of the sun rose above the horizon, the report of a gun was heard from around the point and down the river. It was the first gun from the Confederate River Defense Fleet moving to attack us. Colonel Ellet was standing on the hurricane-deck of the *Queen of the West*. He immediately sprang forward, and, waving his hat to attract my attention, called out: "It is a gun from the enemy! Round out and follow me! Now is our chance!" Without a moment's delay, the *Queen* moved out gracefully, and the *Monarch* followed. By this time our gun-boats had opened their batteries, and the reports of guns on both sides were heavy and rapid.

The morning was beautifully clear and perfectly still; a heavy wall of smoke was formed across the river, so that the position of our gun-boats could only be seen by the flashes of their guns. The *Queen* plunged forward, under a full head of steam, right into this wall of smoke and was lost sight of, her position being known only by her tall pipes which reached above the smoke. The *Monarch*, following, was greeted, while passing the gun-boats, with wild huzzas from our gallant tars. When freed from the smoke, those of us who were on the *Monarch* could see Colonel Ellet's tall and commanding form still standing on the hurricane-deck, waving his hat to show me which one of the enemy's vessels he desired the *Monarch* to attack,—namely, the *General Price,* which was on the right wing of their advancing line. For himself he selected the *General Lovell* and directed the *Queen* straight for her, she being about the middle of the enemy's advancing line.

The two vessels came toward each other in most gallant style, head to head, prow to prow; and had they met in that way, it is most likely that both vessels would have gone down. But at the critical moment the *General Lovell* began to turn; and that moment sealed her fate. The *Queen* came on and plunged straight into the *Lovell's* exposed broadside; the vessel was cut almost in two and disappeared under the dark waters in less time than it takes to tell the story. The *Monarch* next struck the *General Price* a glancing blow which cut her starboard wheel clean off, and completely disabled her from further participation in the fight.

As soon as the *Queen* was freed from the wreck of the sinking *Lovell,* and before she could recover headway, she was attacked on both sides by the enemy's vessels, the *Beauregard* on one side and the *Sumter* on the other. In the mêlée one of the wheels of the *Queen* was disabled so that she could not use it, and Colonel Ellet, while still standing on the hurricane-deck to view the effects of the encounter with the *General Lovell,* received a pistol-ball in his knee, and, lying prone on the deck, gave orders for the *Queen* to be run on her one remaining wheel to the Arkansas shore, whither she was soon followed by the *General Price* in a sinking condition. Colonel Ellet sent an officer and squad of men to meet the *General Price* upon her making the shore, and received her entire crew as prisoners of war. By this time consternation had seized upon the enemy's fleet, and all had turned to escape. The fight had drifted down the river, below the city.

The *Monarch,* as soon as she could recover headway after her conflict with the *General Price,* drove down upon the *Beauregard,* which vessel, after her encounter with the *Queen of the West,* was endeavoring to escape. She was thwarted by the *Monarch* coming down upon her with a well-directed blow which crushed in her side and completely disabled her from further hope of escape. Men on the deck waved a white flag in token of surrender, and the *Monarch* passed on down to intercept the *Little Rebel,* the enemy's flag-ship. She had received some injury from our gun-boats' fire, and was making for the Arkansas shore, which she reached at the moment when the *Monarch*, with very slight headway, pushed her hard and fast aground; her crew sprang upon shore and ran into the thick woods, making their escape. Leaving the *Little Rebel* fast aground, the *Monarch* turned her attention to the sinking *Beauregard,* taking the vessel in tow, and making prisoners of her crew. The *Beauregard* was towed by the *Monarch* to the bar, where she sank to her boiler-deck and finally became a total loss.

The others of the enemy's fleet were run ashore and fired by the crews before they escaped into the adjoining Arkansas swamps. The *Jeff. Thompson* burned and blew up with a tremendous report; the *General Bragg* was secured by our gun-boats before the fire gained headway, and was saved. The *Van Dorn* alone made her escape, and was afterward burned by the enemy at Liverpool Landing, upon the approach of two of our rams in Yazoo River, in order to prevent her from falling into our hands. Two other rebel boats were burned at the same time,—the *Polk* and the *Livingston.* . . .

Colonel Ellet did not rely on heavy ordnance, and did not recommend arming his rams. At the battle of Memphis there were no firearms on board the ram-fleet except a few short carbines and some pocket-revolvers; his reliance was upon the prow of his vessel. He desired, as far as possible, to protect the vulnerable parts of his ship, the boilers and engines, and with simply enough men as crew to handle the boat with certainty and dispatch, to run the gauntlet of any fire that could be precipitated upon him, and drive his ram deep into his unwieldy adversary. At the battle of Memphis the enemy concentrated their fire upon the *Queen of the West* and the *Monarch,* but their missiles passed harmlessly by. Not a splinter was raised off either of the rams, and not a man sustained the slightest injury except Colonel Ellet, whose fatal wound was received from a pistol-ball.

The battle of Memphis was, in many respects, one of the most remarkable naval victories on record. For *two* unarmed, frail, wooden river steamboats, with barely men enough on board to handle the machinery and keep the furnace-fires burning, to rush to the front, between two hostile fleets, and *into* the enemy's advancing line of eight iron-clad, heavily armed, and fully manned steam-rams, sinking one, disabling and capturing three, and carrying consternation to the others, was a sight never before witnessed.

The River Defense Fleet was composed of strong, well-built ocean steamers, well strengthened and protected with railroad iron so as to be almost invulnerable to shot when advancing. The intention was apparent to repeat at Memphis the tactics which had proved so successful at Fort Pillow,—to ram the Union gun-boats at anchor; and had the rams *Queen of the West* and *Monarch* got run through the line of gun-boats and attacked the Defense Fleet as it approached, sinking, disabling, and scattering its vessels, and thus removing the fight half a mile below, the result of the affair might have been very different. The Defense Fleet was advancing up-stream, thus exposing the strongest and best-protected portions of each vessel; the gun-boats, relying upon their guns, were at anchor, with their sterns, their most vulnerable part, pointing down-stream and consequently exposed to the tremendous attack of the enemy. Had the Confederate commanders trusted only to the strength of their vessels, ceased firing, and with every pound of steam on plunged at full speed into our anchored gun-boat fleet, who could doubt what the result would have been?

—ELLET, "Ellet and His Steam-Rams at Memphis"

5. ATTACK AND REPULSE AT BATTERY WAGNER

Throughout the war the Federals tried to capture Charleston; not until Sherman's march through South Carolina forced its evacuation did they succeed. The first major effort came in June 1862, when General Hunter landed on James Island but failed to take the fort of Secessionville (June 16). The second came on April 7, 1863, when an attempt by the Ironsides and eight monitors to break through the harbor defenses and bombard the city was repulsed with heavy loss. The third, and most substantial, was the occupation of Morris Island in the summer of 1863, and the series of land and sea assaults on Battery Wagner that finally forced its surrender.

Early in July General Gillmore, Commander of the Department of the South, landed on the southern end of Morris Island, carried the Confederate lines by assault, and advanced on Fort (or Battery) Wagner, at the northern tip of the island and only a mile from Fort Sumter. Instead of attacking at once Gillmore waited until the following day; by that time the Confederates were ready for him, and repulsed the assault. The second attack came on July 18. The advance was led by Colonel Shaw of the famous 54th Massachusetts (Colored)

Regiment; supporting him were Colonel Barton's 3rd New Hampshire, Colonel Putnam's 7th New Hampshire, Colonel Jackson's 76th Pennsylvania, Colonel Commager's 67th Ohio, and others. The attack was almost—but not quite—successful. After its failure the navy took over. In early September there was a 42-hour bombardment which eventually forced the Confederates to evacuate. Yet Charleston was still impregnable.

We give here the New York Tribune *account of the assault of July 18.*

Morris Island, S. C., July 19, 1863

Again Fort Wagner has been assaulted and again we have been repulsed, and with, I regret to say, a much more formidable loss in killed, wounded, and missing than in the first attempt. . . .

In the assault of the eleventh instant, but one brigade, and that a very small one, under the command of General Strong, were engaged; in that of last evening a whole division, consisting of three full brigades, were drawn out in line to take part in the action, but on account of some misunderstanding of orders, but two actually participated in the fight. . . .

General Gillmore designed to commence the bombardment of the Fort at daylight yesterday morning, but on account of a terrific thunderstorm, which commenced early in the evening and continued until morning, delaying the work of the engineers and dampening the ammunition, the action did not open until half-past twelve. At that hour Admiral Dahlgren signalled that he was ready, and in a few moments the *Montauk,* (his flag-ship,) the *Ironsides,* the *Catskill,* the *Nantucket,* the *Weehawken,* and the *Patapsco* moved into line in the order in which I have named them, and commenced hurling their heaviest shot and shell around, upon, and within the Fort, and, with intervals of but a very few minutes, continued this terrible fire until one hour after the sun had gone down. During all the afternoon the iron fleet lay about one mile off from the Fort, but just at the close of the engagement, and but a few moments before the first assault was made by General Strong, the Admiral ran the *Montauk* directly under the guns of Fort Wagner, and, within two hundred and eighty yards, fired round after round from his fifteen-inch gun, sending, as every shot struck, vast clouds of sand, mud, and timber high up into the air, making one huge sand-heap of that portion of the Fort facing the sea, and dismounting two of the heaviest guns. . . .

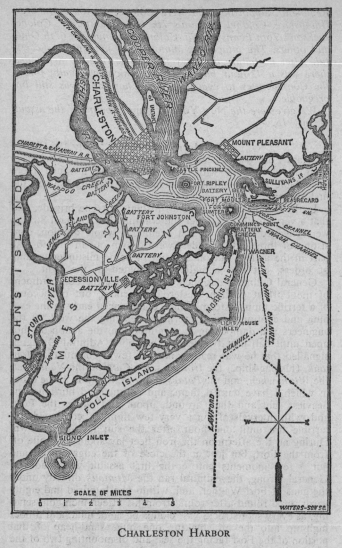

CHARLESTON HARBOR

The firing was almost entirely from our own side. With the most powerful glass, but very few men could be seen in the Fort. At half-past two, a shot from one of our guns on the left cut the halyards on the flag-staff and brought the rebel flag fluttering to the ground.

In a moment, almost before we had begun to ask ourselves whether they had really lowered their flag, and were upon the point of surrendering or not, the old red battle-flag, which the army of the Potomac has so often had defiantly shaken in its face, was run up about ten feet above the parapet, a little cluster of men rallied around it, cheered, waved their hats, and then disappeared, and were not again seen during the day. Fort Sumter, the moment the rebel flag came to the ground, sent a shot over our heads to assure us that it had been lowered by accident and not by design. In this shot she also desired us to distinctly understand that before Fort Wagner surrendered, she herself would have to be consulted. With the exception of this little episode, almost profound silence, so far as the rebel garrison themselves could maintain it, prevailed within the Fort. . . .

For eight hours the monitors and the *Ironsides* have kept up a continuous fire, and Fort Wagner has not yet surrendered. For eight hours fifty-four guns from the land-batteries have hurled their shot and shell within her walls, and still she flaunts the red battle-flag in our face.

"Something must be done, and that, too, quickly, or in a few days we shall have the whole army in Virginia upon us," said an officer high in command. "We *must* storm the Fort to-night and carry it at the point of the bayonet!"

In a few moments signals are made from the top of the look-out, and soon generals and colonels commanding divisions and brigades were seen galloping to the headquarters of the Commanding General. . . . Officers shout, bugles sound, the word of command is given, and soon the soldiers around, upon, and under the sand-hills of Morris Island spring from their hiding-places, fall into line, march to the beach, are organized into new brigades, and in solid column stand ready to move to the deadly assault.

Not in widely extended battle-line, with cavalry and artillery at supporting distances, but in solid regimental column, on the hard ocean beach, for half a mile before reaching the Fort, in plain view of the enemy, did these three brigades move to their appointed work.

General Strong, who has so frequently since his arrival in this department braved death in its many forms of attack, was assigned to the command of the First brigade. Colonel Putnam of the Seventh New-Hampshire . . . took command of the Second, and General Stevenson the Third, constituting the reserve. The Fifty-fourth Massachusetts, (colored regiment,) Colonel Shaw, was the advanced regiment in the First brigade, and the Second South-Carolina, (Negro,) Colonel Montgomery, was the last regiment of the reserve. . . .

Just as darkness began to close in upon the scene of the afternoon and the evening, General Strong rode to the front and ordered his brigade . . . to advance to the assault. At the instant, the line was seen slowly advancing in the dusk toward the Fort, and before a double-quick had been ordered, a tremendous fire from the barbette guns on Fort Sumter, from the batteries on Cumming's Point, and from all the guns on Fort Wagner, opened upon it. The guns from Wagner swept the beach, and those from Sumter and Cumming's Point enfiladed it on the left. In the midst of this terrible shower of shot and shell they pushed their way, reached the Fort, portions of the Fifty-fourth Massachusetts, the Sixth Connecticut, and the Forty-eighth New-York dashed through the ditches, gained the parapet, and engaged in a hand-to-hand fight with the enemy, and for nearly half an hour held their ground, and did not fall back until nearly every commissioned officer was shot down. . . .

When the brigade made the assault General Strong gallantly rode at its head. When it fell back, broken, torn, and bleeding, Major Plimpton of the Third New-Hampshire was the highest commissioned officer to command it. General Strong, Colonel Shaw, Colonel Chatfield, Colonel Barton, Colonel Green, Colonel Jackson, all had fallen; and the list I send you will tell how many other brave officers fell with them. . . . It must be remembered, too, that this assault was made in the night—a very dark night—even the light of the stars was obscured by the blackness of a heavy thunder-storm, and the enemy could be distinguished from our own men only by the light of bursting shell and the flash of the howitzer and the musket. The Fifty-fourth Massachusetts, (Negro,) whom copperhead officers would have called cowardly if they had stormed and carried the gates of hell, went boldly into battle, for the second time, commanded by their brave Colonel, but came out of it led by no higher officer than the boy, Lieutenant Higginson.

The First brigade, under the lead of General Strong, failed to take the Fort. It was now the turn of Colonel Putnam, commanding the Second brigade, composed of the Seventh

New-Hampshire, the Sixty-second Ohio, Colonel Vorhees, the Sixty-seventh Ohio, Colonel Commager, and the One Hundredth New-York, Colonel Dandy, to make the attempt. But alas! the task was too much for him. Through the same terrible fire he led his men to, over, and into the Fort, and for an hour held one half of it, fighting every moment of that time with the utmost desperation, and, as with the First brigade, it was not until he himself fell killed, and nearly all his officers wounded, and no reënforcements arriving, that his men fell back, and the rebel shout and cheer of victory was heard above the roar of Sumter and the guns from Cumming's Point. . . .

Without a doubt, many of our men fell from our own fire. The darkness was so intense, the roar of artillery so loud, the flight of grape and canister shot so rapid and destructive, that it was absolutely impossible to preserve order in the ranks of individual companies, to say nothing of the regiments.

More than half the time we were in the Fort, the fight was simply a hand-to-hand one, as the wounds received by many clearly indicate. Some have sword-thrusts, some are hacked on the head, some are stabbed with bayonets, and a few were knocked down with the butt-end of muskets, but recovered in time to get away with swollen heads. There was terrible fighting to get into the Fort, and terrible fighting to get out of it. The cowardly stood no better chance for their lives than the fearless. Even if they surrendered, the shell of Sumter were thickly falling around them in the darkness, and, as prisoners, they could not be safe, until victory, decisive and unquestioned, rested with one or the other belligerent.

The battle is over; it is midnight; the ocean beach is crowded with the dead, the dying, and the wounded. It is with difficulty you can urge your horse through to Lighthouse Inlet. Faint lights are glimmering in the sandholes and rifle-pits to the right, as you pass down the beach. In these holes many a poor wounded and bleeding soldier has lain down to his last sleep. Friends are bending over them to staunch their wounds, or bind up their shattered limbs, but the deathly glare from sunken eyes tells that their kind services are all in vain. —"The Attack on Fort Wagner, *New York Tribune* Account"

6. FARRAGUT DAMNS THE TORPEDOES AT MOBILE BAY

With the fall of New Orleans and the conquest of much of the Tennessee-Mississippi area by Federal arms, Mobile Bay assumed a position of primary importance to Confederate economy. Farragut had wanted to attack Mobile early in 1863, but had been held to Mississippi River duty by the demands of the Vicksburg and Port Hudson campaigns. After the successful reduction of Port Hudson he sailed for New York for a rest; then in January 1864 he was ordered back to the Gulf and authorized to reduce Mobile. This task required the support of land forces, and not until August 1864 were these available. Early on the morning of August 5 Farragut gave the signal for the attack, and his flotilla steamed up the broad bay, the Brooklyn *in the lead.*

John Kinney, who tells the story of that famous day, was lieutenant and signal officer on the flagship Hartford.

Except for what Farragut had already accomplished on the Mississippi, it would have been considered a foolhardy experiment for wooden vessels to attempt to pass so close to one of the strongest forts on the coast; but when to the forts were added the knowledge of the strength of the ram and the supposed deadly character of the torpedoes, it may be imagined that the coming event impressed the person taking his first glimpse of naval warfare as decidedly hazardous and unpleasant. So daring an attempt was never made in any country but ours, and was never successfully made by any commander except Farragut, who, in this, as in his previous exploits in passing the forts of the Mississippi, proved himself one of the greatest naval commanders the world has ever seen. . . .

After the reconnoissance the final council of war was held on board the *Hartford*, when the positions of the various vessels were assigned, and the order of the line was arranged. Unfortunately Captain (now Rear-Admiral) Thornton A. Jenkins was absent, his vessel, the *Richmond*, having been unavoidably delayed at Pensacola, whither she had gone for coal and to escort the monitor *Tecumseh*. Had he been present he certainly would have been selected to take the lead, in which event the perilous halt of the next day would not have occurred. Much against his own wish Admiral Farragut yielded to the unanimous advice of his captains and gave up his original determination of placing his flagship in the advance, and, in the uncertainty as to the arrival of the *Richmond*, assigned the *Brooklyn*, Captain Alden, to that position. . . .

It was the admiral's desire and intention to get underway by daylight, to take advantage of the inflowing tide; but a dense fog came on after midnight and delayed the work of forming the line.

It was a weird sight as the big ships "balanced to partners," the dim outlines slowly emerging like phantoms in the fog. The vessels were lashed together in pairs, fastened side by side by huge cables. All the vessels had been stripped for the fight, the top-hamper being left at Pensacola, and the starboard boats being either left behind or towed on the port side. The admiral's steam-launch, the *Lovall*, named after his son, steamed alongside the flag-ship on the port side.

It was a quarter of six o'clock before the fleet was in motion. Meantime a light breeze had scattered the fog and left a clear, sunny August day. The line moved slowly, and it was an hour after starting before the opening gun was fired. This was a 15-inch shell from the *Tecumseh*, and it exploded over Fort Morgan. Half an hour afterward the fleet came within range and the firing from the starboard vessels became general, the fort and the Confederate fleet replying. The fleet took position across the entrance to the bay and raked the advance vessels fore and aft, doing great damage, to which it was for a time impossible to make effective reply. Gradually the fleet came into close quarters with Fort Morgan, and the firing on both sides became terrific. The wooden vessels moved more rapidly than the monitors, and as the *Brooklyn* came opposite the fort, and approached the torpedo line, she came nearly alongside the armored monitor. To have kept on would have been to take the lead, with the ram *Tennessee* approaching and with the unknown danger of the torpedoes underneath. At this critical moment the *Brooklyn* halted and began backing and signaling with the army signals. The *Hartford* was immediately behind and the following vessels were in close proximity, and the sudden stopping of the *Brooklyn* threatened to bring the whole fleet into collision, while the strong inflowing tide was likely to carry some of the vessels to the shore under the guns of the fort. . . .

Nearly every man had his watch in his hand awaiting the first shot. To us, ignorant of everything going on above, every minute seemed an hour, and there was a feeling of great relief when the boom of the *Tecumseh's* first gun was heard. Presently one or two of our forward guns opened, and we could hear the distant sound of the guns of the fort in reply. Soon the cannon-balls began to crash through the deck above us, and then the thunder of our whole broadside of nine Dahlgren guns kept the vessel in a quiver. But as yet no wounded were sent down, and we knew we were still at comparatively long range. In the intense excitement of the occasion it seemed that hours had passed, but it was just twenty minutes from the time we went below, when an officer shouted down the hatchway: "Send up an army signal officer immediately; the *Brooklyn* is signaling."

In a moment the writer was on deck, where he found the situation as already described. Running on to the forecastle, he hastily took the *Brooklyn's* message, which imparted the unnecessary information, "The monitors are right ahead; we cannot go on without passing them."

The reply was sent at once from the admiral, "Order the monitors ahead and go on."

But still the *Brooklyn* halted, while, to add to the horror of the situation, the monitor *Tecumseh*, a few hundred yards in the advance, suddenly careened to one side and almost instantly sank to the bottom, carrying with her Captain Tunis A. M. Craven and the greater part of his crew, numbering in all 114 officers and men. . . . Meantime the *Brooklyn* failed to go ahead, and the whole fleet became a stationary point-blank target for the guns of Fort Morgan and of the rebel vessels. It was during these few perilous moments that the most fatal work of the day was done to the fleet.

Owing to the *Hartford's* position, only her few bow guns could be used, while a deadly rain of shot and shell was falling on her, and her men were being cut down by scores, unable to make reply. The sight on deck was sickening beyond the power of words to portray. Shot after shot came through the side, mowing down the men, deluging the decks with blood, and scattering mangled fragments of humanity so thickly that it was difficult to stand on the deck, so slippery was it. The old expressions of the "scuppers running blood," "the slippery deck," etc., give but the faintest idea of the spectacle on the *Hartford*. The bodies of the dead were placed in a long row on the port side, while the wounded were sent below until the surgeons' quarters would hold no more. A solid shot coming through the bow struck a gunner on the neck, completely severing head from body. One poor fellow lost both legs by a cannon-ball; as he fell he threw up both arms, just in time to have them also carried away by another shot. At one gun, all the crew on one side were swept down by a shot which came crashing through the bulwarks. A shell burst between the two forward guns in charge of Lieutenant Tyson, killing and wounding fifteen men. The mast upon which the writer was perched was twice struck, once slightly, and again just below the foretop by a heavy shell, from a rifle on the Confederate gun-boat *Selma*. . . . Looking out over the water, it was easy to trace the course of every shot, both from the guns of the *Hartford* and from the Confederate fleet.

Another signal message from the *Brooklyn* told of the sinking of the *Tecumseh*, a fact known already, and another order to "go on" was given and was not obeyed.

Soon after the fight began, Admiral Farragut, finding that the low-hanging smoke from the guns interfered with his view from the deck, went up the rigging of the mainmast as far as the futtock-shrouds, immediately below the maintop. The pilot, Martin Freeman, was in the top directly overhead, and the fleet-captain was on the deck below. Seeing the admiral in this exposed position, where, if wounded, he would be killed by falling to the deck, Fleet-Captain Drayton ordered Knowles, the signal-quartermaster, to fasten a rope around him so that he would be prevented from falling.

Finding that the *Brooklyn* failed to obey his orders, the admiral hurriedly inquired of the pilot if there was sufficient depth of water for the *Hartford* to pass to the left of the *Brooklyn*. Receiving an affirmative reply, he said: "I will take the lead," and immediately ordered the *Hartford* ahead at full speed. As he passed the *Brooklyn* a voice warned him of the torpedoes, to which he returned the contemptuous answer, "Damn the torpedoes." This is the current story, and may have some basis of truth. But as a matter of fact, there was never a moment when the din of the battle would not have drowned any attempt at conversation between the two ships, and while it is quite probable that the admiral made the remark it is doubtful if he shouted it to the *Brooklyn*.

Then was witnessed the remarkable sight of the *Hartford* and her consort, the *Metacomet*, passing over the dreaded torpedo ground and rushing ahead far in advance of the rest of the fleet, the extrication of which from the confusion caused by the *Brooklyn's* halt required many minutes of valuable time. The *Hartford* was now moving over what is called the "middle ground," with shallow water on either side, so that it was impossible to move except as the channel permitted. Taking advantage of the situation, the Confederate gun-boat *Selma* kept directly in front of the flagship and raked her fore and aft, doing more damage in reality than all the rest of the enemy's fleet. The other gun-boats, the *Gaines* and the *Morgan*, were in shallow water on our starboard bow, but they received more damage from the *Hartford's* broadsides than they were able to inflict. Meanwhile the ram *Tennessee*, which up to this time had contented herself with simply firing at the approaching fleet, started for the *Hartford*, apparently with the intention of striking her amidships. She came on perhaps for half a mile, never approaching nearer than a hundred yards, and then suddenly turned and made for the fleet, which, still in front of the fort, was gradually getting straightened out and following the *Hartford*. This change of course on the part of the ram has always been a mystery. The captain of the ram, in papers published since the war, denies that any such move was made, but it was witnessed by the entire fleet, and is mentioned by both Admiral Farragut and Fleet-Captain Drayton in their official reports.

The *Hartford* had now run a mile inside the bay, and was suffering chiefly from the raking fire of the *Selma*, which was unquestionably managed more skillfully than any other Confederate vessel. Captain (now Admiral) Jouett, commanding the *Hartford's* escort, the *Metacomet*, repeatedly asked permission of the admiral to cut loose and take care of the *Selma*, and finally, at five minutes past eight, consent was given. In an instant the cables binding the two vessels were cut, and the *Metacomet*, the fastest vessel in the fleet, bounded ahead. The *Selma* was no match for her, and, recognizing her danger, endeavored to retreat up the bay. But she was speedily overhauled, and when a shot had wounded her captain and killed her first lieutenant she surrendered. Before this the *Gaines* had been crippled by the splendid marksmanship of the *Hartford's* gunners, and had run aground under the guns of the fort, where she was shortly afterward set on fire, the crew escaping to the shore. The gunboat *Morgan*, after grounding for a few moments on the shoals to the east of Navy Cove, retreated to the shallow water near the fort, whence she escaped the following night to Mobile. The *Hartford*, having reached the deep water of the bay, about three miles north of Dauphine Island, came to anchor.

Let us now return to the other vessels of the fleet, which we left massed in front of Fort Morgan by the remarkable action of the *Brooklyn* in stopping and refusing to move ahead. When the ram *Tennessee* turned away from the *Hartford*, as narrated, she made for the fleet, and in their crowded and confused condition it seemed to be a matter of no difficulty to pick out whatever victims the Confederate commander

(Admiral Franklin Buchanan) might desire, as he had done in 1861 when commanding the *Merrimac* in Hampton Roads. Before he could reach them the line had been straightened, and the leading vessels had passed the fort. . . .

Whatever damage was done by the *Tennessee* to the fleet in passing the fort was by the occasional discharge of her guns. She failed to strike a single one of the Union vessels, but was herself run into by the *Monongahela*, Captain Strong, at full speed. . . . The *Monongahela* was no match for the *Tennessee*, but she had been strengthened by an artificial iron prow, and being one of the fastest—or rather, *least slow*—of the fleet, was expected to act as a ram if opportunity offered. Captain Strong waited for no orders, but seeing the huge ram coming for the fleet left his place in the line and attacked her. . . .

At last all the fleet passed the fort, and while the ram ran under its guns the vessels made their way to the *Hartford* and dropped their anchors, except the *Metacomet, Port Royal, Kennebec,* and *Itasca.* After the forts were passed, the three last named had cut loose from their escorts and gone to aid the *Metacomet* in her struggle with the *Selma* and *Morgan.* . . .

The *Tennessee,* after remaining near Fort Morgan while the fleet had made its way four miles above to its anchorage,— certainly as much as half an hour,—had suddenly decided to settle at once the question of the control of the bay. Single-handed she came on to meet the whole fleet, consisting now of ten wooden vessels and the three monitors. At that time the *Tennessee* was believed to be the strongest vessel afloat, and the safety with which she carried her crew during the battle proved that she was virtually invulnerable. Fortunately for the Union fleet she was weakly handled, and at the end fell a victim to a stupendous blunder in her construction—the failure to protect her rudder-chains.

The spectacle afforded the Confederate soldiers, who crowded the ramparts of the two forts,—the fleet now being out of range,—was such as has very rarely been furnished in the history of the world. To the looker-on it seemed as if the fleet was at the mercy of the ram, for the monitors, which were expected to be the chief defense, were so destitute of speed and so difficult to manoeuvre that it seemed an easy task for the *Tennessee* to avoid them and sink the wooden vessels in detail.

Because of the slowness of the monitors, Admiral Farragut selected the fastest of the wooden vessels to begin the attack.

While the navy signals for a general attack of the enemy were being prepared, the *Monongahela* (Captain Strong) and the *Lackawanna* (Captain Marchand) were ordered by the more rapid signal system of the army to "run down the ram," the order being immediately repeated to the monitors.

The *Monongahela,* with her prow already somewhat weakened by the previous attempt to ram, at once took the lead, as she had not yet come to anchor. The ram from the first headed for the *Hartford,* and paid no attention to her assailants, except with her guns. The *Monongahela,* going at full speed, struck the *Tennessee* amidships—a blow that would have sunk almost any vessel of the Union navy, but which inflicted not the slightest damage on the solid iron hull of the ram. (After the surrender it was almost impossible to tell where the attacking vessel had struck.) Her own iron prow and cutwater were carried away, and she was otherwise badly damaged about the stern by the collision.

The *Lackawanna* was close behind and delivered a similar blow with her wooden bow, simply causing the ram to lurch slightly to one side. As the vessels separated the *Lackawanna* swung alongside the ram, which sent two shots through her and kept on her course for the *Hartford,* which was now the next vessel in the attack. The two flag-ships approached each other, bow to bow, iron against oak. It was impossible for the *Hartford,* with her lack of speed, to circle around and strike the ram on the side; her only safety was in keeping pointed directly for the bow of her assailant. The other vessels of the fleet were unable to do anything for the defense of the admiral except to train their guns on the ram, on which as yet they had not the slightest effect.

It was a thrilling moment for the fleet, for it was evident that if the ram could strike the *Hartford* the latter must sink. But for the two vessels to strike fairly, bows on, would probably have involved the destruction of both, for the ram must have penetrated so far into the wooden ship that as the *Hartford* filled and sank she would have carried the ram under water. Whether for this reason or for some other, as the two vessels came together the *Tennessee* slightly changed her course, the port bow of the *Hartford* met the port bow of the ram, and the ships grated against each other as they passed. The *Hartford* poured her whole port broadside against the ram, but the solid shot merely dented the side and bounded into the air. The ram tried to return the salute, but owing to defective primers only one gun was discharged. This sent a shell through the berth-deck, killing five men and wounding eight. The muzzle of the gun was so close to the *Hartford* that the powder blackened her side.

The admiral stood on the quarter-deck when the vessels came together, and as he saw the result he jumped on to the port-quarter rail, holding to the mizzen-rigging, a position from which he might have jumped to the deck of the ram as she passed. Seeing him in this position, and fearing for his safety, Flag-Lieutenant Watson slipped a rope around him and secured it to the rigging, so that during the fight the admiral was twice "lashed to the rigging," each time by devoted officers who knew better than to consult him before acting. Fleet-Captain Drayton had hurried to the bow of the *Hartford* as the collision was seen to be inevitable, and expressed keen satisfaction when the ram avoided a direct blow.

The *Tennessee* now became the target for the whole fleet, all the vessels of which were making toward her, pounding her with shot, and trying to run her down. As the *Hartford* turned to make for her again, we ran in front of the *Lackawanna*, which had already turned and was moving under full headway with the same object. She struck us on our starboard side, amidships, crushing halfway through, knocking two port-holes into one, upsetting one of the Dahlgren guns, and creating general consternation. For a time it was thought that we must sink, and the cry rang out over the deck: "Save the admiral! Save the admiral!" The port boats were ordered lowered, and in their haste some of the sailors cut the "falls," and two of the cutters dropped into the water wrong side up, and floated astern. But the admiral sprang into the starboard mizzen-rigging, looked over the side of the ship, and, finding there were still a few inches to spare above the water's edge, instantly ordered the ship ahead again at full speed, after the ram.

The unfortunate *Lackawanna*, which had struck the ram a second blow, was making for her once more, and, singularly enough, again came up on our starboard side, and another collision seemed imminent. And now the admiral became a trifle excited. He had no idea of whipping the rebels to be himself sunk by a friend, nor did he realize at the moment that the *Hartford* was as much to blame as the *Lackawanna*. Turning to the writer he inquired. "Can you say 'For God's sake' by signal?"

"Yes, sir," was the reply.

"Then say to the *Lackawanna*, 'For God's sake get out of our way and anchor!' "

In my haste to send the message, I brought the end of

my signal flag-staff down with considerable violence upon the head of the admiral, who was standing nearer than I thought, causing him to wince perceptibly. It was a hasty message, for the fault was equally divided, each ship being too eager to reach the enemy, and it turned out all right, by a fortunate accident, that Captain Marchand never received it. The army signal officer on the *Lackawanna*, Lieutenant Myron Adams (now pastor of Plymouth Congregational Church in Rochester, N.Y.) had taken his station in the foretop, and just as he received the first five words, "For God's sake get out" —the wind flirted the large United States flag at the masthead around him, so that he was unable to read the conclusion of the message.

The remainder of the story is soon told. As the *Tennessee* left the *Hartford* she became the target of the entire fleet, and at last the concentration of solid shot from so many guns began to tell. The flag-staff was shot away, the smoke-stack was riddled with holes, and finally disappeared. The monitor *Chickasaw*, Lieutenant-Commander Perkins, succeeded in coming up astern and began pounding away with 11-inch solid shot, and one shot from a 15-inch gun of the *Manhattan* crushed into the side sufficiently to prove that a few more such shots would have made the casemate untenable. Finally, one of the *Chickasaw's* shots cut the rudder-chain of the ram and she would no longer mind her helm. At this time, as Admiral Farragut says in his report, "she was sore beset. The *Chickasaw* was pounding away at her stern, the *Ossipee* was approaching her at full speed, and the *Monongahela*, *Lackawanna*, and this ship were bearing down upon her, determined upon her destruction." From the time the *Hartford* struck her she did not fire a gun. Finally the Confederate admiral, Buchanan, was severely wounded by an iron splinter or a piece of shell, and just as the *Ossipee* was about to strike her the *Tennessee* displayed a white flag, hoisted on an improvised staff through the grating over her deck. The *Ossipee* (Captain Le Roy) reversed her engine, but was so near that a harmless collision was inevitable.

Suddenly the terrific cannonading ceased, and from every ship rang out cheer after cheer, as the weary men realized that at last the ram was conquered and the day won.

—KINNEY, "Farragut at Mobile Bay"

7. LIEUTENANT CUSHING TORPEDOES THE *ALBEMARLE*

In a war memorable for many deeds of daring, there were few more spectacular than the destruction of the Confederate ram Albemarle *by young Lieutenant William B. Cushing. A "bilged" midshipman, Cushing had managed to get into the navy as master's mate, then proceeded to distinguish himself by one heroic deed after another. He captured numerous prizes, destroyed saltworks along the Atlantic coast, captured enemy officers and couriers, and in the fall of 1864 conceived and carried through the plan to torpedo the* Albemarle. *This formidable vessel, which had already destroyed several Federal ships, was then lying at Plymouth, North Carolina, some eight miles up the Roanoke River.*

Cushing himself tells us how he attacked and sank her. For this act, of which the captain of the Albemarle *said, "a more gallant thing was not done during the war," Cushing was made lieutenant commander, at twenty-two, and given a formal vote of thanks by Congress.*

Finding some boats building for picket duty, I selected two, and proceeded to fit them out. They were open launches, about thirty feet in length, with small engines, and propelled by a screw. A 12-pounder howitzer was fitted to the bow of each, and a boom was rigged out, some fourteen feet in length, swinging by a goose-neck hinge to the bluff of the bow. A topping lift, carried to a stanchion inboard, raised or lowered it, and the torpedo was fitted into an iron slide at the end. This was intended to be detached from the boom by means of a heel-jigger leading inboard, and to be exploded by another line, connecting with a pin, which held a grape shot over a nipple and cap. The torpedo was the invention of Engineer Lay of the navy, and was introduced by Chief-Engineer Wood. Everything being completed, we started to the southward, taking the boats through the canals to Chesapeake Bay. My best boat having been lost in going down to Norfolk, I proceeded with the other through the Chesapeake and Albemarle canal. Half-way through, the canal was filled up, but finding a small creek that emptied into it below the obstruction, I endeavored to feel my way through. Encountering a mill-dam, we waited for high water, and ran the launch over it; below she grounded, but I got a flat-boat, and, taking out gun and coal, succeeded in two days in getting her through. Passing with but seven men through the canal, where for thirty miles there was no guard or Union inhabitant, I reached the sound, and ran before a gale of wind to Roanoke Island.

In the middle of the night I steamed off into the darkness, and in the morning was out of sight. Fifty miles up the sound I found the fleet anchored off the mouth of the river, and awaiting the ram's appearance. Here, for the first time, I disclosed to my officers and men our object, and told them that they were at liberty to go or not, as they pleased. These, seven in number, all volunteered. One of them, Mr. Howarth of the *Monticello*, had been with me repeatedly in expeditions of peril.

The Roanoke River is a stream averaging 150 yards in width, and quite deep. Eight miles from the mouth was the town of Plymouth, where the ram was moored. Several thousand soldiers occupied town and forts, and held both banks of the stream. A mile below the ram was the wreck of the *Southfield*, with hurricane deck above water, and on this a guard was stationed. Thus it seemed impossible to surprise them, or to attack with hope of success.

Impossibilities are for the timid: we determined to overcome all obstacles. On the night of the 27th of October we entered the river, taking in tow a small cutter with a few men, whose duty was to dash aboard the wreck of the *Southfield* at the first hail, and prevent a rocket from being ignited.

We passed within thirty feet of the pickets without discovery, and neared the vessel. I now thought that it might be better to board her, and "take her alive," having in the two boats twenty men well armed with revolvers, cutlasses, and hand-grenades. To be sure, there were ten times our number on the ship and thousands near by; but a surprise is everything, and I thought if her fasts were cut at the instant of boarding, we might overcome those on board, take her into the stream, and use her iron sides to protect us afterward from the forts. Knowing the town, I concluded to land at the lower wharf, creep around, and suddenly dash aboard from the bank; but just as I was sheering in close to the wharf, a hail came, sharp and quick, from the ironclad, and in an instant was repeated. I at once directed the cutter to cast off, and go down to capture the guard left in our rear, and, ordering all steam, went at the dark mountain of iron in front of us. A heavy fire was at once opened upon us, not only from the ship, but from men stationed on the shore. This did not disable us, and we neared them rapidly. A large fire now blazed upon the bank, and by its light I discovered the unfortunate fact that there was a circle of logs around the *Albemarle*, boomed well out from her side, with the very intention of preventing the action of torpedoes. To examine them more closely, I ran alongside until amidships, received the enemy's fire, and sheered off for the purpose of turning, a hundred yards away, and going at the booms squarely, at right angles, trusting to their having been long enough in the water to have become slimy—in which case my boat, under full headway, would bump up against them and slip over into the pen with the ram. This was my only chance of success, and once over the obstruction my boat would never get out again. As I turned, the whole back of my coat was torn out by buckshot, and the sole of my shoe was carried away. The fire was very severe.

In a lull of the firing, the captain hailed us, again demanding what boat it was. All my men gave comical answers, and mine was a dose of canister from the howitzer. In another instant we had struck the logs and were over, with headway nearly gone, slowly forging up under the enemy's quarterport. Ten feet from us the muzzle of a rifle gun looked into our faces, and every word of command on board was distinctly heard.

My clothing was perforated with bullets as I stood in the bow, the heeljigger in my right hand and the exploding-line in the left. We were near enough then, and I ordered the boom lowered until the forward motion of the launch carried the torpedo under the ram's overhang. A strong pull of the detaching-line, a moment's waiting for the torpedo to rise under the hull, and I hauled in the left hand, just cut by a bullet.

The explosion took place at the same instant that 100 pounds of grape, at 10 feet range, crashed among us, and the dense mass of water thrown out by the torpedo came down with choking weight upon us.

—CUSHING, "The Destruction of the 'Albemarle'"

8. THE CONFEDERATES REPULSE AN ATTACK ON FORT FISHER

With the fall of Mobile and the effective bottling up of Charleston, Wilmington, on the Cape Fear River, was the only major port still in Confederate hands, and all through 1864

*it was the chief haven of blockade-runners. With the advance
of Sherman northward through the Carolinas it became important to capture the Cape Fear entrance and Wilmington
in order to afford a supply base for the Union armies. The
mouth of the Cape Fear was controlled by Fort Fisher, whose
ramparts faced both the land and the sea. The first attack on
Fort Fisher came on December 24, 1864, from a fleet of 60
vessels under Admiral Porter.*

*The attack, as the Confederate commander, Colonel William
Lamb, here tells us, was a failure. Yet the Confederate defense, too, was something of a failure. While the defenders of
the fort acquitted themselves gloriously, General Bragg with
3,500 men at near-by Wilmington made no move to strike at
the troops that General Butler had landed for the attack but
allowed them to get off unmolested.*

Saturday, December 24, was one of those perfect winter
days that are occasionally experienced in the latitude of the
Cape Fear. The gale which had backed around from the northeast to the southwest had subsided the day before, and was
followed by a dead calm. The air was balmy for winter, and
the sun shone with almost Indian summer warmth, and the
deep blue sea was calm as a lake, and broke lazily on the bar
and beach.

A grander sight than the approach of Porter's formidable
armada towards the fort was never witnessed on our coast.
With the rising sun out of old ocean, there came upon the
horizon, one after another, the vessels of the fleet, the grand
frigates leading the van, followed by the ironclads,—more
than fifty men-of-war, heading for the Confederate stronghold. At nine o'clock the men were beat to quarters, and
silently the detachments stood by their guns. On the vessels
came, growing larger and more imposing as the distance
lessened between them and the resolute men who had rallied
to defend their homes. The *Minnesota, Colorado,* and *Wa-
bash,* came grandly on, floating fortresses, each mounting
more guns than all the batteries on the land, and the two first,
combined, carrying more shot and shell than all the magazines
in the fort contained. From the left salient to the mound
Fort Fisher had 44 heavy guns, and not over 3600 shot and
shell, exclusive of grape and shrapnel. The Armstrong gun
had only one dozen rounds of fixed ammunition, and no other
projectile could be used in its delicate grooves. The order
was given to fire no shot until the Columbiad at headquarters
fired, and then each gun that bore on a vessel could be fired

every thirty minutes, and not oftener except by special order; unless an attempt was made to cross the bar, when every gun bearing on it should be fired as rapidly as accuracy would permit, the smooth bores at ricochet.

Before coming within range, the wooden ships slowed down and the great *Ironsides* and three monitors slowly forged ahead, coming within less than a mile of the northeast salient, the other ships taking position to the right and left, the line extending more than a mile. As the *Ironsides* took her position she ran out her starboard guns, a flash was seen from the forward one, then a puff of white smoke, a deep boom was heard and over our heads came an 11-inch shell, which I saw distinctly in its passage across our flag-staff, past which it exploded harmlessly with a sharp report. . . .

This was the commencement of the most terrific bombardment from the fleet which war had ever witnessed. Ship after ship discharged its broadsides, every description of deadly missile, from a 3-inch rifle-bolt to a 15-inch shell flying widely into and over the fort until the garrison flag-staff was shattered. Most of the firing seemed directed towards it, and as it stood in the centre of the parade, all these bolts fell harmless as to human life, many of the shells, especially the rifle-shots, going over the fort and into the river in the rear. The dead calm which prevailed in nature caused the smoke to hang around the hulls of the vessels, so enveloping them as to prevent the effect of the shots our gunners were allowed to fire from being seen. It was two hours after the bombardment commenced before the flag was shot away, and in that time, although thousands of shot and shell were hurled at us, I had heard of no casualty in the works. For those two hours I had remained on the parapet of the sea face watching intently for any effort to cross the bar, and in all that time only one shell had exploded near enough to endanger my life. In the rear of the flag-staff the wooden quarters of the garrison were situated, and these were soon set on fire by the bursting shells and more than half of them were consumed. The day being balmy, most of the men had left their overcoats and blankets in their bunks and these were consumed. There was quite a quantity of naval stores,—tar and pitch near these quarters,—and they took fire and made an imposing bonfire in sympathy with the occasion.

As soon as the garrison flag was shot away, finding the staff so split and shivered that it could not be raised, I sent word to Captain Munn to raise the flag on the mound. It seems the halyards had gotten unreeved and it was necessary to climb the staff to fasten the flag. Private Christopher C. Bland volunteered for the service, and climbed the staff under heavy fire and secured the battle-flag to the masthead. At once a terrific fire was poured on the mound and the lower end of the flag having been cut loose, again that heroic soldier repeated the daring act amid the cheers of the garrison, and securely fastened the flag where it floated in triumph, although torn and rent by fragments of shell, until the victory was won. While this was being done I went to the left salient and planted a company battle-flag on the extreme left. My two hours' experience had taught me that the fleet would concentrate a heavy fire on it, and I wanted to put it where it would do the most good by causing the least harm. For five hours this tremendous hail of shot and shell was poured upon the devoted works, but with little effect. At 5:30 P.M the fleet withdrew. . . .

In the first day's fight I had about one half of the quarters burned, three gun carriages disabled, a light artillery caisson exploded, large quantities of the earthworks torn and ploughed up, with some revetments broken and splintered, but not a single bomb proof or magazine injured. Only twenty-three men wounded, one mortally, three seriously and nineteen slightly.

Never, since the invention of gunpowder, was there so much harmlessly expended, as in the first day's attack on Fort Fisher. All was quiet during the night, but next morning, Christmas Day, at about ten o'clock, the great fleet again moved in towards the fort, being reënforced by another monitor and some additional wooden ships of war. At half-past ten the *Ironsides* opened and the fleet commenced an incessant bombardment, if possible, more noisy and furious than that of the preceding day. At about two o'clock several of the frigates came up to the bar and lowered boats, apparently to sound the entrance, but a heavy fire was immediately directed against them and they were promptly driven out. At half-past three a very gallant attempt was made by a number of barges to sound the Carolina shoals, south of the mound. A few shots from Battery Buchanan, the naval battery in my command, first cut the flag from a barge and then cut the barge in two, causing the remainder, after rescuing their comrades, to retreat rapidly.

My two 7-inch Brooke rifles both exploded in the afternoon of this day. Being manned by a detachment of sailors and situated opposite to the bar I had given the officer in charge discretion to fire upon the vessels which had approached the bar, and his fire had been more rapid than from any other guns, and with this disastrous result, the explosion wounding a number of men.

Strange as it may appear, no attempt to pass the fort was made by any of the fleet, and none except the armored vessels came within a mile of the heaviest guns. Whether the smoke obscured the fort or the gunners were untrained, it is hard to account for the wild firing of these two days. If they had tried to miss the guns on the sea face they could not have succeeded better, no gun or carriage on that face being injured by the fire of the fleet; the only two guns disabled were the two Brooke rifles, which exploded. All the disabled guns were on the land face, which was enfiladed by the fleet as well as subjected to the direct fire of the armored ships, which came within half a mile of the fort. With the exception of the Brooke Battery, and some special firing on vessels, the firing of the fort was slower and more deliberate than on the previous day, only 600 shot and shell being expended. The temptation to concentrate the whole of the available fire of the fort on a single frigate and drive her out or destroy her was very great, as I found the garrison were disappointed at having no trophy for the first day's engagement, but I had a limited supply of ammunition, and did not know when it could be replenished. Already on the first day I had expended nearly one sixth of my supply in merely keeping the men in heart by an occasional shot. I could easily have fired every shot and shell away the first day. Admiral Porter expended nearly all of his ammunition in the two days' bombardment. The *Minnesota* fired 1982 shots and the *Colorado* 1569 shots, a total of these two frigates of 3551, about as many as we had in all the batteries of Fort Fisher. On both days I fired the last gun to let our naval visitors know that we had another shot in the locker. In the bombardment the second day, most of the remaining quarters were destroyed, more of the earthworks were displaced, but none seriously damaged, and five guns were disabled by the enemy. The greatest penetration noticed (from 15-inch shell) was five feet perpendicularly.

During the day a large fleet of transports were seen up the beach, and the Federals landed a large force at Battery Anderson, three miles from the fort. At 4:30 P.M. sharpshooters were seen on our left flank and they fired upon our gunners from the old quarters across the causeway, and killed a young courier, who had been, without my knowledge, sent out of the fort, capturing his horse. I had two pieces of artillery run out of the sallyport, and a few discharges of canister stopped the annoyance. At this time, on the 25th, my effective force had been increased to 921 regulars and 450 Junior Reserves, total 1371. At 5:30 P.M. a most furious enfilading fire against the land face and palisade line commenced, certainly never surpassed in warfare, 130 shot and shell per minute, more than two every second. I ordered my men to protect themselves behind the traverses, and removed all extra men from the chambers, with the order the moment the firing stopped, to rally to the ramparts without further orders.

As soon as this fire commenced, I saw a heavy line of skirmishers advancing on our works. Just as the naval fire ceased, the guns were manned and opened with grape and canister, and as it was becoming too dark to see the advance from the ramparts, I threw 800 men and boys behind the palisades, which had been scarcely injured. I never shall forget the gallant youths whom I rallied that night to meet the enemy. I had ordered all to man the parapets as soon as the naval fire ceased, as I supposed it would be followed by an assault. I thought the Junior Reserves were coming up too slowly and I called out rather impatiently, "Don't be cowards, boys," when one manly little officer rushed over the work followed by his companions, shouting, "We are no cowards, colonel," and manned the palisades. I ordered them not to fire until the enemy were within a few feet of the palisades, but the whistle of bullets from Butler's skirmish line so excited them that in spite of my orders they kept up a fusilade until the Federals retired.

I was determined to meet the enemy at the palisade, feeling confident the few who reached it would be easily captured or repulsed. I had the land guns, heavy and light, manned, with orders to fire grape and canister whenever they saw an advance in force, and the operators stood ready, upon my order, to explode some of the sub-terra torpedoes. I stood upon the parapet to the left of the centre sallyport, after giving directions in person to the officers on the land front. The fleet had ceased except an occasional shell from the ironclads down this face. The Federal sharpshooters were firing wildly in the darkness at our ramparts, but the bullets which were few and far between, went harmlessly over our heads. My plan was to open with grape and canister on the assaulting column, and when its front reached the palisade, to open the infantry fire and explode a line of torpedoes in their rear to stop the reënforcing line. I am confident this would have resulted in a repulse of the main body and the capture of the first line. But Butler, with wise discretion, determined not to assault. There were not enough Federal troops landed to have stormed our palisade that Christmas night. If the assaulting column could have reached the comparatively uninjured palisades through the fire of canister and grape, the explosion and infantry fire would have resulted in their capture or destruction.

My only uneasiness was from a boat attack in the rear between the Mound and Battery Buchanan, where a thousand sailors and marines could have landed with little opposition at that time and attacked us in the rear. About 3 A.M. it was reported that such an advance was being made and I sent Major Reilly with two companies to repulse them, following shortly after in person with a third company to reënforce him. A heavy wind and rain storm had arisen at midnight, and if such a movement was contemplated, it was abandoned.

Two prisoners from the 142nd New York were captured in our front at night, and next morning a number of new graves were found. Our casualties for the second day were: killed, 3; wounded, mortally, 2; severely, 7; slightly, 26. Total for the two days, 3 killed and 61 wounded.

—LAMB, "The Defence of Fort Fisher"

9. "IT BEAT ANYTHING IN HISTORY"

General Lee had informed the defenders of Fort Fisher that they must hold it at all costs; otherwise he could not continue to subsist his army. For the same reason Grant was determined to reduce it. The repulse of December 24, therefore, was not accepted as final, and preparations were made for a renewal of the attack on a grander scale. On the morning of January 13, 1865, "the most formidable armada the world had ever known"—the words are those of Colonel Lamb—sailed over the horizon, 60 men-of-war under Admiral Porter and transports carrying 8,500 troops under General Terry. To beat off this force Colonel Lamb had some 1,900 men, 44 guns, and inadequate ammunition; that evil genius of the Confederacy, Braxton Bragg, kept his army of 3,500 men safely at Wilmington. The bombardment opened on the thirteenth, and continued without pause through

*the fourteenth. On the fifteenth an assaulting column attacked
the fort from the river shore, and overwhelmed its gallant
defenders. Thus fell the last available Confederate port.*

Our narrator is again the "boy cannoneer," Augustus Buell.

I wouldn't have missed seeing that bombardment of Fort
Fisher for 10 years of my life. It beat anything in history
for weight of ordnance used—even greater than the bombardment of the Sebastopol forts by the English and French
fleets, because the guns we used were so much heavier. I
cannot describe the discharges of those 13 and 15-inch Rodman guns of the monitors, or the explosion of their great
shells in the air over the fort or among its traverses. To me
it seemed like firing meteors out of volcanoes. I had hitherto
thought that the long percussion shell bolt of a four-and-a-
half-inch Rodman siege gun, which I had "gunned" a couple
of times in cannonades in the redan in the early part of the
great siege was a big thing, but now I hauled down my
colors. I would watch the turrets of the monitors through
my glass. They would turn their iron backs on the enemy to
load, and I could distinctly see the big rammer staves come
out of the ports. Then they would wheel round on a line with
the fort, there would be two puffs of blue smoke about the
size of a thunder cloud in June, and then I could see the big
shell make a black streak through the air with a tail of
white smoke behind it—and then would come over the water,
not the quick bark of a field gun, but a slow, quivering,
overpowering roar like an earthquake, and then, away among
the Rebel traverses, there would be another huge ball of
mingled smoke and flame as big as a meeting house. . . .

Imagine a cold, bright day in the middle of January; a low,
sandy coastline, with a dull surf combing up on the beach; a
tremendous fort of the most elaborate construction, with
ramparts in some places 30 feet high; huge bastions every
little way; deep-throated embrasures from which frowned
the muzzles of seven, eight and 10-inch Armstrong and
Brooke rifled cannon and Columbiads; and the doomed flag
of the gallant Confederacy floating defiantly from its tall staff!

Look, then, seaward, and see 60 steam men-of-war
formed in a great arc of a circle, all steaming slowly to their
anchors and rolling great volumes of smoke from their fun-
nels. Inside of this outer arc five or six of those low, black,
sullen monitors "in line abreast," as the sailors called it,
slowly and steadily creeping toward the fort, no visible sign
of life about them, except now and then you could see an

officer's head come up over the breastwork or barbet on top of the turret.

The sullen monitors never said a word till their noses touched the beach, which was as close as they could get to their antagonist, and then—well, the like of it was never seen. From where our transport was anchored it looked as if the *Canonicus,* which was considerably nearer to the fort than any other ship, must be within 400 yards of the northeast main bastion. I kept my glass trained on her all the time. I could see the fire fly from her iron turret, deck and sides when the big bolts from the Rebel guns struck her. It did not seem possible that anything made by human hands could stand it. At this moment the three single-turreted monitors —*Canonicus, Saugus* and *Mahopac*—were in a bunch together, the *Canonicus* in the center and ahead, not 1,200 feet from the great bastion! On one flank, a little farther from the fort, was the double-turreted *Monadnock,* and on the other, still farther out, was a great, enormous mass of iron, flame and smoke, which the old Quartermaster told us was the famous *New Ironsides,* of which we had read so much in the stories of Fort Sumter. The *Ironsides* was a "broadsider," and she had 11-inch guns, of which she carried eight or nine on each side. As her guns were lighter than those of the monitors and mounted in the ordinary way, she could fire much faster than they could, and so she was pretty much a solid mass of flame all the time.

The bombardment lasted from 10 A.M. till past 2 in the afternoon. Meantime quite a force of sailors and marines had been landed below the fort, but they were not at first in sight from our anchorage. By 2 o'clock the fire from the heavy guns of the fort had ceased. Many of them were dismounted, and the shells from the fleet had driven the Confederate Cannoneers to take shelter in their bombproofs. The fleet now suddenly ceased firing and began to blow their steam whistles, which made a din almost equal to the cannonade. This was the signal for assault. At this time the infantry nearest the river had gotten up within 80 or 100 yards of the fort, and in order to get a clear view of the assault the sailors on the transport began to mount into the rigging. "Old Sig" took his station in the maintop, together with First Officer Hanscomb, and by permission of this officer I climbed up too. The ship was rolling considerably, which made the maintop a ticklish place for a landsman. . . .

The right of the line of men-of-war was now hauled in or shortened, the vessels of the right division falling into a second line astern of the center division. Probably 15 minutes elapsed between the blowing of the whistles and the grand advance of the infantry against the north face of the fort. They did not encounter so heavy a fire of musketry at first as I expected to see, but the sailors and marines who were assaulting the sea face got cold lead in big doses. From where we were it looked as if the enemy was concentrating his whole defense on the sea face. In less time than it takes to write it the infantry had mounted the parapet nearest the river and jumped down into the works. We, of course, supposed that this would finish the business, and momentarily expected the tokens of surrender. But we little understood the nature of the fort. It was so traversed and retrenched on the inside that it really amounted to a line of small redoubts inside of one large fortress, and the continuous angry crackle of musketry, with dense volumes of smoke rolling up from the inside, told that the garrison was defending every inch of the works with desperate resolution. At the time this looked like useless slaughter, though in the light of subsequent history it appears that the gallant garrison was holding out in the vain hope that Hoke's column from Wilmington would make a diversion in their favor; though they must have had a queer idea of what would have been involved in an attempt to advance infantry over that narrow sandspit, swept as it was from sea to river by the guns of 60 men-of-war!

However, the struggle inside the great fort went on until it assumed the proportions of a regular battle, lasting until after dark. The monitors kept throwing a shell now and then, but it was dangerous business as our troops had cleaned out about half the enemy's traverses and they were slowly working their way through the others. Darkness did not end the combat, but the fitful flashes kept lighting up the crest of the long sand parapet and revealing the outlines of the traverses and retrenchments inside. The monitors and *New Ironsides* also opened again with shell against the south end of the sea face, from which our sailors and marines had been repulsed, and for half or three-quarters of an hour the sight was indescribably grand. But about this time the wind lulled, so that the smoke did not drift away, and the fort and the monitors lay enveloped in a huge pall, which, added to the gloom of the night, gave a weird effect to the flashes of the 15-inch guns and the blaze of bursting shells. This lasted till about 9 o'clock at night, when the musketry ceased inside the fort, and soon after the ships began signaling with different-colored rockets, which made another beautiful spectacle. There was not much sleep that night. Shortly after the fort surrendered—say about 11 o'clock.

—BUELL, *"The Cannoneer"*

VIII

The Blockade and the Cruisers

WE ARE *not wholly unfamiliar with the subject of this chapter. Our review of fighting along the coast and inland waters introduced us to the blockade, and our survey of British-American relations to the delicate problem of the Confederate cruisers. We record here something of the story of the blockade itself—as distinct from the attack on coastal ports —of blockade-running, and of Confederate warfare on Union shipping on the high seas.*

Lincoln had formally blockaded the whole coast of the Confederacy from the Chesapeake Bay to the Rio Grande by two proclamations of April 1861. We need not rehearse here the vexatious issue of the legality of his proclamations either in American constitutional law or in international law. Suffice it to say that the constitutionality of the blockade was sustained in the Prize Cases, and that foreign governments respected the blockade. More relevant is the question of the effectiveness of the blockade itself. And that is a very difficult question to answer.

To bottle up a dozen major ports and almost 200 minor ports and inlets the Union had, at the outbreak of the war, less than 20 vessels. By 1865 this number had been increased to over 600—and its task correspondingly diminished by the capture of all major ports. The Confederacy, of course, began at once to evade the blockade, and to persuade other nations to co-operate in this, or to break it by intervention. It had no navy with which to challenge Union control of the seas and coastal waters; the cruisers it built abroad were designed rather to prey on Union commerce than to attack Union men-of-war. Four categories of ships engaged in blockade-running: those owned by the Confederate government; those owned by state governments; those owned by private individuals or groups of speculators; and foreign ships. Of these the third and fourth categories were the most important, though government-owned blockade-runners gave a good account of themselves. It has been estimated that altogether some 600 ships were engaged, at one time or another, in the lucrative and exciting business of blockade-running, but this estimate is palpably too low; that there were, altogether, some 8,000 violations of the blockade; and that blockade-runners brought in altogether over 600,000 small arms, 550,000 pairs of shoes, and large quantities of meat, coffee, saltpeter, lead, and other items. At the same time substantial quantities of supplies were brought in from Mexico, across the Rio Grande, and there was at all times a lively trade with the North: General Sherman said that Cincinnati furnished more goods to the Confederacy than Charleston!

All this would indicate that the blockade was but loosely enforced, and it cannot be denied that it was pretty ineffective in 1861 and even in 1862. Thereafter, however—what with the fall of New Orleans and of Fort Royal and the sealing up of other harbors—it became increasingly effective, and the South felt the pinch seriously. It is estimated that the chances of capture were one in ten in 1861, but one in three by 1864, and with the capture of Wilmington in January 1865 blockade-running practically ceased.

What all this adds up to is that the blockade was a decisive factor in Union victory. We cannot say that without it the Confederacy would have won, but it is clear that without it the war would have been greatly prolonged and might have ended in a stalemate. Yet it must be kept in mind that Confederate susceptibility to the blockade was enhanced by several factors, and that the blockade need not have been as injurious as it actually was. First, the Confederacy was unprepared to take advantage of the feebleness of the blockade in 1861; as the Confederates did not anticipate a long war there was no long-range buying program. Second, the blockade sent prices skyrocketing, and the Confederacy was unable to buy all that it might have obtained had it taxed more successfully or controlled prices or raised money abroad. Third, blockade-running was largely a private enterprise, and shipowners imported luxuries rather than war essentials; not until 1864 did the government assume control over it, requiring that every blockade-runner have a permit and allot at least one half of its cargo space to military essentials. Fourth, imports through Mexico and Texas were large—Galveston, for example, remained in Confederate hands—but the Federal victories on the Mississippi nullified this immense advantage.

Lacking a navy, the Confederacy early authorized letters of marque and set about outfitting privateers. Privateering had been outlawed by the Declaration of Paris, of 1856, but the United States was not a signatory to this declaration, and the Confederacy could thus claim some legal right to ignore it. There were perhaps a dozen privateers, and altogether they captured or destroyed 60 Union vessels. Far more important, for offensive purposes, were the cruisers, or commerce destroyers. As we have already seen the Confederate government sent Captain James Bulloch to Britain, at the outbreak of the war, to arrange for the purchase or construction of cruisers and rams. This service he performed with brilliant success. Altogether the Confederacy acquired 18 cruisers, of which the Alabama, the Florida, the Shenandoah, the Georgia, the Sumter, and the Tallahassee were most effective. The results of the depredations of these commerce destroyers upon the American merchant marine were disastrous; not for two generations did the American fleet regain its place on the high seas, and as late as 1910 American-flag merchant ships totaled only one third the tonnage of 1860.

We have given in this chapter something of the story of the blockade and the blockade-runners; a glimpse of privateerings; and an account of war on the high seas.

1. THE UNITED STATES NAVY BLOCKADES THE CONFEDERACY

This general account of the Union blockade is self-explanatory. It is, however, worth underlining one point that our author makes: that the blockade of the Confederacy was "an undertaking without precedent in history." The British blockade of the continent during the Napoleonic Wars had been largely a paper affair and had not presented a task comparable to that which confronted the Navy Department in

1861. It is appropriate to recall, too, what Wait takes for granted, that Gideon Welles was one of the ablest of American Secretaries of the Navy, and that the Navy Department was, throughout the war, well run.

Horatio Wait was a paymaster in the United States Navy.

At the beginning of the war in 1861, a perplexing question arose as to whether it would be best for the government to declare all the Southern ports of entry to be closed, or to proclaim a blockade. . . . The urgency of the case caused President Lincoln to act promptly. On April 19, 1861, six days after the surrender of Fort Sumter, he issued a proclamation declaring a blockade of the entire coast of the Confederacy, from South Carolina to Texas; and on April 27 extended it to cover Virginia and North Carolina, making a coast-line of over three thousand miles to be blockaded, greater in extent than the Atlantic coast of Europe—an undertaking without precedent in history. . . .

When Mr. Lincoln issued this proclamation we had only forty-two ships in commission in our navy. Most of them were absent on foreign stations, and only one efficient warship, the *Brooklyn,* was available for immediate service. The days of paper blockades had long since passed away. The universally recognized rule of international law on this subject was that "blockades, to be binding, must be effectual. There must be a squadron lying off the harbor to be blockaded, and it must be strong enough to constitute an actual blockade of the port. The neutral must have had due notice of its existence, and to affect a neutral vessel she must have been guilty of an act of violation, by passing, or attempting to pass, in or out of the port, with a cargo laden after the commencement of the blockade. The neutral must be ready to prove himself that which he professes to be; therefore he is subject to the right of visitation and search."

A more serious difficulty now presented itself. How was it possible to undertake such a blockade as this, along such a vast extent of coast, when so few ships of any kind were available, without its being open to the charge of being a mere paper blockade? In the early part of the century European powers had attempted to enforce paper blockades, but the same nations were now the first to make merry over the subject of our paper blockade. Some of the most prominent European statesmen publicly declared it a "material impossibility to enforce it." To avoid any chance of technical complications, a special notice was given by our vessels at the entrance of each port actually closed by them, in addition to the general diplomatic notice, so that for a time one warning was allowed every ship touching at a blockaded port before she was liable to capture. Thus each port was brought under the full operation of the proclamation only when it was actually blockaded by one or more armed vessels.

By degrees, as the blockading force was increased, and the blockade became more extended and stringent, it was assumed that the general notice rendered the special notice unnecessary; it was finally discontinued entirely, and capture took place without warning. The magnitude of the task of establishing and maintaining the blockade was not realized by the people generally, public attention being absorbed by the raising of many large armies from the body of the people.

When the Secretary of the Navy asked the principal shipping merchants and shipowners of New York to aid him in procuring vessels for the blockade, it is related that their committees decided that thirty sailing-ships would be needed. As it took over six hundred ships, mostly steamers, to do the work, it is manifest that they had a very faint conception of what was to be done. There were twenty-eight old ships of war lying dismantled at the various navy-yards. Those that were worth repairing were fitted for sea as rapidly as possible. All the available merchant vessels that could be made to carry a battery, including tugs and old New York ferry-boats, were purchased and converted into fighting ships as hastily as the limited facilities of the Northern ports would permit. The scanty resources of the navy-yards were inadequate. All the private ship-yards were crowded with work. There were not enough skilled workmen to meet this sudden demand, and the naval officers found it necessary personally to direct the unskilled artisans, or to assist with their own hands in fitting these nondescript vessels for the mounting and working of heavy guns. As fast as the vessels could be purchased, altered, and equipped, they were stationed along the coast or sent to sea. Many such vessels, by the tact and skill of the officers in charge of them, were made to do good service. One of the most important prizes captured, the steamer *Circassian*, was taken near the harbor of Havana by one of the old Fulton Ferry boats.

The lack of men was as great an embarrassment as the want of vessels. Three hundred and twenty-two officers of the old navy joined the insurgent forces, many of them having already distinguished themselves in service. One of these, Commander John M. Brooke, rendered very important serv-

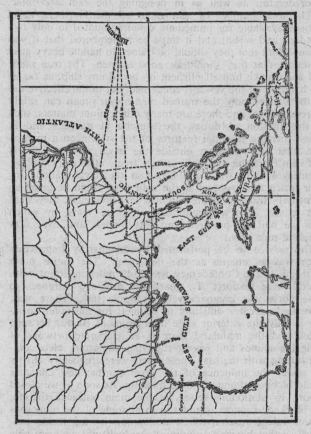

THE BLOCKADED COAST

ices to the Southerners by converting the ten-inch columbiads captured by them into rifled guns. They proved to be
very effective pieces, and were said to be the best converted
guns ever made. He also aided in devising the simplest and
best of the many kinds of torpedoes and fuses used by the
Confederates, as well as in designing the ram *Merrimac*.

The total number of seamen at all the Northern naval
stations available for immediate detail amounted to only two
hundred and seven; and it must be remembered that it was
as important that they should be trained to handle heavy guns
at sea as that they should be good seamen. The true sailor
will soon make himself efficient on board any ship, as far as
the handling of the vessel is concerned; but in the effective use
of the battery only the trained man-o'-war's-man can safely
be relied upon; and there are many other minor matters, such
as the division of duties, the exercise at quarters and in
boats, forming essential features of the system on a man-o'-
war, that are unknown outside the naval service. Officers
and men from the merchant service freely offered themselves.
Gunnery schools were established at the naval stations for
their instruction. As fast as the volunteers could be given an
elementary training in the handling of heavy guns, they were
sent to sea. This was continued for three years, by which
time we had six hundred and fifty vessels and over fifty
thousand men afloat.

The service to be performed by this hastily improvised
force was as unique as the fleet itself. The entire outer
coast-line of the Confederacy was 3549 miles in extent, with
several large seaports. To guard the ordinary entrances to
these ports was comparatively a simple task. There was,
however, a greater difficulty to be met; for the outer coast-
line is only the exterior edge of a series of islands between
which and the mainland there is an elaborate network of
navigable sounds and passages, having numerous inlets communicating with the sea. These inlets were frequently changing under the influence of the great storms; new channels
would be opened and old ones filled up. As soon as we closed
a port, by stationing vessels at the main entrance thereto,
the blockade-runners would slip in at some of the numerous
remote inlets, reaching their destination by the inside passages; so that blockade-running flourished until we were able
to procure as many blockaders as there were channels and
inlets to be guarded. The extreme diversity of the services
required of these blockading vessels made it difficult to obtain ships that could meet the varying necessities. They

must be heavy enough to contend with the enemy's rams, or they would be driven away from the principal ports. They must be light enough to chase and capture the swift block-ade-runners. They must be deep enough in the water to ride out in safety the violent winter gales, and they must be of such light draft as to be able to go near enough to the shal-low inlets to blockade them efficiently.

The blockading fleets of all the important harbors were composed of several very heavy ships, with a few vessels of the lighter class; the rest of the fleet represented some of the other classes needed. But it was impossible to do this along the entire coast, and it sometimes happened that the Con-federate ironclads perversely attacked the lighter vessels, as in the case of the rams at Charleston selecting for their vic-tims the *Mercedita* and the *Keystone State,* instead of the heavier ships; while, on the other hand, the swift blockade-runners disclosed themselves most frequently to the ponder-ous and slow-moving ships that were least able to catch them. . . .

Many of the islands controlled by foreign governments, and lying conveniently near our coast, had good harbors that afforded admirable places of rendezvous for the blockade-runners, where they could safely refit, and remain unmolested until a favorable time came for them to slip out and make a quick run over to the forbidden port; and if unsuccessful in their illicit attempt, they could return as quickly to the protection of the neutral port. As soon as the attention of the naval authorities was drawn to the port of Nassau as a place likely to become the main depot of the contraband trade, Lieutenant-Commander Temple was sent over there priv-ately, in the guise of a civilian, to ascertain the attitude of the officials, the state of public sentiment, and to obtain all the information possible as to the prospects of the blockade-running business. While there he managed to be present at a dinner attended by the local diplomats. There were many indications that the feeling of hostility to the United States was very general. When the old French consul was called upon to express his views, he jumped up, overflowing with an intense desire to express himself in a vigorous manner; but in spite of his profound emotions, all he could manage to utter was: "Ze American people zey sink zey are somewhat, but zey cannot!" This terse presentation of his views was re-ceived with such uproarious applause that Temple was no longer in doubt as to which way the wind blew in that place. . . .

Supplies were brought to the South from various sources, but principally from European ports. At the beginning of the war the blockade-running was carried on from Chesapeake Bay to the mouth of the Rio Grande, by vessels of all sorts, sizes, and nationalities. The steamers formerly engaged in the coasting-trade, that had been interrupted in their regular business by the war, were at first the most successful. The small sailing-vessels did well for some time before the blockade became vigorous; but as the number of our warships increased, the earlier groups of blockade-runners were either captured, destroyed, or drawn off. This diminished the volume of supplies to the Confederates just at the time when the demand was greatly increased by the emergencies of warfare, causing general distress and embarrassment in the Confederacy. Prices reached an unprecedented height. Cotton was as low as eight cents a pound in the Confederacy, as high as sixty cents a pound in England, and over one dollar a pound in New York. The moment this state of affairs became known, the science, ingenuity, and mechanical skill of the British seemed to be directed to the business of violating our blockade. Stock companies were formed, by whom the swiftest steamers in the European merchant service were quickly freighted with the supplies that would bring the highest prices in the Confederacy. Officers of rank in the royal navy, under assumed names; officers of the Confederate navy, who had but just resigned from the United States navy; and adventurous spirits from all quarters, flocked to this new and profitable, though hazardous, occupation. The Confederate government also embarked in the business, procuring swift steamers from English builders, officered with Confederate naval officers, and sailing under the British ensign. They also shipped merchandise in other vessels on government account. . . .

When the blockade-running was at its height, in 1863, a Confederate officer stated that the arrivals and departures were equal to one steamer a day, taking all of the Confederate ports together. Prior to this no such attempts had ever been made to violate a blockade. The industrial necessities of the principal maritime nations stimulated them to unusual efforts, in return for which they looked forward to a rich harvest. The British especially had abundant capital, the finest and swiftest ships ever built, manned by the most energetic seamen. They felt confident that they could monopolize the Southern cotton and the markets of the Confederacy; but when it was found that neither swift steamers, skilled officers, nor desperate efforts could give security to their best investments of capital, and that the perils to their beautiful vessels and precious cargoes increased as fast as their efforts to surmount them, ultimately becoming even greater in proportion than the enormous gains of the traffic when successful, they were at last driven off from our coast entirely, and kept at bay, though armed and supported by the greatest of foreign powers. They finally gave up the business, admitting that the blockade was a success. A Confederate officer stated that when Fort Fisher fell their last port was gone, and blockade-running was at an end.

This signal defeat of that extraordinary development of our Civil War has been spoken of as one of the great moral lessons of our struggle. After the war British officers frankly stated to our naval officers that they considered the blockade and its enforcement the great fact of the war. This was the first time in the history of naval warfare that a steam navy had been kept at sea for so long a period. The Confederates menaced the blockading fleets with nine ironclads which would have been a match for any ironclads in the French or English navy afloat at that time; therefore it becomes manifest that a fleet which could hold in check ironclads, as well as shut out blockade-runners that were the swiftest steamers built at that time, must have combined speed and power to an extent never before displayed in naval warfare. . . .

During the war our navy captured or destroyed 1504 blockade-runners, besides causing many valuable cargoes to be thrown overboard by the long-continued and close pursuit of fugitives, who escaped capture by resorting to this expedient to lighten the vessels. A Confederate officer stated that all the approaches to Wilmington harbor were as thickly paved with valuable merchandise as a certain place is said to be with "good intentions." This assertion would apply to some other harbors.

The value of prizes captured was $31,000,000. The most valuable prize taken was the English steamer *Memphis*, which brought $510,000. She was captured early in the war by the steamer *Magnolia*. The captor was herself a prize-vessel that had been bought by our government and fitted out as a gunboat. The least valuable was a sloop captured by the gunboat *Tahoma*, called the *Alligator*, which brought $50. Many of the most important prizes were taken by mere chance, or when least expected; while many a long and hard chase resulted in the overhauling of an empty vessel, the cargo having been thrown overboard in the efforts to escape.

Before the refinements of the blockade-running system began, the men-o'-war as well as the contraband vessels were all painted the conventional black; but as black objects are readily seen on the water at night, the blockade-runners were soon painted various neutral tints. Our naval authorities at once caused experiments to be made with boats painted different colors. The tint that was least conspicuous under the greatest varieties of conditions was selected, and called "Union color." It was a bluish gray; and a formula for its preparation, together with the necessary materials, was at once distributed among the blockading fleets. It was very difficult to see a vessel of this color.

—WAIT, "The Blockade of the Confederacy"

2. THE *ROBERT E. LEE* RUNS THE BLOCKADE

The Robert E. Lee *was one of the most famous of all the blockade-runners. A Clyde-built iron steamer she was reputed to be the fastest afloat. Unlike most of the blockade-runners, she was owned by the Confederate government. Altogether the* Lee *ran the blockade 21 times—mostly out of Wilmington—before she was finally captured.*

John Wilkinson, who here tells his own story, was one of more than 300 naval officers who resigned, in 1861, to go with the Confederacy. He first saw duty on a shore battery in Virginia; then fought at the Battle of New Orleans, where he was captured. After his exchange he went to England, bought the ship which he christened Robert E. Lee, *and earned a reputation as the boldest of blockade-runners. In 1864 he was engaged in the attempt to capture Johnson's Island in Lake Erie; later he commanded the blockade-runner* Chickamauga.

The *Lee* continued to make her regular trips either to Nassau or Bermuda, as circumstances required, during the summer of 1863; carrying abroad cotton and naval stores, and bringing in "hardware," as munitions of war were then invoiced. Usually the time selected for sailing was during the "dark of the moon," but upon one occasion, a new pilot had been detailed for duty on board, who failed in many efforts to get the ship over the "rip," a shifting sand bar a mile or more inside the true bar. More than a week of valuable time had thus been lost, but the exigencies of the army being at that time more than usually urgent, I determined to run what appeared to be a very great risk.

The tide serving at ten o'clock, we succeeded in crossing the rip at that hour, and as we passed over New Inlet bar, the moon rose in a cloudless sky. It was a calm night too, and the regular beat of our paddles through the smooth water sounded to our ears ominously loud. As we closely skirted the shore, the blockading vessels were plainly visible to us, some at anchor, some under way; and some of them so near to us that we saw, or fancied we saw, with our night glasses, the men on watch on their forecastles; but as we were inside of them all, and invisible against the background of the land, we passed beyond them undiscovered. The roar of the surf breaking upon the beach, prevented the noise of our paddles from being heard. The *Lee's* head was not pointed seaward, however, until we had run ten or twelve miles along the land so close to the breakers that we could almost have tossed a biscuit into them, and no vessel was to be seen in any direction.

Discovery of us by the fleet would probably have been fatal to us, but the risk was not really so great as it appeared; for, as I had been informed by a blockade-runner who had been once captured and released, being a British subject, the vigilance on board the blockading fleet was much relaxed during the moonlit nights. The vessels were sent to Beaufort to coal at these times. My informant was an officer of the British Navy, and was the guest, for a few days after his capture, of Captain Patterson then commanding the blockading fleet off the Cape Fear. Speaking of the arduous service, P. remarked to him, that he never undressed nor retired to bed, during the dark nights; but could enjoy those luxuries when the moon was shining. On this hint I acted.

It was about this time that I adopted an expedient which proved of great service on several occasions. A blockade-runner did not often pass through the fleet without receiving one or more shots, but these were always preceded by the flash of a calcium light, or by a blue light; and immediately followed by two rockets thrown in the direction of the block-ade-runner. The signals were probably concerted each day for the ensuing night, as they appeared to be constantly changed; but the rockets were invariably sent up. I ordered a lot of rockets from New York. Whenever all hands were called to run through the fleet, an officer was stationed along-side of me on the bridge with the rockets. One or two min-utes after our immediate pursuer had sent his rockets, I would direct ours to be discharged at a right angle to our course. The whole fleet would be misled, for even if the vessel which had discovered us were not deceived, the rest of the fleet would be baffled. . . .

We were ready to sail for Nassau on the 15th of August, 1863, and had on board, as usual, several passengers. . . .

We passed safely through the blockading fleet off the New Inlet Bar, receiving no damage from the few shots fired at us, and gained an offing from the coast of thirty miles by day-light. By this time our supply of English coal had been ex-hausted, and we were obliged to commence upon North Carolina coal of very inferior quality, and which smoked terribly. We commenced on this fuel a little after daylight. Very soon afterwards the vigilant look-out at the mast-head called out "Sail ho!" and in reply to the "where away" from the deck, sang out "Right astern, sir, and in chase."

The morning was very clear. Going to the mast-head I could just discern the royal of the chaser; and before I left there, say in half an hour, her top-gallant sail showed above the horizon. By this time the sun had risen in a cloudless sky. It was evident our pursuer would be alongside of us by mid-day at the rate we were then going. The first orders given were to throw overboard the deck-load of cotton and to make more steam. The latter proved to be more easily given than executed; the chief engineer reporting that it was impos-sible to make steam with the wretched stuff filled with slate and dirt. A moderate breeze from the north and east had been blowing ever since daylight and every stitch of canvas on board the square-rigged steamer in our wake was draw-ing.

We were steering east by south, and it was clear that the chaser's advantages could only be neutralized either by bring-ing the *Lee* gradually head to wind or edging away to bring the wind aft. The former course would be running toward the land, besides incurring the additional risk of being inter-cepted and captured by some of the inshore cruisers. I began to edge away, therefore, and in two or three hours enjoyed the satisfaction of seeing our pursuer clew up and furl his sails. The breeze was still blowing as fresh as in the morning, but we were now running directly away from it, and the cruiser was going literally as fast as the wind, causing the sails to be rather a hindrance than a help. But she was still gaining on us.

A happy inspiration occurred to me when the case seemed hopeless. Sending for the chief engineer I said "Mr. S., let us try cotton, saturated with spirits of turpentine." There were on board, as part of the deck load, thirty or forty barrels of "spirits." In a very few moments, a bale of cotton was ripped open, a barrel tapped, and buckets full of the saturated material passed down into the fire-room. The result exceeded our expectations. The chief engineer, an excitable little Frenchman from Charleston, very soon made his appearance on the bridge, his eyes sparkling with triumph, and reported a full head of steam. Curious to see the effect upon our speed, I directed him to wait until the log was hove. I threw it myself, nine and a half knots. "Let her go now sir!" I said. Five minutes afterwards, I hove the log again, *thirteen and a quarter*. We now began to hold our own, and even to gain a little upon the chaser; but she was fearfully near, and I began to have visions of another residence at Fort Warren, as I saw the "big bone in the mouth" of our pertinacious friend, for she was near enough us at one time for us to see distinctly the white curl of foam under her bows, called by that name among seamen. I wonder if they could have screwed another turn of speed out of her if they had known that the *Lee* had on board, in addition to her cargo of cotton, a large amount of gold shipped by the Confederate Government?

There continued to be a very slight change in our relative positions till about six o'clock in the afternoon, when the chief engineer again made his appearance, with a very ominous expression of countenance. He came to report that the burnt cotton had choked the flues, and that the steam was running down. "Only keep her going till dark, sir," I replied, "and we will give our pursuer the slip yet." A heavy bank was lying along the horizon to the south and east; and I saw a possible means of escape.

At sunset the chaser was about four miles astern and gaining upon us. Calling two of my most reliable officers, I stationed one of them on each wheel-house, with glasses, directing them to let me know the instant they lost sight of the chaser in the growing darkness. At the same time, I ordered the chief engineer to make as black a smoke as possible, and to be in readiness to cut off the smoke by closing the dampers instantly, when ordered. The twilight was soon succeeded by darkness. Both of the officers on the wheel house called out at the same moment, "We have lost sight of her," while a dense column of smoke was streaming far in our wake. "Close the dampers," I called out through the speaking tube, and at the same moment ordered the helm "hard a starboard." Our course was altered eight points, at a right angle to the previous one. I remained on deck an hour, and then retired to my state-room with a comfortable sense of security.

  —WILKINSON, *The Narrative of a Blockade-Runner*

3. THE *ROB ROY* RUNS THE BLOCKADE OUT OF HAVANA

Cuba, the Bahamas, and Bermuda were the most important islands from which the blockade-runners operated. The chief ports here—especially Havana and Nassau—were friendly, transshipment to vessels bound for the British Islands convenient, and the run either to the Atlantic ports of Savannah, Charleston, and Wilmington, or to such Gulf ports as Galveston, relatively easy. The risks, to be sure, were great—but so were the profits. A captain received—so Thomas Scharf of the Confederate Navy tells us—$5,000 a month, and officers and seamen in proportion. Two successful trips usually paid the cost of the vessel; after that everything was profit, and some blockade runners made 30 or 40 trips before capture.

William Watson, who here tells of blockade-running into Galveston, is our old friend from the campaigns in Arkansas —a Scotsman who enlisted in the Confederate Army and, after capture and exchange, went into blockade-running. He appears to be the only chronicler who has left us narratives of both land and sea campaigns.

It was already into the month of April [1864], and it was a very bad time to make a trip, owing to the lengthened days and the prevailing calms. There would be no chance of good steady winds before September, and there would be on the Texas coast about three hours more daylight each day than in winter, and the danger of capture would be very great.

On the other hand, I opined that to lay here (Havana) heavy loss was certain. The vessel not being coppered, the sea-worms would penetrate her bottom, unless often docked and painted; expenses were high, and it was almost impossible to avoid being victimized by the numerous harpies who regarded blockade runners as a legitimate prey to pick at; and I felt that if I was to lose what little I had, I would rather lose it under the guns of an honest cruiser, than have it wheedled away from me by the flattery of pretended friends; so I determined to venture a trip if I could make arrangements to do so.

The vessel was taken to the ship-yard and put on the slip-dock to be thoroughly examined, caulked, and otherwise put in the best sailing trim preparative for another voyage.

As I have already said, specie money was not to be had in the Confederate States and it was not to the interest of the blockade runners to run a heavy risk on the inward trip, by taking in a valuable cargo, and many had run in with light cargoes, knowing that they could always obtain a cargo of cotton cheap, or a freight outward at very high rates.

This, however, had now been stopped by the Confederate authorities, and stringent rules had been enforced whereby all vessels entering a Confederate port must take in a full and valuable cargo.

To obtain this cargo was what I desired either as freight or on the vessel's account, and as a large part of the money we had left would be expended in the repairs of the vessel, it would be necessary—if we could not get a freight—to get some one to take a share in the adventure, and as there were so many merchants and speculators who sympathized excessively with the Confederate States and took great interest in furnishing them with supplies, I thought there would be no difficulty in making an engagement.

Applying to several of them, I found their terms to be all about the same; which was, that they were exceedingly wishful to sell me goods for a cargo, but none willing to take a share in the adventure or run any risk. . . .

I may here say that up to this time blockade running by steamers had been confined almost entirely to the Atlantic ports, while nearly the whole trade into the Gulf States had been done by sailing craft, mostly light-draught schooners. When Charleston and the other ports on the Atlantic were captured, or so closely invested that entrance to them was almost impossible, many of those steamers came to Havana to try what could be done between that port and the Gulf States, and the basis for blockade running was transferred from Nassau to Havana.

Steamers, however, were not much in favour at Havana for blockade-running purposes, and it was considered by some that their utility for this trade was more ideal than real, but of this I will speak hereafter.

Havana having now become the principal centre for blockade running, a crowd of speculators soon found their way to the place, who bought up the goods in the limited market, and ran them up to a high figure to sell to blockade runners, representing them, of course, as consignments recently got out from Europe specially selected for the Confederate market. And while trumpeting their zeal for the Confederate cause, they took special care to pocket large profits without running any risk. While to those who actually ran the blockade and incurred the risk and danger, but little accrued. . . .

About the same time my old friend Mr. R. M—— came to the yard and took a look at the *Rob Roy* as she lay on the ways.

He asked me if I had made any arrangements for a trip yet. I said I had not. He said I might come and see him the following day, and he would make me an offer.

On the following day I called upon him. He asked what value I now placed upon the vessel. I said 5,000 dollars when repaired and fitted out ready for sea.

He then said that his offer was that he would furnish a cargo equal in value to that amount, which cargo he would guarantee would satisfy the requirements of the Confederate Government as to inward cargo, and purchase much more cotton than the vessel could carry out, and the surplus would be invested in cotton bonds, which were still worth something in Havana. He would then become owner of half of the vessel, and I would be owner of half of the cargo. We would then be equal partners in the vessel and cargo, each paying his half of the disbursements, out of which he would allow me for my services as captain 500 dollars, to be paid in advance before sailing, and 7 dollars for every bale of cotton when landed in a neutral port.

The cargo which he had to put on board consisted chiefly of arms, which the Confederate Government in Texas stood much in want of at that time.

This offer I accepted, and I asked him to make a memorandum of it in writing, which he did, and handed it to me.

I then got a list of the cargo he proposed to furnish. It consisted of 200 Enfield rifles with bayonets and accoutrements, 400 Belgium muskets with bayonets, 400 cavalry swords, six cases of saddlery and accoutrements, twenty-five boxes of ammunition, a large box of cavalry currycombs and horse brushes, and several bales and cases of blankets, clothing, boots and shoes, hardware, and other goods. Besides this it was good policy to have a good supply of some things which were much esteemed by the Southern people, but which the blockade had cut off and made extremely rare, and in some parts almost unknown, such as tea, coffee, cheese, spices, etc., also thread, needles, and such furnishings. Brandies and wines as well as all spirituous liquors were forbidden to be taken in, but they were received with great thankfulness if given as donations for the use of the hospitals. All these might be entered as ship stores.

This cargo, although valuable, was far from filling up the hold of the schooner, and as I knew that a good inward cargo had great weight with the authorities in the Confederacy, I sent word to Mr. Helm, the Confederate States Consul, that I would sail in a few days for Texas, and I would take free of freight any goods which he might wish to send in.

I received a reply thanking me for the offer, and saying that he would send by my vessel 400 guns. He also said that he had some important despatches to send to General Magruder, which he would confide to my care. . . .

I was now thinking over what port I would try to enter. I was a little sick with the Brazos River on account of the troubles I had had there on last trip, and the entrance to it now was generally blockaded, and it would be impossible to enter during the day, and the bar was dangerous to enter at night without a pilot.

Captain Dave had determined to make for St. Louis Pass at the west end of Galveston Island. . . .

It was impossible, however, for the *Rob Roy* to enter there, and on the advice of Captain M. I determined to shape for Galveston, and take my chance of getting past the fleet.

Captain M. was well acquainted with all the shallow entrances to Galveston Bay, and he gave me some information as to how a light draught vessel like the *Rob Roy* might enter from the eastward or windward side. . . .

We were now all ready to sail, and I only waited for a favourable opportunity.

There were two Federal gunboats which lay between us and the Moro Castle, and which we should have to pass on the way out to sea, and I was pretty certain that they knew we had a cargo of arms on board, but they were to a considerable extent powerless, and we were cleared for Belize, Honduras.

As no vessels were allowed to leave or enter Havana harbour between sunset and sunrise, the best time to leave was just about sunset, so that if any cruisers were lying in the offing we could come to, under the guns of the Moro, until it got quite dark, and then put to sea.

Captain Dave had determined to sail at the same time that we sailed, and as I had been laughing at his vessel, he wished to bet with me a case of brandy that he would arrive in Texas before me if not captured. I did not, however, take the bet, as I intended to creep along cautiously.

I was now well manned and prepared, and my policy was —when it became calm to take down all sail, and make the vessel as inconspicuous as possible; keep a sharp look-out from the mast-head, and if anything appeared on the horizon to get out the sweeps and pull away in the opposite direction before we were observed.

Everything being now ready we got what we called the mail on board. This consisted of letters for people in Texas and other parts of the Confederate States, west of the Mississippi River from all parts of the world. . . .

We now awaited a favourable wind, and were wishful to get away, as Havana is a very bad place for a vessel's bottom fouling, and every day we lay was injuring the sailing qualities of the vessel. . . .

At last a steady breeze sprang up from the south, which freshened towards the afternoon, and we stood down the bay just before sunset.

We passed the two Federal cruisers as they lay at anchor. We saw the officers scrutinizing us with their glasses, but as neither of the vessels had steam up, it was impossible that they could follow us that night.

—WATSON, *The Adventures of a Blockade Runner*

4. BLOCKADE-RUNNERS SUPPLY CHARLESTON

Here is a short account of what blockade-running meant to a city. Charleston was pretty well bottled up, from early in the war; yet swift blockade-runners managed to get past the Federal ships and keep the city supplied with necessities— and with luxuries. This account describes the situation in 1864.

During those long wearisome days and weeks when the city was under fire almost the only event of joy which would occur would be the arrival of some one of these blockade-runners. The business was finally reduced to a science. Even in the darkest night the cunning craft would work their way in or out through the tortuous channels of the harbor. When outward-bound the captain generally went down to Sullivan's Island upon the evening of sailing to learn the disposition of the Union fleet and plan the course of his exit. Lights also were always prearranged along the shores of the island, or suspended from boats in the harbor, in order to indicate the channel.

The most dangerous point, and that which demanded the exercise of the greatest skill to avoid, was a narrow tongue of land which ran out from Sullivan's Island just opposite Sumter, and which was known as the Breakwater Jetty. Here the channel is not only very narrow but takes a sudden turn, and it was in making this turn that the vessel was in danger of getting aground. The Union artillerists after a while learned many of the cunning arts of the blockade-runner, and whenever they saw a light from the opposite shore of Morris Island, which they supposed was intended for the guidance of a vessel, they would immediately open fire. They had a way too of sending out picket-boats which would quietly allow the vessel to pass till it had rounded the jetty and return became impossible, and then by means of rockets would signalize the fleet outside.

The chase of a blockade-runner was the most exciting thing imaginable. Like a hunted deer it would speed through the water, its fierce avenger after it, every beam from stem to stern quivering through the violent pulsations of its great iron heart, and the dash of the paddles as in their lightning-like revolutions they would strike the water. Sometimes not only was one half of the cargo thrown overboard, but every combustible thing that could be laid hold of crowded into the furnaces to increase the steam. Some of these blockade-runners were very successful. I knew of one which had run the gauntlet no less than nineteen times, and had consequently proved a mine of wealth to its owners. When a vessel had once run the blockade it was considered to have paid for itself, and every subsequent trip was consequently clear gain. The captain generally cleared on each round trip ten thousand dollars in gold, and the pilot and mate in proportion.

To be at all connected with or interested in a blockade-runner was in those days esteemed in Charleston a signal piece of good fortune. It insured at least a partial supply of the comforts and luxuries of life; for the ladies an occasional new silk dress, the envy and admiration of the streets; for the gentlemen a good supply of Bourbon—a box or two of cigars, or a larder filled with Stilton cheese or West India fruits. By-and-by came an edict from Richmond forbidding the importation of luxuries of this kind, and restricting the cargo of a vessel entirely to those articles which the country needed in its military operations, or which contributed to the supply of the actual necessities of the people. One half of the cargo of the vessel going out was also required to be devoted to government account, and one half of the cargo of the vessel coming in. This, of course, greatly curtailed the profits of the owners, but still immense fortunes continued to be made on both sides of the water.

—Peck, "Four Years Under Fire at Charleston"

5. CONFEDERATE PRIVATEERS HARRY NORTHERN MERCHANTMEN

The Confederacy early had recourse to letters of marque, and altogether William M. Robinson, foremost authority on Confederate privateering, lists some 64 privateers of various boats, and others. These did considerable damage to Union shipping during the first year of the war, but with the rapid growth of the United States Navy and the successful establishment of the blockade, the privateer became ineffective. Privateering had been outlawed by the Declaration of Paris, but the United States was not a signatory to this Declaration and therefore in no position to protest Confederate privateering. Yet at first Federal authorities tried to treat captured privateersmen as pirates, and there was a notable trial of the crew of the Jeff Davis *for piracy. The Confederacy quickly put a stop to that policy by the threat of retaliation.*

We give here two brief excerpts illuminating the story of privateering. The first introduces us to the Ivy, *one of the earliest and most successful of the privateers, later taken into the Confederate Navy. The second is the story of the capture of the* John Welsh *by the famous* Jefferson Davis, *and is told by the master of the* John Welsh, Captain Fitfield.

A. The *Ivy* Prowls Outside New Orleans

Last Friday I left New Orleans for this place and boat for a little privateering—to assist in annoying the enemy's commerce; but the enemy's commerce has ceased almost to spread its wings in this latitude. On board the *Ivy* are guns and men enough to accomplish great destruction, were we called on to open with our cannon. Our human fighting material is constituted of good bone, sinew and pluck, and some of the crew having entered the privateer service with only one intent—commendable revenge on the North.

Today we succeeded in sighting a vessel of the largest dimensions, and full rigged, which proved to be the *Sarah E. Pettigrew,* which, to our sorrow, was without a cargo, there being in her hold only two or three thousand sacks of salt, from Liverpool. We soon had a prize crew on her broad decks, greatly to the muddled surprise of her officers and crew. After the formality of taking possession, your correspondent being among the boarders—we do not pay weekly —I overhauled the flag-bag, and soon had bunting in plenty for a pretty Southern Confederacy flag, which was immediately set afloat to flutter defiance to all who don't like us. The *Ivy's* capacity enables her to do her own towing, and after she had cruised around in the Gulf two or three hours to overhaul other sails, she returned to us and we turned our prows toward Pass à L'Outre, near where the *Pettigrew* now lies, awaiting to be towed to your city. The privateer *Calhoun* gave chase for the same vessel, but the *Ivy* was too fast for her.

We lie in or near the river every night, but start out soon after midnight, and keep a sharp lookout for any speck on the horizon, and when the cry of "sail-ho!" is heard the *Ivy's* "tendrils" don revolvers, swords, knives and rifles with great excitement and good nature. We have exceedingly good times and "duff" but I fear all will be closed with the appearance of the blockading force.

—Letter by M. Repard in *Daily Delta*

B. The *Jefferson Davis* Takes a Prize off Delaware

At 8:30 the privateer tacked and stood N. W., at the same time setting a French ensign, and from the fact of her having French-cut hempen sails we supposed she was a French merchant brig. In answer to her colors we set the Stars and

Stripes, and thought no more of the stranger. At 9 o'clock, to our surprise, she fired a shot across our bows, when we took in the studding sails and hove the *John Welsh* to. We then supposed her to be a French man-of-war brig; but her ports were closed and the guns covered up, while but few men were to be seen on her decks.

She came within musket shot of us, and lowered a boat which was manned by expert seamen and contained Lieutenant Postell, late of the United States Navy. Just before the boat came alongside the French flag was hauled down and the Confederate flag run up. In about two minutes afterwards the armed crew was on our deck. After inquiring after my health, Lieutenant Postell desired me to show him the brig's papers. I invited him into the cabin, and after showing them, I stated the cargo was Spanish property. Said he, "You are our prize, and the Spaniards had no business to ship their cargoes in American bottoms." He then came on deck and ordered four of my men to go in the privateer's boat, and told the remainder of the crew to pack up their things and stand by to do as ordered. They immediately set to work and broke out the ship's stores and took about eight months' provisions on board of the privateer, leaving only enough to take the prize-crew back with the vessel. This occupied about five hours.

I was transferred with the remainder of my crew on board of the privateer, and they took my boat and sent theirs on board of the *John Welsh*, as mine was the best. A prize-crew corresponding in appearance and number was then put on board in charge of Prize-Master Stevens, and she was ordered to go South but I was not allowed to know of her destination. I think they will palm themselves off as the genuine crew if they fall in with the Federal cruisers. After the work of transferring the stores had been completed, Capt. Coxetter mustered all hands aft and said to them, "Boys, if you molest the crew of that brig or their things to the value of a rope yarn, I will punish you to the utmost of my power. Do you understand? Now go forward." Turning to his officers he said, "Gentlemen, I desire that you do everything in your power to make the stay of these gentlemen as agreeable as possible." He then invited me to dine with him in his cabin while my mate was taken into the officer's mess.

—CAPTAIN FITFIELD, in the *Charleston Mercury*

6. THE *GEORGIA* FIRES THE *BOLD HUNTER*

The Georgia *was one of the most successful of the commerce destroyers purchased or built in England. A swift and powerful ship of 600 tons, she was purchased by Commodore Matthew F. Maury, at Dumbarton, Scotland; obtained her guns and ordnance from the* Alar, *off the French coast, and embarked upon a brief but highly successful career as commerce destroyer. Altogether she captured and destroyed at least nine American ships.*

Here is James Morgan's account of the burning of one of them, the misnamed Bold Hunter. *Morgan was a midshipman on the* Georgia; *later he served in the Egyptian Army, engaged in journalism in South Carolina, went to Australia as consul general and helped build the Statue of Liberty.*

On October 9, 1863, in a light breeze and after a lively chase we brought to, with our guns, the splendid American full-rigged ship *Bold Hunter,* of Boston, from Dundee, bound to Calcutta with a heavy cargo of coal. We hove to leeward of her and brought her captain and crew over to our ship, where as usual the crew were placed in irons and below decks. Being short of coal and provisions we proceeded to supply our wants from the prize. This was easy so far as the provisions were concerned, but when it came to carrying the coal from one ship to the other in our small boats, in something of a seaway, that was another matter. After half a dozen trips one of our boats came very near being swamped, and the wind and sea rapidly rising, we give it up as a bad job. This was about two bells (1 P.M.) in the afternoon watch. We signalled our prize-master to set fire to the *Bold Hunter* and also to come aboard the *Georgia* at once, which he did.

We had hardly finished hoisting our boats to the davits when a great cloud of smoke burst from the hatches of the *Bold Hunter,* coming from the thousands of tons of burning coal in her hold. The wind had by this time increased to a gale and the sea was running very high. As before mentioned, the wind was very light when we captured the ship and she had hove to with all sail set, even to her royals. The flames leaped from her deck to her tarry rigging and raced up the shrouds and backstays and burned away her braces—her yards swung around, her sails filled, and the floating inferno, like a mad bull, bore down on us at full speed, rushing through the water as though she was bent on having her revenge.

To avoid a collision, the order was given on the *Georgia* to go ahead at full speed. The gong in the engine-room sounded, the engine turned the screw, and the screw began to churn the water under our counter. The engine made two or three revolutions—then there was a crash—followed by yells as the engineers and oilers rushed on to the deck accompanied by a shower of lignum-vitæ cogs and broken glass from the engine-room windows. The order to make sail was instantly given, but before the gaskets which confined the furled sails to the yardarms could be cast off, the burning ship was upon us.

She had come for us with such directness that one could easily have imagined that she was being steered by some demon who had come out of the inferno which was raging in her hold. We stood with bated breath awaiting the catastrophe which seemingly was about to overtake us. The *Bold Hunter* was rated at over three thousand tons, and had inside her a burning cargo of coal of even greater weight—the *Georgia* was scarcely one-sixth her size. Onward rushed the blazing ship, presenting an awesome spectacle, with the flames leaping about her sails and rigging, while a huge mass of black smoke rolled out of her hatches. High above our heads her long, flying jib-boom passed over our poop deck as she arose on a great wave and came down on our quarter, her cutwater cleaving through the *Georgia's* fragile plates as cleanly as though they had been made out of cheese. The force of the impact pushed the *Georgia* ahead, and for a moment we congratulated ourselves that we had escaped from the fiery demon whose breath was scorching us.

But the *Bold Hunter* was not yet satisfied with the injuries she had inflicted. Recovering from the recoil she again gathered way and struck us near the place she had previously damaged, but fortunately this was a glancing blow which had the effect only of wrenching off our port quarter davits and reducing the boat which was slung to them to kindling wood.

Not yet satisfied, the apparently infuriated inanimate object made a third attempt to destroy the *Georgia*, this time, fortunately, missing her mark and passing a few yards to leeward of us. Her sails having burned, she soon lost headway and helplessly lay wallowing in the trough of the sea while the fire ate through her sides, and her tall masts, one after the other, fell with a great splash into the sea. Before she went down surrounded by a cloud of steam, we had a good view through the great holes burned in her sides of the fire raging inside her. I imagine it was a very realistic imitation

of what hell looks like when the forced draughts are turned
on in honour of the arrival of a distinguished sinner.

—MORGAN, *Recollections of a Rebel Reefer*

7. THE *KEARSARGE* SINKS THE *ALABAMA* OFF CHERBOURG

*With the possible exception of the duel between the
Monitor and the Merrimac, the fight between the Kearsarge
and the Alabama is the most famous naval battle of the Civil
War. The Alabama was the most notorious of the cruisers
that James Bulloch had had built at Liverpool for the Confederacy.*

*Captained by the brilliant Raphael Semmes and outfitted
at the Azores, in midsummer 1862, she embarked on a career
of destruction unparalleled in modern naval annals. Within
two years Semmes captured or destroyed over 80 merchantmen and one warship. In June 1864 his battered ship put in
at the harbor of Cherbourg for repairs. There the U. S. S.
Kearsarge, commanded by Captain John A. Winslow, caught
up with her. Semmes accepted the challenge and steamed out
to battle and destruction.*

*After the battle Semmes, now a rear admiral, returned to
Richmond to take command of the James River Squadron.
With the end of the war he served as professor of moral
philosophy at Louisiana State University; then engaged in
journalism and law. Commodore Winslow, whose career before this battle had been unspectacular, later commanded the
Gulf Squadron.*

*The story of the famous battle is told here by John Kell,
executive officer of the Alabama.*

Soon after our arrival at Cherbourg an officer was sent on
shore to ask permission of the port admiral to land our prisoners of the two captured ships. This being obtained without
trouble or delay, Captain Semmes went on shore to see to
the docking of the ship for repairs. Cherbourg being a naval
station and the dock belonging to the government, permission
had to be obtained of the emperor before we could do anything. The port admiral told us "we had better have gone into
Havre, as the government might not give permission for repairs to a belligerent ship." The emperor was absent from

Paris at some watering place on the coast, and would not return for some days.

Here was an impediment to our plans which gave us time for thought, and the result of such thought was the unfortunate combat between the *Alabama* and the *Kearsarge*. The latter ship was lying at Flushing when we entered Cherbourg. Two or three days after our arrival she steamed into the harbor, sent a boat on shore to communicate, steamed outside and stationed off the breakwater. While Captain Semmes had not singled her out as an antagonist, and would never have done so had he known her to be chain-clad (an armored ship), he had about made up his mind that he would cease fleeing before the foe, and meet an equal in battle when the opportunity presented itself. Our cause was weakening daily, and our ship so disabled it really seemed to us our work was almost done! We might end her career gloriously by being victorious in battle, and defeat against an equal foe we would never have allowed ourselves to anticipate.

As soon as the *Kearsarge* came into the harbor Captain Semmes sent for me to come to his cabin, and abruptly said to me: "Kell, I am going out to fight the *Kearsarge*. What do you think of it?" We then quietly talked it all over. We discussed the batteries, especially the *Kearsarge's* advantage in 11-inch guns. I reminded him of our defective powder, how our long cruise had deteriorated everything, as proven in our target-practice off the coast of Brazil on the Ship *Rockingham*, when certainly every third shot was a failure even to explode. I saw his mind was fully made up, so I simply stated these facts for myself. I had always felt ready for a fight, and I also knew that the brave young officers of the ship would not object, and the men would be not only willing, but anxious, to meet the enemy! To all outward seeming the disparity was not great between the two ships, barring the unknown (because concealed) chain armor.

The *Kearsarge* communicated with the authorities to request that our prisoners be turned over to them. Captain Semmes made an objection to her increasing her crew. He addressed our agent, Mr. Bonfils, a communication requesting him to inform Captain Winslow, through the United States Consul, that "if he would wait until the *Alabama* could coal ship he would give him battle." We began to coal and at the same to make preparation for battle. We overhauled the magazine and shell rooms, gun equipments, etc.

The *Kearsarge* was really in the fullest sense of the word a man-of-war, stanch and well built; the *Alabama* was made for flight and speed and was much more lightly constructed than her chosen antagonist. The *Alabama* had one more gun, but the *Kearsarge* carried more metal at a broadside. The seven guns of the *Kearsarge* were two 11-inch Dahlgrens, four 32-pounders, and one rifled 28-pounder. The *Alabama's* eight guns were six 32-pounders, one 8-inch and one rifled 100-pounder. The crew of the *Alabama* all told was 149 men, while that of the *Kearsarge* was 162 men.

By Saturday night, June 18th, our preparations were completed. Captain Semmes notified the admiral of the port that he would be ready to go out and meet the *Kearsarge* the following morning. Early Sunday morning the admiral sent an officer to say to us that "the ironclad Frigate *Couronne* would accompany us to protect the neutrality of French waters." . . .

Between 9 and 10 o'clock, June 19th, everything being in readiness, we got under way and proceeded to sea. We took the western entrance of the harbor. The *Couronne* accompanied us, also some French pilot-boats and an English steam yacht, the *Deerhound*, owned by a rich Englishman (as we afterward learned), who with his wife and children, was enjoying life and leisure in his pleasure yacht. The walls and fortifications of the harbor, the heights above the town, the buildings, everything that looked seaward, was crowded with people. About seven miles from the land the *Kearsarge* was quietly awaiting our arrival.

Officers in uniforms, men at their best, Captain Semmes ordered them sent aft, and mounting a gun-carriage made them a brief address:

"Officers and seamen of the *Alabama:* You have at length another opportunity to meet the enemy, the first that has presented to you since you sank the *Hatteras.* In the meantime you have been all over the world, and it is not too much to say that you have destroyed and driven for protection under neutral flags one-half of the enemy's commerce, which at the beginning of the war covered every sea. This is an achievement of which you may well be proud, and a grateful country will not be unmindful of it. The name of your ship has become a household word wherever civilization extends. Shall that name be tarnished by defeat? [An outburst of Never! Never!] The thing is impossible. Remember that you are in the English Channel, the theatre of so much of the naval glory of our race. The eyes of all Europe are at this moment upon you! The flag that floats over you is that of a young Republic that bids defiance to her enemies, whenever and wherever found! Show the world that you know how to uphold it. Go to your quarters!"

We now prepared our guns to engage the enemy on our starboard side. When within a mile and a-quarter he wheeled, presenting his starboard battery to us. We opened on him with solid shot, to which he soon replied, and the action became active. To keep our respective broadsides bearing we were obliged to fight in a circle around a common center, preserving a distance of three quarters of a mile. When within distance of shell range we opened on him with shell. The spanker gaff was shot away and our ensign came down. We replaced it immediately at the mizzen masthead.

The firing now became very hot and heavy. Captain Semmes, who was watching the battle from the horse block, called out to me, "Mr. Kell, our shell strike the enemy's side, doing little damage, and fall off in the water; try solid shot." From this time we alternated shot and shell.

The battle lasted an hour and ten minutes. Captain Semmes said to me at this time (seeing the great apertures made in the side of the ship from their 11-inch shell, and the water rushing in rapidly), "Mr. Kell, as soon as our head points to the French coast in our circuit of action, shift your guns to port and make all sail for the coast." This evolution was performed; righting the helm, hauling aft the fore-trysail sheet, and pivoting to port, the action continuing all the time without cessation,—but it was useless, nothing could avail us.

Before doing this, and pivoting the gun, it became necessary to clear the deck of parts of the dead bodies that had been torn to pieces by the 11-inch shells of the enemy. The captain of our 8-inch gun and most of the gun's crew were killed. It became necessary to take the crew from young Anderson's gun to make up the vacancies, which I did, and placed him in command. Though a mere youth, he managed it like an old veteran.

Going to the hatchway, I called out to Brooks (one of our efficient engineers) to give the ship more steam, or we would be whipped.

He replied she "had every inch of steam that was safe to carry without being blown up!"

Young Matt O'Brien, assistant engineer, called out, "Let her have the steam; we had better blow her to hell than to let the Yankees whip us!"

The chief engineer now came on deck and reported "the furnace fires put out," whereupon Captain Semmes ordered me to go below and "see how long the ship could float."

I did so, and returning said, "Perhaps ten minutes."

"Then, sir," said Captain Semmes, "cease firing, shorten sail, and haul down the colors. It will never do in this nine-teenth century for us to go down and the decks covered with our gallant wounded."

This order was promptly executed, after which the *Kearsarge* deliberately fired into us five shots! In Captain Winslow's report to the Secretary of the Navy he admits this, saying, "Uncertain whether Captain Semmes was not making some ruse, the *Kearsarge* was stopped."

Was this a time,—when disaster, defeat and death looked us in the face,—for a ship to use a ruse, a Yankee trick? I ordered the men to "stand to their quarters," and they did it heroically; not even flinching, they stood every man to his post. As soon as we got the first of these shot I told the quartermaster to show the white flag from the stern. It was done. Captain Semmes said to me, "Dispatch an officer to the *Kearsarge* and ask that they send boats to save our wounded —ours are disabled." Our little dingey was not injured, so I sent Master's Mate Fulham with the request. No boats com-ing, I had one of our quarter boats (the least damaged one) lowered and had the wounded put in her. Dr. Galt came on deck at this time, and was put in charge of her, with orders to take the wounded to the *Kearsarge*. They shoved off in time to save the wounded.

When I went below to inspect the sight was appalling! As-sistant Surgeon Llewellyn was at his post, but the table and the patient on it had been swept away from him by an 11-inch shell, which made an aperture that was fast filling with water. This was the last time I saw Dr. Llewellyn in life. As I passed the deck to go down below the stalwart seaman with death's signet on his brow called to me. For an instant I stood beside him. He caught my hand and kissed it with such rever-ence and loyalty,—the look, the act, it lingers in my memory still! I reached the deck and gave the order for "every man to save himself, to jump overboard with a spar, an oar, or a grating, and get out of the vortex of the sinking ship."

As soon as all were overboard but Captain Semmes and I, his steward, Bartelli, and two of the men—the sailmaker, Alcott, and Michael Mars—we began to strip off all super-fluous clothing for our battle with the waves for our lives. Poor, faithful-hearted Bartelli, we did not know he could not swim, or he might have been sent to shore—he was drowned. The men disrobed us, I to my shirt and drawers, but Captain Semmes kept on his heavy pants and vest. We together gave our swords to the briny deep and the ship we loved so well! The sad farewell look at the ship would have wrung the stoutest heart! The dead were lying on her decks, the surging, roaring waters rising through the death-wound in her side. The ship agonizing like a living thing and going down in her brave beauty, settling lower and lower, she sank fathoms deep—lost to all save love, and fame, and memory! . . .

The next thing that I remember, a voice called out, "Here's our first lieutenant," and I was pulled into a boat, in the stern sheets of which lay Captain Semmes as if dead. He had received a slight wound in his hand, which with the struggle in the water had exhausted his strength, long worn by sleeplessness, anxiety and fatigue. There were several of our crew in the boat. In a few moments we were alongside a steam yacht, which received us on her deck, and we learned it was the *Deerhound*, owned by an English gentleman, Mr. John Lancaster, who used it for the pleasure of himself and family, who were with him at this time, his sons having preferred going out with him to witness the fight to going to church with their mother, as he afterwards told us.

In looking about us I saw two French pilot boats rescuing the crew, and finally two boats from the *Kearsarge*. I was much surprised to find Mr. Fulham on the *Deerhound*, as I had dispatched him in the little dingey to ask the *Kearsarge* for boats to save our wounded. Mr. Fulham told me that "our shot had torn the casing from the chain armor of the *Kearsarge*, indenting the chain in many places." This now explained Captain Semmes' observation to me during the battle —"our shell strike the enemy's side and fall into the water." Had we been in possession of this knowledge the unequal battle between the *Alabama* and the *Kearsarge* would never have been fought, and the gallant little *Alabama* have been lost by an error. She fought valiantly as long as there was a plank to stand upon.

History has failed to explain, unless there were secret orders forbidding it, why the *Kearsarge* did not steam into the midst of the fallen foe and generously save life! The *Kearsarge* fought the battle beautifully, but she tarnished her glory when she fired on a fallen foe and made no immediate effort to save brave living men from watery graves! Both heroic commanders are now gone—before the great tribunal where "the deeds done in the body" are to be accounted for but history is history and truth is truth!

Mr. Lancaster came to Captain Semmes and said: "I think every man is saved, where shall I land you?"

He replied, "I am under English colors; the sooner you land me on English soil the better."

The little yacht, under a press of steam, moved away for Southampton. Our loss was nine killed, twenty-one wounded and ten drowned. That afternoon, the 19th of June, we were landed in Southampton and received with every demonstration of kindness and sympathy.

—KELL, *Recollections of a Naval Life*

IX

Chickamauga and Chattanooga

WITH *the fall of Vicksburg and Port Hudson the whole central
Mississippi Valley fell under Union control and the fighting
shifted to the margins—to Arkansas and the Red River in the
West, to eastern Tennessee on the East. After Stones River
Bragg had retired to Tullahoma while Rosecrans made his
headquarters at Murfreesboro. Not until after Vicksburg did
Rosecrans feel justified in advancing on Chattanooga. Under
his command was an army of some 60,000, divided into three
corps under Thomas, McCook and Crittenden, and a reserve
corps under Granger. General Braxton Bragg commanded some
40,000 Confederates—over 10,000 of them cavalry—and
reinforcements were soon on their way from the Army of
Northern Virginia.*

*Again a word about geography is necessary. There was no
more formidable theater of operations in the Civil War than
that around Chattanooga. Chattanooga was the gateway to
the East; it stood on a great bend of the Tennessee River,
and on it converged the Memphis & Charleston and the
Nashville & Chattanooga railroads. If the Confederates could
hold it they would be able to use it as a base for offensive
operations in Tennessee and Kentucky; if the Federals took it
they could advance from it into Georgia. The Federals enjoyed numerical superiority, but the Confederates were favored by terrain. Between Chattanooga and Murfreesboro lay
the great Cumberland plateau, a rugged mountainous area,*

heavily wooded and crisscrossed with streams and ravines. Chattanooga itself lay on the eastern side of a sharp bend of the Tennessee which then swerved north again and flowed in a great bend toward the southwest. This great bend was dominated by Raccoon Mountain, while immediately to the south of the city itself lay the long Lookout Mountain and to the east and south the Missionary Ridge. Southward toward Ringgold and Dalton stretched a series of heavily wooded hills and valleys cut by gorges and ravines.

Rosecrans decided to cross the Tennessee below Chattanooga. As he advanced Bragg drew back into Chattanooga. By the end of August the so-called Tullahoma campaign—a wholly bloodless one—was over, and by September 4 the Federals were across the Tennessee and below Chattanooga. If Rosecrans succeeded in cutting Bragg's communications to Atlanta, Bragg would be lost, so on September 9 he evacuated Chattanooga and retired southeastward to Chickamauga Creek. Rosecrans advanced on him in three columns, each separated from the other by mountain ridges and the two flanks some 40 miles apart. This was the moment for Bragg to strike. With that fatuousness which characterized all of his military operations, he failed to do so. He was waiting for Longstreet's division, which—because Burnside had moved into Knoxville—had to go the long way around through Augusta and Atlanta. Thus the golden opportunity to smash the Army of the Cumberland passed. Between September 13 and 17 Rosecrans succeeded in concentrating his scattered forces west of Chickamauga Creek.

Since—by waiting for Longstreet—Bragg had thrown away the chance to destroy Rosecrans' army piecemeal, he should have waited until both of Longstreet's divisions arrived, and then assumed the defensive. Instead he brought on battle when only half of the reinforcements had come up. There was some preliminary fighting on September 18. On the nineteenth-twentieth came the battle itself. It was, as our accounts tell us, a Confederate victory, but a curiously inconclusive one. Bragg drove in the Union right and sent it hurtling back to Rossville; he attacked the Union left and curled it up on the center. But at the center stood Thomas, who here earned his name, the Rock of Chickamauga, and when Thomas' situation was most desperate Granger came to his rescue. The Union army was beaten, but not destroyed. It retired to Chattanooga—its original objective—and Bragg invested the city.

Now, for the first time in the war, a large Federal army was besieged. Could Bragg starve it into surrender? Again we must have recourse to our maps. Railroad communications with Chattanooga from the north and the west ran through the town of Bridgeport, on the Tennessee. But Confederate batteries on Raccoon Mountain dominated Bridgeport, and Confederate guns and sharpshooters controlled the winding Tennessee. The only supply route was down the Sequatchie Valley and across the rugged Walden's Ridge; this route was raided by Wheeler and churned into mud by the autumn rains. By the end of October the situation of Rosecrans' army was critical.

Washington had already taken alarm. Rosecrans was removed and General Thomas put in temporary command. Burnside was ordered to go to his support; Grant was instructed to hurry up reinforcements; Hooker was started, with two divisions, from Virginia. During October and November Grant and Hooker converged on the Chattanooga region. Meantime Bragg did nothing effective; instead he detached Longstreet for an attack on Knoxville. By the end of October Hooker had opened the "cracker line" to Chattanooga and Thomas' army was saved. Then Grant assumed the offensive. He sent Sherman on a wide swing from Brown's Ford to the northern end of Missionary Ridge. On the twenty-fourth Hooker carried Lookout Mountain. The next day Sherman and Thomas assaulted the Confederates all along Missionary Ridge, drove them from their entrenchments, and sent them flying toward Dalton. It was one of the most spectacular victories of the war. It was also one of the most consequential. For now the Confederacy had been squeezed into the Atlantic coastal states. And with Burnside at Knoxville and Grant and Sherman at Chattanooga the way was open into Georgia and the Carolinas.

1. THE FEDERALS OPPOSE HOOD WITH DESPERATION

By September 18 Bragg had most of his army west of the Chickamauga; that day Hood arrived with three brigades. There was sharp fighting on the flanks on the eighteenth but the main attack came on the nineteenth. Thomas brought on the battle that day by attacking Forrest's dismounted cavalrymen, on the Confederate right. Soon the engagement was general. Hood struck with fury at the Union center, and *pushed it back across the Lafayette road. Negley's division counterattacked and restored the Federal position, and night fell without decisive fighting.*

Captain James R. Carnahan of the 86th Indiana Volunteers here tells us how his men fought with desperation to hold Hood's assault.

Noonday has passed, when suddenly from out the woods to our front and left onto the open field, dashes an officer, his horse urged to its greatest speed toward our command. The men see him coming, and in an instant they are aroused to the greatest interest. "There come orders," are the words that pass from lip to lip along that line. . . . He reaches our line, and is met by our brigade commander, Colonel Geo. F. Dick, as anxious to receive the orders as he is to give them. The command comes in quick, sharp words: "The general presents his compliments, and directs that you move your brigade at once to the support of General Beard [Baird]. Take the road moving by the flank in 'double quick' to the left and into the woods, and go into line on the left of General Beatty's brigade. I am to direct you. Our men are hard pressed." The last sentence was all that was said in words as to the condition of our troops, but it told that we had read aright before he had spoken.

Scarce had the order been delivered when the command to "take arms" is heard along the line, and to drivers and cannoneers to mount. It scarcely took the time required to tell it for our brigade to get in motion, moving off the field, the artillery taking the wagon road, the infantry alongside. It was a grand scene as we moved quickly into place, closing up the column, and waiting but a moment for the command. The guns are at a right shoulder, and all have grown eager for the order—"Forward." The bugle sounds the first note of the command. Now, look along that column; the men are leaning forward for the start; you see the drivers on the artillery teams tighten the rein in the left hand, and, with the whip in the uplifted right arm, rise in their stirrups; and, as the last note of the bugle is sounded, the crack of the whips of thirty-six drivers over the backs of as many horses, and the stroke of the spurs, sends that battery of six guns and its caissons rattling and bounding over that road, while the infantry alongside are straining every nerve as they hasten to the relief of the comrades so hard pressed.

The spirits of the men grow higher and higher with each moment of the advance. The rattling of the artillery and the

hoof-beats of the horses add to the excitement of the onward
rush, infantry and artillery thus side by side, vieing each
with the other which shall best do his part. Now, as we come
nearer, the storm of the battle seems to grow greater and
greater. On and yet on we press, until, reaching the designated
point, the artillery is turned off to the left, on to a ridge,
and go into position along its crest, while the lines of the
infantry are being formed to the right of the road over which
we have just been hurrying.

Our lines are scarcely formed, and the command to move
forward given, when the lines which are in advance of us
are broken by a terrific charge of the enemy, and are driven
back in confusion onto our line—friend and foe so inter-
mingled that we can not fire a shot without inflicting as much
injury on our men as upon the enemy.

Our artillery, on the crest of the ridge back of us, have
unlimbered and gone into action, and their shells are now
flying over our heads in the woods, where the enemy's lines
had been. Confusion seems to have taken possession of our
lines, and, to add to it, the lines of our right have been
broken and the enemy are sweeping past our flank. The order
is given to fall back on line with the artillery. Out of the
wood, under the fire of our cannon, the men hasten. Now on
the crest of that ridge, without works of any kind to shelter
them, our troops are again hastily formed, and none too
soon. Down the gentle slope of that ridge, and away to our
right and left and front stretches an open field, without tree
or shrub to break the force of the balls. In our front, and at
the edge of the field, two hundred yards away, runs the road
parallel with our lines; beyond the road the heavy timber
where the Confederate lines are formed, and well protected
in their preparations for their charge.

Scarce had our lines been formed, when the sharp crack
of the rifles along our front, and the whistling of the balls
over our heads, give us warning that the advance of the
enemy has begun, and in an instant the shots of the skirmishers are drowned by the shout that goes up from the
charging column as it starts down in the woods. Our men are
ready. The Seventh Indiana Battery—six guns—is on the
right of my regiment; Battery M, Fourth United States
Artillery, is on our left. The gunners and every man of those
two batteries are at their posts of duty, the tightly drawn lines
in their faces showing their purpose there to stand for duty
or die. Officers pass the familiar command of caution along
the line—"Steady, men, steady." The shout of the charging

foe comes rapidly on; now they burst out of the woods and onto the road. As if touched by an electric cord, so quick and so in unison was it, the rifles leap to the shoulder along the ridge where waves the stars and stripes.

Now the enemy are in plain view along the road covering our entire front; you can see them, as with cap visors drawn well down over their eyes, the gun at the charge, with short, shrill shouts they come, and we see the colors of Longstreet's corps, flushed with victory, confronting us. Our men recognize the gallantry of their foe, and their pride is touched as well. All this is but the work of an instant, when, just as that long line of gray has crossed the road, quick and sharp rings out along our line the command, "Ready," "Fire!" It seems to come to infantry and artillery at the same instant, and out from the rifles of the men and the mouths of those cannons leap the death-dealing bullet and canister; again and again, with almost lightning rapidity, they pour in their deadly, merciless fire, until along that entire ridge it had become almost one continuous volley. Now that corps that had known little of defeat begins to waver; their men had fallen thick and fast about them. Again and yet again the volleys are poured into them, and the artillery on our right and left have not ceased their deadly work. No troops can long withstand such fire; their lines waver; another volley, and they are broken, and now fall back in confusion. The charge was not long in point of time, but was terrible in its results to the foe.

Along the entire line to our right and left we can hear the battle raging with increased fury. We are now on the defensive; and all can judge that the lull in our front is only the stillness that forbodes the more terrible storm that is to come. A few logs and rails are hastily gathered together to form a slight breastwork. Soon the scattering shots that began to fall about us gave us warning that our foe was again moving on us. Again we are ready, now laying behind our hastily prepared works. Again we hear the shout, as on they come with more determination than before. But with even greater courage do our men determine to hold their lines. The artillery is double shotted with canister. Again the command, "Fire!" and hotter, fiercer than before the battle rages along our front. Shout is answered with shout, shot by shots tenfold, until again our assailants break before our fire and are again forced back.

But why repeat further the story of that Saturday afternoon. Again and again were those charges repeated along our line, only to be hurled back—broken and shattered. It did seem as though our men were more than human. The artillerymen worked as never before. Their guns—double shotted—had scarce delivered their charges, and, before the gun could complete its recoil, was caught by strong arms, made doubly strong in that fever-heat of battle; was again in position, again double shotted, and again fired into the face of the foe. The arms bared, the veins standing out in great strong lines, the hat or cap gone from the head, the eye starting almost from the socket, the teeth set, the face beaded with perspiration, balls falling all about them, those men of the Seventh Indiana Battery and Battery M seemed to be supernaturally endowed with strength.

Their comrades of the infantry vied with them in acts of heroism, and daring, and endurance. They shouted defiance at the foe with every shot; with face and hands begrimed in the smoke and dust and heat of the battle; with comrades falling about them, the survivors thought only of vengeance. All the horses on two of the guns of the Seventh Indiana Battery are shot down; another charge is beginning; those two guns might be lost; they must be gotten back. Quick as thought, a company of infantry spring to the guns, one hand holding the rifle, the other on the cannon, and, with the shot falling thick and fast in and about them, drag the guns over the brow of the ridge and down into the woods, just in the rear of our lines, and hasten back again to take their places in line, ready to meet the on-coming charge. An artilleryman is shot down; a man from the infantry takes his place and obeys orders as best he can. When the charge begins our men are lying down. Now, in the midst of it, so great has become the excitement, so intense the anxiety, all fear and prudence vanishes, and the men leap to their feet, and fire and load, and fire and load, in the wildest frenzy of desperation. They have lost all ideas of danger or the strength of the assailants. It was this absolute *desperation* of our men that held our lines.

—CARNAHAN, "Personal Recollections of Chickamauga"

2. THOMAS STANDS LIKE A ROCK AT CHICKAMAUGA

During the night of the nineteenth Longstreet came up with two more brigades, and Bragg prepared to renew the battle by a series of attacks on the attenuated Union line, from north to south. The crisis came in the afternoon of the twentieth. Fierce Confederate attacks upon the Union left led Rosecrans to weaken his right. Through some misunderstanding General Wood withdrew his division, near the center, and into the gap thus created Longstreet hurled his fresh brigades like a thunderbolt. The whole Union line cracked and broke; the right crumbled and retreated toward Rossville; the left was in desperate danger. It was then that Thomas earned for himself the title "Rock of Chickamauga" —Thomas who during the whole war never left the battlefield and never lost an engagement. It was Stones River over again, but without the artillery, without even ammunition, for at one time Thomas was forced to rely on the bayonet to hurl back the Confederate attacks. Just as the situation appeared most desperate Gordon Granger came pounding up with his reserve division and saved the day.

The story of the break-through is told here by a Confederate general, and the story of Thomas' stand by a brigadier attached to Rosecrans' staff. D. H. Hill was one of Lee's greatest lieutenants and needs neither introduction nor celebration. Thruston was a brigadier general in the Army of the Cumberland.

A. LONGSTREET BREAKS THE FEDERAL LINE

The heavy pressure on Thomas caused Rosecrans to support him by sending the divisions of Negley and Van Cleve and Brannan's reserve brigade. In the course of these changes, an order to Wood, which Rosecrans claims was misinterpreted, led to a gap being left into which Longstreet stepped with the eight brigades which he had arranged in three lines to constitute his grand column of attack. Davis's two brigades, one of Van Cleve's, and Sheridan's entire division were caught in front and flank and driven from the field. Disregarding the order of the day, Longstreet now gave the order to wheel to the right instead of the left, and thus take in reverse the strong position of the enemy. Five of McCook's brigades were speedily driven off the field. He estimates their loss at forty per cent. Certainly that flank march was a bloody one. I have never seen the Federal dead lie so thickly on the ground, save in front of the sunken wall at Fredericksburg.

But that indomitable Virginia soldier, George H. Thomas, was there and was destined to save the Union army from total rout and ruin, by confronting with invincible pluck the forces of his friend and captain in the Mexican war. Thomas had ridden to his right to hurry up reënforcements, when he discovered a line advancing, which he thought at first was the expected succor from Sheridan, but he soon heard that it was a rebel column marching upon him. He chose a strong position on a spur of Missionary Ridge, running east and west, placed upon it Brannan's division with portions of two brigades of Negley's; Wood's division (Crittenden's) was placed on Brannan's left. These troops, with such as could be rallied from the two broken corps, were all he had to confront the forces of Longstreet, until Steedman's division of Granger's corps came to his relief about 3 P.M. Well and nobly did Thomas and his gallant troops hold their own against foes flushed with past victory and confident of future success. His new line was nearly at right angles with the line of log-works on the west side of the Rossville road, his right being an almost impregnable wall-like hill, his left nearly an inclosed fortification. Our only hope of success was to get in his rear by moving far to our right, which overlapped the Federal left.

Bushrod Johnson's three brigades in Longstreet's center were the first to fill the gap left by Wood's withdrawal from the Federal right; but the other five brigades under Hindman and Kershaw moved promptly into line as soon as space could be found for them, wheeled to the right, and engaged in the murderous flank attack. On they rushed, shouting, yelling, running over batteries, capturing trains, taking prisoners, seizing the headquarters of the Federal commander, at the Widow Glenn's, until they found themselves facing the new Federal line on Snodgrass Hill. Hindman had advanced a little later than the center, and had met great and immediate success. The brigades of Deas and Manigault charged the breastworks at double-quick, rushed over them, drove Laiboldt's Federal brigade of Sheridan's division off the field down the Rossville road; then General Patton Anderson's brigade of Hindman, having come into line, attacked and beat back the forces of Davis, Sheridan, and Wilder in their front, killed the hero and poet General Lytle, took 1100 prisoners, 27 pieces of artillery, commissary and ordnance trains, etc. Finding no more resistance on his front and left, Hindman wheeled to the right to assist the forces of the center. The divisions of Stewart, Hood, Bushrod Johnson, and Hindman came together in front of the new stronghold of the Federals.

It was now 2:30 P.M. Longstreet with his staff, was lunching on sweet-potatoes. A message came just then that the commanding general wished to see him. He found Bragg in rear of his lines, told him of the steady and satisfactory progress of the battle, that sixty pieces of artillery had been reported captured (though probably the number was over-estimated), that many prisoners and stores had been taken, and that all was going well. He then asked for additional troops to hold the ground gained, while he pursued the two broken corps down the Dry Valley road and cut off the retreat of Thomas. Bragg replied that there was no more fight in the troops of Polk's wing, that he could give Longstreet no reënforcements. . . .

Some of the severest fighting had yet to be done. . . . Hindman and Bushrod Johnson organized a column of attack upon the front and rear of the stronghold of Thomas. . . . It began at 3:30 P.M. A terrific contest ensued. The bayonet was used, and men were killed and wounded with clubbed muskets. A little after 4, the enemy was reënforced, and advanced, but was repulsed by Anderson and Kershaw.

—HILL, "Chickamauga—The Great Battle of the West"

B. THOMAS HOLDS THE HORSESHOE RIDGE

The furious initial attack on the Federal left, on the morning of the 20th, although repulsed, unfortunately led to changes in Rosecrans's army materially affecting the results of the general conflict. Thomas, discovering his position turned and his front assaulted, hurried messengers to Rosecrans for assistance. Two aides, in rapid succession, called for reënforcements. All was still on the Federal right. The fight was raging with grand fury on the left.

Rosecrans felt that his apprehensions of the morning were to be realized. The Confederates were doubtless massing on his left. They had reached the much-coveted Chattanooga road. McCook was at once notified that Thomas was heavily pressed, that the left must be held at all hazards, and that he must be ready to reënforce Thomas at a moment's warning. Five minutes later came the order to hurry Sheridan's two brigades to the left. Negley's troops, replaced by Wood, had started. Van Cleve, with two brigades, was also sent to aid Thomas. McCook was now left with one of Sheridan's brigades and two of Jefferson C. Davis's, all depleted by Saturday's losses. They were unable to form a connected front, but joined Wood on their left. Captain Kellogg, of Thomas's staff, hurrying along the line with orders, unfortunately reported to Rosecrans that he had noticed "Brannan was out of line, and Reynolds's right exposed."

Turning to an aide Rosecrans directed him to order Wood "to close up on Reynolds as fast as possible and support him." In fact, Reynolds was *not* needing help, and Brannan was in position on his right, but slightly in rear. Wood, whose left connected with Brannan's right, passed to the rear of Brannan to reach Reynolds's position; thus a wide gap was left in the Union line. McCook had already called up Wilder to strengthen his front, and sent for the main cavalry to protect the right. The right had unexpectedly become, as it were, the *rear* of the army.

Unhappily for the National army, Bragg was *not* now massing his forces on our left. He had just been defeated and repulsed there. Bragg's main plan had failed; but in the quiet forest, within almost a stone's-throw of our right, and in the still overclouding mist, were Longstreet and Buckner, with the left wing of the Confederate army massed in battle array, impatiently awaiting the signal for attack.

Longstreet's troops were placed in column of brigades at half distance,—a masterpiece of tactics. Hood, a soldier full of energy and dash, was to lead the column, his own division being massed five brigades deep, with the brigades of Kershaw and Humphreys as additional supports.

The order to advance came at last. The deep Confederate lines suddenly appeared. The woods in our front seemed alive. On they came like an angry flood. They struck McCook's three remaining brigades, the remnants of the Federal right. Under the daring personal exertions of McCook and Davis, they made a gallant but vain resistance. The massed lines of the enemy swarmed around their flanks. Pouring through the opening made by Wood's withdrawal, they struck his last brigade as it was leaving the line. It was slammed back like a door, and shattered. Brannan, on Wood's left, was struck in front and flank. His right was flung back; his left stood fast. Sheridan, hastening to the left with two brigades, was called back, and rushed to the rescue. His little force stayed the storm for a time. Wave after wave of Confederates came on; resistance only increased the multitude. Brannan's artillery, attacked in flank, rushed to the rear for clearer ground, and, with the Confederates at their heels, suddenly plunged into Van Cleve marching to the aid of Thomas. Disorder ensued; effective resistance was lost. The Reserve Artillery of the center, well posted in rear, unable to manœuvre in the undergrowth, hedged around by infantry a half hour before, was now without immediate support. The sudden rush of Longstreet's compact column through the forest had foiled all plans. The astonished artillerists were swept from their guns. General Negley, with one of his brigades isolated in rear, shared the general fate of the right.

When Longstreet struck the right, Rosecrans was near McCook and Crittenden. Seeing our line swept back, he hurried to Sheridan's force for aid. With staff and escort he recklessly strove to stem the tide. They attempted to pass to the left through a storm of canister and musketry, but were driven back.

All became confusion. No order could be heard above the tempest of battle. With a wild yell the Confederates swept on far to their left. They seemed everywhere victorious. Rosecrans was borne back in the retreat. Fugitives, wounded, caissons, escort, ambulances, thronged the narrow pathways. He concluded that our whole line had given way, that the day was lost, that the next stand must be made at Chattanooga. McCook and Crittenden, caught in the same tide of retreat, seeing only rout everywhere, shared the opinion of Rosecrans, and reported to him for instructions and coöperation.

Briefly, this is the story of the disaster on our right at Chickamauga: We were overwhelmed by numbers; we were beaten in detail. Thirty minutes earlier Longstreet would have met well-organized resistance. Thirty minutes later our marching division could have formed beyond his column of attack. . . .

The sound of battle had lulled. No Union force was in sight. A Confederate line near by was advancing against the position. Harrison, dismounting his men, dashed at the enemy in a most effective charge. Wilder, coming up on our right, also attacked. Wilder had two regiments armed with the same repeating-rifles. They did splendid work. Longstreet told Wilder after the war that the steady and continued racket of these guns led him to think an army corps had attacked his left flank. Bragg, cautious by nature, hesitated. By the time he was ready to turn Longstreet's force against Thomas, valuable time had elapsed.

Brannan, partly knocked out of line, had gathered his division on a hill at right angles to his former position, and a half mile in rear of Reynolds. General Wood came up with Harker's brigade and part of George P. Buell's, and posted them near Brannan's left. Some of Van Cleve's troops joined them, and fragments of Negley's.

General Thomas, ignorant of these movements and of the disaster to the right of the Union army, had again been attacked by Breckinridge and Forrest. They were again in Baird's rear with increased force. Thomas's reserve brigades, Willich, Grose, and Van Derveer, hurried to meet the attack. After a fierce struggle the Confederates were beaten back. Thomas, expecting the promised assistance of Sheridan, had sent Captain Kellogg to guide him to the left. Kellogg, hurrying back, reported that he had been fired on by a line of Confederates advancing in the woods in rear of Reynolds, who held the center of our general line.

The men in gray were coming on the right instead of Sheridan! Wood and Harker hoped the force advancing in the woods on their new front was a friendly one. The National flag was waved; a storm of bullets was the response. It was Stewart and Bate coming with their Tennesseeans. They had finally forced their way across the ragged edge of the Federal right, and were following Hood. Fortunately Thomas had just repulsed Breckinridge's attack on his left, and Stanley, Beatty, and Van Derveer had double-quicked across the "horseshoe" to our new right. They did not come a moment too soon. The improvised line of Federals thus hastily formed on "Battery Hill" now successfully withstood the assault of the enemy. The Union line held the crest. Longstreet was stayed at last. Gathering new forces, he soon sent a flanking column around our right. We could not extend our line to meet this attack. They had reached the summit, and were coming around still farther on through a protected ravine. For a time the fate of the Union army hung in the balance. All seemed lost, when unexpected help came from Gordon Granger and the right was saved.

—THRUSTON, "The Crisis at Chickamauga"

3. CHATTANOOGA UNDER SIEGE

After Chickamauga the Federals retired into Chattanooga; thus the army that had set out to capture the city ended by being caught in its own net. So serious was the situation that Grant himself came on to take charge of its relief. The immediate task was for Hooker to move into the area enclosed by the great bend of the Tennessee, between Bridgeport and Chattanooga; the second for Thomas to get control

*of Brown's Ferry. Then the two could link up. Had Bragg
been on the alert neither of these movements could have
succeeded, for Raccoon Mountain and Lookout Mountain
commanded both approaches. Bragg however failed to build
up adequate strength in this region south and west of Chattanooga. On October 26 Hooker crossed the Tennessee at
Bridgeport and moved overland toward Brown's Ferry, and
some of Thomas' forces captured Brown's Ferry and the
heights above it.*

*The war correspondent, W. F. G. Shanks, who was with
the Army of the Cumberland, here tells what life was like
during the siege and how the siege was raised by opening
the "cracker line."*

The siege of Chattanooga was the only one which any one
of the Union armies suffered or sustained. It is a singular fact,
worthy of mention just here, that the troops of the Union
never abandoned a siege once begun, nor surrendered a position regularly invested, and were compelled to surrender
all those fortresses in which they were besieged. The Union
armies invested and finally captured Yorktown, Fort Donelson,
Corinth, Vicksburg, Island No. 10, Port Hudson, Petersburg, Atlanta, Mobile, Savannah, Charleston, Fort Fisher,
Wilmington, and many other points of lesser importance and
held by mere detachments, not, like those mentioned, gar-
risoned by entire armies. The rebels besieged Nashville, Knoxville, Chattanooga, and other minor positions held by fragments of armies and failed in all. They came nearest to success
at Chattanooga. . . .

If there was little of beauty or elegance in the place when
our troops retreated into it from Chickamauga, there was a
great deal less a fortnight subsequently. Like many another
Southern town Chattanooga grew suddenly old; one might
say it turned gray during the brief but dark night of the
siege. General Saint Clair Morton, the chief of Rosecrans's
engineers, had no mercy; he had no idea of economy either.
As one of his fellow-officers once said of him, "if Morton
needed a certain quantity of earth for a fort, the fact that
it was a gold mine would make no difference to him; he
would only say, 'Gold dust will resist artillery—it will do.'"
So laying out his line of works Morton budged from his
course not an inch to spare the town. Residences were turned
into block-houses; black bastions sprang up in former vine-
yards; rifle-pits were run through the grave-yards; and soon
a long line of works stretched from the river above to the

river below the city, bending crescentlike around it, as if it were a huge bow of iron, and rendering it impregnable. For a fortnight the whole army worked on the fortifications, and it became literally a walled city.

Not alone from the fact that it was shut in by the mud walls of these impregnable fortifications was the town an intrenched camp, and the engineers alone did not despoil Chattanooga of its small modicum of beauty. The winter-quarters of the troops, composed of small dog-kennel-shaped huts, built of boards and roofed over with the shelter-tents with which the soldiers were provided, were scattered all over the town in valley and on hill-side, and it was not difficult to imagine it again the little Indian town of huts and wigwams which Hanging Bird had described. The camps of soldiers were not cantonments in the proper sense of the term. The immediate presence and threatening proximity of the enemy rendered it necessary to safety and discipline that the troops should encamp in the regular order of regiments and brigades, so as to be prepared to form at the sound of alarm, ready to repulse or to make an attack. Instead, therefore, of camping indiscriminately in houses as they stood, the men tore down the houses and fences, and of the frame-work built their huts, and of the bricks their chimneys and fire-places.

The veteran soldier is very ingenious, and makes himself happy on very little; and the quarters of those at Chattanooga during the siege possessed all the "modern improvements." They had curious modes of making themselves comfortable. The rebels used to call our men, when working on forts, rifle-pits, etc., "beavers in blue." The veteran was a regular beaver when building his house. He would buy, beg, or steal from the quarter-master (a species of theft recognized by the camp code of morals as entirely justifiable) the only tool he needed, an axe. With this he would cut, hew, dig, drive—any thing you like, in fact. With his axe he would cut the logs for his cabin—miniature logs, two inches in diameter—trim them to the proper length, and drive the necessary piles. With his axe he would cut the brushwood or the ever-green, and thatch his roof or cover it with his shelter-tent. With his axe he would dig a mud-hole in which to make his plaster for filling the crevices of the logs, and thus shut out the cold. Doors, chimneys, benches, chairs, tables, all the furniture of his commodious house, he would make with the same instrument.

When all was finished he would sit down to enjoy himself,

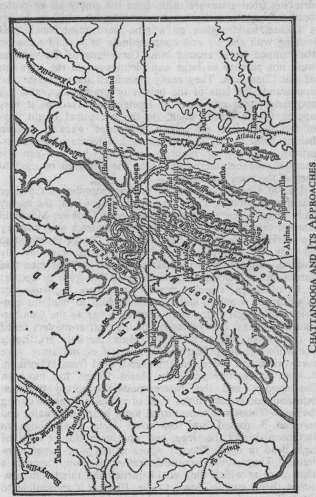

CHATTANOOGA AND ITS APPROACHES

sleeping on good clean straw, dining off a wooden table, drinking from glassware made from the empty ale or porter bottles from the suttler's tent, combing his whiskers before a framed looking-glass on a pine-board mantel-shelf, and looking with the air and contentedness of a millionaire on the camped world around him. These huts of the veterans were not perhaps so large and picturesque as the wigwams of the Cherokees. They really resembled more in size and appearance the huts of the beaver or prairie-dogs, and this comparison did not seem so foreign or forced as it may appear to the reader when, on the occasional bright days of the bleak siege, the gallant "war dogs" were to be seen issuing forth to bay a deep-mouthed welcome to the enter-prising news-boy or faithful postman, who had run the gauntlet of rebel sharpshooters or the embargo of mud to furnish the news from home.

Life in Chattanooga during the two months of the siege was dreary enough. There was no fighting to do; the enemy daily threw a few shells from the top of Lookout Mountain into our camps, but they were too wise to attack with infantry the works which soon encircled the city. Bragg preferred to rely for the final reduction of the garrison upon his ally Famine, and a very formidable antagonist did our men find him in the end. Bragg held the railroad line from Bridgeport to Chattanooga, thereby preventing its use by Rosecrans as a line of supplies, and compelling him to haul his pro-visions in wagon trains from Stevenson across the Cumber-land Mountains. Every exertion of the quarter-masters failed to fully supply the army by this route, the only practicable one while the siege lasted. The animals of the army were overworked and ill-fed, and thousands died from exhaustion. It was almost impossible to obtain forage for those in Chattanooga, and the quarter-masters reported that ten thousand horses and mules died of actual starvation during the siege. Thousands were turned loose in the mountains and perished. I passed over the route from Chattanooga to Stevenson during the siege, and was never out of sight of these dead or dying "heroes whose names were never men-tioned." They would frequently gather in groups around a small pool at which they could quench the thirst that con-sumed them, and lie down to die. Finding it impossible to obtain forage for an animal which I had in Chattanooga, and which had been latterly subsisting on the pine-board fence to which his halter was attached, I turned the poor animal loose to graze near a small stream in the town. He was too exhausted to stray away from it; lying down he picked the few blades of grass within his reach, stretched his neck to the pool for the few drops of water which it gave, and at length gave up the ghost.

The other heroes in the beleaguered town hardly suffered less. Famine became a familiar fiend; they laughed in his face, as crowds will laugh in the face of great dangers and disasters, but it was a very forced laugh. The trains of supplies for the army were frequently twenty days on the route from Stevenson, only sixty miles distant, and as the trains were not numerous naturally the supplies in the town did not increase. And many of these trains frequently came in *empty*. They could not carry full loads across the mountains with skeletons for horses; each train had to be guarded, and the guards had to be supplied from the train whose safety they secured. Most of these guards were men from the besieged city, they had been on quarter rations of fat bacon and mouldy hard bread for weeks, and they did not lose the opportunity to satisfy the cravings of their appetites when guarding the trains. It was all nonsense for quarter-masters in charge to tell them they ought to remember their starving comrades in the besieged city, to appeal to their patriotism, and to talk about discipline; if there are any periods when discipline, patriotism, and sympathy are entirely sunk in a soldier's breast they are when he is thoroughly demoralized by defeat or reckless from hunger. So it frequently happened that the guards of a train eat it *in transitu*. After the third week of the siege the men were put on quarter rations, and only two or three articles were supplied in this meagre quantity. The only meat to be had was bacon, "side bacon" or "middling," I think it is called, and a slice about the size of the three larger fingers of a man's hand, sandwiched between the two halves of a "Lincoln Platform," as the four inches square cake of "hard bread" was called, and washed down by a pint of coffee, served for a meal.

Men can not dig fortifications and fight very long on such rations; and the whole army was half famished. I have often seen hundreds of soldiers following behind the wagon trains which had just arrived, picking out of the mud the crumbs of bread, coffee, rice, etc., which were wasted from the boxes and sacks by the rattling of the wagons over the stones. Nothing was wasted in those days, and though the inspectors would frequently condemn whole wagon loads of provisions as spoiled by exposure during the trip, and order the contents to be thrown away, the soldiers or citizens always found some use for it.

The hundreds of citizens who were confined in the town at the same time suffered even more than the men. They were forced to huddle together in the centre of the town as best they could, and many of the houses occupied by them during the siege surpassed in filth, point of numbers of occupants, and general destitution, the worst tenement-house in New York city. . . .

The siege which was thus conducted was raised by strategy—the strategy of the same man who had captured the city, though he did not execute the movements. The enemy which was in reality investing the town was Famine: the way to defeat him was to find a shorter line of supplies by which the besieged army might be fed. A close study of the map had shown to Rosecrans that if Bragg could be driven from a small peninsula of land near Chattanooga, and on the south side of the Tennessee River, a very short route could be opened by the river to Bridgeport, and that by means of a couple of boats which the soldiers had built the army could be fed. Hooker's corps from the Army of the Potomac had arrived at Bridgeport on Oct. 20, and with this force the peninsula could be seized. But before he could get ready for the movement Rosecrans was relieved of the command, and General Thomas assumed control, with General Grant in chief command. In the mean time the troops in Chattanooga were on the eve of starvation. "We are issuing," said General Gordon Granger, "quarter rations for breakfast only." But Thomas, on assuming command, and being urged by Grant to hold on to the strong-hold at all hazards, had telegraphed in reply, "I will hold the town until we starve;" and the men cheerfully agreed to starve a while longer.

On the arrival of General Grant the movements which Rosecrans had planned were begun. Two columns to seize the peninsula started simultaneously—the one from Bridgeport under General Hooker, the other from Chattanooga under General W. F. Smith. Hooker moved overland along the railroad and seized upon Wauhatchie and three small hills near the mouth of Lookout Creek. Smith, with his command in pontoon boats, on the night of October 26, 1863, dropped down the Tennessee River, running past the rebel batteries to Brown's Ferry, where a prominent and commanding peak of hills on the peninsula was seized, and the boats were soon transformed into a pontoon bridge across the river at that point. General Hooker's position, which was only won after two very desperate engagements, one of which was fought at midnight, covered a road to Kelley's Ferry, a landing-place on the west side of the all-important peninsula; and the result of the whole operation was that a short and good road, only seven miles in length, was obtained from Chattanooga by way of Brown's Ferry to Kelley's Ferry; at which latter place the steamboats built by the troops landed supplies from Bridgeport. Supplies by this route could be very easily carried through in a day, and the army was very soon on full rations again.

—SHANKS, "Chattanooga, and How We Held It"

4. HOOKER WINS THE "BATTLE ABOVE THE CLOUDS"

As soon as the peril of the Federal position at Chattanooga was clear, Halleck ordered General Hooker to proceed west with two corps of the Army of the Potomac. Hooker arrived at Bridgeport early in October and, as we have seen, crossed the river into the Raccoon Mountain region on October 26. After he had cleared this area of Confederates, his next task was to seize control of Lookout Mountain, lying directly south of Chattanooga. Early on the morning of November 24 his forces, 10,000 strong, began their attack. Bragg, with characteristic imbecility, had less than 2,000 men posted here; these put up a stiff resistance but were overwhelmed.

The story of the "Battle above the Clouds" is told by Major Joseph Fullerton of the Army of the Cumberland.

The morning of November 24th opened with a cold, drizzling rain. Thick clouds of mist were settling on Lookout Mountain. At daybreak Geary's division, and Whitaker's brigade of Cruft's division, marched up to Wauhatchie, the nearest point at which Lookout Creek, swelled by recent rains, could be forded, and at 8 o'clock they crossed. The heavy clouds of mist reaching down the mountain-side hid the movement from the enemy, who was expecting and was well prepared to resist a crossing at the Chattanooga road below. As soon as this movement was discovered, the enemy withdrew his troops from the summit of the mountain, changed front, and formed a new line to meet our advance, his left resting at the palisade, and his right at the heavy works in the valley, where the road crossed the creek. Having crossed at Wauhatchie, Whitaker's brigade, being in the advance, drove back the enemy's pickets, and quickly ascended the mountain till it reached the foot of the palisade. Here, firmly attaching its right, the brigade faced left in front, with its left joined to Geary's division. Geary now moved along the side of the mountain, and through the valley, thus covering the crossing of the rest of Hooker's command. In the meantime Grose's brigade was engaging the enemy at the lower road crossing, and Woods' brigade of Osterhaus's division was building a bridge rather more than half a mile farther up the creek. Geary, moving down the valley, reached this point at 11 o'clock, just after the bridge was finished, and as Osterhaus's division and Grose's brigade were crossing.

Hooker's command, now united in the enemy's field, was ready to advance and sweep around the mountain. His line, hanging at the base of the palisades like a great pendulum, reached down the side of the mountain to the valley, where the force that had just crossed the creek was attached as its weight. Now, as, at the command of Hooker, it swung forward in its upward movement, the artillery of the Army of the Cumberland, on Moccasin Point, opened fire, throwing a stream of shot and shell into the enemy's rifle-pits at the foot of the mountain, and into the works thickly planted on the "White House" plateau. At the same time the guns planted by Hooker on the west side of the creek opened on the works which covered the enemy's right. Then followed a gallant assault by Osterhaus and Grose. After fighting for nearly two hours, step by step up the steep mountain-side, over and through deep gullies and ravines, over great rocks and fallen trees, the earthworks on the plateau were assaulted and carried, and the enemy was driven out and forced to fall back. He did so slowly and reluctantly, taking advantage of the rough ground to continue the fight.

It was now 2 o'clock. A halt all along the line was ordered by General Hooker, as the clouds had grown so thick that further advance was impracticable, and as his ammunition was almost exhausted and more could not well be brought up the mountain. But all the enemy's works had been taken. Hooker had carried the mountain on the east side, had opened communication with Chattanooga, and he commanded the enemy's line of defensive works in Chattanooga Valley.

At 2 o'clock Hooker reported to General Thomas and informed him that he was out of ammunition. Thomas at once sent Carlin's brigade from the valley, each soldier taking with him all the small ammunition he could carry. At 5 o'clock Carlin was on the mountain, and Hooker's skirmishers were quickly supplied with the means of carrying on their work.

In the morning it had not been known in Chattanooga, in Sherman's army, or in Bragg's camp, that a battle was to be fought. . . . Soon after breakfast, Sherman's men at the other end of the line, intent on the north end of Missionary Ridge, and Thomas's men in the center, fretting to be let loose from their intrenchments, were startled by the sound of artillery and musketry firing in Lookout Valley. Surprise possessed the thousands who turned their anxious eyes toward the mountain. The hours slowly wore away; the roar of battle increased, as it came rolling around the point of the mountain, and the anxiety grew. A battle was being fought just before and above them. They could hear, but could not see how it was going. Finally, the wind, tossing about the clouds and mist, made a rift that for a few minutes opened a view of White House plateau. The enemy was seen to be in flight, and Hooker's men were in pursuit! Then went up a mighty cheer from the thirty thousand in the valley that was heard above the battle by their comrades on the mountain.

As the sun went down the clouds rolled away, and the night came on clear and cool. A grand sight was old Lookout that night. Not two miles apart were the parallel campfires of the two armies, extending from the summit of the mountain to its base, looking like streams of burning lava, while in between, the flashes from the skirmishers' muskets glowed like giant fire-flies.

—FULLERTON, "The Army of the Cumberland at Chattanooga"

5. THE ARMY OF THE CUMBERLAND CARRIES MISSIONARY RIDGE

Grant's plan was strategically simple but tactically complex. His purpose was to assault Bragg all along the line, drive him from his entrenchments, and, if possible, cut off his retreat and destroy him. To achieve this he planned a three-pronged operation. Sherman was to cross the Tennessee on pontoons, march up the tongue of land in front of Chattanooga, cross over to the east, and attack Bragg at the northern tip of Missionary Ridge. Once this attack was under way Thomas was to launch an attack on the center. If and when these had succeeded Hooker was to strike from the south. The attack jumped off at dawn of November 25, and all went as planned except that Sherman was held and thrown back while Thomas' supporting attack achieved victory.

What Pickett's charge is to the Confederacy, Thomas' attack of November 25 on Missionary Ridge is to the North, one of those moments of gallantry that seem suspended in time and are ever present and ever real. The Confederates had constructed three rows of entrenchments on rugged boulder-strewn Missionary Ridge. When Grant saw that Sherman was in trouble he asked Thomas to create a diversion by carrying the first line of entrenchments; Thomas' men carried them, and kept going to the top.

Here are two accounts of this great dramatic event. The first is by William Morgan, a lieutenant in the 23rd Kentucky Infantry, part of Hazen's brigade. The second comes from our old acquaintance, Major Connolly of the 123rd Illinois Volunteers.

A. "FIRST ONE FLAG, THEN ANOTHER, LEADS"

From the position occupied by my regiment, Orchard Knob was in view and all eyes were leveled in that direction. Suddenly a commotion was discernible on Orchard Knob. Officers were seen mounting their horses and riding towards the several commands. Then every man in the line knew the crucial hour had come. Intense excitement seemed to stir every soldier and officer. Excitement is followed by nervous impatience.

Time moves slowly. Here and there a soldier readjusts his accouterments or relaces his shoes. All know that many will never reach the enemy's works, yet not a countenance shows fear. The delay is becoming unbearable.

At last the first boom of the signal is heard. Men fall in and dress without command. Another gun, and nervous fingers play with gunlocks. Another and another, and each man looks into the eyes of his comrade to ascertain if he can be relied upon. The examination must have been satisfactory, for, just as the report of the fifth gun breaks upon their ears, the line is moving without a word of command from anyone, and when the sixth gun is fired the troops are well on the way, with colors unfurled and guns at "right shoulder shift." All sensations have now given way to enthusiasm. It is a sight never to be forgotten. Fifteen to twenty thousand men in well-aligned formation, with colors waving in the breeze, almost shaking the earth with cadenced tread, involuntarily move to battle.

The troops have scarcely left the rifle-pits when the guns upon the ridge open upon them. Our heavy guns in Fort Wood and the field batteries vigorously respond. We see the enemy in the rifle-pits, at the base of the ridge, looking over the works, with guns in hand, prepared to deliver fire. Why do they hesitate? We are in range. They are evidently waiting so that every shot will tell. From the enemy's lower lines now comes a storm of bullets and the air is filled with every sound of battle. The noise is terrible. Our artillery is exploding shells along the top of the ridge, and a caisson is seen to burst off to the right.

Now all feeling seems to have changed to one of determination. A terrific cheer rolls along the line. Not a rifle has yet been fired by the assaulting column. The quick step has been changed to the "double quick." Another cheer, and the enemy's first line of work at the base of the ridge is ours, together with many of his troops. Shelter is sought on the reverse side of the enemy's works, but the fire from the hilltop makes protection impossible.

Over fifty cannon, supported by veterans of many battle-fields, covered by well-built fortifications, are sending down a rain of shell, shrapnel, and rifle-bullets. The bursting projectiles seem to compress the air and one's head feels as if bound with iron bands. Unable to return the enemy's fire, the delay drives the men to desperation. To remain is to be annihilated; to retreat is as dangerous as to advance. Here and there a man leaps the works and starts towards the hilltop; small squads follow. Then someone gave the command, "Forward!" after a number of men began to advance. Officers catch the inspiration. The mounted officers dismount and stone their horses to the rear. The cry, "Forward!" is repeated along the line, and the apparent impossibility is undertaken. . . .

But little regard to formation was observed. Each battalion assumed a triangular shape, the colors at the apex surrounded by the strongest men, the flanks trailing to the rear.

First one flag passes all others and then another leads. One stand of colors, on our left, is particularly noticeable. The bearer is far ahead of his regiment and advances so rapidly that he draws the enemy's concentrated fire. Then another color-bearer dashes ahead of the line and falls. A comrade grasps the flag almost before it reaches the ground. He, too, falls. Then another picks it up, smeared with his comrade's blood, waves it defiantly, and, as if bearing a charmed life, he advances steadily towards the top. Up, up he goes, his hat pulled over his eyes, his head bent forward as if facing a storm of rain and wind. The bullets whistle about him, splintering the staff. Onward he goes, followed by the admiring cheers of his comrades, who press close behind.

As far advanced as any, Hazen's brigade struggles slowly upward. Willich's brigade on Hazen's left was somewhat in advance, but his left has met a resistance it cannot apparently overcome. On the right, Sheridan's left is considerably in the rear. This is the result of someone recalling it after it had advanced about one-fourth the way up the ridge, but before it had retreated very far the order was countermanded, and now it is forging to the front. The advance of Hazen's brigade is approaching the Rebel works. The enemy is sweeping the face of the hill with a rain of bullets, and his artillery fire crashes along the hillside from vantage-point on both flanks, killing and maiming with all the destruction of double-shotted guns. The men push upward.

Colonel Langdon, who has held his place close to the colors of his consolidated battalion, has reached a sheltered place about twenty yards from the top. Halting the colors there until he had collected about 200 men, he ordered them to fix bayonets. It is hard to tell now whose command is the most advanced. All are losing men rapidly, but not a man lags. Turchin, away to the left, closes with the enemy. His advance has evidently been stopped. Colonel Langdon rises to his feet and is shot, but before he falls he gives the command, "Forward!" The men leap forward, fire into the faces of the enemy, and the colors of the 1st Ohio and 23d Kentucky, fifty minutes after the firing of the signal-guns are planted on the works, quickly followed by the entire brigade. Of the eight corporals composing the color guard of the consolidated battalion, all fell on the hillside, and of the two sergeants who started with the colors, one is dead and the other wounded. Willich's brigade, having overcome all resistance, is over the works and his troops with a portion of Hazen's are moving along the ridge to the left. Hazen personally directs his troops along the ridge to the right, two guns taken are turned upon the enemy on our right, and discharged by firing muskets over the vent until primers could be procured.

Hooker, all this time, has been closing in on the enemy's extreme left and rear. Thus attacked on the flank, with its center pierced, a panic pervades the enemy's line, and gives Sheridan, who has had one of the steepest and highest points to climb, his opportunity, of which he promptly takes advantage. At every point now the enemy's lines begin to melt away except near Bragg's headquarters, in front of Sheridan's center. Suddenly they too give up the fight, abandon their works, and roll down the eastern slope, followed by Sheridan's division. Now cheer upon cheer greets "Old Glory" as it dots the ridge at every point and waves in triumph in the bright rays of the western sun, and the campaign, begun by the Army of the Cumberland three months before, is ended.

The loss in Hazen's brigade was 530 killed and wounded, more than one-half the loss of the entire division. It captured, during this battle, about 400 prisoners, large quantities of small-arms, sixteen to eighteen pieces of artillery, and two stands of colors, and was the first to plant its colors on the ridge.

—MORGAN, "Hazen's Brigade at Missionary Ridge"

B. "AMID THE DIN OF BATTLE 'CHICKAMAUGA' COULD BE HEARD"

Chattanooga, Dec. 7, 1863

Dear wife: . . . On Monday, Nov. 23rd our Division was ordered to move out just in front of the fortifications. We did so, and the rebels, as they looked down on us from Lookout Mountain and Mission Ridge, no doubt thought we had come out for a review. But Sheridan's Division followed us out and formed in line with us. Wonder what the rebels thought then? "Oh, a Yankee review; we'll have some fun shelling them directly." But out came Wood's Division, then Cruft's Division, then Johnson's Division, then Howard's entire Corps of "Potomacs." "What can those Yankee fools mean," Bragg must have thought, as he sat at the door of his tent on Mission Ridge and watched the long lines of blue coats and glistening guns marching around in the valley below him, almost within gun shot of his pickets, and yet not a gun fired. All was peace in Chattanooga valley that day.

The sun shone brightly, the bands played stirring airs; tattered banners that had waved on battle fields from the Potomac to the Mississippi streamed out gaily, as if proud of the battle scars they wore. Generals Grant and Hooker, and Sherman and Thomas and Logan and Reynolds and Sheridan and scores of others, with their staffs, galloped along the lines, and the scene that spread out around me like a vast panorama of war filled my heart with pride that I was a soldier and member of that great army. But what did it all mean? Bragg, from his mountain eyrie, could see what we were doing just as well as Grant who was riding around amongst us. The rebels thought they had us hemmed in so that we dared not move, and so near starved that we could not move. Two o'clock came, and all was yet quiet and peaceful, gay as a holiday review; we could see crowds of rebels watching us from Mission Ridge and Lookout Mountain, but three o'clock came, and a solitary shot away over on our left, among Wood's men, made every fellow think: "Hark"! A few moments and another shot, then a rat-tat-tat-tat made almost every one remark: "Skirmishing going on over there." Wood's line moved forward, a few volleys, still Wood's line moved forward, and Sheridan's started forward, heavy work for a few minutes then all was quiet; two important hills were gained; cheer after cheer rang out in the valley and echoed and reverberated through the gorges of Lookout and Mission Ridge; still it was only 5 o'clock Monday afternoon. The bands commenced playing and the valley was again peaceful, but we all knew there was "something up," and Bragg must have thought so too. We lay there all night, sleeping on our arms.

Tuesday morning, Nov. 24th, broke bright and beautiful; the sun rose clear; but for whom was it a "sun of Austerlitz"? Grant or Bragg? We talked of Austerlitz and Waterloo at headquarters that morning. During the night the moon was almost totally eclipsed. We talked of that also. It was considered a bad omen among the ancients, on the eve of battle; we concluded also that it was ominous of defeat, but not for us; we concluded that it meant Bragg because he was perched on the mountain top, nearest the moon. Daylight revealed the hills which Wood and Sheridan had won the day before, bristling with cannon of sufficient calibre to reach Bragg's eyrie on Mission Ridge. About 9 o'clock in the morning some 30 heavy guns opened on Mission Ridge. It appeared then that we were to advance right down the valley and attack the rebel centre, but, hark! Away off on our right—3 miles away, on the opposite side of Lookout—we hear firing. What can that mean? Suddenly the cannon, with which we have been pounding away at Mission Ridge, are silent, and all eyes are turned westward toward Lookout Mountain. The sounds of battle increase there but it is on the other side of the mountain from us and we can see nothing, but the word passes around: "Hooker is storming Lookout"! My heart grows faint. Poor Hooker, with his Potomac boys are to be the forlorn hope! What? Storm that mountain peak 2400 feet high, so steep that a squirrel could scarcely climb it, and bristling all over with rebels, bayonets and cannon? Poor boys! far from your quiet New England homes, you have come a long way only to meet defeat on that mountain peak, and find your graves on its rugged sides! Lookout Mountain will only hereafter be known as a monument to a whole Corps of gallant New Englanders who died there for their country! But hold! Some one exclaims: "The firing comes nearer, our boys are getting up"! All eyes are turned toward the Mountain, and the stillness of death reigns among us in the valley, as we listen to the sounds of battle on the other side of the Mountain while all was quiet as a Puritan sabbath on our side of it. How hope and despair alternated in our breasts! How we prayed for their success and longed to assist them, can only be known by those of us who, in that valley, stood watching that afternoon and listening to the swelling diapason of their battle. But the firing actually did grow nearer, manifestly our men were drving them; Oh! now if they only can continue it, but we fear they cannot! I have a long telescope with which I can distinctly see everything on our side of the mountain. I scan the mountain with it closely and continuously, but not a soul can I see. After hours of anxious suspense I see a single rebel winding his way back from the firing and around to our side of the mountain.

I announce to the crowd of Generals standing around: "There goes a straggler"! and in an instant everybody's glass is to his eye, but no more stragglers are seen, still the battle rages, and the little gleam of hope, that solitary straggler raised in our breasts, dies out. Minutes drag like hours, the suspense is awful, but look! look! Here comes a crowd of stragglers! here they come by hundreds, yes by thousands! The mountain is covered with them! They are broken, running! There comes our flag around the point of the mountain! There comes one of our regiments on the double quick! Oh! such a cheer as then went up in the valley! Manly cheeks were wet with tears of joy, our bands played "Hail to the Chief," and 50 brazen throated cannon, in the very wantonness of joy, thundered out from the fortifications of Chattanooga, a salute to the old flag which was then on the mountain top. The work was done. Lookout was ours, never again to be used as a perch by rebel vultures. Didn't we of the old Army of the Cumberland feel proud though? It was one of the regiments that fought at Chickamauga that carried that first flag to the mountain top. It was a brigade of the old Chickamauga army that led the storming party up the mountain. A straggling skirmish fire was kept up along our (the Eastern) side of the mountain, which we could trace by the flashes of the guns, until 11 o'clock at night, but then all became quiet, and again we passed the night in line of battle, sleeping on our arms.

Bragg, no doubt, thought Hooker would continue to press forward across the valley from Lookout and attack his left on Mission Ridge in the morning, so he prepared for that during the night, by moving troops from his right to his left, to meet the anticipated attack of the morning, but Sherman, with his Vicksburg veterans, had all this time been lying concealed behind the hills on the North side of the Tennessee river, just North of the northern end of Mission Ridge, where Bragg's right was, awaiting the proper moment to commence his part of the stupendous plan. The time was now come.

Lookout was ours; now for Mission Ridge! Before daylight of Wednesday Nov. 25th, Sherman had his pontoons across the river, about 3 miles north of Chattanooga, and under cover of a dense fog, crossed his whole Corps and took possession of the northern extremity of Mission Ridge, finding nothing there but a few pickets, and there he fell to work fortifying. By this time Bragg saw his mistake. The attack of Wednesday was to be on his right, at the North end of Mission Ridge, instead of his left at the South end of the Ridge, so he hurriedly countermarched his troops back from his left to his right. When the fog rose, about ten o'clock in the morning, Sherman attempted to carry the summit of the Ridge but was repulsed; again he tried it but was again repulsed, still again he tried it and was repulsed. This time the fighting was all to the left of where we were instead of to the right, as it had been the day before. Sherman, after terrible fighting, had been repulsed in three successive efforts to crush the enemy's right on the top of the Ridge, and an order came for our Division to move up the river to his support. We started. The enemy could see us from the top of the Ridge, and quickly understood (or thought they did) our design, so they commenced shelling us, as our long line of 20 regiments filed along, but we moved along until we came to where a thin strip of woodland intervened between us and the Ridge. Sheridan's Division followed us and did the same. The enemy supposed of course that we were moving on up the river to the support of Sherman, but we were not; we halted and formed line of battle in that strip of woodland, facing Mission Ridge.

This, I confess, staggered me; I couldn't understand it; it looked as though we were going to assault the Ridge, and try to carry it by storm, lined and ribbed as it was with rifle pits, and its topmost verge crowded with rebel lines, and at least 40 cannon in our immediate front frowning down on us; we never could live a moment in the open spaces of 600 yards between the strip of woods in which we were formed, and the line of rifle pits at the base of the mountain, exposed as we would be to the fire of the 40 cannon massed, and from five to eight hundred feet immediately above us, also to the infantry fire from the rifle pits. I rode down along the line of our Division, and there I found Woods Division formed on our right and facing the Ridge just as we were; I rode on and came to Sheridan's Division formed on Woods right and facing the same. Here was a line of veteran troops nearly two miles long, all facing Mission Ridge, and out of sight of the enemy. The purpose at once became plain to me, and I hurried back to my own Division, and on asking Gen.——he replied: "When 6 guns are fired in quick succession from Fort Wood, the line advances to storm the heights and carry the Ridge if possible. Take that order to Col.——" (commanding the third brigade of our Division) "and tell him to move forward rapidly when he hears the signal." I communicated the order at once and that was the last I saw of the brigade commander, for he was killed just as he reached the summit of the Ridge.

A few moments elapse, it is about half past three o'clock P.M., when suddenly, 6 guns are rapidly fired from Fort Wood. "Forward"! rings out along that long line of men, and forward they go, through the strip of woods, we reach the open space, say 600 yards, between the edge of the woods and the rifle pits at the foot of the Ridge. "Charge"! is shouted wildly from hundreds of throats, and with a yell such as that valley never heard before, the three Divisions (60 regiments) rushed forward; the rebels are silent a moment, but then the batteries on top of the Ridge, open all at once, and the very heavens above us seemed to be rent asunder; shells go screaming over our heads, bursting above and behind us, but they hurt nobody and the men don't notice them; about midway of the open space a shell bursts directly over my head, and so near as to make my horse frantic and almost unmanageable; he plunges and bursts breast strap and girth and off I tumble with the saddle between my legs. My orderly catches my

horse at once, throws the blanket and saddle on him, gives
me a "leg lift" and I am mounted again, without girth, but
I hold on with my knees and catch up with our madcaps at
the first rifle pits, over these we go to the second line of pits,
over these we go, some of the rebels lying down to be run
over, others scrambling up the hill which is becoming too
steep for horses, and the General and staff are forced to abandon the direct ascent at about the second line of rifle pits; the
long line of men reach the steepest part of the mountain, and
they must crawl up the best way they can 150 feet more
before they reach the summit, and when they do reach it,
can they hold it? The rebels are there in thousands, behind
breastworks, ready to hurl our brave boys back as they
reach their works.

One flag bearer, on hands and knees, is seen away in advance of the whole line; he crawls and climbs toward a rebel
flag he sees waving above him, he gets within a few feet of it
and hides behind a fallen log while he waves his flag defiantly
until it almost touches the rebel flag; his regiment follows
him as fast as it can; in a few moments another flag bearer
gets just as near the summit at another point, and his regiment soon gets to him, but these two regiments dare not go
the next twenty feet or they would be annihilated, so they
crouch there and are safe from the rebels above them, who
would have to rise up, to fire down at them, and so expose
themselves to the fire of our fellows who are climbing up the
mountain.

The suspense is greater, if possible, than that with which
we viewed the storming of Lookout. If we can gain that Ridge;
if we can scale those breastworks, the rebel army is routed,
everything is lost for them, but if we cannot scale the works
few of us will get down this mountain side and back to the
shelter of the woods. But a third flag and regiment reaches
the other two; all eyes are turned there; the men away above
us look like great ants crawling up, crouching on the outside
of the rebel breastworks. One of our flags seems to be moving; look! look! look! Up! Up! Up! it goes and is planted
on the rebel works; in a twinkling the crouching soldiers are
up and over the works; apparently quicker than I can write
it the 3 flags and 3 regiments are up, the close fighting is
terrific; other flags go up and over at different points along
the mountain top—the batteries have ceased, for friend and
foe are mixed in a surging mass; in a few moments the
flags of 60 Yankee regiments float along Mission Ridge
from one end to the other, the enemy are plunging down

the Eastern slope of the Ridge and our men in hot pursuit, but darkness comes too soon and the pursuit must cease; we go back to the summit of the Ridge and there behold our trophies—dead and wounded rebels under our feet by hundreds, cannon by scores scattered up and down the Ridge with yelling soldiers astraddle them, rebel flags lying around in profusion, and soldiers and officers completely and frantically drunk with excitement. Four hours more of daylight, after we gained that Ridge would not have left two whole pieces of Bragg's army together.

Our men, stirred by the same memories, shouted "Chickamauga"! as they scaled the works at the summit, and amid the din of battle the cry "Chickamauga"! "Chickamauga"! could be heard. That is not *fancy* it is *fact*. Indeed the plain unvarnished facts of the storming of Mission Ridge are more like romance to me now than any I have ever read in Dumas, Scott or Cooper. On that night I lay down upon the ground without blankets and slept soundly, without inquiring whether my neighbors were dead or alive, but, on waking found I was sleeping among bunches of dead rebels and Federals, and within a few rods of where Bragg slept the night before, if he slept at all.

—"Major Connolly's Letters to His Wife"

6. "THE DISASTER ADMITS OF NO PALLIATION"

Poor Braxton Bragg! He had come out of the Mexican War with a great reputation, he had won Jefferson Davis' admiration and confidence, as early as February 1861 he had been commissioned brigadier general in the new Confederate Army. But he was stiff-necked, arrogant, and quarrelsome, unpopular alike with officers and with rank and file. Victories might have made these traits bearable, but Bragg could not win victories or—if he did, as at Chickamauga—could not exploit them. After Chattanooga he asked to be relieved of his command; Davis brought him back to Richmond as military advisor.

Headquarters Army of Tennessee
Dalton, Ga., December 1, 1863
His Excellency, JEFFERSON DAVIS,
President Confederate States, Richmond:
Mr. President: I send by Lieutenant Colonel Urquhart a

plain, unvarnished report of the operations at Chattanooga, resulting in my shameful discomfiture. The disaster admits of no palliation, and is justly disparaging to me as a commander. I trust, however, you may find upon full investigation that the fault is not entirely mine. Colonel Urquhart will inform you on any point not fully explained in the report. I fear we both erred in the conclusion for me to retain command here after the clamor raised against me. The warfare has been carried on successfully, and the fruits are bitter. You must make other changes here, or our success is hopeless. Breckinridge was totally unfit for any duty from the 23rd to the 27th—during all our trials—from drunkenness. The same cause prevented our complete triumph at Murfreesborough. I can bear to be sacrificed myself, but not to see my country and my friends ruined by the vices of a few profligate men who happen to have an undue popularity. General Hardee will assure you that Cheatham is equally dangerous.

May I hope, as a personal favor, that you will allow my friend Colonel Urquhart to continue with me as a part of my personal staff? He has never acted in any other capacity, and is almost a necessity in enabling me to bring up my records. I shall ever be ready to do all in my power for our common cause, but feel that some little rest will render me more efficient than I am now.

Most respectfully and truly, yours,

BRAXTON BRAGG,
General, &c.
—*War of the Rebellion . . . Official Records*

7. BURNSIDE HOLDS OUT AT KNOXVILLE

Everywhere in the West that fall and winter of 1863 saw Confederate fortunes wane. While Rosecrans was organizing his army for the Tullahoma campaign, Burnside led the Army of the Ohio into East Tennessee. The purpose of his campaign was both military and political: to cut the railroad connection between Tennessee and Virginia, and to rescue the loyal Unionists of the mountainous region of eastern Tennessee. Bragg promptly sent a corps, under General Buckner, to contest this area with him, and later sent reinforcements under Longstreet. Burnside withdrew into the fortifications of Knoxville and there awaited attack.

What happened is here told by Major Burrage of the 35th Massachusetts Volunteers. Henry S. Burrage was a student at the Newton Theological Seminary when the war broke out. He enlisted as a private and rose to a majority; he fought in Tennessee, was wounded at Cold Harbor, and captured at Petersburg. After the war he had a long and distinguished career as clergyman and historian.

On November 13, Burnside received information that Longstreet had reached the Tennessee River at Hough's Ferry, a few miles below Loudon; and at once informing General Grant, he advised a concentration of his forces in East Tennessee for the purpose of giving battle, but expressed the opinion that the concentration should be neither in the neighborhood of Loudon nor at Kingston, but at Knoxville; thus drawing the enemy further away from Bragg, so far in fact that in case Bragg should order Longstreet to return because his assistance was needed at Chattanooga, he could not be recalled in season to render it. To this General Grant made reply: "It is of the most vital importance that East Tennessee should be held. Take immediate steps to that end. Evacuate Kingston if you think best."

Thrown thus upon his own resources, General Burnside's plan plainly was this—to draw Longstreet up the valley, checking his advance as much as possible and making Knoxville as secure as the circumstances would admit, until Grant, having grappled with Bragg at Chattanooga, should be able to send reënforcements compelling Longstreet to withdraw. . . .

At the time of the arrival of the troops on the morning of November 17, Knoxville was by no means in a defensible condition. The bastion-work occupied by Benjamin's and Buckley's batteries was not only unfinished, but was little more than begun. It required the labor of two hundred Negroes four hours to clear a place for the guns. There was also a fort in process of construction on Temperance Hill. But the work all along the line was now hurried forward with eagerness and even enthusiasm. As fast as the troops were placed in position, they commenced the construction of rifle-pits in their front, but with only a meagre supply of either spades or shovels. Though wearied by three days of marching and fighting, the troops gave themselves to the work with the energy of fresh men. As helpers, both citizens and contrabands were pressed into the service. Many of the former were loyal to the Union cause and devoted themselves to their tasks with a zeal that evinced the interest they felt in making good the defence of the town; but some of them were bitter rebels, and, as Captain Poe well remarked, "worked with a very poor grace, which blistered hands did not tend to improve." The contrabands engaged in the work with that heartiness which throughout the war characterized their labors for the Union cause. . . .

Longstreet did not leave Campbell's Station until the morning of November 17. McLaws' division led the column, and reached the vicinity of Knoxville about noon. General Burnside had ordered General Shackelford to dismount his cavalry command under General Sanders and take position on the Kingston Road a mile or more in front of the Union line of defence on that side of Knoxville. This he did, and during the forenoon of the 17th General Sanders strengthened his position in all possible ways, so that when McLaws approached, he found Sanders' little force blocking his further progress. "Part of our line," says Longstreet, "drove up in fine style and was measurably successful, but other parts, smarting under the stiff musket-fire, hesitated and lay down under such slight shelter as they could find, but close under fire,—so close that to remain inactive would endanger repulse." With such stubbornness did General Sanders contest the approach of McLaws that the latter was compelled at length to bring up his artillery; and only by the combined assault of infantry and artillery was Sanders dislodged from his position. After his men fell back, the enemy pressed forward and established lines within rifle range of our own. McLaws' division formed the Confederate right, his right extending to the river. When Jenkins came up late in the afternoon, he continued the line from McLaws' left and extending to the Tazewell Road; while Hart's and Wheeler's cavalry continued the Confederate line to the Holston River. . . .

Meanwhile Burnside's men were devoting themselves with all diligence to the labor of strengthening and completing their works around the town. For the most part, in campaigns hitherto, they had been the attacking party. So it had been at Fredericksburg, where the Ninth Corps had last faced Longstreet. Here, they were behind defensive works, and it was evident that they regarded the more advantageous position with contentment and even satisfaction. When the main line had been made reasonably secure, the usual devices in the way of obstruction received attention, such as the construction of abatis, chevaux-de-frise, to which were added wire entanglements extending from the stumps of trees, especially in front of Fort Sanders. Along a portion of the line another obstacle was formed by erecting dams on First and Second creeks, and throwing back the water. The whole constituted a series of obstructions which could not be passed in the face of a heavy fire without great difficulty and a fearful loss of life. On November 21, General Burnside telegraphed to General Grant: "We have a reasonable supply of ammunition, and the command is in good spirits. The officers and men have been indefatigable in their labors to make this place impregnable."

But the question of food-supplies was a serious one. When the siege commenced, there was in the commissary department at Knoxville little more than a day's ration for the whole of Burnside's force. Should the enemy gain possession of the south bank of the Holston, the means of subsistence for the troops at Knoxville would be cut off. Thus far Longstreet's attempts to close this part of East Tennessee to the Union forces had failed, and the whole country from the French Board to the Holston was open to our foraging parties. . . .

At length, foiled in these attempts to seize the south bank of the Holston, Longstreet commenced the construction of a raft at Boyd's Ferry, about six miles above Knoxville. Floating this down the swift current of the river, he hoped to carry away Burnside's pontoon-bridge and thus break his communication with the country from which he was obtaining his subsistence supplies. To thwart this plan, Captain Poe commenced the construction of a boom one thousand feet in length, composed of iron bars borne up by wooden floats. This was stretched across the river above the bridge. Afterwards a boom of logs, fastened end to end by chains, was constructed further up the river. This boom was fifteen hundred feet in length. . . .

November 23, in the evening, there was a Confederate attack on the Union pickets in front of the left of the Second Division, Ninth Corps. In falling back, the pickets fired the buildings on the abandoned ground to prevent their use by the enemy's sharpshooters. Among the buildings destroyed were the arsenal and the machine-shops near the railway station. The light of the blazing buildings illuminated the town. On the following day, November 24, the Twenty-first Massachusetts and Forty-eighth Pennsylvania, under the command of Lieutenant-Colonel Hawkes of the Twenty-first, charging the Confederate line at this point, drove it back and reoccupied the abandoned position. Early in the morning of the same day also, an attack was made by the Second Michigan—numbering one hundred and ninety-seven men —on the advanced parallel which the enemy had so constructed as to envelop the northwest bastion of Fort Sanders. The works were gallantly carried, but before the supporting columns could come up, the men of the Second Michigan were repulsed by Confederate reënforcements. The Union loss, amounting to sixty-seven, included Major Byington, commanding the Second Michigan, who was left on the field mortally wounded. In anticipation of an attack that night at some point on the Union intrenchments, orders were issued that neither officers nor men, on either the outer or inner lines, should sleep. . . .

November 27 all was quiet along the lines until evening, when cheers and the strains of band-music enlivened the enemy's camps. Had reënforcements arrived, or had Grant met with reverses at Chattanooga? . . . Colonel Giltner, with his cavalry from Virginia, had reported, the first of approaching additions to Longstreet's command. As yet no word had come from Bragg to Longstreet, though there were rumors that a battle had been fought at Chattanooga. The brigades of Johnson were not yet up, and the artillery and infantry coming from Virginia were a five or six days' march away; but General Leadbetter was impatient, and an order was given by Longstreet for an assault on Fort Sanders on November 28. The weather on that day, however, proved unfavorable.

Within the Union lines it was believed that the crisis of the siege was approaching. . . . On the night of the 27th, on our left we could hear chopping across the Holston on the knob which a few days before, as Longstreet tells us, had been selected as commanding the fort and the line from the fort to the river. His men were now clearing away the trees in front of the earthwork they had constructed at that point. Would they attack at daybreak? So we thought, connecting the chopping sounds with the sound of cheering and of music in the earlier part of the night; but the morning opened as quietly as any of its predecessors. Late in the afternoon the enemy seemed to be placing troops in position in front of our lines covering Fort Sanders; and our men stood in the trenches awaiting an attack. The day passed, however, without further demonstrations.

The regiment with which I was connected was in the line between Fort Sanders and the river, and opposite the Powell house. About eleven o'clock in the evening there was a sound of heavy musketry on our right. It was a dark, cloudy night; and at the distance of only a few feet it was impossible to distinguish any object. The firing soon ceased, with the exception of an occasional shot on the picket-line. An attack had evidently been made at some point, but precisely where, or with what success, was as yet unknown. Reports soon came in. The enemy first had driven in the pickets in front of Fort Sanders, and then had attacked our line still further to the left, which also was obliged to fall back. Later we learned that the enemy had advanced along the whole line and established themselves as near as possible to our works.

It was now evident that Longstreet intended to make an attack at some point in our intrenched position. But where? All the remainder of that long, cold night—our men were without overcoats largely—we stood in the trenches pondering that question. Might not this demonstration in front of Fort Sanders be only a feint designed to draw our attention from other parts of the line where the principal blow was to be struck? So some thought. Gradually the night wore away.

In the morning, a little after six o'clock, but while it was still dark, the enemy opened a furious fire of artillery. This was directed mostly against Fort Sanders; but several shells struck the Powell house in rear of Battery Noble. Roemer immediately responded from College Hill, but Benjamin and Buckley in Fort Sanders reserved their fire. In about twenty minutes the enemy's fire slackened, and in its place rose the well-known rebel yell in front of the fort. Then followed the rattle of musketry, the roar of cannon, and the bursting of shells. The yells died away, and then rose again. Now the roar of musketry and artillery was redoubled. It was a moment of the deepest anxiety along our brigade front and to the right of the fort. Our straining eyes were fixed upon the latter's dim outlines. The enemy had reached the ditch and were now endeavoring to scale the parapet. Whose will be the victory—oh whose? The yells again died away, and then followed three loud Union cheers from our men in the fort— "Hurrah! hurrah! hurrah!" How those cheers thrilled as we stood almost breathless in the trenches! They told us in language that could not be misunderstood that Longstreet had been repulsed and that the victory was ours. Peering through the morning mist toward the fort only a short distance away —a glorious sight—we saw that our flag was still there! . . .

The assault was made by three of McLaws' brigades,— Wofford's, Humphreys', and Bryan's,—with his fourth brigade in reserve. . . . In support were the two brigades of

Buckner's division commanded by General B. R. Johnson,—
they had arrived the day before,—and General Jenkins was
ordered to advance his three brigades in echelon on the left of
McLaws. The brigades were formed for attack in columns
of regiments, and were directed to move with fixed bayonets
and without firing.

When the artillery fire slackened on that cold gray morning the order for the charge was given. The salient of the
northwest bastion of Fort Sanders was the point of attack.
McLaws' columns were much broken in passing the abatis.
But the wire entanglements proved a greater obstacle. Whole
companies were prostrated. Benjamin now opened his triple-
shotted guns. Nevertheless the weight of the attacking force
carried the men forward, and in about two minutes from the
time the charge was commenced they had reached the ditch
around the fort, and were endeavoring to scale the parapet.
The guns, which had been trained to sweep the ditch, now
opened a most destructive fire. Lieutenant Benjamin also took
shells in his hands and lighting the fuse tossed them over the
parapet into the crowded ditch. "It stilled them down," he
said.

One of the Confederate reserve brigades, with added yells,
now came up in support, and in the crowded ditch the
slaughter was renewed. With desperate valor some of the
men in the ditch endeavored to scale the parapet and even
planted their flags upon it, but were swept off by the muskets
of the Seventy-ninth New York (Highlanders) and of the
Twenty-ninth Massachusetts. At length, satisfied of the hopelessness of their task, the survivors in the ditch surrendered.
They represented eleven regiments and numbered nearly three
hundred. Among them were seventeen commissioned officers.
Over two hundred dead and wounded, including three colonels, lay in the ditch alone. . . . Our loss in the fort was
eight men killed and five wounded, a total of thirteen.

To us of the Ninth Corps, as well as to Longstreet's men,
this assault on Fort Sanders was Fredericksburg reversed.
There, we were the attacking party. Now, we were behind a
fortified line with artillery well placed, and we had an object-
lesson as to the great advantage one has in a good position,
strongly defended, over one who is in the attacking
force. . . .

Never was a victory more complete and achieved at so
slight a cost.

—BURRAGE, "Burnside's East Tennessee Campaign"

X

Atlanta and the March to the Sea

WITH *Chattanooga in Federal hands and the Confederates in retreat, the way was open to the east, and to the inauguration of that giant pincers movement that in the end strangled the Confederacy. The Mississippi was under Federal control; in all the vast area between that river and the Appalachians only Alabama and part of Mississippi was still held by the Confederates. What Grant—now general of all the Union armies —planned for the spring of 1864 was a knockout blow: Meade to strike southward toward Richmond, Butler to move up from the James River, Sigel to advance from western Virginia, Sherman to capture Atlanta and "get into the interior of the enemy's country . . . inflicting all the damage you can against their war resources."*

Sherman's march from Atlanta to the sea is probably the best known of all Civil War campaigns—and it scarcely rose to the dignity of a campaign. It was more nearly a glorified picnic, for Hardee, who took over the scattered forces left in Georgia, was unable to offer any effective opposition. But the campaign from Chattanooga to Atlanta was a different matter. It is just 100 miles between these two cities, a rugged mountainous country, crisscrossed by rivers and valleys— poor country in which to subsist a large army. And confronting Sherman was now Joseph E. Johnston, one of the most resourceful of all Confederate commanders, and a master of Fabian tactics.

After the debacle at Chattanooga Bragg had withdrawn to Dalton. There he was supplanted by Johnston, who reorganized the stricken army, brought its strength up to about 60,000, and infused it with a new fighting spirit. Sherman, placed in command of the Grand Army of the West by Grant, reorganized his forces into three unequal armies, commanded by Thomas, Schofield, and McPherson. There was plenty of time for this reorganization: winter had set in, the roads were churned into mud, and not until April was Sherman ready to resume the offensive.

His advance was co-ordinated with Grant's offensive in the Wilderness, and jumped off on May 7. From Dalton to Atlanta is about 85 miles. It took Sherman two months to make that distance, and another two months to take Atlanta. If this seems like a long time it should be remembered that Grant enjoyed greater numerical superiority than Sherman, fought in less difficult country and closer to his bases, and found himself at the end of four months as far from Richmond as ever.

All the way from Dalton to Atlanta it was parry and thrust. Johnston would get astride the railroad, or a valley; Sherman would slide around his flank; threatened from the rear, Johnston would retire. Twice Sherman brought Johnston to battle, but both times on Johnston's terms, and both times was repulsed. Johnston was no Lee but he was the best retreater in either army. In the end the government, and public opinion, took alarm. Was Johnston going to give up Atlanta without a fight? So Davis feared, Davis who had never fully trusted him. Finally Johnston was removed from command and General Hood put in his place. A superb fighter, never happy except in battle, bearing his stump of a leg like a badge of honor, Hood was as impetuous as he was brave. He was expected to take the offensive, and he did. The results were disastrous. On September 1 Hood evacuated Atlanta. It was the first great Union victory of the year, and one that had important effects on the election that November.

What next? Where was Sherman to go? His communications were now stretched to the breaking point; Wheeler and Forrest operated in his rear. What he did was to get Grant's consent to abandon his communications and advance eastward into the heart of Georgia.

But meantime what of Hood? That general was no longer strong enough to oppose Sherman's mighty army. He decided, instead, to move westward and thus force Sherman either

*to return or lose Tennessee. His mind was bemused with even
more ambitious plans. If Sherman marched eastward he
would swing into Tennessee, reconquer Kentucky, and advance to the rescue of Lee!*

*But the day for all that was past. Sherman dispatched
Thomas and Schofield back to Tennessee with forces which,
eventually, aggregated about 50,000. And in due course of
time, as we shall see, Thomas took care of Hood.*

*Meantime Sherman was marching to the sea. Never was
such a march! If to Sherman's soldiers it was a picnic, to the
Negroes it was the "day of Jubilo." But to the South it was
such devastation and ruin as had never before been known in
American warfare. Sherman cut through Georgia like a giant
scythe, leaving a swath of ruined towns and plantations and
railroads and bridges 60 miles wide. On December 10 he
reached Savannah. He captured the city; swung north
through South Carolina; burned Columbia; and continued on
to the end.*

1. GENERAL SHERMAN TAKES COMMAND

*When Grant went to Washington to assume command
of all the Union armies, he appointed Sherman to the command of the armies in the West. Though something was to be
said for appointing Thomas to this position, Sherman's
claims were strong. It was not only that he had had a long
and brilliant military career, but that, however unlike in
character and temperament, he and Grant understood each
other perfectly and worked together like a well-trained
team. Indeed the great strategic plan for the destruction of
the Confederacy, elaborated in the spring of 1864, was in all
probability as much Sherman's as Grant's. After the war
Sherman succeeded to Grant's position as commanding general of all the armies of the United States.*

*John Chipman Gray, who gives us here a perspicacious
picture of General Sherman, was barely out of the Harvard
Law School when he was commissioned lieutenant in the
41st Massachusetts Volunteers. He served in the Peninsular
campaign, and was then appointed judge advocate with the
rank of major. He was later Story Professor of Law at the
Harvard Law School and a lifelong student of the Civil War.*

General Sherman is the most American looking man I ever saw, tall and lank, not very erect, with hair like a thatch, which he rubs up with his hands, a rusty beard trimmed close, a wrinkled face, sharp, prominent red nose, small, bright eyes, coarse red hands; black felt hat slouched over the eyes (he says when he wears anything else the soldiers cry out, as he rides along, "Hallo, the old man has got a new hat"), dirty dickey with the points wilted down, black, old-fashioned stock, brown field officer's coat with high collar and no shoulder-straps, muddy trowsers and one spur. He carries his hands in his pockets, is very awkward in his gait and motion, talks continually and with immense rapidity, and might sit to *Punch* for the portrait of an ideal Yankee. He was of course in the highest spirits and talked with an openness which was too natural not to be something more than apparent. In striving to recall his talk, I find it impossible to recall his language or indeed what he talked about, indeed it would be easier to say what he did not talk about than what he did. I never passed a more amusing or instructive day, but at his departure I felt it a relief and experienced almost an exhaustion after the excitement of his vigorous presence.

He has Savannah securely invested, his left rests securely on the Savannah River, his right at Fort McAllister, his line is within the 3 mile post from the city; he intends to throw a division across the Savannah to prevent the escape of Hardie [sic] from the city, and says he shall take his own time about reducing the city, unless he is hurried by despatches from General Grant; he has 60,000 men with him and only wishes there were more men in Savannah; he says the city is his sure game and stretches out his arm and claws his bony fingers in the air to illustrate how he has his grip on it. There is a "whip the creation" and an almost boastful confidence in himself which in an untried man would be very disgusting, but in him is intensely comic. I wish you could see him, he is a man after your own heart, like Grant he smokes constantly, and producing 6 cigars from his pocket said they were his daily allowance, but judging at the rate he travelled through them while he was on our boat, he must often exceed it. He scouted the idea of his going on ships and said he would rather march to Richmond than go there by water; he said he expected to turn North toward the latter end of December, at the same time the sun did, and that if he went through South Carolina, as he in all probability should, that his march through that state would be one of the most horrible things in the history of the world, that the devil himself could not restrain his men in that state; and I do not think that he (that is Sherman, not the devil) would try to restrain them much. He evidently purposes to make the South feel the horrors of war as much as he legitimately can, and if the men trespass beyond the strict limits of his orders he does not inquire into their cases too curiously. He told with evident delight how on his march he could look 40 miles in each direction and see the smoke rolling up as from one great bonfire.

> —Letter of John Chipman Gray to John Ropes,
> December 14, 1864

2. SHERMAN MARCHES FROM CHATTANOOGA TO ATLANTA

We begin our account of the Atlanta campaign with a general survey by its chief architect, then turn to some of its more striking episodes. There is no better account of the first phase of the campaign than that by Sherman himself. Different as Sherman was from Grant, his Memoirs have much the same qualities as those of Grant—simplicity, lucidity, and objectivity. Sherman is concerned to make clear, here, that the campaign for Atlanta was a very tough affair. He was fighting in difficult terrain, with long lines of communications, and against an able and resourceful opponent.

I now turn with a feeling of extreme delicacy to the conduct of that other campaign from Chattanooga to Atlanta, Savannah, and Raleigh, which with liberal discretion was committed to me by General Grant in his minute instructions of April 4th and April 19th, 1864. To all military students these letters must be familiar, because they have been published again and again, and there never was and never can be raised a question of rivalry or claim between us as to the relative merits of the manner in which we played our respective parts. We were as brothers—I the older man in years, he the higher in rank. We both believed in our heart of hearts that the success of the Union cause was not only necessary to the then generation of Americans, but to all future generations. We both professed to be gentlemen and professional soldiers, educated in the science of war by our generous Government for the very occasion which had arisen. Neither of us by nature was a combative man; but with honest hearts and a clear purpose to do what man could we embarked on that campaign, which I believe, in its strategy, in its logistics, in its grand and minor tactics, has added new luster to the old science of war. Both of us had at our front generals to whom in early life we had been taught to look up,—educated and experienced soldiers like ourselves, not likely to make any mistakes, and each of whom had as strong an army as could be collected from the mass of the Southern people,—of the same blood as ourselves, brave, confident, and well equipped; in addition to which they had the most decided advantage of operating in their own difficult country of mountain, forest, ravine, and river, affording admirable opportunities for defense, besides the other equally important advantage that we had to invade the country of our unqualified enemy and expose our long lines of supply to the guerrillas of an "exasperated people." Again, as we advanced we had to leave guards to bridges, stations, and intermediate depots, diminishing the fighting force, while our enemy gained strength by picking up his detachments as he fell back, and had railroads to bring supplies and reënforcements from his rear. I instance these facts to offset the common assertion that we of the North won the war by brute force, and not by courage and skill.

On the historic 4th day of May, 1864, the Confederate army at my front lay at Dalton, Georgia, composed, according to the best authority, of about 45,000 men, commanded by Joseph E. Johnston, who was equal in all the elements of generalship to Lee, and who was under instructions from the war powers in Richmond to assume the offensive northward as far as Nashville. But he soon discovered that he would have to conduct a defensive campaign. Coincident with the movement of the Army of the Potomac, as announced by telegraph, I advanced from our base at Chattanooga with the Army of the Ohio, 13,559 men; the Army of the Cumberland, 60,773, and the Army of the Tennessee, 24,465—grand total, 98,797 men and 254 guns.

I had no purpose to attack Johnston's position at Dalton in front, but marched from Chattanooga to feign at his front and to make a lodgment in Resaca, eighteen miles to his rear, on "his line of communication and supply." The movement was partly, not wholly, successful but it compelled Johnston to let go Dalton and fight us at Resaca where, May 13th-16th, our loss was 2747 and his 2800. I fought offensively and defensively, aided by earth parapets. He then fell back to Calhoun, Adairsville, and Cassville, where he halted for the battle of the campaign; but, for reasons given in his memoirs, he continued his retreat behind the next spur of mountains to Allatoona.

Pausing for a few days to repair the railroad without attempting Allatoona, of which I had personal knowledge acquired in 1844, I resolved to push on toward Atlanta by way of Dallas; Johnston quickly detected this, and forced me to fight him, May 25th-28th, at New Hope Church, four miles north of Dallas, with losses of 3000 to the Confederates and 2400 to us. The country was almost in a state of nature —with few or no roads, nothing that a European could understand; yet the bullet killed its victim there as surely as at Sevastopol.

Johnston had meantime picked up his detachments, and had received reënforcements from his rear which raised his aggregate strength to 62,000 men, and warranted him in claiming that he was purposely drawing us far from our base, and that when the right moment should come he would turn on us and destroy us. We were equally confident, and not the least alarmed. He then fell back to his position at Marietta, with Brush Mountain on his right, Kenesaw his center, and Lost Mountain his left. His line of ten miles was too long for his numbers, and he soon let go his flanks and concentrated on Kenesaw. We closed down in battle array, repaired the railroad up to our very camps, and then prepared for the contest. Not a day, not an hour, not a minute was there a cessation of fire. Our skirmishers were in absolute contact, the lines of battle and the batteries but little in rear of the skirmishers; and thus matters continued until June 27th, when I ordered a general assault, with the full coöperation of my great lieutenants, Thomas, McPherson, and Schofield, as good and true men as ever lived or died for their country's cause; but we failed, losing 3000 men, to the Confederate loss of 630. Still, the result was that within three days Johnston abandoned the strongest possible position and was in full retreat for the Chattahoochee River. We were on his heels; skirmished with his rear at Smyrna Church on the 4th day of July, and saw him fairly across the Chattahoochee on the 10th, covered and protected by the best line of field intrenchments I have ever seen, prepared long in advance. No officer or soldier who ever served under me will question the generalship of Joseph E. Johnston. His retreats were timely, in good order, and he left nothing behind. We had advanced into the enemy's country 120 miles, with a single-track railroad, which had to bring clothing, food, ammunition, everything requisite for 100,000 men and 23,000

FROM CHATTANOOGA TO ATLANTA

animals. The city of Atlanta, the gate city opening the interior of the important State of Georgia, was in sight; its protecting army was shaken but not defeated, and onward we had to go, —illustrating the principle that "an army once on the offensive must maintain the offensive."

We feigned to the right, but crossed the Chattahoochee by the left, and soon confronted our enemy behind his first line of intrenchments at Peach Tree Creek, prepared in advance for this very occasion. At this critical moment the Confederate Government rendered us most valuable service. Being dissatisfied with the Fabian policy of General Johnston, it relieved him, and General Hood was substituted to command the Confederate army [July 18th]. Hood was known to us to be a "fighter," a graduate of West Point of the class of 1853, No. 44, of which class two of my army commanders, McPherson and Schofield, were No. 1 and No. 7. The character of a leader is a large factor in the game of war, and I confess I was pleased at this change, of which I had early notice. I knew that I had an army superior in numbers and *morale* to that of my antagonist; but being so far from my base, and operating in a country devoid of food and forage, I was dependent for supplies on a poorly constructed railroad back to Louisville, five hundred miles. I was willing to meet the enemy in the open country, but not behind well-constructed parapets.

Promptly, as expected, General Hood sallied from his Peach Tree line on the 20th of July, about midday, striking the Twentieth Corps (Hooker), which had just crossed Peach Tree Creek by improvised bridges. The troops became commingled and fought hand to hand desperately for about four hours, when the Confederates were driven back within their lines, leaving behind their dead and wounded. These amounted to 4796 men, to our loss of 1710. We followed up, and Hood fell back to the main lines of the city of Atlanta. We closed in, when again Hood, holding these lines with about one-half his force, with the other half made a wide circuit by night, under cover of the woods, and on the 22d of July enveloped our left flank "in air," a movement that led to the hardest battle of the campaign. He encountered the Army of the Tennessee,—skilled veterans who were always ready to fight, were not alarmed by flank or rear attacks, and met their assailants with heroic valor. The battle raged from noon to night, when the Confederates, baffled and defeated, fell back within the intrenchments of Atlanta. Their losses are reported 8499 to ours of 3641; but among these was McPherson, the commander of the Army of the Tennessee. Whilst this battle was in progress, Schofield at the center and Thomas on the right made efforts to break through the intrenchments at their fronts, but found them too strong to assault.

The Army of the Tennessee was then shifted, under its new commander (Howard), from the extreme left to the extreme right, to reach, if possible, the railroad by which Hood drew his supplies, when, on the 28th of July, he repeated his tactics of the 22d, sustaining an overwhelming defeat, losing 4623 men to our 700. These three sallies convinced him that his predecessor, General Johnston, had not erred in standing on the defensive. Thereafter the Confederate army in Atlanta clung to its parapets.

> —SHERMAN, "The Grand Strategy of the War
> of the Rebellion"

3. JOHNSTON HALTS SHERMAN AT NEW HOPE CHURCH

Only rarely, and then when he thought his position peculiarly favorable, could Johnston afford the offensive. New Hope Church (May 25-28) was one of those occasions. Here—a few miles north of Dalton—Sherman tried to pass around Johnston's right. Johnston succeeded in stopping this, but at a cost of almost 3,000 men; nothing daunted, Sherman then slid off on Johnston's left and continued his advance.

Here Johnston himself describes the engagement at New Hope Church.

In the mean time Jackson had given information of General Sherman's march toward the bridges near Stilesboro', and of the crossing of the leading Federal troops there on the 23d [May]. In consequence of this intelligence, Lieutenant-General Hardee was ordered to march that afternoon, by New Hope Church, to the road leading from Stilesboro', through Dallas, to Atlanta; and Lieutenant-General Polk to move to the same road, by a route farther to the left. Lieutenant-General Hood was instructed to follow Hardee on the 24th. . . . On the 25th the latter reached New Hope Church, early in the day. Intelligence was received from General Jackson's troops soon after, that the Federal army was near —its right at Dallas, and its line extending toward Alatoona.

Lieutenant-General Hood was immediately instructed to form his corps parallel with the road by which he had marched, and west of it, with the centre opposite to the church; Lieutenant-General Polk to place his in line with it, on the left, and Lieutenant-General Hardee to occupy a ridge extending from the ground allotted to Polk's corps, across the road leading from Dallas toward Atlanta—his left division, Bate's, holding that road.

As soon as his troops were in position, Lieutenant-General Hood, to "develop the enemy," sent forward Colonel Bush Jones, with his regiment and Austin's sharpshooters, in all about three hundred men. After advancing about a mile, this detachment encountered Hooker's corps. Having the written order of his corps commander to hold his ground after meeting the enemy, Colonel Jones resisted resolutely the attack of the overwhelming Federal forces. But, after a gallant fight he was, of course, driven back to his division—Stewart's.

An hour and a half before sunset, a brisk cannonade was opened upon Hood's centre division, Stewart's, opposite to New Hope Church. Major-General Stewart regarding this as the harbinger of assault, leaped upon his horse and rode along his line, to instruct the officers and encourage the men. He soon found the latter to be superfluous, from the confident tone in which he was addressed by his soldiers, and urged by them to lay aside all anxiety, and trust, for success, to their courage. Such pledges were well redeemed. The enemy soon appeared—Hooker's corps—in so deep order that it presented a front equal only to that of Stewart's first line—three brigades. After opening their fire, the Federal troops approached gradually but resolutely, under the fire of three brigades and sixteen field-pieces, until within fifty paces of the Confederate line. Here, however, they were compelled first to pause, and then to fall back, by the obstinate resistance they encountered. They were led forward again, advancing as resolutely, and approaching as near to the Confederate line as before, but were a second time repulsed by the firmness of their opponents, and their deliberate fire of canister-shot and musketry. The engagement was continued in this manner almost two hours, when the assailants drew off.

In this action a few of the men of Clayton's and Baker's brigades were partially sheltered by a hasty arrangement of some fallen timber which they found near their line. The other brigade engaged, Stovall's, had no such protection. Nothing entitled to the term "breastworks" had been constructed by the division. . . .

The Federal troops extended their intrenched line so rapidly to their left, that it was found necessary in the morning of the 27th to transfer Cleburne's division of Hardee's corps to our right, where it was formed on the prolongation of Polk's line. Kelly's cavalry, composed of Allen's and Hannon's Alabama brigades, together less than a thousand men, occupied the interval, of half a mile, between Cleburne's right and Little Pumpkin-Vine Creek. Martin's division (cavalry) guarded the road from Burnt Hickory to Marietta, two miles farther to the right; and Humes's the interval between Kelly's and Martin's divisions.

Between five and six o'clock in the afternoon, Kelly's skirmishers were driven in by a body of Federal cavalry, whose advance was supported by the Fourth Corps. This advance was retarded by the resistance of Kelly's troops fighting on foot behind unconnected little heaps of loose stones. As soon as the noise of this contest revealed to Major-General Cleburne the manoeuvre to turn his right, he brought the right brigade of his second line, Granberry's, to Kelly's support, by forming it on the right of his first line; when the thin line of dismounted cavalry, that had been bravely resisting masses of infantry gave place to the Texan brigade.

The Fourth Corps came on in deep order, and assailed the Texans with great vigor, receiving their close and accurate fire with the fortitude always exhibited by General Sherman's troops in the actions of this campaign. They had also to endure the fire of Govan's right, including two pieces of artillery, on their right flank. At the same time, Kelly's and a part of Humes's troops, directed by General Wheeler, met the Federal left, which was following the movement of the main body, and drove back the leading brigade, taking thirty or forty prisoners. The united force continued to press forward, however, but so much delayed by the resistance of Wheeler's troops as to give time for the arrival, on that part of the field, of the Eighth and Ninth Arkansas regiments under Colonel Bancum, detached by General Govan to the assistance of the cavalry. This little body met the foremost of the Federal troops as they were reaching the prolongation of Granberry's line, and, charging gallantly, drove them back, and preserved the Texans from an attack in flank which must have been fatal. Before the Federal left could gather to overwhelm Bancum and his two regiments, Lowry's brigade, hurried by General Cleburne from its position as left of his second line, came to join them, and the two, formed abreast of Granberry's brigade, stopped the advance of the enemy's left, and successfully resisted its subsequent attacks.

The contest of the main body of the Fourth Corps with Granberry's brigade was a very fierce one. The Federal troops approached within a few yards of the Confederates, but at last were forced to give way by their storm of well-directed bullets, and fell back to the shelter of a hollow near and behind them. They left hundreds of corpses within twenty paces of the Confederate line.

When the United States troops paused in their advance, within fifteen paces of the Texan front rank, one of their color-bearers planted his colors eight or ten feet in front of his regiment, and was instantly shot dead; a soldier sprang forward to his place, and fell also, as he grasped the color-staff; a second and third followed successively, and each received death as speedily as his predecessors; a fourth, however, seized and bore back the object of soldierly devotion.

About ten o'clock at night, Granberry ascertained that many of the Federal troops were still in the hollow immediately before him, and charged and drove them from it, taking two hundred and thirty-two prisoners, seventy-two of whom were severely wounded.

—JOHNSTON, *Narrative of Military Operations*

4. JOE JOHNSTON GIVES WAY TO HOOD

It was a fortunate day for Sherman when President Davis removed Johnston from command and appointed Hood to his place. Confronted by heavy numerical superiority Johnston had no alternative but to retreat; that he conducted his retreat in a masterly fashion is now generally admitted. Davis, however, had never fully trusted Johnston: the distrust probably dated from Johnston's protest, in 1861, against an appointment which made him only fourth in rank in the Confederate Army. Davis' suspicion of Johnston was deepened when Johnston failed either to rescue Pemberton or to strike the Federal army during the Vicksburg campaign. Johnston's appointment to Bragg's command, in December 1863, was welcomed by the officers and men of the Army of Tennessee; his dismissal was generally regarded as a calamity. When Lee was made commander in chief of Confederate armies, in

February 1865, he promptly reappointed Johnston to command of what was left of his army.

We have here Davis' explanation of his dismissal of Johnston, and Johnston's defense of his strategy.

A. President Davis Removes General Johnston
before Atlanta

When it became known that the Army of Tennessee had been successively driven from one strong position to another, until finally it had reached the earthworks constructed for the exterior defense of Atlanta, the popular disappointment was extreme. The possible fall of the "Gate City," with its important railroad communication, vast stores, factories for the manufacture of all sorts of military supplies, rolling-mill and foundries, was now contemplated for the first time at its full value, and produced intense anxiety far and wide. From many quarters, including such as had most urged his assignment, came delegations, petitions, and letters, urging me to remove General Johnston from the command of the army, and assign that important trust to some officer who would resolutely hold and defend Atlanta.

While sharing in the keen sense of disappointment at the failure of the campaign which pervaded the whole country, I was perhaps more apprehensive than others of the disasters likely to result from it, because I was in a position to estimate more accurately their probable extent. On the railroads threatened with destruction, the armies then fighting the main battles of the war in Virginia had for some time to a great degree depended for indispensable supplies, yet I did not respond to the wishes of those who came in hottest haste for the removal of General Johnston; for here again, more fully than many others, I realized how serious it was to change commanders in the presence of the enemy. This clamor for his removal commenced immediately after it became known that the army had fallen back from Dalton, and it gathered volume with each remove toward Atlanta. Still I resisted the steadily increasing pressure which was brought to bear to induce me to revoke his assignment, and only issued the order relieving him from command when I became satisfied that his declared purpose to occupy the works at Atlanta with militia levies and withdraw his army into the open country for freer operations, would inevitably result in the loss of that important point, and where the retreat would cease could not be foretold. If the Army of Tennessee was found to be unable to hold positions of great strength like those at Dalton, Reseca, Etowah, Kenesaw, and on the Chattahoochee, I could not reasonably hope that it would be more successful in the plains below Atlanta, where it would find neither natural nor artificial advantages of position. As soon as the Secretary of War showed me the answer which he had just received in reply to his telegram to General Johnston, requesting positive information as to the General's plans and purposes, I gave my permission to issue the order relieving General Johnston and directing him to turn over to General Hood the command of the Army of Tennessee. I was so fully aware of the danger of changing commanders of an army while actively engaged with the enemy, that I only overcame the objection in view of an emergency, and in the hope that the impending danger of the loss of Atlanta might be averted.

—DAVIS, *Rise and Fall of the Confederate Government*

B. GENERAL JOHNSTON JUSTIFIES HIMSELF

Macon, Ga., September 1st, 1864

My Dear Maury:

I have been intending ever since my arrival at this place to pay a part of the epistolary debt I owe you. But you know how lazy it makes one to have nothing to do, and so with the hot weather we have been enduring here, I have absolutely devoted myself to idleness. I have been disposed to write more particularly of what concerns myself—to explain to you, as far as practicable, the operations for which I was laid on the shelf, for you are one of the last whose unfavorable opinion I would be willing to incur.

You know that the army I commanded was that which, under General Bragg, was routed at Missionary Ridge. Sherman's army was that which routed it, reinforced by the Sixteenth and Twenty-third Corps. I am censured for not taking the offensive at Dalton—where the enemy, if beaten, had a secure refuge behind the fortified gap at Ringgold, or in the fortress of Chattanooga, and where the odds against us were almost ten to four. At Resaca he received five brigades, near Kingston three, and about 3500 cavalry; at New Hope Church one; in all about 14,000 infantry and artillery. The enemy received the Seventeenth Corps and a number of garrisons and bridge guards from Tennessee and Kentucky that had been relieved by "hundred-day men."

I am blamed for not fighting. Operations commenced about

the 6th of May; I was relieved on the 18th of July. In that time we fought daily, always under circumstances so favorable to us as to make it certain that the sum of the enemy's losses was five times ours, which was 10,000 men. Northern papers represented theirs up to about the end of June at 45,000. Sherman's progress was at the rate of a mile and a quarter a day. Had this style of fighting been allowed to continue, is it not clear that we would soon have been able to give battle with abundant chances of victory, and that the enemy, beaten on this side of the Chattahoochee, would have been destroyed? It is certain that Sherman's army was stronger, compared with that of Tennessee, than Grant's, compared with that of Northern Virginia. General Bragg asserts that Sherman's army was stronger than Grant's. It is well known that the army of Virginia was much superior to that of Tennessee.

Why, then, should I be condemned for the defensive while General Lee was adding to his great fame by the same course? General Bragg seems to have earned at Missionary Ridge his present high position. People report at Columbus and Montgomery that General Bragg said that my losses had been frightful; that I had disregarded the wishes and instructions of the President; that he had in vain implored me to change my course, by which I suppose is meant assume the offensive.

As these things are utterly untrue, it is not to be supposed that they were said by General Bragg. The President gave me no instructions and expressed no wishes except just before we reached the Chattahoochee, warning me not to fight with the river behind us and against crossing it, and previously he urged me not to allow Sherman to detach to Grant's aid. General Bragg passed some ten hours with me just before I was relieved, and gave me the impression that his visit to the army was casual, he being on his way further west to endeavor to get us reinforcements from Kirby Smith and Lee. I thought him satisfied with the state of things, but not so with that in Virginia. He assured me that he had always maintained in Richmond that Sherman's army was stronger than Grant's. He said nothing of the intention to relieve me, but talked with General Hood on the subject, as I learned after my removal. It is clear that his expedition had no other object than my removal and the giving proper direction to public opinion on the subject. He could have had no other object in going to Montgomery. A man of honor in his place would have communicated with me as well as with Hood on the subject. Being expected to assume the offensive, he attacked on the 20th, 22d, and 28th of July, disastrously, losing more men than I had done in seventy-two days. Since then his defensive has been at least as quiet as mine was.

Very truly yours,

J. E. JOHNSTON

Major-General MAURY

—MAURY, *Recollections of a Virginian*

5. HARDEE WINS AND LOSES THE BATTLE OF ATLANTA

Atlanta proved a hard nut to crack. Hood had been appointed because he was an aggressive fighter, and he promptly took the offensive. On July 20 he struck Thomas at Peachtree Creek, but was repulsed with heavy losses. Nothing daunted he tried again two days later, this time assaulting the left of the Union line, at Decatur (the Battle of Atlanta).

After Peachtree Creek Sherman sent McPherson eastward toward Decatur to cut off Hood's communications with the east and north. Hood withdrew into the defenses of Atlanta; supposing him in retreat McPherson set out "in pursuit." By a night march Hood—with Wheeler's cavalry—caught McPherson unprepared and assaulted him flank and rear. For a time disaster threatened. McPherson was killed; his army all but routed. But the Federals rallied and in the end inflicted a heavy defeat on their attackers. Confederate losses were between 7,000 and 8,000; Union less than 4,000.

Richard Tuthill, who here tells the story, was an officer of the 1st Michigan Light Artillery.

Hardee had struck us "endways," and his men could be plainly seen occupying the works from which ours had just been driven. The battery of regulars, near the end of our line, had been captured; and Lieutenant Justin of our battery had only been able to save his guns by the exercise of great coolness and quickness of movement. No sooner had the regulars been captured than we heard the booming of their guns, and saw their shot ploughing through our line in direct enfilade.

Some one may then have ordered a change of position. I have heard it said that such an order was given. At the same time, I beg leave respectfully to doubt it. The truth is that there was no time to give orders, and I saw neither general nor staff officer there to give them. All I know is, that we limbered up our guns, and sullenly—for we were much inclined to stay where we were—moved back. Our boys loved their black steel guns, and could not endure the thought of losing one of them. The Third Ohio Battery, in our division, had twenty-pounder Parrotts,—too heavy for field service,—and had to leave at least one of them behind, though it was afterward retaken. At least twice, as we were falling back a distance of not more than two or three hundred yards, as it seems to me, we unlimbered our guns and fired at the enemy. Then the infantry would move away from us, and we would limber up and fall back a little farther, to keep on a line with them.

It is hard now to recall the sensations of twenty-five years ago, but I never can forget thinking, "Can it be possible that the Third Division, victor in a hundred battles, has at last met defeat? Is it going to leave the field while as yet few have been killed or wounded? Better, ten thousand times better, that the entire division die fighting, than to have word sent back home that without serious losses in killed and wounded, it gave up the field." "It is better, sir," said Sir Colin Campbell, "that every man of her Majesty's Guards should lie dead upon the field than that they should now turn their backs upon the enemy." Such I know were my thoughts, and such I soon, from their action, learned was the thought of that glorious and never-conquered phalanx; for in their action their country and history can read their stern, brave thoughts and high determination.

Seeing then, for the first time since the fight began, our Chief of Artillery, Captain Williams,—as nonchalant a man as I ever saw in a place of great danger,—I rode to his side and said to him, "For God's sake, Captain, let us stop falling back and fight!" By that time we had reached a position about on a line drawn at right angles to the line occupied by us when the attack was first made, running toward the east from the top of Leggett's Hill.

Captain Williams replied to my remark, "All right! stop where you are!"

It was just the place to form a line of battle. Some general officer may have given an order to stop there. My own belief always has been that the boys did it of their own accord. They had been in so many fights that they did not need a general to tell them where and when to stop running and begin shooting.

Some distance to the rear of us was a rail fence. Consternation, I have been told, fell upon General Sherman, as with his glass he saw half of Leggett's division drop their guns and run to the rear. But when he saw them stop at the rail fence, and each man of them pick up two, three, and even four rails, and run back, carrying them to the place where they had left their guns, he understood what it meant, and smiled grimly. The operation was repeated; the rails were placed lengthways along their front; with bayonets, knives, and the tin plates taken from their haversacks, the earth was dug up and the rails covered, until, in less time, as it appeared to me, than it was possible to have done the same work with pick and shovel, a very fair protection for men lying on their bellies was made.

In front of us lay an open field, containing, I should think, not more than twenty acres. Beyond this were woods. Pat Cleburne's Texans,—whom Force's brigade had driven from this selfsame hillside the day before,—desperate and mad, were to make an attempt to wipe out the disgrace of their former defeat. Their line well formed, they emerged from their concealment in the woods, and yelling as only the steer-drivers of Texas could yell, charged upon our division. On the top of the hill, in the apex of the angle of the line of works facing Atlanta and our new line, was a four-gun battery of twenty-four-pounder howitzers, commanded by its boy captain, Cooper. This was Battery D, of the First Illinois Artillery, better known as "McAllister's Battery." Our six guns were also near this point, and distributed along the line for a short distance to the east of it. On came the Texans; but they were met by a continuous volley of musketry and shrapnel, shell and canister from our six-rifled Rodmans and Cooper's howitzers. It seemed as if no man of all the host who were attacking us could escape alive; and yet, still yelling, they persisted in their desperate undertaking. Their line was re-formed, and again and again they attempted the impossible,—to drive the Third Division from the line it had decided to hold.

Many of the enemy reached our line; some got across it; many were bayonetted, many killed with clubbed muskets; hand-to-hand conflicts were frequent. But not one inch did the Third Division give way. The boys obeyed Logan's well-remembered command to them at Champion Hill,—"Give them the cold steel! give them hell!"

The smell of powder was everywhere; the smoke from the guns was so dense that though a July sun was shining, there was the appearance of a dense fog. Only as the breath of a passing breeze blew the smoke away could the movements of the enemy be discerned clearly; but his unearthly *yell* could be heard above the sound of muskets and cannon. The day being very warm, men and line officers were for the most part without other clothing than hats and shoes, woollen shirts and trousers. I had left my coat and all my traps, including my letters, at the spot where I had suspended my letter-writing, and never again recovered them.

The exact sequence of events that afternoon I cannot give; nor do I believe any man can, or ever could, do so. Some time during the fight, firing was heard from the direction of Atlanta. General Cheatham's corps—as we now know—made fierce attack upon the Seventeenth and Fifteenth corps from our west front. The smoke was so dense that the men could not at first see whence this attack came. It was remarked that our own men farther to the right, thinking the enemy had taken the position on the hill, were firing upon us. General Force called for a flag. Some frightened young officer, thinking it time to give up when we were being attacked at the same moment from all sides, and that what Force wanted was a flag of truce, ran hither and thither to get a white handkerchief, or shirt, or anything that would answer the purpose. The talk among our boys was that that quiet Christian gentleman—now Judge Force of the Law Court of Cincinnati—was then betrayed into saying, *"Damn* you, sir! I don't want a flag of *truce;* I want the American flag!" If he did say it, we are sure that as in Uncle Tobey's case, "The accusing spirit which flew up to Heaven's chancery with the oath blushed as he gave it in; and the recording angel, as he wrote it down, dropped a tear upon the word and blotted it out forever."

A flag was soon obtained and planted upon the highest point in our earthworks, and there it remained. General Force himself was struck down by a minie-ball, which entered just at the lower outer corner of the eye, passed through his head, and came out near the base of the brain. The blood gushed from his eyes, nose, and mouth; but he uttered no moan, nor a word of complaint. The bones of his mouth were shattered, and he could not, in fact, speak. But from his eyes flashed a spirit unconquered and unconquerable,—the spirit of a soldier *sans peur et sans reproche.*

The attack made by Cheatham's corps from Atlanta was repulsed bloodily by Frank Blair's heroic men. But beyond the bushy ravine of which I have spoken as separating the Fifteenth Corps, where its line had been weakened by sending troops to strengthen our line fronting to the south, Cheatham had succeeded in breaking through, and was rushing in and forming in line of battle in the works from which our men had been driven. Some one asked that a part of our battery be at once sent to the ravine to shell this forming line. There was at that time comparative quiet in our immediate front, and my section of the battery hurried to the point indicated. The Confederates were there in plain sight. De Gress' battery of four twenty-pounder Parrotts had been captured, all of its horses killed, and its guns turned upon us. Taking a position on the edge of the ravine, the boys of my section poured into the forming line of the enemy an enfilading fire of short-range canister—"canned hell-fire," as they used to call it—that no living thing could withstand.

> —TUTHILL, "An Artilleryman's Recollection
> of the Battle of Atlanta"

6. "YOU MIGHT AS WELL APPEAL AGAINST THE THUNDER-STORM"

Even after Peachtree Creek and the Battle of Atlanta, Hood was able to put up a stiff fight for Atlanta. Sherman fell back on his now familiar tactics of flanking the Confederates, trying to cut their supply lines to the south and the east. Late July and early August witnessed a number of stiff cavalry engagements, as Hood tried to break up these extensive flanking movements. Convinced, finally, that Hood could not be defeated by these tactics, Sherman settled down to investing Atlanta. On August 25 he put his whole army in motion to encircle the city. With his communications cut, Hood evacuated Atlanta and moved south and west, and on September 1 Sherman wired Lincoln, "Atlanta is ours, and fairly won." Already the bombardment of Atlanta had started numerous fires; when Sherman was ready to leave it for further campaigning, he ordered it destroyed. This required the evacuation of its inhabitants. Southerners looked on this as inhuman; Sherman thought it a necessary military measure, and the evacuation warning a gesture of courtesy.

What is most interesting about this letter, explaining the necessity of evacuation, is that it gives Sherman's theory of war. That Sherman inflicted heavier damage on the South than any other Union general is doubtless true; it is equally

*true that no other Union general was so sympathetic to
the South or understood it so well.*

Headquarters Military Division of the Mississippi
in the Field, Atlanta, Georgia, September 12, 1864
JAMES M. CALHOUN, Mayor, E.E. RAWSON and S.C. WELLS,
representing City Council of Atlanta.

Gentlemen: I have your letter of the 11th, in the nature of
a petition to revoke my orders removing all the inhabitants
from Atlanta. I have read it carefully, and give full credit to
your statements of the distress that will be occasioned, and
yet shall not revoke my orders, because they were not designed to meet the humanities of the case, but to prepare for
the future struggles in which millions of good people outside of Atlanta have a deep interest. We must have peace,
not only at Atlanta, but in all America. To secure this, we
must stop the war that now desolates our once happy and
favored country. To stop war, we must defeat the rebel armies
which are arrayed against the laws and Constitution that all
must respect and obey. To defeat those armies, we must
prepare the way to reach them in their recesses, provided
with the arms and instruments which enable us to accomplish our purpose. Now, I know the vindictive nature of
our enemy, that we may have many years of military operations from this quarter; and, therefore, deem it wise and pru-
dent to prepare in time. The use of Atlanta for warlike purposes
is inconsistent with its character as a home for families.
There will be no manufactures, commerce, or agriculture
here, for the maintenance of families, and sooner or later
want will compel the inhabitants to go. Why not go now,
when all the arrangements are completed for the transfer,
instead of waiting till the plunging shot of contending armies
will renew the scenes of the past month? Of course, I do
not apprehend any such thing at this moment, but you do not
suppose this army will be here until the war is over. I cannot
discuss this subject with you fairly, because I cannot impart
to you what we propose to do, but I assert that our military
plans make it necessary for the inhabitants to go away, and
I can only renew my offer of services to make their exodus
in any direction as easy and comfortable as possible.

You cannot qualify war in harsher terms than I will. War
is cruelty, and you cannot refine it; and those who brought
war into our country deserve all the curses and maledictions a
people can pour out. I know I had no hand in making this
war, and I know I will make more sacrifices to-day than any

of you to secure peace. But you cannot have peace and a division of our country. If the United States submits to a division now, it will not stop, but will go on until we reap the fate of Mexico, which is eternal war. The United States does and must assert its authority, wherever it once had power; for, if it relaxes one bit to pressure, it is gone, and I believe that such is the national feeling. This feeling assumes various shapes, but always comes back to that of Union. Once admit the Union, once more acknowledge the authority of the national Government, and, instead of devoting your houses and streets and roads to the dread uses of war, I and this army become at once your protectors and supporters, shielding you from danger, let it come from what quarter it may. I know that a few individuals cannot resist a torrent of error and passion, such as swept the South into rebellion, but you can point out, so that we may know those who desire a government, and those who insist on war and its desolation.

You might as well appeal against the thunder-storm as against these terrible hardships of war. They are inevitable, and the only way the people of Atlanta can hope once more to live in peace and quiet at home, is to stop the war, which can only be done by admitting that it began in error and is perpetuated in pride.

We don't want your Negroes, or your horses, or your houses, or your lands, or any thing you have, but we do want and will have a just obedience to the laws of the United States. That we will have, and if it involves the destruction of your improvements, we cannot help it.

You have heretofore read public sentiment in your newspapers, that live by falsehood and excitement; and the quicker you seek for truth in other quarters, the better. I repeat then that, by the original compact of government, the United States had certain rights in Georgia, which have never been relinquished and never will be; that the South began war by seizing forts, arsenals, mints, custom-houses, etc., etc., long before Mr. Lincoln was installed, and before the South had one jot or tittle of provocation. I myself have seen in Missouri, Kentucky, Tennessee, and Mississippi, hundreds and thousands of women and children fleeing from your armies and desperadoes, hungry and with bleeding feet. In Memphis, Vicksburg, and Mississippi, we fed thousands upon thousands of the families of rebel soldiers left on our hands, and whom we could not see starve. Now that war comes home to you, you feel very different. You deprecate its horrors, but did not feel them when you sent car-loads of soldiers and ammunition, and moulded shells and shot, to carry war into Kentucky and Tennessee, to desolate the homes of hundreds and thousands of good people who only asked to live in peace at their old homes, and under the Government of their inheritance. But these comparisons are idle. I want peace, and believe it can only be reached through union and war, and I will ever conduct war with a view to perfect an early success.

But, my dear sirs, when peace does come, you may call on me for any thing. Then will I share with you the last cracker, and watch with you to shield your homes and families against danger from every quarter.

Now you must go, and take with you the old and feeble, feed and nurse them, and build for them, in more quiet places, proper habitations to shield them against the weather until the mad passions of men cool down, and allow the Union and peace once more to settle over your old homes at Atlanta. Yours in haste,

W.T. SHERMAN, *Major-General commanding*
—Memoirs of General William T. Sherman

7. SHERMAN MARCHES FROM ATLANTA TO THE SEA

Sherman's great decision was to break his own line of communications, and live off the country. Dispatching Schofield to Knoxville and Thomas to Nashville, to take care of Hood, he set out with what was left of his army, some 62,000 men, into the heart of the Confederacy.

Once again he is the best historian of his own achievements.

About 7 A.M. of November 16th [1864] we rode out of Atlanta by the Decatur road, filled by the marching troops and wagons of the Fourteenth Corps; and reaching the hill, just outside of the old rebel works, we naturally paused to look back upon the scenes of our past battles. We stood upon the very ground whereon was fought the bloody battle of July 22d and could see the copse of wood where McPherson fell. Behind us lay Atlanta, smoldering and in ruins, the black smoke rising high in air and hanging like a pall over the ruined city. Away off in the distance, on the McDonough road, was the rear of Howard's column, the gun barrels glistening in the sun, the white-topped wagons stretching away to the south, and right before us the Fourteenth Corps, marching steadily and rapidly with a cheery look and swinging pace that made light of the thousand miles that lay between us and Richmond. Some band by accident struck up the anthem of "John Brown's soul goes marching on"; the men caught up the strain, and never before or since have I heard the chorus of "Glory, glory, hallelujah!" done with more spirit or in better harmony of time and place.

Then we turned our horses' heads to the east; Atlanta was soon lost behind the screen of trees and became a thing of the past. Around it clings many a thought of desperate battle, of hope and fear, that now seem like the memory of a dream; and I have never seen the place since. The day was extremely beautiful, clear sunlight, with bracing air, and an unusual feeling of exhilaration seemed to pervade all minds—a feeling of something to come, vague and undefined, still full of venture and intense interest. Even the common soldiers caught the inspiration, and many a group called out to me as I worked my way past them, "Uncle Billy, I guess Grant is waiting for us at Richmond!" Indeed, the general sentiment was that we were marching for Richmond and that there we should end the war, but how and when they seemed to care not; nor did they measure the distance or count the cost in life or bother their brains about the great rivers to be crossed and the food, required for man and beast, that had to be gathered by the way. There was a devil-may-care feeling pervading officers and men that made me feel the full load of responsibility, for success would be accepted as a matter of course, whereas should we fail, this march would be adjudged the wild adventure of a crazy fool. I had no purpose to march direct for Richmond by way of Augusta and Charlotte but always designed to reach the seacoast first at Savannah or Port Royal, South Carolina, and even kept in mind the alternative of Pensacola.

The first night out we camped by the roadside near Lithonia. Stone Mountain, a mass of granite, was in plain view, cut out in clear outline against the blue sky; the whole horizon was lurid with the bonfires of rail ties, and groups of men all night were carrying the heated rails to the nearest trees and bending them around the trunks. Colonel Poe had provided tools for ripping up the rails and twisting them when hot, but the best and easiest way is . . . heating the middle of the iron rails on bonfires made of the crossties and then winding them around a telegraph pole or the trunk of some con-

venient sapling. I attached much importance to this destruction of the railroad, gave it my personal attention, and made
reiterated orders to others on the subject.

The next day we passed through the handsome town of
Covington, the soldiers closing up their ranks, the color-bearers
unfurling their flags, and the band striking up patriotic airs.
The white people came out of their houses to behold the
sight, spite of their deep hatred of the invaders, and the
Negroes were simply frantic with joy. Whenever they heard
my name, they clustered about my horse, shouted and
prayed in their peculiar style, which had a natural eloquence
that would have moved a stone. I have witnessed hundreds,
if not thousands, of such scenes and can now see a poor
girl, in the very ecstasy of the Methodist "shout," hugging
the banner of one of the regiments and jumping up to the
"feet of Jesus."

I remember, when riding around by a bystreet in Covington
to avoid the crowd that followed the marching column, that
some one brought me an invitation to dine with a sister of
Samuel Anderson, who was a cadet at West Point with me; but
the messenger reached me after we had passed the main
part of the town. I asked to be excused and rode on to a
place designated for camp, at the crossing of the Ulco-
fauhachee River, about four miles to the east of the town.
Here we made our bivouac, and I walked up to a plantation house close by, where were assembled many Negroes,
among them an old gray-haired man, of as fine a head as I
ever saw. I asked him if he understood about the war and
its progress. He said he did; that he had been looking for the
"angel of the Lord" ever since he was knee-high, and though
we professed to be fighting for the Union, he supposed that
slavery was the cause and that our success was to be his
freedom. I asked him if all the Negro slaves comprehended
this fact, and he said they surely did. I then explained to
him that we wanted the slaves to remain where they were
and not to load us down with useless mouths, which would
eat up the food needed for our fighting men, that our success
was their assured freedom, that we could receive a few of
their young, hearty men as pioneers, but that if they followed
us in swarms of old and young, feeble and helpless, it would
simply load us down and cripple us in our great task. I think
Major Henry Hitchcock was with me on that occasion and
made a note of the conversation, and I believe that old man
spread this message to the slaves, which was carried from
mouth to mouth to the very end of our journey, and that

it in part saved us from the great danger we incurred of swelling our numbers so that famine would have attended our progress.

It was at this very plantation that a soldier passed me with a ham on his musket, a jug of sorghum molasses under his arm, and a big piece of honey in his hand, from which he was eating, and catching my eye, he remarked *sotto voce* and carelessly to a comrade, "Forage liberally on the country," quoting from my general orders. On this occasion, as on many others that fell under my personal observation, I reproved the man, explained that foraging must be limited to the regular parties properly detailed and that all provisions thus obtained must be delivered to the regular commissaries to be fairly distributed to the men who kept their ranks.

From Covington the Fourteenth Corps [Davis'], with which I was traveling, turned to the right for Milledgeville via Shady Dale. General Slocum was ahead at Madison with the Twentieth Corps, having torn up the railroad as far as that place, and thence had sent Geary's division on to the Oconee to burn the bridges across that stream when this corps turned south by Eatonton for Milledgeville, the common objective for the first stage of the march. We found abundance of corn, molasses, meal, bacon, and sweet potatoes. We also took a good many cows and oxen and a large number of mules. In all these the country was quite rich, never before having been visited by a hostile army; the recent crop had been excellent, had been just gathered and laid by for the winter. As a rule, we destroyed none but kept our wagons full and fed our teams bountifully.

The skill and success of the men in collecting forage was one of the features of this march. Each brigade commander had authority to detail a company of foragers, usually about fifty men, with one or two commissioned officers selected for their boldness and enterprise. This party would be dispatched before daylight with a knowledge of the intended day's march and camp, would proceed on foot five or six miles from the route traveled by their brigade, and then visit every plantation and farm within range. They would usually procure a wagon or family carriage, load it with bacon, cornmeal, turkeys, chickens, ducks, and everything that could be used as food or forage, and would then regain the main road, usually in advance of their train. When this came up, they would deliver to the brigade commissary the supplies thus gathered by the way. Often would I pass these foraging parties at the roadside, waiting for their wagons to come up, and was amused at their strange collections—mules, horses, even cattle, packed with old saddles and loaded with hams, bacon, bags of corn-meal, and poultry of every character and description. Al-though this foraging was attended with great danger and hard work, there seemed to be a charm about it that attracted the soldiers, and it was a privilege to be detailed on such a party. Daily they returned mounted on all sorts of beasts which were at once taken from them and appropriated to the general use, but the next day they would start out again on foot, only to repeat the experience of the day before. No doubt, many acts of pillage, robbery, and violence were com-mitted by these parties of foragers, usually called bummers; for I have since heard of jewelry taken from women and the plunder of articles that never reached the commissary; but these acts were exceptional and incidental. I never heard of any cases of murder or rape, and no army could have carried along sufficient food and forage for a march of three hundred miles, so that foraging in some shape was necessary. The country was sparsely settled, with no magistrates or civil authorities who could respond to requisitions, as is done in all the wars of Europe, so that this system of foraging was simply indispensable to our success. By it our men were well supplied with all the essentials of life and health, while the wagons retained enough in case of unexpected delay, and our animals were well fed. Indeed, when we reached Savan-nah, the trains were pronounced by experts to be the finest in flesh and appearance ever seen with any army.

—*Memoirs of General William T. Sherman*

8. SHERMAN'S "BUMMERS"

The origin of the term "bummer" is a bit obscure; it was with Sherman's March to the Sea that it came into general usage. A bummer, wrote Major Nichols, "is a raider on his own account, a man who temporarily deserts his place in the ranks and starts out upon an independent foraging expedition." The term actually had more general application; cooks, or-derlies, servants, were all called bummers, whether they de-served the name or not.

Here are two descriptions of this peculiar appendage to the Grand Army that marched from Atlanta to the sea. The first is by Captain Henry Dwight of the 20th Ohio Infantry, and an aide to General Force; the second by Daniel Oakey, a captain in the 2nd Massachusetts Volunteers.

A. A GOOD WORD FOR THE BUMMERS

Besides the fighting population of our camps there is a population constitutionally opposed to warfare—cooks, ambulance nurses, stretcher-bearers, shirks, and sometimes surgeons, who all come under the class technically called *bummers.* These are treated by the fighting men with a sort of cool contempt, no matter whether necessity or inclination keeps them to the rear, and they have a hard time. Frequently the rear of the army is a much more dangerous locality than the front line, for the missiles passing over the front line must fall somewhere, and often demoralize whole hosts of "bummers," who build miniature fortifications to live in, and collect together in crowds; for misery loves company. Any favorable ravine thus peopled immediately becomes denominated "Bummer's Roost." Here they spend their days in cooking for their nurses, if they are cooks, or attending to their own business, if their object be to escape duty and danger. Among them originate all sorts of marvelous reports of immense success or terrible disaster. They always know just what General Sherman said about the situation at any given time; and from them start many of the wild stories which penetrate the columns of our best papers.

To watch these cooks, freighted with the precious coffee for the men in the trenches, as they go out to the front three times a day, is amusing. From continually dodging the passing shells or stray bullets their forms become bent and stooping. As they approach the line, the men in the trenches commence shouting, "Hey, bummer! Run quick, bummer!" "A man was killed just there, bummer!" With such encouragements the coffee at last reaches its destination, and being distributed among the eager men the bummer is soon at liberty to hurry back to the "Roost."

—DWIGHT, "How We Fight at Atlanta"

B. "WE WERE PROUD OF OUR FORAGERS"

At length, when we left Savannah and launched cheerily into the untrodden land of South Carolina, the foragers began to assume their wonted spirit. We were proud of our foragers.

They constituted a picked force from each regiment, under an officer selected for the command, and were remarkable for intelligence, spirit, and daring. Before daylight, mounted on horses captured on the plantations, they were in the saddle and away, covering the country sometimes seven miles in advance. Although I have said "in the saddle," many a forager had nothing better than a bit of carpet and a rope halter; yet this simplicity of equipment did not abate his power of carrying off hams and sweet-potatoes in the face of the enemy. The foragers were also important as a sort of advance guard, for they formed virtually a curtain of mounted infantry screening us from the inquisitive eyes of parties of Wheeler's cavalry, with whom they did not hesitate to engage when it was a question of a rich plantation.

When compelled to retire, they resorted to all the tricks of infantry skirmishers, and summoned reënforcements of foragers from other regiments to help drive the "Johnnies" out. When success crowned their efforts, the plantation was promptly stripped of live stock and eatables. The natives were accustomed to bury provisions, for they feared their own soldiers quite as much as they feared ours. These subterranean stores were readily discovered by the practiced "Yankee" eye. The appearance of the ground and a little probing with a ramrod or a bayonet soon decided whether to dig. Teams were improvised; carts and vehicles of all sorts were pressed into the service and loaded with provisions. If any antiquated militia uniforms were discovered, they were promptly donned, and a comical procession escorted the valuable train of booty to the point where the brigade was expected to bivouac for the night. The regimentals of the past, even to those of revolutionary times, were often conspicuous.

On an occasion when our brigade had the advance, several parties of foragers, consolidating themselves, captured a town from the enemy's cavalry, and occupied the neighboring plantations. Before the arrival of the main column hostilities had ceased; order had been restored, and mock arrangements were made to receive the army. Our regiment in the advance was confronted by a picket dressed in continental uniform, who waved his plumed hat in response to the gibes of the men, and galloped away on his bareback mule to apprise his comrades of our approach. We marched into the town and rested on each side of the main street. Presently a forager, in ancient militia uniform indicating high rank, debouched from a side street to do the honors of the occasion. He was mounted on a raw-boned horse with a bit of carpet for a saddle. His old plumed chapeau in hand, he rode with gracious dignity through the street, as if reviewing the brigade. After him came a family carriage laden with hams, sweet-potatoes, and other provisions, and drawn by two horses, a mule, and a cow, the two latter ridden by postilions.

At Fayetteville, North Carolina, the foragers as usual had been over the ground several hours before the heads of column arrived, and the party from my regiment had found a broken-down grist-mill. Their commander, Captain Parker, an officer of great spirit and efficiency, and an expert machinist, had the old wheel hoisted into its place and put the mill in working order. Several parties from other regiments had been admitted as working members, and teams of all sorts were busy collecting and bringing in corn and carrying away meal for distribution. This bit of enterprise was so pleasing to the troops that plenty of volunteers were ready to relieve the different gangs, and the demand was so great as to keep the mill at work all night by the light of pine-knot fires and torches.

—OAKEY, "Marching Through Georgia and the Carolinas"

9. "THE HEAVENS WERE LIT UP WITH FLAMES FROM BURNING BUILDINGS"

Here is how the March to the Sea affected its victims. Dolly Lunt was a Maine girl, distantly related to Charles Sumner, who before the war went to Covington, Georgia, to teach school, and there married a planter, Thomas Burge. At the time Sherman's army swept through Georgia she was a widow, still managing the plantation. Her short but moving diary has been rescued from oblivion by Julian Street.

November 19, 1864

Slept in my clothes last night, as I heard that the Yankees went to neighbor Montgomery's on Thursday night at one o'clock, searched his house, drank his wine, and took his money and valuables. As we were not disturbed, I walked after breakfast, with Sadai, up to Mr. Joe Perry's, my nearest neighbor, where the Yankees were yesterday. Saw Mrs. Laura [Perry] in the road surrounded by her children, seeming to be looking for some one. She said she was looking for her husband, that old Mrs. Perry had just sent her word that the Yankees went to James Perry's the night before, plundered his house, and drove off all his stock, and that she must drive hers into the old fields. Before we were done talking, up came Joe and Jim Perry from their hidingplace. Jim was very much excited. Happening to turn and look behind, as we stood there, I saw some blue-coats coming down the hill. Jim immediately raised his gun, swearing he would kill them anyhow.

"No, don't!" said I, and ran home as fast as I could, with Sadai.

I could hear them cry, "Halt! Halt!" and their guns went off in quick succession. Oh God, the time of trial has come!

A man passed on his way to Covington. I hallooed to him, asking him if he did not know the Yankees were coming.

"No—are they?"

"Yes," said I; "they are not three hundred yards from here."

"Sure enough," said he. "Well, I'll not go. I don't want them to get my horse." And although within hearing of their guns, he would stop and look for them. Blissful ignorance! Not knowing, not hearing, he has not suffered the suspense, the fear, that I have for the past forty-eight hours. I walked to the gate. There they came filing up.

I hastened back to my frightened servants and told them that they had better hide, and then went back to the gate to claim protection and a guard. But like demons they rush in! My yards are full. To my smoke-house, my dairy, pantry, kitchen, and cellar, like famished wolves they come, breaking locks and whatever is in their way. The thousand pounds of meat in my smoke-house is gone in a twinkling, my flour, my meat, my lard, butter, eggs, pickles of various kinds— both in vinegar and brine—wine, jars, and jugs are all gone. My eighteen fat turkeys, my hens, chickens, and fowls, my young pigs, are shot down in my yard and hunted as if they were rebels themselves. Utterly powerless I ran out and appealed to the guard.

"I cannot help you, Madam, it is orders."

As I stood there, from my lot I saw driven, first, old Dutch, my dear old buggy horse, who has carried my beloved husband so many miles, and who would so quietly wait at the block for him to mount and dismount, and who at last drew him to his grave; then came old Mary, my brood mare, who for years had been too old and stiff for work, with her three-year-old colt, my two-year-old mule, and her last little baby colt. There they go! There go my mules, my sheep, and, worse than all, my boys [slaves]!

Alas! little did I think while trying to save my house from

plunder and fire that they were forcing my boys from home at the point of the bayonet. One, Newton, jumped into bed in his cabin, and declared himself sick. Another crawled under the floor,—a lame boy he was,—but they pulled him out, placed him on a horse, and drove him off. Mid, poor Mid! The last I saw of him, a man had him going around the garden, looking, as I thought, for my sheep, as he was my shepherd. Jack came crying to me, the big tears coursing down his cheeks, saying they were making him go. I said:

"Stay in my room."

But a man followed in cursing him and threatening to shoot him if he did not go; so poor Jack had to yield. . . .

My poor boys! My poor boys! What unknown trials are before you! How you have clung to your mistress and assisted her in every way you knew. . . .

Their cabins are rifled of every valuable, the soldiers swearing that their Sunday clothes were the white people's, and that they never had money to get such things as they had. Poor Frank's chest was broken open, his money and tobacco taken. He had always been a money-making and saving boy; not infrequently has his crop brought him five hundred dollars and more. All of his clothes and Rachel's clothes, which dear Lou gave her before her death and which she had packed away, were stolen from her. Ovens, skillets, coffee-mills, of which we had three, coffee-pots—not one have I left. Sifters all gone!

Seeing that the soldiers could not be restrained, the guard ordered me to have their remaining possessions brought into my house, which I did, and they all, poor things, huddled together in my room, fearing every movement that the house would be burned.

A Captain Webber from Illinois came into my house. Of him I claimed protection from the vandals who were forcing themselves into my room. . . .

He felt for me, and I give him and several others the character of gentlemen. I don't believe they would have molested women and children had they had their own way. He seemed surprised that I had not laid away in my house, flour and other provisions. I did not suppose I could secure them there, more than where I usually kept them, for in last summer's raid houses were thoroughly searched. In parting with him, I parted as with a friend.

Sherman himself and a greater portion of his army passed my house that day. All day, as the sad moments rolled on, were they passing not only in front of my house, but from behind; they tore down my garden palings, made a road through my back-yard and lot field, driving their stock and riding through, tearing down my fences and desolating my home—wantonly doing it when there was no necessity for it.

Such a day, if I live to the age of Methuselah, may God spare me from ever seeing again!

As night drew its sable curtains around us, the heavens from every point were lit up with flames from burning buildings. Dinnerless and supperless as we were, it was nothing in comparison with the fear of being driven out homeless to the dreary woods. Nothing to eat! I could give my guard no supper, so he left us. I appealed to another, asking him if he had wife, mother, or sister, and how he should feel were they in my situation. A colonel from Vermont left me two men, but they were Dutch, and I could not understand one word they said.

My Heavenly Father alone saved me from the destructive fire. My carriage-house had in it eight bales of cotton, with my carriage, buggy, and harness. On top of the cotton were some carded cotton rolls, a hundred pounds or more. These were thrown out of the blanket in which they were, and a large twist of the rolls taken and set on fire, and thrown into the boat of my carriage, which was close up to the cotton bales. Thanks to my God, the cotton only burned over, and then went out. Shall I ever forget the deliverance? . . .

The two guards came into my room and laid themselves by my fire for the night. I could not close my eyes, but kept walking to and fro, watching the fires in the distance and dreading the approaching day, which, I feared, as they had not all passed, would be but a continuation of horrors.

LUNT, *A Woman's Wartime Journal*

10. ELIZA ANDREWS COMES HOME THROUGH THE BURNT COUNTRY

This is what Georgia looked like after the Yankees were through with it, as seen by a Georgia girl, Eliza Andrews. The War-Time Diary of a Georgia Girl, from which this brief excerpt is taken, is one of the best of all Confederate diaries.

December 24, 1864.—About three miles from Sparta we struck the "burnt country," as it is well named by the natives, and then I could better understand the wrath and desperation of these poor people. I almost felt as if I should like to hang a Yankee myself. There was hardly a fence left standing all the way from Sparta to Gordon. The fields were trampled down and the road was lined with carcasses of horses, hogs, and cattle that the invaders, unable either to consume or to carry away with them, had wantonly shot down, to starve out the people and prevent them from making their crops. The stench in some places was unbearable; every few hundred yards we had to hold our noses or stop them with the cologne Mrs. Elzey had given us, and it proved a great boon. The dwellings that were standing all showed signs of pillage, and on every plantation we saw the charred remains of the ginhouse and packing screw, while here and there lone chimney stacks, "Sherman's sentinels," told of homes laid in ashes. The infamous wretches! I couldn't wonder now that these poor people should want to put a rope round the neck of every red-handed "devil of them" they could lay their hands on. Hayricks and fodder stacks were demolished, corncribs were empty, and every bale of cotton that could be found was burnt by the savages. I saw no grain of any sort except little patches they had spilled when feeding their horses and which there was not even a chicken left in the country to eat. A bag of oats might have lain anywhere along the road without danger from the beasts of the field, though I cannot say it would have been safe from the assaults of hungry man.

Crowds of soldiers were tramping over the road in both directions; it was like traveling through the streets of a populous town all day. They were mostly on foot, and I saw numbers seated on the roadside greedily eating raw turnips, meat skins, parched corn—anything they could find, even picking up the loose grains that Sherman's horses had left. I felt tempted to stop and empty the contents of our provision baskets into their laps, but the dreadful accounts that were given of the state of the country before us made prudence get the better of our generosity.

Before crossing the Oconee at Milledgeville we ascended an immense hill, from which there was a fine view of the town, with Governor Brown's fortifications in the foreground and the river rolling at our feet. The Yankees had burnt the bridge; so we had to cross on a ferry. There was a long train of vehicles ahead of us, and it was nearly an hour before our turn came; so we had ample time to look about us. On our left was a field where thirty thousand Yankees had camped

SAVANNAH TO BENTONVILLE

hardly three weeks before. It was strewn with the debris they had left behind, and the poor people of the neighborhood were wandering over it, seeking for anything they could find to eat, even picking up grains of corn that were scattered around where the Yankees had fed their horses. We were told that a great many valuables were found there at first, plunder that the invaders had left behind, but the place had been picked over so often by this time that little now remained except tufts of loose cotton, piles of half-rotted grain, and the carcasses of slaughtered animals, which raised a horrible stench. Some men were plowing in one part of the field, making ready for next year's crop.

— ANDREWS, *The War-Time Journal of a Georgia Girl*

11. THE BURNING OF COLUMBIA

Sherman reached Columbia, capital of South Carolina, on February 17. That night the city burned. Whether "Sherman burned Columbia" or not is still hotly debated. Sherman himself denied responsibility for the conflagration, but he did say that "having utterly ruined Columbia, the right wing began its march northward." Perhaps the fire was started by accident; perhaps by the Confederates burning their cotton; perhaps by Negroes; perhaps by soldiers out of control.

We have here two accounts of the tragedy. The first comes from George Nichols, whose Story of the Great March *was the most widely read of contemporary Civil War narratives; the second from Henry Hitchcock, whom we have already met.*

A. "A Scene of Shameful Confusion"

Columbia, February 17th [1865]—It is with a feeling of proud exultation that I write the date of Columbia. We have conquered and occupy the capital of the haughty state that instigated and forced forward the treason which has brought on this desolating war. The city which was to have been the capital of the Confederacy if Lee and the Rebel hosts had been driven from Richmond is now overrun by Northern soldiers. The beautiful capitol building bears the marks of Yankee shot and shell, and the old flag which the Rebels in-

sulted at Sumter now floats freely in the air from the house-
tops of the central city of South Carolina. . . .

General Sherman and General Howard were the first to
cross the bridge, and entered the city, followed by their
staffs. A scene of shameful confusion met their eyes. On
every side were evidences of disorder; bales of cotton scattered here and there; articles of household furniture and
merchandise of every description cast pell-mell in every direction by the frightened inhabitants, who had escaped from a
city which they supposed was doomed to destruction. . . .

The three or four days' notice of our approach enabled
the government officials to remove most of the material belonging to the branch of the Treasury Department which was
located at this point; yet large quantities of paper for printing Confederate notes and bonds, with type, printing-presses,
etc., has fallen into our hands. This loss is irreparable to the
Rebel government.

The arsenal was found well stocked with shot, shell, fixed
ammunition, powder, Enfield rifles, carbines, and other material of war. A full battery of four rifled English Blakely
guns, which were in a battery commanding the bridge, was
also taken, with caissons and other material. Connected with
the arsenal are shops full of costly machinery for the manufacture of arms and ammunition, with founderies for all
sorts of castings. A little way down the river there is a large
powder-mill. All of this will be thoroughly destroyed. . . .

The store-houses are filled with all sorts of supplies—flour,
meal, bacon, corn, harness, hardware, etc.—while cotton is
found in every direction. As there is no treasury agent of our
government to appropriate this costly material for somebody's
benefit, I doubt if a very correct record of the quantity will
be made before it is burned. . . .

I began to-day's record early in the evening, and while
writing I noticed an unusual glare in the sky, and heard a
sound of running to and fro in the streets, with the loud
talk of servants that the horses must be removed to a safer
place. Running out, I found, to my surprise and real sorrow,
that the central part of the city, including the main business
street, was in flames, while the wind, which had been blowing
a hurricane all day, was driving the sparks and cinders in
heavy masses over the eastern portion of the city, where the
finest residences are situated. These buildings, all wooden, were
instantly ignited by the flying sparks. In half an hour the
conflagration was raging in every direction, and but for a

providential change of the wind to the south and west, the whole city would in a few hours have been laid in ashes.

As it is, several hundred buildings, including the old State House, one or two churches, most of the carved work stored in the sheds round about the new capitol, and a large number of public store-houses, have been destroyed. In some of the public buildings the Rebels had stored shot, shell, and other ammunition, and when the flames reached these magazines we had the Atlanta experience over again—the smothered boom, the huge columns of fire shooting heavenward, the red-hot iron flying here and there. But there was one feature, pitiable indeed, which we did not find at Atlanta. Groups of men, women, and children were gathered in the streets and squares, huddled together over a trunk, a mattress, or a bundle of clothes. Our soldiers were at work with a will, removing household goods from the dwellings which were in the track of the flames, and here and there extinguishing the fire when there was hope of saving a building. General Sherman and his officers worked with their own hands until long after midnight, trying to save life and property. The house taken for headquarters is now filled with old men, women, and children who have been driven from their homes by a more pitiless enemy than the detested "Yankees."

Various causes are assigned to explain the origin of the fire. I am quite sure that it originated in sparks flying from the hundreds of bales of cotton which the Rebels had placed along the middle of the main street, and fired as they left the city. Fire from a tightly-compressed bale of cotton is unlike that of a more open material, which burns itself out. The fire lies smouldering in a bale of cotton long after it appears to be extinguished; and in this instance, when our soldiers supposed they had extinguished the fire, it suddenly broke out again with the most disastrous effect.

There were fires, however, which must have been started independent of the above-named cause. The source of these is ascribed to the desire for revenge from some two hundred of our prisoners, who had escaped from the cars as they were being conveyed from this city to Charlotte, and, with the memories of long sufferings in the miserable pens I visited yesterday on the other side of the river, sought this means of retaliation. Again, it is said that the soldiers who first entered the town, intoxicated with success and a liberal supply of bad liquor, which was freely distributed among them by designing citizens, in an insanity of exhilaration set fire to unoccupied houses.

Whatever may have been the cause of the disaster, the direful result is deprecated by General Sherman most emphatically; for however heinous the crimes of this people against our common country, we do not war against women and children and helpless persons.
        —NICHOLS, *The Story of the Great March*

B. MAJOR HITCHCOCK EXPLAINS THE BURNING
OF COLUMBIA

Fayetteville, North Carolina, Sunday, March 12, 1865

One word about Columbia. It was not burned by orders, but expressly against orders and in spite of the utmost effort on our part to save it. Everything seemed to conspire for its destruction. The streets were full of loose cotton, brought out and set on fire *by the rebels* before they left,—I saw it when we rode into town. A gale of wind was blowing all that day and that night, and the branches of the trees were white with cotton tufts blown about everywhere. The citizens themselves—like idiots, madmen,—brought out large quantities of liquor as soon as our troops entered and distributed it freely among them, even to the guards which Gen. Howard had immediately placed all over the city as soon as we came in. This fact is unquestionable, and was one chief cause of what followed. Here in Fayetteville a lady has told Gen. Sherman that Gen. Joe Johnson told her, yesterday morning, that the burning of Columbia was caused by liquor which the people there gave our soldiers. Besides there were 200 or 300 of "our prisoners" who had escaped from rebel hands before, and when we reached Columbia burning to revenge themselves for the cruel treatment they had received; and our own men were fully aware of the claims of Columbia to eminence as the "cradle of secession." In that same town, in 1861, a woman, a school-teacher from New England, was *tarred and feathered* and sent North "for abolition sentiments."

The result of all this was that partly by accident, from the burning cotton, partly by design by our escaped prisoners, and by our drunken men, fire was started in several places, —and once started, with the furious wind blowing, it was simply impossible to put it out. *Nothing was left undone,*—I speak advisedly—to prevent and stop it; Gen. Howard, Sherman, and other Generals and their staffs, and many other officers and hundreds of men were up and at work nearly all night, trying to do it, but in vain. The guard was changed—

three times as many men were on guard as were ever on guard at any one time in Savannah where perfect order was preserved; our own officers shot our men down like dogs wherever they were found riotous or drunk—in short no effort was spared to stop it; and but for the liquor it might perhaps have been stopped. This is the truth; and Wade Hampton's letter to Sherman—it will be in the New York Herald if not already published North—charging him with sundry crimes at Columbia is a tissue of lies.

—HITCHCOCK, "Letters and Diaries"

12. GENERAL SHERMAN THINKS HIS NAME MAY LIVE

We have already read Sherman's statement to the Mayor of Atlanta on the iron necessities of war. Here is an explanation*—and a prophecy—directed to his wife. On the death of his father, Sherman had been practically adopted by Senator Ewing of Ohio. In 1850 he married Ewing's daughter, Ellen. His war letters to his wife are among the most revealing and touching of Civil War letters.

Savannah, January 5, 1865

John writes that I am in everybody's mouth and that even he is known as my brother, and that all the Shermans are now feted as relatives of me. Surely you and the children will not be overlooked by those who profess to honor me. I do think that in the several grand epochs of this war, my name will have a prominent part, and not least among them will be the determination I took at Atlanta to destroy that place, and march on this city, whilst Thomas, my lieutenant, should dispose of Hood. The idea, the execution and strategy are all good, and will in time be understood. I don't know that you comprehend the magnitude of the thing, but you can see the importance attached to it in England where the critics stand ready to turn against any American general who makes a mistake or fails in its execution. In my case they had time to commit themselves to the conclusion that if I succeeded I would be a great general, but if I failed I would be set down a fool. My success is already assured, so that I

* Reprinted from *Home Letters of General Sherman* edited by M. A. De Wolfe Howe; copyright 1909 by Charles Scribner's Sons, 1937 by M. A. De Wolfe Howe; used by permission of the publishers.

will be found to sustain the title. I am told that were I to go north I would be feted and petted, but as I have no intention of going, you must sustain the honors of the family. I know exactly what amount of merit attaches to my own conduct, and what will survive the clamor of time. The quiet preparation I made before the Atlanta Campaign, the rapid movement on Resaca, the crossing the Chattahoochee without loss in the face of a skillful general with a good army, the movement on Jonesboro, whereby Atlanta fell, and the resolution I made to divide my army, with one part to take Savannah and the other to meet Hood in Tennessee are all clearly mine, and will survive us both in history. I don't know that you can understand the merit of the latter, but it will stamp me in years to come, and will be more appreciated in Europe than in America. I warrant your father will find parallel in the history of the Greeks and Persians, but none on our continent. For his sake I am glad of the success that has attended me, and I know he will feel more pride in my success than you or I do. Oh that Willy were living! how his eyes would brighten and his bosom swell with honest pride if he could hear and understand these things. . . .

You will doubtless read all the details of our march and stay in Savannah in the papers, whose spies infest our camps, spite of all I can do, but I could tell you thousands of little incidents which would more interest you. The women here are, as at Memphis, disposed to usurp my time more from curiosity than business. They have been told of my burning and killing until they expected the veriest monster, but their eyes were opened when Hardee, G. W. Smith and McLaws, the three chief officers of the Rebel army, fled across the Savannah river consigning their families to my special care. There are some very elegant people here, whom I knew in better days and who do not seem ashamed to call on the 'Vandal Chief.' They regard us just as the Romans did the Goths and the parallel is not unjust. Many of my stalwart men with red beards and huge frames look like giants, and it is wonderful how smoothly all things move, for they all seem to feel implicit faith in me not because I am strong or bold, but because they think I know everything. It seems impossible for us to go anywhere without being where I have been before. My former life from 1840 to 1846 seems providential and every bit of knowledge then acquired is returned, tenfold. Should it so happen that I should approach Charleston on that very ground where I used to hunt with

Jim Poyas, and Mr. Quash, and ride by moonlight to save day-time, it would be even more strange than here where I was only a visitor.

—Howe, ed., *Home Letters of General Sherman*

XI

XI

The Wilderness

IN FEBRUARY 1864 *U. S. Grant was made lieutenant general and placed in command of all the armies of the United States. For the first time it was possible to organize a unified plan of operations against the Confederacy, and this Grant promptly proceeded to do. Grant might have stayed in Washington to supervise all the complex operations which his plan involved; he preferred to accompany Meade in the crucial campaign against Lee. Thus at last these two great military chieftains were to meet in battle, a battle which ended with Lee's surrender at Appomattox just a year later. In the campaigns of 1864-65 Grant enjoyed most of the advantages. He had a numerical superiority of about two to one, and no difficulty in getting reinforcements when needed. He could count on simultaneous attacks from other quarters which would drain the Confederacy of man power, war matériel, and—in the end—the will to resist. If he did not enjoy interior lines of communication he did have command of the seas and the assistance of the navy. His armies were well fed, well clothed, and well equipped, and never lacked for munitions. As he took, and held, the offensive, he had the initiative. Lee had only the advantage of geography, and of his own military genius. The terrain over which the armies fought was well adapted to defensive operations; Lee knew it intimately; he could draw on some help from Richmond and from Beauregard on the James. But by 1864 death, disease, and desertion had reduced the Army of Northern Virginia to a point well below its strength of earlier years, and the blockade and the capture of Confederate arsenals had reduced its fighting*

364

strength. Its soldiers were hungry, ill-clad, ill-shod, and battle-weary; they knew that they could not count on reinforcement or replacement, and they knew, too, that things were going badly almost everywhere else in the Confederacy. That for a year they held off Grant's mighty hosts is a tribute to their fortitude, their fighting qualities, and their devotion to their heroic leader.

The strategy of Grant's campaign against Lee is simple enough. His objective was not so much Richmond as Lee's army; his policy to hammer away at it until it was decimated. Lee's task was to keep Grant away from Richmond and to inflict such losses upon him that he would abandon the offensive or that the North would despair of victory and turn Lincoln out at the fall elections. With almost anyone else Lee's strategy might have worked, but in Grant he had an opponent who never knew when he was licked.

The Wilderness campaign was really one prolonged battle, from May 4, when Grant crossed the Rapidan, to June 14, when he crossed the James. The details of this battle are confusing but the general pattern is clear. To get to Richmond Grant had to whip Lee's army, or destroy it; Lee's job was to tangle him up in the Wilderness and destroy him. Imagine a diagonal line of about sixty miles, stretching roughly south-easterly from Germanna Ford on the Rapidan to Cold Harbor, just ten miles east of Richmond. Grant smashed at Lee's line, was held and thrust back, and then slid down the diagonal with Lee racing on a parallel line to stop him. Attack, repulse, slide, attack, repulse, slide—that is the tactical story of the Battle of the Wilderness, Spotsylvania, Hanover Court House, and Cold Harbor. No single battle in this campaign reached the dimensions of Gettysburg or Shiloh, but collectively they constituted the most costly campaign of the war and they embraced, too, the hottest fighting of the war. Grant's losses in the Wilderness campaign came to about 55,000; Lee's are unknown, but were probably about half that number.

Who won the Battle of the Wilderness? That is hard to say. On the face of it the victory was Lee's. He had prevented Grant from breaking his lines, had saved Richmond, had forced Grant to abandon the campaign of the direct attack from the north and fall back on siege, and had inflicted on Grant losses almost as large as the whole of Lee's own army. Yet Grant had largely achieved his own primary objective. He had so punished Lee that the Army of Northern Virginia never really recovered. He had thus prepared the way for the subsequent attack on Richmond from the south. And he

*ended his campaign with more men in his army than he had
when he crossed the Rapidan.*

1. U. S. GRANT PLANS HIS SPRING CAMPAIGN

*Here is Grant's own statement of the grand strategy which
he formulated for the spring of 1864; it has all his characteristic sparseness of phrase and his objectivity.*

The Union armies were now divided into nineteen departments, though four of them in the West had been concentrated into a single military division. The Army of the
Potomac was a separate command, and had no territorial
limits. There were thus seventeen distinct commanders. Before
this time these various armies had acted separately and inde-
pendently of each other, giving the enemy an opportunity,
often, of depleting one command, not pressed, to reënforce
another more actively engaged. I determined to stop this. To
this end I regarded the Army of the Potomac as the center,
and all west to Memphis, along the line described as our
position at the time, and north of it, the right wing; the
Army of the James, under General Butler, as the left wing, and
all the troops south as a force in rear of the enemy. Some of
these last were occupying positions from which they could
not render service proportionate to their numerical strength.
All such were depleted to the minimum necessary to hold
their positions as a guard against blockade-runners; when
they could not do this, their positions were abandoned altogether. In this way ten thousand men were added to the
Army of the James from South Carolina alone, with General
Gillmore in command. It was not contemplated that Gillmore
should leave his department; but as most of his troops were
taken, presumably for active service, he asked to accompany
them, and was permitted to do so. Officers and soldiers on
furlough, of whom there were many thousands, were ordered
to their proper commands; concentration was the order of
the day, and the problem was to accomplish it in time to
advance at the earliest moment the roads would permit.

As a reënforcement to the Army of the Potomac, or to act
in support of it, the Ninth Army Corps, over twenty thousand
strong, under General Burnside, had been rendezvoused at
Annapolis, Maryland. This was an admirable position for such

a reënforcement. The corps could be brought at the last moment as a reënforcement to the Army of the Potomac, or it could be thrown on the sea-coast, south of Norfolk, to operate against Richmond from that direction. In fact, up to the last moment Burnside and the War Department both thought the Ninth Corps was intended for such an expedition.

My general plan now was to concentrate all the force possible against the Confederate armies in the field. There were but two such, as we have seen, east of the Mississippi River and facing north: the Army of Northern Virginia, General Robert E. Lee commanding, was on the south bank of the Rapidan, confronting the Army of the Potomac; the second, under General Joseph E. Johnston, was at Dalton, Georgia, opposed to Sherman, who was still at Chattanooga. Besides these main armies, the Confederates had to guard the Shenandoah Valley—a great storehouse to feed their armies from—and their line of communications from Richmond to Tennessee. Forrest, a brave and intrepid cavalry general, was in the West, with a large force, making a larger command necessary to hold what we had gained in middle and west Tennessee. We could not abandon any territory north of the line held by the enemy, because it would lay the Northern States open to invasion. But as the Army of the Potomac was the principal garrison for the protection of Washington, even while it was moving on to Lee, so all the forces to the West, and the Army of the James, guarded their special trusts when advancing from them as well as when remaining at them— better, indeed, for they forced the enemy to guard his own lines and resources, at a greater distance from ours and with a greater force, since small expeditions could not so well be sent out to destroy a bridge or tear up a few miles of railroad track, burn a storehouse, or inflict other little annoyances. Accordingly I arranged for a simultaneous movement all along the line.

Sherman was to move from Chattanooga, Johnston's army and Atlanta being his objective points. General George Crook, commanding in West Virginia, was to move from the mouth of the Gauley River with a cavalry force and some artillery, the Virginia and Tennessee railroad to be his objective. Either the enemy would have to keep a large force to protect their communications or see them destroyed, and a large amount of forage and provisions, which they so much needed, would fall into our hands. Sigel, who was in command in the valley of Virginia, was to advance up the valley, covering the North from an invasion through that channel as well while advancing as by remaining near Harper's Ferry. Every mile he advanced also gave us possession of stores on which Lee relied. Butler was to advance by the James River, having Richmond and Petersburg as his objective. Before the advance commenced I visited Butler at Fort Monroe. This was the first time I had ever met him. Before giving him any order as to the part he was to play in the approaching campaign I invited his views. They were very much such as I intended to direct, and as I did direct, in writing, before leaving. . . .

Banks in the Department of the Gulf was ordered to assemble all his troops at New Orleans in time to join in the general move, Mobile to be his objective.

—Personal Memoirs of U. S. Grant

2. COLONEL PORTER DRAWS A PORTRAIT OF GENERAL GRANT

This portrait of Grant is, as might be expected, a friendly one. Horace Porter left Harvard to enter West Point, and graduated third in rank in the class of 1860. He was appointed chief ordnance officer of the Army of the Potomac and then to the same position in the Army of the Cumberland, where he first made Grant's acquaintance. In November 1863 he was recalled for duty in Washington, and in April 1864 appointed aide-de-camp to Grant. He was at Grant's side all through the Wilderness and Petersburg campaigns, and his book, Campaigning with Grant, is perhaps the best description of that chapter of Grant's military career. After the war Porter had a long and distinguished career in business and public affairs. He was vice-president of the Pullman Company, Ambassador to France, American delegate to the Hague Tribunal, and active in Republican politics and in social life.

A description of General Grant's personal appearance at this important period of his career may not be out of place here, particularly as up to that time the public had received such erroneous impressions of him. There were then few correct portraits of him in circulation. Some of the earliest pictures purporting to be photographs of him had been manufactured when he was at the distant front, never stopping in one place long enough to be "focused." Nothing daunted, the practisers of that art which is the chief solace of the vain had photographed a burly beef-contractor, and spread the pictures broadcast as representing the determined, but rather robust, features of the coming hero, and it was some time before the real photographs which followed were believed to be genuine. False impressions of him were derived, too, from the fact that he had come forth from a country leather store, and was famous chiefly for striking sledge-hammer blows in the field, and conducting relentless pursuits of his foes through the swamps of the Southwest. He was pictured in the popular mind as striding about in the most approved swash-buckler style of melodrama.

Many of us were not a little surprised to find in him a man of slim figure, slightly stooped, five feet eight inches in height, weighing only a hundred and thirty-five pounds, and of a modesty of mien and gentleness of manner which seemed to fit him more for the court than for the camp. His eyes were dark-gray, and were the most expressive of his features. Like nearly all men who speak little, he was a good listener; but his face gave little indication of his thoughts, and it was the expression of his eyes which furnished about the only response to the speaker who conversed with him. When he was about to say anything amusing, there was always a perceptible twinkle in his eyes before he began to speak, and he often laughed heartily at a witty remark or a humorous incident.

His mouth, like Washington's, was of the letter-box shape, the contract of the lips forming a nearly horizontal line. This feature was of a pattern in striking contrast with that of Napoleon, who had a bow mouth, which looked as if it had been modeled after a front view of his cocked hat. The firmness with which the general's square-shaped jaws were set when his features were in repose was highly expressive of his force of character and the strength of his will-power. His hair and beard were of a chestnut-brown color. The beard was worn full, no part of the face being shaved, but, like the hair, was always kept closely and nearly trimmed. Like Cromwell, Lincoln, and several other great men in history, he had a wart on his cheek. In his case it was small, and located on the right side just above the line of the beard.

His face was not perfectly symmetrical, the left eye being a very little lower than the right. His brow was high, broad, and rather square, and was creased with several horizontal wrinkles, which helped to emphasize the serious and somewhat careworn look which was never absent from his countenance. This expression, however, was in no wise an indication of his nature, which was always buoyant, cheerful, and hopeful. His voice was exceedingly musical, and one of the clearest in sound and most distinct in utterance that I have ever heard. It had a singular power of penetration, and sentences spoken by him in an ordinary tone in camp could be heard at a distance which was surprising.

His gait in walking might have been called decidedly unmilitary. He never carried his body erect, and having no ear for music or rhythm, he never kept step to the airs played by the bands, no matter how vigorously the bass drums emphasized the accent. When walking in company there was no attempt to keep step with others. In conversing he usually employed only two gestures; one was the stroking of his chin beard with his left hand; the other was the raising and lowering of his right hand, and resting it at intervals upon his knee or a table, the hand being held with the fingers close together and the knuckles bent, so that the back of the hand and fingers formed a right angle. When not pressed by any matter of importance he was often slow in his movements, but when roused to activity he was quick in every motion, and worked with marvelous rapidity.

He was civil to all who came in contact with him, and never attempted to snub any one, or treat anybody with less consideration on account of his inferiority in rank. With him there was none of the puppyism so often bred by power, and none of the dogmatism which Samuel Johnson characterized as puppyism grown to maturity. . . .

Throughout this memorable year (1864-5), the most important as well as the most harassing of his entire military career, General Grant never in any instance failed to manifest those traits which were the true elements of his greatness. He was always calm amid excitement, and patient under trials. He looked neither to the past with regret nor to the future with apprehension. When he could not control he endured, and in every great crisis he could "convince when others could not advise." His calmness of demeanor and unruffled temper were often a marvel even to those most familiar with him. In the midst of the most exciting scenes he rarely raised his voice above its ordinary pitch or manifested the least irritability. Whether encountered at noonday or awakened from sleep at midnight, his manner was always the same; whether receiving the report of an army commander or of a private soldier serving as a courier or a scout, he listened with equal deference and gave it the same strict attention. He could not only discipline others, but he could discipline himself. If he had lived in ancient days he might, in his wrath, have

broken the two tables of stone: he never would have broken
the laws which were written on them. The only manifestation
of anger he had indulged in during the campaign was upon
the occasion . . . when he found a teamster beating his horses
near the Totopotomoy.

He never criticized an officer harshly in the presence of
others. If fault had to be found with him, it was never made
an occasion to humiliate him or wound his feelings. The only
pointed reprimand he ever administered was in the instance
mentioned in the battle of the Wilderness, when an officer left
his troops and came to him to magnify the dangers which
were to be feared from Lee's methods of warfare. The fact
that he never "nagged" his officers, but treated them all with
consideration, led them to communicate with him freely and
intimately; and he thus gained much information which otherwise he might not have received. To have a well-disciplined
command he did not deem it necessary to have an unhappy
army. His ideas of discipline did not accord with those of the
Russian officer who, one night in the Moscow campaign,
reprimanded a soldier for putting a ball of snow under his
head for a pillow, for the reason that indulgence in such un-
called-for luxuries would destroy the high character of the
army.

It was an interesting study in human nature to watch the
general's actions in camp. He would sit for hours in front of
his tent, or just inside of it looking out, smoking a cigar
very slowly, seldom with a paper or a map in his hands, and
looking like the laziest man in camp. But at such periods his
mind was working more actively than that of any one in the
army. He talked less and thought more than any one in the
service. He studiously avoided performing any duty which
some one else could do as well or better than he, and in this
respect demonstrated his rare powers of administration and
executive methods. He was one of the few men holding high
position who did not waste valuable hours by giving his
personal attention to petty details. He never consumed his
time in reading over court-martial proceedings, or figuring up
the items of supplies on hand, or writing unnecessary letters
or communications. He held subordinates to a strict account-
ability in the performance of such duties, and kept his own
time for thought. It was this quiet but intense thinking, and
the well-matured ideas which resulted from it, that led to the
prompt and vigorous action which was constantly witnessed
during this year, so pregnant with events.

PORTER, *Campaigning with Grant*

3. PRIVATE GOSS DESCRIBES THE BATTLE
OF THE WILDERNESS

Though the entire campaign from early May to mid-June is generally described as the Wilderness, it is the fighting of May 5 and 6 that is called the Battle of the Wilderness. As was so often the case in the war, neither commander wanted to bring on a general engagement that day. Grant much preferred to get out of the Wilderness, if he could, and in any event he had not yet brought Burnside up to his army; Lee was waiting for Longstreet, who, starting on the fourth, made a spectacular march of 35 miles in one day. Warren's corps, however, ran into Ewell at the Old Wilderness Tavern, and the two tangled up. Then Heth's division, of A. P. Hill's corps, advancing up the Orange Plank Road, ran into Getty, of Hancock's corps. The fighting that day was fierce but inconclusive, and it was renewed the next day on a larger scale.

Warren Goss, who here tells the story of the fighting on the fifth and the sixth, we have met before.

Leading our right column on the morning of the 5th [May, 1864], Warren's corps resumed its prescribed march towards Parker's Store, which is on the Orange plank road. . . . Early in the morning, Ewell began his march on the same road by which Griffin was advancing. They met. The Union skirmishers were driven in. The intelligence of the meeting was conveyed to Grant, and orders suspending the movements prescribed to the different corps were at once given.

Grant and Meade both arrived at the Wilderness Tavern shortly after the initial encounter. Meade was heard to say: "They have left a division here to fool us while they concentrate and prepare a position towards the North Anna, and what I want is to prevent those fellows getting back to Mine Run." Grant, with this misconception, at once ordered an attack to brush away or capture this obtruding force.

The attack was opened by Griffin's division, which at first swept everything in its front. It had simply encountered the van of Ewell's column. . . . The disordered van of Ewell's column re-formed on a wooded hill, and resumed at once the offensive. It so happened that the right of Warren's Corps was at this time uncovered. Wright's division of the Sixth Corps, which should have covered this flank, had not come up, owing to the dense underbrush through which it was compelled to move. On this exposed flank Ewell directed his attack. On Griffin's left was Wadsworth's division. This advanced, but while beating through the dense undergrowth encountered a terrible fire from an unseen enemy. It illustrates the difficulty that beset troops operating in this tangled region, that there being no other guides, their directions were given them by the points of the compass. The orders were to advance due west. For some unknown reason Wadsworth advanced northwest, and this brought the fire of the enemy on his flank. Under this terrible flank fire the division broke in disorder. The best way to retreat was for each man to get to the rear, and not stand on the order of his going. The division of Wadsworth finally reformed in the rear and did good service during the fight which followed. . . .

In this abrupt encounter began the battle of the Wilderness. The opening was not auspicious. Warren had lost three thousand men. The enemy was in force in our front. . . .

The encounter . . . awakened Grant to the fact that the Army of Northern Virginia was in his front. He countermanded the previously ordered marches, and at once accepted Lee's challenge to battle. Here in the gloomy forest, with dogged resolution, he prepared to grapple with the enemy in this blind wrestle to the death. He at once recalled Hancock's corps from its march to Shady Grove Church. Our corps had advanced about ten miles when the order reached us, and at eleven o'clock we began our return march up the Brock road. . . .

Getty had already begun the fight before our arrival. Cheers went up from our sweat-begrimed, dusty veterans, as they came up at about three o'clock and formed in double line of battle in front of the Brock road. The road was very narrow, and densely wooded on both sides. Here we began to construct rifle-pits, by piling up logs and throwing up the soil against them. For this purpose men used their tin drinking-cups, bayonets, and caseknives, as well as the few shovels and picks which accompanied each division on pack-mules. We had not completed our rifle-pits when an order came to move on the enemy.

The scene of savage fighting with the ambushed enemy, which followed, defies description. No one could see the fight fifty feet from him. The roll and crackle of the musketry was something terrible, even to the veterans of many battles. The lines were very near each other, and from the dense underbrush and the tops of the trees came puffs of smoke, the "*ping*" of the bullets, and the yell of the enemy. It was a blind and bloody hunt to the death, in bewildering thickets, rather than a battle.

Amid the tangled, darkened woods, the *"ping! ping! ping!"* the *"pop! pop! pop!"* of the rifles, and the long roll and roar of musketry blending on our right and left, were terrible. In advancing it was next to impossible to preserve a distinct line, and we were constantly broken into small groups. The underbrush and briars scratched our faces, tore our clothing, and tripped our feet from under us, constantly.

On our left, a few pieces of artillery, stationed on cleared high ground, beat time to the steady roar of musketry. On the Orange plank road, Rickett's battery, or Kirby's, familiar to us in so many battles, was at work with its usual vigor, adding to the uproar.

"We are playing right into these devils' hands! Bushwhacking is the game! There ain't a tree in our front, twenty feet high, but there is a reb up that tree!" said Wad Rider. Two, three, and four times we rushed upon the enemy, but were met by a murderous fire and with heavy loss from concealed enemies. As often as we rushed forward we were compelled to get back. . . .

The uproar of battle continued through the twilight hours. It was eight o'clock before the deadly crackle of musketry died gradually away, and the sad shadows of night, like a pall, fell over the dead in these ensanguined thickets. The groans and cries for water or for help from the wounded gave place to the sounds of the conflict. . . . Thus ended the first day's fighting of the Army of the Potomac under Grant.

Our lines now faced westward. Burnside's corps had arrived early in the morning, and the formation was north and south in the following order: Sedgwick on the right, then Warren's, Burnside's and Hancock's corps, in the order named. The orders given for the battle were very simple. They were these: "Attack along the entire line at five o'clock."

There was no opportunity for grand maneuvers on this difficult field. It so happened that the commanders of both armies had aggressively determined to assume the offensive early on the morning of the 6th. The plan of the Confederate commander was to overwhelm our left and compel us to retreat to the Rapidan. Longstreet had, however, not yet arrived to participate in the fight, and Lee could not deliver his decisive blow until he came up. Pending his arrival he determined to call our attention from our left by a movement against our right. It thus fell out that Lee began his movement before the hour of attack designated by Grant.

Before five o'clock the roar of musketry on our right told
that Sedgwick was attacked by the enemy. Then Hancock
and Warren joined in the attack, and the whole line was
engaged. . . . The enemy were at once attacked with such
vigor that their lines were broken at all points, and they were
driven confusedly through the woods. Their dead and wounded
lay thick in the jungle of scrub-oaks, pines, and underbrush,
through which we rushed upon them. Squads of prisoners
constantly going to the rear exchanged rough but good-
natured salutations with our men. . . .

By six o'clock the rebel lines had been driven a mile and
a half and were broken and disordered. The advance of our
corps through swamps and tangled thickets, in this hot encounter, had broken our own lines. A proper formation of
the ranks, or any control by the officers in command, in this
tangled region, seemed impossible. In this disorganized condition a portion of our lines, under Birney, was brought to a
stand by the firm resistance of the enemy. It had encountered
the van of Longstreet's corps hastening to the fight. A halt was
ordered, and the lines which had become irregular, and the
brigades and regiments confusedly mixed, were reorganized.

Longstreet had, meanwhile, begun to form on the plank
road, and when a further advance was attempted by the
Union lines, they met this new force, and the fighting became
fierce and bloody. Hancock had promptly informed Meade
of the presence of some of Longstreet's men on his front.
Neither was aware that he had met the entire force of that
general. Intelligence had been gathered from prisoners the
night previous, which led to the inference that he was moving to attack the Union left. Expecting him in this direction
proved to be a great hindrance to Hancock. It was for this
that he had allowed his left, under Gibbon, to remain on the
Brock road. . . .

At eleven o'clock the firing died away. Burnside though
constantly ordered, had not attacked. Longstreet, meanwhile, was preparing for a decisive onslaught on our front.
His first blow fell on Frank's brigade of Hancock's command,
which was soon swept away by the whirlwind of attack, then
struck Mott's division and scattered it like leaves before the
wind. Hancock answered to this by attempting to swing
back his left to the plank road, and unite with his right, which
was still holding its advance position.

On the right of Hancock, Wadsworth's division fought with
heroic firmness. It charged the enemy several times, but was
finally driven back in disorder. In this encounter General

Wadsworth, while in the rear and centre of his lines cheering his men, fell mortally wounded. In the confusion which followed he was abandoned to the enemy, and died next day within their lines.

It was impossible to maneuver on account of the obstructive undergrowth, where no one could see a hundred paces in any direction. The roar of musketry alone disclosed the position of the foe, and the movements were generally learned only by actual collisions. Under these circumstances, general officers could hold but little control of their lines.

The troops fell back, in the confusion caused by the difficult field on which they fought, and re-formed in two lines behind their old intrenchments on the Brock road. Before this the tempest of the attack had ceased as suddenly as it began.

Longstreet, at the head of the assaulting column, was desperately wounded. He had, by mistake, been fired on by his own men when the tempest was at its height. This caused the halt in the attack. Lee now took command of this part of the line in person, and cautiously postponed further battle until more perfect dispositions of his troops were made. This lull in the storm lasted until four o'clock. The attack was then resumed. Then the Confederate columns came dashing on through the undergrowth until within a hundred yards of our lines. Here they halted and opened fire. Protected by their breastworks, for a time our men received but little harm. . . .

Flames sprang up in the woods in our front, where the fight of the morning had taken place. With crackling roar, like an army of fire, it came down upon the Union line. The wind drove the blinding smoke and suffocating heat into our faces. This, added to the oppressive heat of the weather, was almost unendurable. It soon became terrible. The line of fire, with resistless march, swept the thickets before its advance, then reaching out its tongue of flame, ignited the breastworks composed of resinous logs, which soon roared and crackled along their entire length. The men fought the enemy and the flames at the same time. Their hair and beards were singed and their faces blistered.

At last, blinded by the smoke and suffocated by the hot breath of the flames, with the whole length of their intrenchments a crackling mass of fire, they gave way and fell back to the second line of log intrenchments. With a shout the rebel column approached the road and attempted to seize the abandoned position. The impartial flames in turn drove them back.

The fire soon consumed the logs, and the rebels planted their colors there.

The fire swept on and reached our second line of intrenchments. This, like the first, was soon consumed. The men formed at some places eight and ten ranks deep, the rear men loading the muskets for the front ranks, and thus undauntedly kept up the fight while the logs in front of them were in flames. Finally blistered, blinded, and suffocating, they gave way. The enemy yelled with exultation. They rushed forward and attempted to place their colors on this line of our defense. Their triumph was brief, for the last line of log defences was soon consumed like the first. Then, with a shout resembling the rebel yell, our men charged the enemy, and swept them back from the field. At sunset our pickets were advanced half a mile without opposition.

During the conflict our men had exhausted their ammunition and had been obliged to gather cartridges from the dead and wounded. Their rifles, in many instances, became so hot by constant firing, that they were unable to hold them in their hands. The fire was the most terrible enemy our men met that day, and few survivors will forget this attack of the flames on their lines. . . .

After sundown the Confederates made an attack on the right of Burnside's corps, creating considerable confusion. The night prevented them from following up their success. Thus ended this terrible battle, the full details of which were hid in the tangled woods and darkling forests, where its mysteries will never be disclosed.

—Goss, *Recollections of a Private*

4. "TEXANS ALWAYS MOVE THEM"

The battle of the sixth was a near disaster for Lee. Early in the morning the Federals renewed the attack, Sedgwick and Warren smashing at Ewell but making no headway against his breastworks. Meantime the fighting shifted to the Union right, where Hancock was trying to break through Hill's corps. At midafternoon Wadsworth's division rolled up Hill's right flank while Birney's division struck on the left; the Confederate line broke and the victorious Federals poured through. But Longstreet's veterans were already coming up, Gregg's Texans in the van. Lee rallied them, and they dashed in and saved the day for the Confederacy. This is the first of the "Lee to the Rear" episodes. The author of this stirring account is unknown.

As we stood upon this hill, Lee excited and in close consultation with Longstreet—our batteries thundering into the Wilderness below, the roar of musketry from the undergrowth below—our men retreating in a disorganized mass, and the Yankees pressing on and within musket shot, almost, of the hill upon which stood our idolized chief, indeed was an exciting time, and the emergency called for *immediate* and *determined* action upon the part of the Confederate General. Lee was equal to the hour. Action must *not* be delayed, for in less than five minutes the enemy would be upon the hill. Longstreet's corps as it then stood in one mingled mass upon the plank road, could not be thrown in, and time must be allowed for it to reform, and place itself in line of battle. The cannon thundered, musketry rolled, stragglers were fleeing, couriers riding here and there in post-haste, minnies began to sing, the dying and wounded were jolted by the flying ambulances, and filling the road-side, adding to the excitement the terror of death. The "Texas brigade," was in front of Fields' division—while "Humphrey's brigade" of Mississippians led the van of Kershaw's division.

The consultation ended. Gen. Gregg and Gen. Humphrey were ordered to form their brigades in line of battle, which was quickly done, and we found ourselves near the brow of the hill, Gregg on the left—Humphrey on the right. "Gen. Gregg prepare to move," was the order from Gen. L.

About this time, Gen. Lee, with his staff, rode up to Gen. Gregg—"General what brigade is this?" said Lee.

"The Texas brigade," was General G's. reply.

"I am glad to see it," said Lee. "When you go in there, I wish you to give those men the cold steel—they will stand and fire all day, and never move unless you charge them."

"That is my experience," replied the brave Gregg.

By this time an aid from General Longstreet rode up and repeated the order, "advance your command, Gen. Gregg." And now comes the point upon which the interest of this "o'er true tale" hangs. *"Attention Texas Brigade"* was rung upon the morning air, by Gen. Gregg, *"the eyes of General Lee are upon you, forward, march."* Scarce had we moved a step, when Gen. Lee, in front of the whole command, raised himself in his stirrups, uncovered his grey hairs, and with an earnest, yet anxious voice, exclaimed above the din and confusion of the hour, *"Texans always move them."*

Reader, for near four years I followed the fortunes of the Virginia army, heard, saw and experienced much that saddened the heart or appealed in one form · or another to human passions, but never before in my lifetime or since, did I ever witness such a scene as was enacted when Lee pronounced these words, with the appealing look that he gave. A yell rent the air that must have been heard for miles around, and but few eyes in that old brigade of veterans and heroes of many a bloody field was undimmed by honest, heartfelt tears. Leonard Gee, a courier to Gen. Gregg, and riding by my side, with tears coursing down his cheeks and yells issuing from his throat exclaimed, "I would charge hell itself for that old man." It was not what Gen. Lee said that so infused and excited the men, as his tone and look, which each one of us knew were born of the dangers of the hour.

With yell after yell we moved forward, passed the brow of the hill, and moved down the declivity towards the undergrowth—a distance in all not exceeding 200 yards. After moving over half the ground we all saw that Gen. Lee was following us into battle—care and anxiety upon his countenance—refusing to come back at the request and advice of his staff. If I recollect correctly, the brigade halted when they discovered Gen. Lee's intention, and all eyes were turned upon him. Five and six of his staff would gather around him, seize him, his arms, his horse's reins, but he shook them off and moved forward. Thus did he continue until just before we reached the undergrowth, not, however, until the balls began to fill and whistle through the air. Seeing that we would do all that men could do to retrieve the misfortunes of the hour, accepting the advice of this staff, and hearkening to the protest of his advancing soldiers, he at last turned round and rode back to a position on the hill.

We reached the undergrowth—entered it with a yell, and in less than 100 yards came face to face with the advancing, triumphant, and sanguine foe—confronted only by a few brave souls who could only fire and yield their ground. The enemy were at least five or six to one of us, and death seemed to be our portion. With only 15 or 20 paces separating us, the contest waxed hot and deadlier. We gave a cheer and tried a charge, but with our handful of men our only success was to rush up to them, shoot them down, and shove them back some 10 or 15 yards. For 25 minutes we held them steady—not a foot did they advance, and at the expiration of that time more than half of our brave fellows lay around us dead, dying and wounded, and the few survivors could stand it no longer. By order of Gen. Gregg, whose manly form was seen wherever danger gloried most—I bore the order to the 5th and 1st Texas, to fall back in order.

After retreating some 50 yards, a most deafening yell was borne upon the breeze, and ere we were prepared to realize its cause, Gen. Longstreet's corps came sweeping by us, reformed, and reinforced by Gen. Anderson's division, and with a valor that stands unrivaled swept everything before them for three long miles—driving, in that long charge, the yankees from four different lines of breastworks that they had thrown up in their rear. The "Battle of the Wilderness" was won—all other fighting by the enemy that day and next was to prevent defeat from terminating in destruction. . . .

The "Texas Brigade" entered the fight 673 strong. We lost in killed and wounded over 450.—Did we or did we not do all that men could? Gen. Gregg entered the fight with at least 12 commissioned and non-commissioned on his staff. Of these, several were killed, some wounded, and only two horses untouched. Gen. G's. horse was pierced by 5 balls—each creating a mortal wound—though he rode him until we fell back—sent him to the rear where he died.

—R.C.——in The Land We Love

5. "THEIR DEAD AND DYING PILED HIGHER THAN THE WORKS"

On the night of May 6, Grant gave up the attempt to smash his way through Lee, and started the first of his sliding movements southward. From the seventh to the tenth he moved his great army down the Germanna Plank Road and the Brock Road toward Spotsylvania Court House. Lee anticipated his move, as he anticipated all of Grant's moves during the campaign, and had his army behind breastworks before Grant reached his objective.

By May 10 the two armies were in position, around Spotsylvania Court House, the Confederate line extending along some convenient heights in a great arc northward to the McCool house—later to be famous—and then swinging back again and stretching over two miles westward, the Union forces concentrated on either side of the angle of the Con-

*federate line. Early on the morning of the tenth Hancock, on
the Union right, threw one division across the little Po River,
where it was savagely attacked by Hill and forced back. The
real battle did not begin, however, until midafternoon, when
Generals Warren and Wright of Hancock's corps led off with
a heavy assault on the Confederate left. A little later General
Upton attacked the apex of the Confederate angle, penetrated
it, and threatened to take the whole Confederate line from
the rear.*

*Once again Lee came up to rally his broken troops; once
again he was prepared to lead the charge in person. This
time it was Gordon and his Georgians who came to the rescue.
This is the second of the "Lee to the Rear" episodes. That
night the Federals drew back, and both sides licked their
wounds.*

Now it is our old friend Robert Stiles who tells the story.

The 10th of May, '64, was pre-eminently a day of battle with
the Army of Northern Virginia. I know, of course, that the
12th is commonly regarded as the pivotal day, the great day,
and the Bloody Angle as the pivotal place, the great place, of
the Spottsylvania fights, and that for an hour or so along
the sides and base of that angle the musketry fire is said to
have been heavier than it ever was at any other place in all
the world, or for any other hour in all the tide of time. But
for frequency and pertinacity of attack and repetition and
constancy of repulse, I question if the left of General Lee's
line on the 10th of May, 1864, has ever been surpassed. I
cannot pretend to identify the separate attacks or to distinguish between them, but should think there must have been
at least a dozen of them. One marked feature was that, while
fresh troops poured to almost every charge, the same muskets in the hands of the same men met the first attack in the
morning and the last at night; and so it was that the men,
who in the early morning were so full of fight and fun that
they leaped upon the breastworks and shouted to the retiring
Federals to come a little closer the next time, as they did not
care to go so far after the clothes and shoes and muskets,
were so weary and worn and heavy at night that they could
scarcely be roused to meet the charging enemy.

The troops supporting the two Napoleon guns of the Howitzers were, as I remember, the Seventh (or Eighth) Georgia
and the First Texas. Toward the close of the day everything
seemed to have quieted down, in a sort of implied truce
There was absolutely no fire, either of musketry or cannon.

Our weary, hungry infantry stacked arms and were cooking their mean and meager little rations. Some one rose up and, looking over the works—it was shading down a little toward the dark—cried out: "Hello! What's this? Why, here come our men on a run, from—no, by Heavens! it's the Yankees!" and before any one could realize the situation or even start toward the stacked muskets the Federal column broke over the little work between our troops and their arms, bayonetted or shot two or three who were asleep before they could even awake, and dashed upon the men crouched over their low fires—with cooking utensils instead of weapons in their hands. Of course they ran. What else could they do?

The Howitzers—only the left, or Napoleon section, was there—sprang to their guns, swinging them around to bear inside our lines, double-shotted them with canister and fairly spouted it into the Federals, whose formation had been broken in the rush and the plunge over the works and who seemed to be somewhat massed and huddled and hesitating, but only a few rods away. Quicker almost than I can tell it our infantry supports, than whom there were not two better regiments in the army, had rallied and gotten to their arms, and then they opened out into a V-shape and fairly tore the head of the Federal column to pieces. In an incredibly short time those who were able to do so turned to fly and our infantry were following them over the intrenchments; but it is doubtful whether this would have been the result had it not been for the prompt and gallant action of the artillery. . . .

When it became evident that the attack had failed, I suggested to the chaplain—who happened to be with the Howitzer guns, perhaps for that sundown prayer meeting which Willy Dame mentioned—that there might be some demand for his ministrations where the enemy had broken over; so we walked up there and found their dead and dying piled higher than the works themselves. It was almost dark, but as we drew near we saw a wounded Federal soldier clutch the pantaloons of Captain Hunter, who at that moment was passing by, frying pan in hand, and heard him ask with intense eagerness: "Can you pray, sir? Can you pray?"

The old captain looked down at him with a peculiar expression, and pulled away, saying, "No, my friend, I don't wish you any harm now, but praying's not exactly my trade."

—STILES, *Four Years Under Marse Robert*

6. SPOTSYLVANIA AND THE BLOODY ANGLE

The heaviest fighting of the Wilderness campaign came on May 12, when Grant came within a hairbreadth of winning the campaign and perhaps the war. The Confederates should have learned from the experience of the tenth that their salient around the McCool house was peculiarly vulnerable, but—probably because the high ground appeared to offer advantages—they failed to straighten their lines. Not only this but they withdrew their artillery from the apex of this salient, an almost fatal move. At dawn on the twelfth Hancock's division launched a large-scale attack on the salient, the brigades marching twenty deep. Within an hour they had breached the Confederate line, and as Hancock hurried up reinforcements, a torrent of blue poured through the break. Yet once again, as we shall see, Lee managed to plug up the gap and save the day.

Here is the story of the fighting of the twelfth as seen from Grant's headquarters; it is told by Horace Porter, whose description of Grant we have already read.

I had been out all night looking after the movements of the troops which were to form the assaulting columns. After they had all been placed in position I started for headquarters, in obedience to instructions, to report the situation to the general-in-chief. . . . By feeling the way for some hours I reached headquarters about daylight the next morning, May 12.

When I arrived the general was up and sitting wrapped in his overcoat close to a camp-fire which was struggling heroically to sustain its life against the assaults of wind and rain. It had been decided to move headquarters a little nearer to the center of the lines, and most of the camp equipage had been packed up ready to start. The general seemed in excellent spirits, and was even inclined to be jocose. He said to me: "We have just had our coffee, and you will find some left for you"; and then, taking a critical look at my drenched and bespattered clothes and famished appearance, added, "But perhaps you are not hungry." To disabuse the chief's mind on this score, I sent for a cup of coffee, and drank it with the relish of a shipwrecked mariner, while I related the incidents of the embarrassments encountered in Hancock's movement, and the position he had taken up. Before I had quite finished making my report the stillness was suddenly broken by artillery-firing, which came from the direction of Burnside's position. A few minutes after came the sound of cheers and the rattle of musketry from Hancock's front, telling that the main assault upon the "angle" had begun. No one could see a hundred yards from our position on account of the dense woods, and reports from the front were eagerly awaited.

It was nearly an hour before anything definite was received, but at 5:30 an officer came galloping through the woods with a report from Hancock saying he had captured the first line of the enemy's works. This officer was closely followed by another, who reported that many prisoners had been taken. Fifteen minutes later came the announcement that Hancock had captured two general officers. General Grant sent Burnside this news with a message saying, "Push on with all vigor." Wright's corps was now ordered to attack on the right of Hancock. Before six o'clock a message from Hancock's headquarters reported the capture of two thousand prisoners, and a quarter of an hour later Burnside sent word that he had driven the enemy back two miles and a half in his front. Hancock called for reinforcements, but Grant had anticipated him and had already ordered troops to his support. The scene at headquarters was now exciting in the extreme. As aides galloped up one after the other in quick succession with stirring bulletins, all bearing the glad tidings of overwhelming success, the group of staff-officers standing about the camp-fire interrupted their active work of receiving, receipting for, and answering despatches by shouts and cheers which made the forest ring.

General Grant sat unmoved upon his camp-chair, giving his constant thoughts to devising methods for making the victory complete. At times the smoke from the struggling camp-fire would for a moment blind him, and occasionally a gust of wind would blow the cape of his greatcoat over his face, and cut off his voice in the middle of a sentence. Only once during the scene he rose from his seat and paced up and down for about ten minutes. He made very few comments upon the stirring events which were crowding so closely upon one another until the reports came in regarding the prisoners. When the large numbers captured were announced, he said, with the first trace of animation he had shown: "That's the kind of news I like to hear. I had hoped that a bold dash at daylight would secure a large number of prisoners. Hancock is doing well."

This remark was eminently characteristic of the Union commander. His extreme fondness for taking prisoners was manifested in every battle he fought. When word was brought to

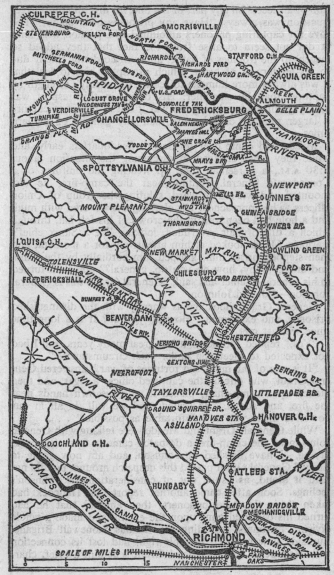

THE WILDERNESS

him of a success on any part of the line, his first and most eager question was always, "Have any prisoners been taken?" The love for capturing prisoners amounted to a passion with him. It did not seem to arise from the fact that they added so largely to the trophies of battle, and was no doubt chiefly due to his tenderness of heart, which prompted him to feel that it was always more humane to reduce the enemy's strength by captures than by slaughter. His desire in this respect was amply gratified, for during the war it fell to his lot to capture a larger number of prisoners than any general of modern times.

Meade had come over to Grant's headquarters early, and while they were engaged in discussing the situation, about 6:30 A.M., a horseman rode up wearing the uniform of a Confederate general. Halting near the camp-fire, he dismounted and walked forward, saluting the group of Union officers as he approached. His clothing was covered with mud, and a hole had been torn in the crown of his felt hat, through which a tuft of hair protruded, looking like a Sioux chief's warlock. Meade looked at him attentively for a moment, and then stepped up to him, grasped him cordially by the hand, and cried, "Why, how do you do, general?" and then turned to his general-in-chief and said, "General Grant, this is General Johnson—Edward Johnson."

General Grant shook hands warmly with the distinguished prisoner, and exclaimed, "How do you do? It is a long time since we last met."

"Yes," replied Johnson; "it is a great many years, and I had not expected to meet you under such circumstances."

"It is one of the many sad fortunes of war," answered General Grant, who offered the captured officer a cigar, and then picked up a camp-chair, placed it with his own hands near the fire, and added, "Be seated, and we will do all in our power to make you as comfortable as possible." . . .

While Generals Grant and Meade were talking with General Johnson by the camp-fire, a despatch came in from Hancock, saying, "I have finished up Johnson, and am now going to Early." General Grant passed this despatch around, but did not read it aloud, as usual, out of consideration for Johnson's feelings. Soon after came another report that Hancock had taken three thousand prisoners; then another that he had turned his captured guns upon the enemy and made a whole division prisoners, including the famous Stonewall Brigade. Burnside now reported that his right had lost its connection with Hancock's corps. General Grant sent him a brief, characteristic note in reply, saying, "Push the enemy with all your might; that's the way to connect." . . .

The battle near the "angle" was probably the most desperate engagement in the history of modern warfare, and presented features which were absolutely appalling. It was chiefly a savage hand-to-hand fight across the breastworks. Rank after rank was riddled by shot and shell and bayonet-thrusts, and finally sank, a mass of torn and mutilated corpses; then fresh troops rushed madly forward to replace the dead, and so the murderous work went on. Guns were run up close to the parapet, and double charges of canister played their part in the bloody work. The fence-rails and logs in the breastworks were shattered into splinters, and trees over a foot and a half in diameter were cut completely in two by the incessant musketry fire. A section of the trunk of a stout oak-tree thus severed was afterward sent to Washington, here it is still on exhibition at the National Museum. We had not only shot down an army, but also a forest.

The opposing flags were in places thrust against each other, and muskets were fired with muzzle against muzzle. Skulls were crushed with clubbed muskets, and men stabbed to death with swords and bayonets thrust between the logs in the parapet which separated the combatants. Wild cheers, savage yells, and frantic shrieks rose above the sighing of the wind and the pattering of the rain, and formed a demoniacal accompaniment to the booming of the guns as they hurled their missiles of death into the contending ranks. Even the darkness of night and the pitiless storm failed to stop the fierce contest, and the deadly strife did not cease till after midnight. Our troops had been under fire for twenty hours, but they still held the position which they had so dearly purchased.

My duties carried me again to the spot the next day, and the appalling sight presented was harrowing in the extreme. Our own killed were scattered over a large space near the "angle," while in front of the captured breastworks the enemy's dead, vastly more numerous than our own, were piled upon each other in some places four layers deep, exhibiting every ghastly phase of mutilation. Below the mass of fast-decaying corpses, the convulsive twitching of limbs and the writhing of bodies showed that there were wounded men still alive and struggling to extricate themselves from their horrid entombment. Every relief possible was afforded, but in too many cases it came too late. The place was well named the "Bloody Angle."

—PORTER, *Campaigning with Grant*

7. "THESE MEN HAVE NEVER FAILED YOU ON ANY FIELD"

Perhaps only once before in the history of the war had the situation been so critical to the Confederacy as it was on the morning of May 12, when the Confederate line broke: that was at Antietam. The Federal advance had not only broken through, it had enveloped General Johnson and taken him and 4,000 men prisoners. Lee tried to rally the fleeing soldiers. "Hold on!" he cried. "We are going to form a new line." But most of the men were panic-stricken, and ran to the rear. Already General Gordon had started his men forward to plug the gap—or at least hold the line. Meeting General Lee Gordon found that Lee was prepared to lead the counterattack himself.

But let Gordon tell the story—the third and the best authenticated of the "Lee to the Rear" episodes.

During the night Hancock had massed a large portion of General Grant's army in front of that salient, and so near to it that, with a quick rush, his column had gone over the breastworks, capturing General Edward Johnson and General George Steuart and the great body of their men before these alert officers or their trained soldiers were aware of the movement. The surprise was complete and the assault practically unresisted. In all its details—its planning, its execution, and its fearful import to Lee's army—this charge of Hancock was one of that great soldier's most brilliant achievements.

Meantime my command was rapidly moving by the flank through the woods and underbrush toward the captured salient. The mist and fog were so heavy that it was impossible to see farther than a few rods. Throwing out in front a small force to apprise us of our near approach to the enemy, I rode at the head of the main column, and by my side rode General Robert Johnson, who commanded a brigade of North Carolinians. So rapidly and silently had the enemy moved inside of our works—indeed, so much longer time had he been on the inside than the reports indicated —that before we had moved one half the distance to the salient the head of column butted squarely against Hancock's line of battle. The men who had been placed in our front to give warning were against that battle line before they knew it. They were shot down or made prisoners. The sudden and unexpected blaze from Hancock's rifles made the dark woodland strangely lurid. General Johnson, who rode immediately at my side, was shot from his horse, severely but not, as I supposed, fatally wounded in the head. His brigade was thrown inevitably into great confusion, but did not break to the rear. As quickly as possible, I had the next ranking officer in that brigade notified of General Johnson's fall and directed him at once to assume command. He proved equal to the emergency. With great coolness and courage he promptly executed my orders.

The Federals were still advancing, and every movement of the North Carolina brigade had to be made under heavy fire. The officer in charge was directed to hastily withdraw his brigade a short distance, to change front so as to face Hancock's lines, and to deploy his whole force in close order as skirmishers, so as to stretch, if possible, across the entire front of Hancock. This done, he was ordered to charge with his line of skirmishers the solid battle lines before him. His looks indicated some amazement at the purpose to make an attack which appeared so utterly hopeless, and which would have been the very essence of rashness but for the extremity of the situation. He was, however, full of the fire of battle and too good a soldier not to yield prompt and cheerful obedience. That order was given in the hope and belief that in the fog and mists which concealed our numbers the sheer audacity of the movement would confuse and check the Union advance long enough for me to change front and form line of battle with the other brigades. The result was not disappointing except in the fact that Johnson's brigade, even when so deployed, was still too short to reach across Hancock's entire front. This fact was soon developed: not by sight, but by the direction from which the Union bullets began to come.

When the daring charge of the North Carolina brigade had temporarily checked that portion of the Federal forces struck by it, and while my brigades in the rear were being placed in position, I rode with Thomas G. Jones, the youngest member of my staff, into the intervening woods, in order, if possible, to locate Hancock more definitely. Sitting on my horse near the line of the North Carolina brigade, I was endeavoring to get a view of the Union lines, through the woods and through the gradually lifting mists. It was impossible, however, to see those lines; but, as stated, the direction from which they sent their bullets soon informed us that they were still moving and had already gone beyond our right. One of those bullets passed through my coat from side to side, just grazing my back.

Jones, who was close to me, and sitting on his horse in a not very erect posture, anxiously inquired: "General, didn't that ball hit you?"

"No," I said; "but suppose my back had been in a bow like yours? Don't you see that the bullet would have gone straight through my spine? Sit up or you'll be killed."

The sudden jerk with which he straightened himself, and the duration of the impression made, showed that this ocular demonstration of the necessity for a soldier to sit up-right on his horse had been more effective than all the ordinary lessons that could have been given. It is but simple justice to say of this immature boy that even then his courage, his coolness in the presence of danger, and his strong moral and mental characteristics gave promise of his brilliant future.

The bullets from Hancock's rifles furnished the informa-tion which I was seeking as to the progress he had made within and along our earthworks. I then took advantage of this brief check given to the Union advance, and placed my troops in line for a counter charge, upon the success or failure of which the fate of the Confederate army seemed to hang. General Lee evidently thought so. His army had been cut in twain by Hancock's brilliant *coup de main*. Through that wide breach in the Confederate lines, which was becoming wider with every step, the Union forces were rushing like a swollen torrent through a broken mill-dam. General Lee knew, as did every one else who realized the momentous import of the situation, that the bulk of the Confederate army was in such imminent peril that nothing could rescue it except a counter-movement, quick, impetuous, and decisive. Lee resolved to save it, and, if need be, to save it at the sacrifice of his own life. With perfect self-poise, he rode to the margin of that breach, and appeared upon the scene just as I had completed the alignment of my troops and was in the act of moving in that crucial counter charge upon which so much depended.

As he rode majestically in front of my line of battle, with uncovered head and mounted on Old Traveller, Lee looked a very god of war. Calmly and grandly, he rode to a point near the centre of my line and turned his horse's head to the front, evidently resolved to lead in person the desperate charge and drive Hancock back or perish in the effort. I knew what he meant; and although the passing moments were of priceless value, I resolved to arrest him in his effort, and thus save to the Confederacy the life of its great leader. I was at the centre of that line when General Lee rode to it. With uncovered head, he turned his face toward Hancock's advancing column.

Instantly I spurred my horse across Old Traveller's front, and grasping his bridle in my hand, I checked him. Then, in a voice which I hoped might reach the ears of my men and command their attention, I called out, "General Lee, you shall not lead my men in a charge. No man can do that, sir. Another is here for that purpose. These men behind you are Georgians, Virginians, and Carolinians. They have never failed you on any field. They will not fail you here. Will you, boys?" The response came like a mighty anthem that must have stirred his emotions as no other music could have done. Although the answer to those three words, "Will you, boys?" came in the monosyllables, "No, no, no; we'll not fail him," yet they were doubtless to him more eloquent because of their simplicity and momentous meaning.

But his great heart was destined to be quickly cheered by a still sublimer testimony of their deathless devotion. As this first thrilling response died away, I uttered the words for which they were now fully prepared. I shouted to General Lee, "You must go to rear." The echo, "General Lee to the rear, General Lee to the rear!" rolled back with tremendous emphasis from the throats of my men; and they gathered around him, turned his horse in the opposite direction, some clutching his bridle, some his stirrups, while others pressed close to Old Traveller's hips, ready to shove him by main force to the rear. I verily believe that, had it been necessary or possible, they would have carried on their shoulders both horse and rider to a place of safety. . . .

I turned to my men as Lee was forced to the rear, and reminding them of their pledges to him, and of the fact that the eyes of their great leader were still upon them, I ordered, "Forward!" With the fury of a cyclone, and almost with its resistless power, they rushed upon Hancock's advancing column. With their first terrific onset, the impetuosity of which was indescribable, his leading lines were shivered and hurled back upon their stalwart supports. In the inextricable confusion that followed, and before Hancock's lines could be reformed, every officer on horseback in my division, the brigade and regimental commanders, and my own superb staff, were riding among the troops, shouting in unison: "Forward, men, forward!"

But the brave line officers on foot and the enthused privates needed no additional spur to their already rapt spirits. Onward they swept, pouring their rapid volleys into Hancock's confused ranks, and swelling the deafening din of battle with their piercing shouts. Like the débris in the track of a storm, the dead and dying of both armies were left in the wake of this Confederate charge. In the meantime the magnificent troops of Ramseur and Rodes were rushing upon Hancock's dissolving corps from another point, and Long's artillery and other batteries were pouring a deadly fire into the broken Federal ranks. Hancock was repulsed and driven out. Every foot of the lost salient and earthworks was retaken, except that small stretch which the Confederate line was too short to cover.

—GORDON, *Reminiscences of the Civil War*

8. GRANT HURLS HIS MEN TO DEATH AT COLD HARBOR

Lee had saved himself by the narrowest of margins at Spotsylvania, but the Federals, too, took heavy punishment. Once more Grant pulled off on one of his sliding movements to the south. This time he headed for Hanover Junction. Lee hurried along parallel with him, and by May 23 had taken position along the North Anna. Grant maneuvered for an attack but found Lee's defenses formidable, and decided to move on. His objective this time was Hanover Town, not far from Richmond. Lee took position on the south bank of the Totopotomy, a branch of the Pamunkey, and not far from Mechanicsville, where he had first met and defeated a Federal army. Then on June 1 the two armies shifted their positions to Cold Harbor, on the north side of the Chickahominy. On June 3 Grant decided on a head-on assault. It was probably the greatest mistake of his military career. Within a few hours he had lost about 10,000 men.

We have met Colonel William Oates before, notably at Gettysburg.

On the 2nd of June [1864] Law was ordered farther down our entrenched line, with his own and Anderson's Georgia brigade, to Cold Harbor, or near it for the purpose of retaking about 300 yards of badly constructed Confederate trenches which the enemy had succeeded in capturing on General Hoke's left. . . .

None of us had slept any. The men worked all night and by day had an excellent line of defensive works completed. When day came details were sent to the rear to fill the canteens at a bold spring of pure water. They had returned, and, just before I could see the sun, I heard a volley in the woods, saw the major running up the ravine in the direction of Anderson's brigade, which lay to the right of Law's, and the skirmishers running in, pursued by a column of the enemy ten lines deep, with arms at a trail, and yelling "Huzzah! huzzah!" I ordered my men to take arms and fix bayonets. Just then I remembered that not a gun in the regiment was loaded. I ordered the men to load and the officers each to take an ax and stand to the works. I was apprehensive that the enemy would be on our works before the men could load.

As Capt. Noah B. Feagin and his skirmishers crawled over the works I thought of my piece of artillery. I called out: "Sergeant, give them double charges of canister; fire, men; fire!" the order was obeyed with alacrity. The enemy were within thirty steps. They halted and began to dodge, lie down, and recoil. The fire was terrific from my regiment, the Fourth Alabama on my immediate right, and the Thirteenth Mississippi on my left, while the piece of artillery was fired more rapidly and better handled than I ever saw one before or since. The blaze of fire from it at each shot went right into the ranks of our assailants and made frightful gaps through the dense mass of men. They endured it but for one or two minutes, when they retreated, leaving the ground covered with their dead and dying. There were 3 men in my regiment killed, 5 wounded. My piece of artillery kept up a lively fire on the enemy where they halted in the woods, with shrapnel shell.

After the lapse of about forty minutes another charge was made by the Twenty-third and Twenty-fifth Massachusetts regiments, in a column by divisions, thus presenting a front of two companies only. Bryan's Georgia brigade came up from the rear and lay down behind Law's. The charging column, which aimed to strike the Fourth Alabama, received the most destructive fire I ever saw. They were subjected to a front and flank fire from the infantry, at short range, while my piece of artillery poured double charges of canister into them. The Georgians loaded for the Alabamians to fire. I could see the dust fog out of a man's clothing in two or three places at once where as many balls would strike him at the same moment. In two minutes not a man of them was standing. All who were not shot down had lain down for protection.

One little fellow raised his head to look, and I ordered him to come in. He came on a run, the Yankees over in the woods firing at him every step ⟨ ⟩ the way, and as he climbed over our works one shot took effect in one of his legs. They evidently took him to be a deserter. I learned from him that there were many more out there who were not wounded. This I communicated to Colonel Perry, who was again in command, General Law having been wounded in the head during the first assault; and thereupon Perry sent a company down a ravine on our right to capture them; they soon brought the colonel who led the charge, and about one hundred other prisoners. The colonel was a brave man. He said he had been in many places, but that was the worst.

This closed their efforts against us on this field for the remainder of that day. The following night they constructed works along the edge of the woods and sharpshooting became incessant. The next day a white flag was displayed and firing was suspended. A Union officer came half-way and met a Confederate staff officer, with a request from Major-General Augur for an armistice for six hours with permission to bury the dead. It was sent to General Lee, who returned it, saying that he did not know General Augur as commander of the Army of the Potomac.

Sharp-shooting was resumed. The stench from the dead between our lines and theirs was sickening. It was so nauseating that it was almost unendurable; but we had the advantage, as the wind carried it away from us to them. The dead covered more than five acres of ground about as thickly as they could be laid. A half hour elapsed, when another white flag was displayed and another request came for an armistice for six hours, with permission to bury the dead in front of our lines, signed this time by General Grant. Lee acceded to the request and hostilities ceased for the six hours. They sent a heavy detail upon the field, and when the time expired they had to get it extended in order to finish burying, although they worked rapidly the whole time. I have no means of knowing the exact number of bodies buried, but from appearances there could not have been less than five or six hundred, and may have been a much greater number. They belonged to Baldy Smith's corps.

—OATES, *The War Between the Union and the Confederacy*

XII

The Siege of Petersburg

THE *Wilderness campaign had decimated Lee's army, but it had not destroyed it, nor had it captured Richmond. What was Grant to do? If he could not take Richmond from the north or the east, he might take it from the south; if he could not destroy Lee's army in battle, he might wear it down by siege. His next move was, therefore, logical enough. Under the protection of his gunboats he threw his army across the James and struck at Richmond from the south. Petersburg was the key to Richmond, and to the whole of eastern Virginia. Through it ran a whole network of railroads connecting with the south and west: the Petersburg & Norfolk, the Weldon, and the Southside. If Grant could cut across these, he would break Richmond's connection with the rest of the Confederacy except for the Richmond & Danville Railroad to the west. And not only would he isolate Richmond; even more important he could cut Lee's army off from its supplies.*

Grant began to ferry his army across the James on June 12; by midnight of the sixteenth the movement was completed. Lee, who had anticipated this movement, was in a dilemma. If he hurried his own army across the James Grant might arrest his movement and assault Richmond with half of his force on the north, the rest on the south; either part would equal the whole of Lee's army. Lee had therefore to move with utmost caution, relying on Beauregard to hold Petersburg as long as possible and feeding him reinforcements as fast as safety permitted. Grant's movement was undoubtedly brilliantly conceived and executed but it should be remembered that it failed of its immediate objective; it neither broke the Confederate lines nor captured Petersburg.

It is often said that Grant's strategy was fundamentally that of McClellan, in 1862, and that Grant's eventual success is a vindication of McClellan. There is neither evidence nor logic to support this. McClellan at no time proposed to attack Richmond from south of the James nor did he, apparently, appreciate the importance of Petersburg as the railway focus of eastern Virginia.

Even before Grant crossed the James he ordered attacks on Richmond from Bermuda Hundred and on Petersburg; neither of these succeeded. Another opportunity to capture Petersburg presented itself on June 15 when W. F. Smith's corps was available for reinforcement of the attack. Once again the opportunity was fumbled. By the sixteenth Beauregard was strong enough to resist attack, and after some ineffectual fighting Grant settled down to besiege Petersburg. His strategy was elementary but sound. With a numerical superiority of two to one, he continued to push his lines ever farther to the west, thus forcing Lee to extend his lines in turn. Eventually Lee was holding 35 miles of defensive works; with his lines stretched thin they were bound to snap somewhere, sooner or later. Because Lee showed the same superb generalship that he had showed in the Wilderness, they did not snap until the following spring, and then it was Sheridan, coming on from the Valley, who broke them.

The siege of Petersburg was the most prolonged of the war—a nine-months affair. It was punctuated by a series of battles, chiefly for the railroads leading to the south and west, and by minor diversionary battles north of the James. While no one of these battles was a major affair, all of them wore down Lee's forces by attrition. At the same time Lee's army was being reduced by sickness and desertion. That Lee was able to sustain this nine-months siege is another tribute to his resourcefulness and fortitude.

1. GRANT'S ARMY CROSSES THE JAMES

Here, in the restrained language characteristic of official reports, is Grant's own summary account of the crossing of the

James, one of the notable operations of the war. For many years historians assumed that Lee was completely deceived by this movement; Douglas S. Freeman has clearly established that Lee anticipated it, prepared for it, and met it as best he could with his inadequate forces. Part of Grant's army was ferried across by ships; part of it crossed on a 2,000-foot pontoon bridge at Wilcox's landing.

From the proximity of the enemy to his defenses around Richmond it was impossible by any flank movement to interpose between him and the city. I was still in a condition to either move by his left flank and invest Richmond from the north side or continue my move by his right flank to the south side of the James. While the former might have been better as a covering for Washington, yet a full survey of all the ground satisfied me that it would be impracticable to hold a line north and east of Richmond that would protect the Fredericksburg railroad—a long, vulnerable line which would exhaust much of our strength to guard, and that would have to be protected to supply the army, and would leave open to the enemy all his lines of communication on the south side of the James. My idea, from the start, had been to beat Lee's army north of Richmond if possible; then, after destroying his lines of communication north of the James River, to transfer the army to the south side and besiege Lee in Richmond or follow him south if he should retreat. After the battle of the Wilderness it was evident that the enemy deemed it of the first importance to run no risks with the army he then had. He acted purely on the defense behind breastworks, or feebly on the offensive immediately in front of them, and where in case of repulse he could easily retire behind them. Without a greater sacrifice of life than I was willing to make, all could not be accomplished that I had designed north of Richmond. I therefore determined to continue to hold substantially the ground we then occupied, taking advantage of any favorable circumstances that might present themselves, until the cavalry could be sent to Charlottesville and Gordonsville to effectually break up the railroad connection between Richmond and the Shenandoah Valley and Lynchburg; and when the cavalry got well off to move the army to the south side of the James River, by the enemy's right flank, where I felt I could cut off all his sources of supply except by the canal. . . .

The Second Corps commenced crossing the James River on the morning of the 14th by ferry-boats at Wilcox's Landing. The laying of the pontoon bridge was completed about midnight of the 14th, and the crossing of the balance of the army was rapidly pushed forward by both bridge and ferry. After the crossing had commenced, I proceeded by a steamer to Bermuda Hundred to give the necessary orders for the immediate capture of Petersburg. The instructions to General Butler were verbal, and were for him to send General Smith immediately, that night, with all the troops he could give him without sacrificing the position he then held. I told him that I would return at once to the Army of the Potomac, hasten its crossing, and throw it forward to Petersburg by divisions as rapidly as it could be done; that we could re-enforce our armies more rapidly there than the enemy could bring troops against us. General Smith got off as directed, and confronted the enemy's pickets near Petersburg before daylight next morning, but, for some reason that I have never been able to satisfactorily understand, did not get ready to assault his main lines until near sundown. Then, with a part of his command only, he made the assault, and carried the lines northeast of Petersburg from the Appomattox River, for a distance of over 2½ miles, capturing fifteen pieces of artillery and 300 prisoners. This was about 7 P.M. Between the line thus captured and Petersburg there were no other works, and there was no evidence that the enemy had re-enforced Petersburg with a single brigade from any source. The night was clear, the moon shining brightly, and favorable to further operations. General Hancock, with two divisions of the Second Corps, reached General Smith just after dark, and offered the service of these troops as he (Smith) might wish, waiving rank to the named commander, who he naturally supposed knew best the position of affairs and what to do with the troops. But instead of taking these troops, and pushing at once into Petersburg, he requested General Hancock to relieve a part of his line in the captured works, which was done before midnight. By the time I arrived the next morning the enemy was in force.

—"Grant's Report covering operations of all armies of the
  U.S. from March, 1864 to May, 1865"

2. BEAUREGARD HOLDS THE LINES AT PETERSBURG

Grant's advance was across the James on June 14, and he ordered an attack on the feebly held Petersburg lines on the fifteenth. For this attack Smith had available some 16,000 men; Beauregard could muster no more than some 3,000. But Smith wasted the day, and before he could be joined by Hancock's corps, which had crossed the river on the fifteenth, Beauregard had rounded up enough reinforcements to hold his lines. On the sixteenth the fighting was renewed but by that time Beauregard had some 14,000 men available for defense. A series of powerful assaults by the Federals took some of the outer lines, and several of the redoubts, but the Confederates held firm on the inner lines, and by the eighteenth Lee had sent across sufficient reinforcements to make Petersburg safe. The fighting from the fifteenth to the eighteenth cost the Federals almost 10,000 in killed, wounded, and missing; there are no figures for Confederate losses, but they were less than half the Federal.

Beauregard himself tells the story of the defense of Petersburg.

The movement of the Army of the Potomac to the south side of the James began on the evening of the 12th of June, and Smith's corps was at Bermuda Hundred in the early afternoon of the 14th. From Point of Rocks it crossed the river that night and was pushed forward without delay against Petersburg. Kautz's cavalry and Hinks's command of colored troops had been added to it.

It was with a view to thwart General Grant in the execution of such a plan that I proposed to the War Department [June 9th] the adoption—should the emergency justify it, and I thought it did—of the bold and, to me, safer plan of concentrating all the forces we could readily dispose of to give battle to Grant, and thus decide at once the fate of Richmond and of the cause we were fighting for, while we still possessed a comparatively compact, well-disciplined, and enthusiastic army in the field.

From Swift Creek, early on June 14th, I telegraphed to General Bragg: "Movement of Grant's across Chickahominy and increase of Butler's force render my position here critical. With my present forces I cannot answer for consequences. Cannot my troops sent to General Lee be returned at once? . . . ." No answer came. Late in the evening of the same day, having further reason to believe that one corps at least of General Grant's army was already within Butler's lines, I telegraphed to General Lee: "A deserter from the enemy reports that Butler has been reënforced by the Eighteenth and a part of the Tenth Army Corps." To this dispatch,

likewise, there came no response. But, as prompt and energetic action became more and more imperative, and as I
could no longer doubt the presence of Smith's corps with
Butler's forces, I sent one of my aides, Colonel Samuel B.
Paul, to General Lee with instructions to explain to him the
exact situation. General Lee's answer to Colonel Paul was
not encouraging. He said that I must be in error in believing
the enemy had thrown a large force on the south side of the
James; that the troops referred to by me could be but a few
of Smith's corps going back to Butler's lines. Strange to say,
at the very time General Lee was thus expressing himself to
Colonel Paul, the whole of Smith's corps was actually assaulting the Petersburg lines. But General Lee finally said that
he had already issued orders for the return of Hoke's division;
that he would do all he could to aid me, and even come himself should the necessity arise.

The Confederate forces opposed to Smith's corps on the
15th of June consisted of . . . a real effective for duty of
2200 only. These troops occupied the Petersburg line on the
left from Battery No. 1 to what was called Butterworth's
Bridge, toward the right, and had to be so stationed as to
allow but one man for every 4½ yards. From that bridge to
the Appomattox—a distance of fully 4½ miles—the line was
defenseless.

Early in the morning—at about 7 o'clock—General Dearing, on the Broadway and City Point roads, reported his regiment engaged with a large force of the enemy. The stand made
by our handful of cavalry, near their breastworks, was most
creditable to themselves and to their gallant commander,
and the enemy's ranks, at that point, were much thinned by
the accurate firing of the battery under Graham. But the
weight of numbers soon produced its almost inevitable result,
and, in spite of the desperate efforts of our men, the cavalry
breastworks were flanked and finally abandoned by us, with
the loss of one howitzer. Still, Dearing's encounter with the
enemy, at that moment and on that part of the field, was of
incalculable advantage to the defenders of our line, inasmuch
as it afforded time for additional preparation and the distribution of new orders by Wise.

At 10 o'clock A.M. the skirmishing had assumed very alarming proportions. To the urgent demands of General Wise for
reënforcements, I was enabled at last to answer that part of
Hoke's division was on the way from Drewry's Bluff and would
be in time to save the day, if our men could stand their ordeal, hard as it was, a little while longer. Then all along the

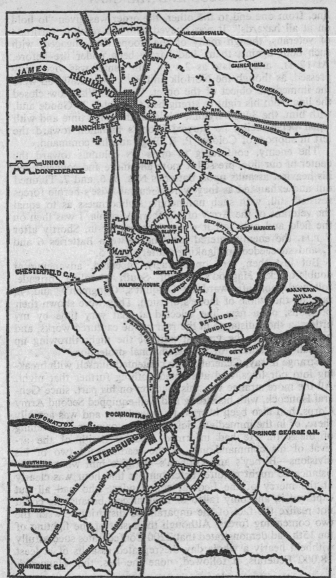

DEFENSES OF RICHMOND AND PETERSBURG

line, from one end to the other, the order was given "to hold on at all hazards!" It was obeyed with the resolute fortitude of veterans, though many of the troops thus engaged, with such odds against them, had hardly been under fire before. At 12 M., and as late as 2 P.M., our center was vigorously pressed, as though the Norfolk and Petersburg Railroad were the immediate object of the onset. General Wise now closed the line from his right to strengthen Colonel J. T. Goode and, with him, the 34th Virginia; while, at the same time and with equal perspicacity, he hurried Wood's battalion toward the left in support of Colonel P. R. Page and his command.

The enemy, continuing to mass his columns toward the center of our line, pressed it more and more and concentrated his heaviest assaults upon Batteries Nos. 5, 6, and 7. Thinned out and exhausted as they were, General Wise's heroic forces resisted still, with such unflinching stubbornness as to equal the veterans of the Army of Northern Virginia. I was then on the field and only left it when darkness set in. Shortly after 7 P.M. the enemy entered a ravine between Batteries 6 and 7, and succeeded in flanking Battery No. 5.

But just then very opportunely appeared, advancing at double-quick, Hagood's gallant South Carolina brigade, followed soon afterward by Colquitt's, Clingman's, and, in fact, by the whole of Hoke's division. They were shown their positions, on a new line selected at that very time by my orders, a short distance in the rear of the captured works, and were kept busy the greatest part of the night throwing up a small epaulement for their additional protection.

Strange to say, General Smith contented himself with breaking into our lines, and attempted nothing further that night. All the more strange was this inaction on his part, since General Hancock, with his strong and well-equipped Second Army Corps, had also been hurried to Petersburg, and was actually there, or in the immediate vicinity of the town, on the evening of the 15th. He had informed General Smith of the arrival of his command and of the readiness of two of his divisions—Birney's and Gibbon's—to give him whatever assistance he might require. Petersburg at that hour was clearly at the mercy of the Federal commander, who had all but captured it, and only failed of final success because he could not realize the fact of the unparalleled disparity between the two contending forces. Although the result of the fighting of the 15th had demonstrated that 2200 Confederates successfully withheld nearly a whole day the repeated assaults of at least 18,000 Federals, it followed, none the less, that Hancock's corps, being now in our front, with fully 28,000 men,—which raised the enemy's force against Petersburg to a grand total of 46,000,—our chance of resistance, the next morning and in the course of the next day, even after the advent of Hoke's division, was by far too uncertain to be counted on, unless strong additional reënforcements could reach us in time. . . .

General Hancock, the ranking Federal officer present, had been instructed by General Meade not to begin operations before the arrival of Burnside's command. Hence the tardiness of the enemy's attack, which was not made till after 5 o'clock P.M., though Burnside had reached Petersburg, according to his own report, at 10 o'clock A.M. [June 16].

The engagement lasted fully three hours, much vigor being displayed by the Federals, while the Confederates confronted them with fortitude, knowing that they were fighting against overwhelming odds, constantly increasing. Birney's division of Hancock's corps finally broke into part of our line and effected a lodgment. The contest, with varying results, was carried on until after nightfall, with advantage to us on the left and some serious loss on the right. It then slackened and gradually came to an end. In the meantime Warren's corps, the Fifth, had also come up, but too late to take a part in the action of the day. Its presence before our lines swelled the enemy's aggregate to about 90,000, against which stood a barrier of not even 10,000 exhausted, half-starved men, who had gone through two days of constant hard fighting and many sleepless nights in the trenches.

Hostilities began early on the 17th. . . . The firing lasted, on the 17th, until a little after 11 o'clock P.M. Just before that time I had ordered all the campfires to be brightly lighted, with sentinels well thrown forward and as near as possible to the enemy's. Then, at about 12:30 A.M., on the 18th, began the retrograde movement, which, notwithstanding the exhaustion of our troops and their sore disappointment at receiving no further reënforcements, was safely and silently executed, with uncommonly good order and precision, though the greatest caution had to be used in order to retire unnoticed from so close a contact with so strong an adversary.

The digging of trenches was begun by the men as soon as they reached their new position. Axes, as well as spades; bayonets and knives, as well as axes,—in fact, every utensil that could be found,—were used. And when all was over, or nearly so, with much anxiety still, but with comparative relief, nevertheless, I hurried off this telegram to General Lee [18th,

12:40 A.M.]: "All quiet at present. I expect renewal of attack in morning. My troops are becoming much exhausted. Without immediate and strong reënforcements, results may be unfavorable. Prisoners report Grant on the field with his whole army." . . .

The evening of the 18th was quiet. There was no further attempt on the part of General Meade to assault our lines. He was "satisfied," as he said in his report, that there was "nothing more to be gained by direct attacks." The spade took the place of the musket, and the regular siege was begun. It was only raised April 2, 1865.

—BEAUREGARD, "Four Days of Battle at Petersburg"

3. "A HURRICANE OF SHOT AND SHELL"

On the night of June 17 Meade issued orders for a general assault of the Confederate lines. These assaults did not get under way early in the morning, as planned, and before they did Beauregard had been strongly reinforced by Anderson's corps and by part of Hill's corps. The Federals hurled themselves desperately against the Confederate lines, but were unable to dent them.

Here is an account of the fighting by Captain Augustus Brown of the 4th New York Artillery.

June 18 [1864]—About nine o'clock orders came to continue the charge. From the fence . . . the ground, covered with some sort of growing grain, sloped gently down for a hundred yards to a narrow belt of trees in which was the dry bed of a little stream, and beyond this belt the grade ascended gradually for some five hundred yards to the rebel works on the brow of the hill, the intervening field being covered with a luxuriant growth of corn about three feet high. Captain Vanderwiel was assigned to command a picket line which was to precede us, and the advance from this point was to be made in two lines of battle, our five companies forming part of the front line. I saw no second line of battle upon our part of the field during the earlier part of the charge, and I certainly was not informed of any in advance. The enemy had posted two pieces of artillery, perhaps more, in what appeared to be angles of its new works, and our battalion very nearly covered the front between these guns.

To those of us who had anxiously watched all the morning the preparations for our reception, and had seen some of the guns moved into position and the troops deployed behind the breastworks, it seemed perfectly evident that the charge would now prove a disastrous failure, but when the order was given, though we felt we were going to almost certain death, these five companies of artillerymen, always accustomed to obey orders, scaled the fence with a cheer, the enemy commencing to fire the moment we left the road. Reaching the belt of timber, we found the picket line halted and firing from behind trees, but the main line pushed on and out into the open cornfield.

One of my men, a good man, too, but for the moment forgetful that the question was not for him or me to decide, stopped behind a tree, and when ordered forward began to argue that we never could carry that breastwork, a proposition in which I heartily concurred, but it being no time or place for the interchange of our views I leveled my revolver at his head and he broke cover instantly. Another of my men had his musket struck by a ball and bent double like a hairpin, but straightening out his arm, which was nearly paralyzed for an instant, he picked up another musket and went on, keeping place in the line. Just at that moment Major Williams received a rifle ball in the shoulder, and falling near me, though I was not the ranking Captain on the field, directed me to assume command of the battalion, and I turned my own company over to Lieutenant Edmonston.

On assuming command, I noticed that the men in the company on the right of my own, whose Captain had allowed them a ration of whiskey just before we started, were dropping into a little ditch just outside of the line of trees, and that the Captain, who was as brave a man as ever lived, but was rather noted for his varied and vigorous vocabulary, was passing up and down the ditch poking them with his sword and with tears streaming down his face, but without an oath, was begging them to get out and keep in line and not disgrace themselves and him. Thinking to shame his men by letting them know that I, the Captain of a rival company, saw them skulking, I shouted to him to get his men out of the ditch and press forward.

I shall never forget the hurricane of shot and shell which struck us as we emerged from the belt of trees. The sound of the whizzing bullets and exploding shells, blending in awful volume, seemed like the terrific hissing of some gigantic furnace. Men, torn and bleeding, fell headlong from the ranks as the murderous hail swept through the line. A splash of blood from a man hit in the cheek struck me in the face. The shrieks of the wounded mingled with the shouts of defiance which greeted us as we neared the rebel works, and every frightful and sickening incident conspired to paint a scene which no one who survived that day will care again to witness.

This part of the charge was made across a portion of an old race course, and the belt of trees which bordered the track at that point and in which lay the dry bed of the little stream, formed a sort of arc with the ends projected toward the enemy, and as the flanks of the battalion came out in full view, and we were within about one hundred and fifty yards of the rebel line, I was astonished to see that there were no troops on either side of us, and looking back, I discovered that my five companies were the only troops of all the charging lines which were in sight, that had obeyed the order and advanced from the sunken road. Then for the first time I understood the fierceness of the fire to which we were being subjected; saw that we were receiving not only the fire from the works in our front, to which we were entitled, but a cross fire from troops and artillery on the right and left of our front which would have been directed toward other parts of the charging lines if we had been supported, and realized that with this little handful of men, being then so rapidly decimated, it was worse than useless to continue the attack. Accordingly I halted the line and gave the order to lie down, the corn being high enough to furnish some little concealment. A general break to the rear would have cost as many lives as the double-quick to the front had done, so I instantly followed my first order with another to the effect that each man should get to the rear as best he could.

When we left the sunken road the Colonel of a regiment on our left whose men, like most of our infantry after six weeks of that sort of strategy, tired of charging a breastwork three times and then going around it, had flatly refused to follow him, joined us with his color-guard and gallantly accompanied us as far as we went, and there planted his flags in the soft earth. He must have discovered the futility of a further advance about the time that I did, for just as I ordered the men down he ordered a retreat, though we were not under his command, and under the combined orders the men at once disappeared in the corn. My orders were intended to embrace the officers of the battalion as well as the men but they were not so understood, and after the men were out of sight there stood the line officers, still targets for the enemy, calmly facing him and awaiting further orders. I shall never forget my thrill of admiration for those brave men as I glanced for an instant up and down the line, but it was no time for a dress parade and I immediately ordered them down and laid down myself.

The sun was blazing straight down upon us and the surface of the ground was very hot, and added to these discomforts, the enemy was firing into the corn in the hope of hitting some of us, which no doubt was done. Although by no means over-charged with physical courage . . . I was not, up to this point, conscious of the slightest apprehension for my own personal safety, my intense anxiety for my men and my fixed determination to go over that breastwork at all hazards having probably banished all other considerations from my mind, but as I lay there broiling in the sun, normal conditions began to return, and it occurred to me that some stray bullet might possibly search me out, and, what seemed even worse,—for there is no measuring the limits and effect of personal vanity, —the reflection forced itself upon me that the rebels, and perhaps some of our own men at the rear, had seen the leader of that charge, an acting Major at least, actually hide in the corn.

That last idea settled it, and reflecting that if I should go directly to the rear I would be an easier mark than if I should go across the fire, and that a wound in the back was not considered ornamental for a soldier, I arose and deliberately walked diagonally to the rear until I came to the continuation of the ditch or runway up which, at its distant lower end, we had filed the night before to build a rifle pit, and dropping into that, worked my way down to the piece of race track just outside of the belt of trees, and crossing that reached our works in safety. Why I was not struck while making that trip is more than I can tell . . . and, as giving some idea of the severity of the fire we faced that day, I may mention that on returning to our lines I counted twenty-four shot and shell marks on the side towards the enemy of a little pine tree not more than eight inches through at the butt, and that the battalion lost, according to the company reports, one hundred and fifteen killed and wounded in this charge.

—BROWN, *The Diary of a Line Officer*

4. THE MINE AND THE BATTLE OF THE CRATER

With the failure of the assaults on the eighteenth, Grant settled down to invest Petersburg, meantime extending his lines as far to the left as he could. During the rest of June, and July, the two armies stood in their entrenchments, sniping at each other and wilting in the broiling sun. So formidable were Confederate defenses that a break-through seemed impossible. In this juncture Colonel Pleasants of the 48th Pennsylvania—a miners' regiment—proposed tunneling under the Confederate lines and breaching them by exploding a mine. The proposal was accepted, responsibility for laying the mine assigned to Colonel Pleasants' division and for breaking through the Confederate lines after the explosion to General Burnside's IX Corps. The mine was exploded at 5:00 a.m. on June 30; Union artillery opened all along the line; General Ledlie's 1st Division, minus its general, surged into the crater —and stopped.

The details of the operation are somewhat confused, but the outcome is clear enough. The attack—well planned as it was—failed. Federal casualties were over 4,000, Confederate around 1,000. General Ledlie resigned; charges were preferred against Burnside, who shortly resigned. Ferrero, whose colored division had borne the brunt of the fighting, was transferred to a post of less responsibility.

John Wise, son of Virginia's Governor Henry S. Wise, was a student at the Virginia Military Institute when he fought in the Battle of New Market; after that engagement—whose history we will read in our next chapter—he came east to fight for the defense of Petersburg. After the war he went into politics, joined the Republican party, and became a cog in the Mahone political machine.

In the whole history of war, no enterprise so auspiciously begun ever resulted in a conclusion more lame and impotent. The Union troops designated for the assault, instead of drawing inspiration from the sight of the breach they had effected, actually appeared to recoil from the havoc. For some time no demonstration followed the explosion; when they finally advanced, it was not with the eagerness of grenadiers or guardsmen, but with rushes and pauses of uncertainty; and when they reached our lines, instead of treating the opening as a mere passageway to their objective point beyond, they halted, peeped, and gaped into the pit, and then, with the stupidity of sheep, *followed their bell-wethers into the crater itself,* where, huddled together, all semblance of organization vanished, and company, regimental, and brigade commanders lost all power to recognize, much less control, their respective troops. Meade, from his position a mile away, was demanding of Burnside why he did not advance beyond the crater to the Blandford cemetery. Burnside, safely in the Union lines, and separated from his assaulting columns, was replying that difficulties existed,—difficulties which he could not specify, for the double reason that he did not know what they were, and that they did not in fact exist. . . .

From our ten-inch and eight-inch mortars in the rear of the line, a most accurate fire was opened upon the troops in the breach; and our batteries to north and south began to pour a deadly storm of shell and canister upon their crowded masses. The situation looked desperate for us, nevertheless, for it was all our infantry could do to hold their lines, and not a man could be spared to meet an advance upon Blandford cemetery heights, which lay before the Union troops. At this juncture, heroic John Haskell, of South Carolina, came dashing up the plank road with two light batteries, and from a position near the cemetery began the most effective work of the day.

Exposed to the batteries and sharpshooters of the enemy, he and his men gave little heed to danger. Haskell, in his impetuous and ubiquitous gallantry, dashed and flashed about: first here, next there, like Ariel on the sinking ship. Now he darted into the covered way to seek Elliott, and implore an infantry support for his exposed guns; Elliott, responding to his appeal, was severely wounded as he attempted with a brave handful of his Carolinians to cover Haskell's position; now Haskell cheered Lampkin, who had already opened with his eight-inch mortars; now he hurried back to Flanner, where he had left him and found him under a fire so hot that in mercy he resolved to retire all his guns but six, and call for volunteers to man them, but that was not the temper of Lee's army: every gun detachment volunteered to remain. Hurrying to the right again, he found but one group of cowards in his whole command, and these he replaced by Hampton Gibbs, and Captain Sam Preston of our brigade, whose conspicuous bravery more than atoned for the first defection; both fell desperately wounded, and were replaced by peerless Hampden Chamberlayne, who left the hospital to hurry to the fight, and won promotion by the brilliancy of his behavior. . .

It was fully six o'clock before General Lee heard the news,
from Colonel Paul, of Beauregard's staff! Colonel Paul lived
in Petersburg, and, being at home that night and learning
of the disaster, galloped out and informed General Lee as he
was sitting down to his breakfast. Before Lee even knew of
the occurrence, General Meade had had time to converse with
prisoners captured at the crater, and to advise Burnside that
Blandford cemetery was unprotected; that none of our troops
had returned from the James; that his chance was *now;* and to
implore him to move forward at all hazards, lose no time in
making formations, and rush for the crest.

General Lee immediately sent Colonel Venable, of his staff,
direct to Mahone, with instructions to come with two brigades
of his division to Blandford cemetery to support the artillery.
The urgency was so great that he did not transmit the order
through General Hill, the corps commander. . . .

Meanwhile, Venable had communicated with Mahone, and
Mahone, always cunning, had retired his two brigades from
the lines so quietly that General Warren, opposite to him, reported that no troops had been withdrawn from his front. The
Virginia and Georgia brigades of Mahone's division were the
troops selected. The message to Mahone was to send them,
but he insisted that he should go with them. They passed
rapidly by way of a ravine from Mahone's position on the
lines covering the Jerusalem plank road to a point in rear of
the crater. The Virginia brigade, commanded by Weisiger,
led. It was now eight o'clock. One cannot but think of what
might have happened during all this time, if Burnside had
acted upon Meade's urgent appeals.

The appearance of this infantry was balm and solace to the
artillery blazing away upon the crest just above them. For
hours they had been fighting there, almost decimated by the
artillery concentrated upon them, and the distant firing of
sharpshooters. They could not have withstood even a feeble
assault of infantry, and had expected it during every minute
they had been engaged: the coming of Mahone was their deliverance. With but an instant's pause in the ravine to strip
for battle, Mahone's division, headed by their gallant little
general, clambered up the slope, crossed the Jerusalem road,
and passed in single file at double-quick into a covered way.
There was no cheering, and no gaudy flaunting of uniforms or
standards; with them, war's work had become too grim and
too real for all that. In weather-worn and ragged clothes, with

hats whose brims could shade their eyes for deadly aim, with bodies hardened down by march and exposure to race-horse lines, they came, not with the look or feelings of mercenaries, but like anxious, earnest men whose souls were in their work, who knew what the crisis was, and who were anxious to perform the task which that crisis demanded. Agile as cats, they sprang across the road and entered the covered way; as they skipped by, many a fellow kissed his hand to the artillerymen to right and left, or strained on tiptoe to catch sight of the ground in front, before entering the sheltered passage. For the first time during the day, a line of infantry was between our guns and the enemy; and the boys at the guns, knowing what reliance could be placed upon Mahone's veterans, took new heart and new courage, and pounded away with redoubled energy.

Venable parted with Mahone at the mouth of the covered way, and, seeking General Lee, informed him that Mahone was up, and proposed to lead his two brigades in person. The general expressed his gratification, and gave a sigh of relief. . . . The ground from the crater sloped to the north and west into a little ravine, into which the covered way, by which Mahone had entered, debouched; in this hollow Mahone formed his troops for battle, the Virginia brigade on the left.

Springing quickly from the covered way, the eight hundred Virginians lay flat upon the ground. The Georgians were forming on their right. Before the Georgians could come into position, the enemy, occupying our gorge line, succeeded in forming an attacking column, and advanced to the assault. Weisiger, commanding the Virginians, was a grim, determined man. Our boys were lying down within one hundred and sixty yards of the works, and saw within them a vast throng of Union troops, and counted eleven Union flags. A gallant Union officer, seizing a stand of Union colors, leaped upon their breastworks and called upon his men to charge. Fully realizing the paucity of his own numbers, and the danger of being overwhelmed by the mass of the enemy if they poured down upon him, Weisiger determined to anticipate the threatened movement by charging. Cautioning his men to reserve their fire, he ordered them forward. Those who saw this assault pronounce it to have been, in many respects, the most remarkable which they ever witnessed. At the command "Forward!" the men sprang to their feet; advanced at a run in perfect alignment; absolutely refrained from firing until within a few feet of the enemy; then, with their guns almost upon the bodies of their foes, delivered a deadly fire, and, rushing upon them with bayonets and clubbed muskets, drove them pell-mell back into the intrenchments which they had just left.

General Lee, when advised of this brilliant assault, remarked, "That must have been Mahone's old brigade." When news came confirming it, he again said, "I thought so." . . .

In the position gained by Mahone's old brigade, nothing intervened between them and the enemy but the pile of breastworks,—they on the outside, the enemy within the crater and gorge line. The fighting by which they established themselves was desperate and hand-to-hand.

Superb Haskell once more came to their rescue: he moved up his little Eprouvette mortars almost to our lines, and, cutting down his charge of powder to an ounce and half, so that his shell scarcely mounted fifty feet, threw a continuous hail of small shell into the pit, over the heads of our men. Our fellows seized the muskets abandoned by the retreating enemy, and threw them like pitchforks into the huddled troops over the ramparts. Screams, groans, and explosions throwing up human limbs made it a scene of awful carnage. Yet the artillery of the enemy searched every spot, and they still had a formidable force of fighting men.

The Georgia brigade, charging a little after Weisiger's, was decimated and repulsed. Our own brigade, which was engaged from first to last and never yielded a foot of ground, lost heavily, and Mahone's brigade, the "immortals" of that day, was almost annihilated. About one o'clock, the Alabama brigade of Mahone's division, under Saunders, arrived upon the scene, formed and charged, and the white flag went up from the crater. Out of it into our lines filed as prisoners eleven hundred and one Union troops, including two brigade commanders, and we captured twenty-one standards and several thousand of small arms. Over a thousand of the enemy's dead were in and about the breach, and his losses exceeded five thousand effective troops, while our lines were reestablished just where they were when the battle began.

—WISE, *The End of an Era*

5. LEE STOPS HANCOCK AT THE GATES OF RICHMOND

Sheridan's offensive in the Valley forced Lee, early in August, to send reinforcements to that threatened area. To prevent the detachment of further reinforcements Grant sent Hancock's corps north of the James to make demonstrations against Richmond and, if possible, capture Chapin's Bluff, on the James River. It was expected that this attack would take Lee by surprise, but surprise was not achieved. Yet the threat to Richmond was a serious one. During the fighting of August 16 two Confederate brigades broke and fled; "not only the day but Richmond seemed to be gone," wrote General C. W. Field.

The confused fighting from August 14 to 18 is here described by Richard Corbin, who had run the blockade in order to serve in the Confederate Army.

Headquarters, Field's Division, Petersburg, Va., August 26, 1864.—My dear mother: Some three weeks have flown by since I wrote to you from the north side of the James River, wither this division had been sent at the time of Grant's grand subterranean operation before Petersburg, the strategy of which was characterized by the fiendish ingenuity of Yankee warfare. . . . As I told you from my headquarters near Chapin's Bluff, we fully expected to pitch into the Yankees immediately on arriving on the north side of the river; but when our division had got into position the enemy had disappeared from our front. As far as the fighting was concerned, we had a little respite, but the staff did not profit much by it, for General Field having been placed ad interim in command of that division of the Richmond defenses, our duties became very onerous; but we were to a certain extent compensated by the importance it gave us, for we literally became monarchs of all we surveyed.

This comparative repose was, however, of short duration. Our scouts, a few days after, brought us the intelligence that the enemy had thrown a pontoon bridge across the river and that a large force was moving across it. We had but few troops with us, but preparations were made for a resolute defense of the line committed to our care. On Sunday they drove our skirmishers in, and in the afternoon they attempted to carry a portion of our intrenchments. For that purpose they hurled against us two divisions of their Second Corps,

which rushed toward our position with yells, banners flying
and bands playing. When they advanced to within about
seven hundred yards of our line two twelve-pounders loaded
with canister blazed away at them. Our artillery is not considered by any means the most efficient branch of our service
and of late has been rather sneered at in this army, but on
this occasion it did terrible execution. The Yanks advanced
in four lines of battle, and a magnificent spectacle it was to
witness that mighty host bearing down upon our thinly-
manned breastworks. Notwithstanding my emotion, I could
not refrain from admiring the sight. Our fire made wide
breaches in their ranks, and after the third discharge the whole
line wavered and fluttered like a flag in the wind; another shell
exploding in their midst, they broke and fled in every direction without retaining a shadow of their former organization.
In their frantic haste to get out of range of our murderous
shots they threw away guns, equipment, and all their warlike
paraphernalia. Deserters told us that they lost very heavily
in that abortive charge. They again renewed the attack, but
with less vigor, on our left, and were driven back with great
loss by our dismounted cavalry. This was the last of that
day's fighting—with the shades of night there came a cessation
of hostilities.

In the morning of Tuesday the Yankees attacked us in
heavy force, but we repulsed them very handsomely. Finding
that these repeated assaults on that part of the line did not
pay, General Hancock felt for a more vulnerable point, which
he discovered on our left. After riding about ever since dawn,
the general and his staff halted in a field in the rear of
Wright's brigade of A. P. Hill's corps. The day was a sultry
one, and the heat, superadded to other exertions, made us so
weary that we got off our horses and lay down for a few
moments on the grass. We had not been there many seconds
when we were aroused by a terrific cannonade followed by
heavy volleys of musketry. We mounted horses in a trice;
presently squads of frightened men came from the front in
anything but a leisurely manner. They informed us that the
whole Yankee army had charged them and that they had
been obliged to give way. The firing increased; the air was
alive with Minié balls; the ground was torn up by shells and
cannonballs, and in a few minutes the whole of Wright's
brigade was stampeding toward us. We strove to rally them
by entreaties and by menaces, and with pistols drawn we
threatened to shoot them if they did not go back, but it was
of no avail; you might as well try to argue with a flock of

affrighted sheep as with a crowd of panic-stricken soldiers.

Up to this time we cannot account for this stampede. The attack, it was true, was sudden and unexpected and the force of the enemy enormous; but the men who were now flying before the Yankees had always beaten them and had invariably borne themselves on every battlefield with distinguished bravery. We are therefore much puzzled to find out what caused them to disgrace the name of their brigade in that manner. . . .

The General, finding that nothing can be got out of these men, decided to fall back, for the Federals were swooping down upon us in overwhelming numbers; it seemed as though forty thousand men would be an underestimate of the force. I was sent by him for reinforcements. I had orders to bring up without delay two brigades of our own division, viz. Laws's Alabama and Binning's Georgians. They came up at a double-quick amid a very galling fire; they were formed right under the guns of the enemy, and then they rushed in with a deafening war-whoop. It was really splendid to witness the dash of these gallant fellows. I was so carried away with enthusiasm that I cantered alongside of them, but, alas! I did not accompany them during the whole of their triumphant advance, for my faithful charger, poor Palmetto, fell under me, pierced in the left hip by a Minié ball. I was a little stunned by the fall, and when I managed to extricate myself from under him our brave boys had beaten back the foe and recaptured the position which they had taken from us. . . .

On the whole, notwithstanding the misbehavior of that brigade of Hill's corps, our achievement was a very brillant one; for with a handful of men, say seven thousand at the outside, we drove back three of the enemy's largest corps; and as usual our division won for itself and its commander golden opinions. General Lee, toward the close of the fight, rode up and congratulated the general on the able manner in which he had handled his troops. At one time it was touch and go, and it required great coolness and skill on the part of our general to parry the attempts of the Yankees to turn our flanks; had they succeeded in accomplishing that, the consequences might have been very serious. The reverse was a very heavy one to the enemy; by sending over the best troops they evidently counted on a success. We had several small artillery and picket engagements during the rest of the week, but finally they sloped off without trumpet or drum, and on Sunday morning Hancock and Company had vamosed.

Desertions from the Yankee army have been so frequent during this campaign that General Lee has desired to encourage them by circulating throughout Grant's army a paper in which kind treatment and protection is promised to those soldiers who come over to us voluntarily. This has produced the desired effect, for deserters flock into our lines at a monstrous rate, and the cry is "still they come."

—[CORBIN], "Letters of a Confederate Officer"

6. THE IRON LINES OF PETERSBURG

Direct assault on the Confederates lines was out of the question; the mine had proved a ghastly failure; attacks north of the James were abortive. Grant fell back on traditional siege operations, meantime striking constantly at the Weldon and the Southside railroads, and persistently pushing his lines westward. Lee's army was stretched to the breaking point; his soldiers were tired, hungry, and dispirited; and he lost as many men by desertion as he gained by recruits and levies.

Here are three letters from a North Carolina soldier who fought through the winter in the iron lines of Petersburg.

Luther Rice Mills to John Mills
                    Trenches Near Crater, Petersburg, Va.
                    Nov. 26th [1864]
Brother John:
   In my short note to you about a week ago I was unable to give you any of the army news &c. for that can only be gathered by observation. We have just passed through a spell of very hard weather. The suffering in the Trenches was much greater than it should have been. Many of the men were entirely destitute of blankets and overcoats and it was really distressing to see them shivering over a little fire made of green pine wood. Duty too is quite heavy. The men have twelve hours of Picket and twelve of Camp Guard every thirty-six hours. The effect that one cold wet night has upon the boys is a little remarkable. They are generally for *peace on any terms* toward the close of a cold wet night but after the sun is up and they get warm they are in their usual spirits. I have never seen our army so *completely whipped*. The men do not seem to fear the winter Campaign so much as they do the

coming of spring. . . . I hardly know what to think of our prospect for next spring. Some men desert from our Brigade nearly every day or two, yet I believe there will be a great many more next spring. Our army however is quite large—perhaps as large as it was last spring. . . . There is a rumor in our camp that our Division will go to Georgia. This I think extremely doubtful. One good decisive victory in the valley or Georgia would do a great deal towards cheering our men up. We have been supplied within the last few days with shoes and blankets and it is to be hoped that our men will do better. We have to carry some men to hospital for frostbites &c. Some have come in off picket crying from cold like children. In fact I have seen men in the trenches with no shoes at all. I saw Capt. John Williams a few days ago but have not been able to see Baldy yet. We are still near the old mine. I suppose that I am now within fifty yards of the spot where I was wounded. I am doing very well. My shoulder does not worry me much.

   Please write soon and give me all the news.

                                        Yours truly
                                          L. R. MILLS

                    Trenches Near Crater, Petersburg Va.
                    Jany. 3rd, 1865
Brother John:
   We are still at our old position—Right of the Brigade extending just beyond Rive's Salient and Left resting near the Blowup. There is a rumor afloat that we will be relieved sometime this month and sent to the rear to rest &c. Everything seems to indicate that we are fixed up here for the winter. Our Division holds the hottest part of the entire lines. The front of Wilcox's Division immediately on our right the enemy can not be seen from the main lines. Here our Picket lines are from 50 to 200 yards from the enemy and a man dares not show his head. We have the biggest rows here some days you ever heard of. The batteries in the rear lines and the enemy's battries get to shelling occasionally and shells fly by as thick as bats in a summer night. After a row last week some men picked up at least 500 pounds of fragments of shells within a hundred yards of my tent. It was an amusing sight to hear our boys taunting and inviting Grant's army to fight with us while they were firing salutes and rejoicing over Sherman's great victory in Georgia. Our men need a good Victory badly. It would do us a great deal of good for Grant to charge our lines. I believe every man would hail such an attack with joy. We are preparing to put out two more lines

of Chevaux de Frise. The spirit of our men is improving
slowly. A good many are deserting to the enemy—more than
come to us. Two men of my company deserted to the enemy
last Christmas night. One was a substitute from Georgetown
and the other from near Wheeling. We get pit coal now
instead of green pine. I guess we will be a little better now.
If I could get a good big cat I could do a great deal better.
We have rats and mice and something else in abundance. We
can say with old Burns

"Ha! Where ye gaun ye crawlie ferties &c."

I saw a man catch a large rat and eat it about a week ago.
What is it that a dirty soldier won't do? The Richmond Examiner says "Coming events cast their shadows before them" but
I have not seen the shadow of that big New Year's Dinner yet.
Perhaps it is not a coming event. . . . One of the men lament-
ing his own hard luck and Younger's good luck said five balls
have struck me this campaign and the one that would have
given me a furlough "I cotch in a blanket." I am in good
health and doing well.

                                          Yours truly
                                          L. R. MILLS

                              Trenches Near Crater, March 2, 1865
Brother John:
  Something is about to happen. I know not what. Nearly
every one who will express an opinion says Gen'l Lee is about
to evacuate Petersburg. The authorities are having all the cotton, tobacco &c. moved out of the place as rapidly as possible.
This was commenced about the 22nd of February. Two thirds
of the Artillery of our Division has been moved out. The Reserved Ordnance Train has been loaded up and is ready to
move at any time. I think Gen'l Lee expects a hard fight on
the right and has ordered all this simply as a precautionary
measure. Since my visit to the right I have changed my opinion about the necessity for the evacuation of Petersburg. If
it is evacuated Johnson's Division will be in a bad situation
for getting out. Unless we are so fortunate as to give the
Yankees the slip many of us will be captured. I would regret
very much to have to give up the old place. The soiled and
tattered Colors borne by our skeleton Regiments is sacred
and dear to the hearts of every man. No one would exchange
it for a new flag. So it is with us. I go down the lines, I see
the marks of shot and shell, I see where fell my comrades,

the Crater, the grave of fifteen hundred Yankees, when I go to the rear I see little mounds of dirt some with headboards, some with none, some with shoes protruding, some with a small pile of bones on one side near the end showing where a hand was left uncovered, in fact everything near shows desperate fighting. And here I would rather "fight it out." If Petersburg and Richmond is evacuated—from what I have seen & heard in the army—our cause will be hopeless. It is useless to conceal the truth any longer. Many of our people at home have become so demoralized that they write to their husbands, sons and brothers that desertion *now* is not *dishonorable*. It would be impossible to keep the army from straggling to a ruinous extent if we evacuate. I have just received an order from Wise to carry out on picket tonight a rifle and ten rounds of Cartridges to shoot men when they desert. The men seem to think desertion no crime & hence never shoot a deserter when he goes over—they always shoot but never hit. I am glad to say that we have not had but four desertions from our Reg't to the enemy. . . . I send you this morning "Five Months in a Yankee prison" by a Petersburg Militiaman.

Write soon.

Yours truly
L. R. MILLS

—HARMON, ed., "Letters of Luther Rice Mills"

XIII

The Valley
in 1864

THE *Valley campaigns of 1864* are among the most interesting in the history of the war. There was no Stonewall Jackson to give them glamour, to be sure, but Jube Early and Phil Sheridan were not bad substitutes. Heretofore the Valley had been, chiefly, the theater for Confederate offensives; this, to some extent, it remained, but the more important offensive operations of 1864 were Federal. The final campaign of 1864 was, too, one of the most decisive of the war, for it deprived Lee's army of its major source of supply and cut it off from the west.

Grant's grand strategy, it will be remembered, called for advances up the Valley by General Sigel and from the west by Generals Averell and Crook to mesh with the major attacks by Meade and Butler. These Valley offensives got under way on time, but accomplished little; not until Sheridan took command was Grant's strategic plan vindicated.

At the end of April Averell and Crook, then along the Kanawha in western Virginia, advanced toward Lynchburg with a view to cutting the important Virginia & Tennessee Railroad. General John Morgan met them and, in a smart action, drove them back to their bases. Meantime Sigel had advanced cautiously up the Valley toward New Market. There, on May 15, he was met by Breckinridge, defeated, and hurled back. General Hunter—next to Butler the most detested of Union commanders—supplanted him and embarked on a program of systematic devastation of the Valley. His military objective was Staunton and the Virginia Central Railroad. Early in June he reached Staunton and then advanced on the town of Lexington, home of Virginia Military Institute, which he put to flames, and of Washington College, which he gutted. Lee hurried Early to the Valley to deal with this menace to his communications; Hunter retreated into western Virginia; and the Confederates were once more in undisputed control of the Valley.

Early seized the opportunity to relieve pressure on Petersburg by striking across the Potomac and at Washington. Swift marches brought him to the outskirts of Washington by July 10; as Federal forces concentrated against him he withdrew to home ground. The bold stroke had achieved its immediate objective; Grant sent large reinforcements to the Valley and appointed Sheridan to temporary command of the whole theater of operations. In two months Sheridan made a national reputation. With a numerical superiority of at least two to one, he was able to seize and hold the offensive. First he struck Early along the Opequon; then at Winchester. These two battles all but destroyed the Confederate forces in the Valley.

Once again Lee was forced to send reinforcements, and once again the intrepid Early took the offensive, scoring what at first seemed a spectacular victory at Cedar Creek. This victory Sheridan turned into defeat. After that there was nothing to stop the deliberate and calculated destruction that Grant ordered and Sheridan willingly executed. By winter the Valley, scene of so many Confederate victories, was firmly in Union hands. And it was from the Valley that Sheridan fianlly rode down to the triumph of Five Forks.

1. V.M.I. BOYS FIGHT AT NEW MARKET

On April 30 General Franz Sigel, in command of the Department of West Virginia, started up the Valley toward Strasburg. Meeting no opposition he pressed on toward New Market. Breckinridge was already on his way to meet him, with a miscellaneous force including the Cadet Corps from the Virginia Military Institute—Stonewall Jackson's school—at Lexington.

John Wise, then a cadet of seventeen, here tells the story

*of the dash from Lexington to New Market and of "the most
glorious day" of his life. The battle was a minor one, but had
far-reaching consequences, for it enabled the Confederates
to hold the Valley long enough to gather the harvest, so
essential to Lee's hungry army.*

On the 10th of May, 1864, the Cadet Corps was the very pink
of drill and discipline, and mustered 350 strong. The plebes
of the last fall had passed through squad and company drill,
and the battalion was now proficient in the most intricate
manœuvre. The broad parade ground lay spread out like a
green carpet. The far-off ranges of the Blue Ridge seemed
nearer in the clear light of spring. The old guard tree, once
more luxuriantly green, sheltered its watching groups of admiring girls and prattling children. . . .

Suddenly the barracks reverberated with the throbbing of
drums; we awoke and recognized the long roll. Lights were
up; the stoops resounded with the rush of footsteps seeking
place in the ranks; the adjutant, by lantern-light, read our
orders amid breathless silence. They told us that the enemy
was in the valley, that Breckinridge needed help, and that
we were ordered to march for Staunton at daybreak—a battalion of infantry and a section of artillery—with three days'
rations. Not a sound was uttered, not a man moved from the
military posture of "parade rest." Our beating hearts told
us that our hour had come at last.

"Parade 's dismissed," piped the adjutant. Then came a wild
halloo, as company after company broke ranks. Again in
fancy I see the excited rush of that gay throng, eager as
greyhounds in the leash, hurrying back and forth, preparing
for the start, forgetful that it would be six hours before they
should march.

Daybreak found us on the Staunton pike after a sleepless
night and a breakfast by candle-light. . . . And now, fairly
started upon our journey, we were plodding on right merrily,
our gallant little battery rumbling behind.

At midday on the 12th of May we marched into Staunton to
the tune of "The girl I left behind me." We were not quite as
fresh or as neat as at the outset, but still game and saucy. . . .

Breckinridge's army, which had hurried up from southwestern Virginia to meet Sigel, soon filled the town and
suburbs. Now and then a bespattered trooper came up wearily
from Woodstock or Harrisonburg to report the steady advance of Sigel with an army thrice the size of our own. Ever
and anon the serious shook their heads and predicted hot

work in store for us. Even in the hour of levity the shadow of impending bloodshed hung over all but the cadet. At evening parade the command came to move down the valley.

Morning found us promptly on the march. A few lame ducks had succumbed and were left behind, but the body of the corps were still elated and eager, although rain had overtaken us. The first day's march brought us to Harrisonburg; the second to Lacy's Springs, within ten miles of New Market. On this day evidences of the enemy's approach thickened on every hand. At short intervals upon the pike, the great artery of travel in the valley, carriages and vehicles of all sorts filled the way, laden with people and their household effects, fleeing from the hostile advance. Now and then a haggard trooper, dispirited by long skirmishing against overwhelming force, would gloomily suggest the power and numbers of the enemy. Towards nightfall, in a little grove by a church, we came upon a squad of Federal prisoners, the first that many of us had ever seen. It was a stolid lot of Germans, who eyed us with curious inquiry as we passed. Laughter and badinage had somewhat subsided when we pitched camp that night in sight of our picket-fires twinkling in the gloaming but a few miles below us down the valley. We learned, beyond doubt, that Franz Sigel and his army were sleeping within ten miles of the spot on which we rested. . . .

The day, breaking gray and gloomy, found us plodding onward in the mud. The exceedingly sober cast of our reflections was relieved by the light-heartedness of the veterans. Wharton's brigade, with smiling "Old Gabe" at their head, cheered us heartily as we came up to the spot where they were cooking breakfast by the road-side. Many were the good-natured gibes with which they restored our confidence. The old soldiers were as merry, nonchalant, and indifferent to the coming fight as if it was a daily occupation. . . .

The mile-posts on the pike scored four miles, three miles, two miles, one mile to New Market. Then the mounted skirmishers crowded past us hurrying to the front. Cheering began in our rear and was caught up by the troops along the line of march. We learned its import as Breckinridge and his staff approached, and we joined in the huzza as that soldierly man, mounted magnificently, dashed past us, uncovered, bowing, and riding like the Cid. Along the crest of the elevation in our front we beheld our line of mounted pickets and the smoldering fires of their night's bivouac. We halted with the realization that one turn in the road would bring us in full view of the enemy's position. Echols's and Wharton's brigades hurried past us. There was not so much banter then. "Forward!" was the word once more, and New Market appeared in sight.

The turn of the road displayed the whole position. A bold range of hills parallel with the mountains divides the Shenandoah Valley into two smaller valleys, and in the eastern-most of these lies New Market. . . .

Orchards skirt the village in these meadows between our position and the town, and they are filled with the enemy's skirmishers. A heavy stone fence and a deep lane run westward from the town and parallel with our line of battle. Here the enemy's infantry was posted to receive our left flank, and behind it his artillery was posted on a slope, the ground rising gradually until, a short distance beyond the town, to the left of the pike, it spreads out in an elevated plateau. The hillsides from this plateau to the pike are gradual and broken by several gullies heavily wooded by scrub-cedar.

It was Sunday morning, and 11 o'clock. In a picturesque little churchyard, right under the shadow of the village spire and among the white tombstones, a six-gun battery was posted in rear of the infantry line of the enemy. The moment we debouched it opened upon us.

Away off to the right, in the Luray Gap of the Massanutten range, our signal corps was telegraphing the position and numbers of the enemy. Our cavalry was moving at a gallop to the cover of the creek to attempt to flank the town. Echols's brigade was moving from the pike at a double-quick by the right flank and went into line of battle across the meadow, its left resting on the pike. Simultaneously his skirmishers were thrown forward at a run and engaged the enemy. Out of the orchards and out on the meadows arose puff after puff of blue smoke as our sharpshooters advanced, the "pop, pop" of their rifles ringing forth excitingly. Thundering down the pike came McLaughlin with his artillery, and wheeling out into the meadows he swung into battery action left, and let fly with all his guns. The cadet section of artillery pressing a little farther forward wheeled to the left, toiled up the slope, and with a plunging fire replied to the Federal battery in the graveyard. At the first discharge of our guns a beautiful wreath of smoke shot upward and hovered over them.

The little town, which a moment before had seemed to sleep so peacefully upon that Sabbath morn, was now wreathed in battle-smoke and swarming with troops hurrying to their positions. We had their range beautifully, and every shell, striking some obstruction, exploded in the streets. Every man of our army was in sight. Every position of the enemy was plainly visible. . . .

My orders were to remain with the wagons at the bend in the pike, unless our forces were driven back; in which case we were to retire to a point of safety. When it became evident that a battle was imminent, a single thought took possession of me, and that was, that I would never be able to look my father in the face again if I sat on a baggage-wagon while my command was in its first, perhaps its only, engagement. He was a grim old fighter, at that moment commanding at Petersburg. . . . If, now that I had the opportunity, I should fail to take part in the fight I knew what was in store for me. Napoleon in Egypt pointed to the Pyramids and told his soldiers that from their heights forty centuries looked down upon them. My oration, delivered from the baggage-wagon, was not so elevated in tone, but equally emphatic. It ran about this wise:

"Boys, the enemy is in our front. Our command is about to go into action. I like fighting no better than anybody else. But I have an enemy in my rear as dreadful as any before us. If I return home and tell my father that I was on the baggage guard when my comrades were fighting I know my fate. He will kill me with worse than bullets—ridicule. I shall join the command forthwith. Any one who chooses to remain may do so."

All the guard followed. The wagon was left in charge of the black driver. Of the four who thus went, one was killed and two were wounded.

We rejoined the battalion as it marched by the left flank from the pike. Moving at double-quick we were in an instant in line of battle, our right near the turnpike. Rising ground in our immediate front concealed us from the enemy. The command was given to strip for action. Knapsacks, blankets, everything but guns, canteens, and cartridge-boxes, were thrown down upon the ground. Our boys were silent then. Every lip was tightly drawn, every cheek was pale; but not with fear. With a peculiar nervous jerk we pulled our cartridge-boxes round to the front and tightened our belts. Whistling rifled-shell screamed over us as, tipping the hillcrest in our own front, they bounded over our heads. Across the pike to our right Patton's brigade was lying down, abreast of us.

"At-ten-tion-n-n! Battalion Forward! Guide—Center-r-rr!" shouted Ship, and off we started. At that moment, from the left of the line, sprang Sergeant-Major Woodbridge, and posted himself forty paces in front of the colors as directing guide. Brave Evans, standing over six feet two, unfurled our colors that for days had hung limp and bedraggled about the staff, and every cadet in the Institute leaped forward, dressing to the ensign, elate and thrilling with the consciousness that "*This is war!*" We reached the hill-crest in our front, where we were abreast of our smoking battery and in full sight and range of the enemy. We were pressing towards him at "arms port" with the light tripping gait of the French infantry. The enemy had obtained our range, and began to drop his shell under our noses along the slope. Echols's brigade rose up and were charging on our right with the rebel yell. . . .

Down the green slope we went, answering the wild cry of our comrades as their musketry rattled out its opening volleys. In another moment we should expect a pelting rain of lead from the blue line crouching behind the stone wall at the lane. Then came a sound more stunning than thunder, that burst directly in my face; lightnings leaped; fire flashed; the earth rocked; the sky whirled round, and I stumbled. My gun pitched forward, and I fell upon my knees. Sergeant Cabell looked back at me sternly, pityingly, and called out, "Close up, men," as he passed on.

I knew no more. When consciousness returned it was raining in torrents. I was lying on the ground, which all about was torn and plowed with shell which were still screeching in the air and bounding on the earth. . . .

From this time forth I may speak of the gallant behavior of the cadets without the imputation of vanity, for I was no longer a participant in their glory. . . .

Bloody work had been done. The space between the enemy's old and new positions was dotted with their dead and wounded —shot as they fled across the open field. But this same exposed ground now lay before, and must be crossed by our own men, under a galling fire from a strong and protected position. The distance was not three hundred yards, but the ground to be traversed was a level green field of young wheat. Again the advance was ordered. Our men responded with a cheer. Poor fellows! they had already been put upon their mettle in two assaults. Exhausted, wet to the skin, muddied to their eyebrows with the stiff clay through which they had pulled,— some of them actually shoeless after their struggle across the plowed ground,—they nevertheless advanced with great grit and eagerness; for the shouting on their right meant victory.

But the foe in our front was far from conquered. As our fellows came on with a dash the enemy stood his ground most courageously. That battery, now charged with canister and shrapnel, opened upon the cadets with a murderous hail the moment they uncovered. The infantry lying behind fence-rails piled upon the ground, poured in a steady, deadly fire. . . .

The men were falling right and left. The veterans on the right of the cadets seemed to waver. Ship, our commandant, fell wounded. For the first time the cadets seemed irresolute. Some one cried out, "Lie down," and all obeyed, firing from the knee—all but Evans, the ensign, who was standing bolt upright. Poor Stanard's limbs were torn asunder and he lay there bleeding to death. Some one cried out, "Fall back, and rally on Edgar's battalion." Several boys moved as if to obey; but Pizzini, orderly of "B" company, with his Italian blood at the boiling-point, cocked his gun and swore he would shoot the first man who ran. Preston, brave and inspiring, with a smile lay down upon his only arm, remarking that he would at least save that. Collona, captain of "D," was speaking words of encouragement and bidding the boys shoot close. The boys were being decimated; manifestly they must charge or retire; and charge it was.

For at that moment, Henry A. Wise, our first captain, beloved of every boy in the command, sprung to his feet, shouted the charge, and led the Cadet Corps forward to the guns. The guns of the battery were served superbly; the musketry fairly rolled. The cadets reached the firm greensward of the farm-yard in which the battery was planted. The Federal infantry began to break and run behind the buildings. Before the order to "Limber up" could be obeyed our boys disabled the trails and were close upon the guns; the gunners dropped their sponges and sought safety in flight. Lieutenant Hanna hammered a burly gunner over the head with his cadet sword. Winder Garrett outran another and attacked him with his bayonet. The boys leaped on the guns, and the battery was theirs; while Evans was wildly waving the cadet colors from the top of a caisson. . . .

We had won a victory,—not a Manassas . . . but, for all that, a right comforting bit of news went up the pike that night to General Lee; for from where he lay, locked in the death grapple with Grant in the Wilderness, his thoughts were, doubtless, ever turning wearily and anxiously towards this flank movement in the valley.

—Wise, "The West Point of the Confederacy"

2. GENERAL HUNTER DEVASTATES THE VALLEY

After New Market Sigel wired that his "retrograde" movement was carried out in good order; Halleck telegraphed in disgust to Grant, "Sigel is in full retreat on Strasburg. He will do nothing but run; never did anything else." He was relieved from command, and David Hunter appointed to his place.

No other Union general, except Butler, was so cordially detested by the South; few did so much to earn that detestation. A veteran of the Mexican War Hunter had replaced Frémont in Missouri, and been replaced, in turn, himself. He had commanded the Department of the South and issued a proclamation freeing the slaves within his lines which Lincoln was forced to repudiate. When he raised a Negro regiment the Confederate Congress proclaimed him a felon and ordered his execution if captured. Perhaps it was no wonder that he was bitter toward the South! When he replaced Sigel he embarked on a plan of systematic destruction of the Valley—a plan which Sheridan was to complete. The destruction itself was justified by those same military considerations that controlled Sherman in Georgia; what embittered Southerners was the animosity which appeared to inspire Hunter and the extent to which he exposed women and children to danger.

General John Imboden, who here describes Hunter's depredations, was a veteran of Jackson's Valley campaign, had covered the retreat at Gettysburg, and was now once more back in his familiar Valley.

From Brownsburg General Hunter proceeded to Lexington. . . . At Lexington he enlarged upon the burning operations begun at Staunton. On his way, and in the surrounding country, he burnt mills, furnaces, storehouses, granaries, and all farming utensils he could find, beside a great amount of fencing, and a large quantity of grain. In the town he burnt the Virginia Military Institute, and all the professors' houses except the superintendent's (General Smith's), where he had his headquarters, and found a portion of the family too sick to be removed. He had the combustibles collected to burn Washington College, the recipient of the benefactions of the Father of his Country by his will; but, yielding to the appeals of the trustees and citizens, spared the building, but destroyed the philosophical and chemical apparatus, libraries and furniture.

He burned the mills and some private stores in the lower part of the town.

Captain Towns, an officer in General Hunter's army, took supper with the family of Governor John Letcher. Mrs. Letcher having heard threats that her house would be burned, spoke of it to Captain Towns, who said it could not be possible, and remarked that he would go at once to headquarters and let her know. He went, returned in a half hour, and told her that he was directed by General Hunter to assure her that the house would not be destroyed, and she might, therefore, rest easy. After this, she dismissed her fears, not believing it possible that a man occupying Hunter's position would be guilty of wilful and deliberate falsehood to a lady. It, however, turned out otherwise, for the next morning, at half-past eight o'clock, his assistant provost marshal, accompanied by a portion of his guard, rode up to the door, and Captain Berry dismounted, rang the door-bell, called for Mrs. Letcher, and informed her that General Hunter had ordered him to burn the house. She replied: "There must be some mistake," and requested to see the order. He said it was verbal. She asked if its execution could not be delayed till she could see Hunter? He replied: "The order is peremptory, and you have five minutes to leave the house."

Mrs. Letcher then asked if she could be allowed to remove her mother's, her sister's, her own and her children's clothing. This request being refused, she left the house. In a very short time they poured camphene on the parlor floor and ignited it with a match. In the meantime Miss Lizzie Letcher was trying to remove some articles of clothing from the other end of the house, and Berry, finding these in her arms, set fire to them. The wardrobe and bureaus were then fired, and soon the house was enveloped in flames.

Governor Letcher's mother, then seventy-eight years old, lived on the adjoining lot. They fired her stable, within forty feet of the dwelling, evidently to burn it, too; but, owing to the active exertions of Captain Towns, who made his men carry water, the house was saved. While Hunter was in Lexington, Captain Mathew X. White, residing near the town, was arrested, taken about two miles, and, without trial, was shot, on the allegation that he was a bushwhacker. During the first year of the war he commanded the Rockbridge Cavalry, and was a young gentleman of generous impulses and good character. The total destruction of private property in Rockbridge county, by Hunter, was estimated and published in the local papers at the time as over $2,000,000. The burning of the

Institute was a public calamity, as it was an educational establishment of great value.

From Lexington he proceeded to Buchanan, in Bottetourt county, and camped on the magnificent estate of Colonel John T. Anderson, an elder brother of General Joseph R. Anderson, of the Tredegar Works, at Richmond. Colonel Anderson's estate, on the banks of the Upper James, and his mansion, were baronial in character. The house crowned a high, wooded hill, was very large, and furnished in a style to dispense that lavish hospitality which was the pride of so many of the old-time Virginians. It was the seat of luxury and refinement, and in all respects a place to make the owner contented with his lot in this world. Colonel Anderson was old—his head as white as snow—and his wife but a few years his junior. He was in no office, and too old to fight—hence was living on his fine estate strictly the life of a private gentleman. He had often, in years gone by, filled prominent representative positions from his county. There was no military or public object on God's earth to be gained by ruining such a man. Yet Hunter, after destroying all that could be destroyed on the plantation when he left it, ordered the grand old mansion, with all its contents, to be laid in ashes.

From Buchanan he proceeded toward Lynchburg, by way of the Peaks of Otter; but on arriving within four miles of the city, where a sharp skirmish occurred between General Crook's command and three brigades under my command, at a place called the Quaker Meeting-House, he ascertained that General Early was in town with Stonewall Jackson's old corps. This was enough for him. That night he began a rapid retreat toward Salem, leaving his cavalry to make demonstrations on Early's lines long enough to give him a good day's start. . . .

I shall conclude this already long narrative by citing a few more instances of Hunter's incendiarism in the Lower Valley. It seems that, smarting under the miserable failure of his grand raid on Lynchburg, where, during a march of over two hundred miles, the largest force he encountered was under Jones at Piedmont, and he routed that, thus leaving the way open to reach Lynchburg within three days, destroy the stores there and go out through West Virginia unmolested, he had failed to do anything but inflict injury on private citizens, and he came back to the Potomac more implacable than when he left it a month before.

His first victim was the Hon. Andrew Hunter, of Charlestown, Jefferson county, his own first cousin, and named after the General's father. Mr. Hunter is a lawyer of great eminence, and a man of deservedly large influence in his county and the State. His home, eight miles from Harper's Ferry, in the suburbs of Charlestown, was the most costly and elegant in the place, and his family as refined and cultivated as any in the State. His offense, in General Hunter's eyes, was that he had gone politically with his State, and was in full sympathy with the Confederate cause. The General sent a squadron of cavalry out from Harper's Ferry, took Mr. Hunter prisoner, and held him a month in the common guard-house of his soldiers, without alleging any offense against him not common to nearly all the people of Virginia, and finally discharged him without trial or explanation, after heaping these indignities on him. Mr. Hunter was an old man, and suffered severely from confinement and exposure. While he was thus a prisoner, General Hunter ordered his elegant mansion to be burned to the ground, with all its contents, not even permitting Mrs. Hunter and her daughter to save their clothes and family pictures from the flames; and, to add to the desolation, camped his cavalry within the inclosure of the beautiful grounds, of several acres, surrounding the residence, till the horses had destroyed them.

—IMBODEN, "Fire, Sword, and the Halter"

3. GENERAL RAMSEUR FIGHTS AND DIES FOR HIS COUNTRY

There was no more gallant figure in the Confederate Army than young Stephen Dodson Ramseur of North Carolina. After graduating from West Point in 1860 he resigned a commission in the U. S. Army to go with his state the following year. His military career was meteoric: within a year he had been promoted from lieutenant to brigadier general. He fought with distinction during the Seven Days; was wounded at Malvern Hill; fought and was wounded again at Chancellorsville; recovered and fought at Gettysburg and in the Wilderness. He led the counterattack that threw Hancock back at the Bloody Angle, and there was wounded a third time. Promoted to major general, at twenty-seven, he joined Early in the Valley campaign and fought with his customary courage at Winchester and Cedar Creek.

In October 1863 Ramseur had married Ellen Richmond, and his letters to his beloved wife give a running account of the war. Those we print here describe the fighting in the

Valley campaign. The day before Cedar Creek Ramseur heard that his baby had been born, and he went into battle wearing a white rose in honor of the daughter he was never to see. He was mortally wounded trying to stem Sheridan's counterattack at Cedar Creek and died the following day. "He was," wrote General Early, "a most gallant and energetic officer whom no disaster appalled, but his courage and energy seemed to gain new strength in the midst of confusion and disorder."

Staunton—Va—June 27th—1864

Have time for only a line—to tell you I am well. We have had hardest march of the war. Couldn't catch Hunter—but we hope yet to strike the Enemy a heavy blow. Do not be uneasy if you fail to hear from us. We are going still further & all communications will be cut. We hope to relieve Richmond & make Yankeedom smart. I may be pardoned for saying to *you* that I am making a reputation as a Maj. Genl. The greatest hardship is being separated from you.

H'dqr'ts Early's Div—July 23rd—1864

Again we have passed thro the ordeal of battle. Caleb [Genl Rs brother in law & aide de camp] & I are both safe wonderful to say. I am greatly mortified at result of battle. My men behaved shamefully. They ran from the enemy. And for the first time in my life, I am deeply mortified at the conduct of troops under my command. Had these men behaved like *my old Brigade* would have done under similar circumstances, a disgraceful retreat would have been a brilliant victory. Caleb & I are both safe wonderful to say. Do not mention to anyone the bad conduct of my troops.

Camp near Bunker Hill. Aug 28th—1864

Last night I rec'd two letters from you. Do you know how precious they are, & how much good they did me? After a long march & a sharp skirmish I had gone to bed, & was thinking of you only, when they were brought to me. I am so glad that you continue cheerful & hopeful through these terrible days. Courage my little wife—maybe I will be permitted to come & see you before long. . . . Do you know that I am beginning to believe that we may very soon have peace! Everybody seems to think that the peace party will carry the election in the north. Oh may these expectations be realized & soon may this terrible war that separates us cease. It is such a happiness to be able to write to you often—

wish I had time to write more fully & more often. Is there anything you want that I can get for you. I have a bottle of fine *Old French* brandy I'll send you by first opportunity, also some money I am anxious to send you by first safe messenger.

Camp near Bunker Hill—Aug 29th—1864

This morning, much to my surprise, we are quiet—how long we will remain so is very doubtful. In fact, I have everything now ready to move. Thus, you see, our life is one of constant action—marching & counter-marching—manoeuvering & sometimes a little fighting. So far we have been very successful. God grant that we may continue to strike telling blows for our bleeding country. I am growing more hopeful about the ending of the War. Every man whose opinion I have asked & who has had an opportunity of learning the feeling of the Yankee people & soldiery, assures me that the north is tired of war & will elect an out & out, unconditional peace man at the Presidential election next November. I trust these opinions may be verified. For myself I think now, as I did several months ago, that everything depends upon the result of operations at Richmond & Atlanta. If we are enabled to baffle all of Grant's movements & to drive back Sherman, it does seem to me that the Yankee nation will be forced to conclude that the task of subjugating the South is more than they can accomplish. At all events we have reason for great thankfulness to the Giver of all Good for his wonderful mercy & care so continually shown toward us during this tremendous campaign. . . . Could we be permitted to see each other for even a short while how we would be encouraged & strengthened. But duty separates us—let us bear it all bravely —& the time will soon come let us hope when we will receive our rich reward—Reunion in peace, independence & happiness! . . .

Nothing new here. Will write as often as I can do not be uneasy if you do not hear regularly. Army movements & irregular mail facilities may prevent.

Camp near Winchester, Sept 6th—1864

This is certainly a time to try our souls! We see in Yankee papers that Sherman has defeated Hood & captured Atlanta. We do not wish to believe this, but are compelled to be apprehensive & anxious. Our hopes for Peace depend upon the success of our armies in the field. Even tho Sherman takes Atlanta, provided he does not destroy nor disorganize Hood's army it will still be alright as long as Gen'l Lee (God bless our old Hero!) & his glorious army continue to baffle the tremendous efforts made to capture Richmond & over run Virginia—so let us be hopeful. Our own accounts may put a different face upon northern news. You will know before this reaches you that McClellan & Pendleton are the nominees of the Chicago Convention. Their Platform is ingeniously contrived to mean either war or peace—so as to catch all of the opponents of the Lincoln administration—& to be governed by events between now & the election. If our armies can hold their own, suffer no crushing disaster before the next election. We may reasonably expect a termination of this war. Let us therefore devote all of our energies to the defense of our country—& persevere in Prayer to the Ruler of Nations. What is the news at home? I am sending you a recpt for apple butter—& as it requires no *store* things—except a few spices, it is one kind of *preserves* we can have! If our army moves forward again, I will get you a circular cloak (forget the technical name) they are "all the rage" now. If we go back up the valley as far as Strasburg soon—(as I think we will before long) & everything promises well, I intend to ask for a furlough to come to see you—dont know tho how things will be. I predict orders for a move before long. . . . We cannot use Confederate money in Maryland—& we have to give six dollars Confed. for *one* Greenback.

Camp near Winchester, Sept. 11th '64

Our campaign, tho a very active & arduous one, I think has been far more free from vexations & trials, upon our patience & endurance than the campaign around Richmond would have been. We have enjoyed a great variety of scenes —have travelled over & sojourned in the most beautiful part of the valley of Va have had pure water, a few vegetables & plenty of fresh meat. Altogether we consider ourselves very fortunate thus far. If we have an active winter campaign, we will not fare so well—tho it will be far more comfortable to campaign there this winter, than to remain in the trenches at Richmond & Petersburg. One great advantage I would have there however, that is I would be so much nearer you. I wish you could see this magnificent Valley—at this beautiful season of the year. Although plantations are ruined—& the blackened remains of once splendid mansions are to be seen on all sides yet nature is triumphant—magnificent meadows, beautiful forests & broad undulating fields rich in grass & clover! Truly it does seem sacreligious to despoil such an Eden! by the ravages of War.

I thank God that my loved ones have not yet known the terror & wretchedness caused by the presence of our mean cowardly foes, Foes who respect not helpless Age nor tender women. Surely a just God will visit upon such a nation the just indignation of His wrath! The Yankees tis true have Atlanta, & Yankee like are making a tremendous glorification over it. But Hoods Army is intact. Sherman is far away from the base of his supplies & it does seem to me that if our army *is at all energetic* his position is obliged to be a very dangerous one to him. I still hope for good news from Ga. At Richmond all efforts of Grants powerful army have heretofore been baffled —by our noble General & his gallant troops. In the "Valley District" we have forced Lincoln to send a heavy force to check our *perigrinations*. We have at least 45,000 or 50,000 men opposed to us. We have offered them battle several times on a fair field. Every offer has been declined. The Yankees hurrying behind their breast works whenever we advance. We are thus accomplishing much good by neutralizing (holding in check) this large force. We are gathering all of the wheat in this wonderfully productive valley enough to supply ourselves & to send large supplies to Gen'l Lee's Army. We have also sent Gen'l Lee several hundred fine beef cattle &c. At this time the Yankees hold less of the territory of this old Commonwealth than at any time since 1862. We learn from gentlemen recently from the North that the Peace party is growing rapidly—that McClellan will be elected & that his election will bring peace, *provided always* that we continue to *hold our own* against the Yankee Armies.

Camp near Winchester, Sept 14th—'64
I wish you could take a peep at my H'dquarters. You would observe two small tents rather the worse for wear, several wagons with their shivering mules—but the interesting & attractive feature would be a flock of ducks & chickens taking shelter under the wagons. We are really growing fat up here, with Yankee money we can buy almost anything for the table except sugar & coffee. . . . We have had no news from Richmond & the West for several days. I do hope that we may be enabled to continue to baffle Grant, & to drive back Sherman. I think everything depends upon this Fall campaign. If we whip the Yankees everywhere, or even, if we can manage to prevent their gaining any important success I surely believe that the Peace party will have grown sufficiently

strong to compel a cessation of hostilities. Whatever course the North follows, *our duty is very plain.* We must fight this fight out—there must be no turning back now—too much precious blood has been shed for the maintainance of our rights! Too great a gulf has opened up between us & our foes! to allow even the thought of re-union to be entertained. No, we can & must bear & suffer all things rather than to give up to Yankees & mercenaries our glorious Birthright. If I can know you are well & hopeful & cheerful I can bear most anything—tho the separation is cruel, when I know how you need me. . . . I need some socks like those you knit for me last winter—would you like to knit me some more?

Camp near Waynesboro—Va. Sept 30th—1864

I have been too busy & too much mortified to write to you for several days. At Winchester after hard fighting, we had prevailed against the largely superior forces in our front & on our right, when the enemy's Cavalry in heavy force broke our Cavalry on the left & created a terrible disorder throughout our lines. We lost my friend Gen'l Rodes. We then fell back to Strasburg (or Fishers Hill). Here the enemy concentrated heavily on our weak point (guarded by our Cavalry) drove everything before them there, & then poured in on our left & rear. I am sorry to say that our men were very much stampeded & did not keep cool nor fight as well as they have here-to-fore done. We then retreated to Port Republic & from there to this point, 12 miles from Staunton. I am daily expecting Gen'l Early to advance. I believe if we could get enough Cavalry to even hold the Yankee Cavalry in check, that our Infantry can drive back Sheridans forces. I cannot tell you . . . how much I have thought of you during this past week. I do hope you have not given up your bright hopeful spirits. Anybody can be hopeful when everything is prosperous. *Adversity calls forth the nobler qualities of our natures.* Continue my beloved to be brave—nothing but Gods mercy has spared our lives. Cease not to pray for us & our Cause. . . .

I still feel confident of the final triumph of our Cause. It may be a long & weary time, but above all things let us never despair of the establishment of our independence. We must steel ourselves for great trials & sacrifice—& have brave hearts for any fate. . . .

I would give *anything* to be with you, but these recent

battles & defeats will make it almost impossible for me to leave this army now.

Camp near Staunton Va Oct. 2nd '64

This is a very lovely quiet Sabbath day. . . . I hope that you have not allowed the bad news from the Army of the Valley District to discourage you. We must bear up bravely in the midst of disaster nor can we always hope to be successful. We must be prepared for any event, with brave hearts for any fate. . . . I hope in a few days we will be enabled to go after the Yankees & drive them down the Valley. At present we are all anxiety to hear from Richmond. We hear all sorts of rumors. I hope and pray Gen'l Lee may be enabled to overcome & drive Grant from before Richmond. Our disaster in the Valley with Hood's at Atlanta make me feel now the War Party will prevail at the North. But tho peace may be a long way off—I feel that surely Justice & Right must finally triumph. We must nerve ourselves to greater exertions & prepare to endure greater privations & hardships—do our duty bravely, hoping for a happy ending of all of our troubles. Surely all true Southrons would prefer anything to submission. How I long for you to be well & happy! May we learn wisdom from our trials. Our movements may prevent my writing frequently now.

Camp near Staunton—Oct 5th '64

After the death of Gen'l Rodes I was assigned the command of his Division. This of course is very pleasing to me. Address y'r letters now "Army of the Valley"—& they will reach me sooner than old address. We have been very quiet for several days, but I expect active service before the month is out. We are very anxious about Richmond. The Yankees are said to be sending a force toward Orange Court House. They seem to stick to McClellan's plan of approaching Richmond from three directions. Everything calls for all the bravery we possess every effort in our power to meet & hurl back our foes—while we fight battles our beloved Wives, Sisters & Mothers must be constant & earnest in prayer that we may have strength courage & wisdom to overcome & drive back our powerful & cruel enemies. These are times calling for great sacrifices. We must bear separation, hardship & danger for the sake of our Country. We must dare & do in the Cause of liberty. We must never yield an inch, nor relax any effort in the defence of our home or the establishment of our nationality. We will do our duty leaving the result to God.

Camp near New Market—Oct 10th '64

I can't help feeling the most intense anxiety & solicitude on your behalf—since our disaster in the Valley, my prospect for a furlough is greatly diminished. I think my duty is plain. I ought not to leave now, even if I could do so—so my Beloved—you must be brave & cheerful without me for awhile —to be separated from you is the hardest trial of my life. . . .

Father writes me that tho discouraged by our late disasters —he is still hopeful as to the final result. I agree with you about your remarks about the "Croakers." I must confess I would be willing to take a musket & fight to the bitter end rather than submit to these miserable Yankees. I feel that they have put themselves beyond the pale of civilization by the course they have pursued in this campaign. This beautiful & fertile valley has been totally destroyed. Sheridan had some of the houses, *all* of the mills & barns, every straw & wheat stack burned. This valley is one great desert. I do not see how these people are to live. We have to haul our supplies from far up the valley. It is rumored that the Yankees are rebuilding the Manassas Gap R. R. If this is true, Sheridan will not give up his hold on the valley, & we will probably remain here for the winter—unless Gen'l Lee becomes so hard pressed that we will have to go to him. My hope now is from Hood. I do hope he may be able to overwhelm Sherman & send reinforcements to our great General Lee. The last private advices I had from Ga. were encouraging. Time is an important element. I believe that Hood can whip Sherman, & I trust he will do it quickly. I have not written you as often recently—because I have been either so constantly occupied or (I must acknowledge it) so much mortified at the recent disasters to our army of the valley that I could not write with any pleasure. There is nothing new to write about right now.

Camp near Strasburg—Va. Oct 17th—1864
My own Darling Wife—

I rec'd late last night through the Signal Corps, the telegram [announcing the birth of his baby]. It has relieved me of the greatest anxiety of my life. I hope that my darling precious wife & our darling babe too are well. . . . I cannot express my feelings. . . . I dont know how I can bear the separation from you much longer. . . . I must see you & be with you & our little Darling & The telegram did not state whether we have a son or a daughter! . . .

Tell Sister Mary for *pity's* sake if not for love's sake to

write me a long letter about my little wife & baby! May God
bless my Darlings & me, & soon reunite us in happiness &
peace—a joyful family. Goodbye, sweetest With love inex-
pressible Yr devoted Husband
            —RAMSEUR, Letters to his fiancée and wife

4. EARLY SURPRISES THE FEDERALS AT
CEDAR CREEK

*After the defeats at Opequon and Strasburg Early's slender
force was shattered, and Sheridan was master of the Valley.
Early retired to Port Republic, where he awaited Kershaw's
brigade, which Lee was hurrying to him, as well as Rosser's
cavalry. With these reinforcements the ever-sanguine Early
resumed the offensive, and Sheridan withdrew beyond New
Market, taking up a position along Cedar Creek, north of
Strasburg. At this juncture Sheridan was called to Washington to confer with Halleck; while at Winchester he heard that
Early had surprised his army at Cedar Creek and inflicted a
heavy defeat upon it.*

*Early had indeed. On October 13 he had begun his advance
northward, taking up a position at Fisher's Hill, just south of
Strasburg. From the summit of this hill he could see the
whole Federal camp spread out along Cedar Creek. On the
nineteenth Early directed Ramseur, Gordon, and Pegram to
cross the Shenandoah and attack the Federals on the flank.
The attack achieved complete surprise and complete initial
success; had it not been for the heroic stand of Getty's division the Union defeat might have turned into a rout.*

*We give here Captain Howard's account of the morning
surprise.*

I was wakened at the first signs of day [October 19, 1864] by
a terrific clap of thunder, and sprang into a sitting position
and listened. The thunder was the tremendous volley that the
enemy was pouring into Crook's devoted camp. The thought
went through my mind like lightning that in some way the
enemy had run against General Crook's corps and were getting punished for their temerity. It never occurred to me at
the instant that it was possible the boot was on the other foot.
I listened for the yell of our men, but, alas, it never came;
instead, the Yi Yi Yi! of the Confederates, and horror of
horrors,—it seemed to me as if our whole left were envel-

oped, enfolded, by this cry. It was like the howls of the wolves
around a wagon train in the early days on the great prairies.
This had taken but a moment. The camp was awake. The
men sprang into line with the celerity of veterans. It was
apparent to everyone from the heavy firing and the yells on
our left that a great calamity impended if it had not already
become a fact.

General Emory rode down in person, ordering the brigade
to cross the pike, to throw a skirmish line into the timber in
Crook's direction, until it met the enemy, and then to hold on
as long as possible.

Away we went on a double quick through the darkness,
the eastern sky at this moment showing the faint gray tinge
of dawn. As we rushed along, the infernal torch on Massa-
nutton, dire omen of impending disaster, still flashed against
the southern sky. The moment the timber was reached the
column came into line on the run, and skirmishers pushed
rapidly forward, followed by the main body. Here we met
the gallant fellows from Crook's camp who had been assailed while lying asleep and who had done the only possible
thing under the circumstances,—run for their lives. They did
not seem excited, only stolidly, doggedly determined to go to
the rear. Many of them were only partly dressed, some
wearing only underclothing, but they generally carried their
muskets. An officer wearing his cap and carrying his naked
sword was attired in a shirt, drawers and shoes. The flash of
a musket showed him to be a man of forty with full beard,
and I think I should recognize his face to-day. They passed
around us, through our ranks, and almost over us, insistent,
determined. They heeded none of our cries to "Turn back!"
"Make a stand!" but streamed to the rear. We had little time
to argue with them.

The skirmish line had not advanced a hundred yards when
it ran in the darkness plump into a body of the enemy; in an
instant the timber was in a blaze of light from the musketry,
and we were in the midst of one of the most fearful struggles
of the war. The enemy were upon us in overwhelming numbers, flushed with victory and with the capture of Crook's
camps. We were a little brigade of four regiments consisting
of the 12th Connecticut, 160th New York, 47th Pennsylvania
and the 8th Vermont. The first two and the 8th Vermont
had been brigaded together back in the Louisiana days when
Godfrey Weitzel commanded us, and in many a bloody fight
had we fought together. It was literally true that we had

never been beaten on any field, but we were to have a new experience.

We were commanded by Colonel Stephen Thomas of the 8th Vermont, . . . the bravest man I have ever known. What Sheridan was to the army under him, Colonel Thomas was to his regiment. Many had been the critical moments in our history when his level head and iron nerve had been our salvation. More than once in the very pinch of a fight, when it seemed as if one straw more would ruin us, had we seen him on his big bay shouting in a voice which rang over the tumult of battle, "Steady, men! Old Vermont is looking at you to-day!" We had never needed him so much as now.

The 8th Vermont was on the left of our line, the most exposed position. We were hotly pressed on our front and left. The timber was ablaze with musketry and the air was filled with the yells of our confident foes. They flung themselves upon us in a mass and for a moment the struggle was hand to hand. Then came the cry "The Colors! The Colors! They've got the Colors!" and with one impulse, as if one mind had moved it, the regiment flung itself into the boiling caldron where the fight for the colors was seething and dragged them out. . . . Again and again the enemy flung many times our number against us, only to be forced back and gather for a fresh trial.

Men fought hand to hand; skulls were crushed with clubbed muskets; bayonets dripped with blood. Men actually clenched and rolled upon the ground in the desperate frenzy of the contest for the flags. Three color bearers were killed, and with one exception every member of the color-guard was killed or wounded. There was not much attempt at order. Not many orders were given. The men realized that they were in a terrible mess and fought like tigers. Stephen Thomas, "Colonel commanding" as we loved to call him, was a very present help in trouble. He raged like a lion and was everywhere present to encourage and hold fast the line. Of course only one result was possible. The time came when valor and devotion proved vain. In a moment, without warning, and as if by common consent we were being swept back, every man for himself and the enemy on every hand. I had received two severe wounds, and though not wholly disabled, was unable to make anything like good time, and I looked with envy on Captain Ford who was just in advance of me running like a buck. In an instant he went down all in a heap, but was up and off again in a second. My mental comment was, "What a lummux to fall down in such a scrape as this!"

It never once entered my mind that he had been hit by one of the bullets of which the air was full. Later in the day I saw him at the hospital, and expressed my disapproval of his clumsiness under such circumstances, to which he replied, "I guess you would fall down if you were shot through both legs." . . . .

Private Robert Sturgeon of my own company was a few yards in advance of me on my right, and I need not say was making good time In an instant a tall bearded fellow in gray bounded out of the mist which overhung the field where daylight was just gaining the supremacy and ordered him to halt. They were not twenty feet apart. Sturgeon's gun was empty and his bayonet lost. He cast a startled glance over his shoulder and ran at the top of his speed. The Confederate's long legs took tremendous strides,—he sprang forward with a rush and gave a vicious lunge with his bayonet. Sturgeon swerved at the moment, but the steel caught him under the left arm, and passed through the cape of his overcoat, through the overcoat itself, through blouse and flannel shirt, between shirt and skin. It left a vivid mark along his side where the cold steel raked, but did not pierce the skin. Sturgeon stopped and threw up his hands dropping his gun. The stalwart in gray was reaching out as if to take him by the collar, when presto! one in blue, pausing in his hot haste for scarcely one second placed the muzzle of his gun hardly a foot from the Confederate's head, fired, blowing the head to fragments, and without a word was gone. Sturgeon, like a good soldier, picked up his gun and ran like a deer.

Farther back Colonel Thomas had chosen a point where he was rallying the men and making some progress toward a line; still further a skirmish line was stretched across the country to stop and collect those who were still able for duty. Challenged here, I pointed to the blood in my shoe and running down my sleeve, and passed on; passed on with greater grief and despair weighing me down than I had ever before in my life felt.

Our campaign, as I have said, had been a great success. The Shenandoah Valley, the great artery of supply, the granary of the rebellion, had the night before seemed firmly and forever in our grasp, and now before the next sunrise, I had seen it taken away from us with the fierce ruthlessness of a hurricane. There was no question about it in my mind. Harper's Ferry was the only point where the shattered army could stand. I had seen the collapse of the Eighth Corps. I had seen our whole left swept away, our camps captured, our artillery taken, our whole army forced out of its works, forced to change its line from front to left, forced far back from its proper position,—sullenly on the defensive, dangerous, but clearly out-matched. The enemy was pressing his victorious columns forward. It would be impossible to withstand him. I pictured the defense we would make of the heights of Harper's Ferry, of the weary months, perhaps years, it would take to retrieve what we had lost, and my heart beat with great throbs of grief as I dragged myself painfully to the rear. General Sheridan I well knew, was absent. . . . Unreasonably I attributed the whole disaster to General Sheridan's absence. Had he been there it could never have happened, and thereby I did injustice to the gallant Wright in command.

Pressing back to get out of danger I threw myself exhausted upon the ground a short distance south of Newtown. The country was full of men, all, it seemed to me, going to the rear; wounded men by themselves; wounded men helped by others; wounded men being carried; men strong and unhurt. Their faces were sullen, despairing, and they were turned to the north. Many halted and rested; some went to sleep, for the exhaustion of a week had been crowded into two hours. Our brigade in its struggle beyond the pike had lost more than one-third of its numbers, and the 8th Vermont, holding the left and most exposed position, had lost more than two-thirds of all the men engaged, and of the sixteen officers who gathered about our camp-fire the evening before, thirteen had been killed and wounded on this horrible hill of sacrifice.

—Howard, "The Morning Surprise at Cedar Creek"

5. SHERIDAN RIDES DOWN THE VALLEY PIKE TO VICTORY AND FAME

The resolute stand by Getty, the confusion in Confederate ranks, and the strong defensive position to which the Federals retired, all persuaded Early to halt his own attack midway. Meantime Sheridan was riding down the Newtown and the Valley Pike from Winchester. By the time he arrived at the battlefield the Federals had steadied and were prepared to repulse Early. Sheridan speedily organized a counterattack which jumped off in midafternoon and was completely successful. Everywhere the Confederate line gave way. "They would not listen to entreaties, threats or appeals of any kind," Early reported "A terror of the enemy's cavalry had seized them and there was no holding them." It was the end of Early—and the beginning of a legend.

Here Sheridan tells his own story.

Toward 6 o'clock the morning of the 19th [October], the officer on picket duty at Winchester came to my room, I being yet in bed, and reported artillery firing from the direction of Cedar Creek. I asked him if the firing was continuous or only desultory, to which he replied that it was not a sustained fire, but rather irregular and fitful. I remarked: "It's all right; Grover has gone out this morning to make a reconnoisance, and he is merely feeling the enemy." I tried to go to sleep again, but grew so restless that I could not, and soon got up and dressed myself. A little later the picket officer came back and reported that the firing, which could be distinctly heard from his line on the heights outside of Winchester, was still going on. I asked him if it sounded like a battle, and as he again said that it did not, I still inferred that the cannonading was caused by Grover's division banging away at the enemy simply to find out what he was up to. However, I went downstairs and requested that breakfast be hurried up, and at the same time ordered the horses to be saddled and in readiness, for I concluded to go to the front before any further examinations were made in regard to the defensive line.

We mounted our horses between half-past 8 and 9, and as we were proceeding up the street which leads directly through Winchester, from the Logan residence, where Edwards was quartered, to the Valley pike, I noticed that there were many women at the windows and doors of the houses, who kept shaking their skirts at us and who were otherwise markedly insolent in their demeanor, but supposing this conduct to be instigated by their well-known and perhaps natural prejudices, I ascribed to it no unusual significance. On reaching the edge of the town I halted a moment, and there heard quite distinctly the sound of artillery firing in an unceasing roar. Concluding from this that a battle was in progress, I now felt confident that the women along the street had received intelligence from the battle-field by the "grapevine telegraph," and were in raptures over some good news, while I as yet was utterly ignorant of the actual situation. Moving on, I put my head downward toward the pommel of my saddle and listened intently, trying to locate and interpret the sound, continuing in this position till we had crossed Mill Creek, about half a mile from Winchester. The result of my efforts in the interval was the conviction that the travel of the sound was increasing too rapidly to be accounted for by my own rate of motion, and that therefore my army must be falling back.

At Mill Creek, my escort fell in behind, and we were going ahead at a regular pace, when, just as we made the crest of the rise beyond the stream, there burst upon our view the appalling spectacle of a panic-stricken army—hundreds of slightly wounded men, throngs of others unhurt but utterly demoralized, and baggage-wagons by the score, all pressing to the rear in hopeless confusion, telling only too plainly that a disaster had occurred at the front. On accosting some of the fugitives, they assured me that the army was broken up, in full retreat, and that all was lost; all this with a manner true to that peculiar indifference that takes possession of panic-stricken men. I was greatly disturbed by the sight, but at once sent word to Colonel Edwards, commanding the brigade in Winchester, to stretch his troops across the valley, near Mill Creek, and stop all fugitives, directing also that the transportation be passed through and parked on the north side of the town.

As I continued at a walk a few hundred yards farther, thinking all the time of Longstreet's telegram to Early, "Be ready when I join you and we will crush Sheridan," I was fixing in my mind what I should do. My first thought was to stop the army in the suburbs of Winchester as it came back, form a new line, and fight there; but as the situation was more maturely considered a better conception prevailed. I was sure the troops had confidence in me, for heretofore we had been successful; and as at other times they had seen me present at the slightest sign of trouble or distress, I felt that I ought to try now to restore their broken ranks, or, failing in that, to share their fate because of what they had done hitherto. . . .

For a short distance I traveled on the road, but soon found it so blocked with wagons and wounded men that my progress was impeded, and I was forced to take to the adjoining fields to make haste. When most of the wagons and wounded were past I returned to the road, which was thickly lined with unhurt men, who, having got far enough to the rear to be out of danger, had halted, without any organization, and began cooking coffee, but when they saw me they abandoned their coffee, threw up their hats, shouldered their muskets, and as I passed along turned to follow with enthusiasm and cheers. To acknowledge this exhibition of feeling I took off my hat, and with Forsyth and O'Keefe rode some distance in advance of my escort, while every mounted officer who saw me galloped out on either side of the pike to tell the men at a distance that I had come back. In this way the news was spread to the stragglers off the road, when they, too, turned their faces to the front and marched toward the enemy, changing in a moment from the depth of depression to the extreme of enthusiasm. I already knew that even in the ordinary condition of mind enthusiasm is a potent element with soldiers, but what I saw that day convinced me that if it can be excited from a state of despondency its power is almost irresistible. I said nothing except to remark, as I rode among those on the road: "If I had been with you this morning this disaster would not have happened. We must face the other way; we will go back and recover our camp."

My first halt was made just north of Newtown, where I met a chaplain digging his heels into the sides of his jaded horse, and making for the rear with all possible speed. I drew up for an instant, and inquired of him how matters were going at the front. He replied, "Everything is lost; but all will be right when you get there"; yet notwithstanding this expression of confidence in me, the parson at once resumed his breathless pace to the rear. At Newtown I was obliged to make a circuit to the left, to get round the village. I could not pass through it, the streets were so crowded, but, meeting on this détour Major McKinley, of Crook's staff, he spread the news of my return through the motley throng there.

When nearing the Valley pike, just south of Newtown I saw about three-fourths of a mile west of the pike a body of troops, which proved to be Ricketts's and Wheaton's divisions of the Sixth Corps had halted a little to the right and rear of these; but I did not stop, desiring to get to the extreme front. Continuing on parallel with the pike about midway between Newtown and Middletown I crossed to the west of it, and a little later came up in rear of Getty's division of the Sixth Corps. When I arrived this division and the cavalry were the only troops in the presence of and resisting the enemy; they were apparently acting as a rear guard at a point about three miles north of the line we held at Cedar Creek when the battle began. General Torbert was the first officer to meet me, saying as he rode up, "My God! I am glad you've come." Getty's division, when I found it, was about a mile north of Middletown, posted on the reverse slope of some slightly rising ground, holding a barricade made with fence-rails, and skirmishing slightly with the enemy's pickets.

Jumping my horse over the line of rails I rode to the crest of the elevation, and there taking off my hat, the men rose up from behind their barricade with cheers of recognition. An officer of the Vermont brigade, Colonel A. S. Tracy, rode out to the front, and joining me, informed me that General Louis A. Grant was in command there, the regular division commander, General Getty, having taken charge of the Sixth Corps in place of Ricketts, wounded early in the action, while temporarily commanding the corps. I then turned back to the rear of Getty's division, and as I came behind it a line of regimental flags rose up out of the ground, as it seemed, to welcome me. They were mostly the colors of Crook's troops, who had been stampeded and scattered in the surprise of the morning. The color-bearers having withstood the panic, had formed behind the troops of Getty. . . . At the close of this incident I crossed the little narrow valley, or depression, in rear of Getty's line, and dismounting on the opposite crest, established that point as my headquarters. In a few minutes some of my staff joined me, and the first directions I gave were to have the Nineteenth Corps and the two divisions of Wright's corps brought to the front, so they could be formed on Getty's division, prolonged to the right; for I had already decided to attack the enemy from that line as soon as I could get matters in shape to take the offensive. Crook met me at this time, and strongly favored my idea of attacking, but said, however, that most of his troops were going. . . .

All this had consumed a good deal of time, and I concluded to visit again the point to the east of the Valley pike, from where I had first observed the enemy, to see what he was doing. Arrived there, I could plainly see him getting ready for attack, and Major Forsyth now suggested that it would be well to ride along the line of battle before the enemy assailed us, for although the troops had learned of my return, but few of them had seen me. Following his suggestion I started in behind the men, but when a few paces had been taken I crossed to the front and, hat in hand, passed along the entire length of the infantry line; and it is from this circumstance that many of the officers and men who then received me with such heartiness have since supposed that that was my first appearance on the field. But at least two hours had elapsed since I reached the ground, for it was after mid-day when this incident of riding down the front took place, and I arrived not later, certainly, than half-past 10 o'clock.

—*Personal Memoirs of P. H. Sheridan*

6. "THE VALLEY WILL HAVE LITTLE IN IT FOR MAN OR BEAST"

After Cedar Creek Sheridan was master of the Valley. He had already embarked on a policy of systematic destruction; now he carried that through almost without opposition. Early, to be sure, did put up a stiff fight at Middletown, on November 9, but without effect. In December, again, Rosser tried to prevent the destruction of the Virginia Central Railway, but again in vain. There was little fighting during the winter, but late in February 1865 Sheridan occupied Staunton and Charlottesville, breaking up the railways leading to the west. Meantime the Valley had suffered the fate of Georgia and South Carolina.

Here is an extract from one of Sheridan's reports to Grant.

Woodstock, October 7, 1864—9 P. M.

I have the honor to report my command at this point to-night. I commenced moving back from Port Republic, Mount Crawford, Bridgewater, and Harrisonburg yesterday morning. The grain and forage in advance of these points up to Staunton had previously been destroyed. In moving back to this point the whole country from the Blue Ridge to the North Mountains has been made untenable for a rebel army. I have destroyed over 2,000 barns filled with wheat, hay, and farming implements; over seventy mills filled with flour and wheat; have driven in front of the army over 4,000 head of stock, and have killed and have issued to the troops not less than 3,000 sheep. This destruction embraces the Luray Valley and Little Fort Valley, as well as the main valley. A large number of horses have been obtained, a proper estimate of which I cannot now make. Lieut. John R. Meigs, my engineer officer, was murdered beyond Harrisonburg, near Dayton. For this atrocious act all the houses within an area of five miles were burned. Since I came into the Valley, from Harper's Ferry up to Harrisonburg, every train, every small party, and every straggler has been bushwacked by people, many of whom have protection papers from commanders who have been hitherto in this valley. From the vicinity of Harrisonburg over 400 wagon-loads of refugees have been sent back to Martinsburg; most of these people were Dunkers and had been conscripted. The people here are getting sick of the war; heretofore they have had no reason to complain, because they have been living in great abundance. I have not been followed by the enemy up to this point, with the exception of a small force of rebel cavalry that showed themselves some distance behind my rear guard to-day. A party of 100 of the Eighth Ohio Cavalry, which I had stationed at the bridge over the North Shenandoah, near Mount Jackson, was attacked by McNeill, with seventeen men; report they were asleep, and the whole party dispersed or captured. I think that they will all turn up; I learn that fifty-six of them have reached Winchester. McNeill was mortally wounded and fell into our hands. This was fortunate, as he was the most daring and dangerous of all the bushwackers in this section of the country. . . . To-morrow I will continue the destruction of wheat, forage, etc., down to Fisher's Hill. When this is completed the Valley, from Winchester up to Staunton, ninety-two miles, will have but little in it for man or beast. In previous dispatches I have used "lower Valley" when I should have said "upper Valley," or, in other words, in my last dispatch I intended to say that the grain and forage from Staunton up to Lexington had been sent to Richmond, and that the grain and forage from Staunton to Strasburg had been left for the wintering of Early's army. Yesterday Colonel Powell captured a guerrilla camp on the mountains, with ten wagons and teams.

> P.H. Sheridan
> *Major-General*

LIEUTENANT-GENERAL GRANT
            —*War of the Rebellion . . . Official Records*

XIV

Lee and Lincoln

SPACE *does not allow us the luxury of portraits of all the distinguished or interesting leaders, military and civilian, of the Union and Confederate causes. We must content ourselves with a presentation of the two men who, at the time and since, seemed to symbolize the two sections and causes, and who, in the end, came to be the common and cherished possession of both. It is one of the happier features of an otherwise tragic war that it left, on the whole, so little bitterness; the sectional animosities of the postwar years were rather a product of Reconstruction than of war itself. It is particularly interesting that the leading figure on each side came to be held in affection by both: this is a circumstance not common in the history of civil wars.*

Condemned by the South and, for that matter, by a substantial part of the North during his own lifetime, Lincoln came eventually to be a completely national figure, transcending section and even time. Lee was always admired, even in the North, and Northern opinion found it possible to respect his decision to go with his state while it respected, too, those Southerners like Thomas and Farragut who remained loyal to the old flag.

Since the war there has developed both a Lincoln and a Lee legend. With Lincoln the legend is almost inextricable from fact, nor is this altogether deplorable. With Lee there was less for the mythmakers to work on; while the Lee legend grows, the facts of his career are available and familiar. With Lincoln the difficulty is to separate fact and myth; with Lee to penetrate behind

the deadly oratory
*Of twenty thousand Lee Memorial Days**

to reality.

That the proud and affectionate recollections of Americans should have worked on both men is a matter of gratification and good fortune. If a nation is to have heroes, it would be difficult to find better ones than these two protagonists of the cause of the Union and the cause of State rights.

Lincoln and Lee represent, in a sense, two persistent currents in American history and two strains in the American character. Just as historical legend has insisted on the Puritan and the Cavalier in the founding of America—and this despite evidence to the contrary—so it has insisted on the contrast of frontier democracy and plantation aristocracy, a contrast, too, that exists in the realm of legend rather than of history. In Lincoln Americans have seen a symbol of equality and freedom; in Lee a symbol of the Cavalier spirit and chivalry. For a wonder both men fitted their legends. In apotheosizing Lincoln and Lee the American people apotheosized what was best in their character rather than what was most typical.

We do not attempt here biographies of either of these leaders; that, after all, is superfluous, for there are biographies enough, and memoirs and volumes of tributes. Our concern is the war, and the relation of these men to the war. Nor do we approach either Lincoln or Lee afresh. Almost every chapter of our history has said something about one or both of them; they do not come to us as strangers. We present them for themselves, to be sure, and as vehicles of much of the character of the contenders, but we present them in relation to the larger contest. It will be sufficient, therefore, if we introduce the chroniclers as they tell their stories.

There is an inescapable difference in these presentations. We have already seen Lee in action: the story of the Army of Northern Virginia is in a sense the story of Lee, and it is enough here to present a few glimpses of the man. He was, as Benét has said, "the prop and pillar of a state," but that role we have already seen him play. With Lincoln the situation is different. Lincoln's character can never cease to interest us, but we must be concerned with what he did, as head of the state, as well as with what he was. We have, designedly, neglected the political scene somewhat in our survey of the

* From *John Brown's Body* in *The Selected Works of Stephen Vincent Benét*, published by Rinehart and Company, Inc. Copyright 1927, 1928 by Stephen Vincent Benét.

war; we present here some aspects of important political chapters in which Lincoln played a commanding role, notably emancipation.

1. ROBERT E. LEE GOES WITH HIS STATE

One of the momentous decisions of the war was a personal one—the decision of R. E. Lee that he could not raise his hand against his own people. No officer in the United States Army had a more brilliant record or a more distinguished career than Lee when, at the age of fifty-four, he resigned from the army to go with his state. He had performed brilliantly a number of difficult engineering assignments, fought gallantly in the Mexican War, served as Superintendent of the West Point Military Academy, and dealt effectively with Indian outbreaks along the Mexican border. Recalled to Washington early in 1861 he was informally offered command of the field forces of the United States. With deep spiritual anguish he refused this offer, resigned his commission, and accepted instead command of the military forces of Virginia. Shortly after he was appointed general in the Confederate Army.

These two letters explain his decision.

A. "MY RELATIVES, MY CHILDREN, MY HOME"

To his Sister, Mrs. Anne Marshall.

Arlington, Virginia
April 20, 1861

My Dear Sister: I am grieved at my inability to see you. . . . I have been waiting for a 'more convenient season,' which has brought to many before me deep and lasting regret. Now we are in a state of war which will yield to nothing. The whole South is in a state of revolution, into which Virginia, after a long struggle, has been drawn; and though I recognize no necessity for this state of things, and would have forborne and pleaded to the end for redress of grievances, real or supposed, yet in my own person I had to meet the question whether I should take part against my native State.

With all my devotion to the Union and the feeling of

loyalty and duty of an American citizen, I have not been able to make up my mind to raise my hand against my relatives, my children, my home. I have therefore resigned my commission in the Army, and save in defense of my native State, with the sincere hope that my poor services may never be needed, I hope I may never be called on to draw my sword. I know you will blame me; but you must think as kindly of me as you can, and believe that I have endeavoured to do what I thought right.

To show you the feeling and struggle it has cost me, I send you a copy of my letter of resignation. I have no time for more. May God guard and protect you and yours, and shower upon you everlasting blessings, is the prayer of your devoted brother,

R. E. LEE

B. "I NEVER DESIRE AGAIN TO DRAW MY SWORD"

To General Scott.

Arlington, Virginia
April 20, 1861

General: Since my interview with you on the 18th inst. I have felt that I ought no longer to retain my commission in the Army. I therefore tender my resignation, which I request you will recommend for acceptance. It would have been presented at once but for the struggle it has cost me to separate myself from a service to which I have devoted the best years of my life, and all the ability I possessed.

During the whole of that time—more than a quarter of a century—I have experienced nothing but kindness from my superiors and a most cordial friendship from my comrades. To no one, General, have I been as much indebted as to yourself for uniform kindness and consideration, and it has always been my ardent desire to merit your approbation. I shall carry to the grave the most grateful recollections of your kind consideration, and your name and fame shall always be dear to me.

Save in defense of my native State, I never desire again to draw my sword.

Be pleased to accept my most earnest wishes for the continuance of your happiness and prosperity, and believe me, most truly yours,

R. E. LEE

—LEE, *Recollections and Letters of General Robert E. Lee*

2. "A SPLENDID SPECIMEN OF AN ENGLISH GENTLEMAN"

Garnet Wolseley was a young lieutenant colonel in the British Army when, in 1862, he slipped away from a tour of duty in Canada to visit the Army of Northern Virginia. We have already enjoyed his portrait of Stonewall Jackson. Lee he admired even more than Jackson and, characteristically, his admiration found expression in extending to Lee the title "English gentleman," which he assumed to be the highest accolade. It was Lord Wolseley who discovered George Henderson and encouraged him to write his classic biography of Stonewall Jackson.

Having presented our letters to the Adjutant-General, we were in turn presented to the Commander-in-Chief. He is a strongly built man, about five feet eleven in height, and apparently not more than fifty years of age. His hair and beard are nearly white; but his dark brown eyes still shine with all the brightness of youth, and beam with a most pleasing expression. Indeed, his whole face is kindly and benevolent in the highest degree. In manner, though sufficiently conversible, he is slightly reserved; but he is a person that, wherever seen, whether in a castle or a hovel, alone or in a crowd, must at once attract attention as being a splendid specimen of an English gentleman, with one of the most rarely handsome faces I ever saw. He had had a bad fall during the Maryland expedition, from which he was not yet recovered, and which still crippled his right hand considerably.

We sat with him for a long time in his tent, conversing upon a variety of topics, the state of affairs being of course the leading one. He talked most freely about the battle of Antietam, and assured us that at no time during that day's fight had he more than thirty-five thousand men engaged. You have only to be in his society for a very brief period to be convinced that whatever he says may be implicitly relied upon, and that he is quite incapable of departing from the truth under any circumstances. . . .

In visiting the headquarters of the Confederate generals, but particularly those of General Lee, any one accustomed to see European armies in the field cannot fail to be struck with the great absence of all the pomp and circumstance of war in and around their encampments. Lee's headquarters consisted of about seven or eight pole tents, pitched with their backs to a stake fence, upon a piece of ground so rocky that it was unpleasant to ride over it—its only recommendation being a little stream of good water which flowed close by the General's tent. In front of the tents were some three or four wheeled wagons, drawn up without any regularity, and a number of horses roamed loose about the field. The servants, who were of course slaves, and the mounted soldiers called "couriers," who always accompany each general of division in the field, were unprovided with tents, and slept in or under the waggons.

Waggons, tents, and some of the horses, were marked U.S., showing that part of that huge debt in the North has gone to furnishing even the Confederate generals with camp equipments. No guard or sentries were to be seen in the vicinity; no crowd of aides-de-camp loitering about, making themselves agreeable to visitors, and endeavouring to save their generals from receiving those who have no particular business. A large farm-house stands close by, which, in any other army, would have been the general's residence, pro tem.: but as no liberties are allowed to be taken with personal property in Lee's army, he is particular in setting a good example himself. His staff are crowded together two and three in a tent: none are allowed to carry more baggage than a small box each, and his own kit is but very little larger. Every one who approaches him does so with marked respect, although there is none of that bowing and flourishing of forage-caps which occurs in the presence of European generals: and whilst all honour him and place implicit faith in his courage and ability, those with whom he is most intimate feel for him the affection of sons to a father. Old General Scott was correct in saying that when Lee joined the Southern cause, it was worth as much as the accession of 20,000 men to the "rebels."

Since, then, every injury that it was possible to inflict, the Northerners have heaped upon him. His house on the Pamunky river was burnt to the ground and the slaves carried away, many of them by force; whilst his residence on the Arlington Heights was not only gutted of its furniture, but even the very relics of George Washington were stolen from it and paraded in triumph in the saloons of New York and Boston. Notwithstanding all these personal losses, however, when speaking of the Yankees, he neither evinced any bitterness of feeling, nor gave utterance to a single violent expression, but alluded to many of his former friends and companions amongst them in the kindest terms. He spoke as a man proud of the victories won by his country, and confident of ultimate

success under the blessing of the Almighty, whom he glorified
for past successes, and whose aid he invoked for all future
operations. He regretted that his limited supply of tents and
available accommodation would prevent him from putting us
up, but he kindly placed at our disposal horses, or a two-
horsed wagon, if we preferred it, to drive about in.
—[WOLSELEY], "A Month's Visit to the Confederate Headquarters"

3. "IT IS WELL WAR IS SO TERRIBLE, OR WE SHOULD GET TOO FOND OF IT"

*Here is another of those little scenes that reveal character:
Lee watching the repulse of the Federals at Fredericksburg.
General Pendleton, who tells the story, was a West Pointer
who had abandoned the army for the Church, was rector of
Grace Church in Lexington, Virginia, when he joined the
Rockbridge Artillery, and rose to be chief of artillery of the
Army of Northern Virginia.*

From prominent points in our line almost the entire scene
could be taken in by the eye. And at one of these, the most
commanding, where we had a few powerful guns, General
Lee remained much of the day, observing the field; only too
indifferent, as was his wont, to danger from the large, numerous, and well-aimed missiles hurled especially thither from
the enemy's heavy batteries across the Rappahannock. Seldom, in all the wars of the world, has a spectacle been presented like that which, from this central elevation, we looked
upon. More than one hundred thousand blue-coated men in
the open plain, with every military appliance, in battle order,
and moving in their respective subdivisions to attack our line.
Although our numbers were certainly not half those of the
enemy, there was misgiving, probably, in no officer or man
as to the result.
    Events in one quarter of the field, as it lay before us,
attracted peculiar interest, and gave occasion to one of those
characteristic remarks of General Lee which told at once of
his capacity for enjoying the excitements of action, and of
the good feeling and strong principle that kept it under control. A large force advanced rapidly to charge our right.
Stonewall Jackson was there, and that he would promptly
hurl them back little doubt was entertained. Still no such as-

sault can be witnessed without earnest interest, if not concern. Nor was the shock received on our side without loss. There fell the heroic General Gregg, of the gallant and now vengeance-suffering State of South Carolina. Presently, however, as was anticipated, the spirited charge was reversed, and blue figures by thousands were seen recrossing, "double quick," with faces to the rear, the space they had traversed, and hundreds of gray pursuers hastening their speed. While younger spectators near us gave expression to their feelings by shouts, clapping of hands, &c., the gratified yet considerate and amiable commander turned to myself, and with beaming countenance said, *"It is well war is so terrible, or we should get too fond of it."*

Not long after an incident occurred which made us shudder for our beloved chief. One of our large guns on that eminence, having to be plied continuously against another portion of the enemy's line, which was advancing to charge that part of our defences held by the good and gallant Georgian, General Tom Cobb, and being, like much hastily-cast Southern ordnance, of insufficient tenacity, finally burst with prodigious violence. None, wonderfully and happily, were struck by its fragments. And, remarkably, those who stood nearest, of whom the individual relating it to you was one, within a little over arm's length, although considerably jarred by the shock, proved to be really in less danger than others farther off. General Lee was standing perhaps fifty feet in the rear, and a large piece of the cannon, weighing, we estimated, about a third of a ton, fell just beyond him. He thus very narrowly escaped death. Like himself, however, he only looked upon the mass calmly for a moment, and then, without a syllable expressive of surprise or concern, continued the business occupying him at the time.

—PENDLETON, "Personal Recollections of General Lee"

4. DR. PARKS'S BOY VISITS LEE'S HEADQUARTERS

Here is a charming vignette of Lee on the road to Gettysburg. It comes from Leighton Parks, the small boy who stood wide-eyed looking at Lee and his lieutenants. Written 40 years later, it is undoubtedly bathed in nostalgia. Yet though the conversations are suspect, the episode itself rings

true enough. The Elizabethtown referred to was a small
Maryland village, no longer on the map.

Before the year was out we learned that the Union troops
had again been driven back to Washington, and, soon after,
that Lee was crossing the river at Williamsport. The report
proved true. First came the cavalry. I had never supposed
so many horses were to be found in the world as I now saw
slowly passing through the street of Elizabethtown. They
kept straight on to the north. I asked many of the soldiers
where they were going. The poor fellows knew nothing;
many of them were too ignorant to know what it meant to
have crossed the Potomac. Had they not crossed many
rivers? What was one more than another? But the officers
laughed gaily and said: "New York." Why not? What could
prevent them? Was not the Army of the Potomac huddled
about the defenses of Washington? "Had not Bobby Lee
stolen a march on the commanding general, whoever that
might be at the moment?" they added with a laugh. Indeed,
the darkest hour of the war had come to the North.

So the troops passed on, thousand after thousand. The
artillery followed the cavalry; then came the infantry. The
impression made by the sight of so many horses was repeated by the hosts of men. It was not only the multitude
that impressed those who saw that march; it was also the
splendid discipline of the army. They were different from the
corps we had seen the year before. These men were well clad
and shod, and they came through the town with flags flying
and bands playing "Dixie," "Dixie," all day long, with
now and then a change to "Maryland, my Maryland" or the
"Bonnie Blue Flag." We became as tired of these as we had
of "Yankee Doodle" or "The Star-Spangled Banner." (But
both armies marched to the tune of "The Girl I Left Behind
Me.") They had the air of men who were used to conquer;
they believed in the men who led them, and they did not
doubt that when they saw the enemy they would drive them
before them again. It was a sight such as few have seen even
of those who took part in the war. Sixty thousand men, it is
said, passed through Elizabethtown on the way to Gettysburg, and I can well believe it. Day after day an unbroken
line passed on due north, and at night the rumble of the
wagons made sleep impossible for nervous people. And who
was not nervous?

Soon after the Confederates began to enter the town I met
a friend of mine, the son of Dr. Doyle, who told me that his

father had just been sent for to see Lee, and that I might go too if I hurried. It is needless to say that I ran as fast as my small legs could carry me, and we found the doctor just starting. Dr. Doyle was a man who had been in communication with the enemy from the beginning of the war, but had so far managed to escape the fate of many innocent men. Two of his sons had been arrested a short time before, and were lying in the jail when their friends arrived and set them free.

The doctor was in his old gig, and, being an immense man, left no room for any one else in it, so we two boys sat on the springs behind. It was on the Williamsport pike, about half a mile from the town, that we met General Lee. He had dismounted and was standing by his horse, a small sorrel mare, which, I was told, it was his custom to ride on the march. His staff was brilliant in gold lace, but he was very simply dressed. No one could have seen that man without being greatly impressed with the dignity of his bearing and the beauty of his face. His hair at this time was almost entirely white, and those who had seen him the year before said he had aged greatly in the short space of time which had elapsed since the battle of Antietam. I could not help thinking of Washington as I looked at that calm, sad face. It has been said since by those who were near him that he had no expectation of conquering the North, and that, at the most, he only hoped to win a great battle on Northern soil in order to affect public opinion in Europe, and lead to the recognition of the Southern Confederacy. However that may be, there was nothing about his bearing which looked like a great hope.

Dr. Doyle drove straight to where he was standing and announced himself as one who was sure of his welcome. General Lee came at once to the gig and thanked him politely for having come so promptly, and began at once to ask about the roads. I was astonished at the familiarity which he showed with the country, and yet he evidently wished to have his map, which he held in his hand, confirmed by an eyewitness. His questions were like those of a lawyer to a witness. What roads ran into the Lightersburg pike? Did the Cavetown pike cross the mountain? What sort of crossing was it? Could cannon be easily brought over it? His right flank, then, was protected by the Blue Ridge until he reached Gettysburg? And on his return should he come that way? Were there good roads running to the river west of the one on which he now stood? Could artillery be moved over them? Was the valley well wooded and watered all the way to Gettysburg? To all of which the answer was "Yes."

Lee had been speaking in a low tone, leaning on the shaft of the gig, with his head under the hood of it, so that we, looking in through the curtain, could see and hear everything. Suddenly Lee saw us and said: "Doctor, are these your boys?"

"One of them is," said the doctor "The other is the son of Dr. Parks. You must have known his father in the old army."

"Is it possible!" said Lee.

Then we were called down and made our bows, and Lee said something that I could not hear; but the doctor answered, "No danger," and then added something at which Lee smiled and said, "Would you boys like to get on that horse?" pointing to his own little mare.

Of course we said, "Yes," and each in turn was lifted by General Lee up to the horse's back. I suspect that that attention was suggested by Dr. Doyle in order to divert our minds from what we had just heard. When we got back to town, he said to me: "Now run home, my boy, and tell your mother that you have seen General Lee and all that he said to you—in fact, all you can remember to have heard him say. It will interest her."

So home I ran, swelling with importance, and told my mother all the questions that General Lee had asked and what Dr. Doyle had said. Of course my mother saw at once the importance of the conversation, and charged me to keep it perfectly quiet. Which I did.

A day or two after this a friend of the family who had been very kind to me asked me if I should not like to go out to General Lee's headquarters? "To-morrow," he said, "you will see a sight that you will be able to tell as long as you live, for Lee's generals are to meet him, and the army is to move."

I boldly asked if he would lend me his horse, and he laughed and consented. So the next morning, dressed in white jacket and trousers, I started off on a brown horse, carrying a basket of raspberries to one of Lee's staff whom my mother had known since he was a lad. I remember my costume from the fact that some of the berries melted, and before I was aware of it they had made a stain on my trousers which no amount of rubbing would remove. This troubled me a good deal because I thought General Lee might think I did not know how to ride; and as I had made up my mind to ask him to let me accompany the army in some capacity not very clear to me, this gave me considerable anxiety. However, I reached the camp without further accident and found Colonel Taylor, to whom I was accredited.

Lee's headquarters were in a hickory grove about three miles from Williamsport. The grove was on the top of a small hill, and near enough to the pike for the general to see the troops as they marched by.

When I reached the camp, Colonel Taylor told me that General Lee was away, but that he would probably return before long. Indeed, it was not many minutes before we heard the trampling of horses and the guard turning out, and, on going to the door of the tent, I saw a splendid sight. First there was Lee himself riding a superb iron-gray horse, and with him were Longstreet, Ewell, and A. P. Hill. Colonel Taylor led me to General Lee and said: "General, this gentleman has brought me some raspberries, and I have asked him to take snack with us."

Lee's back was toward me when the colonel spoke, and I was startled to see how severe he looked as, wheeling sharply, he glanced quickly to right and left and then looked down. Then he smiled very pleasantly and remarked: "I have had the pleasure of meeting your friend before." And then, to my great surprise, this severe-looking man stooped down and, lifting me, kissed me. After this the generals and Colonel Taylor and I went into a large tent for "snack."

I do not remember anything that was said during the meal, nor what we had to eat. I suppose I was a good deal excited, and I know that there was a deal of laughing—I fear at my expense; for they—not Lee, but the others—asked me a great many questions, and then laughed at the answers. I suppose it was a relief to these men, who were carrying such a heavy burden, to have a child to chaff.

After luncheon we went to Lee's tent, and the general took me on his knee and talked to me until some one having taken his attention, Hill beckoned me to come to him, which I did gladly; for, though Lee was gentle, I could not help standing in awe of him in a way that I did not of the others.

When I had been with him for a little while, Longstreet said: "Come, Hill, you've had him long enough; pass him over." So I was dragged over to Longstreet's knee and had my face well rubbed by his great brown beard. And he whispered in my ear that he had a pony he thought would carry my weight, if I should like to join his staff.

But before I could express my joy, Lee suddenly said, "Well, gentlemen," and immediately Colonel Taylor made me a sign. So I got up and said good-by; and I thought then, and think now, that they were sorry to have me go, for I suppose I brought a new element into their life. One of them

—Hill, I think—called to a servant to "bring the captain's horse," at which the man grinned and untied the horse from a tree near by and led him to the front of the tent.

This placed me in a most embarrassing situation; for while I could ride very well for a boy, I was in the habit of mounting my steed by the aid of a fence. Still, I determined to do my best, and, stretching up my leg as high as it would go, managed to touch the stirrup with my toe; but, alas! when I attempted to mount into the saddle I descended to the ground, with my feet very wide apart and my jacket somewhat marked by contact with the horse's flanks. This was greeted with a good-natured laugh, which determined me to mount or die in the attempt. But I was saved either alternative, for before I had time to try again I was lifted lightly into the saddle by Lee himself, who smiled and said: "Give him time, and he'll do for the cavalry yet."

—PARKS, "What a Boy Saw of the Civil War"

5. "A SADNESS I HAD NEVER BEFORE SEEN UPON HIS FACE"

We have already seen something of Lee during and after Gettysburg, and Colonel Fremantle has given us an unforgettable picture of Lee rallying his stricken troops with the assurance that all would come right in the end. Here is perhaps a more intimate picture of Lee the night after the battle. It comes from General John Imboden, who protected the Confederate right in the advance on Gettysburg, and was detached to cover the Confederate retreat after the battle.

When night closed the struggle, Lee's army was repulsed. We all knew that the day had gone against us, but the full extent of the disaster was only known in high quarters. The carnage of the day was generally understood to have been frightful, yet our army was not in retreat, and it was surmised in camp that with to-morrow's dawn would come a renewal of the struggle. All felt and appreciated the momentous consequences to the cause of Southern independence of final defeat or victory on that great field.

It was a warm summer's night; there were few camp-fires, and the weary soldiers were lying in groups on the luxuriant grass of the beautiful meadows, discussing the events of the day, speculating on the morrow, or watching that our horses did not straggle off while browsing. About 11 o'clock a horseman came to summon me to General Lee. I promptly mounted and, accompanied by Lieutenant George W. Mc-Phail, an aide on my staff, and guided by the courier who brought the message, rode about two miles toward Gettysburg to where half a dozen small tents were pointed out, a little way from the roadside to our left, as General Lee's headquarters for the night. On inquiry I found that he was not there, but had gone to the headquarters of General A. P. Hill, about half a mile nearer to Gettysburg. When we reached the place indicated, a single flickering candle, visible from the road through the open front of a common wall-tent, exposed to view Generals Lee and Hill seated on camp-stools with a map spread upon their knees. Dismounting, I approached on foot. After exchanging the ordinary salutations General Lee directed me to go back to his headquarters and wait for him. I did so, but he did not make his appearance until about 1 o'clock, when he came riding alone, at a slow walk, and evidently wrapped in profound thought.

When he arrived there was not even a sentinel on duty at his tent, and no one of his staff was awake. The moon was high in the clear sky and the silent scene was unusually vivid. As he approached and saw us lying on the grass under a tree, he spoke, reined in his jaded horse, and essayed to dismount. The effort to do so betrayed so much physical exhaustion that I hurriedly rose and stepped forward to assist him, but before I reached his side he had succeeded in alighting, and threw his arm across the saddle to rest, and fixing his eyes upon the ground leaned in silence and almost motionless upon his equally weary horse,—the two forming a striking and never-to-be-forgotten group. The moon shone full upon his massive features and revealed an expression of sadness that I had never before seen upon his face. Awed by his appearance I waited for him to speak until the silence became embarrassing, when, to break it and change the silent current of his thoughts, I ventured to remark, in a sympathetic tone, and in allusion to his great fatigue:

"General, this has been a hard day on you."

He looked up, and replied mournfully:

"Yes, it has been a sad, sad day to us," and immediately relapsed into his thoughtful mood and attitude. Being unwilling again to intrude upon his reflections, I said no more. After perhaps a minute or two, he suddenly straightened up to his full height, and turning to me with more animation and excitement of manner than I had ever seen in him before, for he was a man of wonderful equanimity, he said in a voice tremulous with emotion:

"I never saw troops behave more magnificently than Pickett's division of Virginians did to-day in that grand charge upon the enemy. And if they had been supported as they were to have been,—but, for some reason not yet fully explained to me, were not,—we would have held the position and the day would have been ours." After a moment's pause he added in a loud voice, in a tone almost of agony, "Too bad! *Too bad!* OH! TOO BAD!"

I shall never forget his language, his manner, and his appearance of mental suffering. In a few moments all emotion was suppressed, and he spoke feelingly of several of his fallen and trusted officers; among others of Brigadier-Generals Armistead, Garnett, and Kemper of Pickett's division.

—IMBODEN, "The Confederate Retreat from Gettysburg"

6. LEE AND TRAVELLER REVIEW THE ARMY OF NORTHERN VIRGINIA

This picture of a gala military review comes from August 1863, while the army was recuperating after Gettysburg. It is given us by Lee's son, Captain Robert E. Lee, Jr.

During this period of rest, so unusual to the Army of Northern Virginia, several reviews were held before the commanding general. I remember being present when that of the Third Army Corps, General A. P. Hill commanding, took place. Some of us young cavalrymen, then stationed near the Rappahannock, rode over to Orange Court House to see this grand military pageant. From all parts of the army, officers and men who could get leave came to look on, and from all the surrounding country the people, old and young, ladies and children, came in every pattern of vehicle and on horseback, to see twenty thousand of that "incomparable infantry" of the Army of Northern Virginia pass in review before their great commander.

The General was mounted on Traveller, looking very proud of his master, who had on sash and sword, which he very rarely wore, a pair of new cavalry gauntlets, and, I think, a new hat. At any rate, he looked unusually fine, and sat his horse like a perfect picture of grace and power. The infantry was drawn up in column by divisions, with their bright muskets all glittering in the sun, their battle-flags standing straight out before the breeze, and their bands playing, awaiting the inspection of the General, before they broke into column by companies and marched past him in review.

When all was ready, General Hill and staff rode up to General Lee, and the two generals, with their respective staffs, galloped around front and rear of each of the three divisions standing motionless on the plain. As the cavalcade reached the head of each division, its commanding officer joined in and followed as far as the next division, so that there was a continual infusion of fresh groups into the original one all along the lines.

Traveller started with a long lope, and never changed his stride. His rider sat erect and calm, not noticing anything but the gray lines of men whom he knew so well. The pace was very fast, as there were nine good miles to go, and the escort began to become less and less, dropping out one by one from different causes as Traveller raced along without a check.

When the General drew up, after this nine-mile gallop, under the standard at the reviewing-stand, flushed with the exercise as well as with pride in his brave men, he raised his hat and saluted. Then arose a shout of applause and admiration from the entire assemblage, the memory of which to this day moistens the eye of every old soldier.

—LEE, *Recollections and Letters of General Robert E. Lee*

7. "HE LOOKED AS THOUGH HE WAS THE MONARCH OF THE WORLD"

We have already learned how Lee tried to lead the countercharge to close up the gap torn in his lines on the morning of the Battle of the Wilderness, May 6, 1864. Here Colonel Oates, whom we have met before, recalls for us his glimpse of Lee as the Alabamians closed up the gap.

At about 2 o'clock A.M. on the 6th we began to move, and progressed so slowly along the devious neighborhood road that it was daylight when the head of the column reached the Plank Road, about two miles in rear of where the fighting ceased the previous evening and where, just at this moment, it recommenced with great fury. As we hurried to the front we passed quite a number of wounded Confederates lying by the side of the road, and among them Generals Cook, of Georgia, and Kirkland, of North Carolina. In anticipation that his troops would be relieved early the next morning, Hill had not prepared to receive the attack which was made on him.

Longstreet's column reached the scene of action none too soon. Hancock was just then turning Hill's right and driving his men from their position, although they were manfully contesting every inch of ground. Anderson's Georgians was the first brigade of Field's division to engage the enemy. Benning's and the Texas Brigade got into action next on the right or south side of the Plank Road, and were temporarily repulsed. We met General Benning, brought out on a litter severely wounded. Colonel Perry then formed Law's brigade, as it came up in double quick, to the left of the Plank Road with the Fourth Alabama's right resting upon it and the Fifteenth on the left of the brigade and of the line.

To reach our position we had to pass within a few feet of General Lee. He sat his fine gray horse "Traveler," with the cape of his black cloak around his shoulders, his face flushed and full of animation. The balls were flying around him from two directions. His eyes were on the fight then going on south of the Plank Road between Kershaw's division and the flanking column of the enemy. He had just returned from attempting to lead the Texas Brigade in a second charge, when those gallant men and their officers refused to allow him to do so. My friend Col. Van H. Manning, of the Third Arkansas, then in command of the brigade, did that himself, fell severely wounded while leading the charge, and was taken prisoner.

A group of General Lee's staff were on their horses just in rear of him. He turned in his saddle and called to his chief of staff in a most vigorous tone, while pointing with his finger across the road, and said: "Send an active young officer down there." I thought him at that moment the grandest specimen of manhood I ever beheld. He looked as though he ought to have been and was the monarch of the world. He glanced his eye down on the "ragged rebels" as they filed around him in quick time to their place in line, and inquired, "What troops are these?" And was answered by some private in the Fifteenth, "Law's Alabama brigade." He exclaimed in a strong voice, "God bless the Alabamians!" The men cheered and went into line whith a whoop. The advance began.

—Oates, *The War Between the Union and the Confederacy*

8. "THE FIELD RESOUNDED WITH WILD SHOUTS OF LEE, LEE, LEE"

There are altogether, as we pointed out in our chapter on the Wilderness, three "Lee to the Rear" episodes. The third, and best authenticated, is that of May 12, when Hancock broke through the salient, overran Johnson's division, and threatened the whole Confederate line. We give here Colonel Gibson's account of the crisis.

A little after dawn of the 12th [May 1864], I was aroused from a deep sleep by Frank George, one of General Gordon's orderlies, and was told by him that the Yankees had broken through our works and captured Johnson's division; and when I started to say something, he told me not to talk loud, the enemy were very close to us.

I immediately aroused up two or three men near me and told them to arouse the regiment, and tell the men to fall in as quickly and quietly as possible, without any rattling of canteens, as we were near the enemy. . . . The men fell in line about as soon as I could get mounted, and the staff officer came up a few minutes after, and guided us towards the right, and then towards the left, and after we had marched some two or three hundred yards and had come in sight of the line of unoccupied earthworks to our left, he pointed out a little farmhouse some ten or twelve hundred yards distant, and some four or five hundred yards, apparently, in rear of these works extended, as the headquarters of General Lee. He led us some hundred yards or more almost parallel to these unoccupied works, and then stopped, rather closer than the regulations required, as I thought, to a fine looking body of Confederates, dressed in nice, clean uniforms, that contrasted very strongly with the clothing of those of my brigade.

In the rear of these well-dressed troops I saw four mounted men among them; recognized General Robert E. Lee and Major-General John B. Gordon. General Lee rode towards my brigade, and as soon as I had fronted the men I turned towards him saluting for my orders. He paid no attention to me, but wheeled his horse to the right, passed through the vacancy between the brigades, took off his hat and rode Traveler grandly to the front.

He had scarcely got a dozen paces in front of our brigades when General Gordon and an officer on his left, whom I took to be his adjutant, trotted quickly after General Lee, and

Gordon, as soon as he reached him seized Traveler by the
right cheek of his bit, stopped him, and said to General Lee:
"You must not expose yourself; your life is too valuable to
the army and to the Confederacy for you to risk it so wantonly; we are Georgians, we are Virginians, we need no such
encouragement." At this some of our soldiers called out, "No,
No," Gordon continuing, said: "There is not a soldier in the
Confederate army that would not gladly lay down his life to
save you from harm;" but the men did not respond to this
last proposition.

While Gordon was speaking his adjutant rode around the
heads of the horses of the two generals and facing his horse
in a direction opposite that of General Lee's began to tug at
Traveler's bit or bridle rein. Looking through an aperture in
our breastworks I saw a body of the enemy coming from our
left, slowly, and cautiously approaching us.

I called out to General Lee to come back, the enemy were
approaching, and that we could not fight while he was in our
front. A number of our men, especially those of Company A,
called out: "Come back, General Lee; we can't fight while
you are in our front;" and some members of Company A
turned their right shoulders to General Lee and their backs
to me, but I immediately brought these men into line by a
"steady, front!" . . .

On looking out again for the enemy I noticed that they
had drawn very close to our earthworks. I called out to General Lee "To come back, and come quick; that the enemy
were close upon us, and that my men could not fire on the
enemy without shooting him." A number of my men called
out: "Come back, General Lee; we won't fight as long as you
are before us; come back."

The decided call of the men seemed to produce a greater
impression on General Lee than the eloquence of Gordon,
and my curt suggestions. As Traveler could not be easily
turned around with a mounted officer on either side of him,
facing in opposite directions, the adjutant let go Traveler's
bridle, Gordon turned him around to the right, and proudly
started to lead him back, and as he was doing so, I called
out: "Three cheers for General Lee and 'Old' Virginia," but
forgot to add Gordon's name to the list, which were given
with a will. Before the two generals reached the intervening
space between the brigades, Gordon let go his hold of Lee's
bridle and dropped behind a short space, Lee as soon as he
reached the line of the brigades, turned his horse to the right,

close up to mine, and Gordon and his adjutant rode up to the line of the Georgia Brigade.

When General Gordon, amid repeated shouts of "Lee, Lee to the rear!" had approached within eight or ten paces of our line, he found the interval between our two brigades blocked up. A mounted officer had stationed himself on the left of Gordon's brigade, General George Evans commanding. I had remained on the extreme right flank of Early's brigade, where I had placed myself when Lee rode to the front, and the intervening space had been crowded by men of Evans' brigade. Gordon let go his hold of Traveler's bridle, and reined up his horse to fall in behind Lee, and as he did so a member of the Warren Rifles ran forward, seized Lee's horse by the bridle reins, and amid redoubled shouts of "Lee, Lee, Lee to the rear! Lee to the rear!" led him up to the crowd and guided him through the crowders, and I backed my horse to the left to give a freer passage to the riders, and they passed through in single file, and the field of coming carnage resounded with wild shouts of "Lee, Lee, Lee!"

—Account by Colonel J. Catlett Gibson

9. LEE BIDS FAREWELL TO THE ARMY OF NORTHERN VIRGINIA

This moving document needs no introduction. It is relevant, however, to add a word about Lee after the war.

Deeply convinced that the only hope for the South lay in a sincere acceptance of the verdict of Appomattox he devoted himself to healing the wounds of war and training up a generation of young men who might work for the reconstruction of their section. In June 1865 he set an example to others by applying for a presidential pardon; it is mortifying to record that the pardon was never granted. In September 1865 Lee accepted the Presidency of Washington College (now Washington and Lee University), at Lexington, Virginia, and as President inaugurated a series of interesting reforms in the direction of what we would now call progressive education. Stricken with angina pectoris, he died on October 12, 1870, and was buried in Lexington.

In Benét's fine phrase, Lee had known "such glamour as can wear sheer triumph out"; if the cause for which he so valorously fought did not triumph, who can doubt that the admiration and affection in which he came to be held, North as well as South, represented a triumph that has few parallels in history?

Headquarters, Army of Northern Virginia,
April 10, 1865

After four years of arduous service, marked by unsurpassed courage and fortitude, the Army of Northern Virginia has been compelled to yield to overwhelming numbers and resources. I need not tell the survivors of so many hard-fought battles, who have remained steadfast to the last, that I have consented to this result from no distrust of them; but, feeling that valour and devotion could accomplish nothing that could compensate for the loss that would have attended the continuation of the contest, I have determined to avoid the useless sacrifice of those whose past services have endeared them to their countrymen. By the terms of the agreement, officers and men can return to their homes and remain there until exchanged. You will take with you the satisfaction that proceeds from the consciousness of duty faithfully performed; and I earnestly pray that a merciful God will extend to you His blessing and protection. With an increasing admiration of your constancy and devotion to your country, and a grateful remembrance of your kind and generous consideration of myself, I bid you an affectionate farewell.

R. E. LEE, *General*
—LEE, *Recollections and Letters of General Robert E. Lee*

10. NATHANIEL HAWTHORNE CALLS ON PRESIDENT LINCOLN

From 1853 to 1860 Hawthorne had been in England; when he returned to his own country he was bewildered and saddened at the sectional conflict and the war. In the spring of 1862 he visited Lincoln with a delegation from Massachusetts, was disgusted by some of the politicians and lobbyists he saw about the capital, and wrote a caustic article on his observations for the Atlantic Monthly, *"Chiefly about War Matters." The editor was so offended that he added a footnote. "We are compelled to omit two or three pages, in which the author describes the interview, and gives his ideas of the personal appearance and deportment of the President. The sketch . . . lacks reverence, and it pains us to see a gentleman of ripe age . . . falling into the characteristic and most ominous fault of Young America." It is difficult now to understand what it was that worried editor J. T. Fields in this piece, on the whole so perceptive.*

The article as Hawthorne originally wrote it appeared in his Tales, Sketches, and Other Papers.

Nine o'clock had been appointed as the time for receiving the deputation, and we were punctual to the moment; but not so the President, who sent us word that he was eating his breakfast and would come as soon as he could. His appetite, we were glad to think, must have been a pretty fair one; for we waited about half an hour in one of the antechambers, and then were ushered into a reception-room, in one corner of which sat the Secretaries of War and of the Treasury, expecting, like ourselves, the termination of the Presidential breakfast. During this interval there were several new additions to our group, one or two of whom were in a working-garb, so that we formed a very miscellaneous collection of people, mostly unknown to each other, and without any common sponsor, but all with an equal right to look our head-servant in the face.

By and by there was a little stir on the staircase and in the passage-way, and in lounged a tall, loose-jointed figure, of an exaggerated Yankee port and demeanor, whom (as being about the homeliest man I ever saw, yet by no means repulsive or disagreeable) it was impossible not to recognize as Uncle Abe.

Unquestionably, Western man though he be, and Kentuckian by birth, President Lincoln is the essential representative of all Yankees, and the veritable specimen, physically, of what the world seems determined to regard as our characteristic qualities. It is the strangest and yet the fittest thing in the jumble of human vicissitudes, that he, out of so many millions, unlooked for, unselected by any intelligible process that could be based upon his genuine qualities, unknown to those who chose him, and unsuspected of what endowments may adapt him for his tremendous responsibility, should have found the way open for him to fling his lank personality into the chair of state,—where, I presume, it was his first impulse to throw his legs on the council-table and tell the Cabinet Ministers a story. There is no describing his lengthy awkwardness nor the uncouthness of his movement; and yet it seemed as if I had been in the habit of seeing him daily, and had shaken hands with him a thousand times in some village street; so true was he to the aspect of the pattern American, though with a certain extravagance which, possibly, I exaggerated still further by the delighted eagerness with which I took it in. If put to guess his calling and livelihood, I should have taken him for a country schoolmaster as soon as anything else. He was dressed in a rusty black frockcoat and pantaloons, unbrushed, and worn so faithfully that the suit had adapted itself to the curves and angularities of his figure, and had grown to be an outer skin of the man. He had shabby slippers on his feet. His hair was black, still unmixed with gray, stiff, somewhat bushy, and had apparently been acquainted with neither brush nor comb that morning, after the disarrangement of the pillow; and as to a night-cap, Uncle Abe probably knows nothing of such effeminacies. His complexion is dark and sallow, betokening, I fear, an insalubrious atmosphere around the White House; he has thick black eyebrows and an impending brow; his nose is large, and the lines about his mouth are very strongly defined.

The whole physiognomy is as coarse a one as you would meet anywhere in the length and breadth of the States; but withal, it is redeemed, illuminated, softened, and brightened by a kindly though serious look out of his eyes, and an expression of homely sagacity, that seems weighted with rich results of village experience. A great deal of native sense; no bookish cultivation, no refinement; honest at heart, and thoroughly so, and yet, in some sort, sly,—at least, endowed with a sort of tact and wisdom that are akin to craft, and would impel him, I think, to take an antagonist in flank, rather than to make a bull-run at him right in front. But, on the whole, I like this sallow, queer, sagacious visage, with the homely human sympathies that warmed it; and, for my small share in the matter, would as lief have Uncle Abe for a ruler as any man whom it would have been practicable to put in his place.

Immediately on his entrance the President accosted our member of Congress, who had us in charge, and, with a comical twist of his face, made some jocular remark about the length of his breakfast. He then greeted us all round, not waiting for an introduction, but shaking and squeezing everybody's hand with the utmost cordiality, whther the individual's name was announced to him or not. His manner towards us was wholly without pretense, but yet had a kind of natural dignity, quite sufficient to keep the forwardest of us from clapping him on the shoulder and asking him for a story.

—HAWTHORNE, *Tales, Sketches, and Other Papers*

11. JOHN HAY LIVES WITH "THE TYCOON" IN THE WHITE HOUSE

Fresh from Brown University John Hay entered the law office of his uncle, Milton Hay, in Springfield, Illinois. Next door was the office of Lincoln and Herndon, and inevitably Lincoln came to know the young man. A mutual friend, John Nicolay, whom Lincoln had selected as his private secretary, suggested that Hay should go along as assistant private secretary, and Lincoln amiably agreed. For Hay it was the beginning of a distinguished career which led, in the end, to the Secretaryship of State.

While in the White House Hay kept a diary, and it is from this and from his letters to Nicolay that these vivacious extracts are taken

November 13 [1861]. I wish to record what I consider a portent of evil to come. The President, Governor Seward, and I, went over to McClellan's house tonight. The servant at the door said the General was at the wedding of Col. Wheaton at General Buell's, and would soon return. We went in, and after we had waited about an hour, McC. came in and without paying any particular attention to the porter, who told him the President was waiting to see him, went up stairs, passing the door of the room where the President and Secretary of State were seated. They waited about half-an-hour, and sent once more a servant to tell the General they were there, and the answer coolly came that the General had gone to bed.

I merely record this unparalleled insolence of epaulettes without comment. It is the first indication I have yet seen of the threatened supremacy of the military authorities.

Coming home I spoke to the President about the matter but he seemed not to have noticed it specially, saying it was better at this time not to be making points of etiquette & personal dignity.

July 18, 1863. Today we spent 6 hours deciding on Court Martials, the President, Judge Holt, & I. I was amused at the eagerness with which the President caught at any fact which would justify him in saving the life of a condemned soldier. He was only merciless in cases where meanness or cruelty were shown.

Cases of cowardice he was specially averse to punishing

with death. He said it would frighten the poor devils too terribly, to shoot them. On the case of a soldier who had once deserted & reinlisted he indorsed, "Let him fight instead of shooting him."

One fellow who had deserted & escaped after conviction into Mexico, he sentenced, saying, "We will condemn him as they used to sell hogs in Indiana, as they run."

To J. G. NICOLAY.
EXECUTIVE MANSION, WASHINGTON, August 7, 1863

This town is as dismal now as a defaced tombstone. Everybody has gone, I am getting apathetic & write blackguardly articles for the *Chronicle* from which West extracts the dirt and fun & publishes the dreary remains. The Tycoon is in fine whack, I have rarely seen him more serene & busy. He is managing this war, the draft, foreign relations, and planning a reconstruction of the Union, all at once. I never knew with what tyrannous authority he rules the Cabinet, till now. The most important things he decides & there is no cavil. I am growing more and more firmly convinced that the good of the country absolutely demands that he should be kept where he is till this thing is over. There is no man in the country, so wise, so gentle and so firm. I believe the hand of God placed him where he is.

29 September, 1863. . . . Today came to the Executive Mansion as assembly of cold-water men & cold-water women to make a temperance speech at the Tycoon & receive a response. They filed into the East Room looking blue & thin in the keen autumnal air; Cooper, my coachman, who was about half tight, gazing at them with an air of complacent contempt and mild wonder. Three blue-skinned damsels did Love, Purity, & Fidelity in Red, White & Blue gowns. A few invalid soldiers stumped along in the dismal procession. They made a long speech at the Tycoon in which they called Intemperance the cause of our defeats. He could not see it, as the rebels drink more & worse whisky than we do. They filed off drearily to a collation of cold water & green apples, & then home to mulligrubs.

June 5, 1864. For a day or two the House has been full of patriots on the way to Baltimore who wish to pay their respects & engrave on the expectant mind of the Tycoon their images, in view of future contingencies. Among the genuine delegations have come some of the bogus & the irregular ones.

Cuthbert Bullitt is here with Louisiana in his trousers pocket. He has passed thro' New York & has gotten considerably stampeded by the talk of the trading pettifoggers of politics there. He feels uneasy in his seat.

The South Carolina delegation came in yesterday. The Pres^t says "Let them in." "They are a swindle," I said. "They won't swindle me," quoth the Tycoon. They filed in: a few sutlers, cotton-dealers, and Negroes, presented a petition & retired.

Florida sends two delegations: neither will get in. Each attacks the other as unprincipled tricksters.

—DENNETT, ed., *Lincoln and the Civil War in the Diaries and Letters of John Hay*

12. "MY PARAMOUNT OBJECT IS TO SAVE THE UNION"

Lincoln, and his government, were troubled from the beginning by sharp differences of opinion about the proper objectives of the war. Congress went on record, at the very beginning, that the purpose of the war was to save the Union, and not to interfere with the domestic institutions of any state. This, too, was Lincoln's position. But the Radicals were not content. They wanted—understandably enough—to end slavery, and they insisted that this object should be publicly proclaimed, regardless of consequences.

Horace Greeley, the powerful editor of the New York Tribune, was one of the spokesmen for this group. Perhaps the greatest editor in the country, he was erratic and impulsive, and his conduct during the war often troublesome to the administration. What Greeley and his sympathizers overlooked was the effect that an abolitionist program would have on the border states.

Greeley called this letter, which he published in the Tribune, "The Prayer of Twenty Millions." It was certainly not that. Lincoln's reply, justifying his own temperate program, is one of the most notable of his pronouncements.

A. "The Prayer of Twenty Millions"

August 19, 1862

Dear Sir: . . . We complain that the Union cause has suffered, and is now suffering immensely, from mistaken deference to rebel Slavery. Had you, sir, in your Inaugural Address, unmistakably given notice that, in case the rebellion already commenced, were persisted in, and your efforts to preserve the Union and enforce the laws should be resisted by armed force, *you would recognize no loyal person as rightfully held in Slavery by a traitor*, we believe the rebellion would therein have received a staggering if not fatal blow. . . .

On the face of this wide earth, Mr. President, there is not one disinterested, determined, intelligent champion of the Union cause who does not feel that all attempts to put down the rebellion and at the same time uphold its inciting cause are preposterous and futile—that the rebellion, if crushed out to-morrow, would be renewed within a year if Slavery were left in full vigor—that army officers who remain to this day devoted to Slavery can at best be but half-way loyal to the Union—and that every hour of deference to Slavery is an hour of added and deepened peril to the Union. I appeal to the testimony of your ambassadors in Europe. It is freely at your service, not at mine. Ask them to tell you candidly whether the seeming subserviency of your policy to the slaveholding, slavery-upholding interest, is not the perplexity, the despair of statesmen of all parties, and be admonished by the general answer!

I close as I began with the statement that what an immense majority of the loyal millions of your countrymen require of you is a frank, declared, unqualified, ungrudging execution of the laws of the land, more especially of the Confiscation Act. That act gives freedom to the slaves of rebels coming within our lines, or whom those lines may at any time inclose—we ask you to render it due obedience by publicly requiring all your subordinates to recognize and obey it. The rebels are everywhere using the late anti-Negro riots in the North, as they have long used your officers' treatment of Negroes in the South, to convince the slaves that they have nothing to hope from a Union success—that we mean in that case to sell them into a bitter bondage to defray the cost of the war. Let them impress this as a truth on the great mass of their ignorant and credulous bondmen, and the Union will never be restored—never. We cannot conquer ten millions of people united in solid phalanx against us, powerfully aided by Northern sympathizers and European allies. We must have scouts, guides, spies, cooks, teamsters, diggers, and choppers from the blacks of the South, whether we allow them to fight for us or not, or we shall be baffled and repelled. As one of the millions who would gladly have avoided this struggle at any sacrifice but that of principle and honor, but who now feel that the triumph of the Union is indispensable not only to the existence of our country but to the well-being of mankind, I entreat you to render a hearty and unequivocal obedience to the law of the land.

Yours,

HORACE GREELEY.

—MOORE, ed., *The Rebellion Record*

B. "I WOULD SAVE THE UNION"

Executive Mansion, Washington, August 22, 1862

Hon. Horace Greeley:

DEAR SIR: I have just read yours of the nineteenth, addressed to myself through the New-York *Tribune*. If there be in it any statements or assumptions of fact which I may know to be erroneous, I do not now and here controvert them. If there be in it any inferences which I may believe to be falsely drawn, I do not now and here argue against them. If there be perceptible in it an impatient and dictatorial tone, I waive it in deference to an old friend, whose heart I have always supposed to be right.

As to the policy I "seem to be pursuing," as you say, I have not meant to leave any one in doubt.

I would save the Union. I would save it the shortest way under the Constitution. The sooner the National authority can be restored, the nearer the Union will be "the Union as it was." If there be those who would not save the Union unless they could at the same time *save* Slavery, I do not agree with them. If there be those who would not save the Union unless they could at the same time *destroy* Slavery, I do not agree with them. My paramount object in this struggle *is* to save the Union, and is *not* either to save or destroy Slavery. If I could save the Union without freeing *any* slave, I would do it; and if I could save it by freeing *all* the slaves, I would do it; and if I could do it by freeing some and leaving others alone, I would also do that. What I do about Slavery and the colored race, I do because I believe it helps to save this Union; and what I forbear, I forbear because I do *not* believe it would help to save the Union. I shall do *less* whenever I shall believe what I am doing hurts the cause, and I shall do *more* whenever I shall believe doing more will help the cause. I shall try to correct errors when shown to be errors; and I shall adopt new views so fast as they shall appear to be true views. I have here stated my purpose according to my view of *official* duty, and I intend no modification of my oft-expressed *personal* wish that all men, everywhere, could be free.

Yours,

A. LINCOLN.

—MOORE, ed., *The Rebellion Record*

13. "WE SHALL NOBLY SAVE OR MEANLY LOSE THE LAST, BEST HOPE OF EARTH"

Lincoln's own plan for dealing with the slave problem was compensated emancipation. Again and again he presented this to the country, to the border states, to delegations who came to plead with him. There was never much chance that it would have worked, even had Congress adopted it; even when the Confederacy was palpably collapsing, the border states refused to accept the plan.

This eloquent appeal for compensated emancipation was addressed to Congress in the annual message of December 1, 1862.

This plan is recommended as a means, not in exclusion of, but additional to, all others for restoring and preserving the national authority throughout the Union. The subject is presented exclusively in its economical aspect. The plan would, I am confident, secure peace more speedily and maintain it more permanently than can be done by force alone, while all it would cost, considering amounts and manner of payment and times of payment, would be easier paid than will be the additional cost of the war if we rely solely upon force. It is much, very much, that it would cost no blood at all.

The plan is proposed as permanent constitutional law. It cannot become such without the concurrence of, first, two thirds of Congress, and afterwards three fourths of the States. The requisite three fourths of the States will necessarily include seven of the slave States. Their concurrence, if obtained, will give assurance of their severally adopting emancipation at no very distant day upon the new constitutional terms. This assurance would end the struggle now and save the Union forever. . . .

Fellow-citizens, *we* can not escape history. We of this Congress and this administration will be remembered in spite of ourselves. No personal significance or insignificance can spare one or another of us. The fiery trial through which we pass will light us down in honor or dishonor to the latest generation. We *say* we are for the Union. The world will not forget that we say this. We know how to save the Union. The world knows we do know how to save it. We, even *we here,* hold the power and bear the responsibility. In *giving* freedom to the *slave* we *assure* freedom to *the free*—honorable alike in what we give and what we preserve. We shall nobly save or meanly lose the last, best hope of earth. Other means may succeed; this could not fail. The way is plain, peaceful, generous, just—a way which if followed the world will forever applaud and God must forever bless.

—LINCOLN, Annual Message of December 1, 1862

14. LINCOLN BECOMES THE GREAT EMANCIPATOR

Lincoln's Cabinet had been divided, from the beginning, on the advisability of pronouncing officially in favor of emancipation. Yet public opinion in the North was becoming increasingly insistent on some declaration of policy, and the danger of foreign intervention furnished a persuasive argument for rallying English support to the North by making the war openly one for freedom. It did not, however, seem wise to announce an emancipation policy as long as Union arms were unsuccessful; that, as Seward shrewdly remarked, would be like "our last shriek, on the retreat." Lincoln then resolved to issue the proclamation as soon as Union arms had won a victory. Antietam appeared to be such a victory, and on September 22, 1862, Lincoln presented his Cabinet with his decision. The preliminary proclamation was followed by a formal proclamation of January 1, 1863.

We give here Secretary Chase's account of the famous Cabinet meeting, and the official proclamation.

A. SECRETARY CHASE RECALLS A FAMOUS CABINET MEETING

September 22, 1862.—To department about nine. State Department messenger came with notices to heads of departments to meet at twelve. Received sundry callers. Went to the White House. All the members of the cabinet were in attendance. There was some general talk, and the President mentioned that Artemus Ward had sent him his book. Proposed to read a chapter which he thought very funny. Read it and seemed to enjoy it very much; the heads also (except Stanton). The chapter was "High-Handed Outrage at Utica."

The President then took a graver tone and said: "Gentlemen, I have, as you are aware, thought a great deal about the relation of this war to slavery, and you all remember that, several weeks ago, I read to you an order I had prepared upon the subject, which, on account of objections made by some of you, was not issued. Ever since then my mind has been much occupied with this subject, and I have thought all along that the time for acting on it might probably come. I think the time has come now. I wish it was a better time. I wish that we were in a better condition. The action of the army against the rebels has not been quite what I should have liked best. But they have been driven out of Maryland, and Pennsylvania is no longer in danger of invasion. When the rebel army was at Frederick I determined, as soon as it should be driven out of Maryland, to issue a proclamation of emancipation such as I thought most likely to be useful. I said nothing to any one, but I made a promise to myself and (hesitating a little) to my Maker. The rebel army is now driven out, and I am going to fulfill that promise. I have got you together to hear what I have written down. I do not wish your advice about the main matter, for that I have determined for myself. This I say without intending anything but respect for any one of you. But I already know the views of each on this question. They have been heretofore expressed, and I have considered them as thoroughly and carefully as I can. What I have written is that which my reflections have determined me to say. If there is anything in the expressions I use or in any minor matter which any one of you thinks had best be changed, I shall be glad to receive your suggestions. One other observation I will make. I know very well that many others might, in this matter as in others, do better than I can; and if I was satisfied that the public confidence was more fully possessed by any one of them than by me, and knew of any constitutional way in which he could be put in my place, he should have it. I would gladly yield it to him. But though I believe that I have not so much of the confidence of the people as I had some time since, I do not know that, all things considered, any other person has more; and however this may be, there is no way in which I can have any other man put where I am. I am here. I must do the best I can and bear the responsibility of taking the course which I feel I ought to take."

The President then proceeded to read his Emancipation Proclamation, making remarks on the several parts as he went on, and showing that he had fully considered the subject in all the lights under which it had been presented to him.

After he had closed, Governor Seward said: "The general question having been decided, nothing can be said further about that. Would it not, however, make the proclamation more clear and decided to leave out all reference to the act being sustained during the incumbency of the present President; and not merely say that the Government 'recognizes' but that it will maintain the freedom it proclaims?"

I followed, saying: "What you have said, Mr. President, fully satisfies me that you have given to every proposition which has been made a kind and candid consideration. And you have now expressed the conclusion to which you have arrived clearly and distinctly. This it was your right and, under your oath of office, your duty to do. The proclamation does not, indeed, mark out the course I would myself prefer; but I am ready to take it just as it is written and to stand by it with all my heart. I think, however, the suggestions of Governor Seward very judicious, and shall be glad to have them adopted."

The President then asked us severally our opinions as to the modifications proposed, saying that he did not care much about the phrases he had used. Every one favored the modification, and it was adopted. Governor Seward then proposed that in the passage relating to colonization some language should be introduced to show that the colonization proposed was to be only with the consent of the colonists and the consent of the states in which the colonies might be attempted. This, too, was agreed to; and no other modification was proposed. Mr. Blair then said that the question having been decided, he would make no objection to issuing the proclamation; but he would ask to have his paper, presented some days since, against the policy, filed with the proclamation. The President consented to this readily. And then Mr.

Blair went on to say that he was afraid of the influence of the proclamation on the border states and on the army and stated at some length the grounds of his apprehensions. He disclaimed most expressly, however, all objections to emancipation *per se,* saying he had always been personally in favor of it—always ready for immediate emancipation in the midst of slave states, rather than submit to the perpetuation of the system.

—"Diary of S. P. Chase"

B. "Forever Free"

Whereas on the 22d day of September, A.D. 1862, a proclamation was issued by the President of the United States, containing, among other things, the following, to wit:

"That on the 1st day of January, A.D. 1863, all persons held as slaves within any state or designated part of a state the people whereof shall then be in rebellion against the United States shall be then, thenceforward, and forever free; and the executive government of the United States, including the military and naval authority thereof, will recognize and maintain the freedom of such persons and will do no act or acts to repress such persons, or any of them, in any efforts they may make for their actual freedom.

"That the executive will on the 1st day of January aforesaid, by proclamation, designate the states and parts of states, if any, in which the people thereof, respectively, shall then be in rebellion against the United States; and the fact that any state or the people thereof shall on that day be in good faith represented in the Congress of the United States by members chosen thereto at elections wherein a majority of the qualified voters of such states shall have participated shall, in the absence of strong countervailing testimony, be deemed conclusive evidence that such state and the people thereof are not then in rebellion against the United States."

Now, therefore, I, Abraham Lincoln, . . . do, on this 1st day of January, A.D. 1863, . . . order and designate . . . the states and parts of states wherein the people thereof, respectively, are this day in rebellion against the United States. . . .

And by virtue of the power and for the purpose aforesaid, I do order and declare that all persons held as slaves within said designated states and parts of states are, and henceforward shall be, free; and that the executive government of the United States, including the military and naval authorities thereof, will recognize and maintain the freedom of said persons.

And I hereby enjoin upon the people so declared to be free to abstain from all violence, unless in necessary self-defense; and I recommend to them that, in all cases when allowed, they labor faithfully for reasonable wages.

And I further declare and make known that such persons of suitable condition will be received into the armed service of the United States to garrison forts, positions, stations, and other places, and to man vessels of all sorts in said service.

And upon this act, sincerely believed to be an act of justice, warranted by the Constitution upon military necessity, I invoke the considerate judgment of mankind and the gracious favor of Almighty God.

—LINCOLN, "The Emancipation Proclamation"

15. LINCOLN AND HAY FOLLOW THE ELECTION RETURNS

It is almost inconceivable to us, now, that Lincoln should not have been re-elected in 1864. Yet the prospects, in the summer of that year, were dim. Grant was getting nowhere in the Wilderness or at Petersburg; Sherman did not take Atlanta until September and then started on what many critics were pleased to call a "retreat." Frémont was nominated by a group of disgruntled abolitionists and War Democrats, and on August 29 the Democrats nominated McClellan on a platform declaring that the war was a failure. As late as August 23 Horace Greeley wrote that Lincoln's defeat was inevitable and called for another candidate to save the Union. And on August 23 Lincoln presented his Cabinet with a folded sheet of paper, and asked them to sign on the blank side; the other side contained this statement:

"This morning as for some days past, it seems exceedingly probable that this administration will not be re-elected. Then it will be my duty to so cooperate with the President-elect as to save the Union between the election and the inauguration; as he will have secured his election on such ground that he cannot possibly save it afterward."

Yet in the end the tide turned. Atlanta fell and Sherman marched triumphantly to the sea; Farragut won at Mobile Bay; Grant whittled away Lee's army in front of Petersburg.

The election returns of 1864 gave Lincoln 2,216,067, Mc-Clellan 1,808,725 votes, and Lincoln's electoral vote was 212, McClellan's 21.

Once more it is Hay who tells the story of Lincoln and the election.

Nov. 8, 1864. The house has been still and almost deserted today. Everybody in Washington, not at home voting, seems ashamed of it and stays away from the President.

I was talking with him to-day. He said, "It is a little singular that I, who am not a vindictive man, should have always been before the people for election in canvasses marked for their bitterness; always but once; when I came to Congress it was a quiet time. But always besides that the contests in which I have been prominent have been marked with great rancor."

At noon Butler sent a despatch simply saying, "The quietest city ever seen."

Butler was sent to New York by Stanton. The President had nothing to do with it. Thurlow Weed was nervous about his coming, thought it would harm us and even as late as Sunday wrote saying that Butler's presence was on the whole injurious, in spite of his admirable General Order.

Hoffman sent a very cheering despatch giving a rose-coloured estimate of the forenoon's voting in Baltimore. "I shall be glad if that holds," said the President, "because I had rather feared that in the increased vote over that on the Constitution, the increase would rather be against us."

During the afternoon few despatches were received.

At night, at 7 o'clock we started over to the War Department to spend the evening. Just as we started we received the first gun from Indianapolis, showing a majority of 8,000 there, a gain of 1,500 over Morton's vote. The vote itself seemed an enormous one for a town of that size and can only be accounted for by considering the great influx since the war of voting men from the country into the State centres where a great deal of Army business is done. There was less significance in this vote on account of the October victory which had disheartened the enemy and destroyed their incentive to work.

The night was rainy, steamy and dark. We splashed through the grounds to the side door of the War Department where a soaked and smoking sentinel was standing in his own vapor with his huddled-up frame covered with a rubber cloak. Inside a half-dozen idle orderlies, up-stairs the clerks of the telegraph. As the President entered they handed him a despatch from Forney claiming ten thousand Union majority in Philadelphia. "Forney is a little excitable." Another comes from Felton, Baltimore giving us "15,000 in the city, 5,000 in the state. All Hail, Free Maryland." That is superb. A message from Rice to Fox, followed instantly by one from Sumner to Lincoln, claiming Boston by 5,000, and Rice's & Hooper's elections by majorities of 4,000 apiece. A magnificent advance on the chilly dozens of 1862.

Eckert came in shaking the rain from his cloak, with trousers very disreputably muddy. We sternly demanded an explanation. He had slipped, he said, & tumbled prone, crossing the street. He had done it watching a fellow-being ahead and chuckling at his uncertain footing.

Which reminded the Tycoon, of course. The President said, "For such an awkward fellow, I am pretty sure-footed. It used to take a pretty dextrous man to throw me. I remember, the evening of the day in 1858, that decided the contest for the Senate between Mr Douglas and myself, was something like this, dark, rainy and gloomy. I had been reading the returns, and had ascertained that we had lost the Legislature and started to go home. The path had been worn hog-back & was slippery. My foot slipped from under me, knocking the other one out of the way, but I recovered myself & lit square, and I said to myself, 'It's a slip and not a fall.' "

The President sent over the first fruits to Mrs. Lincoln. He said, "She is more anxious than I."

We went into the Secretary's room. Mr. Welles and Fox soon came in. They were especially happy over the election of Rice, regarding it as a great triumph for the Navy Department. Says Fox, "There are two fellows that have been especially malignant to us, and retribution has come upon them both. Hale and Winter Davis."

"You have more of that feeling of personal resentment than I," said Lincoln. "Perhaps I may have too little of it, but I never thought it paid. A man has not time to spend half his life in quarrels. If any man ceases to attack me, I never remember the past against him. It has seemed to me recently that Winter Davis was growing more sensible to his own true interests and has ceased wasting his time by attacking me. I hope for his own good he has. He has been very malicious against me but has only injured himself by it. His conduct has been very strange to me. I came here, his friend, wishing to continue so. I had heard nothing but good of him; he was the cousin of my intimate friend Judge Davis. But he had scarcely been elected when I began to learn of his attacking me on all possible occasions. It is very much the same with Hickman. I was much disappointed that he had failed to be my friend. But my greatest disappointment of all has been with Grimes. Before I came here, I certainly expected to rely upon Grimes more than any other one man in the Senate. I like him very much. He is a great strong fellow. He is a valuable friend, a dangerous enemy. He carries too many guns not to be respected in any point of view. But he got wrong against me, I do not clearly know how, and has always been cool and almost hostile to me. I am glad he has always been the friend of the Navy and generally of the Administration."

Despatches kept coming in all the evening showing a splendid triumph in Indiana, showing steady, small gains all over Pennsylvania, enough to give a fair majority this time on the home vote. Guesses from New York and Albany which boiled down to about the estimated majority against us in the city, 35,000, and left the result in the State still doubtful.

A despatch from Butler was picked up & sent by Sanford, saying that the City had gone 35,000 McC. & the State 40,000. This looked impossible. The State had been carefully canvassed & such a result was impossible except in view of some monstrous and undreamed of frauds. After a while another came from Sanford correcting former one & giving us the 40,000 in the State.

Sanford's despatches all the evening continued most jubilant: especially when he announced that most startling majority of 80,000 in Massachusetts.

General Eaton came in and waited for news with us. I had not before known that he was with us. His denunciations of Seymour were especially hearty and vigorous.

Towards midnight we had supper, provided by Eckert. The President went awkwardly and hospitably to work shoveling out the fried oysters. He was most agreeable and genial all the evening in fact. Fox was abusing the coffee for being so hot—saying quaintly, it kept hot all the way down to the bottom of the cup as a piece of ice staid cold till you finished eating it.

We got later in the evening a scattering despatch from the West, giving us Michigan, one from Fox promising Missouri certainly, but a loss in the first district from that miserable split of Knox & Johnson, one promising Delaware, and one, too good for ready credence, saying Raymond & Dodge & Darling had been elected in New York City.

Capt. Thomas came up with a band about half-past two, and made some music and a small hifalute.

The President answered from the window with rather unusual dignity and effect & we came home.

W. H. L[amon] came to my room to talk over the Chief Justiceship; he goes in for Stanton & thinks, as I am inclined to think, that the President cannot afford to place an enemy in a position so momentous for good or evil.

He took a glass of whiskey and then, refusing my offer of a bed, went out &, rolling himself up in his cloak, lay down at the President's door; passing the night in that attitude of touching and dumb fidelity, with a small arsenal of pistols and bowie knives around him. In the morning he went away leaving my blankets at my door, before I or the President were awake.

> —DENNETT, ed., *Lincoln and the Civil War in the Diaries and Letters of John Hay*

16. LINCOLN REPLIES TO A SERENADE

On November 10, two days after the election, when the returns were in, Lincoln was serenaded at the White House by some enthusiastic countrymen. He took the occasion to make one of the more thoughtful of his short addresses, one which pointed the significance of the election as a commentary on democracy in wartime.

It has long been a grave question whether any government, not too strong for the liberties of its people can be strong enough to maintain its existence in great emergencies. On this point the present rebellion brought our republic to a severe test, and a presidential election occurring in regular course during the rebellion, added not a little to the strain.

If the loyal people united were put to the utmost of their strength by the rebellion, must they not fail when divided and partially paralyzed by a political war among themselves? But the election was a necessity. We cannot have free government without elections; and if the rebellion could force us to forego or postpone a national election, it might fairly claim to have already conquered and ruined us. The strife of the election is but human nature practically applied to the facts of the case. What has occurred in this case must ever recur in similar cases. Human nature will not change. In any future great national trial, compared with the men of this, we shall have as weak and as strong, as silly and as wise, as bad and as good. Let us, therefore, study the incidents of this as philosophy to learn wisdom from, and none of them as wrongs to be revenged. But the election, along with its incidental and undesirable strife, has done good too. It has demonstrated that a people's government can sustain a national election in the midst of a great civil war. Until now, it has not been known to the world that this was a possibility. It shows that, even among candidates of the same party, he who is most devoted to the Union and most opposed to treason can receive most of the people's votes. It shows, also, to the extent yet known, that we have more men now than we had when the war began. Gold is good in its place, but living, brave, patriotic men are better than gold.

But the rebellion continues, and now that the election is over, may not all having a common interest reunite in a common effort to save our common country? For my own part, I have striven and shall strive to avoid placing any obstacle in the way. So long as I have been here I have not willingly planted a thorn in any man's bosom. While I am deeply sensible to the high compliment of a reëlection, and duly grateful, as I trust, to almighty God for having directed my countrymen to a right conclusion, as I think, for their own good, it adds nothing to my satisfaction that any other man may be disappointed or pained by the result.

May I ask those who have not differed with me to join with me in this same spirit toward those who have? And now let me close by asking three hearty cheers for our brave soldiers and seamen and their gallant and skilful commanders.

—*Complete Works of Abraham Lincoln*

17. LINCOLN VISITS THE COLORED SOLDIERS AT CITY POINT

Lincoln got to the army as often as possible, and sometimes to the embarrassment of officers and soldiers alike; Justice Oliver Wendell Holmes once recalled the occasion when he had cried out to the tall, absent-minded President, "Get down, you damn fool," and John Hay tells us of the time when Lincoln waited patiently for McClellan, who had gone up to bed and refused to see him. Probably no visit that Lincoln ever paid to his soldiers was more gratifying than this one that General Porter describes.

On Tuesday, June 21 [1864], a white river-steamer arrived at the wharf, bringing President Lincoln, who had embraced this opportunity to visit for the first time the armies under General Grant's immediate command. As the boat neared the shore, the general and several of us who were with him at the time walked down to the wharf, in order that the general-in-chief might meet his distinguished visitor and extend a greeting to him as soon as the boat made the landing. As our party stepped aboard, the President came down from the upper deck, where he had been standing, to the after-gangway, and reaching out his long, angular arm, he wrung General Grant's hand vigorously, and held it in his for some time, while he uttered in rapid words his congratulations and expressions of appreciation of the great task which had been accomplished since he and the general had parted in Washington.

The group then went into the after-cabin. General Grant said: "I hope you are very well, Mr. President."

"Yes, I am in very good health," Mr. Lincoln replied; "but I don't feel very comfortable after my trip last night on the bay. It was rough, and I was considerably shaken up. My stomach has not yet entirely recovered from the effects."

An officer of the party now saw that an opportunity had arisen to make this scene the supreme moment of his life, in giving him a chance to soothe the digestive organs of the Chief Magistrate of the nation. He said: "Try a glass of champagne, Mr. President. That is always a certain cure for seasickness."

Mr. Lincoln looked at him for a moment, his face lighting up with a smile, and then remarked: "No, my friend; I have seen too many fellows seasick ashore from drinking that very stuff." This was a knockdown for the officer, and in the laugh at his expense Mr. Lincoln and the general both joined heartily.

General Grant now said: "I know it would be a great satisfaction for the troops to have an opportunity of seeing you, Mr. President; and I am sure your presence among them would have a very gratifying effect. I can furnish you a good horse, and will be most happy to escort you to points of interest along the line."

Mr. Lincoln replied: "Why, yes; I had fully intended to go out and take a look at the brave fellows who have fought their way down to Petersburg in this wonderful campaign, and I am ready to start at any time."

General Grant presented to Mr. Lincoln the officers of the staff who were present, and he had for each one a cordial greeting and a pleasant word. There was a kindliness in his tone and a hearty manner of expression which went far to captivate all who met him. The President soon stepped ashore, and after sitting awhile at headquarters mounted the large bay horse "Cincinnati," while the general rode with him on "Jeff Davis." Three of us of the staff accompanied them, and the scenes encountered in visiting Butler's and Meade's commands were most interesting. Mr. Lincoln wore a very high black silk hat and black trousers and frock-coat. Like most men who had been brought up in the West, he had good command of a horse, but it must be acknowledged that in appearance he was not a very dashing rider. On this occasion, by the time he had reached the troops he was completely covered with dust, and the black color of his clothes had changed to Confederate gray. As he had no straps, his trousers gradually worked up above his ankles, and gave him the appearance of a country farmer riding into town wearing his Sunday clothes. A citizen on horseback is always an odd sight in the midst of a uniformed army, and the picture presented by the President bordered upon the grotesque.

However, the troops were so lost in admiration of the man that the humorous aspect did not seem to strike them. The soldiers rapidly passed the word along the line that "Uncle Abe" had joined them, and cheers broke forth from all the commands, and enthusiastic shouts and even words of familiar greeting met him on all sides.

After a while General Grant said: "Mr. President, let us ride on and see the colored troops, who behaved so handsomely in Smith's attack on the works in front of Petersburg last week."

"Oh, yes," replied Mr. Lincoln; "I want to take a look at those boys. I read with the greatest delight the account given in Mr. Dana's despatch to the Secretary of War of how gallantly they behaved. He said they took six out of the sixteen guns captured that day. I was opposed on nearly every side when I first favored the raising of colored regiments; but they have proved their efficiency, and I am glad they have kept pace with the white troops in the recent assaults. When we wanted every able-bodied man who could be spared to go to the front, and my opposers kept objecting to the Negroes,

I used to tell them that at such times it was just as well to be a little color-blind. I think, general, we can say of the black boys what a country fellow who was an old-time abolitionist in Illinois said when he went to a theater in Chicago and saw Forrest playing *Othello*. He was not very well up in Shakspere, and didn't know that the tragedian was a white man who had blacked up for the purpose. After the play was over the folks who had invited him to go to the show wanted to know what he thought of the actors, and he said: 'Wall, layin' aside all sectional prejudices and any partiality I may have for the race, derned ef I don't think the nigger held his own with any on 'em.' " The Western dialect employed in this story was perfect.

The camp of the colored troops of the Eighteenth Corps was soon reached, and a scene now occurred which defies description. They beheld for the first time the liberator of their race—the man who by a stroke of his pen had struck the shackles from the limbs of their fellow-bondmen and proclaimed liberty to the enslaved. Always impressionable, the enthusiasm of the blacks now knew no limits. They cheered, laughed, cried, sang hymns of praise, and shouted in their Negro dialect, "God bless Massa Linkum!" "De Lord save Fader Abraham!" "De day ob jubilee am come, shuah." They crowded about him and fondled his horse; some of them kissed his hands, while others ran off crying in triumph to their comrades that they had touched his clothes. The President rode with bared head; the tears had started to his eyes, and his voice was so broken by emotion that he could scarcely articulate the words of thanks and congratulation which he tried to speak to the humble and devoted men through whose ranks he rode. The scene was affecting in the extreme, and no one could have witnessed it unmoved.

—PORTER, *Campaigning with Grant*

18. "WITH MALICE TOWARD NONE"

Comment on Lincoln's noble second Inaugural Address is as superfluous as comment on his Gettysburg Address. It is, however, relevant to remark that the magnanimous policy which he here suggested for reconstruction was repudiated by Congress during his lifetime and after his death, and that this repudiation embittered sectional relations for half a century.

Fellow countrymen: At this second appearing to take the oath of the presidential office there is less occasion for an extended address than there was at the first. Then a statement somewhat in detail of a course to be pursued seemed fitting and proper. Now, at the expiration of four years, during which public declarations have been constantly called forth on every point and phase of the great contest which still absorbs the attention and engrosses the energies of the nation, little that is new could be presented. The progress of our arms, upon which all else chiefly depends, is as well known to the public as to myself, and it is, I trust, reasonably satisfactory and encouraging to all. With high hope for the future, no prediction in regard to it is ventured.

On the occasion corresponding to this four years ago all thoughts were anxiously directed to an impending civil war. All dreaded it, all sought to avert it. While the inaugural address was being delivered from this place, devoted altogether to *saving* the Union without war, insurgent agents were in the city seeking to *destroy* it without war—seeking to dissolve the Union and divide effects by negotiation. Both parties deprecated war, but one of them would *make* war rather than let the nation survive, and the other would *accept* war rather than let it perish, and the war came.

One eighth of the whole population was colored slaves, not distributed generally over the Union, but localized in the southern part of it. These slaves constituted a peculiar and powerful interest. All knew that this interest was somehow the cause of the war. To strengthen, perpetuate, and extend this interest was the object for which the insurgents would rend the Union even by war, while the government claimed no right to do more than to restrict the territorial enlargement of it. Neither party expected for the war the magnitude or the duration which it has already attained. Neither anticipated that the *cause* of the conflict might cease with or even before the conflict itself should cease. Each looked for an easier triumph and a result less fundamental and astounding. Both read the same Bible and pray to the same God, and each invokes His aid against the other. It may seem strange that any men should dare to ask a just God's assistance in wringing their bread from the sweat of other men's faces, but let us judge not, that we be not judged. The prayers of both could not be answered. That of neither has been answered fully. The Almighty has His own purposes. "Woe unto the world because of offenses; for it must needs be that offenses come, but woe to that man by whom the offense cometh." If we shall suppose that American slavery is one of those offenses which, in the providence of God, must needs come, but which, having continued through His appointed time, He now wills to remove; and that He gives to both North and South this terrible war as the woe due to those by whom the offense came, shall we discern therein any departure from those divine attributes which the believers in a living God always ascribe to Him? Fondly do we hope, fervently do we pray, that this mighty scourge of war may speedily pass away. Yet, if God wills that it continue until all the wealth piled by the bondsman's two hundred and fifty years of unrequited toil shall be sunk, and until every drop of blood drawn with the lash shall be paid by another drawn with the sword, as was said three thousand years ago, so still it must be said, "The judgments of the Lord are true and righteous altogether."

With malice toward none, with charity for all, with firmness in the right as God gives us to see the right, let us strive on to finish the work we are in, to bind up the nation's wounds, to care for him who shall have borne the battle and for his widow and his orphan, to do all which may achieve and cherish a just and lasting peace among ourselves and with all nations.

—LINCOLN, "Second Inaugural Address"

19. ABRAHAM LINCOLN IS ASSASSINATED

Lincoln had gone to Richmond the day after the Confederates had evacuated it—calling, while there, on Mrs. Pickett—and then had returned to Washington in time to make a memorable address on reconstruction. On the evening of April 14 he went to Ford's Theater to see Laura Keene in an English comedy, Our American Cousin. *John Wilkes Booth, brother of the more famous Edwin Booth, had concocted a plot to assassinate all the principal officers of the government; a Southern sympathizer, he thought that this might undo the work of the Union armies and save the South. Entering Lincoln's box he sent a ball through the President's head; then leaped to the stage, shouting,* "Sic semper tyrannis!" *and made good his escape.*

The moving story of Lincoln's death is told by the sorrowing Gideon Welles.

I had retired to bed about half past-ten on the evening of the 14th of April, and was just getting asleep when Mrs. Welles, my wife, said some one was at our door. Sitting up in bed, I heard a voice twice call to John, my son, whose sleeping-room was on the second floor directly over the front entrance. I arose at once and raised a wondow, when my messenger, James Smith, called to me that Mr. Lincoln, the President, had been shot, and said Secretary Seward and his son, Assistant Secretary Frederick Seward, were assasinated. James was much alarmed and excited. I told him his story was very incoherent and improbable, that he was associating men who were not together and liable to attack at the same time. "Where," I inquired, "was the President when shot?" James said he was at Ford's Theatre on 10th Street. "Well," said I, "Secretary Seward is an invalid in bed in his house yonder on 15th Street." James said he had been there, stopped in at the house to make inquiry before alarming me.

I immediately dressed myself, and, against the earnest remonstrance and appeals of my wife, went directly to Mr. Seward's, whose residence was on the east side of the square, mine being on the north. James accompanied me. As we were crossing 15th Street, I saw four or five men in earnest consultation, standing under the lamp on the corner by St. John's Church. Before I had got half across the street, the lamp was suddenly extinguished and the knot of persons rapidly dispersed. For a moment, and but a moment I was disconcerted to find myself in darkness, but recollecting that it was late and about time for the moon to rise, I proceeded on, not having lost five steps, merely making a pause without stopping. Hurrying forward into 15th Street, I found it pretty full of people, especially so near the residence of Secretary Seward, where there were many soldiers as well as citizens already gathered.

Entering the house, I found the lower hall and office full of persons, and among them most of the foreign legations, all anxiously inquiring what truth there was in the horrible rumors afloat. I replied that my object was to ascertain the facts. Proceeding through the hall to the stairs, I found one, and I think two, of the servants there holding the crowd in check. The servants were frightened and appeared relieved to see me. I hastily asked what truth there was in the story that an assassin or assassins had entered the house and assaulted the Secretary. They said it was true, and that Mr. Frederick was also badly injured. They wished me to go up, but no others. . . . As I entered, I met Miss Fanny Seward, with whom I exchanged a single word, and proceeded to the foot of the bed. Dr. Verdi and, I think, two others were there. The bed was saturated with blood. The Secretary was lying on his back, the upper part of his head covered by a cloth, which extended down over his eyes. His mouth was open, the lower jaw dropping down. I exchanged a few whispered words with Dr. V. Secretary Stanton, who came after but almost simultaneously with me, made inquiries in a louder tone till admonished by a word from one of the physicians. We almost immediately withdrew and went into the adjoining front room, where lay Frederick Seward. His eyes were open but he did not move them, nor a limb, nor did he speak. Doctor White, who was in attendance, told me he was unconscious and more dangerously injured than his father.

As we descended the stairs, I asked Stanton what he had heard in regard to the President that was reliable. He said the President was shot at Ford's Theatre, that he had seen a man who was present and witnessed the occurence. I said I would go immediately to the White House. Stanton told me the President was not there but was at the theatre. "Then," said I, "let us go immediately there." . . .

The President had been carried across the street from the theatre, to the house of a Mr. Peterson. We entered by ascending a flight of steps above the basement and passing through a long hall to the rear, where the President lay extended on a bed, breathing heavily. Several surgeons were present, at least six, I should think more. Among them I was glad to observe Dr. Hall, who, however, soon left. I inquired of Dr. H., as I entered, the true condition of the President. He replied the President was dead to all intents, although he might live three hours or perhaps longer.

The giant sufferer lay extended diagonally across the bed, which was not long enough for him. He had been stripped of his clothes. His large arms, which were occasionally exposed, were of a size which one would scarce have expected from his spare appearance. His slow, full respiration lifted the clothes with each breath that he took. His features were calm and striking. I had never seen them appear to better advantage than for the first hour, perhaps, that I was there. After that, his right eye began to swell and that part of his face became discolored.

Senator Sumner was there, I think, when I entered. If not

he came in soon after, as did Speaker Colfax, Mr. Secretary McCulloch, and the other members of the Cabinet, with the exception of Mr. Seward. A double guard was stationed at the door and on the sidewalk, to repress the crowd, which was of course highly excited and anxious. The room was small and overcrowded. The surgeons and members of the Cabinet were as many as should have been in the room, but there were many more, and the hall and other rooms in the front or main house were full. One of these rooms was occupied by Mrs. Lincoln and her attendants, with Miss Harris. Mr. Dixon and Mrs. Kinney came to her about twelve o'clock. About once an hour Mrs. Lincoln would repair to the bedside of her dying husband and with lamentation and tears remain until overcome by emotion.

(April 15.) A door which opened upon a porch or gallery, and also the windows, were kept open for fresh air. The night was dark, cloudy, and damp, and about six it began to rain. I remained in the room until then without sitting or leaving it, when, there being a vacant chair which some one left at the foot of the bed, I occupied it for nearly two hours, listening to the heavy groans, and witnessing the wasting life of the good and great man who was expiring before me.

About 6 A.M. I experienced a feeling of faintness and for the first time after entering the room a little past eleven, I left it and the house, and took a short walk in the open air. It was a dark and gloomy morning, and rain set in before I returned to the house, some fifteen minutes [later]. Large groups of people were gathered every few rods, all anxious and solicitous. Some one or more from each group stepped forward as I passed, to inquire into the condition of the President, and to ask if there was no hope. Intense grief was on every countenance when I replied that the President could survive but a short time. The colored people especially—and there were at this time more of them, perhaps, than of whites —were overwhelmed with grief. . . .

A little before seven, I went into the room where the dying President was rapidly drawing near the closing moments. His wife soon after made her last visit to him. The death-struggle had begun. Robert, his son, stood with several others at the head of the bed. He bore himself well, but on two occasions gave way to overpowering grief and sobbed aloud, turning his head and leaning on the shoulder of Senator Sumner. The respiration of the President became suspended at intervals, and at last entirely ceased at twenty-two minutes past seven. . . .

I went after breakfast to the Executive Mansion. There

was a cheerless cold rain and everything seemed gloomy. On the Avenue in front of the White House were several hundred colored people, mostly women and children, weeping and wailing their loss. This crowd did not appear to diminish through the whole of that cold, wet day; they seemed not to know what was to be their fate since their great benefactor was dead, and their hopeless grief affected me more than almost anything else, though strong and brave men wept when I met them.

—*Diary of Gideon Welles*

XV

The Sunset of the Confederacy

AND so we come to the last chapter of the history of the war, a chapter which none can read without emotion. It is a long and ragged chapter, embracing action in Tennessee, the Carolinas, and Virginia over a period of five months. But it has a coherent pattern—the pattern of Confederate disintegration and collapse.

The closing month of 1864 saw the Confederacy in desperate straits. Sheridan had swept up the Valley, shattering Early's army and closing the door on that storehouse for Lee's army. Thomas destroyed Hood at Nashville, and the pitiful remnants of the once mighty Army of Tennessee were limping into Alabama and Mississippi. Sherman had taken Savannah and turned northward to spread ruin through South Carolina. Grant was hammering at the Petersburg lines, and Lee thrust in vain against the iron ring that the Union commander had forged around him. The blockade, too, was ever tighter. Mobile had fallen in August; Fort Fisher, the last Confederate port, was captured in January. At the beginning of 1865 only two Confederate armies were still in the field as fighting forces: Johnston's forces in the Carolinas, and Lee's Army of Northern Virginia. All through the winter months of 1865 these were decimated by battle, disease, and desertion. With spring came the final blows. Sherman pursued Johnston into North Carolina and shattered him at Bentonville; Sheridan rode down from the Valley to join Grant south of Peters-

burg. Lee abandoned the city he had held for nine grim months, gave up Richmond, and fled along the Appomattox toward the west. It was the end.

In a sense it is true that the Confederacy was not beaten on the battlefield until the very end of the war when, in all theaters of operation, the Union forces held a two-to-one numerical superiority, and enjoyed the inestimable advantage of continuous reinforcement. To this day it is argued that the Confederates succumbed not to the armed might of the North but to other forces. There were enough men to fill the depleted ranks—so it is asserted; there was food enough for the hungry soldiers, and clothing enough in the warehouses; there were arms and munitions sufficient for the needs of the armed forces; there was everything but the will to continue the fight.

But this argument begs the crucial question—why the will to fight had been fatally weakened by 1865? Why did state officials connive with draft evasion? Why did the armies melt away by desertion? Why did the commissary, the transportation system, the economy itself, collapse? A comprehensive answer to these questions would involve a review of the whole war, but a simple answer is not wholly unsatisfactory: these things failed because the Federal armies had overrun most of the South, because they had destroyed so much of the war potential, because they had laid waste the land, killed and wounded the soldiers. The South did not lose because morale was low; morale was low because the South was palpably losing.

The accounts of the collapse of the Confederacy which we include here tell their own story and require little introduction or explanation. What we are witnessing, here, is the working out of the grand strategy that Grant formulated in 1864. Once that strategy had been planned, and backed up with the immense resources available to the North, there was no hope for the South except perhaps in war-weariness and a change of administration in the North. Hood's ambitious attempt to achieve a vast flanking movement against the Union armies was foredoomed to failure; after Atlanta there was nothing left to oppose Sherman; sooner or later the combined armies in Virginia were bound to break Lee's defenses and force him to evacuate Richmond.

Yet to the end two possibilities glimmered in the imaginations of some of the last-ditch Confederates. Lee might have broken away from Petersburg, joined Johnston somewhere in western Virginia or North Carolina, and fought out a last

campaign there. Or Lee and Johnston might have encouraged
their soldiers to make good their escape and wage a long
guerrilla warefare against the invader. Neither possibility
had anything to offer. Even had Lee and Johnston joined
forces there is no likelihood that they could have opposed successfully the combined armies of Sherman and Grant—or, for
that matter, either of them. And guerrilla warfare would
have condemned the South to months and possibly years of
devastating warfare without advancing in any way the cause
of Southern independece.

Lee and Johnston recognized this, and were realistic enough
to know, too, when the end had come. President Davis was
less realistic. As late as April 4 he issued an address to the
people of the Confederacy asserting that "nothing was now
needed to render our triumph certain but the exhibition of
our unquenchable resolve." Even after the surrender of Lee,
Davis wanted to hold out but was dissuaded by Johnston and
Beauregard and by some of his civilian advisers. None can
doubt, now, that these were right in their conclusion that
the verdict of Appomattox was final.

1. THOMAS ANNIHILATES HOOD AT NASHVILLE

It will be remembered that after Atlanta Hood moved into
western Georgia with a view of striking at Sherman's communications. By November Sherman gave up what appeared
to be a futile pursuit, and turned eastward. Hood and Davis
then conceived an ambitious but visionary plan to recover
Tennessee and Kentucky and help Lee in Virginia. Hood was
to strike northward across the Tennessee, destroy Sherman's
communications, advance into Kentucky, and with such recruits as rallied to his banner, move eastward into Virginia.
For this proposed campaign Hood had some 40,000 effectives.

The first part of the operation went according to plan. By
the end of October Hood's army was at Florence, Alabama,
and on November 19 it began its forward movement across
the Tennessee. As yet neither Thomas nor Schofield were
strong enough to oppose Hood, but reinforcements were on
the way. On November 29 Hood caught up with Schofield at
Spring Hill, just south of Franklin; that night while Hood was
asleep Schofield escaped through the Confederate lines to
Franklin where he threw up entrenchments and awaited the

Confederate advance. Hood came up next day, and hurled his divisions against the Union entrenchments in a series of assaults as gallant as those of Gettysburg. He was unable to break Schofield's lines, however, and Franklin proved a costly defeat, Confederate losses running to some 6,000.

After Franklin Schofield withdrew to Nashville, where Thomas was rapidly building up a force strong enough to take the offensive. Hood followed, and on December 2 had his army in position south and east of the city, astride the Franklin Pike and the railroad to Chattanooga. The reinforcements which Grant had arranged for were coming in rapidly, and within a few days Thomas had a force of close to 50,000 men to deal with about half that number under Hood. Grant wanted Thomas to attack at once, but Thomas was, as usual, deliberate; quite rightly he was determined to mount and equip his cavalry before undertaking an offensive which—so he hoped—would require a pursuit. By December 8 Thomas was ready for action; then bad weather intervened and he delayed. Meantime—as General Wilson tells us—Grant had become impatient to the point of ordering Logan to proceed to Nashville to supersede Thomas. On the fourteenth the weather cleared, and Thomas moved out for the kill. Nashville was perhaps the most complete victory of the entire war, for it utterly destroyed Hood's army. Wilson pursued the stricken remnants across the Tennessee; Hood resigned; and the Army of Tennessee was no more.

This account of the battle is by Thomas' brilliant young cavalry commander, General James Wilson.

On December 9, as a result of daily conferences, Thomas ordered me to break camp at Edgefield, to recross the Cumberland with my entire force, and to take position within the defenses of Nashville between the Hillsboro and Harding turnpikes so as to be ready to join in the attack against Hood the next day. But a heavy rain setting in about the time the movement should have begun my orders were countermanded till further notice. Rain, snow, and sleet in abundance followed by intense cold covered the ground that night with such a glare of snow and ice as to render it impossible to move cavalry not especially rough-shod for the occasion. In fact, neither infantry nor cavalry could have made any progress whatever over a battlefield so undulating and broken and so covered with ice and frozen snow as was that which separated our lines from those of the enemy. There cannot be the slightest doubt that the prevailing conditions made it necessary

to suspend operations and were a full justification for every
hour of delay that followed this remarkable storm. It was at
its greatest intensity when Grant telegraphed positive orders
directing Thomas to attack the enemy without further delay,
and it was after it had spent its full force that Thomas, on the
evening of December 10, invited his corps commanders to his
headquarters for the purpose of reciting his orders, making
known his reply, and asking their views as to the action he
had taken entirely on his own responsibility in the emergency
then at hand. . . .

As the others were withdrawing Thomas asked me to remain for further conference, and this I did with great pleasure. As soon as we were alone he said, with much feeling:

"Wilson, the Washington authorities treat me as if I were a
boy. They seem to think me incapable of planning a campaign
or of fighting a battle, but if they will just let me alone till
thawing weather begins and the ground is in condition for
us to move at all I will show them what we can do. I am
sure my plan of operations is correct, and that we shall lick
the enemy, if he only stays to receive our attack." . . .

Everything was astir, breakfast was over, and the cavalry
corps ready to move out by daylight the next morning
[December 15], but, owing to a dense fog which followed the
change in the weather, the cavalry as well as the infantry was
compelled to delay the advance till half past eight, by which
time it had cleared sufficiently to enable each organization to
move against the enemy as directed. In spite, however, of
every precaution, McArthur's division of Smith's corps, instead
of marching to its position on the left by my rear, as
Smith had promised, deliberately crossed my front, thereby delaying not only my advance but the advance of the rest of the
army till nearly ten o'clock. Had the enemy been specially
alert, this unnecessary delay might have greatly deranged
our plan of attack. As it was it cost the entire army an hour
and a half, which, in the short days of December, could ill
be spared, and might have been of inestimable value in our
operations of that afternoon.

Simultaneously with the advance of the infantry, the cavalry
moved out as directed, though Hatch's division was further
delayed after beginning its march by the fact that
McArthur's infantry still blocked its way. Finally having got
a clear road, it advanced rapidly under the cover of a strong
line of skirmishers. Brushing away the enemy's pickets, it soon
encountered Ector's brigade of infantry on the farther side of
Richland Creek, strongly entrenched on commanding ground.

Without a moment's hesitation, Stewart's brigade threw itself headlong against the enemy, broke through his line, and drove him rapidly beyond Harding's House. . . .

Having by this brilliant operation cleared his front and put the enemy's cavalry to flight, Hatch pushed his first brigade by flank rapidly to the left to join his second brigade. This done, the division found itself on the flank of a four-gun battery, posted in a redoubt which formed the left of the enemy's position. Sending his own battery "I," First Illinois Light Artillery, still farther to the right to a position from which it could enfilade the enemy's entrenchments, Hatch threw forward Coon's brigade, dismounted, broke through the enemy's infantry, and captured the redoubt with four guns. Turning the captured guns upon the enemy occupying a

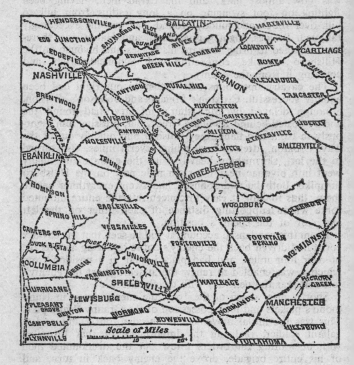

FRANKLIN AND NASHVILLE

higher hill farther on, Hatch promptly threw forward his second brigade, supported by his first, and swept over a second redoubt, capturing four guns and two hundred and fifty prisoners. This operation was conducted in sight of the infantry, which had never seen dismounted cavalry assault a fortified position before. To men less brave and determined than these dismounted horsemen it would have seemed like madness to attack such entrenchments, but armed with magazine carbines the strong line of skirmishers made light of the work before them. In spite of the steep acclivity and of the withering fire both of artillery and musketry, the dismounted cavalrymen swept over the next redoubt and, putting the enemy to flight, captured still another four-gun battery which the enemy abandoned in the valley beyond. It was now almost dark, and the cavalrymen, having been fighting on foot swinging on a long radius from hill to hill, over rough and muddy ground, had become exceedingly fatigued. Besides, night was at hand, and Hatch was, therefore, directed to bring forward his horses and bivouac on the Hillsboro turnpike, connecting with Schofield's right and covering it from the enemy. . . .

The cavalry operations still farther to our right had been equally successful. Croxton's brigade and Johnson's division, although delayed by McArthur's infantry, had found the enemy posted behind Richland Creek, but, pressing him vigorously in front and flank, they brushed him quickly out of the way. Croxton, after following him several miles, also turned to the left, skirmishing heavily with the enemy, and finally went into bivouac near the sixth mile post on the Hillsboro turnpike. Both he and Johnson had swept everything before them, thus making it easy to concentrate the entire mounted force within supporting distance of each other on the left and rear of the enemy's position.

From this condensed account, it will be seen that the cavalry corps had driven back the enemy's entire left wing an average of over four miles, and had placed itself in a position from which it was enabled to renew the attack against the enemy's left and rear the next day with deadly effect. . . .

Shortly after dawn of the 16th, the enemy drove in Hammond's pickets and took possession of the Granny White pike. This was the initial movement of the day, but Hammond, a gallant soldier, realizing the importance of that turnpike, without waiting for orders threw out the dismounted men of his entire brigade, drove the enemy back in turn, and regained firm possession of the turnpike. . . .

But by noon our skirmishers, not less than four thousand in number, had pushed their way slowly through the under-brush and woods up the hills in a curved line from Scho-field's right, across the Granny White pike, to a position parallel with the enemy's line and facing Nashville. There was no longer any uncertainty as to which flank we ought to be on, for all was now going well. Led and directed by their gallant officers, the men of the two divisions, skirmishing heavily, pressed the enemy steadily back from the start at every point.

In the midst of the heaviest fighting, one of our detachments captured a courier from Hood, carrying a dispatch to Chal-mers, directing him "for God's sake to drive the Yankee cavalry from our left and rear or all is lost." Regarding this dispatch as of the first importance, I sent it at once to Thomas without even making a copy of it. Having already informed both Thomas and Schofield by courier of my suc-cess and of the steady progress my troopers were making, I sent three staff officers, one after the other, urging Schofield to attack the enemy in front and finish up the day's work with victory. But nothing whatever was done as yet from the right of the infantry line to support my movement.

Finally, fearing that nothing would be done, and that night would come on again before the enemy could be shaken out of his position, by the efforts of the dismounted cavalry alone, I rode around the enemy's left flank to Thomas's headquarters, which I found on the turnpike about two miles from my own. This was between three and four o'clock, and, as it was a cloudy, rainy day, it was already growing dark. Thomas and Schofield were standing together on the reverse side of a small hill, over the top of which the enemy's line on a still higher elevation could be plainly seen less than a mile away. What was of still more importance was that my dismounted men, with their guidons fluttering in the air, flanked and covered by two batteries of horse artillery, were in plain sight moving against the left and rear of the enemy's line. Shots from their batteries aimed too high but passing over the enemy's heads were falling in front of Schofield's corps. And yet he gave no orders to advance.

Pointing out the favorable condition of affairs, I urged Thomas, with ill-concealed impatience, to order the infantry forward without further delay. Still the stately chieftain was unmoved. Apparently doubting that the situation could be as I represented it, he lifted his field glasses and coolly scanned what I clearly showed him. It was a stirring sight, and, gazing at it, as I thought, with unnecessary deliberation, he finally satisfied himself. Pausing only to ask me if I was sure that the men entering the left of the enemy's works above us were mine, and receiving the assurance that I was dead certain of it, he turned to Schofield and as calmly as if on parade directed him to move to the attack with his entire corps.

Fully realizing that the crisis was now on, I galloped as rapidly as my good gray, Sheridan, could carry me back to my own command, but when I reached its front the enemy had already broken and was in full but disorderly retreat by the only turnpike left in his possession. This was shortly after 4 P.M.

The dismounted troopers had closed in upon the enemy's entrenchments and entered them from the rear before the infantry reached them in front. They had captured fifteen more field guns, thus bringing their score up to twenty-seven for the two days, and had picked up several hundred prisoners. . . . It was now raining heavily, mist was gathering, and dark was closing down like a pall over both victor and vanquished. . . .

Meanwhile, the Confederate commander had committed his final and fatal mistake and had lost out forever. His flank was turned and taken in reverse and his line was irretrievably broken. The most he could hope to do now was to save his army by flight from total destruction and capture. And in this his most potent allies were darkness, rain, snow, sleet, mud, and rising rivers, all of which he was to have in succession for the next two weeks. With the beginning of darkness he was in full retreat along the two turnpikes and we were thundering at his heels.

—WILSON, *Under the Old Flag*

2. "THE LAST CHANCE OF THE CONFEDERACY"

Sherman had entered Savannah on December 21, 1864, and then turned north, through the heart of South Carolina. Against his army of veterans Hardee—now in command of Confederate forces in Georgia and South Carolina—could oppose only delaying actions. Columbia fell on February 18, 1865, and that same day the Confederates evacuated Charleston. By the beginning of March Sherman was into North

*Carolina, moving on Fayetteville and striking toward Raleigh,
the capital of the state.*

*Meantime Grant had decided to open up communications
with Sherman by water, and provide him with a convenient
Atlantic port for a supply base. Wilmington was the last major
port of the Confederacy. It was commanded by Fort Fisher,
and after a desperate struggle Federal amphibious forces captured this fort—and Wilmington—in mid-January. New Bern,
at the mouth of the Neuse River and with direct railroad connections to Goldsboro and Raleigh, was equally important.
Burnside had seized this place in 1862; now Schofield came
on from Tennessee to direct an advance along the Neuse toward Goldsboro and an eventual junction with Sherman
coming up from the south.*

*One of Lee's first acts as commander in chief of the Con-
federate armies had been to restore Joseph Johnston to command of all armies opposing Sherman. Johnston sent Bragg to
hold Schofield and on March 8-10 there was sharp fighting
west of the great Dover Swamp. Bragg retired on Goldsboro,
and Johnston prepared to move out to attack Sherman before
his army and Schofield's could link up. Sherman's Grand Army
of the West was strung out in several columns along many
miles of road, and it was Johnston's plan to strike its van-
guard. The opportunity came at Bentonville on March 19. It
was "the last chance of the Confederacy"—and not a very
good one. Actually even had Johnston succeeded in breaking
Slocum's advance divisions, his position would still have been
hopeless, for Sherman and Schofield together could muster
some 90,000 to his own 35,000.*

*Alexander McClurg, who tells the story of the Battle of
Bentonville, was a Chicago bookdealer who had helped organize the Crosby Guards at the beginning of the war, fought at
Perryville, Chickamauga, and Chattanooga, and marched
with Sherman to the sea and through the Carolinas, as chief
of staff to General J. C. Davis. He later became one of
America's famous booksellers and publishers.*

General Sherman had himself been marching for several
days with the left and exposed wing, and on the night of the
18th his headquarters, as well as those of General Slocum,
who commanded the left wing, had been pitched within the
lines of the Fourteenth Army Corps. On the morning of the
19th . . . when the strains of Old Hundred had ceased,
and the men had had their accustomed breakfast of coffee
and hardtack, varied here and there with a piece of cold

chicken or ham, or a baked sweet potato, foraged from the country, the regiments of the first division—General W. P. Carlin's—of the Fourteenth Corps filed out upon the road, and began the advance. This was about seven o'clock. For the first time almost in weeks, the sun was shining, and there was promise of a beautiful day; and the men strode on vigorously and cheerily.

They found in their front, as they always did, the enemy's cavalry, watching their movements and opposing their advance. But there was of course "nothing but cavalry," and the men pressed on, light-hearted, anticipating the rest they should have at Goldsboro, and then the last march toward Richmond and home. But the cavalry in front were stubborn. They did not yield a foot of ground before it was wrested from them. They were inclined to fight; and the old expression of the Atlanta campaign was brought out for use again: "They don't drive worth a damn." Even the organized parties of foragers, the historical "bummers" of Sherman's army, men who generally made short work of getting through a thin curtain of cavalry, when chickens and pigs and corn and sweet potatoes were on the other side,—even these renowned troopers fell back, dispirited, behind our skirmishers, and lined the roadsides.

At length the whole of the first brigade—General H. C. Hobart's—was deployed and pushed vigorously forward; but still the resistance of the enemy was determined and the advance slow. It began to be evident that they had some reason for this unusual opposition. Ten o'clock came, and we had gained but five miles. General Hobart was hotly engaged. The second brigade—Colonel George P. Buell's—was ordered to make a detour to the left, and take the enemy's line in the flank; but meanwhile our own right flank was becoming exposed to a similar fate, as the enemy overlapped us in that direction, and the third brigade—Lieutenant-Colonel Miles's—was deployed on the right of the first.

Thus the whole of General Carlin's division was now deployed and in line of battle; yet everywhere it found the enemy in front strong and stubborn. The right and left of our line were ordered to advance and develop his strength. They did advance right gallantly, but they soon encountered a strong line of infantry. This was pressed back several hundred yards, after severe fighting; and our men dashed, all unprepared, against a line of earthworks, manned with infantry and strengthened with artillery. The enemy opened upon them such a destructive fire that they were compelled to fall back, with severe loss. Many men and officers and two regimental commanders had fallen, and the whole line was severely shattered; but very important information had been gained. Observations and the reports of prisoners captured left little reason to doubt that General Johnston's whole army was in position in our immediate front, and the persistent fighting of the cavalry had been intended to give time for ample preparation.

It was now about half past one o'clock, and Generals Slocum and Davis were together in consultation, in the woods to the left of the road, when a deserter from the enemy was sent to them by General Carlin. . . . This man told a straight but startling story. It was to the effect that General Johnston's whole army, consisting of over thirty thousand men, had by night marches been concentrated in our immediate front, and was strongly entrenched. He said that General Johnston, accompanied by Generals Hardee and Cheatham and Hoke, had just ridden around among his troops, in the highest spirits, and that he had heard him address a portion of them, telling them that "at last the long-wished-for opportunity had occurred;" that they were "concentrated and in position, while General Sherman's army was scattered over miles of country, separated by almost impassable roads.". . .

The news had come none too soon, for our little command was again preparing to attack. . . . Two divisions and a brigade, with a battery of artillery,—in all, less than ten thousand men,—were face to face with an overwhelming force of the enemy, who had chosen their own ground, strengthened it with field-works, and placed their artillery in position. Confident and prepared, they awaited the order to advance, while we were deceived and surprised.

It was certain that they would lose no time, but attack at once and in overwhelming numbers. Up to this time General Slocum had shared the belief of General Sherman that the force in our front was inconsiderable. He was now thoroughly undeceived, and he went energetically to work to prepare for the most vigorous defensive fighting possible. Every precaution was taken, and the men all along our line were in the act of throwing up hasty field-works, when the attack came upon us like a whirlwind. . . .

Almost immediately I met masses of men slowly and doggedly falling back along the road, and through the fields and open woods on the left of the road. They were retreating, and evidently with good cause; but there was nothing of the panic and rout so often seen on battlefields earlier in the war. They were retreating, but they were not demoralized. Minié-balls were whizzing in every direction, although I was then far from the front line as I had left it only a short time before. Pushing on through these retreating men, and down the road, I met two pieces of artillery,—a section of the 19th Indiana battery,— and was dashing past it, when the lieutenant in command called out, "For Heaven's sake, don't go down there! I am the last man of the command. Everything is gone in front of you. The lieutenant commanding my battery and most of the men and horses are killed, and four guns are captured. These two guns are all we have left."

Checking my horse, I saw the rebel regiments in front in full view, stretching through the fields to the left as far as the eye could reach, advancing rapidly, and firing as they came. Everything seemed hopeless on our centre and left; but in the swampy woods on the right of the road our line seemed still to be holding its position. An overwhelming force had struck Carlin's entire division and Robinson's brigade, and was driving them off the field. The onward sweep of the rebel lines was like the waves of the ocean, resistless. . . . General Morgan's division, on the right, had also been heavily assailed; but it was better situated, and not being at this time out-flanked, it held its position.

One of Morgan's brigades,—that of General Fearing,—being in reserve, had not been engaged. When the left first began to give way, General Davis sent Colonel Litchfield to Fearing, with instructions to hold his brigade in readiness to march in any direction. A few moments later, when the left was falling back, and the rebel line was sweeping after them in hot pursuit, General Davis came plunging through the swamp on his fiery white mare toward the reserve. "Where is that brigade, Litchfield?"

"Here it is, sir, ready to march." It was in column of regiments, faced to the front.

Ordering it swung around to the left, General Davis shouted, "Advance upon their flanks, Fearing! Deploy as you go! Strike them wherever you find them! Give them the best you've got, and we'll whip them yet!" All this was uttered with an emphasis and fire known only upon the field of battle.

The men caught up the closing words, and shouted back, "Hurrah for old Jeff! We'll whip 'em yet!" as they swung off through the woods at a rattling pace. Officers and men, from General Fearing down, were alike inspired with the spirit of their commander, and "We'll whip them yet!" might well be considered their battle-cry. They struck the successful enemy with resistless impetuosity, and were quickly engaged in a desperate conflict. Upon this movement, in all probability, turned the fortunes of the day. It was the right thing, done at the right time.

Seeing at once that, as Fearing advanced, his right flank must in turn become exposed, General Davis sent to General Slocum, begging for another brigade to move in upon Fearing's right and support him. Fortunately, Coggswell's fine brigade of the Twentieth Corps arrived not long after upon the field, and it was ordered to report to General Davis for that purpose. . . . It was splendidly done. The men of these two brigades—Fearing's and Coggswell's—seemed to divine that upon them had devolved the desperate honor of stemming the tide of defeat, and turning it into victory; and magnificently they responded. Finer spirit and enthusiasm could not be shown by troops, and it is no wonder that, after a fierce and bloody contest, the flushed and victorious troops of the enemy, thus taken in the flank, gave way, and in their turn fell back in confusion. So stunned and bewildered were they by this sudden and unexpected attack that their whole line withdrew from all the ground they had gained, and apparently reëntered their works.

And now there was a lull along the whole front, which gave invaluable time for the re-formation of our shattered lines. . . .

To the surprise of every one, a full hour was allowed by the enemy for these new dispositions; and it was about five o'clock before their long line was again seen emerging from the pine woods and swampy thickets in front, and sweeping across the open fields. As soon as they appeared, our artillery opened upon them with most destructive effect. Still they pressed gallantly on, but only to be met with a well-delivered fire from our infantry, securely posted behind hastily improvised field-works, such as our troops were then well skilled in throwing up in a very brief time, and of which they had dearly learned the value. Attack after attack was gallantly met and repulsed, and the golden opportunity of the enemy upon our left was lost. . . .

Morgan's whole division was now stretched out over such an extent of ground that all his troops were in the front line, and he had no men left for a second line or a reserve. As all old troops were wont to do at that time, when in the presence of the enemy, they had at once fallen to build such field-works as could be hastily thrown up with rails and light timber. As one of their officers expressed it, they had often attacked works, but they had rarely had the pleasure of fighting behind them themselves, and they rather enjoyed the prospect. They were there, and they meant to stay. Their skirmishers were heavily engaged from the time they took position, and they found the enemy in front in force, and shielded by well-constructed works. They were fighting more or less severely until about half-past four o'clock in the afternoon, when the enemy attempted to carry their position by assault. The charge was desperate and persistent, and the roar of musketry, as it rolled up from that low wood, was incessant. For half an hour it continued, and the commander of the corps, General Davis, sat uneasily on his horse, a short distance in the rear, and listened to it. . . .

After a while, a slight cessation was noticed in the firing; and by direction of General Davis, I rode forward toward the line to ascertain definitely how matters stood. The ground was swampy, and here and there were openings through the trees, while generally bushes and thickets obstructed the view. I had gone but a few rods, when I caught a glimpse through a vista, obliquely to the left, of a column of men moving to the right, straight across my path and directly in the rear of our line, though out of sight of it. They looked like rebels, and my sharp-sighted orderly, Batterson, said they were "rebs;" but the view was obscured by smoke, and the idea that the enemy could be in that position was preposterous. I hesitated but a moment, and pressed on. A hundred yards further through the bushes, and I broke out suddenly into a large, nearly circular, open space, containing perhaps half an acre. Here the view was not a cheerful one. On the opposite side of the opening, at perhaps twenty-five yards' distance, was a body of unmistakably rebel troops, marching by the flank in column of fours, toward the right. Beyond the column, under a wide-spreading tree, dismounted, stood a group of Confederate officers, whose appearance and uniforms indicated high rank. . . .

Mitchell's brigade had already discovered the intruders in their rear, who at first were thought by them to be reinforcements. . . . Fortunately, all was now quiet in front, and General Morgan quickly got his men to the reverse of their own works. In other words, they were now in front of their works, and prepared to sustain an attack from the rear. . . .

The enemy attacked vigorously, but instead of taking Morgan by surprise, he found him ready. Again the struggle was sharp and bloody, but brief. Nothing could stand that day before the veterans of the old second division. Truly they were enjoying the novelty of fighting behind works. Hardee was repulsed, with severe loss. . . .

Considering the great disaster which was imminent, and which was averted, it is not too much to claim for this engagement that it was one of the most decisive of the lesser battles of the war. When Johnston, with skillful strategy, and with wonderful celerity and secrecy, massed his scattered troops near the little hamlet of Bentonsville, and placed them, unknown to his great adversary, in a strong position directly across the road upon which two "light divisions," as he expressed it, were marching, he proposed to himself nothing less than to sweep these two divisions from the field, in the first furious onset; and then, hurrying on with flushed and victorious troops, to attack, in deep column and undeployed, the two divisions of the Twentieth Corps, which, through heavy and miry roads, would be hastening to the assistance of their comrades. These divisions he expected to crush easily, while General Sherman and the right wing were many miles from the field. Then, with half his army destroyed, with supplies exhausted, and far from any base, he believed General Sherman and his right wing only would no longer be a match for his elated and eager troops.

Never before, in all the long struggle, had fortune and circumstance so united to favor him, and never before had hope shone so brightly. If Sherman's army were destroyed, the Confederacy would be inspired with new spirit, and ultimate success would be at last probable. Doubtless such dreams as these flitted through General Johnston's mind on that Sunday morning, when his well-laid plans seemed so sure of execution. With what a sad and heavy heart he turned at night from the hard-fought field, realizing that the last great opportunity was lost, we can only imagine. As the sun went down that night, it undoubtedly carried with it, in the mind of General Johnston, at least, the last hopes of the Southern Confederacy.

—McClurg, "The Last Chance of the Confederacy"

3. "NOW RICHMOND ROCKED IN HER HIGH TOWERS TO WATCH THE IMPENDING ISSUE"

With the failure of the attack on Fort Stedman Lee's position became critical. On March 26 he notified President

*Davis that Richmond must be abandoned. He himself could
not give up Petersburg at once; it took time to collect supplies
for an army on the move, and to make the necessary dispositions. Yet every hour that he stayed on in the trenches of
Petersburg the situation became more dangerous. Already
Grant had issued orders for a general assault on the twenty-
ninth; already Sheridan had come on from the Valley to the
north bank of the James; already Lincoln and Sherman had
arrived at City Point to witness the grand climax of the campaign and plan for armistice and peace.*

*By the end of March Grant had pushed his lines across the
Weldon Railroad and the Quaker road and along the White
Oak road toward Five Forks. On the twenty-ninth Lee struck
at the Federals at Gravelly Run, but failed to break through.
If the Federal line extended farther west, it could curve northward and cut off Lee's retreat along the Appomattox. This
was precisely what Grant was planning. On the twenty-ninth
Grant sent Sheridan to Five Forks via Dinwiddie Court House,
and Lee started Fitzhugh Lee and Pickett after him. Pickett
and Fitz Lee entrenched at Five Forks; then the two generals
went off to a shad bake. At four in the afternoon of April 1
Sheridan struck. It was the greatest disaster that the Army of
Northern Virginia ever knew; it was the Waterloo of the Confederacy.*

*George Alfred Townsend, with whose remarkable liter-
ary talents we are already familiar, is once again our historian.*

We must start with the supposition that our own men far
outnumbered the Rebels. The latter were widely separated
from their comrades before Petersburg, and the adjustment of
our infantry as well as the great movable force at Sheridan's
disposal, renders it doubtful that they could have returned.
At any rate they did not do so, whether from choice or necessity, and it was a part of our scheme to push them back into
their entrenchments. This work was delegated to the cavalry
entirely, but, as I have said before, mounted carbineers, are
no match for stubborn, bayoneted infantry. So when the
horsemen were close up to the Rebels, they were dismounted,
and acted as infantry to all intents. A portion of them, under
Gregg and Mackenzie, still adhered to the saddle, that they
might be put in rapid motion for flanking and charging purposes; but fully five thousand indurated men, who had seen
service in the Shenandoah and elsewhere, were formed in
line of battle on foot, and by charge and deploy essayed the

difficult work of pressing back the entire Rebel column. This they were to do so evenly and ingeniously, that the Rebels should go no farther than their works, either to escape eastward or to discover the whereabouts of Warren's forces, which were already forming. Had they espied the latter they might have become so discouraged as to break and take to the woods; and Sheridan's object was to capture them as well as to rout them. So, all the afternoon, the cavalry pushed them hard, and the strife went on uninterruptedly and terrifically. . . .

A colonel with a shattered regiment came down upon us in a charge. The bayonets were fixed; the men came on with a yell; their gray uniforms seemed black amidst the smoke; their preserved colors, torn by grape and ball, waved yet defiantly; twice they halted, and poured in volleys, but came on again like the surge from the fog, depleted, but determined; yet, in the hot faces of the carbineers, they read a purpose as resolute, but more calm, and, while they pressed along, swept all the while by scathing volleys, a group of horsemen took them in flank. It was an awful instant; the horses recoiled; the charging column trembled like a single thing, but at once the Rebels, with rare organization, fell into a hollow square, and with solid sheets of steel defied our centaurs. The horsemen rode around them in vain; no charge could break the shining squares, until our dismounted carbineers poured in their volleys afresh, making gaps in the spent ranks, and then in their wavering time the cavalry thundered down. The Rebels could stand no more; they reeled and swayed, and fell back broken and beaten. And on the ground their colonel lay, sealing his devotion with his life.

Through wood and brake and swamp, across field and trench, we pushed the fighting defenders steadily. For a part of the time, Sheridan himself was there, short and broad, and active, waving his hat, giving orders, seldom out of fire, but never stationary, and close by fell the long yellow locks of Custer, sabre extended, fighting like a Viking, though he was worn and haggard with much work. At four o'clock the Rebels were behind their wooden walls at Five Forks, and still the cavalry pressed them hard, in feint rather than solemn effort, while a battalion dismounted, charged squarely upon the face of their breastworks which lay in the main on the north side of the White Oak road. Then, while the cavalry worked round toward the rear, the infantry of Warren, though commanded by Sheridan, prepared to take part in the battle.

The genius of Sheridan's movement lay in his disposition of

the infantry. The skill with which he arranged it, and the
difficult manœuvres he projected and so well executed, should
place him as high in infantry tactics as he has heretofore
shown himself superior in cavalry. The infantry which had
marched at 2½ P.M. from the house of Boisseau, on the
Boydtown plank-road, was drawn up in four battle lines, a
mile or more in length, and in the beginning facing the
White Oak road obliquely; the left or pivot was the division
of General Ayres, Crawford had the center and Griffin the
right. These advanced from the Boydtown plank-road, at ten
o'clock, while Sheridan was thundering away with the cavalry,
mounted and dismounted, and deluding the Rebels with the
idea that he was the sole attacking party; they lay concealed
in the woods behind the Gravelly Run meeting-house, but their
left was not a half-mile distant from the Rebel works, though
their right reached so far off that a novice would have criticized the position sharply. Little by little, Sheridan, extending
his lines, drove the whole Rebel force into their breastworks;
then he dismounted the mass of his cavalry and charged the
works straight in the front, still thundering on their flank. At
last, every Rebel was safe behind his intrenchments. Then the
signal was given, and the concealed infantry, many thousand
strong, sprang up and advanced by echelon to the right.
Imagine a great barndoor shutting to, and you have the
movement, if you can also imagine the door itself, hinge
and all, moving forward also. This was the door:—

AYRES—CRAWFORD—GRIFFIN.

Stick a pin through Ayres and turn Griffin and Crawford
forward as you would a spoke in a wheel, but move your
pin up also a very little. In this way Ayres will advance, say
half a mile, and Griffin, to describe a quarter revolution, will
move through a radius of four miles. But to complicate this
movement by echelon, we must imagine the right when half
was advanced cutting across the centre and reforming, while
Crawford became the right and Griffin the middle of the line
of battle. Warren was with Crawford on this march. Gregory commanded the skirmishers. Ayres was so close to the
Rebel left that he might be said to hinge upon it; and at 6
o'clock the whole corps column came crash upon the full
flank of the astonished Rebels. Now came the pitch of the
battle.

We were already on the Rebel right in force, and thinly
in their rear. Our carbineers were making feint to charge

in direct front, and our infantry, four deep, hemmed in their entire left. All this they did not for an instant note, so thorough was their confusion; but seeing it directly, they, so far from giving up, concentrated all their energy and fought like fiends. They had a battery in position, which belched incessantly, and over the breastworks their musketry made one unbroken roll, while against Sheridan's prowlers on their left, by skirmish and sortie, they stuck to their sinking fortunes, so as to win unwilling applause from mouths of wisest censure.

It was just at the coming up of the infantry that Sheridan's little band was pushed the hardest. At one time, indeed, they seemed about to undergo extermination; not that they wavered, but that they were so vastly overpowered. It will remain to the latest time a matter of marvel that so paltry a cavalry force could press back sixteen thousand infantry; but when the infantry blew like a great barndoor—the simile best applicable—upon the enemy's left, the victory that was to come had passed the region of strategy and resolved to an affair of personal courage. We had met the enemy; were they to be ours? To expedite this consummation every officer fought as if he were the forlorn hope. Mounted on his black pony, the same which he rode at Winchester, Sheridan galloped everywhere, his flushed face all the redder, and his plethoric, but nervous figure all the more ubiquitous. He galloped once straight down the Rebel front, with but a handful of his staff. A dozen bullets whistled for him together; one grazed his arm, at which a faithful orderly rode; the black pony leaped high, in fright, and Sheridan was untouched, but the orderly lay dead in the field, and the saddle dashed afar empty. . . .

The fight, as we closed upon the Rebels, was singularly free from great losses on our side, though desperate as any contest ever fought on the continent. One prolonged roar of rifle shook the afternoon; we carried no artillery, and the Rebel battery, until its capture, raked us like an irrepressible demon, and at every foot of the entrenchments a true man fought both in front and behind. The birds of the forest fled afar; the smoke ascended to heaven; locked in so mad a frenzy, none saw the sequel of the closing day. Now Richmond rocked in her high towers to watch the impending issue, but soon the day began to look gray, and a pale moon came tremulously out to watch the meeting squadrons. Imagine along a line of a full mile, thirty thousand men struggling for life and prestige; the woods gathering about them —but yesterday the home of hermit hawks and chipmonks—

now ablaze with bursting shells, and showing in the dusk the curl of flames in the tangled grass, and, rising up the boles of the pine trees, the scaling, scorching tongues. Seven hours this terrible spectacle had been enacted, but the finale of it had almost come.

It was by all account in this hour of victory when the modest and brave General Winthrop of the first brigade, Ayres division, was mortally wounded. He was riding along the breastworks, and in the act as I am assured, of saving a friend's life, was shot through to the left lung. He fell at once, and his men, who loved him, gathered around and took him tenderly to the rear, where he died before the stretcher on which he lay could be deposited beside the meeting-house door. On the way from the field to the hospital he wandered in mind at times, crying out, "Captain Weaver how is that line? Has the attack succeeded?" . . .

At seven o'clock the Rebels came to the conclusion that they were outflanked and whipped. They had been so busily engaged that they were a long time finding out how desperate were their circumstances; but now, wearied with persistent assaults in front, they fell back to the left, only to see four close lines of battle waiting to drive them across the field, decimated. At the right the horsemen charged them in their vain attempt to fight "out," and in the rear straggling foot and cavalry began also to assemble; slant fire, cross fire, and direct fire, by file and volley rolled in perpetually, cutting down their bravest officers and strewing the fields with bleeding men; groans resounded in the intervals of exploding powder, and to add to their terror and despair, their own artillery, captured from them, threw into their own ranks, from its old position, ungrateful grape and canister, enfilading their breastworks, whizzing and plunging by air line and ricochet, and at last bodies of cavalry fairly mounted their intrenchments, and charged down the parapet, slashing and trampling them, and producing inexplicable confusion. They had no commanders, at least no orders, and looked in vain for some guiding hand to lead them out of a toil into which they had fallen so bravely and so blindly. A few more volleys, a new and irresistible charge, a shrill and warning command to die or surrender, and, with a sullen and tearful impulse, five thousand muskets are flung upon the ground, and five thousand hot, exhausted, and impotent men are Sheridan's prisoners of war.

—TOWNSEND, *Campaigns of a Non-Combatant*

4. "THE MOST SUPERB SOLDIER IN ALL THE WORLD" FALLS AT FIVE FORKS

One by one, in that last bitter year, the Army of Northern Virginia was losing its most dashing leaders. Jeb Stuart had fallen at Yellow Tavern, Robert Rodes at Winchester, Stephen Ramseur at Cedar Creek, General John Pegram, one of the youngest and most brilliant of brigadiers, in the fighting at Petersburg. A. P. Hill, to whom both Jackson and Lee called on their deathbeds, fell the day after Five Forks. One of the most heartbreaking of the losses of Five Forks was that of young William Pegram, the "boy" colonel of artillery—he was just twenty-three—who was admired and beloved as Pelham and Stuart and Ramseur had been.

The tragic event is here recorded by Pegram's adjutant, Gordon McCabe; after the war McCabe became one of the nation's great schoolmasters.

April 1st [1865]. Had nothing to eat, so parched some corn taken from horses' feed. Henry Lee, an old University friend of ours and Ass't Adj't. Gen'l Payne's Brigade, afterwards sent us some meat and bread. At 10 o'clk. we put 3 guns, 1 of Ellett's and Early's section, in position in the centre, and Ellett's other 3 on the right commanding a field. Soon afterwards the enemy's cavalry appeared in front of our right at the distance of 800 yds. We could plainly see them and their pennons flying in the wind. We opened at once with our guns. I told one of the gunners to fire on their colours, on which they were forming. He made a splendid shot, bursting a shell just in front of the colours. The whole line fell back into the woods, but their skirmishers occupied the yard of the Gillem House, and we continued to give them an occasional shot. Skirmishing now broke out in the centre and Col. P[egram] and myself rode down to our guns there. The skirmishing was quite heavy, and Col. ordered Lt. Early to dismount, but he wouldn't, so I wouldn't. We fired a few rounds and the skirmishing soon died out. Col. and myself went back to the right, where we expected the attack to be made. We lay down at the foot of a tree, as everything was now quiet, and he soon fell asleep.

At about 4½ the enemy attacked him, and we mounted and rode rapidly to the centre. When we reached our guns the enemy were only 30 yds. from them, and the infantry fire terrific beyond anything I have ever seen. We were the only mounted officers at that point. The officers, Lts. Hollis and Early, were as cool as on parade, and the men were serving their guns with a precision and rapidity beyond all praise. Pickett's Divn. were fighting well too. We had not been in the battery very long, when Col. P. riding between Lt. Early's guns reeled out of his saddle, shot through his left arm and left side. He cried out, 'Oh, Gordon, I'm mortally wounded, take me off the field.' His last order was, 'Fire your canister low.' I put him on a stretcher and sent him to the rear, and then went back among the guns to give the order. I ran back to the stretcher, and he took my hand and gave me a message for his mother and sisters. He begged me to remain with him, wh. I intended anyhow to do. When I got him to the ambulance, our skirmishers were falling back, square in our rear, and a line of battle pressing them. We were now completely enveloped, our left having been turned and the enemy in our rear. Our guns were carried within 3 minutes, Lt. Early killed and Lt. Hollis captured and the whole line rolled up.

The rout now became general, with the exception of Corse's Brigade, which had not been heavily engaged. This brigade opened to the right and left and let the rout pass through, and then closed up and came off with their integrity of organization unimpaired. I took Col. in my arms and made the ambulance drive between 2 parallel lines-of-battle of the enemy for 4 or 5 hundred yds. I carried him to Ford's Depot on S. S. R. R. about 10 miles from the field. While in the ambulance we prayed together and he was perfectly resigned to die. At about 10 o'clk we reached Ford's and I obtained a bed for him at a Mr Pegram's. I had given him morphine in small quantities until he was easier, and he soon fell into a doze. The enemy advanced on the place about 12 o'clk, and I was left alone with him. I sent off our sabres, horses, spurs, etc. as I felt sure that we w'd be captured. I shall never forget that night of watching. I could only pray. He breathed heavily through the night, and passed into a stupor. I bound up his wounds as well as I knew how and moistened his lips with water. At about Sunday morning April 2nd, he died as gently as possible.

Thus died the truest Christian, the most faithful friend and the most superb soldier in all the world. He was, indeed, my Jonathon, pure in heart, brave in deed, chivalric until it bordered on Quixotism, generous and utterly unselfish, he was the Havelock of the Army of Northern Virginia. I laid him

out, helped to dig his grave, buried him in a blanket, and then
read the Episcopal service over him.

—GORDON, *Memories and Memorials of William Gordon
McCabe*

5. THE CONFEDERATES ABANDON RICHMOND

*After Five Forks the abandonment of Richmond was inev-
itable. To give President Davis time to move government
offices and archives Lee clung to his lines at Petersburg for another day. Early on the morning of April 2 Grant assaulted the
Confederate lines, carrying the first line of entrenchments. Lee
retired to the suburbs of the city; Grant attacked and carried
Forts Gregg and Whitworth—the last strongholds. A final assault was planned for the morning of the third, but that night
Lee's army slipped away and began the race to the west. Meantime the Confederate government had evacuated Richmond;
on the morning of the third the capital was formally surrendered to General Weitzel, and Federal troops moved in to
restore order and put out the flames that were threatening
to destroy the city.*

*We have here two descriptions of the evacuation of Rich-
mond and its occupation by the Federals. The first* comes
from the brilliant Constance Cary, later Mrs. Burton Harrison,
whose husband was private secretary to President Davis. The
second account is by a Yankee—Lieutenant R. B. Prescott,
who was one of the first of the conquerors to enter the
stricken city.*

A. "A GREAT BURST OF SOBBING ALL OVER THE CHURCH"

GRACE STREET, RICHMOND, *April 4, 1865*
MY PRECIOUS MOTHER AND BROTHER:

I write you this jointly, because I can have no idea where
Clarence is. Can't you imagine with what a heavy heart I begin
it—? The last two days have added long years to my life.
I have cried until no more tears will come, and my heart throbs
to bursting night and day. When I bade you good-bye, dear,

* Reprinted from *Recollections Grave and Gay* by Mrs. Burton Harrison; copyright 1911 by Charles Scribner's Sons, 1939 by Fairfax
Harrison; used by permission of the publishers.

and walked home alone, I could not trust myself to give another look after you. All that evening the air was full of farewells as if to the dead. Hardly anybody went to bed. We walked through the streets like lost spirits till nearly daybreak. My dearest mother, it is a special Providence that has spared you this! Your going to nurse poor Bert at this crisis has saved you a shock I never can forget. With the din of the enemy's wagon trains, bands, trampling horses, fifes, hurrahs and cannon ever in my ears, I can hardly write coherently. As you desired, in case of trouble, I left our quarters and came over here to be under my uncle's wing. In Aunt M.'s serious illness the house is overflowing; there was not a room or a bed to give me, but that made no difference, they insisted on my staying all the same. Up under the roof there was a lumber-room with two windows and I paid an old darkey with some wrecks of food left from our housekeeping, to clear it out, and scrub floor and walls and windows, till all was absolutely clean. A cot was found and some old chairs and tables—our own bed linen was brought over, and here I write in comparative comfort, so don't bother about me!

Hardly had I seemed to have dropped upon my bed that dreadful Sunday night—or morning rather—when I was wakened suddenly by four terrific explosions, one after the other, making the windows of my garret shake. It was the blowing up, by Admiral Semmes, by order of the Secretary of the Navy, of our gunboats on the James, the signal for an all-day carnival of thundering noise and flames. Soon the fire spread, shells in the burning arsenals began to explode, and a smoke arose that shrouded the whole town, shutting out every vestige of blue sky and April sunshine. Flakes of fire fell around us, glass was shattered, and chimneys fell, even so far as Grace Street from the scene. . . .

Edith and I . . . set out for the Capital Square, taking our courage in both hands. Looking down from the upper end of the square, we saw a huge wall of fire blocking out the horizon. In a few hours no trace was left of Main, Cary, and Canal Streets, from 8th to 18th Streets, except tottering walls and smouldering ruins. The War Department was sending up jets of flame. Along the middle of the streets smouldered a long pile, like street-sweepings, of papers torn from the different departments' archives of our beloved Government, from which soldiers in blue were picking out letters and documents that caught their fancy. The Custom House was the sole building that defied the fire amongst those environing the Square. The marble Statesman on the Monument looked upon queer doings that day, inside the enclosure from which all green was soon scorched out, or trampled down by the hoofs of cavalry horses picketted at intervals about it. Mr. Reed's Church, Mrs. Stanard's house, the Prestons' house, are all burned; luckily the Lee house and that side of Franklin stand uninjured. General Lee's house has a guard camped in the front yard.

We went on to the head-quarters of the Yankee General in charge of Richmond, that day of doom, and I must say were treated with perfect courtesy and consideration. We saw many people we knew on the same errand as ourselves. We heard stately Mrs.——and the——'s were there to ask for food, as their families were starving. Thank God, we have not fallen to that! Certainly, her face looked like a tragic mask carved out of stone.

A courteous young lieutenant . . . was sent to pilot us out of the confusion, and identify the house, over which a guard was immediately placed. Already the town wore the aspect of one in the Middle Ages smitten by pestilence. The streets filled with smoke and flying fire were empty of the respectable class of inhabitants, the doors and shutters of every house tight closed. . . .

The ending of the first day of occupation was truly horrible. Some Negroes of the lowest grade, their heads turned by the prospect of wealth and equality, together with a mob of miserable poor whites, drank themselves mad with liquor scooped from the gutters. Reinforced, it was said, by convicts escaped from the penitentiary, they tore through the streets, carrying loot from the burnt district. (For days after, even the kitchens and cabins of the better class of darkies displayed handsome oil paintings and mirrors, rolls of stuff, rare books, and barrels of sugar and whiskey.) One gang of drunken rioters dragged coffins sacked from undertakers, filled with spoils from the speculators' shops, howling so madly one expected to hear them break into the Carmagnole. Thanks to our trim Yankee guard in the basement, we felt safe enough, but the experience was not pleasant.

Through all this strain of anguish ran like a gleam of gold the mad vain hope that Lee would yet make a stand somewhere—that Lee's dear soldiers would give us back our liberty.

Dr. Minnegerode has been allowed to continue his daily services and I never knew anything more painful and touching than that of this morning when the Litany was *sobbed out* by the whole congregation.

, A service we went to the same evening of the old Monumental I never shall forget. When the rector prayed for 'the
sick and wounded soldiers and all in distress of mind or body,'
there was a brief pause, filled with a sound of weeping all
over the church. He then gave out the hymn: 'When gathering clouds around I view.' There was no organ and a voice
that started the hymn broke down in tears. Another took it
up, and failed likewise. I, then, with a tremendous struggle
for self-control, stood up in the corner of the pew and sang
alone. At the words, 'Thou Saviour see'st the tears I shed,'
there was again a great burst of crying and sobbing all over
the church. I wanted to break down dreadfully, but I held on
and carried the hymn to the end. As we left the church, many
people came up and squeezed my hand and tried to speak,
but could not. Just then a splendid military band was passing,
the like of which we had not heard in years. The great swell
of its triumphant music seemed to mock the shabby broken-
spirited congregation defiling out of the gray old church
buried in shadows, where in early Richmond days a theatre
with many well-known citizens was burned! That was one of
the tremendous moments of feeling I experienced that week.
  —HARRISON, *Recollections Grave and Gay*

B. "THE POOR COLORED PEOPLE THANKED GOD THAT THEIR SUFFERINGS WERE ENDED"

Every moment the light we had seen over Richmond on
starting became more and more brilliant. Above it hung great
clouds of heavy smoke, and as we drew nearer there arose a
confused murmur now swelling into a loud roar and then
subsiding, and again swelling into a great tumult of excited
voices, while at frequent intervals short, sharp explosions were
heard as of the discharge of field artillery. Weary, breathless,
hungry, begrimed with dust and perspiration, but eager and
excited, we pushed on, and at half-past six o'clock in the
morning I stood with about two-thirds of my men on the
summit of a hill and looked down upon the grandest and
most appalling sight that my eyes ever beheld. Richmond was
literally a sea of flame, out of which the church steeples
could be seen protruding here and there, while over all hung
a canopy of dense black smoke, lighted up now and then
by the bursting shells from the numerous arsenals scattered
throughout the city. I waited here until the stragglers of my
command had come up, then marched down the hill until we
came to a little creek, crossed by a few planks which alone

separated us from the city. Two mounted cavalry-men stood upon this bridge who said that they had been sent there by General Weitzel with orders to allow no one to cross the bridge until he came up. So there was nothing to do but to wait.

The men stacked arms and threw themselves upon the ground. While resting, a rebel iron-clad lying in the James River in full sight blew up with a terrific crash, scattering fragments of iron and timbers all about us, but fortunately no one was hurt. In a few moments more a carriage appeared coming from the city, and stopped directly before us. Beckoning me to approach, the occupant asked if I was in command of the men lying about, and on being answered in the affirmative, he said that he was the mayor of Richmond, and that he wished to make a formal surrender of the city. At the same time he placed in my hands a large package, containing, I presume, official papers, the city seal, keys and other property. I told him that General Weitzel, commanding the department, would be present in a short time and that he would be a proper person to treat with. Even while we were speaking the general and his staff appeared at the top of the hill, and the mayor rode forward to meet him. The whole party shortly returned, and General Weitzel ordered me to follow him into the city.

This I did, but we had not advanced many rods before the smoke became so thick as to make it impossible to see even a few feet in advance, and for this reason, I suppose, I missed the general, he turning to the right towards the upper part of the city, and I to the left towards the river. We had not gone far before I discovered that I had become separated from him and was uncertain how to proceed, when on a lamp-post at a corner I read the words, "Main Street." Thinking this would at least conduct us to the central part of the city and assist in finding the capitol grounds, I turned into it.

The scene that met our eyes here almost baffles description. Pandemonium reigned supreme. Two large iron-clads near by in the river exploded with a deafening crash, the concussion sweeping numbers of people off their feet. The street we were in was one compact mass of frenzied people, and it was only with the greatest difficulty that we were able to force our way along. Had they been hostile our lives would not have been worth a moment's purchase.

But the poor colored people hailed our appearance with the most extravagant expression of joy. They crowded into the ranks and besought permission to carry the soldiers' knap-sacks and muskets. They clapped them on the back, hung about their necks, and "God bless you," and "Thank God, the Yankees have come," resounded on every side. Women, emaciated, barefoot, with but one scanty skirt made from old bags, fell on their knees in the street, and with clasped hands and streaming eyes thanked God that their sufferings were ended at last. Others with little children, wretched little skeletons, clinging to their scanty skirts and crying with hunger and fright, pressed into the ranks and begged most piteously for food. One woman, I distinctly remember, with three little pale, starved girls clinging about her, herself barefoot, bareheaded, thinly and miserably clad, seized my arm with a vise-like grip, and begged for the love of God, for just a morsel for her starving children. They had tasted nothing since Sunday morning, and then only a spoonful of dry meal. I gave her the contents of my haversack, and one man in the ranks, a great, rough, swearing fellow, poured into her lap his entire three days' rations of pork and hard bread, thrust a ten dollar greenback, all the money he possessed, into her hand, swearing like a pirate all the while as a means of relief to his overcharged feelings, their intensity being abun-dantly evident by the tears which coursed rapidly down his cheeks. . . .

The gutters literally ran whiskey. The members of the City Council, foreseeing the mischief that would ensue should the liquor shops be sacked, had rolled all the barrels to the curbstone, knocked in their heads, and emptied their contents into the gutters. The poisonous flood rolled like a river of death rapidly on into the sewers, while the atmosphere fairly reeked with its unsavory odor. The rougher element of the popula-tion, white and black alike, were dipping up the vile stuff with their hands, and pouring it down their throats. The shrill whistle of locomotives sounded loud and frequent in the near distance, as train after train hurried away bearing frantic citizens with what valuables they had time to secure. Bands of thieves and rascals of every degree, broken loose from the penitentiary, were entering the stores on either side the street and stealing whatever they could lay their hands upon, while the entire black population seemed out of doors and crazy with delight. Tumult, violence, riot, pillage, every-where prevailed, and as if these were not enough to illustrate the horrors of war, the roar of the flames, the clanging of bells, and general uproar and confusion were sufficient to appal the stoutest heart.

Fearing violence from some unexpected source in the midst of such fearful scenes, I looked about for some avenue of escape into a less crowded street, where I could more easily keep the soldiers apart from the populace, but none presented itself. At length the heat became so great that we could proceed no further. Our hair and beards were scorched, our clothing smoked, the air we breathed was like a furnace blast, and many of the men, weighed down as they were with musket, knapsacks, blanket, ammunition, and other accoutrements, were well-nigh exhausted. Three fire engines were burning in the street immediately before us. On the sidewalk near by lay the bodies of three young girls· burnt to a crisp. People jumped from the windows of burning buildings; others with wildly waving arms shrieked for help, not daring to take the fatal leap.

On a lamp-post just at my right, I read the words "Fourteenth Street," and turning to a citizen who stood in a porch on the corner, I asked him to direct me to the capitol.

"Turn right up here," he said, "go straight on for two or three streets, and you will see it just on your left." He also added that General Early, at the head of a body of Confederate cavalry, had passed along only a moment before, and with out-stretched hand showed us through the smoke the rearmost rank. . . .

The same tumultuous scenes just described were visible throughout the city. The spacious capitol grounds afforded the only spot of refuge, and these were crowded with women and children, bearing in their arms and upon their heads their most cherished possessions. Piles of furniture lay scattered in every direction, and about them clustered the hungry and destitute family groups, clinging to each other with the energy of despair. One of the most touching sights amid these accumulated horrors, was that of a little girl—a toddling infant—holding her kitten tightly under her arm, a dilapidated rag doll in one hand and grasping her mother's gown with the other, as they sought shelter from the showers of cinders, under the capitol steps.

The constant explosion of ammunition in the arsenals seemed almost like a battle. Many citizens were killed by the flying fragments. Many were burned to death. In one house seventeen people perished from the flames. The sick, the aged, helpless and infirm, left to themselves in the general panic, could only pray for deliverance, which came to them when the flames had stifled their prayers in death.

Seven hundred and fifty thousand loaded shells in the

arsenals, exploding from the heat, tore their way through houses, ploughed up the streets and the gardens, and spread death and destruction on every hand. The whole city jarred and vibrated with horrid sounds, while warehouses, stores, mills, bridges, depots, and dwellings went down by scores and hundreds. The streets leading to the railroad stations were filled with a frantic mob, pushing, struggling, cursing, trampling each other without mercy in their efforts to get away with what plunder they could carry. No troops of either army were in sight, only rebel stragglers, whose long familiarity with similar scenes rendered them, no doubt, the only cool-headed and indifferent spectators of these appalling sights. Over and above all the terrible roar of the conflagration as it leaped from building to building, from street to street, filled the whole city with its scorching breath, and lent added horrors to the scene.

—PRESCOTT, "The Capture of Richmond"

6. THE WHITE FLAG AT APPOMATTOX

On the night of April 2-3, Lee withdrew from Petersburg along the northern bank of the little Appomattox; at the same time Mahone abandoned his lines at Bermuda Hundred, and Ewell retreated from north of the James. The objective of Lee's army was Danville, where they were abundant supplies and from which he might yet hope to link up with Johnston; if he were cut off from Danville he hoped to make Lynchburg and the Valley. Grant, however, was hot in pursuit, Sheridan's cavalry in the lead. Lee planned to concentrate and provision his forces at Amelia Court House, some 30 miles west of Petersburg; when he got there, on April 4 and 5, however, he found no supplies, and a day was lost in foraging for provisions.

Meantime Sheridan's cavalry had reached Jetersville, west of Amelia Court House. Lee turned north, planning to swing around Sheridan and get to Farmville. Meade's infantry came up, however, and at Sayler's Creek inflicted a heavy defeat on the shattered Confederates. By the seventh Lee's army was reduced to two infantry and one cavalry corps, and had lost most of its wagon trains. This diminished force reached Farmville on that day, when it was once again required to fight. That night Lee resumed his retreat toward Lynchburg, but Sheridan raced ahead to Appomattox Court House and blocked his advance.

Already some of his officers were advising surrender, but Lee determined on one final try. He instructed Gordon to move against Sheridan; if he should find only cavalry he was to fight; if he found an army in front of him, he was to abandon the attempt to break through.

Early on the morning of the ninth the dauntless Gordon moved out to the attack. Only Sheridan's cavalry was in front of him, and he assailed it with fury; for a moment he was, miraculously, successful. Then, about 9 a.m. the Union V and XXIV Corps reached the battlefield, and Gordon withdrew.

Already Grant had opened discussions looking to the surrender of the Army of Northern Virginia. With the failure of Gordon to break through, Lee was now ready to discuss surrender.

We give here Joshua Chamberlain's description of the fighting on the morning of the ninth, and the "white flag, earnestly borne, like a wraith of morning mist." Chamberlain we have met in the fighting at Fredericksburg and Gettysburg. A clergyman, and professor at Bowdoin College, he enlisted as lieutenant colonel in the 20th Maine, fought in over 20 engagements, was six times wounded, received the Congressional Medal of Honor for his gallantry, and in the Appomattox campaign commanded two brigades of the V Army Corps. After the war he served as Governor of Maine and President of Bowdoin College.

The darkest hours before the dawn of April 9, 1865, shrouded the Fifth Corps sunk in feverish sleep by the roadside six miles away from Appomattox Station on the Southside Road. Scarcely is the first broken dream begun when a cavalryman comes splashing down the road and vigorously dismounts, pulling from his jacket-front a crumpled note. The sentinel standing watch by his commander, worn in body but alert in every sense, touches your shoulder. "Orders, sir, I think." You rise on elbow, strike a match, and with smarting, streaming eyes read the brief, thrilling note, sent back by Sheridan to us infantry commanders. Like this, as I remember: "I have cut across the enemy at Appomattox Station, and captured three of his trains. If you can possibly push your infantry up here to-night, we will have great results in the morning."

Ah, sleep no more. The startling bugle notes ring out "The General"— "To the march." Word is sent for the men to take a bite of such as they have for food: the promised rations will not be up till noon, and by that time we shall be perhaps too far away for such greeting. A few try to eat, no matter what. Meanwhile, almost with one foot in the stirrup, you take from the hands of the black boy a tin plate of nondescript food and a dipper of miscalled coffee;—all equally black, like the night around. You eat and drink at a swallow; mount, and get to the head of the column before you shout the "Forward." They are there—the men: shivering to their senses as if risen out of the earth, but something in them not of it. Now sounds the "Forward," for the last time in our long-drawn strife. And they move—these men—sleepless, supperless, breakfastless, sore-footed, stiff-jointed, sense-benumbed, but with flushed faces pressing for the front.

By sunrise we have reached Appomattox Station, where Sheridan has left the captured trains. A staff officer is here to turn us square to the right, to the Appomattox River, cutting across Lee's retreat. Already we hear the sharp ring of the horse-artillery, answered ever and anon by heavier field guns; and drawing nearer, the crack of cavalry carbines; and unmistakably, too, the graver roll of musketry of opposing infantry. There is no mistake. Sheridan is square across the enemy's front, and with that glorious cavalry alone is holding at bay all that is left of the proudest army of the Confederacy. It has come at last,—the supreme hour. No thought of human wants or weakness now: all for the front; all for the flag, for the final stroke to make its meaning real—these men of the Potomac and the James, side by side, at the double in time and column, now one and now the other in the road or the fields beside. One striking feature I can never forget,—Birney's black men abreast with us, pressing forward to save the white man's country.

We did not know exactly what was going on. We did know that our cavalry had been doing splendid work all night, and in fact now was holding at bay Lee's whole remaining army. . . .

I was therefore in about the middle of our Fifth Corps column. The boom of the battle thickened ahead of us. We were intent for the front. Suddenly I am accosted by a cavalry officer dashing out of rough wood road leading off to our right. "General, you command this column?"

"Two brigades of it, sir; about half the First Division, Fifth Corps."

"Sir, General Sheridan wishes you to break off from this column and come to his support. The rebel infantry is press-

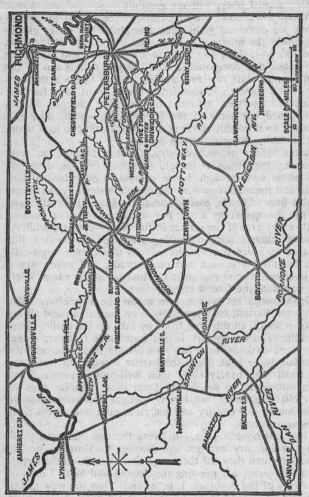

PETERSBURG TO APPOMATTOX

ing him hard. Our men are falling back. Don't wait for orders through the regular channels, but act on this at once."

Of course I obey, without question. . . .

Sharp work now. Pushing through the woods at cavalry speed, we come out right upon Sheridan's battle flag gleaming amidst the smoke of his batteries in the edge of the open field. Weird-looking flag it is: fork-tailed, red and white, the two bands that composed it each charged with a star of the contrasting color; two eyes sternly glaring through the cannon-cloud. Beneath it, that storm-center spirit, that form of condensed energies, mounted on the grim charger, Rienzi, that turned the battle of the Shenandoah,—both, rider and steed, of an unearthly shade of darkness, terrible to look upon, as if masking some unknown powers.

Right before us, our cavalry, Devins' division, gallantly stemming the surges of the old Stonewall brigade, desperate to beat its way through. I ride straight to Sheridan. A dark smile and impetuous gesture are my old orders. Forward into double lines of battle, past Sheridan, his guns, his cavalry, and on for the quivering crest! For a moment it is a glorious sight: every arm of the service in full play,—cavalry, artillery, infantry; then a sudden shifting scene as the cavalry, disengaged by successive squadrons, rally under their bugle-calls with beautiful precision and promptitude, and sweep like a storm-cloud beyond our right to close in on the enemy's left and complete the fateful envelopment.

Ord's troops are now square across the Lynchburg Pike. Ayres and Bartlett have joined them on their right, and all are in for it sharp. In this new front we take up the battle. Gregory follows in on my left. It is a formidable front we make. The scene darkens. In a few minutes the tide is turned; the incoming wave is at flood; the barrier recedes. In truth, the Stonewall men hardly show their well-proved mettle. They seem astonished to see before them these familiar flags of their old antagonists, not having thought it possible that we could match our cavalry and march around and across their pressing columns.

Their last hope is gone,—to break through our cavalry before our infantry can get up. Neither to Danville nor to Lynchburg can they cut their way; and close upon their rear, five miles away, are pressing the Second and Sixth Corps of the Army of the Potomac. It is the end! They are now giving way, but keep good front, by force of old habit. Halfway up the slope they make a stand, with what perhaps they think a good omen,—behind a stone wall. I try a little artillery on them, which directs their thoughts towards the crest behind them, and stiffen my lines for a rush, anxious for that crest myself. My intensity may have seemed like excitement. For Griffin comes up, quizzing me in his queer way of hitting off our weak points when we get a little too serious; accusing me of mistaking a blooming peach tree for a rebel flag, where I was dropping a few shells into a rallying crowd. I apologize —I was a little near-sighted, and hadn't been experienced in long-range fighting. But as for peaches, I was going to get some if the pits didn't sit too hard on our stomachs. . . .

But now comes up Ord with a positive order: "Don't expose your lines on that crest. The enemy have massed their guns to give it a raking fire the moment you set foot there." I thought I saw a qualifying look as he turned away. But left alone, youth struggled with prudence. My troops were in a bad position down here. I did not like to be "the under dog." It was much better to be on top and at least know what there was beyond. So I thought of Grant and his permission to "push things" when we got them going; and of Sheridan and his last words as he rode away with his cavalry, smiting his hands together—"Now smash 'em, I tell you; smash 'em!" So we took this for orders, and on the crest we stood. One booming cannon-shot passed close along our front, and in the next moment all was still.

We had done it,—had "exposed ourselves to the view of the enemy." But it was an exposure that worked two ways. For there burst upon our vision a mighty scene, fit cadence of the story of tumultuous years. Encompassed by the cordon of steel that crowned the heights about the Court House, on the slopes of the valley formed by the sources of the Appomattox, lay the remnants of that far-famed counterpart and companion of our own in momentous history,—the Army of Northern Virginia—Lee's army! . . .

It was hilly, broken ground, in effect a vast amphitheater, stretching a mile perhaps from crest to crest. On the several confronting slopes before us dusky masses of infantry suddenly resting in place; blocks of artillery, standing fast in a column or mechanically swung into park; clouds of cavalry small and great, slowly moving, in simple restlessness;—all without apparent attempt at offense or defence, or even military order.

In the hollow is the Appomattox,—which we had made the dead-line for our baffled foe, for its whole length, a hundred miles; here but a rivulet that might almost be stepped over dry-shod, and at the road crossing not thought worth while to bridge. Around its edges, now trodden to mire, swarms an indescribable crowd: worn-out soldier struggling to the front; demoralized citizen and denizen, white, black, and all shades between,—following Lee's army, or flying before these suddenly confronted terrible Yankees pictured to them as demon-shaped and bent; animals, too, of all forms and grades; vehicles of every description and non-description, —public and domestic, four-wheeled, or two, or one,—heading and moving in every direction, a swarming mass of chaotic confusion.

All this within sight of every eye on our bristling crest. Had one the heart to strike at beings so helpless, the Appomattox would quickly become a surpassing Red Sea horror. But the very spectacle brings every foot to an instinctive halt. We seem the possession of a dream. We are lost in a vision of human tragedy. But our light-twelve Napoleon guns come rattling up behind us to go into battery; we catch the glitter of the cavalry blades and brasses beneath the oak groves away to our right, and the ominous closing in on the fated foe. . . .

Watching intently, my eye was caught by the figure of a horseman riding out between those lines, soon joined by another, and taking a direction across the cavalry front towards our position. They were nearly a mile away, and I curiously watched them till lost from sight in the nearer broken ground and copses between.

Suddenly rose to sight another form, close in our own front,—a soldierly young figure, a Confederate staff officer undoubtedly. Now I see the white flag earnestly borne, and its possible purport sweeps before my inner vision like a wraith of morning mist. He comes steadily on, the mysterious form in gray, my mood so whimsically sensitive that I could even smile at the material of the flag,—wondering where in either army was found a towel, and one so white. But it bore a mighty message,—that simple emblem of homely service, wafted hitherward above the dark and crimsoned streams that never can wash themselves away.

The messenger draws near, dismounts; with graceful salutation and hardly suppressed emotion delivers his message: "Sir, I am from General Gordon. General Lee desires a cessation of hostilities until he can hear from General Grant as to the proposed surrender."

What word is this! so long so dearly fought for, so feverishly dreamed, but ever snatched away, held hidden and aloof; now smiting the senses with a dizzy flash! "Surrender?"

We had no rumor of this from the messages that had been passing between Grant and Lee, for now these two days, behind us. "Surrender?" It takes a moment to gather one's speech. "Sir," I answer, "that matter exceeds my authority. I will send to my superior. General Lee is right. He can do no more." All this with a forced calmness, covering a tumult of heart and brain. I bid him wait a while, and the message goes up to my corps commander, General Griffin, leaving me mazed at the boding change.

Now from the right come foaming up in cavalry fashion the two forms I had watched from away beyond. A white flag again, held strong aloft, making straight for the little group beneath our battle-flag, high borne also,—the red Maltese cross on a field of white, that had thrilled hearts long ago. I see now that it is one of our cavalry staff in lead,—indeed I recognize him, Colonel Whitaker of Custer's staff; and, hardly keeping pace with him, a Confederate staff officer. Without dismounting, without salutation, the cavalryman shouts: "This is unconditional surrender! This is the end!" Then he hastily introduces his companion, and adds: "I am just from Gordon and Longstreet. Gordon says 'For God's sake, stop this infantry, or hell will be to pay!' I'll go to Sheridan," he adds, and dashes away with the white flag, leaving Longstreet's aide with me.

I was doubtful of my duty. The flag of truce was in, but I had no right to act upon it without orders. There was still some firing from various quarters, lulling a little where the white flag passed near. But I did not press things quite so hard. Just then a last cannon-shot from the edge of the town plunges through the breast of a gallant and dear young officer in my front line,—Lieutenant Clark, of the 185th New York,—the last man killed in the Army of the Potomac, if not the last in the Appomattox lines. Not a strange thing for war, —this swift stroke of the mortal; but coming after the truce was in, it seemed a cruel fate for one so deserving to share his country's joy, and a sad peace-offering for us all.

Shortly comes the order, in due form, to cease firing and to halt. There was not much firing to cease from; but "halt," then and there? It is beyond human power to stop the men, whose one word and thought and action through crimsoned years had been but forward. They had seen the flag of truce, and could divine its outcome. But the habit was too strong; they cared not for points of direction, it was forward still,—for-

ward to the end; forward to the new beginning; forward to
the Nation's second birth!

—CHAMBERLAIN, *The Passing of the Armies*

7. GENERAL LEE SURRENDERS AT APPOMATTOX

*The story of the surrender needs no further introduction.
As early as April 7 Grant had suggested to Lee the propriety
of surrender, in order to avoid further bloodshed. Lee, as we
have seen, was not yet ready to give up. But when he found
his sadly decimated army surrounded, on the ninth, he knew
that the end had come. "There is nothing left for me to do but
go and see General Grant," said Lee, "and I would rather die
a thousand deaths." But there was no alternative; that afternoon Lee rode Traveller to the McLean house in Appomattox
Court House and accepted Grant's terms of surrender.*

*We give here Colonel Charles Marshall's account of the
famous scene in the McLean house.*

We struck up the hill towards Appomattox Court House.
There was a man named McLean who used to live on the first
battle field of Manassas, at a house about a mile from Manassas Junction. He did n't like the war, and having seen the first
battle of Manassas, he thought he would get away where
there would n't be any more fighting, so he moved down to
Appomattox Court House. General Lee told me to go forward and find a house where he could meet General Grant,
and of all people, whom should I meet but McLean. I rode
up to him and said, "Can you show me a house where General Lee and General Grant can meet together?" He took me
into a house that was all dilapidated and that had no furniture
in it. I told him it would n't do.

Then he said, "Maybe my house will do!" He lived in a very
comfortable house, and I told him I thought that would suit.
I had taken the orderly along with me, and I sent him back to
General Lee and Babcock, who were coming on behind. I
went into the house and sat down, and after a while General
Lee and Babcock came in. Colonel Babcock told his orderly
that he was to meet General Grant, who was coming on the
road, and turn him in when he came along. So General Lee,
Babcock and myself sat down in McLean's parlour and talked
in the most friendly and affable way.

In about half an hour we heard horses, and the first thing I knew General Grant walked into the room. There were with him General Sheridan, General Ord, Colonel Badeau, General Porter, Colonel Parker, and quite a number of other officers whose names I do not recall.

General Lee was standing at the end of the room opposite the door when General Grant walked in. General Grant had on a sack coat, a loose fatigue coat, but he had no side arms. He looked as though he had had a pretty hard time. He had been riding and his clothes were somewhat dusty and a little soiled. He walked up to General Lee and Lee recognized him at once. He had known him in the Mexican war. General Grant greeted him in the most cordial manner, and talked about the weather and other things in a very friendly way. Then General Grant brought up his officers and introduced them to General Lee.

I remember that General Lee asked for General Lawrence Williams, of the Army of the Potomac. That very morning General Williams had sent word by somebody to General Lee that Custis Lee, who had been captured at Sailor Creek and was reported killed, was not hurt, and General Lee asked General Grant where General Williams was, and if he could not send for him to come and see him. General Grant sent somebody out for General Williams, and when he came, General Lee thanked him for having sent him word about the safety of his son.

After a very free talk General Lee said to General Grant: "General, I have come to meet you in accordance with my letter to you this morning, to treat about the surrender of my army, and I think the best way would be for you to put your terms in writing."

General Grant said: "Yes; I believe it will."

So a Colonel Parker, General Grant's Aide-de-Camp, brought a little table over from a corner of the room, and General Grant wrote the terms and conditions of surrender on what we call field note paper, that is, a paper that makes a copy at the same time as the note is written. After he had written it, he took it over to General Lee.

General Lee was sitting at the side of the room; he rose and went to meet General Grant to take that paper and read it over. When he came to the part in which only public property was to be surrendered, and the officers were to retain their side arms and personal baggage, General Lee said: "That will have a very happy effect."

General Lee then said to General Grant: "General, our

cavalrymen furnish their own horses; they are not Government horses, some of them may be, but of course you will find them out—any property that is public property, you will ascertain that, but it is nearly all private property, and these men will want to plough ground and plant corn."

General Grant answered that as the terms were written, only the officers were permitted to take their private property, but almost immediately he added that he supposed that most of the men in the ranks were small farmers, and that the United States did not want their horses. He would give orders to allow every man who claimed to own a horse or mule to take the animal home.

General Lee having again said that this would have an excellent effect, once more looked over the letter, and being satisfied with it, told me to write a reply. General Grant told Colonel Parker to copy his letter, which was written in pencil, and put it in ink. Colonel Parker took the table and carried it back to a corner of the room, leaving General Grant and General Lee facing each other and talking together. There was no ink in McLean's inkstand, except some thick stuff that was very much like pitch, but I had a screw boxwood inkstand that I always carried with me in a little satchel that I had at my side, and I gave that to Colonel Parker, and he copied General Grant's letter with the aid of my inkstand and my pen.

There was another table right against the wall, and a sofa next to it. I was sitting on the arm of the sofa near the table, and General Sheridan was on the sofa next to me. While Colonel Parker was copying the letter, General Sheridan said to me, "This is very pretty country."

I said, "General, I have n't seen it by daylight. All my observations have been made by night and I have n't seen the country at all myself."

He laughed at my remark, and while we were talking I heard General Grant say this: "Sheridan, how many rations have you?"

General Sheridan said: "How many do you want?" and General Grant said, "General Lee has about a thousand or fifteen hundred of our people prisoners, and they are faring the same as his men, but he tells me his have n't anything. Can you send them some rations?"

"Yes," he answered They had gotten some of our rations, having captured a train.

General Grant said: "How many can you send?" and he replied "Twenty-five thousand rations."

General Grant asked if that would be enough, and General Lee replied "Plenty; plenty; an abundance;" and General Grant said to Sheridan "Order your commissary to send to the Confederate Commissary twenty-five thousand rations for our men and his men."

After a while Colonel Parker got through with his copy of General Grant's letter and I sat down to write a reply. I began it in the usual way: "I have the honor to acknowledge the receipt of your letter of such a date," and then went on to say the terms were satisfactory.

I took the letter over to General Lee, and he read it and said: "Don't say, 'I have the honor to acknowledge the receipt of your letter of such a date'; he is here; just say, 'I accept these terms.' "

Then I wrote:—

HEADQUARTERS OF THE ARMY OF NORTHERN VIRGINIA

April 9, 1865

I received your letter of this date containing the terms of the surrender of the Army of Northern Virginia proposed by you. As they are substantially the same as those expressed in your letter of the 8th instant, they are accepted. I will proceed to designate the proper officers to carry the stipulations into effect.

Then General Grant signed his letter, and I turned over my letter to General Lee and he signed it. Parker handed me General Grant's letter, and I handed him General Lee's reply, and the surrender was accomplished. There was no theatrical display about it. It was in itself perhaps the greatest tragedy that ever occurred in the history of the world, but it was the simplest, plainest, and most thoroughly devoid of any attempt at effect, that you can imagine.

The story of General Grant returning General Lee's sword to him is absurd, because General Grant proposed in his letter that the officers of the Confederate Army should retain their side-arms. Why, in the name of common sense, any-body should imagine that General Lee, after receiving a letter which said that he should retain his side-arms, yet should offer to surrender his sword to General Grant, is hard to understand. The only thing of the kind that occurred in the whole course of the transaction—which occupied perhaps an hour—was this: General Lee was in full uniform. He had on the handsomest uniform I ever saw him wear; and he had on a sword with a gold, a very handsome gold and leather, scabbard that had been presented to him by English ladies. General Grant excused himself to General Lee towards the close of the conversation between them, for not having his side arms with him; he told him that when he got his letter he was about four miles from his wagon in which his arms and uniform were, and he said that he had thought that General Lee would rather receive him as he was, than be detained, while he sent back to get his sword and uniform. General Lee told him he was very much obliged to him and was very glad indeed that he had n't done it.

——Sir Frederick Maurice, ed., *An Aide-de-Camp of Lee*

8. "THE WHOLE COLUMN SEEMED CROWNED WITH RED"

The day after the surrender Grant rode over to Lee's headquarters to discuss with him the formalities of surrender; later that day Meade rode over to pay his respects. Already the leaders of the grand armies were binding up the wounds of war, taking the road to reunion. Formal surrender was arranged for the twelfth, and General Chamberlain was designated to receive it on behalf of Grant. Grant, Meade, and Sheridan had all left Appomattox by that day, but Lee stayed on to the bitter end, though he did not witness the actual stacking of arms.

The description of that ceremony comes, appropriately enough, from Chamberlain himself.

It was now the morning of the 12th of April. I had been ordered to have my lines formed for the ceremony at sunrise. It was a chill gray morning, depressing to the senses. . . . We formed along the principal street, from the bluff bank of the stream to near the Court House on the left,—to face the last line of battle, and receive the last remnant of the arms and colors of that great army which ours had been created to confront for all that death can do for life. . . .

Our earnest eyes scan the busy groups on the opposite slopes, breaking camp for the last time, taking down their little shelter-tents and folding them carefully as precious things, then slowly forming ranks as for unwelcome duty. And now they move. The dusky swarms forge forward into gray columns of march. On they come, with the old swinging route step and swaying battle-flags. In the van, the proud Confederate ensign—the great field of white with canton of star-strewn cross of blue on a field of red, the regimental battle-flags with the same escutcheon following on, crowded so thick, by thinning out of men, that the whole column seemed crowned with red. At the right of our line our little group mounted beneath our flags, the red Maltese cross on a field of white, erewhile so bravely borne through many a field more crimson than itself, its mystic meaning now ruling all.

The momentous meaning of this occasion impressed me deeply. I resolved to mark it by some token of recognition, which could be no other than a salute of arms. Well aware of the responsibility assumed, and of the criticisms that would follow, as the sequel proved, nothing of that kind could move me in the least. The act could be defended, if needful, by the suggestion that such a salute was not to the cause for which the flag of the Confederacy stood, but to its going down before the flag of the Union. My main reason, however, was one for which I sought no authority nor asked forgiveness. Before us in proud humiliation stood the embodiment of manhood: men whom neither toils and sufferings, nor the fact of death, nor disaster, nor hopelessness could bend from their resolve; standing before us now, thin, worn, and famished, but erect, and with eyes looking level into ours, waking memories that bound us together as no other bond;—was not such manhood to be welcomed back into a Union so tested and assured?

Instruction had been given; and when the head of each division column comes opposite our group, our bugle sounds the signal and instantly our whole line from right to left, regiment by regiment in succession, gives the soldier's salutation, from the "order arms" to the old "carry"—the marching salute. Gordon at the head of the column, riding with heavy spirit and downcast face, catches the sound of shifting arms, looks up, and, taking the meaning, wheels superbly, making with himself and his horse one uplifted figure, with profound salutation as he drops the point of his sword to the boot toe; then facing to his own command, gives word for his successive brigades to pass us with the same position of the manual,—honor answering honor. On our part not a sound of trumpet more, nor roll of drum; not a cheer, nor word nor whisper of vain-glorying, nor motion of man standing again at the order, but an awed stillness rather, and breath-holding, as if it were the passing of the dead!

As each successive division masks our own, it halts, the men face inward toward us across the road, twelve feet away; then carefully "dress" their line, each captain taking pains for the good appearance of his company, worn and half starved as they were. The field and staff take their positions in the intervals of regiments; generals in rear of their commands. They fix bayonets, stack arms; then, hesitatingly, remove cartridge boxes and lay them down. Lastly,—reluctantly, with agony of expression,—they tenderly fold their flags, battle-worn and torn, blood-stained, heart-holding colors, and lay them down; some frenziedly rushing from the ranks, kneeling over them, clinging to them, pressing them to their lips with burning tears. And only the Flag of the Union greets the sky!

What visions thronged as we looked into each other's eyes! Here pass the men of Antietam, the Bloody Lane, the Sunken Road, the Cornfield, the Burnside-Bridge; the men whom Stonewall Jackson on the second night at Fredericksburg begged Lee to let him take and crush the two corps of the Army of the Potomac huddled in the streets in darkness and confusion; the men who swept away the Eleventh Corps at Chancellorsville; who left six thousand of their companions around the bases of Culp's and Cemetery Hills at Gettysburg; these survivors of the terrible Wilderness, the Bloody-Angle at Spottsylvania, the slaughter pen of Cold Harbor, the whirlpool of Bethesda Church!

Here comes Cobb's Georgia Legion, which held the stone wall on Marye's Heights at Fredericksburg, close before which we piled our dead for breastworks so that the living might stay and live.

Here too come Gordon's Georgians and Hoke's North Carolinians, who stood before the terrific mine explosion at Petersburg, and advancing retook the smoking crater and the dismal heaps of dead—ours more than theirs—huddled in the ghastly chasm.

Here are the men of McGowan, Hunton, and Scales, who broke the Fifth Corps lines on the White Oak Road, and were so desperately driven back on that forlorn night of March 31st by my thrice-decimated brigade.

Now comes Anderson's Fourth Corps, only Bushrod Johnson's Division left, and this the remnant of those we fought so fiercely on the Quaker Road two weeks ago, with Wise's Legion, too fierce for its own good.

Here passes the proud remnant of Ransom's North Carolinians which we swept through Five Forks ten days ago,—and all the little that was left of this division in the sharp passages at Sailor's Creek five days thereafter.

Now makes its last front A. P. Hill's old Corps, Heth now at the head, since Hill had gone too far forward ever to return: the men who poured destruction into our division at Shepardstown Ford, Antietam, in 1862, when Hill reported the Potomac running blue with our bodies; the men who opened the desperate first day's fight at Gettysburg, where withstanding them so stubbornly our Robinson's Brigades lost 1185 men, and the Iron Brigade alone 1153,—these men of Heth's Division here too losing 2850 men, companions of these now looking into our faces so differently.

What is this but the remnant of Mahone's Division, last seen by us at the North Anna? its thinned ranks of worn, bright-eyed men recalling scenes of costly valor and ever-remembered history.

Now the sad great pageant—Longstreet and his men! What shall we give them for greeting that has not already been spoken in volleys of thunder and written in lines of fire on all the river-banks of Virginia? Shall we go back to Gaines' Mill and Malvern Hill? Or to the Antietam of Maryland, or Gettysburg of Pennsylvania?—deepest graven of all. For here is what remains of Kershaw's Division, which left 40 per cent. of its men at Antietam, and at Gettysburg with Barksdale's and Semmes' Brigades tore through the Peach Orchard, rolling up the right of our gallant Third Corps, sweeping over the proud batteries of Massachusetts—Bigelow and Philips, —where under the smoke we saw the earth brown and blue with prostrate bodies of horses and men, and the tongues of overturned cannon and caissons pointing grim and stark in the air.

Then in the Wilderness, at Spottsylvania and thereafter, Kershaw's Division again, in deeds of awful glory, held their name and fame, until fate met them at Sailor's Creek, where Kershaw himself, and Ewell, and so many more, gave up their arms and hopes,—all, indeed, but manhood's honor.

With what strange emotion I look into these faces before which in the mad assault on Rives' Salient, June 18, 1864, I was left for dead under their eyes! It is by miracles we have lived to see this day,—any of us standing here.

Now comes the sinewy remnant of fierce Hood's Division, which at Gettysburg we saw pouring through the Devil's Den, and the Plum Run gorge; turning again by the left our stubborn Third Corps, then swarming up the rocky bastions of Round Top, to be met there by equal valor, which changed

Lee's whole plan of battle and perhaps the story of Gettysburg.

Ah, is this Pickett's Division?—this little group left of those who on the lurid last day of Gettysburg breasted level crossfire and thunderbolts of storm, to be strewn back drifting wrecks, where after that awful, futile, pitiful charge we buried them in graves a furlong wide, with name unknown!

Met again in the terrible cyclone-sweep over the breastworks at Five Forks; met now, so thin, so pale, purged of the mortal,—as if knowing pain or joy no more. How could we help falling on our knees, all of us together, and praying God to pity and forgive us all!

—CHAMBERLAIN, *The Passing of the Armies*

9. THE STARS AND STRIPES ARE RAISED OVER FORT SUMTER

When the Confederate forces evacuated Charleston in February 1865, and Union troops entered, the first thought of the captors was to hold a ceremonial reraising of the flag over the fort. The event was set for April 14, the anniversary of the surrender four years before, and the flag was hoisted by Robert Anderson, who was in command in 1861.

This moving scene is described by Mary Cadwalader Jones, daughter of a well-known Philadelphia attorney, and granddaughter of Horace Binney.

On March 18, 1865, Edwin M. Stanton, Lincoln's last Secretary of War, wrote to brevet Major General Robert Anderson:

"I have the pleasure of communicating to you the inclosed order of the President, directing the flag of the United States to be raised and planted upon the ruins of Fort Sumter by your hands, on the 14th day of April next, the fourth anniversary of the evacuation of that post by the United States forces under your command."

It was my good fortune to be there. . . .

Sailing from New York in the end of February, 1865, we landed at Hilton Head and reached Charleston by way of Savannah in the last days of March or beginning of April. To one who had never seen the actual effects of war, the city was a melancholy spectacle. Our bombardment had left its marks everywhere, even on church steeples and on gravestones in the cemeteries. One heavy Parrott gun, called by our men the "Swamp Angel" which had been planted in a marsh five miles inland, did a great deal of damage before she burst, and was looked upon by the Charlestonians with a mixture of wrath and amazement.

Every one who could possibly get away had left the city before our troops entered it; the streets were deserted except for our sentries, strolling soldiers and sailors, and bands of Negroes who had floated down on flatboats from distant plantations, many of them never having seen a large town before in their lives. Almost without exception the house and body servants had stuck to their masters and mistresses; these were field hands, and they gaped and laughed like careless children. As their new freedom did not feed them, they lived chiefly on the good-natured charity of our troops and at night camped in the empty cotton warehouses, with the natural result of frequent fires.

Heavy cloth-of-gold roses hung over garden walls and on the porches of closely-shuttered houses; occasionally an old servant would creep furtively from a back door; but there was no sign of ordinary everyday life—the men were all at the war and the women and children either away or in hiding. It had been different in the less aristocratic Savannah, which the Federal troops had occupied since December; when I walked about there, always with an officer or an orderly, the girls would run up their high steps and turn their backs sharply on the hated blue uniform, but if I looked round quickly after I had gone a little farther I usually caught them gazing eagerly at the back of my frock. Fashions were four years old in the Confederacy; it was worth while to run the blockade for rifles or quinine, but not for furbelows. Charleston was, however, too proud and too sad to care about fashions.

The ceremony was to be at noon punctually; four or five thousand people wanted to go, and there was no regular communication between Sumter and the town. The big visiting steamship ferried her own passengers, and the boats belonging to the blockading squadron plied busily to and fro, as temporary landings and steps had been put up on all sides of the fort walls. The entire management was in the hands of the Navy, and everything went like clockwork.

The ceremony began with a short prayer by the old army chaplain who had prayed when the flag was hoisted over Fort Sumter on December 27, 1860. Next a Brooklyn clergyman read parts of several Psalms, expecting the company to read alternate verses, as in church; but that was not very effective, because if any copies were printed, there were not enough of them to go round. Then Sergeant Hart, who had held up the flag when its staff was shot through in the first attack, came forward quietly and drew the selfsame flag out of an ordinary leather mail bag. We all held our breath for a second, and then we gave a queer cry, between a cheer and a yell; nobody started and nobody led it; I never heard anything like it before or since, but I can hear it now. It stopped suddenly, for we saw that a couple of the sailors who had been in the first fight were fastening the flag to its new halyards with a little wreath of laurel on top. General Anderson stood up, bareheaded, took the halyards in his hands, and began to speak. At first I could not hear him, for his voice came thickly, but in a moment he said clearly, "I thank God that I have lived to see this day," and after a few more words he began to hoist the flag It went up slowly and hung limp against the staff, a weather-beaten, frayed, and shell-torn old flag, not fit for much more work, but when it had crept clear of the shelter of the walls a sudden breath of wind caught it, and it shook its folds and flew straight out above us, while every soldier and sailor instinctively saluted.

I don't know just what we did next, but I remember looking on either side of me and seeing my father's eyelids brimming over and that Admiral Dahlgren's lips were trembling. I think we stood up, somebody started "The Star-Spangled Banner," and we sang the first verse, which is all that most people know. But it did not make much difference, for a great gun was fired close to us from the fort itself, followed, in obedience to the President's order, "by a national salute from every fort and battery that fired upon Fort Sumter." The measured, solemn booming came from Fort Moultrie, from the batteries on Sullivan and Folly Islands, and from Fort Wagner. . . . When the forts were done it was the turn of the fleet, and all our warships from the largest—which would look tiny today—down to the smallest monitor, fired and fired in regular order until the air was thick and black with smoke and one's ears ached with the overlapping vibrations.

—JONES, *Lantern Slides*

10. "BOW DOWN, DEAR LAND, FOR THOU HAST FOUND RELEASE"

In July 1865 Harvard College held commemoration services for Harvard men who had given their lives to the preservation of the Union. Altogether 138 Harvard men had been killed, or died, in the Union armies—and 64 in the Confederate armies. James Russell Lowell, then a Professor at Harvard College, was called on to write an appropriate ode. "The ode itself," he said later, "was an improvisation . . . the whole thing came out of me with a rush." It is, by common consent, the finest of Lowell's poems, and probably the most noble and moving poem to come out of the Civil War.

. . . Bow down, dear Land, for thou hast found release!
    Thy God, in these distempered days,
    Hath taught thee the sure wisdom of His ways,
And through thine enemies hath wrought thy peace!
    Bow down in prayer and praise!
No poorest in thy borders but may now
Lift to the juster skies a man's enfranchised brow.
O Beautiful! my Country! ours once more!
Smoothing thy gold of war-dishevelled hair
O'er such sweet brows as never other wore,
    And letting thy set lips,
    Freed from wrath's pale eclipse,
The rosy edges of their smile lay bare,
What words divine of lover or of poet
Could tell our love and make thee know it,
Among the Nations bright beyond compare?
    What were our lives without thee?
    What all our lives to save thee?
    We reck not what we gave thee;
    We will not dare to doubt thee,
But ask whatever else, and we will dare!
    —JAMES RUSSELL LOWELL, "Ode Recited at the
    Harvard Commemoration," July 31, 1865

Bibliography
and Acknowledgments

CHAPTER I. GETTYSBURG

1. General Lee Decides to Take the Offensive.
   The War of the Rebellion . . . Official Records. Ser. I, vol. XXVII, pt. III, 868-869; ser. I, vol. XXVII, pt. III, 880-882; ser. I, vol. XXVII, pt. II, 305.
2. General Lee Invades Pennsylvania.
   Letter of William S. Christian, in Frank Moore, ed., *The Rebellion Record.* New York, 1864. VII, 325.
3. The Armies Converge on Gettysburg.
   Henry J. Hunt, "The First Day at Gettysburg," in *Battles and Leaders of the Civil War.* New York. The Century Co., 1884, 1888. III, 271 ff.
4. Buford and Reynolds Hold Up the Confederate Advance.
   Major Joseph G. Rosengarten, "General Reynolds' Last Battle," in *The Annals of the War, Written by Leading Participants North and South . . . in the Philadelphia Weekly Times.* Philadelphia: The Times Publishing Co., 1879. Pp. 62-64.
5. A Boy Cannoneer Describes Hard Fighting on the First Day.
   Augustus Buell, *"The Cannoneer." Recollections of Service in the Army of the Potomac. By "A Detached Volunteer" in the Regular Artillery.* Washington: The National Tribune, 1890. Pp. 63-73, *passim.*
6. The Struggle for Little Round Top.
   A. General Warren Seizes Little Round Top. "Reminiscences of the 140th Regiment, New York Volunteer Infantry, by Porter Farley," in Blake McKelvey, ed., *Rochester in the Civil War.* Rochester: Rochester Historical Society, 1944. Pp. 218-223. (By permission of Rochester Historical Society.)
   B. Colonel Oates Almost Captures Little Round Top. William C. Oates, *The War Between the Union and the Confederacy and Its Lost Opportunities, with a history of the 15th Alabama Regiment and the forty-eight battles in which it was engaged.* New York: The Neale Publishing Co., 1905. Pp. 210-211, 212, 218-221.

C. The 20th Maine Saves Little Round Top. Theodore Gerrish, *Army Life: A Private's Reminiscences of the Civil War.* Portland, Me.: Hoyt, Fogg & Donham, 1882. Pp. 104-111.
7. High Tide at Gettysburg.
   A. Alexander Gives the Signal to Start. Letter from E. P. Alexander to the Rev. J. Wm. Jones, in *Southern Historical Society Papers,* IV (1877), 102-109, *passim.*
   B. Armistead Falls Beside the Enemy's Battery. James Longstreet, *From Manassas to Appomattox: Memoirs of the Civil War in America.* 2nd ed., rev.; Philadelphia: J. B. Lippincott Co., 1903. Pp. 391-394. (By permission of Mrs. Helen Dortch Longstreet.)
   C. "The Crest Is Safe." Frank Aretas Haskell, *The Battle of Gettysburg.* ("Wisconsin History Commission Reprints," No. 1.) Wisconsin History Commission, November 1908. Pp. 107 ff. (By permission of Wisconsin Historical Commission.)
   D. "All This Will Come Right in the End." [Arthur J. L. Fremantle], "The Battle of Gettysburg and the Campaign in Pennsylvania," *Blackwood's Edinburgh Magazine,* XCIV (1863), 380-382.
8. General Lee Offers to Resign after Gettysburg.
   The War of the Rebellion . . . Official Records. Ser. I, vol. LI, pt. II, 752-753; vol. XXIX, pt. II, 639-640.
9. "Bells Are Ringing Wildly."
   War Letters of William Thompson Lusk. New York: Privately printed, 1911. Pp. 284-285.
10. "A New Birth of Freedom."
    Abraham Lincoln, "The Gettysburg Address," November 19, 1863, Nicolay and Hay, eds., *The Complete Works of Abraham Lincoln.* New York: The Century Co., 1894. II, 439. (By permission of Appleton-Century-Crofts, Inc.)

CHAPTER II. VICKSBURG AND PORT HUDSON

1. "Onward to Vicksburg."
   Edgar L. Erickson, ed., "With Grant at Vicksburg—From the Civil War Diary of Captain Charles E. Wilcox," *Journal of the Illinois State Historical Society,* XXX (January 1938), 463-497, *passim.* (By permission of Illinois State Historical Society.)
2. A Union Woman Suffers through the Siege of Vicksburg.
   George W. Cable, ed., "A Woman's Diary of the Siege of Vicksburg. Under Fire from the Gunboats," *Century Illustrated Magazine,* VIII (1885), 767-775.
3. Vicksburg Surrenders.
   U. S. Grant, "The Vicksburg Campaign," in *Battles and Leaders of the Civil War.* New York: The Century Co., 1884, 1888. III, 530-536.
4. General Banks Takes Port Hudson.
   A. Eating Mules at Port Hudson. *Port Hudson—Its History*

from an Interior Point of View, as Sketched from the Diary of an Officer. St. Francisville, La., 1938. (By permission of Mr. Elrie Robinson.)

B. Blue and Gray Fraternize after the Surrender of Port Hudson. *Ibid.*

5. "The Father of Waters Again Goes Unvexed to the Sea." Letter of Lincoln to James C. Conkling. Nicolay and Hay, eds., *The Complete Works of Abraham Lincoln.* New York: The Century Co., 1894. II, 398-399. (By permission of Appleton-Century-Crofts, Inc.)

6. General Morgan Invades the North.

A. Morgan's Cavalrymen Sweep Through Kentucky. "Journal of Lieutenant-Colonel Alston," in Frank Moore, ed., *The Rebellion Record.* New York, 1864. VII, 358-360.

B. Morgan's Raid Comes to an Inglorious End. James Bennett McCreary, "The Journal of My Soldier Life," *Register of the Kentucky State Historical Society,* XXXIII (July 1935), 198-200. (By permission of Kentucky State Historical Society.)

CHAPTER III. PRISONS, NORTH AND SOUTH

1. Abner Small Suffers in Danville Prison.

Harold A. Small, ed., *The Road to Richmond; The Civil War Memoirs of Major Abner R. Small of the Sixteenth Maine Volunteers. Together with the Diary which he kept when he was a Prisoner of War.* Berkeley: University of California Press, 1939. Pp. 171-176. (By permission of University of California Press.)

2. Suffering in Andersonville Prison.

Eliza Frances Andrews, *The War-Time Journal of a Georgia Girl, 1864-1865.* New York: D. Appleton & Co., 1908. Pp. 76-79.

3. The Bright Side of Libby Prison.

Frank E. Moran, "Libby's Bright Side: A Silver Lining in the Dark Cloud of Prison Life," in W. C. King and W. P. Derby, eds., *Camp-Fire Sketches and Battle-Field Echoes.* Springfield, Mass.: W. C. King & Co., 1887. Pp. 180-181, 183-185.

4. The Awful Conditions at Fort Delaware.

Randolph Abbott Shotwell, "Three Years in Battle," J. G. de Roulhac Hamilton, ed., *The Papers of Randolph Abbott Shotwell.* Raleigh, N. C.: North Carolina Historical Commission, 1931. II, 149-182, *passim.* (By permission of State of North Carolina Department of Archives and History.)

5. The Privations of Life in Elmira Prison.

Marcus B. Toney, *The Privations of a Private.* Nashville, Tenn.: Methodist Episcopal Church South, 1905. Pp. 93-104, *passim.*

CHAPTER IV. BEHIND THE LINES: THE NORTH

1. Washington as a Camp.
   Noah Brooks, "Washington in Lincoln's Time," *Century Illustrated Magazine*, XXVII (November 1894), 140-141. (By permission of Appleton-Century-Crofts, Inc.)
2. Walt Whitman Looks Around in Wartime Washington.
   Emory Halloway, ed., *The Uncollected Poetry and Prose of Walt Whitman*. New York: Doubleday, Page & Co., 1921. II, 21 ff. (By permission of Doubleday & Company, Inc.)
3. Anna Dickinson Sees the Draft Riots in New York City.
   Anna Elizabeth Dickinson, *What Answer?* Boston: Ticknor & Fields, 1868. Pp. 243-256.
4. The Army of Lobbyists and Speculators.
   Régis de Trobriand, *Four Years with the Army of the Potomac*. Trans. by George K. Dauchy. Boston: Ticknor & Co., 1889. Pp. 134-136.
5. Charles A. Dana Helps Stop Frauds in the War Department.
   Charles A. Dana, *Recollections of the Civil War*. New York: D. Appleton & Co., 1898. Pp. 161-164. (By permission of Appleton-Century-Crofts, Inc.)
6. Colonel Baker Outwits Bounty Jumpers and Brokers.
   LaFayette C. Baker, *The Secret Service in the Late War*. Philadelphia: John E. Potter & Co., 1874. Pp. 249-267, *passim*.
7. Confederate Plots Against the North.
   A. A Confederate Plan to Seize Johnson's Island Is Frustrated.
   Hon. H. B. Brown, "The Lake Erie Piracy Case," *The Green Bag*, XXI (April 1909), 143-147.
   B. The Confederates Attempt to Burn New York. John W. Headley, *Confederate Operations in Canada and New York*. New York: The Neale Publishing Co., 1906. Pp. 274-277.

CHAPTER V. BEHIND THE LINES: THE SOUTH

1. A War Clerk Suffers Scarcities in Richmond.
   John B. Jones, *A Rebel War Clerk's Diary at the Confederate States Capital*. Philadelphia: J. B. Lippincott Co., 1866. Vols. I and II, *passim*.
2. Mr. Eggleston Recalls When Money Was Plentiful.
   George Cary Eggleston, *A Rebel's Recollections*. New York, 1874. Pp. 78-84, 100-109.
3. Parthenia Hague Tells How Women Outwitted the Blockade.
   Parthenia Antoinette Hague, *A Blockaded Family: Life in Southern Alabama During the Civil War*. Boston: Houghton, Mifflin & Co., 1888. Pp. 37-42, 100-105.
4. The Confederates Burn Their Cotton.
   Sarah Morgan Dawson, *A Confederate Girl's Diary*, Warrington Dawson, ed. Boston: Houghton Mifflin Co., 1913. Pp. 16-18. (By permission of Mr. Warrington Dawson.)
5. "The Yankees Are Coming."

Testimony of Mrs. Mary A. Ward, *Report of the Committee of the Senate upon the Relations between Labor and Capital, and Testimony Taken by the Committee.* Washington: Government Printing Office, 1885. IV, 334-336.

6. "The Lives Which Women Have Lead Since Troy Fell."
Kate Mason Rowland and Mrs. Morris L. Croxall, eds., *The Journal of Julia LeGrand, New Orleans, 1862-1863.* Richmond: Everett Waddey Co., 1911. Pp. 51-54.

7. "They Must Reap the Whirlwind."
M. A. De Wolfe Howe, ed., *Home Letters of General Sherman.* New York: Charles Scribner's Sons, 1909. Pp. 268-269. (By permission of Charles Scribner's Sons.)

8. Georgia's Governor Laments Davis' Despotism.
Ulrich B. Phillips, ed., "The Correspondence of Robert Toombs, Alexander H. Stephens, and Howell Cobb," *Annual Report of the American Historical Society for the year of 1911.* Washington: Government Printing Office, 1913, II, 605-606. (By permission of American Historical Society.)

9. Peace at Any Price.
J. G. de Roulhac Hamilton, ed., *The Correspondence of Jonathan Worth.* Raleigh, N. C.: North Carolina Historical Commission, 1909. I, 257-258. (By permission of State of North Carolina Department of Archives and History.)

10. "The Man Who Held His Conscience Higher Than Their Praise."
James Petigru Carson, *Life, Letters and Speeches of James Louis Petigru, The Union Man of South Carolina,* Washington: W. H. Loudermilk & Co., 1920. P. 487.

CHAPTER VI. HOSPITALS, SURGEONS, AND NURSES

1. George Townsend Describes the Wounded on the Peninsula.
George Alfred Townsend, *Campaigns of a Non-Combatant, And His Romaunt Abroad During the War.* New York: Blelock & Co., 1866. Pp. 103-118.

2. The Sanitary Commission to the Rescue.
Katherine Wormeley, *The Other Side of the War; With the Army of the Potomac. Letters from the Headquarters of the United States Sanitary Commission during the Peninsular Campaign in Virginia in 1862.* Boston: Ticknor & Co., 1889. Pp. 102-111.

3. Clara Barton Surmounts the Faithlessness of Union Officers.
William E. Barton, *The Life of Clara Barton, Founder of the American Red Cross.* Boston: Houghton Mifflin Co., 1922. I, 277-279. (By permission of Mr. Bruce Barton.)

4. Susan Blackford Nurses the Wounded at Lynchburg.
Charles Minor Blackford, III, ed., *Letters from Lee's Army; or, Memoirs of Life In and Out of the Army in Virginia During the War Between the States. Compiled by Susan Leigh*

Blackford from original and contemporaneous memoirs, correspondence and diaries. New York: Charles Scribner's Sons, 1947. Pp. 259-261. (By permission of Charles Scribner's Sons.)

5. Cornelia Hancock Nurses Soldiers and Contrabands.
   Henrietta Stratton Jaquette, ed., *South After Gettysburg, Letters of Cornelia Hancock from the Army of the Potomac, 1863-1865.* Philadelphia: University of Pennsylvania Press, 1937. Pp. 8-12, 31-32. (By permission of University of Pennsylvania Press.)

6. The Ghastly Work of the Field Surgeons.
   A. The Heartlessness of the Surgeons. Charles Sterling Underhill, ed., *"Your Soldier Boy Samuel"—Civil War Letters of Lieut. Samuel Edmund Nichols, Amherst '65 of the 37th Regiment Massachusetts Volunteers.* Privately printed, 1929. Pp. 50-52. (By permission of Mrs. I. S. Underhill.)
   B. The Horrors of the Wilderness. Augustus C. Brown, *The Diary of a Line Officer.* New York: Privately printed, 1906. Pp. 43-44.

7. The Regimental Hospital.
   Charles Beneulyn Johnson, *Muskets and Medicine, or Army Life in the Sixties.* Philadelphia: F. A. Davis Co., 1917. Pp. 129-134. (By permission of F. A. Davis Company.)

CHAPTER VII. THE COAST AND INLAND WATERS

1. The *Merrimac* and the *Monitor*.
   A. The *Minnesota* Fights for Her Life in Hampton Roads. "Report of Captain Van Brunt," in Frank Moore, ed., *The Rebellion Record.* New York, 1863. IV, 267-268.
   B. The *Monitor* Repels the *Merrimac*. S. D. Greene to His Parents, March 14, 1862, in Lydia Minturn Post, ed., *Soldiers' Letters from Camp, Battle-field and Prison.* New York: Bunce & Huntington, 1865. Pp. 109-113.

2. Commodore Farragut Captures New Orleans.
   Susan Perkins, ed., *Letters of Capt. Geo. Hamilton Perkins, U. S. N. . . . Also a Sketch of His Life.* Concord, N.H.: Privately printed, 1886. Pp. 67-71.

3. New Orleans Falls to the Yankees.
   A. Julia LeGrand Describes the Surrender of New Orleans. Kate Mason Rowland and Mrs. Morris L. Croxall, eds., *The Journal of Julia LeGrand, New Orleans, 1862-1863.* Richmond: Everett Waddey Co., 1911. Pp. 39-43.
   B. General Butler Outrages the Moral Sentiment of the World. General Butler's Order No. 28, in Frank Moore, ed., *The Rebellion Record.* New York, 1863. V, 136.
   C. Palmerston Protests Butler's Proclamation. Palmerston to Charles Francis Adams, *Proceedings of the Massachusetts Historical Society* (Boston), XLV (1911-1912), 257. (By permission of Massachusetts Historical Society.)
   D. "A More Impudent Proceeding Cannot Be Discovered."

Sarah Agnes Wallace and Frances Elma Gillespie, eds., *The Journal of Benjamin Moran, 1857-1865.* Chicago: University of Chicago Press, 1949. II, 1027-1029. (By permission of University of Chicago Press.)

4. Ellet's Steam Rams Smash the Confederate Fleet at Memphis.
   Alfred W. Ellet, "Ellet and His Steam-Rams at Memphis," in *Battles and Leaders of the Civil War.* New York: The Century Co., 1884-1887. I, 453-459.

5. Attack and Repulse at Battery Wagner.
   "The Attack on Fort Wagner. New York 'Tribune' Account," in Frank Moore, ed., *The Rebellion Record.* New York, 1864, VII, 211-214.

6. Farragut Damns the Torpedoes at Mobile Bay.
   John C. Kinney, "Farragut at Mobile Bay," in *Battles and Leaders of the Civil War.* New York: The Century Co., 1884, 1887, 1888. IV, 382 ff.

7. Lieutenant Cushing Torpedoes the *Albemarle.*
   W. B. Cushing, "The Destruction of the 'Albemarle,'" in *Battles and Leaders of the Civil War.* New York: The Century Co., 1884, 1887, 1888. IV, 634-637.

8. The Confederates Repulse an Attack on Fort Fisher.
   William Lamb, "The Defence of Fort Fisher, North Carolina," *Papers of the Military Historical Society of Massachusetts* (Boston), IX (1912), 361-368. (By permission of Military Historical Society of Massachusetts.)

9. "It Beat Anything in History."
   Augustus Buell, *"The Cannoneer." Recollections of Service in the Army of the Potomac. By "A Detached Volunteer" in the Regular Artillery.* Washington: The National Tribune, 1890. Pp. 328-333.

CHAPTER VIII. THE BLOCKADE AND THE CRUISERS

1. The United States Navy Blockades the Confederacy.
   Horatio L. Wait, "The Blockade of the Confederacy," *The Century Illustrated Magazine,* XXXIV (1898), 914-920, *passim.* (By permission of Appleton-Century-Crofts, Inc.)

2. The *Robert E. Lee* Runs the Blockade.
   John Wilkinson, *The Narrative of a Blockade-Runner.* New York: Sheldon & Co., 1877. Pp. 162-171.

3. The *Rob Roy* Runs the Blockade out of Havana.
   William Watson, *The Adventures of a Blockade Runner; or, Trade in Time of War.* London: T. Fisher Unwin, 1892. Pp. 141-159.

4. Blockade-Runners Supply Charleston.
   W. F. G. Peck, "Four Years Under Fire at Charleston," *Harper's New Monthly Magazine,* XXXI (1865), 364.

5. Confederate Privateers Harry Northern Merchantmen.
   A. The *Ivy* Prowls Outside New Orleans. Letter of M.

Repard, in *New Orleans Delta*, May 26, 1861, in William
Morrison Robinson, Jr., *The Confederate Privateers*. New
Haven, Conn.: Yale University Press, 1928. Pp. 45-46. (By
permission of Yale University Press.)
B. The *Jefferson Davis* Takes a Prize off Delaware. Captain
Fitfield, in *The Charleston Mercury*, July 23, 1861, *Ibid.*, 67-
69.

6. The *Georgia* Fires the *Bold Hunter*.
James Morris Morgan, *Recollections of a Rebel Reefer*. Lon-
don: Constable & Co., Ltd., 1918. Pp. 154-156. Boston:
Houghton Mifflin Co., 1917. (By permission of Mrs. Daniel
Hunter Wallace.)

7. The *Kearsarge* Sinks the *Alabama* off Cherbourg.
John McIntosh Kell, *Recollections of a Naval Life, including
the Cruises of the Confederate States Steamers "Sumter" and
"Alabama."* New York: The Neale Publishing Co., 1900. Pp.
244-251.

CHAPTER IX. CHICKAMAUGA AND CHATTANOOGA

1. The Federals Oppose Hood with Desperation.
James R. Carnahan, "Personal Recollections of Chickamauga,"
in *Sketches of War History, 1861-65 . . . Ohio Commandery
of the Military Order of the Loyal Legion of the United
States*. Cincinnati: Robert Clarke & Co., 1888. I, 410-417.

2. Thomas Stands Like a Rock at Chickamauga.
A. Longstreet Breaks the Federal Line. Daniel H. Hill,
"Chickamauga—The Great Battle of the West," in *Battles and
Leaders of the Civil War*. New York: The Century Co., 1884,
1888. III, 657-660.
B. Thomas Holds the Horseshoe Ridge. Gates P. Thruston,
"The Crisis at Chickamauga," in *Battles and Leaders of the
Civil War*. New York: The Century Co., 1884, 1888. III,
663-664.

3. Chattanooga under Siege.
W. F. G. Shanks, "Chattanooga, And How We Held It,"
Harper's New Monthly Magazine, XXXVI (1867-1868), 142-
146, 148-149.

4. Hooker Wins the "Battle above the Clouds."
Joseph G. Fullerton, "The Army of the Cumberland at Chatta-
nooga," in *Battles and Leaders of the Civil War*. New York:
The Century Co., 1884, 1888. III, 721-723.

5. The Army of the Cumberland Carries Missionary Ridge.
A. "First One Flag, Then Another, Leads." William A. Mor-
gan, "Hazen's Brigade at Missionary Ridge," in *War Talks in
Kansas . . . Commandery of Kansas, Military Order of the
Loyal Legion of the United States*. Kansas City, Mo.: Franklin
Hudson Publishing Co., 1906. I, 271-275. (By permission of
Kansas Commandery, Military Order of the Loyal Legion of

the United States.)

B. "Amid the Din of Battle 'Chickamauga' Could Be Heard."
"Major Connolly's Letters to His Wife, 1862-1865," *Transactions of the Illinois State Historical Society*. ("Publications of the Illinois State Historical Library," No. 35.) Springfield, Ill.: 1928. Pp. 298-303. (By permission of Illinois State Historical Society.)

6. "The Disaster Admits of No Palliation."
Braxton Bragg to Jefferson Davis, in *The War of the Rebellion . . . Official Records*. Ser. I, vol. LII, pt. II, 745-746.

7. Burnside Holds Out at Knoxville.
Henry S. Burrage, "Burnside's East Tennessee Campaign," *Papers of the Military Historical Society of Massachusetts* (Boston), VIII (1910), 574-595, *passim*. (By permission of Military Historical Society of Massachusetts.)

CHAPTER X. ATLANTA AND THE MARCH TO THE SEA

1. General Sherman Takes Command.
John Chipman Gray to John Ropes, in Roland Gray, "Memoir of John Chipman Gray," *Proceedings of the Massachusetts Historical Society*, XLIX (1915-1916), 393-394. (By permission of Massachusetts Historical Society.)

2. Sherman Marches from Chattanooga to Atlanta.
W. T. Sherman, "The Grand Strategy of the War of the Rebellion," *Century Illustrated Magazine*, XIII (February 1888), 593-595.

3. Johnston Halts Sherman at New Hope Church.
Joseph E. Johnston, *Narrative of Military Operations, Directed, During the Late War Between the States*. New York: D. Appleton & Co., 1874. Pp. 326-331.

4. Joe Johnston Gives Way to Hood.
A. President Davis Removes General Johnston before Atlanta. Jefferson Davis, *Rise and Fall of the Confederate Government*. New York: D. Appleton & Co., 1881. II, 556-557.
B. General Johnston Justifies Himself. Letter from Johnston to Maury, in Dabney H. Maury, *Recollections of a Virginian*. New York: Charles Scribner's Sons, 1897. Pp. 146-148.

5. Hardee Wins and Loses the Battle of Atlanta.
Richard S. Tuthill, "An Artilleryman's Recollections of the Battle of Atlanta," in *Military Essays and Recollections . . . Military Order of the Loyal Legion, Illinois Commandery*. Chicago: A. C. McClurg & Co., 1891. I, 302-306.

6. "You Might as Well Appeal against the Thunder-Storm."
[William T. Sherman], *Memoirs of General William T. Sherman*. New York: D. Appleton & Co., 1875. II, 125-127.

7. Sherman Marches from Atlanta to the Sea.
[William T. Sherman], *Memoirs of General William T. Sherman*. New York: D. Appleton & Co., 1875. II, 178 ff.

 8. Sherman's "Bummers."
    A. A Good Word for the Bummers. Henry O. Dwight, "How
    We Fight at Atlanta," *Harper's New Monthly Magazine*,
    XXIX (1864), 666.
    B. "We Were Proud of Our Foragers," Daniel Oakey, "March-
    ing Through Georgia and the Carolinas," in *Battles and
    Leaders of the Civil War*. New York: The Century Co., 1884,
    1887, 1888. IV, 672-673.
 9. "The Heavens Were Lit Up with Flames from Burning
    Buildings."
    Dolly Sumner Lunt, *A Woman's Wartime Journal . . . With
    an introduction and Notes by Julian Street*. New York: The
    Century Co., 1918. Pp. 20-32, *passim*. (By permission of Mrs.
    L. D. Bolton.)
10. Eliza Andrews Comes Home through the Burnt Country.
    Eliza Frances Andrews, *The War-Time Journal of a Georgia
    Girl*. New York: D. Appleton & Co., 1908. Pp. 32-33, 38.
11. The Burning of Columbia.
    A. "A Scene of Shameful Confusion." Brevet Major George
    Ward Nichols, Aide-de-Camp to General Sherman, *The
    Story of the Great March, from the Diary of a Staff Officer*.
    New York: Harper & Bros., 1865. Pp. 160-166.
    B. Major Hitchcock Explains the Burning of Columbia. M. A.
    De Wolfe Howe, ed., *Marching with Sherman, Passages from
    the Letters and Campaign Diaries of Henry Hitchcock*. New
    Haven: Yale University Press, 1927. Pp. 265-270. (By permis-
    sion of Yale University Press.)
12. General Sherman Thinks His Name May Live.
    M. A. De Wolfe Howe, ed., *Home Letters of General Sher-
    man*. New York: Charles Scribner's Sons, 1909. Pp. 324-327.
    (By permission of Charles Scribner's Sons.)

CHAPTER XI. THE WILDERNESS

 1. U. S. Grant Plans His Spring Campaign.
    [Ulysses S. Grant], *Personal Memoirs of U. S. Grant*. New
    York: Charles L. Webster & Co., 1886. II, 127 ff.
 2. Colonel Porter Draws a Portrait of General Grant.
    General Horace Porter, *Campaigning with Grant*. New York:
    The Century Co., 1897. Pp. 13-16, 248-250.
 3. Private Goss Describes the Battle of the Wilderness.
    Warren Lee Goss, *Recollections of a Private. A Story of the
    Army of the Potomac*. New York: Thomas Y. Crowell & Co.,
    1890. Pp. 268-277.
 4. "Texans Always Move Them."
    R. C. ————, of 'Hood's Texas Brigade,' "Gen. Lee at the
    'Wilderness,'" in *The Land We Love*, V (1868), 484-486.
 5. "Their Dead and Dying Piled Higher Than the Works."
    Robert Stiles, *Four Years Under Marse Robert*. New York:
    The Neale Publishing Co., 1910. Pp. 253-255, 263-264.

6. Spotsylvania and the Bloody Angle.
   General Horace Porter, *Campaigning with Grant*. New York: The Century Co., 1897. Pp. 101-111.
7. "These Men Have Never Failed You on Any Field."
   General John B. Gordon, *Reminiscences of the Civil War*. New York: Charles Scribner's Sons, 1903. Pp. 275-281. (By permission of Charles Scribner's Sons.)
8. Grant Hurls His Men to Death at Cold Harbor.
   William C. Oates, *The War Between the Union and the Confederacy and Its Lost Opportunities*. New York: The Neale Publishing Co., 1905. Pp. 365-368.

CHAPTER XII. THE SIEGE OF PETERSBURG

1. Grant's Army Crosses the James.
   "Grant's Report covering operations of all armies of the U. S. from March, 1864 to May, 1865," in *The War of the Rebellion . . . Official Records*. Ser. I, vol. XXXVI, pt. I, 22-25.
2. Beauregard Holds the Lines at Petersburg.
   G. T. Beauregard, "Four Days of Battle at Petersburg," in *Battles and Leaders of the Civil War*. New York: The Century Co., 1884, 1887, 1888, IV, 540-544.
3. "A Hurricane of Shot and Shell."
   Captain Augustus C. Brown, *The Diary of a Line Officer*. New York: Privately printed, 1906. Pp. 77-82.
4. The Mine and the Battle of the Crater.
   John S. Wise, *The End of an Era*. Boston: Houghton, Mifflin & Co., 1899. Pp. 357-366.
5. Lee Stops Hancock at the Gates of Richmond.
   [Richard Corbin], "Letters of a Confederate Officer to His Family in Europe during the Last Year of the War of Secession," reprinted by William Abbatt, *Magazine of History*, Extra No. 24, 1913. Pp. 57-62.
6. The Iron Lines of Petersburg.
   George D. Harmon, ed., "Letters of Luther Rice Mills—a Confederate Soldier," *North Carolina Historical Review*, IV (July 1927), 303-308. (By permission of State of North Carolina Department of Archives and History.)

CHAPTER XIII. THE VALLEY IN 1864

1. V.M.I. Boys Fight at New Market.
   John S. Wise, "The West Point of the Confederacy," *Century Illustrated Magazine*, XXXVII (1888-1889), 464-470.
2. General Hunter Devastates the Valley.
   General J. D. Imboden, "Fire, Sword, and the Halter," in *The Annals of the War, Written by Leading Participants North and South . . . in the Philadelphia Weekly Times*. Philadelphia: The Times Publishing Co., 1879. Pp. 177-181.

3. General Ramseur Fights and Dies for His Country.
Letters of Ramseur to his fiancée and wife, Ramseur Manuscripts, University of North Carolina. (By permission of Messrs. Paul W. Schenck, Jr., and David Schenck.)

4. Early Surprises the Federals at Cedar Creek.
Captain S. E. Howard, "The Morning Surprise at Cedar Creek," in *Civil War Papers . . . Massachusetts Commandery, Military Order of the Loyal Legion of the United States.* Boston: Printed for the Commandery, 1900. II, 417-422. (By permission of Massachusetts Commandery, Military Order of the Loyal Legion of the United States.)

5. Sheridan Rides down the Valley Pike to Victory and Fame.
[Philip H. Sheridan], *Personal Memoirs of P. H. Sheridan.* New York: Charles L. Webster & Co., 1888. II, 68-86.

6. "The Valley Will Have Little in It for Man or Beast."
Letter of General Sheridan, in *The War of the Rebellion . . . Official Records,* Ser. I, vol. XLIII, pt. 1, 30-31.

CHAPTER XIV. LEE AND LINCOLN

1. Robert E. Lee Goes with His State.
A. "My Relatives, My Children, My Home." Lee to his sister, Mrs. Anne Marshall, in Robert E. Lee [Jr.], *Recollections and Letters of General Robert E. Lee,* New York: Doubleday, Page & Co., 1904. Pp. 25-26. (By permission of Doubleday & Company, Inc.)
B. "I Never Desire Again to Draw My Sword." Lee to General Scott, Ibid., 24-25.

2. "A Splendid Specimen of an English Gentleman."
[Col. Garnet Wolseley], "A Month's Visit to the Confederate Headquarters," *Blackwood's Edinburgh Magazine,* XCIII (January-June 1863), 18, 20-21.

3. "It Is Well War Is So Terrible or We Should Get Too Fond of It."
W. N. Pendleton, "Personal Recollections of General Lee," *Southern Magazine,* XV (1874), 620-621.

4. Dr. Parks's Boy Visits Lee's Headquarters.
Leighton Parks, "What a Boy Saw of the Civil War; with Glimpses of General Lee," *Century Illustrated Magazine,* LXX (1905), 258-264. (By permission of Appleton-Century-Crofts, Inc.)

5. "A Sadness I Had Never Before Seen upon His Face."
J. D. Imboden, "The Confederate Retreat from Gettysburg," in *Battles and Leaders of the Civil War.* New York: The Century Co., 1884, 1888. III, 420-421.

6. Lee and Traveller Review the Army of Northern Virginia.
Robert E. Lee [Jr.], *Recollections and Letters of General Robert E. Lee.* New York: Doubleday, Page & Co., 1904. Pp. 106-107. (By permission of Doubleday & Company, Inc.)

7. "He Looked as Though He Was the Monarch of the World." William C. Oates, *The War Between the Union and the Confederacy and Its Lost Opportunities*. New York: The Neale Publishing Co., 1905. Pp. 343-344.

8. "The Field Resounded with Wild Shouts of Lee, Lee, Lee." Account by Colonel J. Catlett Gibson, *Southern Historical Society Papers*, XXXI (1903), 200-203. (By permission of Southern Historical Society.)

9. Lee Bids Farewell to the Army of Northern Virginia. Robert E. Lee [Jr.], *Recollections and Letters of General Robert E. Lee.* New York: Doubleday, Page & Co., 1904. Pp. 153-154. (By permission of Doubleday & Company, Inc.)

10. Nathaniel Hawthorne Calls on President Lincoln. Nathaniel Hawthorne, *Tales, Sketches, and Other Papers,* many editions.

11. John Hay Lives with "The Tycoon" in the White House. Tyler Dennett, ed., John Hay, *Lincoln and the Civil War in the Diaries and Letters of John Hay.* New York: Dodd, Mead & Co., 1939. Pp. 34-35, 68-69, 76, 96, 185. (By permission of Dodd, Mead & Company, Inc.)

12. "My Paramount Object Is to Save the Union."
    A. "The Prayer of Twenty Millions." Greeley to Lincoln, in Frank Moore, ed., *The Rebellion Record.* New York, 1871. XII, 480 ff.
    B. "I Would Save the Union." Lincoln to Greeley, *Ibid.*

13. "We Shall Nobly Save or Meanly Lose the Last, Best Hope of Earth." Abraham Lincoln, "Annual Message of Dec. 1, 1862," in James D. Richardson, ed., *Messages and Papers of the Presidents.* New York, 1904. VI, 126 ff.

14. Lincoln Becomes the Great Emancipator.
    A. Secretary Chase Recalls a Famous Cabinet Meeting. J. W. Shuckers, *The Life and Public Services of Salmon Portland Chase.* New York: D. Appleton & Co., 1874. Pp. 453-455.
    B. "Forever Free." Abraham Lincoln, "The Emancipation Proclamation," in James D. Richardson, ed., *Messages and Papers of the Presidents.* New York, 1904. VI, 157 ff.

15. Lincoln and Hay Follow the Election Returns. Tyler Dennett, ed., John Hay, *Lincoln and the Civil War in the Diaries and Letters of John Hay.* New York: Dodd, Mead & Co., 1939. Pp. 232-236. (By permission of Dodd, Mead & Company, Inc.)

16. Lincoln Replies to a Serenade. Nicolay and Hay, eds., *The Complete Works of Abraham Lincoln.* New York: The Century Co., 1894. II, 595-596. (By permission of Appleton-Century-Crofts, Inc.)

17. Lincoln Visits the Colored Soldiers at City Point. General Horace Porter, *Campaigning with Grant.* New York: The Century Co., 1897. Pp. 216-220.

18. "With Malice Toward None."

Abraham Lincoln, "Second Inaugural Address," in James D. Richardson, ed., *Messages and Papers of the Presidents.* New York, 1904. VI, 276-277.
19. Abraham Lincoln Is Assassinated.
    Diary of Gideon Welles. Boston: Houghton Mifflin Co., 1911. II, 283 ff. (By permission of Houghton Mifflin Company.)

CHAPTER XV. THE SUNSET OF THE CONFEDERACY

1. Thomas Annihilates Hood at Nashville.
   James Harrison Wilson, *Under the Old Flag; Recollections of Military Operations in the War for the Union, the Spanish War, the Boxer Rebellion, etc.* New York: D. Appleton & Co., 1912. II, 99-121, *passim.* (By permission of Appleton-Century-Crofts, Inc.)
2. "The Last Chance of the Confederacy."
   Alexander C. McClurg, "The Last Chance of the Confederacy," *Atlantic Monthly,* L (September 1882), 389 ff.
3. "Now Richmond Rocked in Her High Towers to Watch the Impending Issue."
   George Alfred Townsend, *Campaigns of a Non-Combatant, And His Romaunt Abroad During the War.* New York: Blelock & Co., 1866. Pp. 318-326.
4. "The Most Superb Soldier in All the World" Falls at Five Forks.
   Armistead Churchill Gordon, *Memories and Memorials of William Gordon McCabe.* Richmond, Va.: Old Dominion Press, Inc., 1925. I, 164-166. (By permission of Mr. W. Gordon McCabe II and Brigadier General E. R. Warner McCabe.)
5. The Confederates Abandon Richmond.
   A. "A Great Burst of Sobbing All Over the Church." Mrs. Burton Harrison, *Recollections Grave and Gay.* New York: Charles Scribner's Sons, 1916. Pp. 210-219. (By permission of Charles Scribner's Sons.)
   B. "The Poor Colored People Thanked God That Their Sufferings Were Ended." R. B. Prescott, "The Capture of Richmond," in *Civil War Papers . . . Massachusetts Commandery, Military Order of the Loyal Legion of the United States.* Boston: Printed for the Commandery, 1900. I, 64-70. (By permission of Massachusetts Commandery, Military Order of the Loyal Legion of the United States.)
6. The White Flag at Appomattox.
   Joshua Lawrence Chamberlain, *The Passing of the Armies, An Account of the Final Campaign of the Army of the Potomac, Based upon Personal Reminiscences of the Fifth Army Corps.* New York: G. P. Putnam's Sons, 1915. Pp. 230-242.
7. General Lee Surrenders at Appomattox.

Sir Frederick Maurice, ed., *An Aide-de-Camp of Lee; being the Papers of Colonel Charles Marshall*. Boston: Little, Brown & Co., 1927. Pp. 268-274. (By permission of Sir Frederick Maurice.)

8. "The Whole Column Seemed Crowned with Red."
Joshua Lawrence Chamberlain, *The Passing of the Armies, An Account of the Final Campaign of the Army of the Potomac, Based upon Personal Reminiscences of the Fifth Army Corps*. New York: G. P. Putnam's Sons, 1915. Pp. 248, 258-265.

9. The Stars and Stripes Are Raised over Fort Sumter.
Mary Cadwalader Jones, *Lantern Slides*. Boston: Privately printed, 1937. (By permission of Mrs. Max Farrand.)

10. "Bow Down, Dear Land, for Thou Hast Found Release."
James Russell Lowell, "Ode Recited at the Harvard Commemoration," *Poems,* many editions.

Several selections quoted from *John Brown's Body,* in *The Selected Works of Stephen Vincent Benét,* published by Rinehart and Company, Inc. Copyright 1927, 1928 by Stephen Vincent Benét, reprinted by permission of Brandt & Brandt.

Maps, Chattanooga and Its Approaches, from *The Mississippi Valley in the Civil War* by John Fiske, published by Houghton, Mifflin & Co. Copyright 1900, reprinted by permission of Houghton Mifflin Company.

Index

Abner Small Suffers in Danville Prison, 98–101

Abraham Lincoln Is Assassinated, 493–497

Alabama, Sinking of the, 275–281

Albemarle, Sinking of the, 237–239

Alexander, Edward P., quoted, 37–41

Alexander Gives the Signal to Start, 37–41

"All This Will Come Right in the End," 51–53

Alston, Colonel, quoted, 90–94

"*Amid the Din of Battle 'Chickamauga' Could Be Heard*," 307–313

Andrews, Eliza Frances, quoted, 102–103, 354–355

Anna Dickinson Sees the Draft Riots in New York City, 124–130

"Annual Message of December 1, 1862" (Lincoln), 478–479

Antietam (Sharpsburg), Battle of, 2

Appomattox, 469–470, 499, 528–544

Armies Converge on Gettysburg, The, 8–12

Armistead Falls Beside the Enemy's Battery, 42–44

Army of Lobbyists and Speculators, The, 130–132

Army of the Cumberland Carries Missionary Ridge, The, 304–313

Atlanta, Battle of, 2, 146, 329–330, 337–341

Atlanta Campaign, 321–322, 325–344, 367; Resaca, 327; New Hope Church, 327, 330–333; Kenesaw Mountain, 327; Peachtree Creek, 329; Atlanta, 1, 146, 329–330, 337–341

Attack and Repulse at Battery Wagner, 222–227

Awful Conditions at Fort Delaware, The, 107–111

Baker, LaFayette C., quoted, 135–140

Barton, Clara, quoted, 183–186

Battery Wagner, Attack on, 201, 222–227. See also Charleston under Fire

"Battle above the Clouds," see Lookout Mountain

Beaufort, N. C., Capture of, 200

Beaufort, S. C., Capture of, 200

Beauregard, P. G. T., quoted, 399–404

Beauregard Holds the Lines at Petersburg, 398–404

"Bells Are Ringing Wildly," 57–58

Benét, Stephen Vincent, quoted, 168, 451, 469

Bentonville, Battle of, 498, 506–513

Bermuda Hundred, Battle of, 396

Big Black River, Battle of, 62, 74

Big Round Top (Gettysburg), 2, 22, 23, 26, 27–28, 36

Blackford, Susan Leigh, quoted, 185–186

Blockade, 157–161, 199–201, 250–270

Blockade-Runners Supply Charleston, 268–270

Blue and Gray Fraternize after the Surrender of Port Hudson, 87–88

"Bow Down, Dear Land, For Thou Hast Found Release," 547

Boy Cannoneer Describes Hard Fighting on the First Day, A, 16–22

Bragg, Braxton, quoted, 313–314

Brandy Station, Battle of, 5, 8

Bright Side of Libby Prison, The, 103–106

Brooks, Noah, quoted, 117–120

Brown, Augustus C., quoted, 193–194, 404–407

Brown, H. B., quoted, 141–142

Brown, Joseph E., quoted, 169–170

Buell, Augustus, quoted, 16–22, 246–249

Buford and Reynolds Hold Up the Confederate Advance, 13–15

Burning of Columbia, The, 357–361

Burnside Holds Out at Knoxville, 314–320

Burrage, Henry S., quoted, 315–320

Butler, Benjamin, quoted, 214–215

Carnahan, James R., quoted, 285–288

Cedar Creek, Battle of, 421, 432, 439–447

Cemetery Hill, *see* Cemetery Ridge

Chamberlain, Joshua L., quoted, 529–536, 540–544

Champion's Hill, Battle of, 62

Charles A. Dana Helps Stop Frauds in the War Department, 132–134

Charleston under Fire, 200, 222–223, 268–270, 506. *See also* Battery Wagner, Attack on

Chase, Salmon Portland, quoted, 480–482

Chattanooga, Battle of, 282–284, 294–314; Lookout Mountain, 284, 301–303, 308–310; Missionary Ridge, 2, 284, 303–314. *See also* Chattanooga, Siege of

Chattanooga, Siege of, 284, 294–301. *See also* Chattanooga, Battle of

Chattanooga under Siege, 294–301

Chickamauga, Battle of, 282–294

Chickasaw Bluffs, Battle of, 61

Christian, William, quoted, 6–7

Clara Barton Surmounts the Faithlessness of Union Officers, 182–184

Clemens, Samuel, *see* Mark Twain

Cold Harbor, Battle of, 365, 392–394

Colonel Baker Outwits Bounty Jumpers and Brokers, 135–140

Colonel Oates Almost Captures Little Round Top, 27–31

Colonel Porter Draws a Portrait of General Grant, 368–371

Columbia, Capture of, 323, 357–361, 506

Commodore Farragut Captures New Orleans, 208–212

Confederate Plan to Seize Johnson's Island Is Frustrated, A, 141–142

Confederate Plots Against the North, 140–145

Confederate Privateers Harry Northern Merchantmen, 270–272

Confederates Abandon Richmond, The, 521–528

Confederates Attempt to Burn New York, The, 142–145

Confederates Burn Their Cotton, The, 161–163

Confederates Repulse an Attack on Fort Fisher, The, 239–245

Connolly, James A., quoted, 307–313

Corbin, Richard, quoted, 413–416

Cornelia Hancock Nurses Soldiers and Contrabands, 187–191

Crater, Battle of the (Petersburg), 408–412

"Crest Is Safe, The," 44–51

Culp's Hill (Gettysburg), 2, 9, 16, 22, 23

Cushing, William B., quoted, 237–239

Dana, Charles A., quoted, 132–134

Davis, Jefferson, quoted, 55–57, 334–335

Dawson, Sarah Morgan, quoted, 162–163

De Trobriand, Régis, quoted, 130–132

Dickinson, Anna, quoted, 124–130

"Disaster Admits of No Palliation, The," 313–314

Dr. Parks's Boy Visits Lee's Headquarters, 457–462

Dwight, Henry O., quoted, 349

Early Surprises the Federals at Cedar Creek, 439–443

Eating Mules at Port Hudson, 85–87

Eggleston, George Cary, quoted, 154–157

Eliza Andrews Comes Home Through the Burnt Country, 354–357

Ellet, Alfred W., quoted, 217–222

Ellet's Steam Rams Smash the Confederate Fleet at Memphis, 217–222

"Emancipation Proclamation, The," 482–483

"Enemy Were Upon Us, The," 439–443

Fair Oaks, Battle of, *see* Seven Pines, Battle of

Farley, Porter, quoted, 23–26

Farragut Damns the Torpedoes at Mobile Bay, 228–236

"Father of Waters Again Goes Unvexed to the Sea, The," 88–89

Federals Oppose Hood with Desperation, The, 284–288

"Field Resounded with Wild Shouts of Lee, Lee, Lee, The," 467–469

"First One Flag, Then Another, Leads," 304–307

Fisher's Hill, Battle of, *see* Strasburg, Battle of

Fitfield, Captain, quoted, 271–272

Five Forks, Battle of, 498, 514–521

"Forever Free," 482–483

Fort Donelson, Battle of, 201, 217

Fort Fisher, Attack on, 200, 239–249; Capture of, 498, 507. *See also* Wilmington under blockade

Fort Sumter, Stars and Stripes raised over, 544–546

Franklin, Battle of, 2, 500–501

Fredericksburg, Battle of, 456–457

Fremantle, Arthur J. L., quoted, 51–53

Fullerton, Joseph, quoted, 301–303

General Banks Takes Port Hudson, 85–88

General Butler Outrages the Moral Sentiment of the World, 214–215

General Hunter Devastates the Valley, 428–431

General Johnston Justifies Himself, 335–337

General Lee Decides to Take the Offensive, 3–5

General Lee Invades Pennsylvania, 6–7

General Lee Offers to Resign after Gettysburg, 53–57

General Lee Surrenders at Appomattox, 536–540

General Morgan Invades the North, 89–96

General Ramseur Fights and Dies for His Country, 431–439

General Sherman Takes Command, 323–325

General Sherman Thinks His Name May Live, 361–363

General Warren Seizes Little Round Top, 23–26

George Townsend Describes the Wounded on the Peninsula, 174–178

Georgia Fires the Bold Hunter, The, 273–275

Georgia's Governor Laments Davis' Despotism, 168–170

Gerrish, Theodore, quoted, 32–35

Gettysburg, Battle of, 1–59, 146, 187–189, 462–464. *See also* Willoughby Run; Seminary Ridge; Peach Orchard; Little Round Top; Big Round Top; Culp's Hill; Cemetery Ridge

"Gettysburg Address, The," 58–59

Ghastly Work of the Field Surgeons, The, 191–194

Gibson, J. Catlett, quoted, 467–469

Good Word for the Bummer, A, 349

Gordon, John B., quoted, 388–392

Goss, Warren Lee, quoted, 372–377

Grand Gulf, Battle of, 61, 63–68

Grant, U. S., quoted, 79–85, 366–368, 397–398

Grant Hurls His Men to Death at Cold Harbor, 392–394

Grant's Army Crosses the James, 396–398

Gray, John Chipman, quoted, 324–325

"*Great Burst of Sobbing All Over the Church, A,*" 521–524

Greeley, Horace, quoted, 476–477

Greene, S. Dana, quoted, 205–208

Hague, Parthenia, quoted, 157–161

Hancock, Cornelia, quoted, 187–191

Hardee Wins and Loses the Battle of Atlanta, 337–341

Harrison, Constance Cary, quoted, 521–524

Haskell, Frank Aretas, quoted, 44–51

Hawthorne, Nathaniel, quoted, 471–472

Hay, John, quoted, 473–475, 484–487

Headley, John W., quoted, 142–145

Heartlessness of the Surgeons, The, 191–193

"*Heavens Were Lit Up with the Flames from Burning Buildings, The,*" 351–354

"*He Looked as Though He Was the Monarch of the World,*" 465–466

"*He Might Sit for a Portrait of an Ideal Yankee,*" 324–325

High Tide at Gettysburg, 35–53

Hill, Daniel H., quoted, 289–291

Hilton Head, Capture of, 200

Hitchcock, Henry, quoted, 360–361

Holly Springs, Capture of, 61

Hooker Wins the "Battle above the Clouds," 301–303

Horrors of the Wilderness, The, 193–194

Howard, S. E., quoted, 439–443

Hunt, Henry J., quoted, 8–12

"Hurricane of Shot and Shell, A," 404–407

Imboden, John D., quoted, 428–431, 462–464

"I Never Desire Again to Draw My Sword," 453

Iron Lines of Petersburg, The, 416–419

Island No. 10, Battle of, 60, 217

"It Beat Anything in History," 245–249

"It Is Well War Is So Terrible, or We Should Get Too Fond of It," 456–457

Ivy Prowls Outside New Orleans, The, 271

"I Would Save the Union," 477–478

Jackson, Capture of, 61–62

Jefferson Davis Takes a Prize off Delaware, The, 271–272

Joe Johnston Gives Way to Hood, 333–337

John Hay Lives with "The Tycoon" in the White House, 473–475

Johnson, Charles Beneulyn, quoted, 194–198

Johnston, Joseph E., quoted, 330–333, 335–337

Johnston Halts Sherman at New Hope Church, 330–333

Jones, John Beauchamp, quoted, 148–153

Jones, Mary Cadwalader, quoted, 544–546

Julia LeGrand Describes the Surrender of New Orleans, 212–214

Kearsarge Sinks the Alabama off Cherbourg, The, 275–281

Kell, John McIntosh, quoted, 275–281

Kenesaw Mountain, Battle of, 327

Kinney, John, quoted, 228–236

Knoxville, Battle of, 283, 314–320

Lamb, William, quoted, 240–245

"Last Chance of the Confederacy, The," 506–513

Lee, Robert E., quoted, 3–5, 54–55, 452–453, 470

Lee and Traveller Review the Army of Northern Virginia, 464–465

Lee Bids Farewell to the Army of Northern Virginia, 469–470

Lee's Farewell to His Army, quoted, 470

Lee Stops Hancock at the Gates of Richmond, 413–416

LeGrand, Julia, quoted, 166–167, 212–214

Lieutenant Cushing Torpedoes the Albemarle, 237–239

Lincoln, Abraham, quoted, 58–59, 88–89, 477–479, 482–483, 487–488, 492–493

Lincoln and Hay Follow the Election Returns, 483–487

Lincoln Becomes the Great Emancipator, 479–483

Lincoln Replies to a Serenade, 487–488

Lincoln Visits the Colored Soldiers at City Point, 488–491

Little Round Top (Gettysburg), 2, 22–35, 35–36

"Lives Which Women Have Lead Since Troy Fell, The," 166–167

Longstreet, James, quoted, 42–44

Longstreet Breaks the Federal Line, 288–291

Lookout Mountain, Battle of, 284, 301–303, 308–310

Lowell, James Russell, quoted, 547

Lunt, Dolly Sumner, quoted, 351–354

Lusk, William Thompson, quoted, 57–58

McCabe, William Gordon, quoted, 519–521

McClurg, Alexander, quoted, 507–513

McCreary, James Bennett, quoted, 94–96

Major Hitchcock Explains the Burning of Columbia, 360–361

"Man Who Held His Conscience Higher Than Their Praise, The," 171–172

March to the Sea, 2, 146, 321–323, 324–325, 344–363

Marshall, Charles, quoted, 536–540

Marye's Heights, *see* Fredericksburg, Battle of

Memphis, Battle of, 217–222

Merrimac and the Monitor, *The,* 201–208

Merrimac and the *Monitor,* Battle of the, 200, 201–208

Mills, Luther Rice, quoted, 416–418

Mine and the Battle of the Crater, The, 408–412

Minnesota Fights for Her Life in Hampton Roads, The, 202–205

Missionary Ridge, Battle of, 2, 284, 303–314

Mr. Eggleston Recalls When Money Was Plentiful, 153–157

Mobile Bay, Battle of, 200, 228–236, 498

Monitor *Repels the* Merrimac, *The,* 205–208

Monocacy, Battle of, *see* Washington, Early's march on

Moran, Benjamin, quoted, 215–217

Moran, Frank, quoted, 103–106

"More Impudent Proceeding Cannot Be Discovered, A," 215–217

Morgan, James Morris, quoted, 273–275

Morgan, William, quoted, 304–307

Morgan's Cavalrymen Sweep Through Kentucky, 90–94

Morgan's Raid, 89–96

Morgan's Raid Comes to an Inglorious End, 94–96

"Most Superb Soldier in All the World" Falls at Five Forks, The, 518–521

"My Paramount Object Is to Save the Union," 475–478

"My Relatives, My Children, My Home," 452–453

Nashville, Battle of, 498, 500–506

Nathaniel Hawthorne Calls on President Lincoln, 470–472

New Bern, Capture of, 200, 507

"New Birth of Freedom, A," 58–59

New Hope Church, Battle of, 327, 330–333

New Madrid, Battle of, 201, 217

New Market, Battle of (1864), 421, 422–427, 428

New Orleans, Capture of, 60, 162–163, 200, 208–217, 251

New Orleans Falls to the Yankees, 212–217

New York Draft Riots, 124–130

New York Tribune, quoted, 223–227

Nichols, George Ward, quoted, 357–360

Nichols, Samuel Edmund, quoted, 191–193

Norfolk, Battle of, 200

"Now Richmond Rocked in Her High Towers to Watch the Impending Issue," 513–518

Oakey, Daniel, quoted, 349–351

Oates, William, quoted, 27–31, 392–394, 465–466

"Ode Recited at the Harvard Commemoration," quoted, 547

"Onward to Vicksburg," 62–71

Opequon, Battle of, 421, 439

Palmerston, Viscount, quoted, 215

Palmerston Protests Butler's Proclamation, 215

Parks, Leighton, quoted, 458–462

Parthenia Hague Tells How Women Outwitted the Blockade, 157–161

Peace at Any Price, 170–171

Peach Orchard (Gettysburg), 2, 23

Peachtree Creek, Battle of, 329

Peck, W. F. G., quoted, 269–270

Pendleton, W. N., quoted, 456–457

Peninsular Campaign, 174–182; Norfolk, 200

Perkins, George Hamilton, quoted, 208–212

Petersburg, Siege of, 395–419, 498, 499, 514; Crater, Battle of the, 408–412

Petigru Monument, 172

Pittsburg Landing, Battle of, see Shiloh, Battle of

"Poor Colored People Thanked God That Their Sufferings Were Ended, The," 524–528

Porter, Horace, quoted, 368–371, 383–388, 489–491

Port Gibson, Fall of, 61, 62

Port Hudson, Fall of, 60, 62, 77, 85–88, 201, 228

Port Royal, Capture of, 200

"Prayer of Twenty Millions, The," 476–477

Prescott, R. B., quoted, 524–528

President Davis Removes General Johnston before Atlanta, 334–335

Private Goss Describes the Battle of the Wilderness, 372–377

Privations of Life in Elmira Prison, The, 111–115

Ramseur, Stephen Dodson, quoted, 432–439

Raymond, Battle of, 61–62

Red River Campaign, 201

Regimental Hospital, The, 194–198

Repard, M., quoted, 271

Resaca, Battle of, 326

Richmond, Surrender of, 499, 521–528

Roanoke Island, Capture of, 200

Robert E. Lee Goes with His State, 452–453

Robert E. Lee Runs the Blockade, The, 260–264

Rob Roy Runs the Blockade Out of Havana, The, 264–268

Rosengarten, Joseph, quoted, 13–15

"Sadness I Had Never Before Seen upon His Face, A," 462–464

Sanitary Commission to the Rescue, The, 178–182

Savannah, Capture of, 200, 323, 324, 498, 506

"Scene of Shameful Confusion, A," 357–360

"Second Inaugural Address" (Lincoln), 492–493

Secretary Chase Recalls a Famous Cabinet Meeting, 480–482

Seminary Ridge (Gettysburg), 9, 12, 13, 19, 20–21

Shanks, W. F. G., quoted, 295–301

Sheridan, Philip H., quoted, 443–447, 448–449

Sheridan Rides Down the Valley Pike to Victory and Fame, 443–447

Sherman, William T., quoted, 168, 325–330, 342–344, 344–348, 361–363

Sherman Marches from Atlanta to the Sea, 344–348

Sherman Marches from Chattanooga to Atlanta, 325–330

Sherman's "Bummers," 348–351

Shiloh (Pittsburg Landing), Battle of, 2, 201

Shotwell, Randolph Abbott, quoted, 107–111

Small, Abner, quoted, 98–101

"Splendid Specimen of an English Gentleman, A," 454–456

Spotsylvania, Battle of, 365, 383–392, 465–469

Spotsylvania and the Bloody Angle, 383–388

Stars and Stripes Are Raised over Fort Sumter, The, 544–546

Stiles, Robert, quoted, 381–382

Strasburg, Battle of (Fisher's Hill), 436, 438

Struggle for Little Round Top, The, 22–35

Suffering in Andersonville Prison, 101–103

Susan Blackford Nurses the Wounded at Lynchburg, 185–186

"Texans Always Move Them," 377–380

"Their Dead and Dying Piled Higher Than the Works," 380–382

"These Men Have Never Failed You on Any Field," 388–392

"They Must Reap the Whirlwind," 167–168

Thomas Annihilates Hood at Nashville, 500–506

Thomas Holds the Horseshoe Ridge, 291–294

Thomas Stands Like a Rock at Chickamauga, 288–294

Thruston, Gates P., quoted, 291–294

Toney, Marcus B., quoted, 111–115

Townsend, George Alfred, quoted, 174–178, 514–518

20th Maine Saves Little Round Top, The, 32–35

Tullahoma Campaign, 283, 314

Tuthill, Richard, quoted, 337–341

Union Woman Suffers Through the Siege of Vicksburg, A, 71–79

United States Navy Blockades the Confederacy, The, 252–260

U. S. Grant Plans His Spring Campaign, 366–368

Valley Campaign (1864), 367, 396, 420–449; New Market, 420, 421, 428; Washington, Early's march on, 421, 432; Opequon, 421, 439; Winchester, 435–436; Strasburg, 436, 439; Cedar Creek, 421, 431, 439–447

"Valley Will Have Little in It for Man or Beast, The," 448–449

Van Brunt, G. J., quoted, 202–205

Vicksburg, Siege of, 61–62, 69–70, 71–85. *See also* Vicksburg Campaign

Vicksburg Campaign, 1, 57–58, 60–89, 146, 168, 201, 228, 282; Holly Springs, 61; Chickasaw Bluffs, 61; Grand Gulf, 61, 63–68; Port Gibson, 61, 62; Raymond, 61, 62; Jackson, 61–62; Champion's Hill, 62; Big Black River, 62, 74; Vicksburg, Siege of, 62, 69–70, 71–85; Port Hudson, 60, 62, 77, 201, 228

Vicksburg Surrenders, 79–85

V.M.I. Boys Fight at New Market, 421–427

Wait, Horatio L., quoted, 253–260

Walt Whitman Looks Around in Wartime Washington, 120–124

War Clerk Suffers Scarcities in Richmond, A, 147–153

Ward, Mary A., quoted, 163–165

Washington, Early's march on (Battle of Monocacy), 421, 432

Washington as a Camp, 117–120

Watson, William, quoted, 264–268

Welles, Gideon, quoted, 494–497

"We Shall Nobly Save or Meanly Lose the Last, Best Hope of Earth," 478–479

"We Were Proud of Our Foragers," 349–351

White Flag at Appomattox, The, 528–536

Whitman, Walt, quoted, 121–124

"Whole Column Seemed Crowned with Red, The," 540–544

Wilcox, Charles E., quoted, 63–71

Wilderness, Battle of the, 365, 465

Wilderness Campaign, 2, 146, 182–186, 193–194, 364–394, 395, 465–469; Wilderness, Battle of the, 365, 465–466; Spotsylvania, 365, 383–392, 467–469; Cold Harbor, 365, 392–394

Wilkinson, John, quoted, 260–264

Willoughby Run (Gettysburg), 9, 16, 19

Wilmington under blockade, 200, 240; Capture of, 507. *See also* Fort Fisher, Attack on

Wilson, James Harrison, quoted, 501–506

Winchester, Battle of (1863), 5

Winchester, Battle of (1864), 421, 435–436

Wise, John S., quoted, 408–412, 422–427

"With Malice Toward None," 491–493

Wolseley, Lord Garnet, quoted, 454–456

Worth, Jonathan, quoted, 170–171

"Yankees Are Coming, The," 163–165

"You Might as Well Appeal against the Thunder-Storm," 341–344